# The Tibeto-Burman Reproductive System

# The Tibeto-Burman Reproductive System: Toward an Etymological Thesaurus

*James A. Matisoff*

*Comments on Chinese comparanda by Zev J. Handel*

UNIVERSITY OF CALIFORNIA PRESS
Berkeley • Los Angeles • London

University of California Press, one of the most distinguished university presses in the
United States, enriches lives around the world by advancing scholarship in the humanities,
social sciences, and natural sciences. Its activities are supported by the UC Press Foundation
and by philanthropic contributions from individuals and institutions. For more information,
visit http://www.ucpress.edu.

University of California Publications in Linguistics, Volume 139
Editorial Board: Judith Aissen, Andrew Garrett, Larry M. Hyman, Marianne Mithun,
Pamela Munro, Maria Polinsky

University of California Press
Berkeley and Los Angeles, California

University of California Press, Ltd.
London, England

Library of Congress Cataloging-in-Publication Data

Matisoff, James A.
    The Tibeto-Burman reproductive system : toward an etymological thesaurus / by James A.
Matisoff ; comments on Chinese comparanda by Zev J. Handel.
        p.     cm. — (University of California publications in linguistics ; v. 139)
    Includes bibliographical references and index.
    ISBN 978-0-520-09871-8 (pbk. : alk. paper)
    1. Tibeto-Burman languages—History.   2. Tibeto-Burman languages—Etymology.
3. Reconstruction (Linguistics).   4. Comparative linguistics.   I. Title.   II. Series.

PL3551.M37   2008
495'.4009—dc22                                                                    2008037215

Manufactured in the United States of America

The paper used in this publication meets the minimum requirements of
ANSI/NISO Z39.48-1992 (R 1997) (*Permanence of Paper*).

# Grant Support

This research has been supported in part by grants to the *Sino-Tibetan Etymological Dictionary and Thesaurus* project from

* The National Science Foundation (NSF), Division of Behavioral & Cognitive Sciences, Grant Nos. BNS-86-17726, BNS-90-11918, DBS-92-09481, FD-95-11034, SBR-9808952, BCS-9904950, BCS-0345929, and BCS-0712570.

* The National Endowment for the Humanities (NEH), Preservation and Access, Grant Nos. RT-20789-87, RT-21203-90, RT-21420-92, PA-22843-96, PA-23353-99, PA-24168-02, PA-50709-04, and PM-50072-07.

# Table of Contents

# Acknowledgments

This volume may be considered to be a sort of "down payment" or pilot project for a much larger effort: the creation of a computerized etymological thesaurus that will eventually include the entire proto-lexicon of the Tibeto-Burman/Sino-Tibetan family. That has been the ultimate goal of the *Sino-Tibetan Etymological Dictionary and Thesaurus* project (STEDT) since its inception in 1987.

As explained in more detail in the *Introduction* (Section 1, below), progress toward this goal has not been as speedy as we would have liked, due both to the inherent complexity of the project and to the rapidly evolving nature of computer technology. The early years of STEDT were devoted to the creation of our lexical database from a multitude of published and unpublished sources (see the *Appendix of Source Abbreviations*), the necessary prerequisite for assembling cognate sets. Among the heroic "Stedtniks" of that era, special thanks are due to John B. Lowe, Randy J. LaPolla, Zev J. Handel, Jonathan P. Evans, Matthew Juge, and Richard S. Cook, all of whom are now Berkeley Ph.D.'s.

During this period J. B. Lowe devised a pioneering program called "The Tagger's Assistant", that enabled me to etymologize tens of thousands of syllables in our database by labelling them with numerical "tags" that could then be used to assemble them into cognate sets. (That is, each syllable deemed to be a reflex of a particular etymon would be tagged with the same number.) With an eye to the eventual publication of our results, J. B. also solved such essential formatting problems as how to insert footnotes at any point in a printed etymological text, whether on a semantic diagram, an etymon as a whole, or a particular supporting form.[1]

A preliminary version of the book the reader now holds in his/her hands, then called the "Reproductive Fascicle of the Bodypart Volume" of STEDT, was in fact submitted to the *UCPL* Series of the University of California Press in 1998-99. It was provisionally accepted for publication, but only on condition that we could commit to firm deadlines for the publication of subsequent fascicles and volumes until the project was completed.[2] However, since some 80 percent of our laboriously created database, huge as it was, consisted of bodypart terms, we were hardly in a position to make such a commitment.

So I decided to let the thesauric side of STEDT slide for awhile, and to switch the emphasis of the project to *phonologically* presented etyma (the "D" or "dictionary" part

---

[1]See Section 2.9 of the *Introduction*, below.
[2]Thanks are due to the then *UCPL* Series editor, Rose Anne White, for her support at this stage.

of "STEDT"), an effort which culminated in the publication of the *Handbook of Proto-Tibeto-Burman* (2003).

Since that time, several other projects have intervened, but now finally we are again in a position to concentrate fully on semantically based collections of etymologies. The present volume is meant to serve as an example of what the entire *Sino-Tibetan Etymological Dictionary and Thesaurus* would eventually look like in print. However, for the foreseeable future we are planning to switch to an electronic and interactive approach, whereby batches of suggested etyma will be periodically released for feedback from colleagues.[3]

It gives me special pleasure to thank Professor Zev J. Handel of the University of Washington for taking time out between the two halves of his 2007-08 sabbatical year in Korea to update his discussions of the Chinese comparanda in this volume.[4] Zev had originally contributed such comments to the preliminary version of the manuscript some ten years ago, evaluating my suggested Proto-Tibeto-Burman/Old Chinese comparisons in terms of the competing reconstructive systems of leading Sinologists, past and present. These updated comments, presented in a neutral, non-judgmental tone, constitute a precious guide through the minefield of Chinese historical phonology!

The attractive appearance of this book is entirely due to the talent and industry of Dominic Yu, who has been working for the better part of a year to solve the intricate problems of formatting that have presented themselves through the various redactions of the manuscript. Among his accomplishments are the semantic diagrams[5] that grace the beginning of each chapter. Although these are based on the diagrams from the previous draft of this volume (the exception is the WATER/FLUID diagram, which is new), each diagram had to be remade from scratch during the revision process. On the back end, his efforts involved porting the entire database to a web-accessible engine using MySQL, accomplished in conjunction with David R. Mortensen and J. B. Lowe, and simultaneously converting our in-house legacy STEDT Font encoding to Unicode. The final print volume is typeset in X꜔LATEX using Charis SIL as the main font.

I am grateful to the *University of California Publications in Linguistics* (UCPL) series for accepting a book of mine for the fifth time.[6]

The STEDT project has been sponsored from the beginning by the National Endowment for the Humanities and the National Science Foundation. To both agencies I express again my enduring gratitude.[7]

Finally I would like to thank my wife Susan for her constant support, and for having taught me so much about the reproductive system over the past 46 years.

JAM

Berkeley, February 2008

---

[3] As noted in the *Introduction* (*ibid.*), this aspect of our enterprise will be called the *STEDT Root Canal*.
[4] See the *Introduction*, Section 2.8.
[5] See the *Introduction*, Section 2.1.
[6] See Matisoff 1973 (*UCPL* #75), 1988 (#111), 2003 (#135), 2006 (#139).
[7] See *Grant Support*, p. i above.

# Symbols and Abbreviations

## Books, Monographs, Monograph Series[*]

**AHD** *American Heritage Dictionary*

**CISTL** Kitamura, Nishida, and Nagano, eds. (1994)

**CSDPN** Hale (1973)

**CTT** Hyman, ed. (1973)

**GL** Matisoff (1973b/1982)

**GSR** Karlgren (1957)

**GSTC** Matisoff (1985a)

**HCT** Li (1977)

**HPTB** Matisoff (2003)

**HRAF** *Human Relations Area Files* (New Haven)

**NHTBM** Nishi, Matisoff, and Nagano, eds. (1995)

**OED** *Oxford English Dictionary*

**OPWSTBL** *Occasional Papers of the Wolfenden Society on Tibeto-Burman Linguistics*

**PPPB** Luce (1986)

**STC** Benedict (1972)

**TBL** Dai et al., eds. (1992)

**TBT** Weidert (1987)

**TSR** Matisoff (1972a)

**UCPL** *University of California Publications in Linguistics* (Berkeley, Los Angeles, London)

**SELAF** *Société d'Etudes Linguistiques et Anthropologiques de France* (Paris)

**VSTB** Matisoff (1978a)

**ZMYYC** Sun et al., eds. (1991)

## Journals

**AM** *Asia Major* (Leipzig; London; Taipei)

**AO** *Acta Orientalia* (Copenhagen)

**BIHP** *Bulletin of the Institute of History and Philology* (Taipei)

**BMFEA** *Bulletin of the Museum of Far Eastern Antiquities* (Stockholm)

**BSLP** *Bulletin de la Société de Linguistique de Paris* (Paris)

**BSOAS** *Bulletin of the School of Oriental and African Studies* (London)

**GK** *Gengo Kenkyū* (Tokyo)

---

[*]Here listed only by author and date. For full citations see the References, pp. 249-257.

**HJAS** *Harvard Journal of Asiatic Studies* (Cambridge, MA)

**IJAL** *International Journal of American Linguistics* (Chicago)

**JAOS** *Journal of the American Oriental Society* (New Haven)

**JASB** *Journal of the Asiatic Society of Bengal* (Calcutta)

**LTBA** *Linguistics of the Tibeto-Burman Area* (Berkeley; Chico, CA; Melbourne)

**MSOS** *Mitteilungen des Seminars für orientalische Sprachen an der königlichen Friedrich-Wilhelms-Universität zu Berlin* (Berlin)

**TAK** *Tōnan Azia Kenkyū* (Southeast Asian Studies) (Kyoto)

**ZDMG** *Zeitschrift der deutschen morgenländischen Gesellschaft* (Wiesbaden)

# Conferences

**ICSTLL** International Conferences on Sino-Tibetan Languages and Linguistics

**SEALS** Southeast Asia Linguistics Society

# Research Units

**AS** Academia Sinica (Taipei)

**CIIL** Central Institute of Indian Languages (Mysore)

**EFEO** Ecole Française d'Extrême Orient (Hanoi/Paris)

**ILCAA** Institute for the Study of Cultures of Asia and Africa (Tokyo)

**POLA** Project on Linguistic Analysis (Berkeley)

**SIL** Summer Institute of Linguistics (Dallas)

**STEDT** Sino-Tibetan Etymological Dictionary and Thesaurus (Berkeley)

# Languages

**HM** Hmong-Mien ( = Miao-Yao)

**IA** Indo-Aryan

**IE** Indo-European

**Jg.** Jingpho ( = Kachin)

**KC** Kuki-Chin

**LB** Lolo-Burmese

**Lh.** Lahu

**MC** Middle Chinese

**OC** Old Chinese

**PIE** Proto-Indo-European

**PLB** Proto-Lolo-Burmese

**PNN** Proto-Northern Naga

**PST** Proto-Sino-Tibetan

**PTB** Proto-Tibeto-Burman

**ST** Sino-Tibetan

**TB** Tibeto-Burman

**TK**  Tai-Kadai

**WB**  Written Burmese

**WT**  Written Tibetan

# Miscellaneous

> goes to; becomes

< comes from; is derivable from

**A ⋊ B**  A and B are co-allofams; A and B are members of the same word-family

**Clf.**  classifier

**JAM**  James A. Matisoff

**lit.**  literally

**OICC**  "obscure internal channels and connections" (see Ch. III)

**ult.**  ultimately

**WHB**  William H. Baxter

**ZJH**  Zev J. Handel

# Introduction

## 1 The place of this volume in the STEDT project

The Sino-Tibetan (ST) language family, comprising Chinese on the one hand, and the hundreds of Tibeto-Burman (TB) languages on the other, is one of the largest in the world, with well over a billion and a half speakers.[1] Yet the field of ST linguistics is only about 70 years old, and many TB languages remain virtually unstudied. The *Sino-Tibetan Etymological Dictionary and Thesaurus* project (STEDT) was begun in August 1987, with the goal of reconstructing the lexicon of Proto-Sino-Tibetan and Proto-Tibeto-Burman from both the phonological and the semantic point of view.

In a sense the present work is a companion volume to the *Handbook of Proto-Tibeto-Burman* (*HPTB*; Matisoff 2003), where TB/ST roots were discussed, sorted, and analyzed according to their *phonological shapes*, regardless of their meanings. In the present volume, a group of phonologically disparate TB/ST etyma have been assembled according to their *meanings*, all of which have to do with the body's reproductive system.[2]

Even though the number of etyma reconstructed in this volume (nearly 200) is not inconsiderable, they represent only a small fraction of the thousands of roots in the proto-lexicon. Experience has taught us that STEDT's original goal of simultaneously etymologizing the entire vocabulary of the proto-language was unrealistic. As originally conceived, STEDT was to produce a series of large print volumes, each devoted to the exhaustive presentation of the reconstructed roots in a specific semantic area, covering the entire lexicon, approximately as follows:

---

[1] Some scholars, especially in China, consider Sino-Tibetan to include the Tai-Kadai (TK) and Hmong-Mien (HM) ( = Miáo-Yáo) language families as well. While there is definitely a striking typological similarity among Chinese, TK, and HM, this is undoubtedly due to prolonged ancient contact rather than genetic relationship. See Benedict 1975a (*Austro-Thai Language and Culture, with a glossary of roots*).

[2] My ultimate inspiration for a thesaurus-like approach to the proto-lexicon was Buck 1949 (*A Dictionary of Selected Synonyms in the Principal Indo-European Languages: a contribution to the history of ideas*), a copy of which I purchased as a graduate student in the early 1960's, at the then astronomical price of $40. In each section of this great work, arranged Roget-like into semantic categories and subcategories, Buck first lists the forms for each concept in 30-plus modern and ancient IE languages; then he assembles these synonymous forms into etymological groups. Each of these etyma is briefly discussed in terms of breadth of attestation, solidity of the reconstruction, and semantic connections with other areas of the lexicon.

Each volume was in turn to be divided into a number of smaller units called "fascicles". Thus Vol. I *Body Parts* was to comprise the following nine fascicles:

1. *Body (general)*
2. *Head and Face*
3. *Mouth and Throat*
4. *Torso*
5. *Limbs, Joints, and Body Measures*
6. *Diffuse Organs*
7. *Internal Organs*
8. *Secretions and Somatophonics*[3]
9. *Reproductive System*

Despite the limitations of computer technology in the 1980s and 1990s, the STEDT staff and I managed to build up a database of nearly 300,000 forms from some 250 TB languages and dialects, using a wide variety of heterogeneous sources.[4] I spent several years laboriously "tagging" tens of thousands of individual words and syllables in the database with numerals, each of which corresponded to a reconstructed etymon in an ever-growing list of "official STEDT roots".[5] All forms tagged with a certain number could then be assembled into an etymological set supporting the reconstruction. Some 2000 etyma were eventually set up in this manner. As the work proceeded, however, every subpart and sub-subpart of the lexicon expanded and bloomed into a major project, forcing me to gradually lower my sights: first from dealing with the whole lexicon to confining myself to bodyparts; then from dealing with the whole body to confining myself to one of the nine "fascicles" of the bodypart volume as originally planned. I decided to select the Reproductive System as a pilot project, not merely for its prurient interest, but also because this semantic field tends to be neglected in historical linguistic studies, despite the fact that it is particularly rich in metaphorical associations with other areas of the lexicon.

Clearly it would be impractical to continue with print publications in this fashion for a century or so until the entire lexicon is covered. Our approach in the future must be electronic and interactive. Over the next several years, it is planned gradually to release groups of STEDT etymologies on the web, perhaps 25 or so at a time, in one semantic

---

[3]By "somatophonics" I mean sneezes, belches, farts, and the like.

[4]See the section on *Source Abbreviations* below.

[5]For example, the Lahu word **yû-tu-šï** 'navel' was tagged with the numerals "137, 520, 1019", indicating that the first syllable descends from PTB **\*ram** 'belly', the second syllable from PTB **\*du** 'navel' (see #44 in this volume), and the third syllable from PTB **\*sey** 'fruit; small round object'.

field after another. This electronic conduit I would like to call the *STEDT Root Canal*. Colleagues will be invited to comment on roots already reconstructed and to establish new ones.

# 2 Structure of the chapters and sections

The material in each of the nine chapters of this book is presented in a certain order, as outlined in 2.1-2.9.

## 2.1 Semantic diagrams

Each chapter begins with a semantic diagram. These diagrams, called "metastatic flowcharts" in STEDT parlance, were first introduced in Matisoff 1978a (*VSTB*), and have been used subsequently in many of my articles.[6] They are intended to represent the paths of semantic association undergone by etyma, as established by comparative/historical and/or internal synchronic evidence. An association between two points (X,Y) in semantic space may be established either synchronically or diachronically, either on the basis of a single language or comparatively.[7] I rely on three basic types of evidence:[8]

(a) *Synchronic intra-lingual vagueness.* A given daughter language has a single form that means X or Y according to context, e.g. Mikir **artho** means either 'blood vessel' or 'tendon' or 'muscle' or 'nerve'. In many Chin languages reflexes of *m-luŋ can mean either HEART or LIVER.

(b) *Inter-lingual semantic shift of phonological cognates,* i.e. reflexes of the same etymon mean X in Lg. A but Y in Lg. B, e.g.:
  PTB *r-kliŋ 'marrow/brain' > Mikir **arkleŋ** 'marrow', Dimasa **buthluŋ** 'brain';
  PTB *s-pʷik 'bowels/stomach' > Mikir **phek** 'bowels', Lahu ɔ̀-*fɨ*-qō 'stomach'.

(c) *Association via compounding.* Three points (A,B,C) in semantic space are related, such that in some language a compound of two morphemes, A + B, has the meaning C. In other words, an etymon appears as a constituent in compounds, such that part of the meaning of the compound derives from it, e.g.:

  FOOT + EYE → ANKLE (Lahu **khi-mê̠ʔ-šī** < **khi** 'foot' + **mê̠ʔ-šī** 'eye'); similarly Indonesian **mata-kaki** 'ankle' (< **mata** 'eye' + **kaki** 'foot'), which establishes the

---

[6]See, e.g., Matisoff 1980 ("Stars, moon, and spirits"); 1985a ("God and the ST copula"); 1985b ("Arm, hand, wing"); 1988b ("Property, livestock, talent"); 1991a ("Grammatization in Lahu"); 1991b ("Mother of all morphemes"); 1994b ("Buttock and dull"); 2000b ("Three TB word-families"); 2004 ("Areal semantics").

[7]As a desideratum for the future, one can envision three-dimensional semantic diagrams like those used to model molecules in organic chemistry!

[8]See the discussion in *VSTB*: 194-200.

association EYE $\longleftrightarrow$ ANKLE[9]

Certain conventions are observed in the metastatic flowcharts of this volume:

(a) Points in semantic space between which an association has been established are connected by solid lines. If a point is a bodypart, it is labelled in capital letters. An association between two points that are both bodyparts is an "intra-field association", e.g.:

EGG ——————— TESTICLE

WOMB ——————— PLACENTA

(b) If the association crosses into another semantic field (i.e., with respect to this volume, if it is between a bodypart and a non-bodypart), the non-bodypart point is labeled with small letters, e.g.:

PENIS ——————— banana

NAVEL ——————— center

(c) Antonymic associations (cases where the etymon has acquired opposite meanings) are diagrammed by a curved *yin-yang* type of line, e.g.:

PENIS

VAGINA

(d) Compounds are diagrammed by a pitchfork-like symbol, with the two constituents appearing at the points of the fork, and the overall meaning of the compound indicated at the tip of the handle, e.g.:

---

[9]The same formation is found in many other TB languages, e.g.:

|  | FOOT | EYE | ANKLE |
|---|---|---|---|
| Lalung | ia-thong | mi | ia-thong-mi |
| Limbu | lāŋ | mik | lāŋ-mik |
| Lushai | ke | mit | ke-mit |
| Meithei | khu | mit | khu-mit |
| Tangkhul | phei | mik-ra | phei-mik-ra |
| Written Burmese | khre | myak-ci' | khre-myak-ci' |

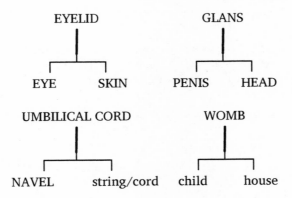

The same convention with respect to capital vs. small letters applies to compounds. In cases where several different combinations of morphemes are attested in compounds with the same meaning, graphic constraints sometimes require geometric reorientations of the pitchfork, e.g.

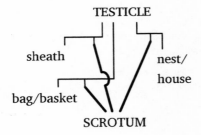

The category of "reproductive bodyparts" is construed broadly to include related verbs (e.g., KISS, SUCK, LOVE, SQUIRT). This volume also includes some non-bodypart terms which frequently appear in compounds with etyma referring to the reproductive system. See especially Ch. IX, "Body fluids".

Deciding how much semantic latitude to allow among putative cognates is definitely an art rather than a science. Here as elsewhere a middle-of-the-road approach is necessary, neither overly conservative nor too wildly speculative. As a positive example of a promising new etymology involving a semantic leap, we may offer *m-t(s)i 'salt / yeast' [HPTB 3.3.1]. Although forms in the daughter languages sometimes mean 'salt' and sometimes 'yeast', the phonological correspondences between both semantic groups of forms are good. On the other hand, the semantic association between 'salt' and 'yeast' has yet to be attested in other language families, even though it has great initial plausibility. Both are efficacious substances that have dramatic effects on the taste of food or drink; their lack renders the food or drink insipid.[10]

---

[10]Yeast is used for brewing liquor rather than for baking bread in East and SE Asia.

## 2.2  Reconstructed PTB etyma

After the semantic chart which begins each chapter, the reconstructed PTB roots of the chapter are presented one after the other, roughly in the order of the strength of their attestation. After preliminary remarks about the distribution of the etymon, the "supporting forms" for the reconstruction are listed, subgroup by subgroup.

The reconstructions all conform to the syllable canon posited for the proto-language,[11]

$$(P^2) \quad (P^1) \quad C_i \quad (G) \quad V \quad (:) \quad (C_f) \quad (s),$$

where the initial consonant ($C_i$) may be preceded by up to two prefixes (with the inner prefix $P^1$ assumed to be historically prior to the outer one ($P^2$); the $C_i$ may optionally be followed by one of four glides (G), */-y-, -r-, -w-, -l-/, and the vowel, which may be long (:), may be followed by a final consonant ($C_f$); if the syllable does contain a $C_f$, it may also (although quite rarely) end with suffixal -s. It should be noted that many daughter TB languages have much simpler canons, e.g. Lahu, where native syllables consist maximally of an initial consonant, a vowel, and a tone:

$$(C_i) \quad \overset{T}{V}$$

No attempt is made to reconstruct tones beyond the subgroup level, since it is far from proven that a single system of tonal contrasts can be set up for PTB.

Reconstructions at the subgroup level (i.e. "meso-reconstructions" like Proto-Lolo-Burmese (PLB), Proto-Northern-Naga (PNN), Proto-Tani) are listed as individual records along with their supporting forms.

A few notational conventions with respect to my PTB reconstructions should be mentioned:

- Variant reconstructed forms are indicated in several ways. They are usually written with the "allofam symbol" ⚔ between them, e.g.: *glim ⚔ *glip BROOD / INCUBATE; *s-riŋ ⚔ *s-r(y)aŋ LIVE / ALIVE / GREEN / RAW / GIVE BIRTH. Sometimes, however, I use an alternative notation with parentheses, e.g.: *(t)si COPULATE/LOVE; this is equivalent to *si ⚔ *tsi. Slashes may also be used, e.g. *p/buk ⚔ *p/bik BORN/GIVE BIRTH; this is equivalent to *puk ⚔ *buk ⚔ *pik ⚔ *bik. Finally, still another way of indicating proto-variation is by means of a "vertical reconstruction", e.g.:

$$* \overset{t}{\underset{d}{}} \text{uŋ NAVEL. This means the same as *tuŋ ⚔ *duŋ.}$$

- Parentheses are especially appropriate for those frequent cases where there is variation or indeterminacy between dental and palatal fricates; in fact that is one of my principal motivations for writing the palatal series as sequences of dental plus -y-, rather than writing them with *hačeks* or grave accents, e.g.:

---

[11] See *HPTB*, pp. 11-13.

| | | |
|---|---|---|
| **\*ts(y)uːŋ** | NAVEL / CENTER | ( = \*tsuːŋ ⪥ \*tšuːŋ) |
| **\*s(y)ok** | DRINK / SUCK / SMOKE | ( = \*sok ⪥ \*šok) |

- Etyma which show variation between initial \*p- and \*w- are reconstructed with the morphophonemic symbol **\*pʷ-,** which is roughly equivalent to treating the stop element as a prefix (**\*p-w-**).[12] Thus, a reconstruction like **\*pʷu** EGG / BIRD / ROUND OBJECT implies the existence of two sub-roots, **\*pu** and **\*wu,** whatever the ultimate explanation for this variation might prove to be.

- In the original version of Benedict 1972 (henceforth *STC*, ca. 1943), Benedict reconstructed two PTB high long vowels **\*-iy** and **\*-uw,** contrasting with the much less frequent short high vowels **\*-i** and **\*-u.** In the published version (1972) he modified the reconstruction of these long vowels to **\*-əy** and **\*-əw,** a practice which I follow myself. Occasionally, however, when the evidence does not permit us to decide between a long and a short high proto-vowel, it is convenient to revert to the earlier notation, with parentheses, e.g. **\*b-ni(y)** 'petticoat' (*STC* #476); **\*sru(w)** 'relative' (*STC* p. 108). There are no such cases among the etyma in this volume, however.

For more discussion of variational patterns in PTB, see "Regularity and variation", section 3.1 below.

Many of the PTB etyma in this volume are here reconstructed for the first time in print, and a good number of the TB/Chinese comparanda are likewise here proposed for the first time. If references are not explicitly given to *STC* and/or *HPTB* in the introductory note for an etymon it may be assumed that the reconstruction is new.[13]

## 2.3   Subgroup names

Tibeto-Burman is an extremely complex language family, with great internal typological diversity, comparable to that of modern Indo-European. This diversity is due largely to millennia of language contact, especially with the prestigious cultures of India and China,[14] but also with the other great language families of Southeast Asia (Austroasiatic, Tai-Kadai, Hmong-Mien), as well as with other TB groups. We are thus faced with what I have described as "an interlocking network of fuzzy-edged clots of languages, emitting waves of mutual influence from their various nuclear ganglia. A mess, in other words."[15] While subgrouping such a recalcitrant family is difficult, there is certainly no need to go so far as van Driem by denying that TB subgroups exist at all, or by claiming that even if they do exist, there are so many of them that there is no point in talking about them![16]

---

[12]For extended discussion of this issue, see Matisoff 2000a.

[13]References to HPTB as labelled with "**H:**" followed by a page number, e.g. **(H:165)** \*wa ⪥ \*wu BIRD / FOWL means that the root is discussed chiefly on page 165 of *HPTB*.

[14]I have called the Indian and Chinese areas of linguistic and cultural influence the *Indosphere* and the *Sinosphere*. See Matisoff 1973.

[15]Matisoff 1978 (*VSTB*), p. 2.

[16]See his review (2003) of G. Thurgood & R.J. LaPolla, eds. (2003), *The Sino-Tibetan Languages.*

In the published version of *STC* (1972), P. K. Benedict wisely refrained from offering a pseudo-precise family-tree model of the higher-order taxonomic relationships in TB, presenting instead a schematic chart where Kachin ( = Jingpho) was conceived as the center of geographical and linguistic diversity in the family. See Fig. 1.

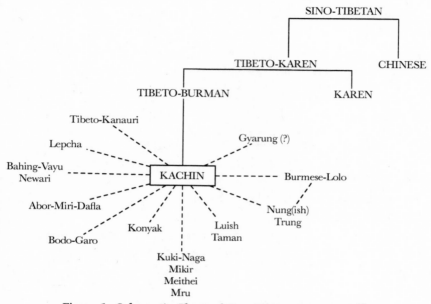

*Figure 1. Schematic Chart of Sino-Tibetan Languages*[17]

A simpler scheme represents the heuristic model now used at STEDT. See Fig. 2.

This diagram differs from *STC* in several respects:[18]

- Karenic is no longer regarded as having a special status, but is now considered to be a subgroup of TB proper.

- Baic, hardly mentioned (under the name "Minchia") in *STC*, but later hypothesized by Benedict to belong with Chinese in the "Sinitic" branch of Sino-Tibetan, is now also treated as just another subgroup of TB, though one under particularly heavy Chinese contact influence. Both Karenic and Baic have SVO word order, unlike the rest of the TB family.

- The highly ramified Kuki-Chin and Naga groups have provisionally been amalgamated with Bodo-Garo ( = Barish) and Abor-Miri-Dafla ( = Mirish) into a supergroup called by the purely geographical name of *Kamarupan*, from the old Sanskrit name for Assam.

- The important Tangut-Qiang languages (deemed to include rGyalrong [ = Gyarung = Jiarong] and the extinct Xixia [ = Tangut]) were hardly known to Western

---

[17]Reproduced from *STC*, p. 6; *VSTB*, p. 3; *HPTB*, p. 4.
[18]See *HPTB*, pp. 5-6.

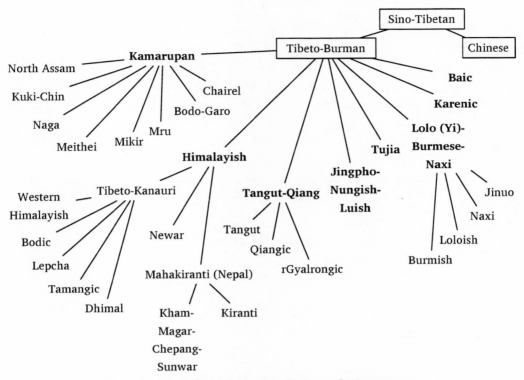

*Figure 2. Simplified STEDT Family Tree of ST Languages*

scholars at the time *STC* was written (ca. 1942-3) or published (1972). It seems doubtful that a special relationship exists between Qiangic and Jingpho, or between Qiangic and Lolo-Burmese, as some Chinese scholars maintain.[19]

• The Nungish and Luish languages are grouped with Jingpho (=Kachin). Jingpho is also recognized to have a special contact relationship with the Northern Naga (=Konyak) group.[20]

• The somewhat idiosyncratic Mikir, Meithei (=Manipuri), and Mru languages are included under Kamarupan.

[19]A supergroup called "Rung" was proposed by Thurgood (1984), into which he placed, among others, some Qiangic languages, Nungish, and Lepcha. This grouping was based partly on shared "protomorphosyntax", and partly on nomenclature, including the *-rong* of *rGyalrong*, the Nungish language *Rawang*, and the Lepcha autonym *Rong*.

[20]The *Linguistic Survey of India* (Grierson and Konow, 1903-28) recognized a "Bodo-Naga-Kachin" group, an idea revived by Burling (1983), whose "Sal" supergroup comprises Bodo-Garo (Barish), Northern Naga (Konyak), and Jingpho (=Kachin). Burling's name for this grouping is derived from the etymon ***sal** 'sun' (ult. < PTB ***tsyar** 'sunshine'), one of a number of roots which is attested chiefly in these languages. See *HPTB*:393-4.

- The Himalayish ( = Himalayan) group is considered to include Bodic (i.e. Tibetanoid) languages, as well as Kanauri-Manchad, Tamang-Gurung-Thakali, Kiranti ( = Rai), Lepcha, and Newar.

- The relatively well-studied Lolo-Burmese group ( = *STC*'s "Burmese-Lolo") is deemed to include the aberrant Jinuo language of Xishuangbanna, Yunnan.[21] The Naxi/Moso language is quite close to LB, but stands somewhat outside the core of the family.[22]

- The mysterious Tujia language of Hunan and Hubei (not mentioned in *STC*) has so far not been assigned to a subgroup.

Still, a schema like Fig. 2 hardly does justice to the complexity of the problem of subgrouping the TB languages. In particular, the "Kamarupan" and "Himalayish" groupings are based more on geographical convenience than on strong constellations of similar characteristics.[23] More detailed subgroupings are certainly possible, as in STEDT Monograph #2,[24] which makes distinctions like the following:

*Kamarupan*
- Abor-Miri-Dafla ( = Mirish)[25]
- Kuki-Chin
- Naga
  · Konyak ( = Northern Naga)
  · Angamoid
  · Central
  · Eastern
  · Southern
  · Southwestern
- Meithei
- Mikir
- Mru
- Bodo-Garo ( = Barish)
- Chairel

---

[21]Chinese scholars have further divided the Loloish languages of China into six nuclei, although no attempt is made in this volume to distinguish them. In a recent talk (Matisoff 2007b) I examined Loloish tonal developments and the fate of the PLB rhyme *-a in terms of this six-way grouping, with inconclusive results.

[22]I have grouped Naxi with Lolo-Burmese proper in a supergroup called "Burmo-Naxi-Lolo" (Matisoff 1991c). On the basis of some shared tonal developments, I have also entertained the idea of a special relationship between Lolo-Burmese and Jingpho, to which I assigned the jocular designation *Jiburish* ( < **Ji**-(ngpho) + -**bur**(mish) + (Lolo)**ish**). See Matisoff 1974, 1991c.

[23]Several scholars have objected to the term Kamarupan, largely on the grounds that it has distinctly Indo-Aryan connotations, which might irritate TB groups. See, e.g. R. Burling, "On *Kamarupan*" (1999; *LTBA* 22.2:169-71), and the reply by Matisoff, "In defense of *Kamarupan*" (1999; *LTBA* 22.2:173-82). The only alternative term suggested so far to refer to these geographically contiguous languages collectively is the verbose "TB languages of Northeast India and adjacent areas".

[24]J. Namkung, ed. (1996), *Phonological Inventories of Tibeto-Burman Languages*, pp. 455-457.

[25]A well-defined subgroup of AMD has been dubbed *Tani* by J. Sun (1993).

*Himalayish*
- Western (Bunan, Kanauri, Manchad/Pattani)
- Bodic (Tibetanoid)
- Lepcha
- Tamangic (incl. Chantyal, Gurung, Tamang, Thakali, Manang, Narphu)
- Dhimalish
- Newar
- Central Nepal Group (Kham, Magar, Chepang, Sunwar)
- Kiranti ( = Rai), including Bahing and Hayu

## 2.4 Language names

Tibeto-Burman languages are notorious for the multiplicity of names by which they are referred to. These may include the name they use for themselves (autonym), as opposed to the name(s) other groups use for them (exonyms). Languages are frequently referred to by the principal town in which they are spoken (loconyms). Some exonyms are now felt to be pejorative, and have been abandoned, thus acquiring the status of "paleonyms" for which "neonyms" have been substituted.[26] A certain Angamoid Naga group call themselves and their language *Memi* (autonym), and their chief village they call *Sopvoma*; but other groups use *Mao* for this village or its people (exonym), and either *Mao* or *Sopvoma* (exonymic loconym) for their language. There is an older term *Imemai* (probably an autonymic paleonym) which refers to the same language and people.

Some names are used in both a broader and a narrower sense, both for a specific language and for a group of languages that share a close contact relationship. The Maru, Atsi, and Lashi[27] (who speak Burmish languages) consider themselves to be "Kachin" in the broad sense, and in this the Jingpho themselves seem to agree, even though the Jingpho language belongs to a different TB subgroup.

In recent years cultural sensitivities have forced the abandonment of many language names that had been well established in the academic literature. The important Central Chin language that used to be called *Lushai* (a name which is said to mean "long-headed") should now properly be called *Mizo*. A Karenic group that used to be known by the Burmese exonym *Taungthu* (lit. "mountain folk") now prefers to be referred to by their autonym *Pa-o*. The Southern Loloish people formerly known by the Tai exonym *Phunoi* (lit. "little people") should now be called by their autonym *Coong*. Speakers of several TB languages of Nepal now object to the Indianized versions of their names with the Indo-Aryan **-i** suffix (e.g. *Newari, Magari, Sunwari*), and prefer to omit the suf-

---

[26]The terminology for the various types of TB language names was developed in Matisoff 1986a: "The languages and dialects of Tibeto-Burman: an alphabetic/genetic listing, with some prefatory remarks on ethnonymic and glossonymic complications." In John McCoy and Timothy Light, eds., *Contributions to Sino-Tibetan Studies*, pp. 1-75. This article was later (1996) expanded into a STEDT Monograph, with the assistance of J.B. Lowe and S. P. Baron.

[27]Referred to as Langsu, Zaiwa, and Leqi in Chinese sources.

fix, even though this can lead to ambiguity between the names of the people and their languages (*Newar, Magar, Sunwar*). The psychological dimensions of these issues are often as fascinating as they are paradoxical. Chinese linguists now feel that the term *Lolo(ish)*, widely used outside of China, is offensive, and insist that the proper respectful term is *Yi*, written with the character 彞 'type of sacrificial wine vessel'. Yet this is only a recent substitution for the homophonous character 夷 'barbarian; savage group on the fringes of the Chinese empire'.

Naturally enough, what is true for the names of individual languages is also true for the names of subgroups. Some of this nomenclatural variation goes back to differences between Benedict and his former collaborator and supervisor Robert Shafer,[28] e.g. Shafer's *Barish* and *Mirish* are the same as Benedict's *Bodo-Garo* and *Abor-Miri-Dafla*, respectively. An important group of at least a dozen TB languages spoken in East Nepal is known either as *Kiranti* or *Rai*.[29] An extreme example of proliferation is furnished by the well-established and non-controversial group I call Lolo-Burmese, which has also been referred to as Burmese-Lolo, Yi-Burmese, Burmese-Yi, Burmese-Yipho, Yipho-Burmese, Yi-Myanmar, Myanmar-Yipho, etc.—and even Myanmar-Ngwi!

Bearing all these complicating factors in mind, an attempt has been made in this volume to use maximally clear and consistent designations for the TB languages and subgroups.

## 2.5   Supporting forms in the individual languages

The forms which support the reconstructions are cited according to the notation of the particular source. Although this policy of "following copy" often leads to redundancy (see 2.7 below), since one and the same form in a given language may be transcribed in a variety of different ways,[30] it seems preferable to a policy of "normalization", which might have the effect of losing some phonetic detail that is captured in one source but not in another.

---

[28]Shafer and Benedict collaborated on the Depression-era *Sino-Tibetan Linguistics* project at Berkeley (1939-40), which aimed to assemble all data then available on TB languages. The direct fruits of this project were Shafer's *Introduction to Sino-Tibetan* (1967-73), 5 vols. (Wiesbaden: Otto Harrassowitz) and the MS of Benedict's *STC*. Benedict produced (1975) an entertaining account of this seminal project in LTBA 2.1:81-92: "Where it all began: memories of Robert Shafer and the *Sino-Tibetan Linguistics* project, Berkeley (1939-40)."

[29]According to K. P. Malla (p.c. 2008), "*Kirāt* is a loose label in Old Indo-Aryan for the cave-dweller, attested in late Vedic texts as well as in the *Mahābhārata*." Rai is "a Nepali word, linked to IA *raaya* 'lord', given to the Khambu chiefs by the Gorkhali rulers in the late 18th century."

[30]Cf. the multiple transcriptions of the Written Burmese form for BREAST/MILK under *s-nəw, #53 below: **no**[1] (ZMYYC:281.39); **nuí** (AW-TBT:327; *STC*:419); **núi** (WSC-SH:48); **nui'** (JAM-Ety; GEM-CNL; PKB-WBRD); **nui.** (GEM-CNL); **nuiw'** (GHL-PPB). For these source abbreviations, see the *Appendix*. Similarly, cf. the many slightly different forms from the Bodic and Tamangic groups that reflect the etymon *tsaŋ NEST/WOMB/PLACENTA (#103 below).

---

## 2.6 Glosses of the supporting forms

In almost all cases, the gloss given in each particular source is preserved, unless it is so awkward or misleading as to require emendation. Even if the glosses in consecutive records are identical, the gloss is repeated for each individual record, instead of using a symbol like the "ditto-mark".

If a gloss is too long to fit onto a single line, it is "wrapped" so that the additional lines are indented under the first one.

## 2.7 Source abbreviations

Each supporting form is ascribed to a particular source. Many forms are cited in more than one source in our database. If the form is not identical in different sources, we include them all. This is especially useful in cases where one or more of the sources might not be totally accurate phonemically, or where subphonemic phonetic detail is provided. When the forms in different sources are identical, the form only appears once, but there are multiple source abbreviations, separated by commas. Forms from well-studied languages (e.g. Written Tibetan, Written Burmese, Jingpho) are likely to appear in several sources used by STEDT.

The STEDT database contains forms from sources of many different kinds, including:

- printed books, monographs, articles, especially dictionaries and grammars of individual languages;
- synonym lists (i.e. groups of forms from different languages with the same meaning, but with no reconstructions provided), e.g. Luce 1986 (PPPB); Sun Hongkai et al. 1991 (ZMYYC); Dai Qingxia, Huang Bufan et al. 1992 (TBL);
- semantically based questionnaires solicited by STEDT from fieldworkers working on particular languages;
- monographs and treatises of an etymological nature, including works which provide reconstructions at the subgroup level, e.g.:

  Proto-Bodo: Burling 1959
  Proto-Karenic: Haudricourt 1942-45/1975, Jones 1961, Burling 1969,
  Benedict 1972 (*STC*), Solnit, in prep.
  Proto-Kiranti: Michailovsky 1991
  Proto-Kuki-Chin: VanBik 2003
  Proto-Lolo-Burmese: Burling 1968, Matisoff 1969/1972, Bradley 1979
  Proto-Northern-Naga: French 1983
  Proto-Tamangic: Mazaudon 1978
  Proto-Tani: Sun Tianshin 1993

The abbreviations used in these source attributions are in general quite transparent,[31]

---

[31] For a complete list of the source abbreviations that appear in this volume, see the *Appendix*.

e.g.:

| | |
|---|---|
| CK-YiQ | Chen Kang, "Yi Questionnaire" |
| JZ-Zaiwa | Xu Xijian, *Outline Grammar (Jiǎnzhì) of Zaiwa* |
| AW-TBT | A. Weidert, *Tibeto-Burman Tonology* |
| GHL-PPB | G. H. Luce, *Phases of Pre-Pagán Burma* |
| JAM:MLBM | J. A. Matisoff, "Mpi and Lolo-Burmese microlinguistics" |
| EJAH:BKD | E. J. A. Henderson, *Bwo Karen Dictionary* |

The abbreviation "JAM-Ety" refers to my own etymological notes compiled in the pre-STEDT era, derived especially from older, classic sources. These specific sources can easily be tracked down from the *Bibliography*.

## 2.8   Chinese comparanda

After the evidence for a TB etymon is presented, one or more Chinese comparanda are often suggested in the interests of pushing the reconstruction further back to the Proto-Sino-Tibetan stage. For all of these comparanda Zev J. Handel has kindly provided comparisons of the Old Chinese reconstructions cited in Karlgren's (1957) system with those of Li Fang-kuei (1971, 1976, 1980) and William Baxter (1992),[32] evaluating the plausibility of the putative TB/Chinese comparison according to each of these systems.[33] Handel's invaluable contributions are marked with his initials "ZJH". Comparisons between TB and OC etyma that are not explicitly ascribed to a particular scholar are original with me, as far as I know.

## 2.9   Notes

Footnotes may appear at virtually any point in the text. They may refer to an entire chapter, to a semantic diagram, to an etymon as a whole, to a specific supporting form, or to a Chinese comparandum.

# 3   Theoretical issues

Implicit in the reconstructions of this volume are my positions on certain theoretical issues.

---

[32]Handel also contributed a detailed comparison of these systems in his *A Concise Introduction to Old Chinese Phonology*, which appeared as Appendix A to *HPTB*, pp. 543-74.

[33]Handel also frequently refers to several other reconstructive systems for OC that are to be found in the literature, e.g. those of W. South Coblin (1986), Axel Schuessler (1987), Laurent Sagart (1999), Gong Hwang-cherng (1990, 1994, 1995, 1997, 2000), and Pan Wuyun (2000).

## 3.1 Regularity and variation

It must be admitted that a lot of guesswork is involved in etymologizing material from hundreds of languages and dialects at once, without having established the "sound laws" in advance. The problems are especially acute when comparing phonologically depleted languages with those having richer syllable canons. When there is a partial phonological similarity between distinct etyma with the same meaning (e.g. *sem and *sak 'mind / breath'; *muːr and *muk 'mouth'; *s-maːy and *s-mel 'face'; *s-r(y)ik and *s(y)ar 'louse'), it is not easy to decide by simple inspection to which etymon we should assign a phonologically slight form in a daughter language (e.g. sɒ 'mind', mɔ 'mouth', hmɛ 'face').

There is a dialectical relationship between synchronic data and sound laws. The "laws" are derived by inference from the data in the first place, but once proto-forms are reconstructed, they can be used to guide us in our hunt for cognates in languages not yet examined (even if they have undergone semantic change). Almost every TB/ST etymology so far proposed presents problems and complications—irregularities—in some language or other, which is par for the course even in the much better known Indo-European family. Part of our task is to indicate where the exceptions, problems, and irregularities lie, in the hope that they can ultimately be explained.[34] The concept of "regularity" itself is by no means simple, nor does it mean the same thing to different scholars.[35]

Those who lack what I have called "Proto-Sprachgefühl"[36] can produce abstract, formulaic reconstructions bristling with strange symbols but devoid of any phonetic or typological plausibility.[37] Given sufficient semantic latitude and proto-forms that are complex enough, one can formulate "sound laws" in such a way that they appear completely regular and exceptionless. At an extreme level we find "megalocomparative" proposals of genetic relationship that turn received notions upside down (e.g. Sino-Mayan, Sino-Caucasian, Sino-Austronesian, Japanese-Dravidian), and which can lead the unwary down fruitless paths, obscuring the differences among cognates, borrowings, and chance resemblances.[38] Various tricks of analysis that I have lumped under the rubric of "proto-form stuffing" can help the Nostraticist or Sino-Mayanist convince

---

[34]The computer can be very useful in deciding between alternative etymologies. Once "sound-laws" have been formulated, computer checking can test whether a particular reconstruction follows the laws, identifying inconsistencies in the reflexes of the same proto-element in a given language. Such a methodology has been applied to the Tamangic languages, using the "reconstruction engine" developed by J.B. Lowe at STEDT in collaboration with Martine Mazaudon and Boyd Michailovsky during their sojourns at Berkeley as visiting scholars (1987-89, 1990-91).

[35]See Matisoff 1992 ("Following the marrow") and 1994a ("Regularity and variation").

[36]See Matisoff 1982.

[37]Recent examples of this genre include Sedláček 1970; Weidert 1975, 1979, 1981, 1987; Peiros & Starostin 1996; Sagart 2007.

[38]See Matisoff 1990a ("On megalocomparison"). Megalocomparison has the apparent advantage of non-falsifiability, since, as Haudricourt has observed, one can never prove that any two languages are not related. But non-falsifiable hypotheses are not scientific. When presented with alternative non-falsifiable proposals it is impossible to choose among them.

himself that his fantastical comparisons are "perfectly regular". Paradigmatically, one can multiply the number of proto-phonemes. If you reconstruct 35 proto-vowels, any anomalous vowel correspondence can be regarded as "regularly reflecting" a separate proto-vowel. Syntagmatically, if you reconstruct etyma like *mrgsla, and the monstrous proto-cluster *mrgsl- occurs only in a single etymon, any set of reflexes in the daughter languages can be said to be "regular".[39]

The time-depth of PST is perhaps 6000 years B.P., about at the limits of the comparative method. We can hardly afford to insist on "perfect regularity" of correspondence among our putative cognates. But instead of resorting to "proto-form stuffing" to try to explain away problems, what is needed is an explicit theory of variational phenomena. TB and ST etyma, like those of other language families, are not independent isolated entities, but stand in complex phonosemantic relationships with each other. It has been recognized for a long time that words in Chinese and TB languages participate in morphophonemic groups of partially resemblant forms that have been called "word families".[40] In Matisoff 1978 (*VSTB*) I developed the notion of the *allofam*, or individual member of a word-family, and advocated the formulation of "allofamic reconstructions" that accommodated all the well-attested variants deemed to descend from the same proto-word-family. The symbol ⋊ was introduced to symbolize an allofamic relationship between variant forms, i.e., "A ⋊ B" means that "A and B are synchronic allofams of each other", while "*A ⋊ *B" means that there is a word-family relationship between A and B at the proto-level.[41]

Needless to say, extreme care must be used in claiming that different forms are variants of the same etymon. Allofamic theory must be applied in a controlled and constrained way.[42] Not everything may be said to vary with everything else! It is sometimes quite difficult to decide whether partially resemblant forms represent separate etyma or whether they are merely allofams of the same word-family. Not only must each proto-allofam fit our canonic template (above 2.2), but the type of variation posited must be abundantly replicated in other examples. This volume does not attempt to conceal such uncertainties, but frequently entertains the possibility that etyma set up as independent might actually be co-allofams, or *vice versa*.

The best attested patterns of variation in ST/TB are all exemplified in the etymologies of this volume. They include the following:

---

[39]This is actually the proto-form offered in Weidert 1981:25 for an etymon meaning 'spirit, ghost, shadow' (reconstructed as *m-hla in *STC* #475). As I have observed (Matisoff 1982:22), "It is always possible and sometimes necessary to invent an *ad hoc* explanation for an anomalous case. It is even true that some such *ad hoc* 'solutions' are more plausible than others. The only harm is in deluding oneself that an explanation which covers only a single case establishes a 'regularity'."

[40]See the pioneering study of Karlgren (1933), "Word families in Chinese".

[41]This symbol ⋊, a combination of > 'goes to' and < 'comes from', is meant to suggest that neither variant is necessarily deemed to have temporal priority, but that both must be set up to account for attested forms.

[42]See the extended discussion in Ch. XII of *HPTB* (pp. 491-534), "Allofamic variation in rhymes".

(a) Voicing vs. voicelessness of the initial consonant:[43]

    *gop ≍ *kop   (11a)   HATCH/INCUBATE/COVER
    *prat ≍ *brat   (75)    BREAK/WEAN
    *tuŋ ≍ *duŋ   (44a)   NAVEL

(b) Variation between fricative and affricate:

    *(t)sum         (45)    NAVEL
    *(t)sip ≍ *(t)sup   (107)   NEST/WOMB/SCROTUM[44]

(c) Presence vs. absence of medial -y-

    *b(y)at   (81)    VAGINA
    *l(y)ap   (151)   COPULATE

A special case of (c) is the alternation between dental and palatal fricatives and affricates:

    *s(y)ok    (61)    DRINK/SUCK/SMOKE
    *dz(y)əw   (56)    BREAST/MILK
    *ts(y)uːŋ   (44b)  NAVEL

(d) Variation between labial stop and labial semivowel:

    *pu ≍ *wu    (1a, 1b)    EGG
    *pam ≍ *wam   (98a, 98b)  WOMB/PLACENTA/NEST

(e) Variation between different prefixes:

    *r-ga ≍ *N-ga ≍ *d-ga ≍ *s-ga   (141)   COPULATE/LOVE/WANT
    *n-tow ≍ *s-tow            (3)     EGG
    *m-ŋal ≍ *l-ŋal          (100)   WOMB/PLACENTA

(f) Variation between -u- and -i- in closed syllables:

    *dul ≍ *dil       (2b)   EGG/TESTICLE
    *m-dzup ≍ *m-dzip  (55)   SUCK/SUCKLE/MILK/KISS
    *tsyur ≍ *tsyir    (66)   MILK/SQUEEZE/WRING

(g) Variation between medial -ya- and -i-:

    *s-riŋ ≍ *s-ryaŋ  (39)   LIVE/ALIVE/GREEN/RAW/GIVE BIRTH
    *s-nik ≍ *s-nyak   (124)  PENIS/COPULATE
    *b-rim ≍ *b-ryam  (46)   NAVEL/UMBILICAL CORD

(h) Alternation between medial -wa- and -u-:

    *tsyul ≍ *tsywal  (105)  WOMB/PLACENTA

---

[43]Nothing is more common in TB word families than variation of voicing in initial consonants, largely due to the pervasive influence of prefixes on the manner of the initial. This is in sharp contrast to the situation in Indo-European, where such variation in manner is quite rare, and is usually not tolerated in PIE reconstructions.
[44]This etymon also illustrates (f), below.

(i) Alternation between final homorganic stops and nasals:

| | | |
|---|---|---|
| *glim ⋊ *glip | (15) | BROOD/INCUBATE EGGS |
| *s-nəwn ⋊ *s-nəwt | (53c) | BREAST/MILK/SUCK |
| *tsiŋ ⋊ *tsik | (78) | VAGINA |

As some of the above examples illustrate, some roots show more than one type of variation. When a posited allofamic reconstruction (e.g. *sir ⋊ *sit (6) EGG) does not fall into a well-attested variational category, I comment on it. Handel makes similar remarks with respect to some of my TB comparisons with OC.

Occasionally, when the phonosemantic variation among the allofams is considerable, and when each variant is amply attested, I split up the presentation of the data into subroots that are designated by the same number but with different lower case letters, e.g.: *p-wu (1) EGG is split into *wu (1a) and *pu (1b); *m/s-la(:)y ⋊ *s-tay (40) NAVEL/CENTER/SELF is split into *m/s-la(:)y (40a) and *s-tay (40b); *m-ley ⋊ *m-li ⋊ *m-ney (114) PENIS is broken down into *m-ley ⋊ *m-li (114a) and *m-ney (114b).

As I put it 35 years ago, "We must steer an Aristotelian middle path between a dangerous speculativism and a stodgy insensitivity to the workings of variational phenomena in language history."[45]


## 3.2 Etymological accuracy and rectification of possible errors

There are all too many ways in which one can make etymological mistakes, and I have been guilty of all of them at one time or another.[46] A rough taxonomy of errors would have to include the following:

- Treating a loanword as native

  I was at first delighted when I ran across the Jingpho form wéʔ-wū 'screw', since its first syllable looked like an excellent match with Lahu ɔ̀-vὲʔ 'id.', for which I then had no etymology. Could this be a precious example of the rare PTB rhyme *-ek? But the screw is hardly an artifact of any great antiquity, and it would be *prima facie* implausible that a root with such a meaning would have existed in PTB. The truth quickly became apparent. The modern Burmese form for 'screw', wéʔ-ʔu (WB wak-ʔu), the obvious source from which both Jingpho and Lahu borrowed these words, means literally "pig-intestine". The semantic association is the corkscrew-like appearance of a pig's small intestine. This etymology is also interesting from the viewpoint of distinguishing native vs. borrowed co-allofams. The usual, native words for 'pig' in Jingpho and Lahu are wàʔ and vàʔ, respectively; but the doublets borrowed from Burmese have front vowels, as in spoken Burmese. Unless a native speaker of Jingpho knows Burmese, s/he is unlikely to realize that the first syllable of wéʔ-wū means 'pig', especially since this syllable is in the high-stopped tone, while 'pig' is low-stopped. The native Lahu speaker

---

[45] Matisoff 1972b ("Tangkhul Naga and comparative TB"), p. 282.
[46] The discussion in this section is adapted from *HPTB*, pp. 538-40.

is even less likely to recognize the source of ɔ̀-vɛ̀ʔ, since the morpheme for 'intestine' has been completely dropped from the original Burmese compound, rather like the way our word *camera* (< Lat. 'room; chamber; vaulted enclosure') is a shortening of the old compound *camera obscura* ("dark chamber").[47]

- Combining reflexes of unrelated roots

When two forms bearing a semantic resemblance in a phonologically depleted language differ only in tone, it is tempting to try to relate them. I once entertained the possibility that such pairs of Lahu forms as **phu** 'silver, money' / **phû** 'price, cost' and **mu** 'high, tall' / **mû** 'sky' were co-allofams, though they can easily be shown to descend from quite separate etyma: **phu** < PTB \*plu (*STC* p. 89) / **phû** < PTB \*pəw (*STC* #41); **mu** < PTB \*mraŋ (*STC* p. 43) / **mû** < PTB \*r-məw (*STC* #488).[48]

- Failure to recognize that separately reconstructed etyma are really co-allofams

An opposite type of error is to overlook the etymological identity between sets of forms, assigning them to separate etyma when they are really co-allofams. Thus *STC* sets up two independent PTB roots, both with the shape \*dyam, one meaning 'full; fill' (*STC* #226) and the other glossed as 'straight' (*STC* #227). Yet it can be shown that the latter root also means 'flat', and that all reflexes of #226 and #227 may be subsumed under a single etymon, with the underlying idea being "perfection in a certain dimension".[49]

Similarly, I was slow to recognize that two roots I had set up separately, PLB \*dzay[2] 'cattle; domestic animal' (Matisoff 1985a #129) and Kamarupan \*tsaːy 'elephant; cattle' (#143) are really one and the same.[50]

- Double-dipping

This embarrassing situation occurs when an author inadvertently assigns the same form in a daughter language to two different etyma, perhaps within the pages of the same book, but more likely in separate articles. At different times I have compared Chinese **chún** 唇 'lip' (OC d̑i̯wən) to both PTB \*dyal and \*m-ts(y)ul, finally deciding in favor of the latter.[51] It is of course perfectly legitimate to change one's mind, as long as one explains why. The best course is to present the alternative etymologies together, inviting the reader to choose between them.

- Misanalyses of compounds

A vast number of words in TB languages are di- or tri-syllabic compounds, a fact

---

[47]There is a difference in detail between the two cases, however: the deleted 'intestine' is the head of the compound "pig-intestine", but the deleted *obscura* is the modifier in the collocation "dark-chamber".
[48]See Matisoff 1973b (*GL*:29); such speculations were debunked in the 2nd Printing (1982) of *GL*, p. 675.
[49]See Matisoff 1988b:4-9.
[50]I have argued that a third root set up in Matisoff 1985a (*GSTC* #106), \*(t)saːy ≍ \*(d)zaːy 'temperament / aptitude /talent', is also related, the common notion being 'property (either material or intellectual)'. See Matisoff 1985a:44-45; 1988b:10-13.
[51]See *HPTB* 9.2.1, 9.22(4), 9.2.4.

which greatly complicates the task of etymologization. Many traps lie in wait for the analyst, leading to potential errors of several kinds.

(a) Wrong segmentation

This can happen when a form in an inadequately transcribed source is not syllabified. The Pochury and Sangtam forms for 'star', transcribed as **awutsi** and **chinghi**, respectively, in the little glossaries compiled by the *Nagaland Bhasha Parishad*,[52] should be segmented as **a-wu-tsi** and **ching-hi**, and not as **a-wut-si** and **chi-nghi**, as I imprudently did in Matisoff 1980:21.

(b) Misunderstanding the meaning of a constituent

A special case of this problem is mistaking an affix for a root, especially likely to occur when no grammatical description exists for a language. Several Naga languages have dissyllabic forms for 'moon' with similar final syllables, e.g. Chang **litnyu**, Konyak **linnyu**, Phom **linnyü**, Sangtam **chonu**, Liangmai **chahiu**. Yet these final elements do not constitute a new root meaning 'moon', as I had originally guessed; rather they represent an abstract formative, ultimately grammaticalized from a root ***n(y)u** 'mother', that occurs in nouns from all sorts of semantic fields (e.g. Chang **chinyu** 'center', **henyu** 'ladder', **lamnyu** 'road', **pinyu** 'snake').[53]

(c) Choosing the wrong syllable of a compound for an etymology

This can happen when two different syllables of a compound are phonologically similar, especially if one is dealing with a poorly known language with depleted final consonants, e.g. forms like Guiqiong Ganzi t∫hə$^{55}$sã$^{55}$ and Ersu ʂ$^{55}$ji$^{55}$ 'otter'. Which syllables are to be ascribed to PTB ***sram**?

## 3.3 Looking toward the future of ST/TB studies

Although I feel that we are entering a new era of etymological responsibility in TB/ST studies—the bar has been raised, as it were—I am not suggesting that we turn our field into a "tough neighborhood" like that of the Indo-Europeanists. In particular I hope we can avoid the *"Gotcha!"* attitude,[54] whereby if a single error, real or fancied, is found in an article or book, the whole work is impugned. This attitude is encapsulated in the dreadful maxim *Falsum in uno, falsum in omnibus.*[55] Historical linguists cannot afford to be too thin-skinned, as long as criticism is fair, constructive, and proportionate. As I

---

[52]Kumar et al., *Hindi Pochury English Dictionary* (1972); *Hindi Sangtam English Dictionary* (1973). Kohima: Linguistic Circle of Nagaland.

[53]See Matisoff 1980 ("Stars, moon, spirits"), p. 35; for the suffixal use of morphemes meaning 'mother', see Matisoff 1991b ("The mother of all morphemes").

[54]Non-American readers might need a word of explanation here. "Gotcha!" is an attempt to render the colloquial pronunciation of "(I've) got you (now)!", a triumphant phrase used by someone who feels he has won an argument.

[55]"If one thing is wrong, it's all wrong."

have said in print, "I ask nothing better than to be corrected."[56] Or again, "We can take comfort from our mistakes. Reconstruction of a proto-lexicon is a piecemeal process. It is hardly surprising that we stumble along from one half-truth to another, as we try to trace the [phonological and] semantic interconnections among our reconstructed etyma. We should not be discouraged if we barge off down blind alleys occasionally, or if the solution to one problem raises as many questions as it answers."[57] After all, a computerized etymological enterprise by its very nature is eminently revisable. The reconstructive process by its very nature is provisional and open-ended. Our STEDT etymologies undergo a constant process of "rectification", and may be roughly divided into three types: (a) those to be accepted as is; (b) those to be accepted with modifications; (c) those to be rejected. As with all scientific hypotheses, our reconstructions are falsifiable in the light of new data or better analyses.

We still have a long way to go before comparative/historical TB studies are as advanced as they deserve to be. Despite the quickening pace of research, our knowledge of the various branches of this multifarious family remains highly uneven. With a few important exceptions mentioned above, reliable reconstructions at the subgroup level are not yet available. Many more roots remain to be reconstructed at all taxonomic levels of the family. Much remains to be done on the Chinese side as well, and we seem destined for a period of flux until the dust settles and competing reconstructions of OC have sorted themselves out.

Nevertheless, it is hard not to be optimistic about the future of TB/ST linguistics, as fieldwork opportunities increase and new generations of talented researchers enter the discipline. Eventually it seems inevitable that scholars throughout the world will share their information more and more, granting mutual access to their databases for the common good. On the other hand, too many TB languages are endangered, and may well disappear before they have been adequately recorded. In any case, "the reconstruction of PTB is a noble enterprise, where a spirit of competitive territoriality is out of place. We should pool our knowledge and encourage each other to venture outside of our specialized niches, so that we begin to appreciate the full range of TB languages...."[58]

---

[56]Matisoff 1985b:422 ("Out on a limb").

[57]Matisoff 1988a:13.

[58]Matisoff 1982:41. There is nothing more satisfying than to have inadequate data on a language of which one has no firsthand knowledge corrected by a specialist in that language. The STEDT project has recently (summer of 2007) benefited tremendously from the kindness of K.P. Malla, who edited all the Newar(i) forms in our database, identifying loanwords, putting verbs into their proper citation forms, and correcting the transcription of vowels and consonants used in our previous sources.

# I. Egg

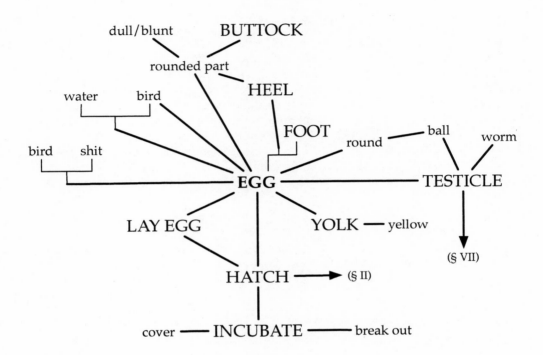

An important associated concept is BIRD, with several distinct roots appearing in compounds for EGG, including **(H:165)** \***wa** ⋉ \***wu** BIRD / FOWL, **(H:386)** \***haːr** BIRD / CHICKEN, **(H:171)** \***bya** ⋉ \***bra** BIRD, **(H:226-7)** \***daw** BIRD, \***s-ŋak** BIRD. It is sometimes hard to distinguish reflexes of \***wa** and \***haːr**; cf. the first syllable in Wancho **ao-ti**, below. Similarly, it is sometimes hard to distinguish reflexes of \***wa** and \***bya**; cf. the first syllable in Bahing **ʔba-di**.

(1)                              \***pʷu**                    **EGG / BIRD / ROUND OBJECT**

This is one of over 30 TB etyma showing interchange between \***p-** and \***w-**, including such important roots as AXE, BAMBOO, BELLY, MAN/HUSBAND, PIG, etc. In this volume, see also **(98)** \***pʷam** WOMB / PLACENTA / NEST / BELLY. These are reconstructed with \***pw-** clusters in the revised version of *STC* (e.g. \***pak** = \***pwak**; see n. 78, pp. 23-4). I originally preferred to treat the stop component as prefixal (e.g. \***p-wak**), but later abandoned this approach in favor of an "extrusional" interpretation, where the [-w-] is considered to be a mere phonetic perseveration of the preceding stop, e.g. *p$^w$ak (see Matisoff 2000a). This extrusion is especially common before the vowel [-a-], but also, as in EGG, occasionally occurs before [-u-]. See also *HPTB*:61-62.

In the following sections, the reflexes of this etymon are presented separately, according to whether they derive from the variant with semivowel (*wu) or stop (*pu) initial.

## (1a)    *wu    EGG / BIRD

This etymon is closely related to one for BIRD, set up as **(H:165) *wa ≍ *wu** BIRD / FOWL. The original version of *STC* sets up *wa for BIRD (*STC* #99), but this is revised to ***(b)wa** (largely because of Bahing **ba** 'fowl') in the indexes (pp. 209, 211). In some languages (e.g. Jingpho and Kadu) a reflex of **(1a) *wu** EGG / BIRD occurs as a prefix in bird-names (**ù-**). Marrison (p. 459) sets up three Proto-Northern Naga allofams for BIRD: ***C-waw**, ***ua**, and ***wa**. It is sometimes difficult to distinguish the reflexes of *wa and *wu. For example, in the following Kamarupan forms, the italicized syllables are to be derived from *wa ≍ *wu BIRD, with another constituent conveying the meaning EGG: Chang **a***okiak*, Chokri **thü***vu*zü, Konyak **a***okiak*, Konyak (Tamlu) *ʌu*ji, Ntenyi **a***wüü*-atsü, Sema **a***u*khu, Tangsa ¹*vu*¹ʈʌi, Tangsa (Moshang) **wu** di, Wancho **a***o*-ti/*ɔ*-ti, Yacham-Tengsa **u**-tü.

These roots have a wide distribution in TB. In Lolo-Burmese (including Jinuo), the root *wu is widely attested with the predominant meanings 'egg; lay egg; hatch'. In Bai this root means 'hatch', while in Northern Naga and Qiang (Mawo, Yadu) it generally means 'bird', occurring as the first element in compounds for 'egg' (see below).

See *HPTB* *ʔu, p. 199.

| 1.3. Naga | | | |
|---|---|---|---|
| Chokri | thü **vu** zü | egg | GEM-CNL |
| 6. Lolo-Burmese | | | |
| *Lolo-Burmese | *ʔu³ | egg | JAM-Ety |
| 6.1. Burmish | | | |
| Achang (Lianghe) | a³¹ **u**³¹ | egg | JZ-Achang |
| Achang (Longchuan) | **u**³⁵ | lay (egg) | JZ-Achang; ZMYYC:785.41 |
| | **u**ʔ³¹ | egg | JZ-Achang; TBL:0450.28; ZMYYC:170.41 |
| Achang (Luxi) | a³¹ **u**³⁵ | egg | JZ-Achang |
| | **u**⁵¹ | lay (egg) | JZ-Achang |
| Achang (Xiandao) | pẓap³⁵ **u**³¹ | duck egg | DQ-Xiandao:575 |
| | **u**³¹ | egg | DQ-Xiandao:573 |
| | **u**³⁵ | lay egg | DQ-Xiandao:2363 |
| | ṣan³¹ **u**³¹ | nit | DQ-Xiandao:418 |
| Bola | pjɛt⁵⁵ **u̱**³⁵ | duck egg | DQ-Bola:575 |
| | **u̱**³⁵ | egg | DQ-Bola:573 |
| Bola (Luxi) | **u̱**³⁵ | egg | TBL:0450.32 |
| Bola | ɣaʔ³¹ **u̱**³⁵ | chicken egg | DQ-Bola:574 |
| Burmese (Spoken Rangoon) | **u̱**⁵³ | egg; lay (egg) | ZMYYC:170.40,785.40 |
| Burmese (Written) | krak **u**' | hen's egg | GEM-CNL |

| | | | | |
|---|---|---|---|---|
| | lə ʔu | scrotum | JAM-Ety | 1 |
| | thɑn³û¹ | nit ("louse-egg") | ZMYYC:163.39 | |
| | û¹ | egg; lay (egg) | TBL:0450.26; ZMYYC:170.39,785.39 | |
| | u' | egg | JAM-Ety | |
| | ə-u' | egg | PKB-WBRD | |
| | ʔu' | egg | ILH-PL:493 | |
| | ʔə ʔu' | egg | JAM-Ety | |
| Hpun (Northern) | ă ʔù'; chó ʔù' | egg | EJAH-Hpun | |
| | lauŋ ú' | scrotum; testicles | EJAH-Hpun | |
| Langsu (Luxi) | au⁵⁵ | egg | TBL:0450.31 | |
| Lashi | u̱⁵³ | egg (of animal) | DQ-Lashi:10.4.16 | |
| Leqi (Luxi) | u̱⁵³ | egg | TBL:0450.33 | |
| Maru [Langsu] | au⁵⁵ | egg; egg (of animal) | ZMYYC:170.43; DQ-Langsu:10.4.16 | |
| | ʃiŋ³⁵au⁵⁵ | nit | ZMYYC:163.43 | |
| Atsi [Zaiwa] | a²¹ u⁵⁵ | egg | JZ-Zaiwa; TBL:0450.30; ZMYYC:170.42 | |

**6.2. Loloish**

| | | | | |
|---|---|---|---|---|
| *Loloish | *u³ | egg | DB-PLolo:86; ILH-PL:493 | 2 |
| Achang (Xiandao) | u³¹ | egg | TBL:0450.29 | |
| Akha (Thai) | ja-uq | egg | ILH-PL:493 | 3 |
| Akha | leh̩ uˆ | scrotum | JAM-Ety | |
| | leh̩ uˆ leh̩ si̩ | scrotum | PL-AETD | |
| | uq | egg | ILH-PL:493 | |
| Akha (Yunnan) | xha wuq | egg | ILH-PL:493 | 4 |
| Bisu | hlə̆ ʔu³³ | testicles | DB-PLolo | 5 |
| | lɛ̀ ʔu | testicles | PB-Bisu:15 | 6 |
| | ʔaŋ ʔu | egg; egg (animal) | DB-Bisu; PB-Bisu:2 | |
| | ʔu | egg | DB-PLolo | |
| Gazhuo | fɣ³³ | lay (egg); egg | DLF-Gazhuo; DQ-Gazhuo:10.4.16; TBL:0450.47 | |
| Hani (Lüchun) | á wu | egg | ILH-PL:493 | |
| Hani (Dazhai) | a⁵⁵ u̱³³ | egg | JZ-Hani; ZMYYC:170.31 | |
| | na³¹ u̱³³ | earlobe | JZ-Hani | |
| | se⁵⁵u̱³³ | nit | ZMYYC:163.31 | |
| | u̱³³ | sit on, hatch (egg) | JZ-Hani; ZMYYC:786.31 | |
| Hani (Lüchun) | (xa³³) u̱³³ | egg | TBL:0450.41 | |
| Hani (Caiyuan) | se⁵⁵ɣ³³ | nit | ZMYYC:163.30 | |
| Hani (Pijo) | vu | egg | ILH-PL:493 | |

---

[1] The first syllable is reduced to schwa in this compound. This atonic syllable is a reduction of **lî** 'penis', and is not to be identified with the first syllable of WB **lin-khu'** 'scrotum', which is ultimately from Skt. *lingam*.

[2] The constriction in the Akha form is unexplained; it is perhaps due to assimilation to the glottal-stop (= zero) initial. This is a Tone *3 etymon in Lolo-Burmese, which is associated with creakiness in any case. The same holds for Achang Longchuan and several Hani forms.

[3] First syllable means "chicken".

[4] First syllable means "animal".

[5] Literally "penis + egg".

[6] Literally "penis + egg".

## I. Egg

| | | | |
|---|---|---|---|
| Hani (Caiyuan) | $\mathbf{v}^{33}$ | egg | JZ-Hani; ZMYYC:170.30 |
| | $\mathbf{\bar{v}}^{33}$ | sit on, hatch (egg) | JZ-Hani |
| | $\mathbf{v}^{33}$ | hatch | ZMYYC:786.30 |
| Hani (Pijo) | ɔ̀ **vu** | egg | ILH-PL:493 |
| Hani (Gelanghe) | $\mathbf{u}^{33}$ | sit on, hatch (egg); egg | JZ-Hani |
| Hani (Wordlist) | al **wuv** | egg | ILH-PL:493 [7] |
| Hani (Shuikui) | $a^{55}\ \mathbf{\bar{v}}^{33}$ | egg | JZ-Hani |
| | $a^{55}\mathbf{v}^{33}$ | egg | ZMYYC:170.32 |
| | $\mathbf{v}^{33\top}$ | hatch | ZMYYC:786.32 |
| | $ʃɛ^{55}\mathbf{v}^{33}$ | nit | ZMYYC:163.32 |
| Hani (Khatu) | à **vu** | egg | ILH-PL:493 |
| | **vu** | egg | ILH-PL:493 |
| Hani (Mojiang) | $(xa^{33})\ \mathbf{v}^{33}$ | egg | TBL:0450.42 |
| *Common Lahu | *\*u:* | egg | DB-PLolo:86 |
| Lahu (Black) | nī-sī-**u** | testicle | JAM-Ety |
| | nī-**u**-té | testicle | JAM-Ety |
| | $se^{33}\mathbf{u}^{33}$ | nit | ZMYYC:163.33 [8] |
| | **u** | egg; lay an egg | JAM-Ety |
| | $\mathbf{u}^{33}$ | egg | ZMYYC:170.33 |
| | $\mathbf{ɣ}^{33}$ | lay (egg) | JZ-Lahu |
| | $ɔ^{31}\ \mathbf{ɣ}^{33}$ | egg | JZ-Lahu |
| | ɔ̀-**u** | egg | JAM-Ety |
| | ɔ̀-**u u** ve | lay an egg | JAM-DL:135 |
| Lahu (Yellow) | $\mathbf{u}^{33}$ | lay (egg) | JZ-Lahu |
| | $ɔ^{31}\ \mathbf{u}^{33}$ | egg | JZ-Lahu |
| Lalo | de-**fu** | testicle | SB-Lalo |
| | **fu** | egg | SB-Lalo |
| | $\mathbf{fu}^{33}$ | egg (of animal) | CK-YiQ:10.4.16 |
| Lipho | $dɛ^{33}\mathbf{fu}^{33}$ | testicle | CK-YiQ:10.3.5 |
| | $\mathbf{fu}^{33}$ | egg | CK-YiQ:10.4.16 |
| Lisu (Northern) | $a^{21}gɤ^{21}ma^{33}\mathbf{fu}^{33}$ | egg capsule of mantis | DB-Lisu |
| | $a^{55}ɣa^{55}\mathbf{fu}^{33}$ | chicken egg | DB-Lisu |
| Lisu (Nujiang) | $e^{55}\ \mathbf{fu}^{44}$ | egg | JZ-Lisu |
| Lisu | $e^{55}\mathbf{fu}^{44}$ | egg | ZMYYC:170.27 |
| Lisu (Putao) | $\mathbf{fo}^{3}$ | egg; tuber; testicles | GHL-PPB:G.80 |
| Lisu (Northern) | $\mathbf{fu}^{33}$ | egg; spawn; reproduce | DB-Lisu |
| | $\mathbf{fu}^{33}gɔ^{21}$ | rotten egg | DB-Lisu |
| Lisu (Nujiang) | $\mathbf{fu}^{44}$ | lay (egg) | JZ-Lisu |
| Lisu | $\mathbf{fu}^{44}$ | lay (egg) | ZMYYC:785.27 |
| | $\mathbf{hu}^{3}$ | egg | DB-PLolo:86 |
| Lisu (Theng-yüeh) | $\mathbf{hu}^{3}$ | egg; tuber; testicles | GHL-PPB:G.80 |
| Lisu (Central) | $\mathbf{hu}^{3}$ | lay (as egg); egg | JF-HLL |
| Lisu (Northern) | $hɤ^{33}\mathbf{fu}^{33}$ | egg of a louse | DB-Lisu |
| | $ji^{55}\mathbf{fu}^{33}$ | egg; spawn | DB-Lisu |
| | $la^{55}\mathbf{fu}^{33}$ | testicle | DB-Lisu [9] |
| Lisu | $xɯ^{44}\mathbf{fu}^{44}$ | nit | ZMYYC:163.27 |

---

[7] The final **-v** is a tonemark in this transcription.
[8] Literally "louse-egg".
[9] Lit. "penis + egg".

| Lisu (Northern) | ɔ̃³³fu³³ | goose egg | DB-Lisu |
|---|---|---|---|
| | ɣa³³fu³³ | chicken egg | DB-Lisu |
| | ɣa³³fu³³ʃɿ³³ | egg yolk | DB-Lisu |
| Lolopho | fɣ³³ | egg (of animal) | DQ-Lolopho:10.4.16 |
| Mpi | ʔuʔ⁴ | egg | DB-PLolo; ILH-PL:493 |
| Nesu | der²¹ fu²¹ | testicle | CK-YiQ:10.3.5 |
| | fu²¹ | egg (of animal) | CK-YiQ:10.4.16 |
| Nusu (Central) | u³³ | lay egg | DQ-NusuB:2363. |
| | u³¹ | egg | DQ-NusuB:573.; TBL:0450.34 |
| Nusu (Central/Zhizhiluo) | u̠³¹ | egg | DQ-NusuA:573. |
| | u̠³¹ u̠³⁵ | lay egg | DQ-NusuA:2363. |
| Nusu (Northern) | fiu³¹ | lay (egg) | JZ-Nusu |
| Nusu (Bijiang) | ɹɑ³¹ʔu³¹ | egg | ZMYYC:170.45 |
| Nusu (Central) | ɹɑ³¹ ʔu³¹ | egg | JZ-Nusu [10] |
| Nusu (Bijiang) | ʂɑ˧⁵⁵u³¹ | nit | ZMYYC:163.45 |
| Nusu (Southern) | ʔu³¹ | egg | JZ-Nusu |
| Nusu (Northern) | ʔu⁵⁵ | egg | JZ-Nusu |
| Nusu (Southern) | ʔu⁵⁵ | lay (egg) | JZ-Nusu |
| Nusu (Bijiang) | ʔu⁵⁵ɑ⁵⁵ | lay (egg) | ZMYYC:785.45 |
| Phunoi | hə-ʔuʔ | egg | JAM-Ety |
| | hə³³ ʔuʔ³³ | egg | DB-Phunoi [11] |
| | shɛ̀ ʔu | testicle | JAM-Ety |
| | sʰɛ¹¹ ʔu³³ | testicles | DB-Phunoi |
| | ʔuʔ | egg | DB-PLolo |
| Yi (Dafang) | fɒ³³ | sit on (egg) | JZ-Yi |
| Yi (Mojiang) | fu²¹ | egg; lay (egg) | ZMYYC:170.26,785.26 |
| Yi (Nanhua) | xu³³ | egg; lay (egg) | TBL:0450.37; ZMYYC:785.24 |
| | xu̠³³; fu̠³³ | egg | ZMYYC:170.24 |
| Yi (Nanjian) | fu³³ | egg; lay (egg) | JZ-Yi; ZMYYC:170.23,785.23 |
| Yi (Weishan) | fu̠³³ | egg | TBL:0450.36 |
| Yi (Xide) | vu̠³³ | hatch | CSL-YIzd; ZMYYC:786.21 |

### 6.3. Naxi

| Naxi (Eastern) | a³¹o¹³ | egg | JZ-Naxi |
|---|---|---|---|

### 6.4. Jinuo

| Jinuo (Baya/Banai) | vu³³ | egg | DQ-JinA:604 |
|---|---|---|---|
| | vu³¹ | incubate | DQ-JinA:1899 |
| | vu³¹ pʰo⁴⁴ | incubate | DQ-JinA:1899.1 |
| Jinuo (Youle) | vu⁴² | sit on (egg) | JZ-Jinuo |
| Jinuo (Buyuan) | vu⁴⁴ | hatch (an egg); hatch, incubate | JZ-Jinuo |
| Jinuo | vu⁴⁴ | egg | TBL:0450.44 |
| Jinuo (Baka) | ɣ³³ | egg | DQ-JinB:604 |
| | ɣ³¹ | incubate | DQ-JinB:1899 |
| Jinuo (Baya/Banai) | ʃe³¹ u³³ | nit | DQ-JinA:441 |
| Jinuo (Baka) | ʃɿ³¹ ɣ³³ | nit | DQ-JinB:441 |
| Jinuo | ɑ³³vu³³ | egg | ZMYYC:170.34 |

[10]First syllable means 'chicken' < *k-rak.
[11]First syllable is 'chicken' < *k-rak.

## I. Egg

| | | | |
|---|---|---|---|
| Jinuo (Youle) | ɑ⁴⁴ **vu**³³ | egg | JZ-Jinuo |
| 8. Bai | | | |
| Bai (Bijiang) | **ue**ꜝ⁴⁴ | hatch | ZMYYC:786.37 |
| Bai (Dali) | **vu̠**⁴⁴ | sit on (egg) | JZ-Bai |
| | **ɣu**⁴⁴ | hatch | ZMYYC:786.35 |
| Bai (Jianchuan) | **vu̠**⁴⁴ | sit on (egg) | JZ-Bai |
| | **vu**⁴⁴ | hatch | ZMYYC:786.36 |

## (1b)          *pu          EGG

This morpheme appears in cognate object constructions, e.g. Bengni **pɯ-pɯ pɯ** 'lay an egg', where the last element is the verb. The noun looks reduplicated in Bengni, but Apatani has **pa-pu** 'egg', with apparently distinct components. Similar cognate objects are characteristic of **(1a) *wu** EGG / BIRD, e.g. Lahu **ɔ̀-u u ve** 'lay an egg', where the noun appears with a prefix.

This root may well be related to a morpheme with a more general meaning of BALL / EGG / ROUND OBJECT (1c, below).

### 1.1. North Assam

| | | | | |
|---|---|---|---|---|
| *Tani | *pɯ | egg | JS-HCST:122 | 12 |
| Padam-Mising [Abor-Miri] | a-**pui** | egg | JAM-Ety | |
| | a-**pɯ** | egg | JS-HCST | |
| Apatani | pa-**pu** | egg | JS-HCST; JS-Tani | |
| | pà-**pu** | egg | JS-Tani | |
| | pà-**pu** pa-xu | egg shell | JS-Tani | |
| | **pù** | lay egg | JS-Tani | |
| | ²pa ¹**pu** | egg | AW-TBT:555 | |
| Bengni | pɯ-**pɯ** | egg | JS-HCST; JS-Tani | |
| | pɯ-**pɯ pɯ** | lay egg | JS-Tani | |
| Bokar Lhoba | pɯ **pɯ:** | egg | ZMYYC:170.51 | |
| Bokar | pɯ-**pɯ** | egg | JS-HCST | |
| | pɯ-**pɯ:** | egg | JS-Tani | |
| Bokar Lhoba | **pɯ:** | lay (egg) | ZMYYC:785.51 | |
| | **pɯ** jak | hen's egg | SLZO-MLD | |
| | pɯ **pɯ:** | egg | SLZO-MLD | |
| Damu | cok-**pɯ** xɯm | lay egg | JS-Tani | 13 |
| | rok-**pɯ** | egg | JS-Tani | |
| | təp-**pɯ** | testicle | JS-Tani | |
| Gallong | pi-**pɤ** | egg | KDG-IGL | |
| | pi: **pi** | egg | KDG-IGL | |
| | ˆɯt-tum ˋa **pɤ** | testicle | AW-TBT:617a | |
| | ˋpɯ **pɤ** | egg | AW-TBT:555 | |
| Tagin | pɯ **pɯ** | egg | KDG-Tag | |

### 1.4. Meithei

| | | | |
|---|---|---|---|
| Meithei | **bu** ri khaw | testicle | CYS-Meithei:10.3.5 |

[12]The first elements in the Bengni, Bokar, Gallong, and Tagin forms are either morphemes meaning 'bird' or 'chicken' (cf. Damu **rok-pɯ**, where **rok** clearly < **\*k-rak** 'chicken'), or else reduplications of the root.

[13]The final nasal in this Damu form is similar to those in Rongmei, Thado, and Mzieme.

| Moyon | bʌ thí | testicle | DK-Moyon:10.3.5 |
|---|---|---|---|

**2.3.1. Kham-Magar-Chepang-Sunwar**

| Sunwar | bo-**phu** | egg | JAM-Ety |
|---|---|---|---|

**3.2. Qiangic**

| Muya [Minyak] | tʰɯ³¹**bu**⁵³ | testicle | SHK-MuyaQ:10.3.5 |
|---|---|---|---|
| Qiang (Mawo) | bʌˈ | testicle | SHK-MawoQ:10.3.5 |
| Qiang (Yadu) | bəˈ | testicles | DQ-QiangN:145 |

**3.3. rGyalrongic**

| rGyalrong | ta **bo** ɕi | testicle | DQ-Jiarong:10.3.5 |
|---|---|---|---|

**5. Tujia**

| Tujia | **phɯe**²¹ | hatch | ZMYYC:786.38 |
|---|---|---|---|

**6.2. Loloish**

| Nusu (Central/Zhizhiluo) | **bɯ**⁵⁵ be³⁵ | testicles | DQ-NusuA:142. |
|---|---|---|---|

**6.3. Naxi**

| Naxi (Lijiang) | **bv**³¹ | hatch | ZMYYC:786.28 |
|---|---|---|---|
| Naxi (Yongning) | **bv**⁵⁵ | hatch | ZMYYC:786.29 |

**6.4. Jinuo**

| Jinuo | **pho**⁵⁵ | hatch | ZMYYC:786.34 |
|---|---|---|---|

**7. Karenic**

| Karen (Sgaw/Hinthada) | di̠³¹ **bo̠**³³ | testicles | DQ-KarenB:145.1 |
|---|---|---|---|

## Chinese comparandum

孵 **fū** 'to hatch (eggs); incubate'

*GSR*: not in 1233        Karlgren: **\*p'i̯ôg**        Li: **\*phjəgw**        Baxter: **\*ph(r)ju**

The earliest attested use of this Chinese character seems to be the Han Dynasty work *Fangyan*. However, it is clearly a later graphic variant of 孚, which is attested writing 'hatch'. Thus although the character may be of later development, the word itself obviously existed at the Old Chinese time period.

Characters with the 孚 phonetic are generally placed in the OC 幽 Yōu rhyme group. However, some members of this phonetic series are found in the Middle Chinese 虞 Yú rhyme, which is not regularly derivable from the OC 幽 Yōu group.

Neither Li nor Baxter specifically discusses the difficulties of reconstructing this set of characters. Baxter (1992:757) does however list a reconstruction for 孚 (square brackets represent irregular development): 孚 **[fú]** < **[phju]** < **\*ph(r)ju**. It is treated as an irregular development from the OC 幽 Yōu group into the MC 虞 Yú rhyme. I have therefore provided a parallel reconstruction for 孵 in the systems of Li and Baxter.

Karlgren reconstructs other characters in this phonetic series with **\*-ug** (equivalent to the OC 侯 Hóu rhyme group), which yields a regular development into MC. However, I have provided a Karlgren-system reconstruction based on the assumption that the word belongs in the 幽 Yōu rhyme group.

The OC-PTB correspondence of finals is regular. PTB *-u and *-əw phonemically differ only in length, and show identical OC correspondences. In open syllables the long vowel *-əw (which could be written /uw/ or /uː/) is more common, and so cognate sets exemplifying this correspondence usually involve that vowel. Examples include 'nine' (TB *d-kəw, OC *kjəgw), 'dove/pigeon' (TB *khəw, OC *kjəgw) and **(102)** *r-bu ⪤ *pru NEST / WOMB / PLACENTA (elsewhere in this volume). It is interesting to note that this correspondence seems to be attested only after grave initials.

As for the mismatch in aspiration of the OC and PTB initials, this raises the broader issue of voicing and aspiration within and across Chinese and TB. PTB is reconstructed with a two-way voicing contrast (e.g. *p vs. *b), while Old Chinese is reconstructed with a three-way voicing and aspiration contrast (e.g. *p vs. *ph vs. *b). Voicing and aspiration correspondences between cognates are notoriously imprecise. This is because of various complex morphological processes, not yet entirely understood, at play in word families on both sides, which can affect voicing and aspiration. On the Chinese side, it has become increasingly clear in recent decades that prefixal elements, such as *s- and various nasals, can voice or devoice root initials. (See for example Baxter and Sagart 1998, Sagart 1999, and Gong 2000.) It has also been argued that Chinese aspiration is mostly, or entirely, a secondary feature. (See Schuessler 2007:58ff for a recent articulation of this view.) Similar processes have been observed in various TB languages and posited for PTB. Because not all of these processes are fully understood, and because of the complex history of individual words and word families, it is not always possible to be sure that one is comparing etymological roots, rather than derived forms, in established OC/PTB cognate sets.

For this reason the correspondence of PTB *p- with OC *ph-, for the comparison under discussion here, must be considered regular, with the assumption that aspiration in the Chinese form is a secondary development. Similarly, mismatches in voicing or aspiration will not be considered impediments in the proposal of Chinese comparanda for PTB etyma elsewhere in this volume. We assume, ultimately, that PTB voiceless initials correspond to Chinese voiceless initials, and that PTB voiced initials correspond to Chinese voiced initials, and that as our understanding of morphological processes on each side improves, these patterns of correlation will become more evident.

[ZJH]

## (1c)   *pu   BALL / EGG / ROUND OBJECT

These forms are undoubtedly related to those meaning "egg", but have acquired or retained the more general meaning of BALL / SMALL ROUND OBJECT. This morpheme appears in several compound body part terms like "eyeball" and perhaps "head" (cf. **(H:477)** *d-bu HEAD). See also the discussion under **(98c)** *pʷam BELLY, where this morpheme occurs as second element in compounds.

### 1.1. North Assam

| | | | |
|---|---|---|---|
| Padam-Mising [Abor-Miri] | mik-**pui** | eyeball ("eye-egg") | JAM-Ety |
| Bengni | ñik-**pɯ** | eyeball | JS-Tani |
| Bokar Lhoba | a **pɯ** | ball | ZMYYC:501.51 |

|  | mik **pɯ** | eyeball | SLZO-MLD |
| Bokar | ə-**pɯ** | ball | JS-Tani |
| Damu | mik-**pɯ** | eyeball | JS-Tani |
| Idu | **po**⁵⁵lo⁵⁵ | ball | ZMYYC:501.50 |

**1.3. Naga**

| Sema | a ye **pu** | star | GEM-CNL |

**1.4. Meithei**

| Meithei | lem **phu** | skull | JAM-Ety |

**2.1.2. Bodic**

| Tsangla (Motuo) | **po**⁵⁵lo¹³ | ball | JZ-CLMenba |
|  | **po** lo | ball | ZMYYC:501.7 |
| Tshona (Wenlang) | **pu**⁵⁵lu⁵⁵ | ball | JZ-CNMenba |
| Tshona (Mama) | meʔ⁵³ pri:¹³ **pu**⁵³ | eyeball | SLZO-MLD |
|  | **po**⁵⁵lo⁵³ | ball | ZMYYC:501.6 |
|  | ɬA⁵⁵ **pu**⁵³ | eye | SLZO-MLD |
| Tibetan (Balti) | **po**:lo· | ball | RAN1975:22 |
|  | **po** lo· | ball | RAN1975:54 |
| Tibetan (Khams:Dege) | **po**⁵⁵lo⁵³ | ball | ZMYYC:501.3 |
| Tibetan (Lhasa) | **po**⁵³lo¹³ | ball | ZMYYC:501.2 |
| Tibetan (Written) | **spo** lo | ball | ZMYYC:501.1 |

**2.1.4. Tamangic**

| Gurung (Ghachok) | miq **phu** | eyeball | JAM-Ety |
|  | mĩq **pʰũ** | eyeball | SIL-Gur:2.A.23 |

**3.2. Qiangic**

| Queyu (Yajiang) [Zhaba] | **pa**⁵⁵lo⁵⁵ | ball | ZMYYC:501.16 |

**4.1. Jingpho**

| Jingpho | **po**³¹luŋ⁵⁵ | ball | ZMYYC:501.47 |

**5. Tujia**

| Tujia | a³⁵ bo⁵⁵ **bu**²¹ | head | CK-TujMQ:2.1 |
|  | a³⁵ la⁵⁵ **bu**²¹ | eyeball | CK-TujMQ:3.4.2 |
| Tujia (Northern) | lo³⁵ **pu**³⁵ | eye | JZ-Tujia |
|  | lo³⁵ **pu**³⁵ pie⁵⁵ tsʰe²¹ | tears | JZ-Tujia |
| Tujia | lo³⁵ **pu**⁵⁵ | eye | CK-TujBQ:3.4 |
|  | lo³⁵ **pu**⁵⁵ pɹie⁵⁵ tsʰe²¹ | tears | CK-TujBQ:3.4.6 |
|  | lo³⁵ **pu**⁵⁵ tʰa⁵⁵ pʰa²¹ | eyelid | CK-TujBQ:3.4.1 |

**6.1. Burmish**

| Burmese (Spoken Rangoon) | **bɔ**⁵⁵lõ⁵⁵ | ball | ZMYYC:501.40 |
| Maru [Langsu] | **pɔ**³³luŋ⁵⁵ | ball | ZMYYC:501.43 |
| Atsi [Zaiwa] | **po**²¹luŋ⁵¹ | ball | ZMYYC:501.42 |

**6.2. Loloish**

| Ahi | ne³³ **bu̱**³³ tsʻɛ²² | eyebrow | LMZ-AhiQ:3.4.3 |
|  | o⁵⁵ ko̱³³ **bu**⁵⁵ | skull | LMZ-AhiQ:2.4 |
| Lahu (Black) | mɛ̂ʔ-qha-**phu** | eyeball | JAM-Ety:DL 1022 |
|  | ú-**phu** | head (in idioms) | JAM-DL:115 |

---

[14]This Balti word is the source of English *polo*!

I. Egg

| Nasu | o$^{33}$ **bu**$^{55}$ | skull | CK-YiQ:2.4 |
|---|---|---|---|
| Nusu (Central) | u$^{33}$ **p$^h$u**$^{55}$ guɔ$^{53}$ | bald person | DQ-NusuB:246. |
| Nusu (Central/Zhizhiluo) | u$^{31}$ **p$^h$u**$^{55}$ | head | DQ-NusuA:96. |
| Nusu (Central) | u$^{31}$ **p$^h$u**$^{55}$ | head | DQ-NusuB:96.; JZ-Nusu |
| Nusu (Central/Zhizhiluo) | u$^{31}$ **p$^h$u**$^{55}$ tɕ$^h$ɚ$^{35}$ | bald person | DQ-NusuA:246. |
| Nusu (Bijiang) | u$^{31}$**phu**$^{55}$ | head | ZMYYC:232.45 |
| Nusu (Northern) | ʔo$^{31}$ **p$^h$u**$^{55}$ | head | JZ-Nusu |
| Nusu (Southern) | ʔo$^{31}$ **p$^h$u**$^{55}$ | head | JZ-Nusu |

6.3. Naxi

| Naxi (Yongning) | **pu$^{33}$pu$^{33}$** | ball | ZMYYC:501.29 |

7. Karenic

| Karen (Sgaw/Hinthada) | mi$^{33}$ bua$^{33}$ **p$^h$o**$^{55}$ | eyeball | DQ-KarenB:104.1 |

8. Bai

| Bai | ŋuĩ$^{33}$ **p$^h$o̠**$^{44}$ | eye | ZYS-Bai:3.4 |

| (2a) | *d(w)əy | EGG / TESTICLE |
|---|---|---|

Especially in Himalayish and Kamarupan, it is often difficult to distinguish *d(w)əy from its probable co-allofam (2b) *dil ≍ *dul EGG / TESTICLE. Thus, Kulung **wa-di** ("bird + egg") looks like Tangsa (N.Naga) **wu-di**, Mikir **vo-ti**, etc., but other Kiranti languages (e.g. Limbu, Athpare) have reflexes with -n, apparently from *-l. Kanauri, Lepcha, and Tibetan retain -l. For now, we are assigning all Himalayish reflexes of this word-family to *dil, though a better Proto-Himalayish reconstruction would be *di-l. Similarly, some Kamarupan languages retain overt reflexes of *-l, but many have forms with open syllables. Our assignment of some Kamarupan forms to (2a) *d(w)əy EGG / TESTICLE rather than (2b) *dil ≍ *dul EGG / TESTICLE remains arbitrary.

Benedict 1939:225 ("Semantic differentiation in Indo-Chinese" HJAS 4:213-229) ana-lyzed compounds like Lushai **ar-tui** 'egg' as "bird + water". *STC* postulates a connec-tion between *twəy 'egg' (*STC* #168) and a general root *ti(y) 'water; moist' (*STC* #55 and pp. 45, 135, 196). (This latter root should actually be set up as (162) *m-t(w)əy ≍ *m-ti WATER / FLUID / LIQUID / SOAK.[15] The proposed connection between EGG and WATER is complicated by the related forms for EGG with final *-l. *STC* (n. 149) admits that Dhimal has different forms for EGG (**tui**) and WATER (**tśi**), and yet a third form in **hna-thi** 'snot'. Elsewhere in *STC* (p. 135, discussing the Karen cognates; and p. 196, in connection with the putative two-tone contrast for PTB), Benedict suggests that the etyma for EGG and WATER do indeed descend from separate allofams, different in both tone and initial at the PTB stage.

There is a further semantic connection between EGG and HEEL (both being smooth and rounded). Cf. Lushai **ar-tui** 'egg' (perhaps "bird-water", **ke-ar-tui** 'heel' ("foot-egg", i.e. "foot-bird-water"). The syllable **-ar-** must be bleached of all avian meaning by the time it gets incorporated into HEEL. See Matisoff 1994b, which also brings BUTTOCK into the same network of semantic associations as HEEL.

---

[15]See also *TSR* #109 *N/ʔ-tit/k 'soak; saturate'.

---

The putative semantic connection between BIRD and WATER is strengthened by compounds of BIRD with other roots for WATER, e.g. < **(H:433)** *k/r/s-wa WATER / RAIN (Tangkhul **tara** 'water', **har-ra** 'egg' (**har** 'bird'), **hai-ra** 'semen').[16] Less clear, but possibly a parallel formation is Muya **vɑ³³ vɑ⁵⁵** 'egg' (**vɑ³³** 'bird'). Cf. also Maring **wa-yui** 'egg', with the second element < **(164)** *rəy WATER / LIQUID.

This root is widely distributed, appearing in Kamarupan, Himalayish, Jingpho-Luish, Karen, and Qiangic (including Tangut), and perhaps in a few Loloish forms (Xide, Nosu) where the initial is palatalized to an affricate.

Seven forms from four Sak-Luish languages (Sak Bawtala, Sak Dodem, Ganan, Kadu) cited in Luce 1986 (Chart L) have the confusing gloss 'Penis/Testicles'. Since there are two phonologically similar etyma in this area, *ti EGG/TESTICLE and **(117)** *ti-k PENIS, these forms have presented serious problems of analysis, and have been re-glossed to mean either 'penis' or 'testicle', but not both. See Etymon Note under **(117)**, below.

See *HPTB* *twəy ≍ *dwəy 'water; egg', p. 195.

## 1.1. North Assam

| | | | |
|---|---|---|---|
| Darang [Taraon] | a:-**tei** | egg | JAM-Ety |
| | grõ-**ti** | heel | JAM-Ety |
| | gɹoŋ⁵³ **ti**⁵⁵ | heel | SLZO-MLD |
| Milang | ci-**ci** | egg | AT-MPB |
| Darang [Taraon] | a:tei | egg | NEFA-Taraon |

## 1.2. Kuki-Chin

| | | | |
|---|---|---|---|
| Khumi (Bangladesh) | **kduy** | testicles | DAP-Chm |
| | yaang **kduy** | male genitals ("penis + testicles") | DAP-Chm |
| Awa Khumi | yã³dü² | testicles | GHL-PPB:P.13 |
| Kom Rem | ər **tui** | egg (of animal) | T-KomRQ:10.4.16 |
| Lai (Hakha) | **ti**⁵ | egg; tuber; testicles | GHL-PPB:G.80 |
| Lailenpi | a´**ti**¹- | testicles | GHL-PPB:P.13 |
| Lakher [Mara] | **ti**-pao | elephantiasis of testicles | JAM-Ety |
| | **ti**-tla | bereft of testicles | JAM-Ety |
| Lushai [Mizo] | ar **tui** | egg | GEM-CNL |
| | ke-ar-**tui** | heel ("foot-chicken-egg") | JAM-Ety; STC:45n149; GEM-CNL |
| | **tui** | egg | JAM-Ety; PB-CLDB:1845 |
| Puiron | maka **tui** | egg | GEM-CNL |
| Thanphum | tə̃ **dui**¹ | testicles | GHL-PPB:P.13 |
| Tiddim | **tui**¹ | egg; tuber; testicles | GHL-PPB:G.80 |
| | tu:i² | egg | PB-CLDB:1845 |
| Tiddim Chin | `tu:i | egg | EJAH-TC |
| Tiddim | `tu:i | egg | JAM-Ety |
| Womatu | yak¹**tui**⁴ | testicles | GHL-PPB:P.13   [17] |

---

[16]See also **(157)** *ra ≍ *wa SEMEN.

[17]For the first syllable, see **(115)** *N-yaŋ PENIS / TESTICLE / STINGER (of bee), below. The final stop arose through assimilation to the stop initial of the second syllable.

# I. Egg

| | | | |
|---|---|---|---|
| Zotung | **tjui**[4] | testicles | GHL-PPB:P.13 |
| 1.3. Naga | | | |
| *Northern Naga | *(C-)wa(w) **təy** | egg | WTF-PNN |
| Chang | au **tei** | egg ("bird-egg") | WTF-PNN:481; GEM-CNL |
| Konyak (Tamlu) | ʌu **ji** | egg | AW-TBT:896 |
| Nocte | (a) **ti** | egg | WTF-PNN:481 |
| | a **ti** | egg | GEM-CNL |
| | [1]ʌ[2]**ti** | its egg; egg | AW-TBT:1190,896 |
| Phom | a **ti** | egg | WTF-PNN:459; GEM-CNL |
| Rongmei | kə **dui** | egg | JAM-Rong |
| | roi **dui** | egg | GEM-CNL |
| Tangsa | [1]vu[1]**ʈʌi** | egg | AW-TBT:896 |
| Tangsa (Moshang) | wu **di** | egg | WTF-PNN:481; STC:45n149; GEM-CNL |
| Wancho | ao **ti** | egg | GEM-CNL |
| | tau-**ci** | egg | JAM-Ety |
| | ɔ **ti** | egg | WTF-PNN:481 |
| Yacham-Tengsa | u **tü** | egg | GEM-CNL |
| 1.4. Meithei | | | |
| Moyon | bʌ **thí** | testicle | DK-Moyon:10.3.5 |
| 1.5. Mikir | | | |
| Mikir | kèng-**tì** | heel | KHG-Mikir:42 |
| | keng **ti** | heel ("foot-egg") | GEM-CNL; JAM-Ety |
| | keŋ-**ti** | heel | STC:45n149 |
| | **ti** | egg | JAM-Ety |
| | **tì** | egg (of animal); testicle | KHG-Mikir:88,88 |
| | vo **ti** | egg | GEM-CNL |
| | wō a-**tì** | egg (of animal) | KHG-Mikir:217 |
| | wò-**tī** | egg (of animal) | KHG-Mikir:glossary p |
| 1.7. Bodo-Garo = Barish | | | |
| Bodo | bi-**dəy** | egg | JAM-Ety; Bhat-Boro |
| | daw **də́y** | egg (hen's); egg | Bhat-Boro |
| Dimasa | dao **di** | egg | GEM-CNL |
| Bodo | dauʔ-**dəi** | egg | JAM-Ety |
| Garo | doʔ-**ci** | egg | JAM-Ety; AW-TBT:1190 |
| Kokborok | bə-**təy** | egg | PT-Kok |
| | tauʔ-**təy** | egg | PT-Kok |
| Lalung | tu **di** | egg | MB-Lal:78     18 |
| 3.1. Tangut | | | |
| Tangut [Xixia] | l **dai**[1] | testicle | MVS-Grin     19 |

---

[18]The first syllable **tu-** of this Lalung form means "bird" (< **(H:226-7)** *daw BIRD). But in the Lalung compound **tu-dar** 'penis', the **tu-** cannot mean 'bird', but is rather to be assigned to **(116a)** *k-tu-k PENIS.

[19]The first element **l-** 'penis' appears in reduced form in this "crypto-compound".

### 3.2. Qiangic

| | | | |
|---|---|---|---|
| Qiang (Mawo) | **zdi** | hatch | ZMYYC:786.8 |

### 4. Jingpho-Nung-Luish

| | | | |
|---|---|---|---|
| Ganan | kăpɔ³ **ti¹** | testicles | GHL-PPB:L.149 |
| | **ti¹** | egg; tuber; testicles | GHL-PPB:G.80 |
| Kadu (Kantu) | kăpɔt³ **ti¹** | testicles | GHL-PPB:L.149 |
| Kadu | **ti¹** | egg; tuber; testicles | GHL-PPB:G.80 |
| | u-**di** | egg | JAM-Ety |
| Sak (Bawtala) | ă¹**tji⁴** | egg; tuber; testicles | GHL-PPB:G.80 |
| | ă tji² **tu⁴** | testicles | GHL-PPB:L.149 |
| Sak | wa-**tí** | egg | JAM-Ety [20] |

### 4.1. Jingpho

| | | | |
|---|---|---|---|
| Jingpho | **di** | egg | JAM-Ety; STC:45n149 |
| | ne-**di** | testicle | JAM-Ety |
| | ne³¹**ti³¹** | scrotum | JCD |
| | **ti** | egg | GEM-CNL |
| | **ti³¹** | egg | JZ-Jingpo; TBL:0450.19; ZMYYC:170.47 |
| | ¹u¹**di** | egg | AW-TBT:896 |

### 6.2. Loloish

| | | | |
|---|---|---|---|
| Nosu | **tɕhi²¹** | egg | CK-YiQ:10.4.16 |
| Yi (Xide) | **tɕhi²¹** | egg | TBL:0450.35; ZMYYC:170.21 |
| | **tɕʰi²¹** | egg | CSL-YIzd; JZ-Yi |

### 7. Karenic

| | | | |
|---|---|---|---|
| *Karen (Pho-Sgaw) | *dìq | egg | RBJ-KLS:81 |
| *Karen | *díq | egg | RBJ-KLS:81 |
| *Karen (Pho) | *díq | egg | RBJ-KLS:81 |
| *Karen (TP) | *díq | egg | RBJ-KLS:81 |
| *Karen (Sgaw) | *díʔ | egg | RBJ-KLS:81 |
| *Karen | *ʔdi | egg | STC:135n367 |
| Bwe | dè-ʔdì | egg | AW-TBT:896 |
| | **đi** | egg; testicle; lay an egg | EJAH-BKD |
| Bwe (Western) | **đi²** | egg; tuber; testicles | GHL-PPB:G.80 |
| Geba | **di²** | egg; tuber; testicles | GHL-PPB:G.80 |
| Karen | **dị³¹** | egg | TBL:0450.50 |
| Pa-O | **dí** | egg; lay eggs | AW-TBT:896; DBS-PaO; RBJ-KLS:81 |
| Pa-O (Northern) | **di¹** | egg; tuber; testicles | GHL-PPB:G.80 |
| Palaychi | **dìq** | egg | RBJ-KLS:81 |
| Pho (Tenasserim) | s'ɔ̌⁴ **đi¹** | egg; tuber; testicles | GHL-PPB:G.80 |
| Pho (Delta) | s'ɔ̌ **đi⁴** | egg; tuber; testicles | GHL-PPB:G.80 |
| Pho (Bassein) | **dì** | egg | AW-TBT:896 |
| | **díʔ** | egg | RBJ-KLS:81 |

---

[20]Sak also has a compound **u-kyi** 'egg', which apparently means "bird-shit", where we interpret the first syllable as meaning 'bird', not 'egg'. Cf. the Jingpho prefix **ù-**, which occurs in many bird-related words, e.g. **ù-dì** 'egg', **ù-mài** 'bird's tail' (more examples in Hanson, pp. 50-53). **(H:165)** *wa ≍ *wu BIRD / FOWL seems related to *wu EGG/BIRD in any case.

| Pho (Moulmein) | díq | egg | RBJ-KLS:81 |
|---|---|---|---|
| | dí? | egg | AW-TBT:896 |
| Sgaw | ²?di | egg | AW-TBT:896 |
| Paku | đi³ | egg; tuber; testicles | GHL-PPB:G.80 |
| Sgaw | đi⁴ | egg; tuber; testicles | GHL-PPB:G.80 |
| Sgaw (Bassein) | dì | egg | RBJ-KLS:81 |
| Karen (Sgaw/Hinthada) | a³¹ di̱³¹ | egg | DQ-KarenB:573.1 |
| | di̱³¹ | egg | DQ-KarenB:573 |
| | di̱³¹ bɔ³³ | testicles | DQ-KarenB:145.1 |
| | di̱³¹ kʰli⁵⁵ | testicles | DQ-KarenB:145 |
| | di⁵⁵ glo³¹ di̱³¹ | castrate | DQ-KarenB:2303.1 |
| | tsʰɔ⁵⁵ di̱³¹ lɔ³³ | lay egg | DQ-KarenB:2468.1 |
| | xɯ⁵⁵ di̱³¹ | incubate | DQ-KarenB:1899.1 |
| Sgaw (Moulmein) | dí? | egg | RBJ-KLS:81 |
| Karen (Sgaw/Yue) | di̱³¹ | lay egg; egg | DQ-KarenA:2468,604 |

9. Sinitic

| Chinese (Mandarin) | chʼï | egg (of an ant) | GSR:590m |
| Chinese (Old/Mid) | dʼi̯ər/dʼi | egg (of an ant) | GSR:590m |

## Chinese comparandum

蚳 chí 'ant egg'

*GSR*: 590m          Karlgren: \*dʼi̯ər          Li: \*drjid          Baxter: \*drjij

This rare character does not appear in Li or Baxter. However, reconstruction in either system is not in doubt based on reconstruction of other characters with the same phonetic and identical Middle Chinese pronunciation (E.g. Baxter 1992:750 坻 chí < drij < \*drjij.) But it is worth noting that at least one character with the same phonetic is placed in the 微 Wēi group by Baxter and reconstructed with \*-ij: 鴟 chī < tsyhij < \*thjij, presumably because it is found rhyming with a 微 Wēi group word (*Shijing* 24.3A). If this character is not simply an exception, then according to Baxter's rhyme group division, characters with the same phonetic are spread across the two rhyme groups. In the absence of rhyming evidence, \*drjij is also a possible reconstruction for 蚳 in Baxter's system.

Assuming the semantics are not problematic,[22] the correspondences are quite sound. Examples of OC \*-id (Li) corresponding to TB \*-əy are numerous, and include 'die' OC 死 \*sjid (Li), TB \*səy; 'four' OC 四 \*sjid (Li), TB \*b-ləy; 'excrement' OC 屎 \*hrjid, TB \*kləy. The TB final \*-i should not be troubling; we would expect this relatively rare PTB final to correspond to OC in the same way as \*-əy (in parallel to TB \*-əw and \*-u; see the discussion of **(1)** \*pʷu EGG / BIRD / ROUND OBJECT). On the correspondence of OC medial \*-r-, see the discussion of 中 under **(44)** \*t/duŋ ⪥ \*ts(y)uːŋ NAVEL / CENTER.

[ZJH]

---

[21] It is the first syllable which is the verb, since Karen is VO.
[22] R. S. Cook (1995:63) offers much evidence that the real meaning of *GSR* 590m is 'scorpion'. [JAM]

## (2b)          *dil ⪰ *dul          EGG / TESTICLE

This etymon is sometimes hard to distinguish from **(2a)** **\*d(w)əy** EGG / TESTICLE, above. It is possible that conflation with an Indo-Aryan root is involved. Jäschke (p. 234) says that WT **thul** is "according to Cunningham a Cashmiri word". The TB cognates are indeed confined to Indospheric branches of TB (Kamarupan and Himalayish).

Some Himalayish forms for HEEL have an element like **-din-** which look as if they could probably come from this etymon for EGG (see the note on Lushai **ke-ar-tui**): these include Kulung **'dhin-di-ri**, and Thulung and Khaling **din-di-ri**. Yet the suspicious similarity among these forms suggest that they might be loans from Nepali.

This is very likely the same etymon as **\*r-tul ⪰ \*r-til** DULL / BUTTOCK / HEEL / ROUNDED PART (*HPTB* p. 419), cf. WT **rtul-po** 'blunt, dull'; Abor-Miri **ko-dun** 'buttock'; Meithei **mə-thun** 'buttock'; Wancho **chi-dun** 'heel' (**chi** 'foot'); Khözha **šú-dò**; Lisu **khi²¹du²¹** 'buttock' (**khi²¹** 'excrement'); Phunoi **pi³³tun¹¹** 'heel'. See Matisoff 1994b[23], and the Chinese comparanda, below. The allofam with medial **-i-** is represented by Jingpho **šətin** 'buttock', **ləthin** 'heel', and also perhaps by WT **rtiŋ-pa** 'heel'.

Benedict apparently had a different theory. He implies a connection between Lushai **til** 'testicle' and Thado **til** 'earthworm; testicle' (cf. also PLB **\*di** 'worm' > WB **ti**, Lisu **bi-di**), which he reconstructs as PTB **\*zril** 'worm' (*STC*, n.121, p. 37). Several Chinese comparanda meaning WORM are offered (n.457, p. 171). It must be said, however, that the semantic association between TESTICLE and WORM is a bit obscure.

**1.1. North Assam**

| | | | |
|---|---|---|---|
| Apatani | ar-**tiŋ** | testicle | JS-Tani |
| | ¹ar²**tiŋ** | testicle | AW-TBT:617a |

**1.2. Kuki-Chin**

| | | | | |
|---|---|---|---|---|
| Anal | à-**dál** | testicle | AW-TBT:617b | |
| Khualsim | tɪl² | testicles | GHL-PPB:P.13 | |
| Kom Rem | ǰəŋ **kəti** mu | testicle | T-KomRQ:10.3.5 | |
| | **kəti** kok | scrotum | T-KomRQ:10.3.4 | 24 |
| | **kəti** sem | castrate (v.) | T-KomRQ:10.3.9 | |
| Lai (Hakha) | til | testicle | KVB-Lai | |
| | til de? | fart around lazily | KVB-Lai | 25 |
| | til⁵ | testicles | GHL-PPB:P.13 | |
| Lakher [Mara] | ti hmô | scrotum | JAM-Ety | 26 |
| Liangmei | mai-**tiŋ**-kha | testicle | AW-TBT:617a | |
| Lothvo (Hiranpi) | θɤ³- | testicles | GHL-PPB:P.13 | |
| | θɤ¹- | testicles | GHL-PPB:P.13 | |
| Lushai [Mizo] | tĭl | testicle | AW-TBT:617b | |
| | til | testicle | JAM-Ety | |
| | til-mu | testicle | JAM-Ety | 27 |
| | tɪl³ | testicles | GHL-PPB:P.13 | |

---

[23]"How dull can you get?: buttock and heel in Sino Tibetan".
[24]EGG + **kok** 'hanging basket'.
[25]Literally, "play with one's testicles".
[26]Second element means 'seed'. See **(132)** **\*s-mu** SEED / TESTICLE / ROUND OBJECT, below.
[27]Second element means 'seed'. See **(132)** **\*s-mu** SEED / TESTICLE / ROUND OBJECT, below.

| Matupi | ti:l⁴ | testicles | GHL-PPB:P.13 |
|---|---|---|---|
| Mera | ti⁶ | testicles | GHL-PPB:P.13 |
| Tha'oa | til² | testicles | GHL-PPB:P.13 |
| Thado | tíl | testicle | THI1972:31 |
| | tīl cáŋ | testicle | THI1972:30 |
| Tiddim | tjɪl³ | testicles | GHL-PPB:P.13 |
| | tsĭl-táŋ | testicle | AW-TBT:617a |
| Xongsai | tɪl² | testicles | GHL-PPB:P.13 |

**1.4. Meithei**

| Moyon | i tír | testicle | DK-Moyon:10.3.5 [28] |
|---|---|---|---|

**1.5. Mikir**

| Mikir | tì a-thijā | scrotum | KHG-Mikir:88 |
|---|---|---|---|
| | ti athija | scrotum | JAM-Ety |

**1.7. Bodo-Garo = Barish**

| Garo (Bangladesh) | ri-sip-il | testicles | RB-GB |
|---|---|---|---|
| Lalung | tu ki ku thi | testicle | MB-Lal:78 |

**2.1.1. Western Himalayish**

| Kanauri | kŏ ṭöl | testicle | JAM-Ety |
|---|---|---|---|
| | kŏ ṭöl ŭ pŏṭō | testicle | JAM-Ety |

**2.1.2. Bodic**

| Baima | li⁵³ dɐ³⁴¹ | testicle | SHK-BaimaQ:10.3.5 |
|---|---|---|---|
| Tibetan (Balti) | tʰul | egg | RAN1975:41 |
| | γo tʰul | testicle | RAN1975:59 |
| Tibetan (Written) | thul | egg; tuber; testicles | GHL-PPB:G.80; JAM-Ety [29] |

**2.1.3. Lepcha**

| Lepcha | a-tí | egg | JAM-Ety |
|---|---|---|---|
| | a-tʻól | testicle | JAM-Ety |

**2.1.4. Tamangic**

| Gurung (Ghachok) | nyiq ri | egg (louse) | SIL-Gur:3.A.88 |
|---|---|---|---|
| Thakali (Tukche) | ne ṭi | egg (louse) | SIL-Thak:3.A.88 |

**2.1.5. Dhimal**

| Dhimal | tui | egg | STC:45n149 |
|---|---|---|---|

**2.3. Mahakiranti**

| *Kiranti | *di:n | testicle | AW-TBT:617b |
|---|---|---|---|
| | *tin | egg | BM-PK7:55 |
| Athpare (Rai) | le wa ḍin | testicle | AW-TBT:617b |

**2.3.2. Kiranti**

| Bahing | din | testicle | JAM-Ety |
|---|---|---|---|
| | ɓa-di | egg | JAM-Ety |
| | ʔba di | egg | BM-PK7:55 |
| Bantawa | din | egg; testicle | BM-PK7:55; JAM-Ety |
| | Din | egg | NKR-Bant |
| | din | egg | WW-Bant:23 |

---

[28]Cf. also Moyon **bʌ-thí**, where the second element is assigned to *dwəy, above.

[29]As mentioned above, Jäschke (p. 234) says that "according to Cunningham [this is] a Cashmiri word".

|            |                |                          |                      |     |
|------------|----------------|--------------------------|----------------------|-----|
|            | li-wa-**din**  | testicle                 | WW-Bant:46           | 30  |
|            | l Ua **Din**   | testicle                 | NKR-Bant             |     |
|            | wa **Din**     | egg of hen               | NKR-Bant             |     |
|            | wa ḍin         | chicken egg              | BM-PK7:55            |     |
|            | ḍin            | egg                      | BM-PK7:55            |     |
| Chamling   | da**î**        | egg                      | BM-PK7:55            |     |
|            | dAyN           | egg                      | WW-Cham:10           |     |
|            | du**î**        | egg                      | BM-PK7:55            |     |
|            | wa- **daî** ma | chicken egg              | BM-PK7:55            |     |
| Dumi       | **ti:**        | egg, testicle            | BM-PK7:55            |     |
| Khaling    | **ti**         | egg                      | BM-PK7:55; JAM-Ety   |     |
|            | **ti** mū-ne   | lay egg                  | AH-CSDPN:03b.14      |     |
| Kulung     | wa **di**      | egg                      | BM-PK7:55; RPHH-Kul  |     |
| Limbu      | le **thim** ba | testicle                 | BM-Lim               | 31  |
|            | lɛ **dhi:m** ba| testicle ("penis-egg")   | AW-TBT:142,617b      |     |
|            | **thi:n**      | egg                      | BM-Lim; BM-PK7:55    |     |
|            | wā **thin**    | egg                      | JAM-Ety              |     |
| Thulung    | **Di**         | egg                      | NJA-Thulung          |     |
|            | le koak **ti** | testicle                 | NJA-Thulung          |     |
|            | ḍi             | egg                      | BM-PK7:55            |     |

## Chinese comparanda

There are several likely Chinese comparanda (*HPTB* pp. 422, 504), including 臀 OC
**\*d'wən** (*GSR* 429b-c) 'buttocks', 殿 OC **\*tiən** (*GSR* 429d) 'rear of an army', 沌 OC
**\*d'wən** (*GSR* 427h) 'confused / stupid', 鈍 OC **\*d'wən** (*GSR* 427i) 'dull', 頓 OC **\*twən**
(*GSR* 427j) 'worn / dull / spoiled'.

[JAM]

As noted above, if this PTB root is related to **\*r-tul ✕ \*r-til** DULL / BUTTOCK / HEEL
/ ROUNDED PART, then it can be compared to the following Chinese word family (see
Coblin 1986:67-68; Gong 1995 set 154; *HPTB* pp. 422, 504):

臀 **tún** 'buttocks'

| *GSR* 429b-c | Karlgren: **\*d'wən** | Li: **\*dən** | Baxter: **\*dun** |
|---|---|---|---|

殿 **diàn** 'rear of an army'

| *GSR* 429d | Karlgren: **\*tiən** | Li: **\*tiənh** | Baxter: **\*tins** |
|---|---|---|---|

沌 **dùn** 'confused / stupid'

| *GSR*: 427h | Karlgren: **\*d'wən** | Li: **\*dənx** | Baxter: **\*dunʔ** |
|---|---|---|---|

鈍 **dùn** 'dull'

| *GSR* 427i | Karlgren: **\*d'wən** | Li: **\*dənh** | Baxter: **\*duns** |
|---|---|---|---|

頓 **dùn** 'worn / dull/ spoiled'

| *GSR* 427j | Karlgren: **\*twən** | Li: **\*tənh** | Baxter: **\*tuns** |
|---|---|---|---|

---

[30]Literally "penis + bird + egg". Cf. also the Athpare form.
[31]With assimilation to **-m**, before the labial suffix.

The correspondence between PTB *-l and OC *-n is regular (see Gong 1995 for numerous examples). The initials and vowels also match well. The voicing alternation and suffixation seen in the Chinese word family are typical, although in this case the morphological function is not clear.

[ZJH]

The following comparanda are offered for PTB *zril EARTHWORM in *STC* p. 171: 蟺 ḍian 148p; 蚓 ḍiĕn 371c; 螾 ḍiən 450j.

[JAM]

蟺 **shàn** 'earthworm'

| | | | |
|---|---|---|---|
| *GSR*: 148p | Karlgren: *ḍian | Li: *djanx | Baxter: *djanʔ |

蚓 **yǐn** 'earthworm'

| | | | |
|---|---|---|---|
| *GSR*: 371c | Karlgren: *ḍiĕn | Li: *rinx | Baxter: *ljinʔ |

螾 **yǐn** 'earthworm'

| | | | |
|---|---|---|---|
| *GSR*: 450j | Karlgren: *ḍiən | Li: *rənx ? | Baxter: *lji/inʔ |

Benedict (*STC* p. 37 note 121 and p. 171 note 457) argues that all three Chinese words are related and 'point... to an original initial such as *zr-'. These in turn are compared to TB *zril 'worm'.[32] Based on this and a handful of other comparisons, Benedict argues for the following developments from PST to Chinese: *zr- > *źr- > *ḍi̯ [33] varying with *zr- > *zy- > *y- > *di̯.

Based on our current understanding of Old Chinese, Benedict's hypothesis is no longer sustainable, at least not in full. *GSR* 148 is a dental series while *GSR* 371 and 450 are lateral series. This and the vowel difference indicate that 蟺 **shàn** is not an allofam of 蚓 **yǐn** and 螾 **yǐn**.[34] As for the latter two, the reconstruction in both Li's and Baxter's systems is difficult. The Middle Chinese forms might be descended from either OC *i or OC *ə (Li)/*i (Baxter). Li and Baxter agree that *GSR* 371 has main vowel *i, but the reconstruction of *GSR* 450 is ambiguous.

Schuessler 2007:574 explicitly relates 蚓 **yǐn** and 螾 **yǐn**, indicating that they are variant graphs used to write the same morpheme. He reconstructs OC *lə/inʔ or *jə/inʔ. While various attested binomial forms for 'earthworm' suggest that *i is the OC vowel, Min dialect forms point to *ə.

As for the initial, it is now generally agreed that it should be *l or *j, not *r.

Looking again at Benedict's comparison with PTB *zril, we note that the vowel and coda correspondences are regular. A comparison of PTB *zr- with OC *l- or *j- looks

---

[32]It is in footnote 121 that Benedict seems to relate TB *zril to Lushai **til** 'testicles', the TB etymon currently under discussion in this volume.

[33]ḍi̯ is mistakenly written *d'i* in *STC*; in Karlgren's reconstruction *d* with an inverted breve above is distinct from *d* followed by an apostrophe, but as far as I can tell Benedict transcribes them identically, perhaps due to typographic limitations.

[34]Peiros and Starostin 1996 v2:156 set 570 relate Chinese 蟺 **shàn** to Lushai **tāl** 'to struggle, wriggle, writhe'. See also Schuessler 2007:453.

doubtful on phonetic grounds, but cannot be dismissed out of hand. Since *zr- is so rare in TB, it is difficult to establish regularity of correspondence.

Whatever the fate of that comparison, Benedict's claim that these Chinese words are ultimately connected to **(2b)** *dil ≍ *dul EGG / TESTICLE now seems quite unlikely to be true.

[ZJH]

(3)                              * $\frac{n}{s}$ -tow                              **EGG**

This etymon appears in Kamarupan (Idu), Loloish, and Qiangic, and looks safe to set up for PTB. There is evidence for both a nasal (Loloish) and a sibilant (Qiangic) prefix.

1.1. North Assam

| | | | |
|---|---|---|---|
| Idu | e **to**-cu | egg | NEFA-PBI; JP-Idu |
| | e **to** cu lo | egg (white) | JP-Idu |
| | e **to** cu mi | egg (yolk) | JP-Idu |
| | e **to** cu roka | egg (shell) | JP-Idu |

3.2. Qiangic

| | | | |
|---|---|---|---|
| Ergong (Daofu) | rɑ **stu** | egg (of animal) | DQ-Daofu:10.4.16 |
| Ergong (Danba) | ẓa **stu** | egg (of animal); egg | SHK-ErgDQ:10.4.16; ZMYYC:170.14 |
| Ersu (Central) | tsɛ$^{55}$ | egg | SHK-ErsCQ |
| Ersu | tsɛ$^{55}$ | egg | ZMYYC:170.18 |
| Pumi (Jinghua) | skhi$^{55}$tsə$^{55}$ | egg | ZMYYC:170.11 |
| | sk$^h$i$^{55}$ tsə$^{55}$ | egg | JZ-Pumi |
| Qiang (Mawo) | tɕi wə **st** | egg | ZMYYC:170.8; JZ-Qiang |
| | wu **stə̣** | egg (of animal) | SHK-MawoQ:10.4.16 |
| Qiang (Taoping) | χtə$^{55}$ | egg | JZ-Qiang; ZMYYC:170.9 |
| Qiang (Yadu) | wə **s** | egg | DQ-QiangN:604 [35] |

6.2. Loloish

| | | | |
|---|---|---|---|
| Ahi | da$^{33}$**tho**$^{22}$ | testicle | CK-YiQ:10.3.5 |
| | dɑ$^{33}$ **t'o**$^{22}$ | testicle | LMZ-AhiQ:10.3.5 |
| | i$^{33}$ **t'o**$^{22}$ | egg (of animal) | LMZ-AhiQ:10.4.16 |
| | **ʈho**$^{22}$ | egg | CK-YiQ:10.4.16 |
| Nasu | t$^h$ọ$^{21}$ | egg (of animal) | CK-YiQ:10.4.16 |
| Noesu | **ndo**$^{55}$ | egg | CK-YiQ:10.4.16 |
| Yi (Dafang) | **ndo**$^{55}$ | egg; lay (egg) | JZ-Yi; ZMYYC:170.22 |
| Yi (Mile) | i$^{33}$**tho**$^{33}$ | egg | ZMYYC:170.25 |

(4)                              **\*dz(y)u**                              **EGG**

This etymon seems confined mostly to Kamarupan, with a likely Himalayish cognate in Kham. The Idu form **e-to-cu** proves that this root is distinct from **(3)** *n/s-tow EGG.

---

[35]Comparison with other Qiangic forms indicates that the final **-s** in Yadu is a truncated verson of **stə** or **stu**. This apocopation of the vowel of second elements in compounds is characteristic of Qiangic. See Benedict (1983), "Qiang monosyllabization: a third phase in the cycle" (*LTBA* 7.2:113-4).

## 1.1. North Assam

| Idu | e to-**cu** | egg | NEFA-PBI; JP-Idu |
|---|---|---|---|
| | e to **cu** lo | egg (white) | JP-Idu |
| | e to **cu** mi | egg (yolk) | JP-Idu |
| | e to **cu** roka | egg (shell) | JP-Idu |

## 1.3. Naga

| Angami (Khonoma) | **dzü** | egg | GEM-CNL |
|---|---|---|---|
| Angami (Kohima) | **dzü**; thevü **dzü** | egg | GEM-CNL |
| | khu$^{55}$nuo$^{31}$**dzü**$^{33}$ | egg (of animal) | VN-AngQ:10.4.16 |
| | pe$^{31}$ra$^{31}$**dzü**$^{33}$ | egg (of animal) | VN-AngQ:10.4.16 |
| Ao (Chungli) | aen **tzü** | egg | GEM-CNL |
| Ao (Mongsen) | an **sü** | egg | GEM-CNL |
| Chokri | (u) **dzü**$^{33}$ | testicle | VN-ChkQ:10.3.5 |
| | **dzü**$^{33}$ | egg (of animal) | VN-ChkQ:10.4.16 |
| | thü vu **zü** | egg | GEM-CNL |
| Khezha | 'e **júɑ** | testicle | SY-KhözhaQ:10.3.5 |
| Khezha | me **juɯ** | egg (of animal) | SY-KhözhaQ:10.4.16 |
| Lotha Naga | E **ju** | egg (of animal) | VN-LothQ:10.4.16 |
| | hono-e **tchhü** | egg | GEM-CNL |
| Mao | ho **dzü** | egg | GEM-CNL |
| Ntenyi | a wüü-a **tsü** | egg | GEM-CNL |
| Rengma | tero **zü** | egg | GEM-CNL |

## 2.3.1. Kham-Magar-Chepang-Sunwar

| Kham | 'bā-**zu**-ri: | egg | JAM-Ety |
|---|---|---|---|
| | 'ba **zu** ri: | egg (non-human) | DNW-KhamQ:1.33 |
| | **zuh** ri: | testicles | DNW-KhamQ |

(5)                    **\*rum ⋊ \*lum**                    **EGG**

This root is attested in Kamarupan, Nungish, and perhaps Qiangic, as well as in Himalayish (Hayu, Tshona). The proto-initial seems to have been **\*r-**, though some reflexes have **l-**. It is possible that there is a connection with **\*s-lum** or **\*z-lum** 'round' (*STC* #143).

## 1.1. North Assam

| Sulung | mə$^{33}$**ri**$^{33}$ | egg | ZMYYC:170.52 |
|---|---|---|---|

## 1.2. Kuki-Chin

| Khoirao | a roi **ghum** | egg | GEM-CNL |
|---|---|---|---|

## 1.4. Meithei

| Meithei | mə **rum** | egg (of animal) | CYS-Meithei:10.4.16 |
|---|---|---|---|
| | ye **rum** | egg | GEM-CNL |

## 2.1.2. Bodic

| Tshona (Wenlang) | k$^h$a$^{55}$ **lum**$^{55}$ | egg | JZ-CNMenba |
|---|---|---|---|
| Tshona (Mama) | khA?$^{53}$**lum**$^{53}$ | egg | ZMYYC:170.6 |
| | k$^h$A?$^{53}$ **lum**$^{53}$ | egg | SLZO-MLD |

---

[36]Note that the Sulong form has the same **mə-** prefix as in Meithei.

| 2.3.2. Kiranti | | | |
|---|---|---|---|
| Hayu | **rum** | brood (of a hen) | BM-Hay:84.113 |
| 3.2. Qiangic | | | |
| Namuyi | ɦɛ⁵⁵ɣo⁵⁵ | egg (of animal); egg | SHK-NamuQ:10.4.16; ZMYYC:170.19 |
| Shixing | rɛ³³ʁo³⁵ | egg | SHK-ShixQ; ZMYYC:170.20 |
| 4.2. Nungic | | | |
| Anong | **lim⁵⁵** | egg | ZMYYC:170.44 |
| Trung [Dulong] | kɑ⁵⁵**lŭm⁵³** | egg | ZMYYC:170.46 |
| Trung [Dulong] (Du-longhe) | kɑ⁵⁵ **lŭm⁵³** | egg | JZ-Dulong |
| Trung [Dulong] (Nujiang) | kʰɑ³¹ **lŭm⁵³** | egg | JZ-Dulong |
| 5. Tujia | | | |
| Tujia | a²¹**le⁵⁵** | egg (of animal) | CK-TujMQ:10.4.16 |
| 9. Sinitic | | | |
| Chinese (Mandarin) | **luǎn** | egg | GSR:179a |
| Chinese (Old) | **C-ronʔ** | egg | WHB-OC:949 |
| | **g-ronʔ** | egg | WHB-OC:557 |
| Chinese (Old/Mid) | **lwân/luân:** | egg | GSR:179a |

## Chinese comparandum

卵 **luǎn** 'egg; testicle'

*GSR*: 179a     Karlgren: **\*lwân**     Li: **\*luanx**     Baxter: **\*g-ronʔ** (557)

In Baxter's system, MC l- is always derived from OC *C-r-, that is, an initial **r** with a prefixed consonant (to be distinguished from *Cr- in which **r** functions as a medial). In other systems, MC l- may descend from simple initial *r-. Baxter gives two separate reconstructions for this word: *g-ronʔ (set 557) and *C-ronʔ (set 949, with C unspecified). There is some reason to suppose that if the prefix *C- is to be reconstructed it would be a velar (Baxter 1992:387).

The correspondence between PTB *r- and Middle Chinese l- is well-attested. Although both the Chinese and PTB forms have a rounded vowel and a nasal final, the correspondences are problematic. No generally accepted OC/PTB cognates show an *-n/*-m correspondence. OC *ua (Li) / *o (Baxter) generally corresponds to PTB *o, not *u. (For example, 'remove', OC 脱 *hluat (Li), PTB *hlot.) We would expect PTB rhyme *-um to correspond to OC *-əm (Li) (see examples in Gong 1995).

Gong 1995 (set 41) compares Chinese 卵, which he reconstructs *ruanx, with Written Tibetan **sro-ma** 'nit' (see **(20)** *s-row EGG / NIT, below), following Benedict 1976:190. Schuessler 2007:369 makes the same comparison, citing PTB *(s-)rwa rather than

---

[37]We are provisionally assigning the second syllable of the Namuyi and Shixing forms to this etymon, but the second syllables of Pumi ʐɑ¹¹qu⁵⁵, rɛ³⁵ ku⁵⁵ to **(7)** *s/r-go-ŋ EGG / TESTICLE, below. The first syllables of all these compounds mean 'fowl', from **(H:317)** *k-rak FOWL.

**s-row.** For this comparison to hold, a nominalizing *-n suffix must be posited for the Chinese form (Schuessler 2007:74-75).

[ZJH]

(6)           **\*sir ≍ \*sit**           **EGG**

This root is not widely attested, though identical reflexes occur as the last syllables of compounds in Geman, Miju, and Hayu. The Monpa forms in **-r** are of uncertain affiliation, since **-r** and **-t** do not usually cooccur in TB word-families.

1.1. North Assam

| | | | |
|---|---|---|---|
| Kaman [Miju] | kré-sît | egg | AW-TBT:1190 |
| | kɹai⁵⁵sit⁵⁵ | egg | ZMYYC:170.48 |
| | kɹɑi⁵⁵ sit⁵⁵ | egg | SLZO-MLD |

2.1.2. Bodic

| | | | |
|---|---|---|---|
| Tsangla (Motuo) | ser kʰum | egg | SLZO-MLD |
| Tshona (Mama) | sir⁵⁵ sir⁵⁵ mo⁵³ | egg | SLZO-MLD |

2.3.2. Kiranti

| | | | |
|---|---|---|---|
| Hayu | kuŋ sit | egg | BM-Hay:84.229 |

(7)           **\* $\frac{s}{r}$ -go-ŋ**           **EGG / TESTICLE**

WT has a doublet with and without the final nasal. It looks as if the nasal-finalled variant is due to assimilation to a following syllable **-ŋa (8) \*s-ŋa** EGG / HATCH in WT, but other languages have a nasal final even before other consonants (Tsangla [Monpa] **khong-lung**, Hayu **kuŋ-luŋ**). This etymon also appears in Qiangic, but some of these forms may be loans from Tibetan. The rGyalrong forms in **-m** are of uncertain affiliation. The **-m** makes them look somewhat like the second syllables of some Monpa Tsangla forms with dental initials, though we are referring these to ((9) **\*t-lam** EGG / TESTICLE. This root also occurs in Bai (where it means 'testicle'), in scattered Kamarupan languages, and in Lolo-Burmese.

The Newar forms **i khẽ, khec-, kheː, khẽ jɔ, khẽ** 'egg' are similar to the second syllable of Yakha **liːgeŋ** 'testicle' (**li** 'penis'), and should probably be set up as a separate etymon, perhaps **\*keŋ**.

1.3. Naga

| | | | |
|---|---|---|---|
| Sema | au khu | egg | GEM-CNL |

1.7. Bodo-Garo = Barish

| | | | |
|---|---|---|---|
| Lalung | tu ki ku thi | testicle | MB-Lal:78 |

2.1.2. Bodic

| | | | |
|---|---|---|---|
| Tsangla (Central) | go tham | egg | EA-Tsh:87 |
| | khong lung | testicle | SER-HSL/T:34 4 |
| Tsangla (Motuo) | go-tham | egg | ZMYYC:170.7 |
| | go tʰam | egg | SLZO-MLD |
| | ko¹³ tʰam⁵⁵ | egg | JZ-CLMenba |

| | ser kʰum | egg | SLZO-MLD | |
|---|---|---|---|---|
| Tsangla (Tilang) | goi-tʰam | egg | JZ-CLMenba | |
| Tibetan (Amdo:Bla-brang) | ḥgoŋ wa | egg | ZMYYC:170.4 | |
| Tibetan (Amdo:Zeku) | goŋ-wæ | egg | JS-Amdo:218 | |
| | rgoŋ ŋwa | egg | ZMYYC:170.5 | |
| Tibetan (Batang) | gõ²³¹ŋa¹³ | egg (of animal) | DQ-Batang:10.4.16 | |
| Tibetan (Jirel) | go-ngā | egg | JAM-Ety | |
| Tibetan (Khams:Dege) | go¹³ŋa⁵³ | egg | ZMYYC:170.3 | |
| Tibetan (Lhasa) | ko¹³ŋɑ¹³ | egg | ZMYYC:170.2 | |
| Spiti | gõ-ŋa | egg (of animal) | CB-SpitiQ:10.4.16 | |
| Tibetan (Written) | sgo ŋa | egg | ZMYYC:170.1 | 38 |
| | sgo-ña ~ sgoñ (-ña) | egg | JAM-Ety | |
| | sgo-ŋa | egg | ZLS-Tib:6 | |
| | sgo.nga | egg | JS-Tib:218 | |
| | sgo ña | egg | GEM-CNL | |

## 2.1.4. Tamangic

| Tamang (Sahu) | kʰo syop | egg white | SIL-Sahu:7.13 | |
|---|---|---|---|---|

## 2.2. Newar

| Newar | gwa | Clf. for round objects | KPM-pc | |
|---|---|---|---|---|
| | mikh ā-gwa(l) | eyeball | JAM-Ety | |

## 2.3.2. Kiranti

| Bahing | kɔ lɔ | egg; testicle | JAM-Ety | 39 |
|---|---|---|---|---|
| Hayu | kuŋ-luŋ | egg | JAM-Ety | |
| | kuŋ sit | egg | BM-Hay:84.229 | |

## 3.2. Qiangic

| Ergong (Northern) | lʁo³³ | testicle | SHK-ErgNQ:10.3.5 | |
|---|---|---|---|---|
| | lʁo³³ ɕip⁵³ | scrotum | SHK-ErgNQ:10.3.4 | 40 |
| | zgo³³ŋa³³ | egg (of animal) | SHK-ErgNQ:10.4.16 | |
| Muya [Minyak] | kuɯ⁵³ | testicle | SHK-MuyaQ:10.3.5 | |
| Pumi (Jiulong) | zɑ¹¹qu⁵⁵ | egg | TBL:0450.10 | |
| Pumi (Lanping) | qu⁵⁵ | egg | TBL:0450.09 | |
| | zɑ¹³qu⁵⁵ | egg | TBL:0450.09 | |
| Pumi (Taoba) | rɐ³⁵ ku⁵⁵ | egg | JZ-Pumi; ZMYYC:170.10 | 41 |
| Queyu (Yajiang) [Zhaba] | gõ³⁵ŋa⁵³ | egg (of animal); egg | SHK-ZhabQ:10.4.16; ZMYYC:170.16 | |
| Zhaba (Daofu County) | ʂkui¹³ | egg | TBL:0450.14 | |

## 3.3. rGyalrongic

| rGyalrong | ta gam | egg (of animal); egg | DQ-Jiarong:10.4.16; ZMYYC:170.12 | |
|---|---|---|---|---|
| rGyalrong (NW) | tan gum | egg (of animal) | SHK-rGNWQ:10.4.16 | |

---

[38]The first syllable of WT **sgo-pur** 'foreskin (vulg.)' does not appear to descend from this etymon, but seems rather to mean 'door; aperture, outlet'. However, Jäschke does not include this under compounds with **sgo** 'door' (114-6), but rather lists it as a separate head-entry (p. 116). The meaning of the second syllable **-pur** is unclear, though there might be a connection with **ḥp'ur-ba** 'wrap up, envelop'.

[39]The second element of this Bahing form apparently means 'stone', as in the Monpa and Hayu forms.

[40]Literally, TESTICLE + NEST.

[41]See the note about the Namuyi and Shixing forms under (5) *rum ✕ *lum EGG, above.

| | | | |
|---|---|---|---|
| rGyalrong (Northern) | taŋ **gom** | egg (of animal) | SHK-rGNQ:10.4.16 |
| rGyalrong (Eastern) | ta **gam** | egg (of animal) | SHK-rGEQ:10.4.16 |
| | tə **rgo** | testicle | SHK-rGEQ:10.3.5 |
| | tə **rgo** pok cço | scrotum | SHK-rGEQ:10.3.4 |
| rGyalrong (NW) | tə **rgu** | testicle | SHK-rGNWQ:10.3.5 |
| | tə **rgu** tɕʰim | scrotum | SHK-rGNWQ:10.3.4 [42] |

### 6.2. Loloish

| | | | |
|---|---|---|---|
| Ugong | ní **khû** | testicle | DB-Ugong:10.3.5 |
| Yi (Mile) | **ko**$^{33}$ | lay (egg) | ZMYYC:785.25 |

### 6.3. Naxi

| | | | |
|---|---|---|---|
| Naxi (Yongning) | **ko**$^{55}$ | egg | ZMYYC:170.29 |
| Naxi (Western) | **kv**$^{33}$ | egg | JZ-Naxi |
| Naxi (Lijiang) | **kv**$^{33}$ | egg | ZMYYC:170.28 |
| Naxi (Eastern) | **kv**$^{31}$ | lay (egg) | JZ-Naxi |
| Naxi (Western) | **kv**$^{31}$ | lay (egg) | JZ-Naxi |
| Naxi (Lijiang) | **kv**$^{31}$ | lay (egg) | ZMYYC:785.28 |
| Naxi | **kv̩**$^{33}$ | egg | TBL:0450.45 |

### 8. Bai

| | | | |
|---|---|---|---|
| Bai | **kuã**$^{33}$ | testicle | ZYS-Bai:10.3.5 |
| | **kuã**$^{33}$ lõ$^{21}$ | scrotum | ZYS-Bai:10.3.4 |

## (8)  *s-ŋa  EGG / HATCH

This root is confined to Tibetan, where it always seems to occur in binomes after re-flexes of **(7)** *s/r-go-ŋ EGG / TESTICLE. It also appears in Qiangic, although these forms look like loans from Tibetan.

### 2.1.2. Bodic

| | | | |
|---|---|---|---|
| Tibetan (Amdo:Bla-brang) | ḥgoŋ **wa** | egg | ZMYYC:170.4 |
| Tibetan (Amdo:Zeku) | goŋ-**wæ** | egg | JS-Amdo:218 |
| | rgoŋ **ŋwa** | egg | ZMYYC:170.5 |
| Tibetan (Batang) | gõ$^{231}$**ŋa**$^{13}$ | egg (of animal) | DQ-Batang:10.4.16 |
| Tibetan (Jirel) | go-**ngā** | egg | JAM-Ety |
| Tibetan (Khams:Dege) | go$^{13}$**ŋa**$^{53}$ | egg | ZMYYC:170.3 |
| | **ŋa**$^{13}$ | hatch | ZMYYC:786.3 |
| Tibetan (Lhasa) | ko$^{13}$**ŋɑ**$^{13}$ | egg | ZMYYC:170.2 |
| Spiti | gõ-**ŋa** | egg (of animal) | CB-SpitiQ:10.4.16 |
| Tibetan (Written) | sgo-**n̊a** ~ sgoň (-n̊a) | egg | JAM-Ety |
| | sgo-**ŋa** | egg | ZLS-Tib:6 |
| | sgo.**nga** | egg | JS-Tib:218 |
| | sgo ň**a** | egg | GEM-CNL |

### 3.1. Tangut

| | | | |
|---|---|---|---|
| Tangut [Xixia] | **nge**$^{1}$ | testicle | MVS-Grin |

### 3.2. Qiangic

| | | | |
|---|---|---|---|
| Ergong (Northern) | zgo$^{33}$**ŋa**$^{33}$ | egg (of animal) | SHK-ErgNQ:10.4.16 |
| Ergong (Danba) | z**ŋa** | hatch | ZMYYC:786.14 |

---

[42]Literally "testicle" + "house" (< PTB *k-yim).

| | | | |
|---|---|---|---|
| Queyu (Yajiang) [Zhaba] | gō³⁵ŋa⁵³ | egg (of animal); egg | SHK-ZhabQ:10.4.16; ZMYYC:170.16 |

## (9)           *t-lam           EGG / TESTICLE

This root is attested in Himalayish (including Tsangla), Abor-Miri-Dafla, and also perhaps in Chang Naga. The Lepcha and rGyalrong forms are good evidence for prefixal **t-**, which seems to have preempted the root-initial in all the other forms.

| 1.1. North Assam | | | | |
|---|---|---|---|---|
| Padam-Mising [Abor-Miri] | 'et-**tum** | testes and scrotum | JAM-Ety | |
| Damu | tǝp-pɯ | testicle | JS-Tani | |
| Gallong | ˆɯt-**tum** ˋa pɤ | testicle | AW-TBT:617a | |
| **1.3. Naga** | | | | |
| Chang | **tam** laŋ | testicle | WTF-PNN:540 | 43 |
| **2.1.1. Western Himalayish** | | | | |
| Bunan | khuar **tum** | egg (of animal) | SBN-BunQ:10.4.16 | |
| **2.1.2. Bodic** | | | | |
| Tsangla (Central) | go **tham** | egg | EA-Tsh:87 | |
| Tsangla (Motuo) | go-**tham** | egg | ZMYYC:170.7 | |
| | go tʰam | egg | SLZO-MLD | |
| | ko¹³ tʰam⁵⁵ | egg | JZ-CLMenba | |
| Tsangla (Tilang) | goi-tʰam | egg | JZ-CLMenba | |
| **2.1.3. Lepcha** | | | | |
| Lepcha | tălam | scrotum, testicles | JAM-Ety | |
| | tălam să tăblyóṅ | scrotum | JAM-Ety | |
| | tălam t'yeṅ | testicle | JAM-Ety | 44 |
| | tălam pot | testicle | JAM-Ety | 45 |
| **3.3. rGyalrongic** | | | | |
| rGyalrong | tǝ **lem** | scrotum | DQ-Jiarong:10.3.4 | |
| rGyalrong (Eastern) | tǝ **lam** ndzi̤ | foreskin | SHK-rGEQ:10.3.3 | |
| | tǝ **lam** tʃi | semen | SHK-rGEQ:10.3.7 | |

## (10)           *krak ≋ *kwak           EGG / TESTICLE

This etymon appears in only a few Kamarupan and Himalayish languages. Thulung reflects medial *-w- rather than *-r-. This root is quite distinct from the coincidentally nearly homophonous etymon **(H:317)** *k-rak FOWL (cf. Bokar **po-rok** 'chicken', WB **krak** 'id.'), despite the fact that many languages have an association between 'chicken' and 'penis' (cf. Spanish *polla* 1. 'chicken' 2. [*Slang*] 'penis').

---

[43]The second syllable of this Chang form is referred by W. T. French (p. 540) to PNN **\*C-ruŋ** 'round (of body parts)'. This binome is thus not a dimidation of a sesquisyllabic combination of prefix *t- plus root-initial *l- (as in Lepcha). Besides no final -ŋ occurs anywhere else in the set.

[44]According to Mainwaring/Grünwedel 1898:164, **t'yeṅ** actually means 'the chief or most precious part', as in **să-bŭr t'yeṅ** 'the musk bag or gland of the musk-deer'.

[45]The last syllable **pot** means "fruit, ball".

### 1.3. Naga

| | | | | |
|---|---|---|---|---|
| Konyak | ao **kiak** | egg | GEM-CNL | 46 |

### 1.7. Bodo-Garo = Barish

| | | | | |
|---|---|---|---|---|
| Deuri | du-**jā**² | egg | Deuri | 47 |
| | du **ja** | egg | WBB-Deuri:65 | |

### 2.3.1. Kham-Magar-Chepang-Sunwar

| | | | |
|---|---|---|---|
| Chepang (Eastern) | **krak** | testicle | RC-ChepQ:10.3.5 |
| | **krak** pun | scrotum | RC-ChepQ:10.3.4 |

### 2.3.2. Kiranti

| | | | |
|---|---|---|---|
| Thulung | le **koak** ti | testicle | NJA-Thulung |

## (11a)     *gop ⪰ *kop     HATCH / INCUBATE / COVER

This etymon, with velar stop or fricative initial reflexes, seems clearly to have an allo-famic relationship to **(11b)** ***ʔup** COVER / INCUBATE / HATCH. Other TB etyma showing variation between velar and zero (= glottal stop) initial include NEEDLE ***kap** (but WB **ʔap**), HOUSE ***kyim** (but WB **ʔim**), etc. See *STC* pp. 25-6, Matisoff 1997, and *HPTB* p. 57.

This etymon, which seems to include both simplex and causative allofams (thus the variation in voicing) is widely attested, occurring in Kamarupan, Himalayish, Jingpho, and perhaps Karenic. There is a good Chinese comparandum, 蓋, meaning 'cover; lid' (below).

See *HPTB* ***ʔup** ⪰ ***gup**, pp. 57, 369.

### 0. Sino-Tibetan

| | | | |
|---|---|---|---|
| *Sino-Tibetan | ***gap**/kap | cover | WSC-SH:59 |
| *Tibeto-Burman | ***gab**/khab | cover | WSC-SH:59 |

### 1.1. North Assam

| | | | | |
|---|---|---|---|---|
| Apatani | **gúŋ** | hatch | JS-Tani | |
| | **guʔ** | brood | JS-Tani | |
| Bengni | **gup** | hatch | JS-Tani | |
| Bokar | **gup** | hatch | JS-Tani | |
| | **kup**-lup | cover up | JS-Tani | |
| | me:-**kap** | cover with the hand | JS-Tani | |
| | pam-**kap** | cover up | JS-Tani | |
| Damu | cok-pɯ **xɯm** | lay egg | JS-Tani | 48 |
| Gallong | porok-ape **gup**-nam | hatch | KDG-IGL | |
| Milang | ci-ci **gup**-le-ma | hatch | AT-MPB | |

### 1.2. Kuki-Chin

| | | | |
|---|---|---|---|
| Thado | xú **xùm** | cover | THI1972:61 |

---

[46] The first element means "bird".

[47] The first element means "bird".

[48] The final nasal in this Damu form is similar to those in Rongmei, Thado, and Mzieme.

# (11a) *gop ⪥ *kop HATCH / INCUBATE / COVER

## 1.3. Naga

| | | | |
|---|---|---|---|
| *Northern Naga | *kup | cover / shut | WTF-PNN:472 |
| | *ku:p | cover / shut | WTF-PNN:472 |
| Ao (Chungli) | küp bang | cover | GEM-CNL |
| Chang | kap | cover | GEM-CNL |
| Konyak | küp | cover | GEM-CNL |
| Nocte | ka hap | cover | GEM-CNL |
| Phom | küp | cover | GEM-CNL |
| Rongmei | gum | cover | GEM-CNL |
| Tangsa (Yogli) | a hip | cover | GEM-CNL |
| Mzieme | gum | cover | GEM-CNL |

## 1.5. Mikir

| | | | |
|---|---|---|---|
| Mikir | kup | cover | GEM-CNL |

## 2.1.2. Bodic

| | | | |
|---|---|---|---|
| Kaike | kap pā | covered | AH-CSDPN:12c.14 |
| Tibetan (Written) | sgab-pa | cover | WSC-SH:59 |

## 2.1.4. Tamangic

| | | | |
|---|---|---|---|
| *Tamang | *<sup>A</sup>gap | cover (v.) | MM-Thesis:142 |
| | *<sup>Bh</sup>ŋup | brood | MM-Thesis:6 |
| Gurung | kā:q bā: | covered | AH-CSDPN:12c.14 |
| Gurung (Ghachok) | ka:q ba: | covered | SIL-Gur:12.C.14 |
| Tamang (Risiangku) | ³kap | cover (n.) / lid | MM-Thesis:142 |
| Tamang (Sahu) | ³kap | cover, lid | MM-Thesis:142 |
| Tamang (Taglung) | ³kap-pa | cover | MM-Thesis:142 |
| Thakali | kahp-ci-wa | covered | AH-CSDPN:12c.14 |
| Thakali (Marpha) | go<sup>ɦ</sup>-wa | cover (v.) | MM-Thesis:142 |
| | ³ko<sup>ɦ</sup> | cover (n.) / lid | MM-Thesis:142 |
| Thakali (Tukche) | kɔhp | cover / lid | SIL-Thak:6.A.58 |
| | kɔhp-ci-wɔ | covered | SIL-Thak:12.C.14 |
| | kɔhp-lɔ | cover | SIL-Thak:7.B.1.34 3 |
| | ³kəp | cover (n.) / lid | MM-Thesis:142 |
| | ³kəp-lə | cover (v.) | MM-Thesis:142 |

## 2.3.1. Kham-Magar-Chepang-Sunwar

| | | | |
|---|---|---|---|
| Kham | kap sio | covered | AH-CSDPN:12c.14 |
| Magar | hup-ke | covered | AH-CSDPN:12c.14 |

## 2.3.2. Kiranti

| | | | |
|---|---|---|---|
| Dumi | khop nɨ | cover, cap | SVD-Dum |
| | kop mɨt nɨ | cover someone with a blanket | SVD-Dum |
| Kulung | khəpp-u | cover (with a lid) | RPHH-Kul |
| | kupp-u | brood (eggs) | RPHH-Kul |
| Limbu | khapt- | cover (e.g. so. with a blanket), to roof | SVD-LimA |

## 4.1. Jingpho

| | | | |
|---|---|---|---|
| Jingpho | gàp | cover / top | JAM-TJLB:327 |
| | mə gàp | cover | JAM-TJLB:327 |

## 6.1. Burmish

| | | | |
|---|---|---|---|
| Achang (Xiandao) | xup⁵⁵ | incubate | DQ-Xiandao:1834 |

27

6.2. Loloish

| | | | |
|---|---|---|---|
| Nusu (Central/Zhizhiluo) | ɣɔ³¹ | incubate | DQ-NusuA:1834. |
| Nusu (Central) | ɣɔ⁵³ | incubate | DQ-NusuB:1834. |

7. Karenic

| | | | |
|---|---|---|---|
| *Karen (Pho) | *ɣwýq | brood (eggs) | RBJ-KLS:356 |
| *Karen (Sgaw) | *ɣý | brood (eggs) | RBJ-KLS:356 |
| *Karen (Pho-Sgaw) | *ɣỳh | brood (eggs) | RBJ-KLS:356 |
| Pa-O | khɔ́ʔ | brood, sit on eggs | DBS-PaO; RBJ-KLS:356 |
| Pho (Bassein) | ɣỳ | brood (eggs) | RBJ-KLS:356 |
| Pho (Moulmein) | ɣúʔ | brood (eggs) | RBJ-KLS:356 |
| Sgaw (Bassein) | hý | brood (eggs) | RBJ-KLS:356 |
| Karen (Sgaw/Hinthada) | xɯ⁵⁵ | incubate | DQ-KarenB:1899 |
| | xɯ⁵⁵ di̱³¹ | incubate | DQ-KarenB:1899.1 |
| Sgaw (Moulmein) | ɣý | brood (eggs) | RBJ-KLS:356 |

9. Sinitic

| | | | |
|---|---|---|---|
| Chinese (Middle) | ɣâp | cover | WSC-SH:59 |
| Chinese (Old) | gap | cover | WSC-SH:59 |
| | kabh | cover | WSC-SH:59 |
| | kaps | cover; conceal | WHB-OC:1731,1825 |
| | ʔjap | cover | WSC-SH:59 |

## Chinese comparandum

蓋 **hé** 'to cover, thatch' ≍ **gài** 'a cover, lid'

*GSR*: 642q   Karlgren: *\*gâp* / *\*kâb* > *\*kâd*   Li: *\*gap* / *\*kabh* > *\*kadh*   Baxter: *\*fikap* / *\*kaps* > *\*kats* (1732, 1731)

These two related words perhaps derive from an unattested root **\*kap**. The noun has an **\*-s** suffix, which derives a passive noun from a transitive verb (i.e. 'the thing that is used to cover' > 'a lid'). In the verb form, Baxter's **\*fikap** develops as **\*gap**, the notation suggesting morphological derivation from a root with initial **\*k-**. While voicing derivation is a well-known Old Chinese morphological process, it usually derives intransitives from transitive verbs, so the function here is not clear.

The only difficulty with the TB comparison is the vowel. While Baxter's six-vowel system permits the possibility of reconstructing **\*fikop** or **\*gop** for the verb, the noun must be reconstructed with **\*a** to account for subsequent sound changes, and this forces a reconstruction of **\*a** in the verb as well.

It is possible that OC **\*a** corresponds regularly to PTB **\*o** before bilabial codas. Unfortunately, there are very few proposed cognate sets that would help us establish or refute such a possibility.

[ZJH]

## (11b)                         **\*ʔup**                         **COVER / INCUBATE / HATCH**

This is *STC* #107, which cites forms from Jingpho, Mikir, Written Burmese, and Lushai. This etymon is most likely an allofam of **(11a) \*gop** ≍ **\*kop** HATCH / INCUBATE / COVER.

See *HPTB* \*ʔup ✕ \*gup, pp. 57, 369.

**0. Sino-Tibetan**

| | | | |
|---|---|---|---|
| *Tibeto-Burman | \*up | cover | STC:107 |

**1.2. Kuki-Chin**

| | | | |
|---|---|---|---|
| Lushai [Mizo] | up | shelter | STC:107 |
| Tiddim | op³ | brood over eggs | PB-TCV |

**1.5. Mikir**

| | | | |
|---|---|---|---|
| Mikir | up | cover | STC:107 |

**2.1.4. Tamangic**

| | | | |
|---|---|---|---|
| *Tamang | \*ᴬu | cover | MM-Thesis:3 |
| | \*ᴬup | cover | MM-Thesis:5 |
| | \*ᴮup | brood | MM-Thesis:6 |
| Gurung (Ghachok) | hu ba | cover | SIL-Gur:6.B.2.11 |
| | uh ba | cover | SIL-Gur:7.B.1.34 |
| Gurung | ³u- = uh ba | cover (v.) | MM-Thesis:5 |
| Manang (Prakaa) | ²ʔuː- | cover | HM-Prak:0797 |
| | ³uː- | cover | MM-Thesis:5 |
| Tamang (Sahu) | 'up-pā(p) | brood (hens) | AH-CSDPN:03b.16 |
| | 'wah-pa | cover | SIL-Sahu:18.A.34 |
| | ²up=pa = 'up-pa | brood | MM-Thesis:6 |

**4.1. Jingpho**

| | | | |
|---|---|---|---|
| Jingpho | úp ✕ wúp | cover | STC:107 |

**6.1. Burmish**

| | | | |
|---|---|---|---|
| Achang (Longchuan) | up⁵⁵ | sit on, hatch (egg) | JZ-Achang; ZMYYC:786.41 |
| Bola | ɣaʔ³¹ ap⁵⁵ | incubate | DQ-Bola:1834 |
| Burmese (Spoken Rangoon) | wuʔ⁴⁴ | hatch | ZMYYC:786.40 |
| Burmese (Written) | up | cover; rule over | GEM-CNL; PKB-WBRD; STC:107 |
| | wɑp | hatch | ZMYYC:786.39 |
| Hpun (Northern) | àʔ | incubate | EJAH-Hpun |
| Maru [Langsu] | ap⁵⁵ | hatch | ZMYYC:786.43 |
| Atsi [Zaiwa] | up⁵⁵ | sit on (egg); hatch | JZ-Zaiwa; ZMYYC:786.42 |

**6.2. Loloish**

| | | | |
|---|---|---|---|
| Lisu (Northern) | fu³⁵ | cover up; boil in a covered pot | DB-Lisu |
| Lisu (Central) | ū'³ | cover (house with roof) | JF-HLL |

**6.4. Jinuo**

| | | | |
|---|---|---|---|
| Jinuo (Buyuan) | vu¹³ | cover (muffle) | JZ-Jinuo |

**7. Karenic**

| | | | |
|---|---|---|---|
| Palaychi | hùq | brood (eggs) | RBJ-KLS:356 |
| Karen (Sgaw/Yue) | u̲ʔ⁵⁵ | incubate | DQ-KarenA:1899 |

## (12)  *pʷum  EGG / SIT ON EGGS / HATCH / TESTICLE

This well-attested etymon occurs in Kamarupan, Himalayish, and Jingpho-Nung, with a variety of ovoid meanings.

The Hill Miri and Sunwar forms reflect a variant *pup, perhaps to be explained in terms of assimilation to the initial.

A couple of other Himalayish languages, Magar and Manang (Prakaa), seem to reflect still another variant, *puŋ. The zero (ʔ-) initial in Chepang is unexplained.

It is not clear whether this root is to be related to (1) *pʷu EGG / BIRD / ROUND OBJECT.

See *HPTB* *pʷum, p. 57.

1.1. North Assam

| | | | |
|---|---|---|---|
| Miri, Hill | pɯp | egg | IMS-HMLG |

1.2. Kuki-Chin

| | | | |
|---|---|---|---|
| Liangmei | marui **bum** | egg | GEM-CNL |

1.3. Naga

| | | | |
|---|---|---|---|
| Zeme | nrui **bum** | egg | GEM-CNL |

2.1.2. Bodic

| | | | |
|---|---|---|---|
| Kaike | kã **pum** | egg | JAM-Ety |

2.1.4. Tamangic

| | | | |
|---|---|---|---|
| *Tamang | *ᴮpʰum | egg | MM-Thesis:653 |
| Gurung | ²pʰũ = pʰũq | egg | MM-Thesis:653 |
| Manang (Gyaru) | gar³ **bum**² | testicles | YN-Man:042-08 |
| | pɯm² | egg | YN-Man:076 |
| Manang (Prakaa) | ²pʰuŋ | egg | MM-Thesis:653 |
| | ¹pʰuŋ | egg | HM-Prak:0061 |
| Tamang | 'phum | egg | AW-TBT:555 |
| Tamang (Risiangku) | ²pʰum | egg; testicle | MM-TamRisQ:10.4.16; MM-Thesis:653 |
| Tamang (Sahu) | 'mi: phum | eyeball | JAM-Ety |
| | 'phum | egg | JAM-Ety |
| | 'phum 'phum-pā(m) | lay egg | AH-CSDPN:03b.14 |
| | 'pʰum ki 'mar | egg | SIL-Sahu:7.11 |
| | ²pʰum | egg | MM-Thesis:653 |
| Thakali | phum phum-la | lay egg | AH-CSDPN:03b.14 |
| Thakali (Syang) | ⁵⁴pʰum | egg | MM-Thesis:653 |
| | ⁵⁵pʰum | egg | MM-Thesis:653 |
| Thakali (Tukche) | naka pʰum | egg | SIL-Thak:7.A.10 |
| | phum | egg | JAM-Ety |
| | pʰum | egg | SIL-Thak:1.33 |
| | pʰum nahŋ-ri-we tɔr | egg white | SIL-Thak:7.A.12 |
| | ᴴpʰum | egg | MM-Thesis:653 |

2.3.1. Kham-Magar-Chepang-Sunwar

| | | | |
|---|---|---|---|
| Chepang | ʔum | egg; egg (louse) | JAM-Ety; SIL-Chep:1.33,3.A.88 |

|  |  |  |  |
|---|---|---|---|
|  | ʔum ʔot.sā | lay egg | AH-CSDPN:03b.14 |
| Chepang (Eastern) | ʔum | egg (of birds, insects) | RC-ChepQ:10.4.16 |
| Kham | pum-nyā | brood (hens) | AH-CSDPN:03b.16 |
| Magar | pung-khe | brood (hens) | AH-CSDPN:03b.16 |
| Sunwar | pup-cā | brood (hens) | AH-CSDPN:03b.16 |

**4.1. Jingpho**

| Jingpho | phum⁵⁵ | hatch | ZMYYC:786.47 |

**4.2. Nungic**

| Anong | bɯm³¹ | hatch | SHK-Anong |
|  | bɯm³⁵ | hatch | ZMYYC:786.44 |
| Trung [Dulong] | sɯ³¹bɯm⁵⁵ | hatch | ZMYYC:786.46 |
| Trung [Dulong] (Nujiang) | pɔm⁵⁵ | birth, give (to child) | JZ-Dulong |

**6.1. Burmish**

| Burmese (Written) | phuṁ | cover | GEM-CNL |
|  | phûṁ | cover, cover up | PKB-WBRD |
|  | ə-phûṁ | cover of a vessel | PKB-WBRD |

**6.2. Loloish**

| Lahu (Black) | phɛ⁵³ | hatch | ZMYYC:786.33 [49] |

**7. Karenic**

| Bwe | phɛ-tha | hatch out, to open up | EJAH-BKD |

## (13)                                   *pay                                   HATCH

The basic meaning of this etymon seems to be 'break out'. It is reconstructed in *STC* #254 as **be ~ *pe** 'broken; break', though the present reconstruction with *-ay* seems preferable.

This root is possibly related to Proto-Kuki-Chin **paːy** CONCEIVE / PREGNANT (Tiddim ˊpaːi/ˆpaːi; Lushai **păi**). See *GSTC* #140; *HPTB*:210.

**1.2. Kuki-Chin**

| Lushai [Mizo] | peʔ | break; be broken; broken (off) | AW-TBT:319; JAM-GSTC:074; RJL-DPTB:75; STC:254 |

**1.7. Bodo-Garo = Barish**

| Dimasa | bai | break; get broken | GEM-CNL; RJL-DPTB:75; STC:254 |
|  | do-phai | break with an instrument | JAM-GSTC:074; STC:254 |
|  | ga bai | broken | JAM-GSTC:074; STC:254 |

---

[49]This Lahu form in -ɛ shows the regular reflex of the *-um rhyme, but the meaning is basically 're-lease, come forth' rather than 'cover, incubate'. The same seems to be true of the Bwe form (**phɛ-tha**). For now we include them here, however.

| | phai | hatch | JAM-GSTC:074; STC:254 |
|---|---|---|---|
| | sa **bai** | break | GEM-CNL; JAM-GSTC:074; STC:254 |
| Garo | **be** | break; broken | JAM-GSTC:074; RJL-DPTB:75; STC:254 |
| | **be?**-a | broken (off) | AW-TBT:319 |
| | **pe** | break down | JAM-GSTC:074; STC:254 |

### 2.3.1. Kham-Magar-Chepang-Sunwar

| | | | |
|---|---|---|---|
| Kham | **phay**-nyā | hatch | AH-CSDPN:03b.17 |

### 6.1. Burmish

| | | | |
|---|---|---|---|
| Burmese (Written) | **pai'** | broken off; chipped; crumble; hare-lipped | PKB-WBRD |
| | **phai'** | break off a small piece from a larger; crumble; break off a piece | JAM-GSTC:074; PKB-WBRD |

### 7. Karenic

| | | | |
|---|---|---|---|
| Pa-O | ?ə **pé** pá? | hatch | DBS-PaO |

## (14)                    *s-mu                    HATCH / BROOD ON EGGS

This root is solidly attested, but almost exclusively in Loloish. There also seems to be a good Gallong cognate. The very-low tone in Lahu **mū** (Matisoff 1988a, p. 1005), as well as the Lalo form **?mò**, point to a Proto-Loloish *?- prefix, ultimately from prefixal *s-.

The constriction in Yi Mojiang is perhaps due to the *?- prefix.

See *HPTB* PLB *?-mu², pp. 112, 180.

### 1.1. North Assam

| | | | |
|---|---|---|---|
| Gallong | **mɯ**-nam | brood | KDG-IGL |

### 6.2. Loloish

| | | | |
|---|---|---|---|
| *Loloish | ***?-mu²** | hatch | JAM-II |
| Lahu (Black) | **mū** | brood; sit on eggs | JAM-DL:1005 |
| | **mɣ³¹** | hatch (a chick) | JZ-Lahu |
| Lahu (Yellow) | **mɣ¹¹** | hatch (a chick) | JZ-Lahu |
| Lalo | **?mò** | incubate / sit on egg | SB-Lalo |
| Lisu (Central) | **mū⁴** | hatch | JF-HLL |
| Lisu | **mu⁵⁵** | hatch | ZMYYC:786.27 |
| Lisu (Northern) | **mɣ⁵⁵** | hatch | DB-Lisu |
| Yi (Mile) | **mu⁵⁵** | hatch | ZMYYC:786.25 |
| Yi (Mojiang) | **mṵ³³** | hatch | ZMYYC:786.26 |
| Yi (Nanhua) | **mɯ⁵⁵** | hatch | ZMYYC:786.24 |
| Yi (Nanjian) | **mṵ²¹** | sit on, hatch (egg) | JZ-Yi |
| | **m̩(ṵ)²¹** | hatch | ZMYYC:786.23 |

## (15)        *glim ⪴ *glip        BROOD / INCUBATE (eggs)

This root is attested mainly in Himalayish. The Jinuo and Bola forms also look related, though more evidence is needed to establish this etymon for Lolo-Burmese.

**2.3.2. Kiranti**

| | | | |
|---|---|---|---|
| Bahing | glyp dzi | brood (of a hen) | BM-Bah |
| Dumi | gɨm nɨ | brood (eggs) | SVD-Dum |
| Khaling | glam-ne | brood (hens) | AH-CSDPN:03b.16 |
| Thulung | ghleom- | brood; to hatch; to keep sthg warm | NJA-Thulung |

**6.1. Burmish**

| | | | |
|---|---|---|---|
| Bola | kʰja³⁵ | lay egg | DQ-Bola:2363 |

**6.4. Jinuo**

| | | | |
|---|---|---|---|
| Jinuo (Baka) | kʰlo⁴⁴ | lay egg | DQ-JinB:2468 |
| Jinuo (Baya/Banai) | kʰlɔ⁴⁴ | lay egg | DQ-JinA:2468 |

## (16)        *puk ⪴ *buk        HATCH / EGG

This etymon, which quite distinct from **(1b)** *pu EGG, seems to be confined to Himalayish. It is perhaps to be identified with **(30)** *p/buk ⪴ *p/bik BORN / GIVE BIRTH, below.

**1.3. Naga**

| | | | |
|---|---|---|---|
| Tangkhul | huk | hatch | Bhat-TNV:90 |

**2.1.2. Bodic**

| | | | |
|---|---|---|---|
| Tsangla (Motuo) | buŋ | hatch | ZMYYC:786.7 |

[50]

**2.1.4. Tamangic**

| | | | |
|---|---|---|---|
| Gurung (Ghachok) | phuq | egg | JAM-Ety |
| Gurung | phuq phuq-bā | lay egg | AH-CSDPN:03b.14 |
| Gurung (Ghachok) | pʰũq | egg | SIL-Gur:1.33 |

**2.3.1. Kham-Magar-Chepang-Sunwar**

| | | | |
|---|---|---|---|
| Chepang | bhyuk.sā | hatch | AH-CSDPN:03b.17 |
| | bʰyuk-sa | hatch | SIL-Chep:3.B.17 |
| Sunwar | 'pu:k-cā | hatch | AH-CSDPN:03b.17 |

## (17)        *du        BROOD / INCUBATE (eggs)

This root, like **(19)** *naŋ BROOD / INCUBATE (eggs), seems confined to the Tamang-Gurung-Thakali branch of Himalayish.

**2.1.4. Tamangic**

| | | | |
|---|---|---|---|
| *Tamang | *ᴬduː | brood | MM-Thesis:514 |
| Tamang (Sahu) | 'nakca Tʰo-pa | brood | SIL-Sahu:14.16 |
| Thakali | tun-la | brood (hens) | AH-CSDPN:03b.16 |
| Thakali (Tukche) | tuh-lɔ | brood | SIL-Thak:3.B.16 |
| | ³tu-lə | brood | MM-Thesis:514 |

---

[50]The final nasal in this form in unexplained.

## (18) *a           HATCH / LAY EGG

This beautifully minimalist root (minimal both from the point of view of its phonological shape and the paucity of languages in which it is attested) seems unimpeachable, occurring both in Kamarupan and Loloish with exactly the same meaning.

First reconstructed in Matisoff 1996, "Primary and secondary laryngeal initials in Tibeto-Burman", 7.1 (p. 42).

1.1. North Assam

| | | | |
|---|---|---|---|
| Darang [Taraon] | $a^{53}$ | lay (egg) | ZMYYC:785.49 |
| Idu | $aŋ^{55}a^{55}$ | hatch | ZMYYC:786.50 |
| | $a^{55}$ | lay (egg) | ZMYYC:785.50 |

6.2. Loloish

| | | | |
|---|---|---|---|
| Nusu (Bijiang) | $ʔu^{55}a^{55}$ | lay (egg) | ZMYYC:785.45 |

## (19) *naŋ           BROOD / INCUBATE (eggs)

This root, like (17) above, is confined to the Tamang-Gurung-Thakali branch of Himalayish. It may well be related to (29) *naŋ GIVE BIRTH, below.

2.1.4. Tamangic

| | | | |
|---|---|---|---|
| *Tamang | *$^{Bh}$naŋ | brood | MM-Thesis:576 |
| Gurung (Ghachok) | naqga nõq ba | brood | SIL-Gur:3.B.16 |
| Gurung | nāq gā noq bā | brood (hens) | AH-CSDPN:03b.16 |
| | $^{2}$nõ- | brood | MM-Thesis:576 |
| Thakali | cahca nāng-la | hatch | AH-CSDPN:03b.17 |
| Thakali (Tukche) | cɔh cɔ naŋ-lɔ | hatch | SIL-Thak:3.B.17 |

## (20) *s-row           EGG / NIT

This etymon is set up in *STC* #278 (and note 201), where the Tibetan, Jingpho, and rGyalrong forms are cited.

Possibly to be compared with this etymon is Chinese 卵 (Mand. **luǎn**) 'ovum; egg; spawn', perhaps with the collective *-n suffix. See note under (5) *rum ✕ *lum EGG for an alternative etymology.

See *HPTB* *s-row, p. 224.

0. Sino-Tibetan

| | | | |
|---|---|---|---|
| *Tibeto-Burman | *(s-)row | nit | STC:278 |

1.2. Kuki-Chin

| | | | |
|---|---|---|---|
| Lushai [Mizo] | hrū | egg | JHL-Lu:186 |

1.3. Naga

| | | | |
|---|---|---|---|
| Tangkhul | rɯ | egg | Bhat-TNV:88 |

2.1.2. Bodic

| | | | |
|---|---|---|---|
| Tibetan (Central) | sro-ma | nit | STC:278 |

| Tibetan (Western) | sro-ma | nit | STC:278 |
|---|---|---|---|
| **2.1.4. Tamangic** | | | |
| Tamang (Sahu) | ru | egg | SIL-Sahu:1.33 |
| **2.3.1. Kham-Magar-Chepang-Sunwar** | | | |
| Magar | mi-rhu | egg | JAM-Ety |
| | rhu-ke | lay egg | AH-CSDPN:03b.14 |
| **3.2. Qiangic** | | | |
| Shixing | ra³³ʁu⁵⁵ | egg | TBL:0450.17 |
| **3.3. rGyalrongic** | | | |
| rGyalrong | dẓə ru | egg (louse) | STC:64n201 |
| **4.1. Jingpho** | | | |
| Jingpho | tsíʔ-rù | nit | STC:278 |
| **6.2. Loloish** | | | |
| Namuyi | ɦæ˪⁵⁵ʁuo⁵⁵ | egg | TBL:0450.46 |
| Yi (Wuding) | ɬu̱² | egg | TBL:0450.38 |

\* \* \*

The English work *yolk* (< OE *geolca*) is an allofam of *yellow* (< OE *geolu*) < PIE **\*ghel-** 'shine; shiny object' [*AHD*:2029]. Similarly, TB words for YOLK typically contain a morpheme meaning YELLOW, e.g. Lahu **ğâʔ-u-ši** 'yolk of hen's egg' < (H:317) **\*k-rak** FOWL + (1a) **\*wu** EGG / BIRD + **ši** 'yellow/gold' < PLB (H:191) **\*s-rwəy¹** ≍ **\*s-rwe¹** GOLD / YELLOW. See *HPTB*:191.

# II. Birth

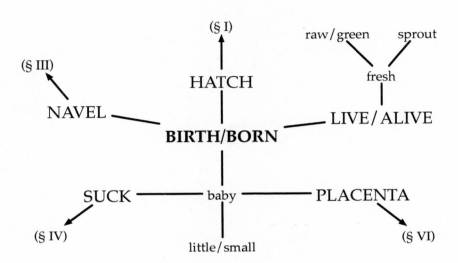

## (21)                     *braŋ                     BORN / BIRTH

This well-attested root occurs in Kamarupan, Himalayish, and Lolo-Burmese, and probably in Karenic and Qiangic as well. It is reconstructed in *STC* #135, which only lists the WT and Lushai forms. The Jingpho forms **pràt, šəpràt** 'bear, give birth' do not belong in this set, since **-ŋ ≍ -t** is not an established pattern of variation in TB word-families.[1]

The Himalayish forms with high vowels (Tamangic **-u/-i**, Pattani **-i**) are tentatively assigned to this etymon.

See *HPTB* **\*braŋ**, p. 264.

| 0. Sino-Tibetan | | | |
|---|---|---|---|
| *Tibeto-Burman | *braŋ | born, give birth | STC:135 |
| **1.1. North Assam** | | | |
| Idu | bɹa⁵⁵ | birth, give | SHK-Idu:10.4.15 |
|  | bɹɑ⁵⁵ | birth, give | ZMYYC:774.50 |
| **1.2. Kuki-Chin** | | | |
| Lushai [Mizo] | **piang** | birth, give | GEM-CNL |
|  | **piaŋ** | born, be | STC:135 |
| **1.5. Mikir** | | | |
| Mikir | ke **plang** | birth, give | GEM-CNL |

---

[1] As a longshot, we might relate these Jingpho forms to **(75) \*prat ≍ \*brat** BREAK / WEAN, below.

2.1.1. Western Himalayish

| Pattani [Manchati] | zir pʰi | born, be / to rise | DS-Patt |

2.1.2. Bodic

| Tibetan (Written) | ḥbraŋ-ba | birth, give | STC:135 |

2.1.4. Tamangic

| *Tamang | *^Apʰju: | born, be | MM-Thesis:673 |
| Gurung | phi bāq | birth, give (animals?) | AH-CSDPN:03b.46 |
| Gurung (Ghachok) | pʰi baq | born, be | SIL-Gur:2.B.2.11 |
| Gurung | ¹pʰi- = pʰi baq | born, be | MM-Thesis:673 |

2.3.2. Kiranti

| Limbu | po:ŋ ma? | born, be | SVD-LimA:491 |

3.2. Qiangic

| Namuyi | e˩³³ba³⁵ | birth, give | SHK-NamuQ:10.4.15 |
| | ə˩³³ba³⁵ | birth, give | ZMYYC:774.19 |
| Qiang (Mawo) | pæ˩ (?æ zæ pæ˩) | birth, give | SHK-MawoQ:10.4.15 |

6. Lolo-Burmese

| *Lolo-Burmese | *b(r)aŋ³ | born / birth | JAM-DL:p.857 | 2 |

6.1. Burmish

| Achang (Xiandao) | pɔ³⁵ | birth, give | DQ-Xiandao:2227 |

6.2. Loloish

| Ahi | a³³ bɑ⁵⁵ zo²¹ bu³³ | birth, give | LMZ-AhiQ:10.4.15 |
| Akha | baw-eu | be born | PL-AETD:73-74 |
| | bɔ | born, be | ILH-PL:265 |
| Hani (Gelanghe) | bɔ³³ | birth, give | JZ-Hani |
| Hani (Shuikui) | pɣ³³ | birth, give | JZ-Hani |
| *Common Lahu | *paw: | born, be | DB-PLolo:597 |
| Lahu (Black) | pɔ | born, be; give birth to | JAM-DL |
| | pɔ³³ | birth, give | JZ-Lahu; ZMYYC:774.33 |
| Nesu | ba²¹ | birth, give | CK-YiQ:10.4.15 |
| Nusu (Southern) | pʰa̱⁵³ | birth, give | JZ-Nusu |

7. Karenic

| Bwe | ɔ phlɛ | born, be | EJAH-BKD |
| | ɔ phlɛ-la | born, be | EJAH-BKD |
| Karen (Sgaw/Hinthada) | o̱³¹ pʰlɛ³¹ a³¹ pʰo⁵⁵ | birth, give | DQ-KarenB:2320 |
| Karen (Sgaw/Yue) | o̱³¹ pʰlɛ³¹ | birth, give | DQ-KarenA:2320 |

(22)            **\*hu**           **BORN / BIRTH / REAR**

This excellent root, with a relatively rare laryngeal proto-initial, appears in Kamarupan, Lolo-Burmese, and Qiangic, with a range of meanings including 'be pregnant'; 'give birth'; 'bring up, rear (a child)'; 'nourish, feed', covering the whole range of parental

---

[2]This etymon is mistakenly reconstructed as Proto-Loloish *baw³ in Bradley 1979 (DB-PL) #597, on the basis of WB paw 'to appear'.

responsibility from conception to childhood. It is reconstructed in Matisoff 1985a (note 69, p. 38) and in Matisoff 1988a (p. 1071), and discussed in the context of TB laryngeal-initial etyma in general in Matisoff 1997 "Primary and secondary laryngeals in TB" (section 5.3).

See *HPTB* ***hu**, p. 58.

### 1.1. North Assam

| | | | | |
|---|---|---|---|---|
| Padam-Mising [Abor-Miri] | u | raise (child) | JAM-II | [3] |
| Bokar | ho: | birth, give | JS-Tani | |

### 1.4. Meithei

| | | | |
|---|---|---|---|
| Meithei | əŋaŋ **u** nə bə | birth, give | CYS-Meithei:10.4.15 |

### 3.2. Qiangic

| | | | |
|---|---|---|---|
| Qiang (Mawo) | χu | birth, give | JZ-Qiang; ZMYYC:774.8 |

### 6.2. Loloish

| | | | | |
|---|---|---|---|---|
| Gazhuo | za²¹ ni²⁴ za²¹ **fʏ³³** | birth, give | DQ-Gazhuo:10.4.15 | |
| Lahu (Black) | cê **hu** ve | raise animals | JAM-DL:1072 | |
| | **hu** | support; nourish; rear | JAM-DL:1071 | |
| | yâ **hu** ve | be pregnant; raise a child | JAM-DL:1259 | |
| Lipho | xo³³ | birth, give | CK-YiQ:10.4.15 | |
| Lisu | h'ū⁴ | born, be | DB-PLolo:597 | |
| Lisu (Nujiang) | he³³ | birth, give (human) | JZ-Lisu | |
| Lisu | he³³ | birth, give | ZMYYC:774.27 | |
| Lisu (Nujiang) | he̠⁴² | birth, give (animal) | JZ-Lisu | |
| Lisu (Northern) | hĩ³³gu³³ | birth place | DB-Lisu | [4] |
| Lisu (Central) | hỹ³³gu⁴⁴ | birth place | DB-Lisu | |
| Lisu (Northern) | hø̃³³ | birth, give ; support; feed and educate; raise | DB-Lisu | |
| | hø̃³³gu³³ | birth place | DB-Lisu | |
| | hø̃ʔ²¹la³³ | birth, give | DB-Lisu | |
| Lisu (Central) | h'ū⁴ | birth, give | JF-HLL | |
| | h'ū⁴ ta¹ law³ | born, be | JF-HLL | |
| Luquan | ʔhʏ¹¹ | raise, bring up (child) | MXL-Lolo | |
| Yi (Nanjian) | hu⁵⁵ | birth, give | JZ-Yi | |
| Yi (Xide) | hu⁵⁵ | birth, give | JAM-II | |

### 9. Sinitic

| | | | |
|---|---|---|---|
| Chinese (Old) | xu(ʔ)s | love | WHB-OC:737b |
| | xuʔ | good | WHB-OC:1566 |

---

[3] J. H. Lorrain (1907:229) glosses this word as 'to bring up; to tend; to rear; to keep; to support; to feed (as child, etc.).'

[4] The nasalization in some of the Lisu forms is due to rhinoglottophilia. See Matisoff 1975.

## Chinese comparandum

好 **hǎo** 'good' ⤲ **hào** 'love, like'[5]

*GSR*: 1044a    Karlgren: *χôg    Li: *həgwx / *həgwh    Baxter: *xuʔ / *xu(ʔ)s (737)

The word for 'love, like' is a putative form derived from 'good' through *-s suffixa-tion. This presents some semantic difficulty for the OC-PTB comparison, since the basic meaning of the PTB root is closer to that of the derived Chinese transitive verb.

Corroborated as it is by other etyma (e.g. **(1)** *pʷu EGG / BIRD / ROUND OBJECT, **(102)** *r-bu ⤲ *pru NEST / WOMB / PLACENTA), the correspondence TB *-u with OC *-əgw (Li)/*-u (Baxter) is well attested. The initial correspondence is difficult to eval-uate because there are so few proposed cognates involving words with OC *h- (Li)/*x-(Baxter) or PTB *h-. Of these several (such as Gong 1995 set 142 comparing OC 鼾 *xan 'snore' to PTB *hal 'snore') are clearly onomatopoetic. In other cases Gong has derived OC *x- from earlier *skh-, facilitating comparison with Written Tibetan forms having initial velars (see Gong 2000). Nevertheless, there is no specific reason to doubt the validity of the initial correspondence.

[ZJH]

**(23)**　　　　　**\*ʔ-bu ⤲ \*pu**　　　　**BORN / BIRTH / BUD / BLOOM**

The basic meaning of this root seems to be 'bloom, open up (as a flower), bud', thence 'give birth'. It is reconstructed in *STC* #260 as 'open, bud', with reflexes offered from WT, Nung, Jingpho, WB, and Mikir. The semantic connection between this root for 'open, bloom' and 'bear a child' was first suggested by W. T. French (1983:455), who reconstructs Proto-Northern Naga *ʔ-bəw. *STC* reconstructs both voiceless- and voiced-initial allofams (*bu ⤲ *pu), which we can now interpret as reflecting a simplex/causative opposition ('bloom' vs. 'cause to bud' [i.e. 'give birth']). A PLB reconstruction *ʔpu² (equivalent to *ʔbu²) is given in Matisoff 1988a (p. 831), with the glottalization in-ferred from the very-low tone of the Lahu reflex **pū**. This reinforces French's PNN re-construction with *ʔ-, as does the *a-chung* [ḥ] in the WT reflex (ḥbu). The Phom form **bəʔ** cited by French (*loc. cit.*) has been reanalyzed as belonging under **(30)** *p/buk ⤲ *p/bik BORN / GIVE BIRTH [q.v.].

See *HPTB* *s-bu, p. 184.

| | | | | |
|---|---|---|---|---|
| 0. Sino-Tibetan | | | | |
| *Tibeto-Burman | *bu ⤲ pu | open / bud | STC:260 | |
| 1.1. North Assam | | | | |
| Apatani | a-**pú** | blossom | JS-Tani | |
| | o-**bu** | birth, give | JS-Tani | 6 |
| | o-**bu**-nɯ | birth | JS-Tani | |
| | ó-hó **bu** | birth, give | JS-Tani | |

---

[5]This comparison is correctly cited in *HPTB* (p. 58), although by an unfortunate error the Chinese character 愛 is given instead of 好. [JAM]

[6]Apatani preserves reflexes of both the voiceless and voiced allofams of this etymon; cf. **pù** 'bloom', alongside **bu** 'give birth'.

|  | pù | bloom | JS-Tani |
|---|---|---|---|
| Gallong | ao be-nam | birth | KDG-IGL |

**1.3. Naga**

| *Northern Naga | *ʔ-bəw | bear a child | WTF-PNN:455 |
|---|---|---|---|
| Chokri | pü | birth, give | GEM-CNL |
| Konyak | pu | birth, give | GEM-CNL; WTF-PNN:455 |
| Ntenyi | pfüa | birth, give | GEM-CNL |

**1.5. Mikir**

| Mikir | iŋ pú | bud / swell | AW-TBT:264 |
|---|---|---|---|
|  | iŋ pu | open, dilate | STC:260 |
|  | phu | bud | STC:260 |

**2.1.2. Bodic**

| Tibetan (Written) | ḥbu-ba | open (of flowers) | STC:260 |
|---|---|---|---|

**2.2. Newar**

| Newar | bu-ye | be born | JAM-II |
|---|---|---|---|
|  | bwui:ke | birth, give | AH-CSDPN:03b.46 |

**2.3.2. Kiranti**

| Hayu | pho ku | birth, give; bear a child | BM-Hay:84.101 |
|---|---|---|---|
| Khaling | 'bu-ne | birth, give | AH-CSDPN:03b.46 |

**3.2. Qiangic**

| Shixing | bu$^{35}$ | bloom | ZMYYC:789.20 |
|---|---|---|---|

**4.1. Jingpho**

| Jingpho | pu | bloom, bud | STC:260 |
|---|---|---|---|
|  | pṵ$^{31}$ | bloom | ZMYYC:789.47 |
|  | ə pu | blossom, bud | STC:260 |

**4.2. Nungic**

| Anong | nam-phu | blossom, bud | STC:260 |
|---|---|---|---|
|  | phu | open | STC:260 |
| Trung [Dulong] | pɯ$^{31}$ɟu$^{53}$ | birth, give | ZMYYC:774.46 |

**5. Tujia**

| Tujia (Northern) | kha$^{55}$phu$^{55}$phu$^{21}$ | bloom | JZ-Tujia |
|---|---|---|---|
| Tujia | phu$^{21}$ | bloom | ZMYYC:789.38 |
| Tujia (Southern) | tsu$^{33}$pu$^{35}$do$^{55}$ | bloom | JZ-Tujia |

**6. Lolo-Burmese**

| *Lolo-Burmese | *ʔbu$^{2}$ | bloom | JAM-DL:831 |
|---|---|---|---|

**6.1. Burmish**

| Achang (Lianghe) | ɑ$^{31}$po$^{31}$po$^{31}$ | bloom | JZ-Achang |
|---|---|---|---|
| Achang (Xiandao) | pʰo$^{31}$ | birth, give (pig) | DQ-Xiandao:2362 [7] |
| Burmese (Written) | ăphù | bud, swelling | STC:260 |
|  | phù | bud / swell into protuberance | AW-TBT:264; STC:260 |
| Maru [Langsu] | pu$^{55}$ | bloom | ZMYYC:789.43 |

[7]Contrast Achang Xiandao pɔ$^{35}$ 'give birth' < (21) *braŋ BORN / BIRTH.

| Atsi [Zaiwa] | pau²¹ | birth, give | JZ-Zaiwa; |
|---|---|---|---|
| | | | ZMYYC:774.42 |
| | po⁵⁵ | bloom | ZMYYC:789.42 |

### 6.2. Loloish

| Ahi | bu²² | birth, give | CK-YiQ:10.4.15 |
|---|---|---|---|
| Hani | by²¹ | bloom | JAM-DL:831 |
| Hani (Pijo) | phu | open | ILH-PL:429 |
| Lahu (Black) | pū | bloom | JAM-DL:831 |
| Lisu | bu²¹ | bloom | JAM-DL:831 |
| Noesu | bo²¹ | birth, give | CK-YiQ:10.4.15 |
| Sani [Nyi] | a²¹ nɯ⁴⁴ bu²¹ | birth, give | YHJC-Sani:25.4 |
| | bu²¹ | birth, give | YHJC-Sani |
| Yi (Mile) | bu³³ | birth, give (taboo) | ZMYYC:774.25 |

### 6.4. Jinuo

| Jinuo (Youle) | po³³ | bloom | JZ-Jinuo |
|---|---|---|---|
| Jinuo | pɔ³³ | bloom | ZMYYC:789.34 |

### 7. Karenic

| Karen (Sgaw/Hinthada) | o̩³¹ phlɛ³¹ a³¹ pho⁵⁵ | birth, give | DQ-KarenB:2320 |
|---|---|---|---|
| | phui⁵⁵ | birth, give (to piglet) | DQ-KarenB:2467 |
| Karen (Sgaw/Yue) | phui⁵⁵ | birth, give (pig) | DQ-KarenA:2467 |

## (24)  *s-kya-y  BORN / GIVE BIRTH

This newly established root seems quite solid. The Barish forms (esp. Dimasa, Kokborok) point to a diphthongal prototype, while most Loloish (including Jinuo) and Qiangic forms seem to reflect a monophthong. (*-a > -i is a common Qiangic development.) The Himalayish evidence is mixed: Bantawa has -a, but WT and Pattani have -e (presumably from *-ay). There is evidence from Bahing for alternation between voiced and voiceless initial stops, reflecting a distinction between simplex ('be born') vs. causative ('give birth').

### 1.7. Bodo-Garo = Barish

| Deuri | je | born, be | WBB-Deuri:72 |
|---|---|---|---|
| | je¹ | born, be | Deuri |
| Dimasa | ha dźai | birth, give | STC:65n206 |
| | ha jai | birth, give | GEM-CNL |
| Garo | at tśi | birth, give | STC:65n206 |
| Kokborok | a-čay | born, be | PT-Kok |
| Lalung | chonja ha je na | birth, give (twins) | MB-Lal:85 |
| | ha je o sa | birth, give | MB-Lal:27 |
| | ha je na | born, be | MB-Lal:27 |

### 2.1.1. Western Himalayish

| Pattani [Manchati] | ze pi | birth | DS-Patt |
|---|---|---|---|

### 2.1.2. Bodic

| Tsangla (Motuo) | ke | birth, give | ZMYYC:774 |
|---|---|---|---|
| Tibetan (Amdo:Bla-brang) | htɕe | birth, give | ZMYYC:774.4 |
| Tibetan (Amdo:Zeku) | rcçe | birth, give | ZMYYC:774.5 |
| Tibetan (Batang) | xhɛʔ⁵³ | birth, give | DQ-Batang:10.4.15 |
| Tibetan (Khams:Dege) | çe⁵³ | birth, give | ZMYYC:774.3 |

| | | | |
|---|---|---|---|
| Tibetan (Lhasa) | ce?⁵³ | birth, give | ZMYYC:774.2 |
| Spiti | ṭu ke ze | birth, give | CB-SpitiQ:10.4.15 |
| Tibetan (Written) | skje | birth, give | ZMYYC:774.1 |

### 2.3.1. Kham-Magar-Chepang-Sunwar

| | | | |
|---|---|---|---|
| Sunwar | 'giy-cā | birth, give (animals?) | AH-CSDPN:03b.46 |

### 2.3.2. Kiranti

| | | | |
|---|---|---|---|
| Bahing | gi gi (moeba) | born, be | BM-Bah |
| | kik- | birth, give | BM-Bah |
| Bantawa | cha tokt- | birth, give | WW-Bant:18 |
| | chas- | birth, give | WW-Bant:18 |

### 3.2. Qiangic

| | | | |
|---|---|---|---|
| Ergong (Northern) | vʝjə⁵³ | birth, give | SHK-ErgNQ:10.4.15 |
| Ergong (Danba) | ŋʐɛ | birth, give | SHK-ErgDQ:10.4.15; ZMYYC:774.14 |
| Ergong (Daofu) | ɬŋɑ ?ʐa | birth, give | DQ-Daofu:10.4.15 |
| Ersu (Central) | dzɿ⁵⁵ | birth, give | SHK-ErsCQ |
| Ersu | dzɿ⁵⁵ | birth, give | ZMYYC:774.18 |
| Pumi (Jinghua) | khə¹³dzə⁵⁵ | birth, give | ZMYYC:774.11 |
| | kʰə¹³ dzə⁵⁵ | birth, give | JZ-Pumi |
| Pumi (Taoba) | khə³⁵ʑɛ³⁵ | birth, give | ZMYYC:774.10 |
| | kʰə³⁵ ʑɛ⁵⁵ | birth, give | JZ-Pumi |
| Qiang (Yadu) | ?i tɕi | birth, give | DQ-QiangN:2227 |
| Shixing | ji³⁵ | birth, give | SHK-ShixQ; ZMYYC:774.20 |
| Queyu (Yajiang) [Zhaba] | tə³⁵ tɕe⁵³ | birth, give | SHK-ZhabQ:10.4.15; ZMYYC:774.16 |

### 3.3. rGyalrongic

| | | | |
|---|---|---|---|
| rGyalrong (Northern) | ccʰo scci | birth, give | SHK-rGNQ:10.4.15 |
| rGyalrong | kə sccə | birth, give | ZMYYC:774.12 |
| rGyalrong (Eastern) | nɐ scci | birth, give | SHK-rGEQ:10.4.15 |

### 6.2. Loloish

| | | | |
|---|---|---|---|
| Lahu (Yellow) | dʐa⁵⁵ | birth, give | JZ-Lahu |
| Lalo | tjhỳ | birth, give (of animals) | SB-Lalo |
| Noesu | ʐe³³ | birth, give | CK-YiQ:10.4.15 |
| Nusu (Central/Zhizhiluo) | tsa⁵⁵ | birth, give; birth, give (to piglet) | DQ-NusuA:2227.,2362. |
| Nusu (Central) | tsa⁵⁵ | birth, give; birth, give (to piglet) | DQ-NusuB:2227.,2362. |
| Nusu (Northern) | tsɑ³⁵ | birth, give | JZ-Nusu |
| Yi (Mojiang) | tshɛ⁵⁵ | birth, give | ZMYYC:774.26 |
| Yi (Nanhua) | dzʌ³³ | birth, give | ZMYYC:774.24 |
| Yi (Nanjian) | tɕʰy²¹ | birth, give | JZ-Yi |
| Yi (Xide) | a³⁴-dzi³³ | birth, give | CSL-YIzd |

### 6.3. Naxi

| | | | |
|---|---|---|---|
| Naxi (Western) | tɕi³³xə³¹ | birth, give | JZ-Naxi |
| Naxi (Lijiang) | tɕi³³xə³¹ | birth, give | ZMYYC:774.28 |

---

[8]The final velar stop in this form is unexplained.

# II. Birth

### 6.4. Jinuo

| Jinuo (Baya/Banai) | tʃa³¹ | birth, give; birth, give (to piglet) | DQ-JinA:2320,2467 |
|---|---|---|---|
| Jinuo (Baka) | tʃa³¹ | birth, give; birth, give (to piglet) | DQ-JinB:2320,2467 |
| Jinuo | tʃa⁴² | birth, give | ZMYYC:774.34 |
| Jinuo (Youle) | tʃɑ⁴² | birth, give | JZ-Jinuo |

## (25)    *b-na                    BEAR A CHILD / BORN

This root is widespread in Naga languages, where it is always accompanied by a labial prefix. The Tamangic cognates show no evidence of the prefix. This etymon seems unrelated to (29) *naŋ GIVE BIRTH.

### 1.3. Naga

| Angami (Khonoma) | peno | birth, give | GEM-CNL |
|---|---|---|---|
| Angami (Kohima) | penuo | birth, give | GEM-CNL |
| | pe³¹nuo³³ | birth, give | VN-AngQ:10.4.15 |
| Chokri | mü³¹nou³³ | birth, give | VN-ChkQ:10.4.15 |
| Lotha Naga | ngaro vana | birth, give | VN-LothQ:10.4.15 |
| Mao | mono | birth, give | GEM-CNL |
| Sema | punu | birth, give | GEM-CNL |
| Mzieme | mna | birth, give | GEM-CNL |

### 2.1.4. Tamangic

| *Tamang | *ᴬna | born, be | MM-Thesis:537 |
|---|---|---|---|
| Manang (Prakaa) | ²nə- | born, be | HM-Prak:0395 |
| | ³nʏ- | born, be | MM-Thesis:537 |
| Tamang (Risiangku) | ³na | put down (e.g. a load); give birth, be born; care for (a child); raise, rear | MM-Thesis |
| Tamang (Sahu) | ²kola ³na-pa | born, be | MM-Thesis:537 |
| Thakali | nah-la | birth, give (animals?) | AH-CSDPN:03b.46 |
| Thakali (Marpha) | na⁶¹¹-wa¹¹ | birth, give / lay down | MM-Thesis:541 |
| Thakali (Tukche) | nɔh-lɔ | birth, give; born, be; birth, give (animals) | SIL-Thak,2.B.2.11,3.B.46 |
| | nɔh-lɔ tɔn-lɔ | birth, give | SIL-Thak:2.B.2.11a |
| | ³nə-lə; nɔh-lɔ | birth, give | MM-Thesis:537 |

## (26)    *mun          GIVE BIRTH / CONCEIVE / CREATE

This root is reconstructed for Proto-Kiranti by Michailovsky (1991). The Burmese form definitely appears cognate. It is possible that this etymon should be reconstructed with the PTB rhyme *-ul, as suggested by apparently parallel examples: (H:388) *mul BODY HAIR ( > WB mwê); (H:385) *b-ru:l SNAKE ( > WB mrwe).

| | | | |
|---|---|---|---|
| 2.3. Mahakiranti | | | |
| *Kiranti | **\*mun-** | created | BM-PK7:39 |
| 2.3.2. Kiranti | | | |
| Bahing | **mun-** | conceived (of a child) | BM-PK7:39 |
| Bantawa | **mun-** | birth, give | BM-PK7:39 |
| Chamling | **mun**-a | originate, to be born | BM-PK7:39 |
| Dumi | **mɨn-** | conceived (of a child) | BM-PK7:39 |
| Thulung | **mun-** | created | BM-PK7:39 |
| 6.1. Burmish | | | |
| Burmese (Spoken Rangoon) | **mwe⁵⁵** | birth, give | ZMYYC:774.40 |
| Burmese (Written) | **mwê** | bear, bring forth | PKB-WBRD |
| | **mwe:** | birth, give | GEM-CNL |
| | **mwe³** | birth, give | ZMYYC:774.39 |

## (27)        *pwa        BORN / BIRTH

This root is solidly established for Lolo-Burmese. The Pa-O (Karenic) form may be a borrowing from Burmese.

| | | | |
|---|---|---|---|
| 6.1. Burmish | | | |
| Achang (Luxi) | **pa³¹** | birth, give (to child) | JZ-Achang |
| Burmese (Written) | **phwâ** | bear, bring forth | PKB-WBRD |
| Atsi [Zaiwa] | **vo⁵⁵** | birth, give (child); birth, give | JZ-Zaiwa; ZMYYC:774.42 |
| 6.2. Loloish | | | |
| Nusu (Bijiang) | **phuɔ⁵³** | birth, give | ZMYYC:774.45 |
| Nusu (Central) | **pʰuɔ⁵³** | birth, give | JZ-Nusu |
| 7. Karenic | | | |
| Pa-O | **phwā** | born, be; birth, give (humans only) | DBS-PaO |

## (28)        *g-sow        REAR (child) / BEAR (child)

The WT form is the key to this reconstruction, although no other Himalayish cognates have been found so far. This etymon seems to be widespread in Loloish, with probable reflexes also in Kamarupan, Nungish (Dulong), and Qiangic (Muya).

| | | | |
|---|---|---|---|
| 1.1. North Assam | | | |
| Damu | **ço-tuŋ-xo** | birth, give (calves) | JS-Tani |
| Milang | miu-**cu**-ma | birth of a boy | AT-MPB |
| | or-mi **cu**-ma | birth of a girl | AT-MPB |
| 1.3. Naga | | | |
| Ao (Chungli) | a **so** | birth, give | GEM-CNL |
| Ao (Mongsen) | **so** | birth, give | GEM-CNL |

---

[9]Zaiwa treats the labial stop in this etymon as a prefix, so that it reflects an immediate prototype **\*wa.**

| | | | |
|---|---|---|---|
| Sangtam | **su** ro | birth, give | GEM-CNL |
| Yimchungrü | **zü** pe | birth, give | GEM-CNL |

**2.1.2. Bodic**

| | | | |
|---|---|---|---|
| Tibetan (Written) | **gso**-ba | feed, nourish; bring up, rear | HAJ-TED:590 |

**3.2. Qiangic**

| | | | |
|---|---|---|---|
| Muya [Minyak] | mɯ⁵⁵zɯ⁵⁵ | birth, give | SHK-MuyaQ:10.4.15; ZMYYC:774.15 |

**4.2. Nungic**

| | | | |
|---|---|---|---|
| Trung [Dulong] | pɯ³¹ʝu⁵³ | birth, give | ZMYYC:774.46 |

**6.1. Burmish**

| | | | |
|---|---|---|---|
| Achang (Lianghe) | ʂu³¹ | birth, give (to child) | JZ-Achang |

**6.2. Loloish**

| | | | |
|---|---|---|---|
| Ahi | ʐu̱³³ | birth, give | CK-YiQ:10.4.15 |
| Hani (Caiyuan) | tsu⁵⁵ | birth, give | JZ-Hani; ZMYYC:774.30 |
| Nasu | ʐo̱²¹ | birth, give | CK-YiQ:10.4.15 |
| Nosu | ʐu̱³³ | birth, give | CK-YiQ:10.4.15 |
| Sani [Nyi] | kɯ³³ ʐo̱⁴⁴ | born, be | YHJC-Sani:263.2 |
| | ʐo̱³³ | birth, give | JAM-II |
| | ʐo̱⁴⁴ | birth, give | CK-YiQ:10.4.15 |
| | ʐu̱⁴⁴ | grow, be born | MXL-SaniQ:346.1 |
| Yi (Sani) | ʐu̱⁴⁴ | birth, give to | TBL:1620.39 |
| Yi (Dafang) | a³³ŋa⁵⁵ ʐo³³ | birth, give | JAM-II |
| | ʐɔ³³ | born, be; grow (up); birth, give | JZ-Yi; ZMYYC:774.22 |
| Yi (Mile) | ʐu̱³³ | birth, give (polite term) | ZMYYC:774.25 |
| Yi (Xide) | ɕu̱³³ | birth, give | CSL-YIzd |
| | ʐu̱³³ | birth, give | JZ-Yi |

**6.3. Naxi**

| | | | |
|---|---|---|---|
| Naxi (Yongning) | dʑu¹³ | birth, give | ZMYYC:774.29 |
| Naxi (Eastern) | tɕu³¹ | birth, give | JZ-Naxi |

## (29)                      *naŋ                      GIVE BIRTH

This root is attested in a few widely separated languages: Kaman [Miju], Guiqiong (Qiangic), and Tujia. It is perhaps to be related to **(19)** *naŋ BROOD / INCUBATE (eggs), but seems quite distinct from **(25)** *b-na BEAR A CHILD / BORN.

**1.1. North Assam**

| | | | |
|---|---|---|---|
| Kaman [Miju] | xɑ³¹**naŋ**⁵⁵ | birth, give | ZMYYC:774.48 |

**3.2. Qiangic**

| | | | |
|---|---|---|---|
| Guiqiong | nɔ̃³⁵ | birth, give | SHK-GuiqQ; ZMYYC:774.17 |

**5. Tujia**

| | | | |
|---|---|---|---|
| Tujia | nũ⁵⁵ | birth, give | CK-TujBQ:10.4.15 |
| Tujia (Northern) | nũ⁵⁵ | birth, give (to child) | JZ-Tujia |

---

[10]a³³ŋa⁵⁵ means 'child'. See **(37)** *m/s-ŋa-y CHILD / BIRTH / SMALL, below.

(30)   $*\begin{smallmatrix} p \\ b \end{smallmatrix} uk \asymp *\begin{smallmatrix} p \\ b \end{smallmatrix} ik$   **BORN / GIVE BIRTH**

This root may well be related to **(16)** **\*puk** ⩵ **\*buk** HATCH / EGG.

| | | | | |
|---|---|---|---|---|
| **1.1. North Assam** | | | | |
| Bengni | (ku:) **buŋ** | birth, give | JS-Tani | 11 |
| **1.3. Naga** | | | | |
| Chang | **puk** | birth, give | GEM-CNL | |
| Lotha Naga | **pok** | birth, give | GEM-CNL | |
| Phom | **büh** | birth, give | GEM-CNL | |
| | **bə?** | birth, give | WTF-PNN:455 | 12 |
| **1.4. Meithei** | | | | |
| Meithei | **pok** | birth, give | GEM-CNL | |
| | əŋaŋ **pok** pə | birth, give | CYS-Meithei:10.4.15 | 13 |
| **2.1.2. Bodic** | | | | |
| Tsangla (Motuo) | **phok** | bloom | ZMYYC:789.7 | |
| | **pʰek**⁵⁵ | birth, give (of an animal) | JZ-CLMenba | |
| **2.3.2. Kiranti** | | | | |
| Bantawa | **puk-** | birth, give (medical) | WW-Bant:59 | |
| Chamling | **puk-**(a) | birth, give (animal) | WW-Cham:29 | |
| Dumi | **bɨk** nɨ | birth, give (of non-humans) | SVD-Dum | |
| **6.1. Burmish** | | | | |
| Hpun (Northern) | ăsă **phó?** | birth, give | EJAH-Hpun | 14 |

(31)   **\*wat**   **GIVE BIRTH**

This splendid little root is well-established in Himalayish (Chepang, Dumi), with likely cognates in Barish (Lalung) and Karenic.

| | | | |
|---|---|---|---|
| **1.7. Bodo-Garo = Barish** | | | |
| Lalung | ha je **o** sa | birth, give | MB-Lal:27 |
| **2.3.1. Kham-Magar-Chepang-Sunwar** | | | |
| Chepang | co? **?o.**sa | birth, give (animals?); birth, give | AH-CSDPN:03b.46; SIL-Chep:3.B.46 |
| | **?ot**-sa | birth, give | SIL-Chep:2.B.2. 11. |
| | ?um **?ot.**sā | lay egg | AH-CSDPN:03b.14 |
| Chepang (Eastern) | co? **?ot** na? | birth, give | RC-ChepQ:10.4.15 |

---

[11] The final nasal in the Bengni form is unexplained.

[12] W.T. French (1983:455) assigned this Phom form to PNN **\*?-bəw**; see **(23)** **\*?-bu** ⩵ **\*pu** BORN / BIRTH / BUD / BLOOM above.

[13] **əŋaŋ** means 'child'. Cf. Lhoba **aŋa:**, Yi (Dafang) **a³³ŋa⁵⁵**, as well as set **(37)** **\*m/s-ŋa-y** CHILD / BIRTH / SMALL.

[14] **ăsă** means "child".

2.3.2. Kiranti

| | | | |
|---|---|---|---|
| Dumi | **waːt** nɨ | bear (children, offspring); yean, calve, whelp | SVD-Dum |
| Limbu | ku-hiŋ **wEt** | alive | BM-Lim |

7. Karenic

| | | | |
|---|---|---|---|
| Karen (Sgaw/Hinthada) | o̱³¹ pʰlɛ³¹ a³¹ pʰo⁵⁵ | birth, give | DQ-KarenB:2320 |
| Karen (Sgaw/Yue) | o̱³¹ pʰlɛ³¹ | birth, give | DQ-KarenA:2320 |

(32)  \*to $^{k}_{ŋ}$  **GIVE BIRTH (of animals)**

This sparsely attested root seems to be associated especially with animal births. It appears in Himalayish, Damu (Abor-Miri-Dafla) and Mikir.

1.1. North Assam

| | | | |
|---|---|---|---|
| Damu | meː-**təŋ** xo | birth, give (babies) | JS-Tani |
| | ço-**tuŋ**-xo | birth, give (calves) | JS-Tani |

1.5. Mikir

| | | | |
|---|---|---|---|
| Mikir | ching **thòk**- | birth, give (animals) | KHG-Mikir:68 |

2.1.4. Tamangic

| | | | |
|---|---|---|---|
| Tamang (Sahu) | 'Tʰok-pa | birth, give (animals) | SIL-Sahu:14.46 |

2.3.2. Kiranti

| | | | |
|---|---|---|---|
| Bantawa | cha **tokt**- | birth, give | WW-Bant:18 |

(33)  **\*ra**  **GIVE BIRTH**

This etymon is so far attested only in a few Naga (Sangtam, Tangkhul) and Burmish (Bola, Maru) languages.

1.3. Naga

| | | | |
|---|---|---|---|
| Sangtam | su **ro** | birth, give | GEM-CNL |
| Tangkhul | pha **ra** | birth, give | GEM-CNL |

6.1. Burmish

| | | | |
|---|---|---|---|
| Bola | ɣa³⁵ | birth, give | DQ-Bola:2227 |
| Maru [Langsu] | ɣɔ⁵⁵ | birth, give | DQ-Langsu:10.4.15; ZMYYC:774.43 |

(34)  **\*sut**  **GIVE BIRTH**

This etymon is worth setting up, even though it only occurs for sure in two widely separated languages, one Himalayish (Yakha) and one Burmish (Lashi). The affiliation of the Karen form is uncertain, though it possibly reflects an allofam **\*sit**.

2.3.2. Kiranti

| | | | |
|---|---|---|---|
| Yakha | **sut** keːri | birth, give | TK-Yakha:10.4.15 |

| 6.1. Burmish | | | |
|---|---|---|---|
| Lashi | su:t⁵⁵ | birth, give | DQ-Lashi:10.4.15 |
| 7. Karenic | | | |
| Karen (Sgaw/Yue) | si?⁵⁵ sa³¹ | birth, give | DQ-KarenA:2320.1 |

| (35) | **\*kak ≍ \*gak** | | **LIFE / BORN** |
|---|---|---|---|

This root has so far been discovered only in two languages, in the Naga (Tangkhul) and Kiranti (Thulung) groups. The Thulung allofams with voiced vs. voiceless initials reflect a simplex/causative distinction: 'be born' (with **g-**) / 'give birth' (with **k-**).

| 1.3. Naga | | | |
|---|---|---|---|
| Tangkhul | **khak** | breath / life | JAM-Ety |
| | **khak**-kasui | breath / life | JAM-Ety |
| | **khak**-khā | breath / life | JAM-Ety |
| 2.3.2. Kiranti | | | |
| Thulung | **gəks-** | born, be | NJA-Thulung |
| | **gək** siu ma | childbirth, woman in | NJA-Thulung |
| | **kəks-** | birth, give | NJA-Thulung |

| (36) | IA **\*ǰan** | | **GIVE BIRTH** |
|---|---|---|---|

This is an Indo-Aryan root, borrowed into the Hayu language of Nepal (cf. Nepali **jan-ma** 'birth', **jan-manu** 'be born'. Two Tamangic languages have superficially similar forms: Chantyal **yā-wā** 'give birth' and Tamang (Sahu) **'kola yaŋ-pa** 'be born', **nah 'yahm-pa** 'give birth', but these are actually object + verb expressions meaning literally "find a baby", from an unrelated Tamangic root meaning 'find' (M. Mazaudon, p.c. 2008).

| 2.3.2. Kiranti | | | |
|---|---|---|---|
| Hayu | **jā:**sa | birth, give; bear a child | BM-Hay:84.59 |
| X. Non-TB | | | |
| Nepali | **jan** manu | born, be | AH-CSDPN:02b2.11 |

| (37) | \* $\frac{m}{s}$ -ŋa-y | | **CHILD / BIRTH / SMALL** |
|---|---|---|---|

This etymon has a range of meanings from 'small' to 'child' to 'give birth'. Most reflexes descend from a diphthongal prototype in **\*-ay**, but occasionally from monophthongal **\*-a** (e.g. Yi Dafang **a³³ ŋa⁵⁵** [see **\*g-sow** above], and Bokar Lhoba **a-ŋa:**), so that this is a good candidate for a putative PTB palatal suffix, one of the functions of which is to mark diminutives. See Matisoff 1995.

Chinese 兒 'child' (Mand. **ér**) is a plausible comparandum.

| 1.1. North Assam | | | |
|---|---|---|---|
| Bokar | a-ŋa: | baby | JS-HCST |

| Bokar Lhoba | a **ŋa:** | child | SLZO-MLD | |
|---|---|---|---|---|
| **1.4. Meithei** | | | | |
| Meithei | ə-**ŋaŋ** | child | CYS-Meithei:10.4.15 | 15 |
| **1.7. Bodo-Garo = Barish** | | | | |
| Bodo | ma **ŋáy** | small | JAM-GSTC:111; RJL-DPTB:211 | |
| **3.3. rGyalrongic** | | | | |
| rGyalrong (NW) | ta lŋa kʰ**ŋɛ**tʰi | birth, give | SHK-rGNWQ:10.4.15 | |
| **4.1. Jingpho** | | | | |
| Jingpho | chi **ngai** | birth, give | GEM-CNL | |
| | šə**ŋài** | birth, give | JAM-GSTC:111 | |
| | ʃa³¹ **ŋai³¹** | birth, give | RJL-DPTB:211 | |
| | ʃă³¹**ŋai³¹** | birth, give | ZMYYC:774.47 | |
| | ʃa¹ **ŋai³¹** | birth, give (to child) | JZ-Jingpo | |
| | ʔ**ŋāi** | birth, give | JAM-GSTC:111 | |
| **6.1. Burmish** | | | | |
| Achang (Lianghe) | **ŋɛ⁵⁵** | small | RJL-DPTB:211 | |
| Achang (Luxi) | **ŋəi³¹** | small | JZ-Achang; RJL-DPTB:211 | |
| Burmese (Spoken Rangoon) | **ŋɛ²²** | small | ZMYYC:801.40 | |
| Burmese (Written) | **ṅay** | small | GEM-CNL | |
| | **nây** | small | ILH-PL:120 | |
| | **ŋɑj²** | small | ZMYYC:801.39 | |
| Maru [Langsu] | **ŋai³¹** | small | ZMYYC:801.43 | |
| **6.2. Loloish** | | | | |
| Yi (Dafang) | a³³**ŋa⁵⁵** | child | ZMYYC:295.22 | |
| Yi (Mojiang) | **ŋɛ⁵⁵** | small | ZMYYC:801.26 | |
| **9. Sinitic** | | | | |
| Chinese (Old) | **ngje** | child; son | WHB-OC:1452,352 | |

## Chinese comparandum

兒 **ér** 'child'

*GSR*: 873a-d          Karlgren: *\**ńi̯ĕg**          Li: *\**ngrjig**          Baxter: *\**ngje** (1452)

In Li's system, *-rj- is reconstructed to account for the palatalization of the velar initial in Middle Chinese. This palatalizing medial is no longer accepted by most scholars today. In Baxter's system, medial *-r- blocks palatalization, and must be omitted.

The TB/Chinese correspondences look good. We would expect *a vocalism in Chinese, but *i (Li)/*e (Baxter) could be the result of an original *a fusing irregularly with the palatal suffix. As seen in **(40b)** *s-tay NAVEL / ABDOMEN / CENTER / SELF and **(140)** *ŋ-(w)a:y COPULATE / MAKE LOVE / LOVE / GENTLE), TB *-ay may correspond to OC *-əd (Li)/*-ij (Baxter), and there is some evidence that OC *-ig (Li)/*-e (Baxter) also can correspond to this same TB final. Consider, for example, 'crab' (*STC* #51), TB **\*d-kay**, which is likely cognate to OC 蟹 **\*grigx** (Li) (see *STC* p. 166, *GSR* 861d).

---

[15]The final nasal perhaps arose by assimilation to the syllable initial.

Schuessler (2007:225) believes that this is an area word, with connections to forms in Austroasiatic and Miao-Yao.

[ZJH]

## (38)        *kruŋ        LIVE / BORN / GREEN / SPROUT

This root is reconstructed in *STC* #382, which cites the WT, Jingpho, Bodo, and Dimasa forms. The Bai and Lolo-Burmese forms look cognate, but the relationship of the Jinuo form to this set is uncertain. The semantic range of this etymon, which extends from the notion of birth to that of sprouting, greenness, freshness, is parallelled by another root **(39) *s-riŋ ⪤ *s-r(y)aŋ** LIVE / ALIVE / GREEN / RAW / GIVE BIRTH (q.v.).

See *HPTB* **\*kruŋ**, pp. 285, 288.

| | | | |
|---|---|---|---|
| 0. Sino-Tibetan | | | |
|   *Tibeto-Burman | **\*kruŋ** | alive | STC:382 |
| | | | |
| 1.7. Bodo-Garo = Barish | | | |
|   Bodo | ga **khraŋ** | fixed, firm, healthy | STC:382 |
|   Dimasa | ga **khraŋ** | green | STC:382 |
| | | | |
| 2.1.2. Bodic | | | |
|   Tshona (Wenlang) | **kʰroŋ**⁵⁵ | birth, give (to child) | JZ-CNMenba |
|   Tshona (Mama) | **khroŋ**⁵³ | birth, give | ZMYYC:774.6 |
|   Tibetan (Written) | **'khruŋ**-ba | be born; shoot, sprout, grow (of seeds and plants) | STC:382 |
| | | | |
| 2.1.4. Tamangic | | | |
|   Tamang (Sahu) | **kʰrui** la-pa | live | SIL-Sahu:13.B.32 |
| | | | |
| 2.3.1. Kham-Magar-Chepang-Sunwar | | | |
|   Chepang | **jhuŋ**-sa | born, be | SIL-Chep:2.B.2.11,2.B.2.11 |
| | | | |
| 4.1. Jingpho | | | |
|   Jingpho | **khruŋ** | live, be alive | STC:382 |
| | mə **kruŋ** | fresh sprouts, new twigs | STC:382 |
| | | | |
| 6.1. Burmish | | | |
|   Bola | **kɔ̃**⁵⁵ | life; life-span | DQ-Bola:193,194 |
| | | | |
| 6.2. Loloish | | | |
|   Lolopho | **gɤ**³³ **lɤ**⁴⁴ | alive / be living | DQ-Lolopho:1.12 |
| | | | |
| 6.4. Jinuo | | | |
|   Jinuo (Baya/Banai) | **a**⁴⁴ **kʰʌ**⁴⁴ | life | DQ-JinA:201 |
|   Jinuo (Baka) | **a**⁴⁴ **kʰʌ**⁴⁴ | life | DQ-JinB:201 |
| | | | |
| 8. Bai | | | |
|   Bai | **kɤ̠**⁴² | alive / be living | ZYS-Bai:1.12 |

## (39)    *s-riŋ ⪥ *s-r(y)aŋ    LIVE / ALIVE / GREEN / RAW / GIVE BIRTH

This etymon constitutes a large set in *STC* (#404), where it was originally reconstructed with *-a- ⪥ *-i- variation at the PTB level: *s-riŋ ⪥ *s-raŋ. Benedict later changed the reconstruction to *śriŋ (n. 252, n.128), explaining the -a- in WB **hraŋ** as being 'conditioned by the initial cluster'. I find this revision unconvincing, and prefer to posit vocalic variation at the proto-level.[16] There is an excellent Chinese comparandum, 生, reconstructed in *GSR* #812a-d as OC *sĕng/MC ṣɒng. But here too Karlgren notes an irregular vocalic development from OC to MC (one would have expected MC ṣeng). The semantic fit between the TB forms and Chinese is extraordinarily good.

This root is perhaps to be reconstructed *tsiŋ at the PLB level (cf. Lahu **chê**).

See *HPTB* *s-riŋ ⪥ *s-r(y)aŋ, pp. 29, 78, 282, 283, 307, 506, 528.

| | | | |
|---|---|---|---|
| **0. Sino-Tibetan** | | | |
| *Sino-Tibetan | *sring | live / bear | WSC-SH:104 |
| *Tibeto-Burman | *s-raŋ | live | AW-TBT:199 |
| | *s-ring(*A) | live / bear | WSC-SH:104 |
| | *s-riŋ | live | AW-TBT:199 |
| | *s-riŋ ~ *s-raŋ | live / alive / green / raw | STC:404 |
| | *s-riŋ ~ s-raŋ | live / bear / be born / fresh (e.g. greens) | ACST:812a-d |
| | *śriN | live | BM-PK7:109 |
| | *śriŋ | live / alive / green / raw | ACST:812a-d |
| **1.1. North Assam** | | | |
| Darang [Taraon] | a³¹ suŋ⁵⁵ | alive, live; birth, give | SLZO-MLD; ZMYYC:774.49 |
| Kaman [Miju] | kɯ³¹ ɹăŋ³⁵ | alive, live | SLZO-MLD |
| Idu | suŋ⁵⁵ | alive / be living | SHK-Idu:1.12 |
| Milang | ɟuŋ-dom-pi | live | AT-MPB |
| **1.2. Kuki-Chin** | | | |
| Anal | rhìn | fresh / green / unripe | AW-TBT:199 |
| Kom Rem | ə kə riŋ | alive / be living | T-KomRQ:1.12 |
| Lakher [Mara] | ³ə¹hrɒ | fresh / green / unripe | AW-TBT:199 |
| Lushai [Mizo] | hrìn | fresh, green, unripe | AW-TBT:199 |
| | hríŋ | fresh / green / unripe | AW-TBT:199 |
| | hriŋ | fresh, green | STC:404 |
| | hriŋʔ | birth, give | STC:404 |
| **1.3. Naga** | | | |
| *Northern Naga | *criŋ | alive | WTF-PNN:449    [17] |

---

[16]This is similar to the *-ya- ⪥* -i- variation found in several roots, notably EYE and PHEASANT. See *STC* pp. 84-5, *VSTB* pp. 40-1.

[17]W.T. French (1983:449-50) sets up no fewer than four allofams of this root at the Proto-Northern Naga level.

|  | *C$_{VL}$-raŋ | alive | WTF-PNN:449 |
|---|---|---|---|
|  | *C$_{VL}$-rin | alive | WTF-PNN:450 |
|  | *ryən | alive | WTF-PNN:449 |
| Angami Naga | ²hri | live | AW-TBT:199 |
|  | ²ke³hri | life | AW-TBT:199 |
| Chang | laŋ | live, living | WTF-PNN:449 |
|  | sʌ̀ŋ-dúɪ̃ŋ- | green | AW-TBT:199 |
| Konyak | a yin | life | WTF-PNN:450 |
| Konyak (Tamlu) | kʌ-húɪ̃ŋ | green | AW-TBT:199 |
| Konyak (Wakching) | ʌ-húɪ̃ŋ | green | AW-TBT:199 |
| Mao | ¹hrɯ | live | AW-TBT:199 |
| Nocte | hiŋ | live | WTF-PNN:449 |
|  | ¹ʌ²hin(?) | green | AW-TBT:199 |
| Phom | yaŋ ñu | live | WTF-PNN:449 |
|  | yem ñu | live | WTF-PNN:450 |
|  | yem(bəm) | life | WTF-PNN:450 |
| Rengma (Northern) | ¹ga³hã | live | AW-TBT:199 |
| Tangsa (Moshang) | a ta roŋ | live | WTF-PNN:449 |
| Wancho | a raŋ | alive; raw | WTF-PNN:449 |
|  | a zaŋ | live | WTF-PNN:449 |
|  | e zaŋ | green | WTF-PNN:449 |
| Zeme | ¹ke¹riŋ | fresh / green / unripe | AW-TBT:199 |

### 1.4. Meithei

|  |  |  |  |
|---|---|---|---|
| Meithei | hiŋ | alive | STC:404 |
|  | hiŋ bə | alive / be living | CYS-Meithei:1.12 |
| Moyon | lríŋ | alive / be living | DK-Moyon:1.12 |
|  | nǽ nríŋ | birth, give | DK-Moyon:10.4.15 |

### 1.5. Mikir

|  |  |  |  |
|---|---|---|---|
| Mikir | reŋ | live, come to life | STC:404 |
|  | reŋ-seŋ | green, verdant | STC:404 |

### 1.7. Bodo-Garo = Barish

|  |  |  |  |
|---|---|---|---|
| Atong | raŋ-sət- | breath / life | JAM-Ety |
| Bodo | gɤ táŋʔ | green | AW-TBT:199 |
| Dimasa | ga thaŋ | alive, living; green, unripe | STC:404 |
| Bodo | haŋ-sur | breath / life | JAM-Ety |
| Garo | ga thaŋ | green | STC:404 |
|  | raŋ-sit- | breath / life | JAM-Ety |
|  | taŋ-sek | green | AW-TBT:199 |
|  | taŋ-sik | green | AW-TBT:199 |
|  | thaŋ | live | STC:108n304 |
| Khiamngan | ¹²a³saŋ²¹ña | green | AW-TBT:199 |
| Kokborok | mə-tʰaŋ | keep alive | PT-Kok |
|  | tʰaŋ | alive, live | PT-Kok |
| Meche | mo ʈaŋ | green | AW-TBT:199 |

### 2.1.1. Western Himalayish

|  |  |  |  |
|---|---|---|---|
| Kanauri | kə tsiŋ | fresh, green, raw, unripe | STC:404 |
|  | riṅ sā | breath / life | JAM-Ety |
|  | sā sӧṅ | breath / life | JAM-Ety |

## II. Birth

|  |  |  |  |
|---|---|---|---|
|  | sa sən | breath | DS-Kan:30 |
|  | śöng | live, alive | WSC-SH:104 |
|  | śöŋ | live, be alive | STC:404 |
| Pattani [Manchati] | šiŋ mi | alive / be living | STP-ManQ:1.12 |
|  | sring | live, alive | WSC-SH:104 |
|  | sriŋ | live, be alive | STC:404 |

### 2.1.2. Bodic
| Chamba Lahuli * | sriŋ ⋨ śiŋ | live, be alive | STC:404 |
| Tsangla (Motuo) | sik | birth, give | ZMYYC:774.7 |
|  | siŋ⁵⁵ | birth, give (to child) | JZ-CLMenba |

### 2.1.4. Tamangic
| Thakali (Tukche) | mih li | life | SIL-Thak:10.A.12 |

### 2.3.2. Kiranti
| *SE Kiranti | *hiŋ- | live | BM-PK7:109 |
| Bahing | seli | alive | BM-Bah [18] |
| Bantawa | hïŋ- | alive | BM-PK7:109 |
|  | hUN | alive | NKR-Bant |
| Chamling | hing-a | sit; to rest, to remain | BM-PK7:109 |
| Kulung | hiŋŋ-u | care for; care for (children) | BM-PK7:109; RPHH-Kul |
| Limbu | hiŋ- | live | BM-PK7:109 |
|  | ku-hiŋ wEt | alive | BM-Lim |
| Yakha | wə hiŋ glik | alive / be living | TK-Yakha:1.12 |

### 4.1. Jingpho
| Jingpho | tsiŋ | grass; grassy; fresh | STC:404 |

### 4.2. Nungic
| Anong | məśiŋ | green (color) | STC:404 |
|  | śin | grass | STC:404 |
|  | əthiŋ | unripe, uncooked | STC:404 |

### 6. Lolo-Burmese
| *Lolo-Burmese | *tsiŋ² | live | JAM-II |

### 6.1. Burmish
| Bola | ŋji⁵⁵ jɛʔ⁵⁵ | life | DQ-Bola:976 |
| Burmese (Written) | hrang | live, alive | WSC-SH:104 |
|  | hraŋ | live; to live, be alive | AW-TBT:199; PKB-WBRD; STC:404 |
|  | ə-hraŋ | alive | PKB-WBRD |
| Lashi | tə³¹ tsə⁵⁵ | alive / be living | DQ-Lashi:1.12 |

### 6.2. Loloish
| Gazhuo | sɣ²⁴ | alive / be living | DQ-Gazhuo:1.12 |
| Hani (Dazhai) | zi⁵⁵ | life | JZ-Hani |
| Hani (Shuikui) | ɔ³¹ zi⁵⁵ | life | JZ-Hani |
| Lahu (Black) | chê | live, dwell, stay | JAM-DL:542-3 |
| Sani [Nyi] | sɿ⁴⁴ | alive | MXL-SaniQ:354.4 |
|  | zɿ³³ çæ³³ | long life | MXL-SaniQ:356.1 |

---

[18]I am interpreting the syllable se- as deriving from prefixal *s-, and -li as coming from the major syllable *-riŋ. For the same last element see the Thakali (Tukche) form mih-li 'life' (mih 'person').

| Phunoi | hnã⁵⁵ ce¹¹ ɲiʔ⁵⁵ | live | DB-Phunoi | 19 |
|---|---|---|---|---|
| | ʔã⁵⁵ cɑ³³ | live | DB-Phunoi | |
| **8. Bai** | | | | |
| Bai | xæ̃⁵⁵ | alive / be living | ZYS-Bai:1.12 | |
| **9. Sinitic** | | | | |
| Chinese (Middle) | ʂɐng | live, life; bear, be born | WSC-SH:104 | |
| | ʂɒŋ | live / bear / be born / fresh (e.g. greens) | ACST:812a-d | |
| Chinese (Old) | sěŋ | live / bear / be born / fresh (e.g. greens) | ACST:812a-d | |
| | śrěŋ | live / bear / be born / fresh (e.g. greens) | ACST:812a-d | |
| | sring | live / bear | WSC-SH:104 | |
| | srjeng | be born; live, be alive; be fresh | WHB-OC:130,1497,1912,303,573 | |

## Chinese comparandum

生 **shēng** 'live; bear, born; fresh'

*GSR*: 812a          Karlgren: **\*sěng**          Li: **\*sring**          Baxter: **\*srjeng** (130)

For the reconstruction of **-j-** in Baxter's system, see Baxter 1992:580-581. The development to Middle Chinese is regular in Baxter's system, while it is irregular in Li's system.

This is a long-recognized cognate (see e.g. *STC* #404). The Chinese initial and coda correspond to the Tibeto-Burman. In Li's reconstruction, the main vowel \*i is also a perfect match for the TB vowel. Baxter's OC system does not permit a final **-ing** reconstruction. Baxter postulates developments \*-ing > \*-in and \*-ing > \*-eng (depending on dialect) predating the Old Chinese period (1992:299,563). In this case the comparative evidence points to \*-ing > \*-eng, and Baxter's reconstruction is also a perfect match for the Tibeto-Burman.

Other Chinese members of the word family (such as 青 **qīng** 'green; color of living things') apparently reflect PST allofams with vowel **\*a** and/or lacking medial **\*r**. See Schuessler (2007:431, 459-460) for tables comparing Chinese and Tibeto-Burman allofams.

Schuessler (2007:76, 460) further argues that this etymon derives from PST **\*sri** 'to be, exist'.

[ZJH]

---

[19]The cognacy of these two Phunoi forms is uncertain, but **ce¹¹ ⋉ ca³³** perhaps reflects \*-iŋ ⋉ \*-aŋ.

# III. Navel

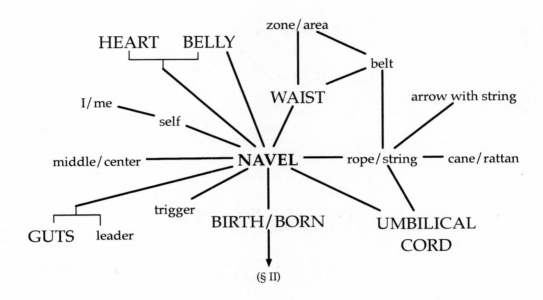

(40)          $*\begin{smallmatrix}m\\s\end{smallmatrix}$ -la(ː)y ≍ *s-tay          **NAVEL**

A root *laːy is set up in *STC* #287 with the meaning MIDDLE/CENTER, on the basis of WB **ălai** and Lushai **lai**.[1] Elsewhere, *STC* presents two additional roots: *s-tay 'navel' (*STC* #299), based on WT **lte-ba**, Jingpho **dài ~ šədāi**, Garo **ste**; and *tay 'self' (*STC* #284), based on Jingpho **dāi** (also **dāidāi**) and Lushai **tei**. Yet Benedict himself implies by a cross-reference (p. 65) that these latter two roots are really one and the same. I wish to go a step further to claim that all three *STC* roots (#284, #287, #299) are co-allofamic.

The interchange of **l-** with dental stops occurs in several other TB roots, including TONGUE and ARROW (and this phenomenon is known from other language families as well, notably Indo-European, where by coincidence TONGUE is also one of the best examples (cf. Latin *lingua* vs. pGmc *tungōn-*), alongside TEAR (cf. Latin *lacrima* vs. pGmc *tahr-* ≍ *tagr-*), BROTHER-IN-LAW (cf. Latin *lēvir* vs. Lithuanian *dieverìs*), etc.[2]

---

[1]This root, widespread in Chin languages, is also used in an ethno-geographical sense. The glossonym *Lai* is used broadly for a group of languages in the *central* subdivision of the Chin area in Burma, and more narrowly for the language of Hakha, its most important town.

[2]See Matisoff 1990b ("The dinguist's dilemma: **l/d** interaction in Sino-Tibetan"), presented at ICSTLL

There is strong evidence for both a nasal and a sibilant prefix with this root (occasionally with both together, as in the Ashö Sandoway form **ă`hmlai**¹ 'navel' < **\*s-m-laːy**). However, the appearance of a cluster like **tl-** in TB words for SELF or NAVEL does not by itself indicate the co-allofamy of the stop and lateral prototypes, since **tl-** is frequently the reflex of **\*sl-** (especially in Kuki-Chin and other Kamarupan languages), so that these forms could be referred directly to **\*s-laːy**. See the Lakher (Mara), Miju, Bantawa, and Kham forms below.

In forms like Ao ²**tɯ** ²**pɯ** ²**la**, Rengma ¹**a** ²**bvɯ** ³**li**, it might be plausible to treat the second syllables like dimidiations (syllabizations) of the labial prefix **\*bV-** ⋊ **\*mV-**, since in that position many other languages have elements with unstressed vowels (transcribed **pə-**, **mə-**, **pü-**, etc.). On the other hand, when the quality of the vowel in such a syllable is clearly [**u**], it seems preferable to analyze this element as descending from **\*s-bu-k** BELLY / STOMACH / CAVE or **\*poŋ/n** BELLY / CENTER. This is especially clear in Himalayish: cf. the Bantawa and Kham reflexes.

Both the lateral- and stop-initialled variants of this etymon are widely attested in TB. In the following sections, the reflexes are divided between the two allofams.

The semantic scope of this etymon is already quite broad, but I would like to claim that there is also a genuine phonosemantic connection with a root meaning BELT / ZONE / WAIST (see below).

There is an interesting Dumi compound **saːkhil tim** 'navel' composed of **saːkhil** 'viscera, guts' < **khil** 'feces', plus **tim** 'head, leader': i.e. the navel is viewed in Dumi as the leader of the intestines. See van Driem 1993:415.

See *HPTB* **\*laːy** ⋊ **\*m/s-taːy**, pp. 52, 210.

(40a)  **\* m/s -la(ː)y**  **NAVEL / CENTER / SELF**

Reflexes of this allofam occur in Kamarupan, Himalayish, and Lolo-Burmese, as well as in Tujia.

0. Sino-Tibetan

| | | | |
|---|---|---|---|
| \*Tibeto-Burman | \*laːy | navel; middle, center | AW-TBT:214; JAM-GSTC:062; STC:287 |

1.1. North Assam

| | | | |
|---|---|---|---|
| Padam-Mising [Abor-Miri] | ai | self | JAM-GSTC:071 |
| Kaman [Miju] | pɑ³¹ tɯ³¹ lɑi⁵⁵ | center | SLZO-MLD |

#23, Univ. of Texas, Arlington, still unpublished in English, but translated into Chinese (2006) by 蘇玉玲 邱彥遂 李岳儒 Sū Yùlíng et al., as 漢藏語和其他語言中邊音的塞音化 *Hàn-Zàng-yǔ hé qí tā de yǔyán zhōng biānyīn de sèyīnhuà* in Chinese Phonology 聲韻論叢 [*Shēngyùn lùncóng*] (Taipei) 14:45-65. See also the discussion in *HPTB*, pp. 50-53.

³For now we are including this Abor-Miri form for 'self' with zero-initial in this set, along with several zero-initial forms meaning 'I/me' from Naga languages. One can imagine a scenario whereby the \*s-l cluster became a voiceless lateral \*hl-, thence a plain \*h-, then zero. (Such was the fate, e.g. of the voiceless PLB resonants \*hl-, \*hr-, \*hy-, which all became h- in Lahu.) Cf. also the Tangkhul reflexes in h-.

| | | | | |
|---|---|---|---|---|
| | tlái | navel / center | AW-TBT:214 | 4 |
| 2. Kuki-Chin | | | | |
| shö [Sho] (Sandoway) | ă`hmlɑi¹ | navel | GHL-PPB:N.16 | 5 |
| hualsim | lai³ | navel | GHL-PPB:N.16 | |
| wa Khumi | lɛ³lun⁴ | navel | GHL-PPB:N.16 | |
| humi (Ahraing) | lɑɛ² | navel | GHL-PPB:N.16 | |
| | lɑɛ⁴ [lɛŭ⁴] | navel | GHL-PPB:N.16 | |
| om Rem | məlǝi | navel | T-KomRQ:5.7.1 | |
| | mʌláai | navel / center | AW-TBT:214 | |
| | nǝi mǝlǝi rui | umbilical cord | T-KomRQ:10.4.12 | |
| ai (Hakha) | lai⁵ | navel | GHL-PPB:N.16 | |
| ailenpi | mə´pǒlɛ⁴ri¹ | navel | GHL-PPB:N.16 | |
| akher [Mara] | (pa-)lia-ri | umbilical cord | JAM-Ety | |
| | palia | navel | JAM-Ety | |
| | tlai | oneself, self | JAM-GSTC:071 | |
| | ²pǝ¹liǝ | navel / center | AW-TBT:214 | |
| angmei | cha la | navel | GEM-CNL | |
| othvo (Hiranpi) | pǒ`liɛ¹ | navel | GHL-PPB:N.16 | |
| ushai [Mizo] | láai | navel / center | AW-TBT:214 | |
| | lai | navel; middle; center | GEM-CNL; JAM-Ety; JAM-GSTC:062; STC:287 | |
| | lai¹ | navel | GHL-PPB:N.16 | |
| aram | puk la | navel | GEM-CNL | |
| aring | palai | navel | GEM-CNL | |
| atupi | buŋ⁴lai⁴ | navel | GHL-PPB:N.16 | |
| era | pǒ⁵lɛ⁶ | navel | GHL-PPB:N.16 | |
| uiron | ai | I | GEM-CNL | |
| ha'oa | lai¹ | navel | GHL-PPB:N.16 | |
| hanphum | nɑi¹nŭ³ | navel | GHL-PPB:N.16 | |
| iddim | lai¹ | navel; middle | GHL-PPB:N.16 | |
| Vomatu | lai⁴ | navel | GHL-PPB:N.16 | |
| ongsai | lai³ | navel | GHL-PPB:N.16 | |
| otung | la⁵rwi⁴ | navel | GHL-PPB:N.16 | |
| 3. Naga | | | | |
| ngami Naga | ⁵u³luo | navel / center | AW-TBT:214 | |
| ngami (Khonoma) | lo | navel | GEM-CNL | |
| ngami (Kohima) | (u) lou³³ | navel | VN-AngQ:5.7.1 | |
| | u lo | navel | GEM-CNL | |
| o (Chungli) | te pela | navel | GEM-CNL | |
| o (Mongsen) | tü püla | navel | GEM-CNL | |
| o Naga | ²tɯ²pɯ²la | navel / center | AW-TBT:214 | |
| hokri | (u) lou³³ | navel | VN-ChkQ:5.7.1 | |

---

[4]The tl- cluster in this Miju form looks like a reduction of the disyllabic sequence tɯ-lai (previous ord). This disyllabic form in turn is susceptible of two interpretations. Either it is a two-morpheme uence where the first element is < *du NAVEL/UMBILICAL CORD (i.e. < *du-la:y; see below), more plausibly it, as well as the first consonant in the monosyllabic form tlái, is simply a reflex of *s- prefix (*s-la:y > tlái, or *s-la:y > tɯ-lai). See also the Bantawa, Kham, and Lakher (Mara) lexes with tl- in this section, as well as the WT form with lt-, under (40b) *s-tay NAVEL / ABDOMEN ENTER / SELF.

[5]This form attests to the simultaneous presence of the *s- and *m- prefixes with this root: *s-m-lay.

III. Navel

| | | | | |
|---|---|---|---|---|
| Khezha | pəló | navel | SY-KhözhaQ:5.7.1 | |
| Lotha Naga | ai | I | GEM-CNL | |
| | Nla | navel | VN-LothQ:5.7.1 | |
| | nna | navel | GEM-CNL | |
| | [1]n[1]la | navel / center | AW-TBT:214 | |
| Mao | ai | I | GEM-CNL | |
| Rengma | nnu | navel | GEM-CNL | |
| Rengma (Northern) | [1]a[2]bvɯ[3]li | navel / center | AW-TBT:214 | |
| Rengma (Southern) | [4]n[4]lu | navel / center | AW-TBT:214 | |
| Rongmei | ai | I | GEM-CNL | |
| | la | navel | GEM-CNL | |
| Sema | a pfo la | navel | GEM-CNL | |
| Tangkhul | hai zo | navel | GEM-CNL; JAM-Ety | 6 |
| | hay toŋ | navel | JAM-GSTC:071 | |
| | hay zo | navel | JAM-GSTC:071 | |
| Zeme | mi la ria | navel | GEM-CNL | |
| | [3]mi[1]n[1]la | navel / center | AW-TBT:214 | |

### 1.7. Bodo-Garo = Barish

| | | | | |
|---|---|---|---|---|
| Bodo | a má tù~ a máy tu | navel | JAM-Ety | 7 |
| Dimasa | ho tha mai | navel | GEM-CNL | 8 |
| Khiamngan | [23]lɪʔ | navel / center | AW-TBT:214 | |
| Meche | u-tu-mɣi | navel | AW-TBT:15 | |

### 2.1.1. Western Himalayish

| | | | |
|---|---|---|---|
| Bunan | rè | umbilical cord | SBN-BunQ:10.4.12 |
| Pattani [Manchati] | re | navel | STP-ManQ:5.7.1 |
| | ré(h) | navel | DS-Patt |

### 2.1.2. Bodic

| | | | |
|---|---|---|---|
| Sherpa | lhyeq | navel | JAM-Ety |

### 2.3.1. Kham-Magar-Chepang-Sunwar

| | | | |
|---|---|---|---|
| Chepang | ləyʔ | self | SIL-Chep:13.B.28 |
| Kham | 'pū:h təli | navel | DNW-KhamQ:2.A.38 |
| | pūh tali | navel | JAM-Ety |

### 2.3.2. Kiranti

| | | | |
|---|---|---|---|
| Bantawa | chum buy tli | navel | AW-TBT:214 | 9 |
| | chum bu li | middle; navel | AW-TBT:214; WW-Bant:21 |
| | tshum-bu li | navel | JAM-Ety |
| Hayu | sʊ li pʊŋ | navel | BM-PK7:129 |

---

[6]The **h-** in these Tangkhul forms apparently descends from the lateral cluster **\*s-l**. Cf. the forms from Abor-Miri and Naga languages with zero initial.

[7]We are assuming preemption by the nasal prefix in this Bodo form, as well as in Dimasa **ho-tha-mai**.

[8]We are assuming preemption by the labial prefix in this Dimasa form, as well as in Bodo **a-má(y)-tu**.

[9]The **tl-** in the last syllable seems to be the reflex of the **\*s-l** cluster (cf. the Lakher and Miju forms with similar initials). If the second syllable **-bu(y)-** were really just a fully vocalized reflex of a labial prefix **\*bV-**, this form would reflect a doubly-prefixed prototype like **\*b-s-lay** (cf. the Ashö Sandoway **hmlai** < **\*s-m-lay**). On the other hand, the second syllable seems to descend from a separate etymon (perhaps **\*s-bu-k** BELLY / STOMACH / CAVE or **\*poŋ/n** BELLY / CENTER), especially in view of Kham forms like **pū:h-tali**.

60

| 5. Tujia | | | |
|---|---|---|---|
| Tujia (Northern) | lo³⁵ li⁵⁵ | center | JZ-Tujia |
| Tujia | mɯe²¹ tʰi⁵⁵ kʰu⁵⁵ li⁵⁵ | navel | CK-TujBQ:5.7.1 |
| 6.1. Burmish | | | |
| Burmese (Written) | **ălai** | middle, center, navel | STC:287 |
| | a **lay** | middle | GEM-CNL |
| | ə **lai** | navel / center | AW-TBT:214 |
| | ʔə **lai** | middle, center | JAM-Ety |
| 6.2. Loloish | | | |
| Lahu (Black) | khâʔ-**le** | trigger of crossbow | JAM-DL:p.369; JAM-GSTC:062 |
| | **le** | trigger | JAM-GSTC:062 |
| | nâʔ-**le** | trigger; trigger of gun | JAM-DL:p.751; JAM-GSTC:062 |

10

# (40b)  *s-tay  NAVEL / ABDOMEN / CENTER / SELF

I regard this root as a co-allofam of **(40a)** ***m/s-la(:)y** NAVEL / CENTER / SELF. Both *STC* #299 ***s-tay** 'navel' and *STC* #284 ***tay** 'self' are to be subsumed under this stop-initialled allofam. Reflexes occur widely in TB: Kamarupan, Himalayish, Jingpho, Karenic, Qiangic (including Tangut), Bai, and Tujia, as well as occasionally in Loloish.

There is also an excellent Chinese comparandum 臍 (Mand. **qí**), *GSR* 593f ***dz'iər/dz'iei**, perhaps < ***s-tay** via ****zday**. This comparison has been suggested several times, including by Weidert (*TBT* #843).

See *GSTC* #62 and #71, and *HPTB* pp. 52, 208, 217.

| 0. Sino-Tibetan | | | |
|---|---|---|---|
| *Tibeto-Burman | ***s-tay** | navel | AW-TBT:738 |
| | ***s-tăy** | self / navel | JAM-GSTC:071 |
| | ***s-tay** | navel, abdomen | STC:299 |
| | ***s-ta[:]y** | navel, abdomen | WTF-PNN:525 |
| | ***tay** | self | STC:284 |
| 1.2. Kuki-Chin | | | |
| Lushai [Mizo] | **tei** | self | STC:284 |
| 1.3. Naga | | | |
| *Northern Naga | ***taːy** | navel | JAM-GSTC:071; WTF-PNN:525 |
| Ao (Chungli) | **te** pela | navel | GEM-CNL |
| Ao (Mongsen) | **tü** püla | navel | GEM-CNL |
| Ao Naga | ²**tɯ**²pɯ²la | navel / center | AW-TBT:214 |
| Nocte | po **te** | navel | WTF-PNN:525; JAM-GSTC:071 |
| | ²po¹**te** | navel | AW-TBT:15 |
| | ³po¹**te** | navel / center | AW-TBT:214 |
| Mzieme | ka **tei** | self | GEM-CNL |

---

[10] The trigger is, as it were, the navel of a gun or crossbow. See Matisoff 1988a, p. 1373.

### 1.5. Mikir

| Mikir | ce tè | navel; center | AW-TBT:15,214 | |
|---|---|---|---|---|
| | che te | navel | GEM-CNL; JAM-Ety | |
| | che tè | navel | KHG-Mikir:60 | |
| | che tè a-charàng | umbilical cord | KHG-Mikir:60 | 11 |
| | che te acharang | umbilical cord | JAM-Ety | |

### 1.6. Mru

| Mru | **dai** | navel | JAM-Ety; |
|---|---|---|---|
| | | | JAM-GSTC:071 |

### 1.7. Bodo-Garo = Barish

| Bodo | u **də́y** | abdomen / belly | JAM-Ety |
|---|---|---|---|
| Garo | **ste** | abdomen | JAM-GSTC:071; |
| | | | STC:96n276 |

### 2.1.1. Western Himalayish

| Bunan | por **tsi** | navel | SBN-BunQ:5.7.1 | 12 |
|---|---|---|---|---|

### 2.1.2. Bodic

| Baima | $te^{13}$ $te^{35}$ | navel | SHK-BaimaQ:5.7.1 | |
|---|---|---|---|---|
| Bumthang | **ti** wit | navel | AW-TBT:738 | |
| Dzongkha | **ti**-u: | navel | AW-TBT:738 | |
| Kaike | **Tya** | navel | JAM-Ety | |
| Tsangla (Central) | phu **chi** | navel | SER-HSL/T:33 13 | |
| Tsangla (Motuo) | $pu^{55}$ $ti^{55}$ ma | navel | JZ-CLMenba | |
| Sakka Trokpa | **tĩ**-a | navel | AW-TBT:738 | |
| Tibetan (Amdo:Zeku) | **htɛ** | navel | JS-Amdo:627 | |
| Tibetan (Balti) | ɫ**ti** ya· | navel | RAN1975:77 | |
| Tibetan (Batang) | $tia^{55}$ | navel | DQ-Batang:5.7.1 | |
| Tibetan (Jirel) | **teq** | navel | JAM-Ety | |
| Jirel | **teq** | navel | JAM-GSTC:071 | |
| Tibetan (Sherpa:Helambu) | **tẽ** gah | navel | B-ShrpaHQ:5.7.1 | |
| Spiti | **tiya** | navel | CB-SpitiQ:5.7.1 | |
| Tibetan (Written) | **lte** | navel | JAM-Ety | |
| | **lte**-ba | navel; center; abdomen | AW-TBT:214,738; | 13 |
| | | | JAM-GSTC:071; |
| | | | STC:299; JS-Tib:627; |
| | | | GEM-CNL |

### 2.1.4. Tamangic

| Chantyal | põ **ti** | navel | NPB-ChanQ:5.7.1 | |
|---|---|---|---|---|
| Gurung (Ghachok) | pa **diq** | navel | JAM-Ety; | |
| | | | SIL-Gur:2.A.38 | |
| Manang (Gyaru) | $bi^1$ $dɛ^1$ | navel | YN-Man:039 | |
| Manang (Prakaa) | ²pi **te** | navel | HM-Prak:0027 | |
| Tamang (Bagmati) | pe **te** | navel | AW-TBT:738 | |
| Tamang (Risiangku) | ²pe **te** | navel, umbilical cord | MM-TamRisQ:5.7.1, 10. | |
| Tamang (Sahu) | 'pe **te** | navel; umbilical cord | AW-TBT:738; JAM-Ety; | |
| | | | SIL-Sahu:2.36 | |

[11] The last element **charang** means 'pipe, tube' (Walker 1925:24).

[12] The first syllable of this form is to be compared to the second syllable of Bahing **sy-pyr** 'navel'. See **(46) *bryam ≍ *brim** NAVEL / UMBILICAL CORD, below.

[13] The **lt-** cluster in the WT form looks like a metathesized version of the **tl-** cluster found in Kham, Bantawa, Lakher (Mara), and Miju (above), further justifying the treatment of **\*s-lay** and **\*s-tay** as co-allofams of the same etymon.

|  | -Ti | self | SIL-Sahu:12.E.28 |
|---|---|---|---|
| **2.1.5. Dhimal** | | | |
| Dhimal | bo **dhi** | navel | JK-Dh |
| **2.2. Newar** | | | |
| Newar (Dolakhali) | ṭẽ bu ri | navel | CG-Dolak |
| Newar | te pu | navel | JAM-Ety |
|  | te pu ca | navel | SH-KNw:5.7.1 |
| Newar (Kathmandu) | te pɔ ca | navel | CG-Kath |
| **2.3.1. Kham-Magar-Chepang-Sunwar** | | | |
| Chepang | **toi** | navel | AW-TBT:15 |
|  | **toy** | navel | AW-TBT:738 |
|  | **toyʔ** | navel | JAM-Ety; JAM-GSTC:071; SIL-Chep:2.A.38 |
|  | **toyʔ**-ru | umbilical cord | SIL-Chep:2.A.39; JAM-Ety |
| Chepang (Eastern) | **toy** | navel | RC-ChepQ:5.7.1 |
| Magar | me-pe **de** | navel | JAM-Ety |
|  | me-pe ɹe | navel | AW-TBT:738 |
| **3.1. Tangut** | | | |
| Tangut [Xixia] | (ɣɔfi) **tefi** | navel | NT-SGK:191 |
|  | **tefi** | navel | NT-SGK:106-061 |
|  | **tɿn²** | navel | MVS-Grin |
|  | ʔo **tɿ̃** | navel | DQ-Xixia:5.7.1 |
| **4.1. Jingpho** | | | |
| Jingpho | **dāi** | navel; self | JAM-Ety; JAM-GSTC:071 |
|  | **dai** | self | STC:284 |
|  | **dài ~ śədāi** | navel | JAM-GSTC:071 |
|  | **dai ⚭ śədai** | navel, abdomen | STC:299 |
|  | **dāi-dāi** | self | JAM-Ety |
|  | **shadai** | navel | GEM-CNL |
|  | **shədāi** | navel | JAM-Ety |
|  | ¹**šə²dai** | navel; center | AW-TBT:214,843 |
| **5. Tujia** | | | |
| Tujia (Southern) | tu³⁵ **di²¹** ŋã³³ | navel | JZ-Tujia |
| **6.2. Loloish** | | | |
| Nosu | tɕho²¹bu²¹**di³³** | navel | CK-YiQ:5.7.1 |
| Yi (Xide) | tɕʰɔ³³-bu²¹-**di³³** | navel | CSL-YIzd |
| **7. Karenic** | | | |
| *Karen (Sgaw) | ***dé*** | navel | RBJ-KLS:143 |
| *Karen (Pho) | ***dè'*** | navel | RBJ-KLS:143 |

[14]K. P. Malla (p.c. 2007) analyzes this form as consisting of **te** 'navel' plus **pu** 'seed, round thing' plus **ca** (preferably **chaa**) 'diminutive morpheme; child'. The last element also appears in compounds like **ma-chaa** 'a child' and **khi-chaa** 'a dog'.

[15]The sibilant prefix might be a reduction of PTB ***sya** 'flesh; animal'. This prefix occurs productively with body parts in a number of other TB languages (e.g. Nung **sərö** 'bone', WT **skra** 'hair', Dimasa **salai** 'tongue', WT **snabs** 'snot', etc.).

| | | | |
|---|---|---|---|
| *Karen (TP) | *dè' | navel | RBJ-KLS:143 |
| *Karen | *dəi' | navel | RBJ-KLS:143 |
| *Karen (Pho-Sgaw) | *dəih | navel | RBJ-KLS:143 |
| Bwe | -dí mú | navel | EJAH-BKD |
| Bwe (Western) | dɪ¹ | navel | GHL-PPB:F.19 |
| Bwe | ʔdí-phlɔ́ | navel | AW-TBT:843 |
| Geba | ă di¹ | navel | GHL-PPB:F.19 |
| Pa-O (Northern) | pă de⁶ | navel | GHL-PPB:F.19 |
| Pa-O | pɔ́ʔ de | navel | JAM-Ety; RBJ-KLS:143 |
| Palaychi | dìq bòq | navel | JAM-Ety; RBJ-KLS:143 |
| Pho | dé | navel | AW-TBT:843 |
| Pho (Tenasserim) | ə̃ de⁵ | navel | GHL-PPB:F.19 |
| Pho (Delta) | ə di² | navel | GHL-PPB:F.19 |
| Pho (Bassein) | dé | navel | JAM-Ety; JAM-GSTC:071; RBJ-KLS:143 |
| Pho (Moulmein) | de | navel | AW-TBT:843; JAM-Ety; JAM-GSTC:071; RBJ-KLS:143 |
| Sgaw | de¹ | navel | GHL-PPB:F.19 |
| Paku | de¹bɔ² | navel | GHL-PPB:F.19 |
| Sgaw | ⁴ʔde | navel | AW-TBT:843 |
| Sgaw (Bassein) | dé | navel | JAM-Ety; RBJ-KLS:143 |
| Karen (Sgaw/Hinthada) | di⁵⁵ bɔ³³ | navel | DQ-KarenB:123 |
| Sgaw (Moulmein) | dé | navel | JAM-Ety; RBJ-KLS:143 |
| Karen (Sgaw/Yue) | de̠⁵⁵ | navel | DQ-KarenA:123 |
| | de̠⁵⁵ bo̠⁵⁵ | umbilical cord | DQ-KarenA:148 |

**8. Bai**

| | | | |
|---|---|---|---|
| Bai | jõ²¹ fv̠ᵢ⁴⁴ te̠⁴⁴ | navel | ZYS-Bai:5.7.1 |

**9. Sinitic**

| | | | |
|---|---|---|---|
| Chinese (Mandarin) | ts'i | navel | GSR:593f |
| Chinese (Old) | dz'iei | navel | AW-TBT:843 |
| Chinese (Old/Mid) | dz'iər/dz'iei | navel | GSR:593f |

## Chinese comparanda

臍 qí 'navel'

*GSR*: 593f       Karlgren: *dz'iər       Li: *dziəd       Baxter: *dzij

The initial correspondence of OC *dz- to PTB *s-t- could be explained by metathesis, as discussed in Bodman 1969[16]. Baxter (1992:229-30) allows for the general developments *St- > ts- and *Sd- > dz-, where *S is a metathesizing prefix. This prefix is usually reconstructed when phonetic series evidence suggests an original stop initial. Within *GSR* 593, however, there is no evidence for original dental stops. Nevertheless, Schuessler (2007:421) admits the possibility, suggesting possible pre-Old Chinese forms *dz(l)əi < *s-d(l)əi.

---

[16]"Tibetan *sdud* 'folds of a garment', the character 卒, and the *st- hypothesis." *Bulletin of the Institute of History and Philology*, Academia Sinica 39:327-45.

On the apparent mismatch between the voiceless PTB initial and the voiced OC initial, see the discussion under **(1b)** ***pu** EGG.

For a discussion of the correspondence between OC *-ij and TB *-ay, see **(140)** ***ŋ-(w)aːy** COPULATE / MAKE LOVE / LOVE / GENTLE.

[ZJH]

There also seems to be a phonosemantic connection between the stop-initialled allofam *s-tay and a PTB root *taːy meaning BELT/ZONE/WAIST, first reconstructed in Matisoff 1985a (*GSTC* #95) on the basis of WT **sde** 'part, portion (e.g. of a country), province, district, territory, zone', Lahu **de** 'belt of land between the high rain-forest and the plains; large expanse of terrain', Luquan Lolo **nt$^h$e$^{11}$** 'plain, flat expanse', Lushai **tai** 'waist', Mikir **daykha** 'middle, intermediate'. This implies that WT **lte-ba** 'navel' is a co-allofam of WT **sde** 'zone'.

A very likely Chinese comparandum is 帶 OC *tâd 'girdle, sash', Mand. **dài** 'belt, zone'. For the semantics, cf. Eng. *zone* < Gk. *zōnē* 'girdle' < PIE *yōs-nā (*yōs 'to gird').

[JAM]

帶 **dài** 'belt, sash'

| *GSR*: 315a | Karlgren: *tâd | Li: *tadh | Baxter: *tats (p. 753) |
|---|---|---|---|

This word is reconstructed with a final stop by both Baxter and Li. As Schuessler (2007:72) notes, there is reason to think that some of the words reconstructed by Baxter in *-ts should be revised to *-s. 帶 is one of the words that Schuessler so revises, supporting the comparison made here (Schuessler 2007:203).

The comparison of PTB *-ay with either OC *-as or *-ats is still problematic, as I know of no other examples of such a correspondence. It must be noted, however, that a regular pattern of correspondence between OC and PTB *-ay has not yet emerged. The most commonly attested correspondences are with OC *-aj or *-ij on the one hand (as with 臍, above), and OC *-e on the other (see **(37)** ***m/s-ŋa-y** CHILD / BIRTH / SMALL).

[ZJH]

## (41)         *kyak         NAVEL / UMBILICAL CORD / ROPE

This root is abundantly attested in Lolo-Burmese and in Qiangic. It is reconstructed as PLB *ʔkyak in *TSR* #58, with the meaning ROPE/STRING; *TSR* also tentatively assigns several forms for NAVEL to this etymon.

There are two Chinese candidates for relationship to this etymon: 弋 *GSR* 918a-b **dịək / ịək** 'shoot with arrow with string attached; such an arrow' 矰 繳 *GSR* 1258e **t̂ịak / tśịak** [OC form not cited in *GSR*] 'string attached to arrow'. *STC* (p. 176) attempts to relate these Chinese words to PTB *b-la 'arrow' [*STC* #449], via a hypothetical intermediate form **pliak. I consider this to be far-fetched phonologically and unsatisfying semantically. The semantic association between an umbilical cord and an arrow with string attached is irresistible. The metaphor is still alive today, e.g. in spacecraft, where the lifeline attaching a space-walking astronaut to the mother ship is commonly called an *umbilical cord*. For more discussion of these Chinese words, see ZJH's note below.

See *HPTB*, pp. 318, 319.

### 1.1. North Assam

| | | | |
|---|---|---|---|
| *Tani | *kri-ni | navel | JS-HCST:268 |
| Padam-Mising [Abor-Miri] | ki-ni | navel | JAM-Ety; JS-HCST |
| | ki-nyo | navel | JAM-Ety |
| Apatani | kʰrjɯ-nə | navel | JS-Tani |
| | kʰrə-nə | navel | JS-Tani |
| | xrjɯ-nɯ | navel | JS-HCST |
| | xɯ-nɯ | navel | JS-Tani |
| Bengni | ki-ni | navel | JS-HCST; JS-Tani |
| Bokar | kiː-niː | navel | JS-HCST |
| Idu | i ci-be | navel | NEFA-PBI |
| | i ci bɤ | navel | JP-Idu |

### 1.2. Kuki-Chin

| | | | |
|---|---|---|---|
| Liangmei | cha la | navel | GEM-CNL |

### 1.4. Meithei

| | | | |
|---|---|---|---|
| Meithei | cə niŋ | navel | CYS-Meithei:5.7.1 |

### 3.2. Qiangic

| | | | |
|---|---|---|---|
| Ergong (Northern) | vəu¹³ tʰya³³ | umbilical cord | SHK-ErgNQ:10.4.12 |
| | vəu⁵³ tʰya¹³ | navel | SHK-ErgNQ:5.7.1 |
| Ergong (Danba) | wɯ tɕʰi | navel | SHK-ErgDQ:5.7.1 |
| Muya [Minyak] | vi³³tsʰa⁵³ | navel | SHK-MuyaQ:5.7.1 |
| Qiang (Mawo) | pu ʂ | navel | JS-Mawo |
| | pʌ tʃə̩ | navel | SHK-MawoQ:5.7.1 |
| Qiang (Yadu) | pu tʂu̩ | navel | DQ-QiangN:123 |

### 3.3. rGyalrongic

| | | | |
|---|---|---|---|
| rGyalrong (Eastern) | pok tʃʰu | navel | SHK-rGEQ:5.7.1 |
| rGyalrong | tə pok tɕʰu | navel | DQ-Jiarong:5.7.1 |
| rGyalrong (Northern) | tə po tɕʰak | navel | SHK-rGNQ:5.7.1 |
| | tə pu cɕʰak | umbilical cord | SHK-rGNQ:10.4.12 |
| rGyalrong (NW) | tə wu tɕʰak | umbilical cord | SHK-rGNWQ:10.4.12 |
| | tə ɣ tɕʰak | navel | SHK-rGNWQ:5.7.1 |

### 6. Lolo-Burmese

| | | | |
|---|---|---|---|
| *Lolo-Burmese | *kyakᴴ, ʔkyakᴴ | navel | JAM-MLBM:75 |
| | *ʔkyak | rope; string; navel | JAM-TSR:58,58 |

### 6.1. Burmish

| | | | |
|---|---|---|---|
| *Burmese | *khyak | navel | JO-PB |
| Achang (Lianghe) | tshaʔ⁵⁵ | navel | JZ-Achang |
| Achang (Longchuan) | tɕhi³¹ tɔt⁵⁵ | navel | JZ-Achang |
| Achang (Luxi) | tɕha⁵¹ | navel | JZ-Achang |
| Achang (Xiandao) | tʂʰɔʔ⁵⁵ tʰoŋ³¹ | navel; umbilical cord | DQ-Xiandao:120,145 |
| Arakanese | hcoʼ | navel | JO-PB |
| Bola | tʃʰaʔ⁵⁵ | navel; umbilical cord | DQ-Bola:120,145 |
| Burmese (Modern) | kʻyak | navel | GHL-PPB:V.118 |

17

18

---

[17]This is a contraction of the other Mawo form pʌtʃə̩.

[18]The first constituent looks like a contraction of tə wu 'belly'. See previous record tə wu tɕʰak 'umbilical cord'.

| | | | |
|---|---|---|---|
| Burmese (Standard Spoken) | hce' | navel | JO-PB |
| Burmese (Written) | khyak | navel | GEM-CNL; JAM-Ety; JAM-MLBM:75; JO-PB; PKB-WBRD |
| | khyak-krûi | umbilical cord | JAM-Ety |
| | k'yak | navel | GHL-PPB:V.118 |
| Hpun (Northern) | shɛ̀ʔ shú, shɛ̀ əshú | navel | EJAH-Hpun |
| Intha | hye' | navel | JO-PB |
| Lashi | tʃhɔʔ⁵⁵ | navel | DQ-Lashi:5.7.1 |
| Maru [Langsu] | chó' | navel | JO-PB |
| | tʃhɔʔ⁵⁵ | navel | DQ-Langsu:5.7.1 |
| Tavoyan | hyi' | navel | JO-PB |
| Atsi [Zaiwa] | tʃhoʔ⁵⁵ | navel | JZ-Zaiwa |

### 6.2. Loloish

| | | | |
|---|---|---|---|
| *Loloish | *(C-k)yak[H] | navel | DB-PLolo:120A |
| Ahi | tše 44 | rope / string | JAM-TSR:58 |
| | tɕhe³³bu²¹duɯ⁵⁵luɯ⁵⁵ | navel | CK-YiQ:5.7.1 |
| | tʂ'i²¹ bu̠²¹ duɯ⁵⁵ luɯ⁵⁵ | navel | LMZ-AhiQ:5.7.1 |
| Akha (Yunnan) | á tjaq / á tsaq | rope | ILH-PL:451 |
| Akha | a-ca H-HS | rope / string | JAM-TSR:58 |
| Akha (Thai) | á tjáq | rope, string, cord | ILH-PL:451 |
| Akha | caˆ tah˯ | navel | JAM-Ety |
| | caˆ uˇ | umbilical cord | JAM-Ety |
| | tjaq | rope | ILH-PL:451 |
| Gazhuo | tɣ³⁵ tshɳ³⁵ jɛ³²³ | navel | DQ-Gazhuo:5.7.1 |
| Hani (Lüchun) | à tjaq | rope | ILH-PL:451 |
| Hani (Dazhai) | a⁵⁵tsa̠³³ | rope | ZMYYC:422.31 |
| Hani (Pijo) | tjhɔ | rope | ILH-PL:451 |
| | tə̀ tjhɔ | rope | ILH-PL:451 |
| Hani (Gelanghe) | a⁵⁵tɕa³³ | rope | JZ-Hani |
| Hani (Wordlist) | al zav | rope | ILH-PL:451 |
| Hani (Shuikui) | a⁵⁵tʃha³³ | rope | ZMYYC:422.32 |
| Hani (Khatu) | tjhɔ | rope | ILH-PL:451 |
| | tsɣ̀ tjhɔ | rope | ILH-PL:451 |
| Lahu (Black) | câʔ | rope / string | JAM-TSR:58 |
| | ɣ̈û(~ ɣ̈ɔ̂)-tu-câʔ | umbilical cord | JAM-DL:1138 |
| | ɔ̀-pi-câʔ | strap; sash; belt | JAM-DL:p. 817 |
| | ɣû-tu-šī-câʔ | umbilical cord | JAM-DL:1129 |
| Lahu (Yellow) | tsa⁶khɛ¹ | rope | JZ-Lahu |
| Lalo | hí-tshí | rope | SB-Lalo |
| | tɕhi³³ pa³³ tʂa³³ | umbilical cord | CK-YiQ:10.4.12 |
| | tɕhi̠³³ ma³³ du̠²¹ | navel | CK-YiQ:5.7.1 |
| | ʂa⁵⁵ ku̠⁵⁵ tʂa³³ | backbone / spine | CK-YiQ:5.5.4 [19] |
| Lipho | tshe⁵⁵du²¹ | navel | CK-YiQ:5.7.1 |
| Lisu (Central) | chi¹-hchya⁵ | self | JF-HLL |
| Lisu (Putao) | ch'ɛ²du⁵ | navel | GHL-PPB:V.118 |
| Lisu (Central) | hchi³ ra⁵ | rope | JF-HLL |
| Lisu | hchi³-ra⁵ | rope / string | JAM-TSR:58 |

---

[19]Note the similarity between the last two syllables and the Lahu forms ɔ̀-ku-câʔ 'vein, sinew, tendon' and ɔ̀-ku-ɔ̀-câʔ 'every bone in the body'.

| | | | |
|---|---|---|---|
| Lisu (Central) | hchya⁴-du⁵ | navel | JF-HLL |
| Lisu (Theng-yüeh) | hchya⁴du⁵ | navel | GHL-PPB:V.118 |
| Lisu (Nujiang) | tʃʰɛ³⁵ du³¹ | navel | JZ-Lisu |
| Lisu (Northern) | tɕhæ³⁵du²¹ | navel | DB-Lisu |
| | tɕi⁵⁵tɕhæ²¹ | self; individual | DB-Lisu |
| Lolopho | tshe̱⁴⁴ dʋ³¹ | navel | DQ-Lolopho:5.7.1 |
| Luquan | tʂa 22s | rope / string | JAM-TSR:58 |
| Mpi | tɕeʔ⁴-thuŋ² | navel | JAM-MLBM:75; DB-PLolo |
| Nasu | tsʰa̱²¹ bi²¹ du³³ | navel | CK-YiQ:5.7.1 |
| | tʂa 32s | rope / string | JAM-TSR:58 |
| | tʂʰa̱²¹ | umbilical cord | CK-YiQ:10.4.12 |
| Nesu | tsʰ̩³³ bi²¹ tu⁵⁵ | navel | CK-YiQ:5.7.1 |
| Noesu | tʂha³³bi²¹du³³ | navel | CK-YiQ:5.7.1 |
| Nosu | tɕho̱²¹bu²¹di³³ | navel | CK-YiQ:5.7.1 |
| Nusu (Central/Zhizhiluo) | tsʰɛ³¹ | navel | DQ-NusuA:120. |
| | tsʰɛ¹ | umbilical cord | DQ-NusuA:145. |
| Nusu (Bijiang) | tɕhi⁵⁵tɕha³¹ | self | ZMYYC:979.45 |
| Nusu (Central) | tʂʰa̱⁵³ | navel; umbilical cord | DQ-NusuB:120.,145. |
| Sani [Nyi] | tše 44 | rope / string | JAM-TSR:58 |
| | tɕhe³³bu²¹du⁵⁵ | navel | YHJC-Sani |
| | tɕhe³³tʂɒ³³ | umbilical cord | YHJC-Sani |
| | tɕhe⁴⁴bu²¹du⁵⁵ | navel | CK-YiQ:5.7.1 |
| | tɕhe⁴⁴tʂa³³ | umbilical cord | CK-YiQ:10.4.12 |
| | tɕʰe³³ tʂa³³ | umbilical cord | YHJC-Sani:233.1 |
| Phunoi | mə̆ chàʔ | navel | JAM-Ety |
| | mə chà | navel | DB-PLolo |
| | mə cʰaʔ¹¹ | navel | DB-Phunoi |
| Ugong | cɔ̆ʔ | navel | DB-Ugong:5.7.1 |
| | cɔ̆ʔ ʔéŋ/ cɔ̆ʔ khlí | navel lint | DB-Ugong |
| Woni | tsʻa 33 | rope / string | JAM-TSR:58 |
| Yi (Dafang) | tsa³³ | rope | ZMYYC:422.22 |
| Yi (Mile) | ni̠⁵⁵tɕe³³ | rope | ZMYYC:422.25 |
| Yi (Mojiang) | tɕe³³ | rope | ZMYYC:422.26 |
| Yi (Nanhua) | tʂʌ³³vɛ²¹ | rope | ZMYYC:422.24 |
| Yi (Nanjian) | pɑ³³tɕe³³ | rope | ZMYYC:422.23 |
| Yi (Xide) | tɕʰɔ³³-bu²¹-di³³ | navel | CSL-YIzd |

### 6.4. Jinuo

| | | | |
|---|---|---|---|
| Jinuo (Baya/Banai) | tʃʰa³¹ to⁴⁴ | navel; umbilical cord | DQ-JinA:123,148 |
| | tʃʰa³¹ to⁴⁴ lo⁴⁴ | umbilical cord | DQ-JinA:148.1 |
| Jinuo (Youle) | tʃʰɑ⁴² to⁴⁴ lo⁴⁴ | navel | JZ-Jinuo |

### 9. Sinitic

| | | | |
|---|---|---|---|
| Chinese (Old/Mid) | t̂i̯ak/tśi̯ak | string attached to arrow | ACST:1258e |

## Chinese comparanda

弋 **yì** 'shoot arrow (with string attached)'

| | | | |
|---|---|---|---|
| *GSR:* 918a | Karlgren: **\*di̯ək** | Li: **\*rək** | Baxter: **\*ljɨk** (467) |

---

[20]The Sani forms **tɕhe³³tʂɒ³³**, **tɕhe⁴⁴tʂa³³**, **tɕʰe³³ tʂa³³** are puzzling, since either syllable is a plausible reflex of this root. Perhaps two Sani variants have developed, one (with aspirated initial) < **\*kyak**, meaning 'navel'; and the other (with unaspirated initial) < **\*gyak**, meaning 'cord'.

[21]The second element means 'shit'.

There is considerable disagreement about the reconstruction of words with MC initial **j-** which appear in phonetic series with words having dental initials. While Karlgren's *****d-** is no longer accepted, variations of *****r-**, *****l-**, and *****j-** are proposed by a number of scholars.

This Chinese word does not appear to be directly cognate to the PTB form, as there is no evidence of a velar initial. Gong (2001) revives Benedict's (*STC* p. 176) comparison with PTB *****b-la** 'arrow', reconstructing OC *****blək**, with the regular development *****bl-** > *****l-**. Gong's system would also admit the possibility of reconstructing *****glək**.

A more likely candidate for cognacy is 繳 **zhuó** (see below).

Cf. 射 **shè** 'shoot with bow', OC *****mljaks** (Baxter 1992 sets 1357, 1393, with revision of *****L-** to *****ml-**), which may also be etymologically related to 弋 and/or PTB *****b-la**.

繳 **zhuó** 'string attached to arrow'

| *GSR*: 1258e | Karlgren: -- | Li: *****krjakw ?** | Baxter: *****kjewk ?** |
|---|---|---|---|

This character has two Middle Chinese readings, one with velar initial and no coda, and one with palatal initial and velar coda. Based on internal Chinese evidence, the Old Chinese reconstruction cannot be determined with certainty. Karlgren placed this word in series 1258, which is not a phonetic series at all but a collection of words that Karlgren deemed unreconstructible for lack of evidence. Other characters that appear to have the same phonetic element appear in *GSR* 1162, all of which are reconstructed as open syllables with velar initial.

The character 激 **jī** 'dam up and cause (water) to rush up', found in *GSR* 1162 and apparently sharing a phonetic element with 繳, is reconstructed 激 *****kewk** by Baxter and *****kiakw** by Li, suggesting that in Baxter's system 繳 should be reconstructed *****kjewk** and *****kew?** to account for the two Middle Chinese pronunciations. An *****a** vocalism in Baxter's system cannot be completely discounted, but it would make it difficult to explain the subsequent palatalization of the initial velar in one of the Middle Chinese forms.

All of the possible Old Chinese reconstructions present problems in terms of the Chinese/PTB vowel correspondence. Old Chinese coda *****-kw** (Li)/*****-wk** (Baxter) regularly corresponds to TB rounded vowels.

Given the difficulty of determining the Old Chinese reconstruction of 繳, this proposed cognate set must be considered tentative.

[ZJH]

## (42)        *du        NAVEL / UMBILICAL CORD

The stronghold of this etymon is Lolo-Burmese (including Jinuo), but cognates also occur in Kamarupan, Himalayish, and Tujia.

The second syllable of the Kaman [Miju] form **pɑ³¹ tɯ³¹ lɑi⁵⁵** is probably just a reflex of the *****s-** prefix in **(40a) *m/s-la(:)y** NAVEL / CENTER / SELF, above. See note on Kaman [Miju] **tlái** (*ibid.*).

### 1.4. Meithei

| | | | |
|---|---|---|---|
| Meithei | khoi **dou** | navel | GEM-CNL |

### 1.7. Bodo-Garo = Barish

| | | | |
|---|---|---|---|
| Bodo | a má **tu**~ a máy **tu** | navel | JAM-Ety |
| Garo (Bangladesh) | gan-**du**-ri | navel | RB-GB |
| Meche | u-**tu**-mɤi | navel | AW-TBT:15 |

### 2.1.4. Tamangic

| | | | |
|---|---|---|---|
| Gurung (Ghachok) | **thu** | umbilical cord | JAM-Ety |
| | **tʰu** | umbilical cord | SIL-Gur:2.A.39 |

### 5. Tujia

| | | | |
|---|---|---|---|
| Tujia | mɯe$^{13}$ tɕi$^{55}$ **dɯ**$^{35}$ | navel | CK-TujMQ:5.7.1 |
| Tujia (Southern) | **tu**$^{35}$ di$^{21}$ ŋã$^{33}$ | navel | JZ-Tujia |

22

### 6.2. Loloish

| | | | |
|---|---|---|---|
| Ahi | tɕhe̞$^{33}$bu$^{21}$**dɯ**$^{55}$lɯ$^{55}$ | navel | CK-YiQ:5.7.1 |
| | tʂ'i$^{21}$ bu̞$^{21}$ **dɯ**$^{55}$ lɯ$^{55}$ | navel | LMZ-AhiQ:5.7.1 |
| Gazhuo | ty$^{35}$ tshŋ$^{35}$ jɛ$^{323}$ | navel | DQ-Gazhuo:5.7.1 |
| Lahu (Nyi) | g'awˇ **tu**: shi̱ | navel | DB-Lahu:120 |
| Lahu (Bakeo) | g'u̮ˇ **tu**: shi̱ | navel | DB-Lahu:120 |
| Lahu (Shehleh) | g'u̮ **tu**: | navel | DB-Lahu:120 |
| *Common Lahu | ***tu**: | navel | DB-PLolo:120B |
| Lahu (Banlan) | u̮ˇ **tu**: shi̱ | navel | DB-Lahu:120 |
| Lahu (Black) | ğû(~ ğɔ́)-**tu**-câʔ | umbilical cord | JAM-DL:1138 |
| | ğû(~ ğɔ́)-**tu**-šī | navel | JAM-DL:1138 |
| | ɣû-**tu**-šī-câʔ | umbilical cord | JAM-DL:1129 |
| | ɣu$^{53}$ tɣ$^{33}$ si$^{11}$ | navel | JZ-Lahu |
| Lahu (Yellow) | ʔu$^{55}$ **tu**$^{33}$ ɕi?$^{21}$ | navel | JZ-Lahu |
| Lalo | tɕʰi̠$^{33}$ mɑ$^{33}$ **du̠**$^{21}$ | navel | CK-YiQ:5.7.1 |
| Lipho | tshe$^{55}$**du**$^{21}$ | navel | CK-YiQ:5.7.1 |
| Lisu (Putao) | ch'ɛ$^{2}$**du**$^{5}$ | navel | GHL-PPB:V.118 |
| Lisu (Central) | hchya$^{4}$-**du**$^{5}$ | navel | JF-HLL |
| Lisu (Theng-yüeh) | hchya$^{4}$**du**$^{5}$ | navel | GHL-PPB:V.118 |
| Lisu (Nujiang) | tʃʰɛ$^{35}$ **du**$^{31}$ | navel | JZ-Lisu |
| Lisu (Northern) | tɕhæ$^{35}$**du**$^{21}$ | navel | DB-Lisu |
| Lolopho | tshe$^{44}$ **dɣ**$^{31}$ | navel | DQ-Lolopho:5.7.1 |
| Nasu | tsʰa̠$^{21}$ bi$^{21}$ **du**$^{33}$ | navel | CK-YiQ:5.7.1 |
| Nesu | tsʰŋ̍$^{33}$ bi$^{21}$ **tu**$^{55}$ | navel | CK-YiQ:5.7.1 |
| Noesu | tʂha$^{33}$bi$^{21}$**du**$^{33}$ | navel | CK-YiQ:5.7.1 |
| Sani [Nyi] | tɕhe$^{33}$bu$^{21}$**du**$^{55}$ | navel | YHJC-Sani |
| | tɕhe$^{44}$bu$^{21}$**du**$^{55}$ | navel | CK-YiQ:5.7.1 |

### 6.3. Naxi

| | | | |
|---|---|---|---|
| Naxi (Western) | **dɣ**$^{31}$me$^{33}$ | belly | JZ-Naxi |

### 6.4. Jinuo

| | | | |
|---|---|---|---|
| Jinuo (Baya/Banai) | tʃʰa$^{31}$ **to**$^{44}$ | navel; umbilical cord | DQ-JinA:123,148 |
| | tʃʰa$^{31}$ **to**$^{44}$ lo$^{44}$ | umbilical cord | DQ-JinA:148.1 |
| Jinuo (Youle) | tʃʰɑ$^{42}$ **to**$^{44}$ lo$^{44}$ | navel | JZ-Jinuo |

---

[22]The first two syllables mean "belly".

## Chinese comparandum

肚 **dù** 'stomach'

*GSR*: not in 62          Karlgren: **\*d'o**          Li: **\*dagx**          Baxter: **\*laʔ** or **\*daʔ**

There is also a variant with a voiceless initial, meaning 'animal stomach used as food'. *GSR* 62 is reconstructed as a lateral-initial series by Baxter, but since the character is not attested until late, it is possible that this word had a dental initial, and that the character used to write it was created after the change \*l- > \*d- had taken place, making 土 **\*hlaʔ** > **\*thaʔ** a suitable phonetic element.

The difficulty with this comparison lies in the vowel, as we would expect to find PTB \*a corresponding with OC \*a, as in Chinese 吾 **\*ngag** (Li)/**\*nga** (Baxter) and PTB **\*ŋa** 'first person pronoun' (STC #406), and Chinese 魚 **\*ngjag** (Li)/**\*ng(r)ja** (Baxter) and PTB **\*ŋya** 'fish' (STC #189).

[ZJH]

(43)                            **\*ni(n)**                            **NAVEL**

This relatively rare root appears in Kamarupan, Himalayish, and Nungish. It is quite possible that it is related to **(H:347) \*s/k-niŋ** BRAIN / HEART / MIND, *STC* #367. The Dulong compounds look as if they could mean "belly-heart", although the usual Dulong word for 'heart' is **ɹɯ³¹ mɔ̆ʔ⁵⁵**. Cf. also Meithei **puk-ning** 'heart' (Marrison 1967:120), where BELLY + HEART apparently means 'heart', not 'navel'.

| | | | |
|---|---|---|---|
| **1.1. North Assam** | | | |
| *Tani | \*kri-**ni** | navel | JS-HCST:268 |
| Padam-Mising [Abor-Miri] | ki-**ni** | navel | JAM-Ety; JS-HCST |
| | ki-**nyo** | navel | JAM-Ety |
| Apatani | kʰrjɯ-**nə** | navel | JS-Tani |
| | kʰrə-**nə** | navel | JS-Tani |
| | xrjɯ-**nɯ** | navel | JS-HCST |
| | xɯ-**nɯ** | navel | JS-Tani |
| Bengni | ki-**ni** | navel | JS-HCST; JS-Tani |
| Bokar | ki:-**ni:** | navel | JS-HCST |
| **1.2. Kuki-Chin** | | | |
| Thanphum | nɑi¹**nɯ̃³** | navel | GHL-PPB:N.16 |
| **1.4. Meithei** | | | |
| Meithei | cə **niŋ** | navel | CYS-Meithei:5.7.1 |
| **2.3.2. Kiranti** | | | |
| Limbu | **nim**-rōk | navel | JAM-Ety |
| **4.2. Nungic** | | | |
| Trung [Dulong] | pu⁴⁴ **ñin⁴²** | navel | JAM-Ety |
| | pu⁵⁵**ɲin⁵⁵** | navel | JAM-Ety |
| Trung [Dulong] (Du-longhe) | pu⁵⁵ **ɲin⁵⁵** | navel | JZ-Dulong |

(44)  $*\begin{smallmatrix}t\\d\end{smallmatrix}$ uŋ ⪰ *ts(y)uːŋ  **NAVEL / CENTER**

This etymon was originally set up as **\*tsyuːŋ** in *STC* #390, on the basis of Lushai, Bodo, and Dimasa forms. Benedict later revised this to **\*tuːŋ** (*STC* n. 63, p.17), and specifically banished WT **gźuŋ** as probably not cognate. This reconstruction was also adopted in *HPTB* pp. 287, 310. It seems clear that the most ancient version of this root had a simple or palatalized dental stop, as witnessed by the certain Chinese cognate 中 *GSR* #1007a-e **ti̯ông/t̯i̯ung** 'middle' (see below). From an early date, however, many languages developed a sibilant or affricate initial before this medial vowel -u-, in a manner reminiscent of a phenomenon in modern Japanese, where the phonemic syllable /tu/ has come to be pronounced [tsɯ]. The same variation between stop and (af)fricate initials before -u- is to be found in 'mortar' PTB **\*(t)sum**, with most reflexes pointing unambiguously to PTB **\*tsum** (e.g. WB **chum**, Lahu **chɛ**, Lushai **sum**), while Jingpho **thùm** reflects **\*tum**. See also **(45) \*(t)sum** NAVEL, below.

For convenience I am here assigning the reflexes of this etymon into two allofamic roots, according to whether they have retained a stop initial **(44a)** or have undergone initial frication **(44b)**.

The semantic range of this word-family includes the notion of CENTER (as does the phonologically unrelated root **(40a) \*m/s-la(ː)y** NAVEL / CENTER / SELF [q.v.]).

(44a)  $*\begin{smallmatrix}t\\d\end{smallmatrix}$ uŋ  **NAVEL**

To this more conservative allofam we assign reflexes with dental stop initials.
See *HPTB* **\*tuːŋ**, pp. 287, 310.

| 0. Sino-Tibetan | | | |
|---|---|---|---|
| *Tibeto-Burman | *tuuŋ | middle | RJL-DPTB:208 |
| 1.3. Naga | | | |
| Tangkhul | hay **toŋ** | navel | JAM-GSTC:071 |
| | kui **tuŋ** yāŋ | center of skull | JAM-Ety [23] |
| 4.2. Nungic | | | |
| Anong (Rawang) | mə **duŋ** | perpendicular; straighten | STC:17n63 |
| | ə **duŋ** | in; middle | ACST:1007a-e; RJL-DPTB:208; STC:17n63 |
| Trung [Dulong] | a **tuŋ** | middle | RJL-DPTB:208; STC:17n63 |
| | a³¹**duŋ**⁵⁵ | middle | ZMYYC:56.46 |
| | a **tuŋ** | middle | ACST:1007a-e |
| Trung [Dulong] (Dulonghe) | a³¹ **duuŋ**⁵⁵ | middle | RJL-DPTB:208 |
| | a³¹ **duŋ**⁵⁵ | middle | JZ-Dulong |

[23] The first syllable is part of the Tangkhul word for 'skull': **mi-kui** or **ā-kui-ra**.

| Trung [Dulong] (Nujiang) | a³¹ **duuŋ**⁵⁵ | middle | RJL-DPTB:208 | |
| | ɑ³¹ **duŋ**⁵⁵ | middle | JZ-Dulong | |
| 6.1. Burmish | | | | |
| Achang (Xiandao) | tʂʰɔʔ⁵⁵ **tʰoŋ**³¹ | navel; umbilical cord | DQ-Xiandao:120,145 | |
| 6.2. Loloish | | | | |
| *Loloish | *ʔ-**doŋ**¹ | navel | DB-PLolo:120B | |
| Akha | caˆ **tah**˯ | navel | JAM-Ety | |
| Bisu | sa **tɔ̀ŋ** | navel | DB-PLolo | 24 |
| | ʃa **tɔŋ** | navel | PB-Bisu:15 | |
| | ça **tɔŋ** | navel | PB-Bisu:15 | |
| | ça **tɔ̀ŋ** sàj | umbilical cord | PB-Bisu:16 | 25 |
| Mpi | tɕeʔ²⁴-**thuŋ**² | navel | JAM-MLBM:75; DB-PLolo | |
| 9. Sinitic | | | | |
| Chinese | **tḭ̂ôŋ** / **t̂ḭuŋ** | middle | STC:17n63 | |
| Chinese (Mandarin) | **jong** jian | middle | JS-Ch:485 | |
| Chinese (Old) | **k-ljung** | middle | WHB-OC:1641 | |
| Chinese (Old/Mid) | **tḭəŋ**/**t̂ḭuŋ** | middle | ACST:1007a-e | |
| | **tjôŋ** | middle | RJL-DPTB:208 | |
| | **t̂juŋ** | middle | RJL-DPTB:208 | |

# Chinese comparandum

中 **zhōng** 'middle, center'

*GSR*: 1007a-e      Karlgren: *ti̯ôŋ[26]      Li: *trjəngw      Baxter: *k-ljung (477, 1641)

There are at least two competing etymologies for this Chinese word, one relating it to Tibetan **gźung** 'middle, midst' (e.g. Bodman 1980:123 set 240, Coblin 1986:53) and the other the one proposed here (e.g. *STC* p. 182).

Baxter (1992:525) follows Bodman, reconstructing *k-l- rather than *trj- to match Tibetan **gźung** and to explain the use of the character as a sound gloss for 宮 *k(r)jung in the Eastern Han.

The original comparison in *STC* seemed suspect because of the irregular correspondence between the stop initial in Chinese and the sibilant initial in Tibeto-Burman, but the revised PTB etymon makes a good match. If we consider the possibility of reconstructing *r-tjung, as proposed in Handel 1998, then there is no mismatch in the medial.

For another example of the same final correspondence, compare **(93)** *guŋ ⪤ *kuŋ HOLE / ORIFICE / ROUNDED PART with Chinese 孔 (elsewhere in this volume).

[ZJH]

---

[24]The first syllable probably means 'flesh' < PTB *sya.

[25]The last syllable is a borrowing from Thai **săaj** 'cord, string'. This morpheme, interestingly enough, occurs in reduced form in the Thai word for 'navel', **sədɨɨ**. Cf. Li Fang Kuei 1977:92.

[26]*HPTB* pp. 287, 310 incorrectly cites *GSR*'s reconstruction as *tḭəŋ. This was corrected in L. Sagart's review of *HPTB* (2006:217) to *t̂ḭuŋ, which is also incorrect: this is Karlgren's MC form. [JAM]

## (44b)  *ts(y)u:ŋ                          NAVEL / CENTER

### 1.2. Kuki-Chin

| | | | |
|---|---|---|---|
| Lushai [Mizo] | tśhu:ŋ | inside (of anything); inside | STC:17n63,390; ACST:1007a-e |
| Tiddim | suŋ | inside; middle | ACST:1007a-e; RJL-DPTB:208; STC:17n63 |

### 1.3. Naga

| | | | |
|---|---|---|---|
| *Northern Naga | *dzu:ŋ | navel | WTF-PNN:525 |
| Ao (Chungli) | te tsung da | middle | GEM-CNL |
| | tiong | middle | GEM-CNL |
| Ao (Mongsen) | tiyung ko | middle | GEM-CNL |
| Chang | shung | navel | GEM-CNL |
| | šuŋ | navel | WTF-PNN:525 |
| Mao | to tsü | middle | GEM-CNL |
| Wancho | sung | navel | GEM-CNL |
| | suŋ | navel | WTF-PNN:525 |

### 1.7. Bodo-Garo = Barish

| | | | |
|---|---|---|---|
| Bodo | siŋ | middle | RJL-DPTB:208 |
| Deuri | u-jū² | navel | Deuri |
| Dimasa | bising | among | GEM-CNL |
| | bisiŋ | inside; within; middle | ACST:1007a-e; RJL-DPTB:208; STC:17n63,390 |

### 2.1.2. Bodic

| | | | |
|---|---|---|---|
| Tsangla (Motuo) | bar zuŋ | center | SLZO-MLD |
| Tibetan (Written) | gźuŋ | middle | STC:17n63 |

## (45)                    *(t)sum                          NAVEL

This root is virtually confined to Himalayish. The Konyak form with initial h- is also probably related. Note the two Thulung forms, which may be co-allofams; theom seems to fit better phonologically, despite the semantic divergence.

### 1.3. Naga

| | | | |
|---|---|---|---|
| Konyak | hum bo | navel | GEM-CNL |

### 2.3.2. Kiranti

| | | | |
|---|---|---|---|
| Bantawa | chum buy tli | navel | AW-TBT:214 |
| | chum bu li | middle; navel | AW-TBT:214; WW-Bant:21 |
| | tshum-bu li | navel | JAM-Ety |
| | tshum bu ri | umbilical cord | JAM-Ety |
| Hayu | suq wo | navel | BM-Hay:84.146 (fo |
| | su li puŋ | navel | BM-PK7:129 |
| Limbu | nā sum bro | navel | JAM-Ety |
| | sām brok pā | navel | JAM-Ety |
| Thulung | byu syu ma | navel | JAM-Ety |
| | theom | belly | BM-PK7:90; NJA-Thulung |
| Yakha | phok su kəli:k | navel | TK-Yakha:5.7.1 |

## (46)         **\*bryam ≍ \*brim**         **NAVEL / UMBILICAL CORD**

This etymon is mostly confined to Himalayish, though there is an excellent Moyon cognate. The initial labial stop may be a reduction of one of several etyma for 'belly' that begin with a labial (probably **\*s-bu-k** BELLY / STOMACH / CAVE), as illustrated by the disyllabic Moyon doublet and the Lepcha form, so that this root should perhaps be reconstructed **\*b-ryam ≍ \*b-rim**.

| | | | |
|---|---|---|---|
| 1.4. Meithei | | | |
| Moyon | **bræ ~ bʌræ** | navel | DK-Moyon:5.7.1 |
| 2.1.1. Western Himalayish | | | |
| Bunan | **por** tsi | navel | SBN-BunQ:5.7.1 |
| 2.1.3. Lepcha | | | |
| Lepcha | băk-**lim** | navel | JAM-Ety |
| 2.1.4. Tamangic | | | |
| Thakali (Tukche) | 'prih-**khum** | navel | JAM-Ety |
| | 'prih-**kʰum** | navel | SIL-Thak:2.A.38 |
| 2.3.2. Kiranti | | | |
| Bahing | sy **pym** | navel | BM-PK7:129; JAM-Ety |
| | sy **pyr** | navel | BM-Bah |
| Khaling | '**baram** | navel | BM-PK7:130 |
| | **baram** | navel; umbilical cord | JAM-Ety |
| Kulung | **birim** | navel | BM-PK7:130 |
| | **birim_** | navel | RPHH-Kul |
| Thulung | **biurium** | navel, umbilical cord | BM-PK7:130; NJA-Thulung |

## (47)                 **\*br(w)ak**                 **NAVEL**

This etymon appears fairly solid, though it has so far been unearthed only in three scattered languages (Himalayish, Karenic, and Qiangic).

| | | | |
|---|---|---|---|
| 2.3.2. Kiranti | | | |
| Limbu | nā sum **bro** | navel | JAM-Ety |
| | nim-**rōk** | navel | JAM-Ety |
| | sām **brok** pā | navel | JAM-Ety |
| 3.3. rGyalrongic | | | |
| rGyalrong (Eastern) | pǝktʃʰu **sprak** | umbilical cord | SHK-rGEQ:10.4.12 |
| 7. Karenic | | | |
| Bwe | ʔdí-**phlɔ́** | navel | AW-TBT:843 |

## (48)                   **\*koy**                   **NAVEL**

This root has only been discovered in two Kamarupan languages of Manipur, Meithei and Puiron, but the semantic and phonological correspondence is perfect. However, since Meithei (also known as Manipuri) is the dominant TB language of Manipur, the Puiron form may well be borrowed from it.

| 1.2. Kuki-Chin | | | |
|---|---|---|---|
| Puiron | **koi** | navel | GEM-CNL |
| 1.4. Meithei | | | |
| Meithei | **khôi** | navel | JAM-Ety |
| | **khoi** dou | navel | GEM-CNL |

## (49)          *zo          NAVEL / UMBILICAL CORD

This root is of restricted distribution, but the Lepcha form certainly looks related to the
Meluri and Tangkhul ones, which might be enough to set it up for PTB.

| 1.2. Kuki-Chin | | | | |
|---|---|---|---|---|
| Meluri | a bo **zü** | navel | GEM-CNL | |
| 1.3. Naga | | | | |
| Tangkhul | hai **zo** | navel | GEM-CNL; JAM-Ety | 27 |
| | hay **zo** | navel | JAM-GSTC:071 | |
| 2.1.3. Lepcha | | | | |
| Lepcha | 'ayeň-**zo** | umbilical cord | JAM-Ety | 28 |

## (50)          *bi          STRING / STRAP / BELT

This etymon basically means 'string, strap, belt', but also occurs in compounds for UM-
BILICAL CORD. It has been discovered in Himalayish and Lolo-Burmese.

| 1.1. North Assam | | | |
|---|---|---|---|
| Padam-Mising [Abor-Miri] | rí-**bí**, ri-**bui** | creeper of any sort; cane, wire, rope, string | JAM-GSTC:053 |
| 2.2. Newar | | | |
| Newar | **pi** | umbilical cord | JAM-Ety; SH-KNw:10.4.12 |
| 2.3.1. Kham-Magar-Chepang-Sunwar | | | |
| Chepang (Eastern) | **pay?** ra | umbilical cord | RC-ChepQ:10.4.12 |
| Kham | **bi** kha | umbilical cord | JAM-Ety |
| | **bi** khə | umbilical cord | DNW-KhamQ:2.A.39 |
| | **bi** kʰə | umbilical cord | DNW-KhamQ:2.A.39 |
| 6.2. Loloish | | | |
| Hani (Pijo) | lɔ **phfi** | belt | ILH-PL:410 |
| | lɔ **phi** | belt | ILH-PL:410 |
| Lahu (Black) | gú-**pi** | string coiled around an object | JAM-DL:p. 817 |
| | ɠò?-**pi** | needle and thread | JAM-DL:p.817 |
| | ɔ-**pi**-câ? | strap; sash; belt | JAM-DL:p. 817 |

---

[27]The **h-** in these Tangkhul forms apparently descends from the lateral cluster **\*s-l**. Cf. the forms from
Abor-Miri and Naga languages with zero initial. See the note under **(40a)** **\*m/s-la(:)y** NAVEL / CENTER
/ SELF above.

[28]The first constituent means "child".

## (51)            *rup ⋇ *rip            CORD / STRING

This root is set up to account for certain Himalayish forms with final -p and high vowel, as well as the Chepang morpheme -ru. Forms from the Angamoid branch of the Naga group are also included.

1.3. Naga

| | | | |
|---|---|---|---|
| Angami (Khonoma) | ke **ro** | rope | GEM-CNL |
| Angami (Kohima) | ke **ro** | rope | GEM-CNL |
| Chokri | kü **ro** | rope | GEM-CNL |

2.1.4. Tamangic

| | | | |
|---|---|---|---|
| Gurung (Ghachok) | **ruq** | string | SIL-Gur:8.A.34 |
| Thakali (Tukche) | **rʰup** | string | SIL-Thak:8.A.34 34 |

2.3.1. Kham-Magar-Chepang-Sunwar

| | | | |
|---|---|---|---|
| Chepang | toyʔ-**ru** | umbilical cord | SIL-Chep:2.A.39; JAM-Ety |

2.3.2. Kiranti

| | | | |
|---|---|---|---|
| Khaling | hi **rip** | blood vessel / vein / artery | JAM-Ety |
| Thulung | so: **rip** | tendon, vein | BM-PK7:124 |

## (52)          *s-rwəy          OICC / CORD / STRING / CANE / RATTAN

The basic meaning of this etymon seems to be 'cord, string'. It also appears in a large number of compounds referring to "OICC's" (obscure internal channels and connections), such as NERVE, VEIN, MUSCLE, SINEW. In addition it appears in compounds for UMBILICAL CORD, thence by extension to NAVEL itself. For the concept of "OICC's", see *VSTB* pp. 184-5.

*STC* sets up two roots with the meaning 'cane, rattan', *STC* #478 *rey and *STC* #201 *s-rwi(y), which I am collapsing into a single set. The meaning of this etymon ranges from 'string, cord' to 'OICC' to the specific plants 'cane, rattan'.

Several Himalayish forms which look superficially as if they descend from this morpheme are actually loans from Sanskrit *nālī ~ nāḍī* 'any tubular vessel or vein of the body' (Monier-Williams:537): Sunwar **nā:ri** 'nerve', Newar **hi *nu(li)*** 'blood vessel; vein; artery' (**hi** 'blood' < PTB *s-hywəy),[29] Bahing **sā:ti** 'vein, blood vessel', Bantawa **tshum-bu*ri*** 'umbilical cord', Khaling **'sö *ri*** 'nerve'. A couple of Barish forms, Bodo **na-ri** and Lalung **na-ti** 'navel' (Balawan 1965:42), are also probably borrowings from this Sanskrit word, despite the semantic difference. Note that **r** and **t/d** are frequently confused in Barish languages. (Cf. the language name *Bodo ~ Boro*).

0. Sino-Tibetan

| | | | |
|---|---|---|---|
| *Tibeto-Burman | **\*rey** | cane; rattan; rope; string, thread; rattan, cane | AW-TBT:754; JAM-GSTC:053; RJL-DPTB:151; STC:478 |

---

[29]See *HPTB*:194.

| | *rwi(y) | cane (plant) | STC:201 |
|---|---|---|---|
| **1.1. North Assam** | | | |
| Padam-Mising [Abor-Miri] | rí-bí, ri-bui | creeper of any sort; cane, wire, rope, string | JAM-GSTC:053 |
| | tə rü | cane plant | STC:201 |
| **1.2. Kuki-Chin** | | | |
| Kom Rem | məti rui | sinew / tendon (muscle to bone) | T-KomRQ:8.5 |
| | ru rui | ligament (bone to bone) | T-KomRQ:8.6 |
| | rəlhə rui | nerve | T-KomRQ:8.10 |
| | rətʰə rui | blood vessel / vein / artery | T-KomRQ:8.7.1 |
| Kuki | hrwi | cane plant | STC:201 |
| Lailenpi | mə´pǎlɛ⁴ri¹ | navel | GHL-PPB:N.16 |
| Lakher [Mara] | (pa-)lia-ri | umbilical cord | JAM-Ety |
| | tha-ri | blood vessel; vein; artery; nerve; sinew; tendon | JAM-Ety |
| Lushai [Mizo] | hrwi | cane plant | STC:201 |
| Zotung | la⁵rwi⁴ | navel | GHL-PPB:N.16 |
| **1.3. Naga** | | | |
| *Northern Naga | *rey | cane; rattan; rope | JAM-GSTC:053; WTF-PNN:466 |
| Angami (Khonoma) | ke re | rope | GEM-CNL |
| Chang | li | cane; rattan; rope | GEM-CNL; JAM-GSTC:053 |
| Konyak | wei | cane; rattan; rope | GEM-CNL; JAM-GSTC:053 |
| Nocte | ri | cane; rattan; rope | GEM-CNL; JAM-GSTC:053 |
| Tangkhul | khə rùy | string flowers | JAM-GSTC:176 |
| | ruy | string | Bhat-TNV:98 |
| Tangsa (Moshang) | ri | cane; rattan; rope | GEM-CNL; JAM-GSTC:053 |
| | tag ri | blood | GEM-CNL |
| Wancho | re | cane; rattan; rope; reed | GEM-CNL; JAM-GSTC:053 |
| Zeme | mi la ria | navel | GEM-CNL |
| **1.4. Meithei** | | | |
| Meithei | sing li | blood vessel / vein / artery | JAM-Ety |
| | siŋ li | blood vessel; vein; artery; nerve | CYS-Meithei:8.10,8.7.1 |
| Moyon | šiŋ rí | blood vessel / vein / artery | DK-Moyon:8.7.1 |
| **1.7. Bodo-Garo = Barish** | | | |
| Digaro | tərui ⋈ təroi | cane plant | STC:201 |

| Dimasa | rai | cane; rattan, cane | GEM-CNL; JAM-GSTC:053; RJL-DPTB:151 |
|---|---|---|---|
| Garo | re | string, thread | RJL-DPTB:151 |
| Garo (Bangladesh) | gan-du-ri | navel, belly button | RB-GB |

### 2.3.1. Kham-Magar-Chepang-Sunwar

| Magar | ri | cane | RJL-DPTB:151 |
|---|---|---|---|

### 2.3.2. Kiranti

| Dumi | kəm ri səm | moustache | SVD-Dum |
|---|---|---|---|

### 3.2. Qiangic

| Ergong (Danba) | suɯ ʐi̩ | rope | ZMYYC:422.14 |
|---|---|---|---|
| Namuyi | ʐ̩ɹ$^{55}$ | rope | ZMYYC:422.19 |
| Qiang (Taoping) | sia33 li$^{55}$ | string, thread | RJL-DPTB:151 |

### 4.1. Jingpho

| Jingpho | gin ri | fine thread | RJL-DPTB:151 |
|---|---|---|---|
| | ri | rattan, cane; cord, string | RJL-DPTB:151 |
| | sum$^{33}$ʒi$^{33}$ | rope | ZMYYC:422.47 |
| | sum ri, śiŋ-ri | rope, cord | GEM-CNL |

### 4.2. Nungic

| Anong | ban-ri | rope, string | RJL-DPTB:151 |
|---|---|---|---|
| | sə ri | thread | RJL-DPTB:151 |
| | thə ri | cane | RJL-DPTB:151 |
| Anong (Rawang) | təri | cane | STC:56n185 |
| Anong (Rawang/Lungmi) | təru̯ | cane | STC:56n185 |
| Trung [Dulong] (Du-longhe) | tsuɯ$^{31}$ ri$^{55}$ | string, thread | RJL-DPTB:151 |
| Trung [Dulong] (Nujiang) | puɯ$^{31}$ ɹi$^{53}$ | navel | JZ-Dulong |
| | tsuɯ$^{31}$ ri$^{55}$ | string, thread | RJL-DPTB:151 |

### 6.2. Loloish

| Yi (Xide) | gu$^{33}$ ʐi$^{33}$ | muscle / sinew | JZ-Yi |
|---|---|---|---|
| | gu$^{33}$-ɕi$^{33}$ | muscle | CSL-YIzd |

### 7. Karenic

| Karen (Sgaw/Hinthada) | a$^{31}$ ɣi$^{31}$ | muscle | DQ-KarenB:162 |
|---|---|---|---|
| Karen (Sgaw/Yue) | ɣi$^{31}$ | muscle | DQ-KarenA:162 |

# IV. Breast

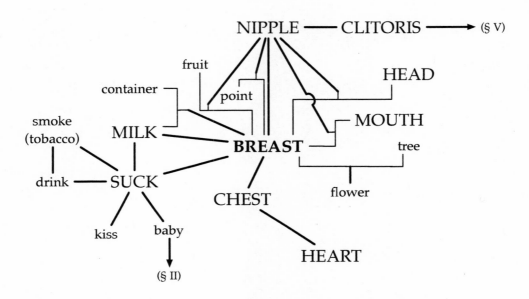

The roots in this chapter refer primarily to the female breast as part of the reproductive system, rather than BREAST in the sense of CHEST (but see **(65) *b(y)at** BREAST / CHEST, below).

**(53)**                    ***s-nəw(-)***                    **BREAST / MILK / SUCK**

This root is reconstructed as ***nəw** in *STC* #419, on the basis of forms from WT, Tsangla, WB, and Lushai. (The rhyme ***-əw** in *STC* is equivalent to Benedict's earlier reconstruction ***-uw**.) The ***s-** in our reconstruction is reflected in the voiceless nasals in Kuki-Chin and Barish languages (including the Lushai form **hnu-te** cited in *STC* #419), the **tă-** prefix in Awa Khumi, and directly in Thanphum **ʃə̌nũ⁵** and WT **snun-pa** 'suckle'.

This root has been frequently combined with dental and velar suffixal elements, both nasals and stops. The reflexes are presented in the following sections according to the particular allofam they represent: the unsuffixed root ***s-nəw** in **(53a)**; forms with dental suffixes (***s-nəwt**, ***s-nəwn**) in **(53b)**; and forms with velar suffixes (***s-nəwk**, ***s-nəwŋ**) in **(53c)**.

This etymon is very widely distributed in ST, appearing in Chinese, Kamarupan, Himalayish, Lolo-Burmese, Karenic, and Qiangic (including Tangut). Many languages have reduplicated forms (e.g. Ergong **nu-nu**), as is to be expected in such a hypocoristic concept as BREAST.

Somewhat similar phonologically is the root *s-nye-n, which is here treated as a separate etymon, below **(54)**.

See *HPTB* *nəw, p. 198.

## (53a)         *s-nəw         BREAST / MILK / SUCK

Despite the phonological similarity of the Newar forms **nu gɔr** (Dolakhali) and **nu gɔ:** (Kathmandu) 'heart' to other Himalayish reflexes of this etymon, K. P. Malla denies their cognacy.

In fact, the semantic connection, between BREAST (of female) and HEART has yet to be demonstrated for Tibeto-Burman.

**0. Sino-Tibetan**

| | | | |
|---|---|---|---|
| *Sino-Tibetan | *njuɤ | breast / nipple / milk | WSC-SH:48 |
| *Tibeto-Burman | *nuw | milk; breast | AW-TBT:327,926; BM-PK7:117; STC:419 |
| | *nuw*C | breast / nipple / milk | WSC-SH:48 |
| | *nəw | breast; milk | ACST:135a; AW-TBT:327,926 |

**1.1. North Assam**

| | | | |
|---|---|---|---|
| Idu | **no** bra | nipple | JP-Idu |
| | **no** ci e co ga | suckle | JP-Idu |
| | **no** ci bra | nipple | JP-Idu |
| | **nu** ci | milk | JP-Idu |
| | **nu** pũ | breasts | NEFA-PBI |
| | ɳo⁵⁵bi³⁵ | breast | SHK-Idu:5.4; ZMYYC:259.50 |
| | ɳo⁵⁵bɹa⁵⁵ | milk | SHK-Idu:5.4.3 |
| | ɳo⁵⁵bɹɑ⁵⁵ | milk | ZMYYC:281.50 |

**1.2. Kuki-Chin**

| | | | | |
|---|---|---|---|---|
| Chiru | ru **nu** | milk / breast | AW-TBT:327 | |
| Khualsim | hnɔi¹ | breasts | GHL-PPB:P.17 | |
| Khumi (Ahraing) | kə̆ **nu**¹ | breasts | GHL-PPB:P.17 | |
| Awa Khumi | tănu⁴ | breasts | GHL-PPB:P.17 | |
| Lailenpi | mə̆ **hnɑu**¹ bɛʔ¹ | breasts | GHL-PPB:P.17 | |
| Liangmei | **n** dui, bui **na** dui | milk | GEM-CNL | 1 |
| Lothvo (Hiranpi) | ă **hnũ**³ | breasts | GHL-PPB:P.17 | |
| Lushai [Mizo] | **hnu**-te | breast, milk | STC:419; WSC-SH:48 | 2 |
| | **hnùu** | breast / milk | LL-PRPL | |
| | **hnu** tê | breast | GEM-CNL | |
| | **hnu** te tui | milk | GEM-CNL | |
| | hnu⁴tɛ³ | breasts | GHL-PPB:P.17 | |
| Maram | ta **na** dui | milk | GEM-CNL | |

---

[1]Note the reduction of this morpheme to a syllabic nasal in **ndui**.

[2]This Lushai form was miscopied from *STC* #419 in Coblin 1986:48, where it is attributed to Written Burmese.

| | | | |
|---|---|---|---|
| Mera | hnəu'[1] | breasts | GHL-PPB:P.17 |
| Paangkhua (??) | ra nuù | breast / milk | LL-PRPL |
| Puiron | se nu | breast | GEM-CNL |
| | se nu tui | milk | GEM-CNL |

### 1.3. Naga

| | | | |
|---|---|---|---|
| Angami Naga | [5]u[1]ñu | breast; milk | AW-TBT:131,327 |
| Angami (Khonoma) | nu | breast; suck | GEM-CNL |
| | nu dzü | milk | GEM-CNL |
| Angami (Kohima) | (u) nou[11] | breast | VN-AngQ:5.4 |
| | (u) nou[11] tia[33] | nipple | VN-AngQ:5.4.1 |
| | nou[31] dzü[55] | milk | VN-AngQ:5.4.3 |
| | nu, nyu | suck | GEM-CNL |
| | nu dzü | milk | GEM-CNL |
| | pe[31] nou[11] | nurse (v.) / suckle | VN-AngQ:5.4.6 |
| | u nu | breast | GEM-CNL |
| Chokri | (u) no[11] | breast | VN-ChkQ:5.4 |
| | (u) no[11] she[55] | nipple | VN-ChkQ:5.4.1 |
| | (u) no[11] ta[33] | nipple | VN-ChkQ:5.4.1 |
| | mü[31] no[11] | nurse (v.) / suckle | VN-ChkQ:5.4.6 |
| | no[31] dzü[35] | milk | VN-ChkQ:5.4.3 |
| | tho no zü | milk | GEM-CNL |
| Chakrü | [1]no | milk / breast | AW-TBT:327 |
| Khezha | [1]e [2]ñu | milk / breast | AW-TBT:327 |
| | 'è ñu | breast | SY-KhözhaQ:5.4 |
| | 'è ñu ké | nipple | SY-KhözhaQ:5.4.1 |
| | 'è ñu jú | milk | SY-KhözhaQ:5.4.3 |
| Mao | o ne dzü | milk | GEM-CNL |
| | [2]o[4]ne | milk / breast | AW-TBT:327 |
| Nocte | ñuʔ-[1]po | milk; breast | AW-TBT:327,131 |
| | ŋu po | milk | WTF-PNN:490 |
| Rengma | nyu ju | breast | GEM-CNL |
| Rongmei | nau dui | milk | GEM-CNL |
| | nou | breast | GEM-CNL |
| | nouh' | suck | GEM-CNL |
| Sangtam | nyi ki | milk | GEM-CNL |
| Yimchungrü | ([1])ñuʔ [1]ge | milk / breast | AW-TBT:327 |
| | niu | breast | GEM-CNL |

### 1.4. Meithei

| | | | |
|---|---|---|---|
| Moyon | næ thén | milk | DK-Moyon:5.4.3 |

### 1.7. Bodo-Garo = Barish

| | | | |
|---|---|---|---|
| Khiamngan | [1]ñaʋʔ | milk / breast | AW-TBT:327 |

### 2.1.1. Western Himalayish

| | | | |
|---|---|---|---|
| Kanauri | nu ni | nipple | DS-Kan:12 |
| Pattani [Manchati] | pa: nu | milk | STP-ManQ:5.4.3 |
| | pa nu | milk | DS-Patt |

### 2.1.2. Bodic

| | | | |
|---|---|---|---|
| Baima | no[35] ne[13] ne[35] | milk | SHK-BaimaQ:5.4.3 |
| | ro[13] nɔ[53] | bosom | SHK-BaimaQ:1.9 |

| | | | | |
|---|---|---|---|---|
| Tsangla (Central) | **nu** | milk; breast | EA-Tsh:90; SER-HSL/T:33 11; STC:419; WSC-SH:48 | |
| | **nu** ma | breast (woman's) | EA-Tsh:11 | |
| Tsangla (Motuo) | **nu** | milk; breast | SLZO-MLD; ZMYYC:259.7,281.7 | |
| | **nu**$^{13}$ | breast; milk | JZ-CLMenba | |
| Tsangla (Tilang) | **nu** | breast; milk | JZ-CLMenba | |
| Tibetan (Amdo:Bla-brang) | **nə** ma | breast | ZMYYC:259.4 | |
| Tibetan (Amdo:Zeku) | **nə** ma | breast | JS-Amdo:96; ZMYYC:259.5 | |
| Tibetan (Batang) | **n̥ə**$^{13}$ ngo$^{55}$ | nipple | DQ-Batang:5.4.1 | |
| Tibetan (Khams:Dege) | **nu**$^{13}$ma$^{53}$ | breast | ZMYYC:259.3 | |
| Tibetan (Written) | **nu** ma | breast; nipple; to suckle; milk | ZMYYC:259.1; GHL-PPB:G.53,U.9,W.75; STC:419; WSC-SH:48 | |
| | **nu**-ŝa | chest / thoracic muscle | JAM-Ety | |
| | **nu**-tog | nipple | ZLS-Tib:47 | |
| | **nu**.ma | breast | JS-Tib:96; GEM-CNL | |
| 2.1.4. Tamangic | | | | |
| *Tamang | *$^{A}$**new** | milk | MM-Thesis:561 | |
| Chantyal | **nu nu** | bosom; breast | NPB-ChanQ:1.9,5.4 | |
| | **nu nu** khwaya-wa | nurse (v.) / suckle | NPB-ChanQ:5.4.6 | |
| | **nu nu**-ye kəpal | nipple | NPB-ChanQ:5.4.1 | 3 |
| Thakali (Marpha) | $^{11}$**ɲu**$^{ɦ}$ | milk | MM-Thesis:561 | |
| 2.1.5. Dhimal | | | | |
| Dhimal | du du **no** si | nipple | JK-Dh | |
| 2.3.1. Kham-Magar-Chepang-Sunwar | | | | |
| Kham | **nwi:** | breast | DNW-KhamQ:1.51 | |
| 2.3.2. Kiranti | | | | |
| Bahing | **nyrs**- | milk | BM-Bah | |
| | **ny** tsy | milk | BM-PK7:117 | 4 |
| Limbu | **nu** | breast, udder, milk | BM-Lim; BM-PK7:117 | |
| | **nu:** | breast / milk | AW-TBT:131 | |
| | **nu** seq | nipple | BM-Lim | |
| Yakha | **nu:** | breast | TK-Yakha:5.4 | |
| | **nu:** uŋmeʔ | nurse (v.) / suckle | TK-Yakha:5.4.6 | |
| | **nu:** ga ɔ cam | nipple | TK-Yakha:5.4.1 | |
| | **nu:** piʔ meʔmana | nurse (v.) / suckle | TK-Yakha:5.4.6 | |
| 3.1. Tangut | | | | |
| Tangut [Xixia] | **new** mbu̥o | breast | DQ-Xixia:5.4 | |
| | **neɯ**$^{1}$ | breast | MVS-Grin | |
| | **nəw** | milk | NT-SGK:204-09y | |
| 3.2. Qiangic | | | | |
| Ergong (Daofu) | **nu** ma | nipple | DQ-Daofu:5.4.1 | |

[3]Literally "breast-head"; **ye** is a genitive particle; **kepal** 'head' is a loan from Nepali.

[4]Bahing **ny-tsy** is glossed as 'nipple' by Hodgson (1857-8); Michailovsky (1991) suggests a connection of the second syllable with an etymon for 'point, tip'.

| | | | |
|---|---|---|---|
| Ergong (Danba) | **nu nu** | breast | SHK-ErgDQ:5.4; ZMYYC:259.14 |
| Ergong (Daofu) | **nu nu** da phra | wean | DQ-Daofu:5.4.7 |
| | **nu nu** sthei | nurse / suckle | DQ-Daofu:5.4.6 |
| Ergong (Northern) | **nəu⁵³** | breast | SHK-ErgNQ:5.4 |
| | **nəu⁵³** tok⁵³ | nipple | SHK-ErgNQ:5.4.1 |
| | **nə³³** | suck | SHK-ErgNQ:5.4.5 |
| Ersu (Central) | **n̠o³³ n̠o³³** | suck | SHK-ErsCQ |
| | **n̠o⁵⁵ n̠o⁵⁵** | milk; breast | SHK-ErsCQ |
| Ersu | **n̠o⁵⁵n̠o⁵⁵** | breast; milk | ZMYYC:259.18,281.18 |
| Guiqiong | **ni⁵⁵ ni⁵⁵** | milk | SHK-GuiqQ; ZMYYC:281.17 |
| | **n̠i⁵⁵ n̠i⁵⁵** wĩ⁵⁵ jɛ̃⁵⁵ | nipple | SHK-GuiqQ |
| Muya [Minyak] | **kʰɯ⁵⁵nɯ⁵⁵** | suck | SHK-MuyaQ:5.4.5 |
| | **nɯ³³nø⁵³** | breast | SHK-MuyaQ:5.4; ZMYYC:259.15 |
| | **nɯ³⁵nø³⁵** | nipple | SHK-MuyaQ:5.4.1 |
| Namuyi | **n̠y³³n̠y⁵⁵** | breast; milk; suck | SHK-NamuQ:5.4,5.4.3,5.4.5; ZMYYC:259.19,281.19 |
| | **n̠y³³n̠y⁵⁵ʁo⁵⁵ba⁵⁵** | nipple | SHK-NamuQ:5.4.1 |
| Pumi (Taoba) | **nɛ³⁵** | milk | JZ-Pumi; ZMYYC:281.10 |
| Qiang (Taoping) | **n̠y⁵⁵ n̠y⁵⁵** | breast | JZ-Qiang |
| | **n̠y⁵⁵ n̠y⁵⁵** tsuə³³ | milk | JZ-Qiang |
| | **n̠y⁵⁵n̠y⁵⁵** | breast | ZMYYC:259.9 |
| | **n̠y⁵⁵n̠y⁵⁵tsuə⁵⁵** | milk | ZMYYC:281.9 |
| Shixing | **niɛ⁵⁵** | milk | SHK-ShixQ; ZMYYC:281.20 |
| | **n̠u⁵⁵ n̠u³³** | breast; nipple | SHK-ShixQ; ZMYYC:259.20 |
| Queyu (Yajiang) [Zhaba] | **nu⁵³** | breast | SHK-ZhabQ:5.4; ZMYYC:259.16 |
| | **nu⁵³** tɕʰi⁵³ | milk | SHK-ZhabQ:5.4.3 |
| | **nu⁵³tɕhi⁵³** | milk | ZMYYC:281.16 |

**3.3. rGyalrongic**

| | | | |
|---|---|---|---|
| rGyalrong (Northern) | kə **nu nu** | suck | SHK-rGNQ:5.4.5 |
| rGyalrong | tə **nu** | breast | DQ-Jiarong:5.4.0; ZMYYC:259.12 |
| rGyalrong (Eastern) | tə **no** | breast | SHK-rGEQ:5.4 |
| | tə **no** ko | nipple | SHK-rGEQ:5.4.1 |
| rGyalrong (NW) | tə **noɣ** | breast | SHK-rGNWQ:5.4 |
| | tə **noɣ** ku | nipple | SHK-rGNWQ:5.4.1 |
| rGyalrong (Northern) | tə **nu** | breast | SHK-rGNQ:5.4 |
| | tə **nu** ku | nipple | SHK-rGNQ:5.4.1 |
| rGyalrong | tə **nu** wa ko | nipple | DQ-Jiarong:5.4.1 |

**6. Lolo-Burmese**

| | | | |
|---|---|---|---|
| *Lolo-Burmese | **\*nəw³** | milk / breast | AW-TBT:327 |

---

[5]It seems to be the first syllable of these Muya forms which belongs in this set, since PTB *-əw most often becomes Muya -ɯ, e.g. 'steal' PTB **\*r-kəw** > WT **rku**, WB **khûi**, Muya **kɯ⁵⁵**; 'sky' PTB **\*r-məw** > WT **rmu-ba** 'fog', WB **mûi(gh)**, Muya **mɯ⁵⁵**.

## 6.1. Burmish

| | | | |
|---|---|---|---|
| Achang (Longchuan) | nau³⁵ | milk | JZ-Achang; ZMYYC:281.41 |
| | nau³⁵ tʂu³⁵ | breast | JZ-Achang; ZMYYC:259.41 |
| Achang (Xiandao) | no³¹ nau³¹ | milk (cow's) | DQ-Xiandao:311 |
| Bola | nau³⁵ | breast | DQ-Bola:118 |
| | nŏ³¹ nau³⁵ | milk (cow's) | DQ-Bola:311 |
| Burmese (Modern) | nui? | breasts | GHL-PPB:U.9 |
| | nui'¹ | breasts; nipple | GHL-PPB:G.53 |
| Burmese (Spoken) | no'² | breasts | GHL-PPB:U.9 |
| Burmese (Spoken Rangoon) | no⁵³ | milk | ZMYYC:281.40 |
| | no⁵³õ²² | breast | ZMYYC:259.40 |
| Burmese (Written) | no¹ | milk | ZMYYC:281.39 |
| | no¹uṁ² | breast | ZMYYC:259.39 |
| | nuí | milk, breast | AW-TBT:327; STC:419 |
| | núi | breast, milk | WSC-SH:48 |
| | nui. | breast | GEM-CNL |
| | nuiw' | breasts; nipple; to suckle | GHL-PPB:G.53,U.9,W.75 |
| | nui' | breast; milk | GEM-CNL; JAM-Ety; PKB-WBRD |
| Danu | no?² | breasts | GHL-PPB:U.9 |
| Hpun (Northern) | ă nù ʀáɪ́ŋ | milk ('breast liquid') | EJAH-Hpun |
| | ă nù, ă nú | breast | EJAH-Hpun |
| Hpun (Metjo) | ă nuh⁴ | breasts; nipple | GHL-PPB:G.53,U.9 |
| Hpun (Northern) | ă nù' s(h)ù' | suck (the breast) | EJAH-Hpun |
| Lashi | nou⁵⁵ | breast | DQ-Lashi:5.4 |
| | nou⁵⁵ jiŋ³¹ | milk | DQ-Lashi:5.4.3 |
| | nou⁵⁵ sɹ̩⁵⁵ | nipple | DQ-Lashi:5.4.1 |
| Lashi (Lachhe') | nɑu² | breasts | GHL-PPB:U.9 |
| | nɑu¹ | breasts | GHL-PPB:U.9 |
| Maru [Langsu] | no?² | breasts | GHL-PPB:U.9 |
| | nuk⁵⁵ | breast; udder (of cow, goat); milk | DQ-Langsu:5.4,5.4.2; ZMYYC:259.43,281.43 [6] |
| | nuk⁵⁵ xək⁵⁵ | colostrum | DQ-Langsu:5.4.4 |
| | nuk⁵⁵ ɣək³¹ | milk | DQ-Langsu:5.4.3 [7] |
| | nuk⁵⁵ ʃ³⁵ | nipple | DQ-Langsu:5.4.1 |
| | nú kàm | milk / breast | AW-TBT:327 |
| Taung-Yo | no?¹ | breasts | GHL-PPB:U.9 |
| Atsi [Zaiwa] | nāu | milk / breast | AW-TBT:327 |

[6]The final **-k** in the Maru form is secondary; **-uk** is the regular Maru reflex of *-əw, as first noted in the original version of *STC* (p. 60 in the published version, 1972) and for the first time in print by Burling 1966 (*Language* 42.3). Thus this form is not to be referred to the stop-finalled allofam (**53c**) *s-nəwk/ŋ BREAST / MILK. Burling's correct observation about the secondariness of the velar stop in the Maru rhyme **-uk** (which is paralleled by the secondary **-t** in Maru **-it** < PTB *-əy), was attacked by Roy Andrew Miller "Once again, the Maru final stops" (1968 paper presented at ICSTLL #1, Yale University). This attack was in turn refuted in *STC*, in the new note 193 (added in 1972).

[7]The second syllable **ɣək³¹** is from PLB *rəy¹ 'water; liquid' (see (**164**) *rəy WATER / LIQUID below). As just noted, final *-əy regularly becomes **-it** in the Maru dialect described in Burling 1968. The unreleased final stop evidently sounds more like a velar in the dialect recorded by Dai Qingxia, who transcribes this rhyme as "-ək".

|  |  |  |  |
|---|---|---|---|
|  | nau$^{55}$ | breast; milk | JZ-Zaiwa; ZMYYC:259.42,281.42 |
|  | nɑu$^1$ | breasts | GHL-PPB:U.9 |

## 6.2. Loloish

|  |  |  |  |
|---|---|---|---|
| *Loloish | *no$^3$ | milk; breast | AW-TBT:327; DB-PLolo:119B,155B |
| Ahi | a$^{33}$nɯ$^{33}$ | milk | CK-YiQ:5.4.3 |
|  | a$^{33}$nɯ$^{33}$o$^{55}$dɯ$^{33}$ | nipple | CK-YiQ:5.4.1 |
|  | a$^{33}$nɯ$^{33}$pi$^{55}$ | breast | CK-YiQ:5.4 |
|  | ɑ$^{33}$ nɯ$^{33}$ | milk | LMZ-AhiQ:5.4.3 |
|  | ɑ$^{33}$ nɯ$^{33}$ ni$^{21}$ | nipple | LMZ-AhiQ:5.4.1 |
|  | ɑ$^{33}$ nɯ$^{33}$ pi$^{55}$ | breast | LMZ-AhiQ:5.4 |
|  | ɑ$^{33}$ nɯ$^{33}$ ŋɯ$^{55}$ | wean | LMZ-AhiQ:5.4.7 |
| Gazhuo | a$^{24}$ ŋ$^{33}$ | milk | DQ-Gazhuo:5.4.3 [8] |
| Hani (Caiyuan) | na$^{55}$ nɣ$^{33}$ | milk; breast | JZ-Hani; ZMYYC:259.30,281.30 |
| Lisu | na$^3$ naw$^3$ | breast | DB-PLolo:119A |
| Lisu (Putao) | no$^2$nʊʔ$^6$ | breasts; nipple | GHL-PPB:G.53,U.9 |
| Lisu (Northern) | nɔ$^{35}$nɔʔ$^{21}$ | milk; breast | DB-Lisu |
| Nusu (Central) | nuɔ$^{55}$ nɯ$^{33}$ nɯ$^{33}$ | milk (cow's) | DQ-NusuB:311. |
| Nusu (Central/Zhizhiluo) | nɔ$^{55}$ nɯ$^{35}$ nɯ$^{31}$ | milk (cow's) | DQ-NusuA:311. |
| Nusu (Northern) | nə̃$^{31}$ nə̃$^{55}$ | breast | JZ-Nusu |
| Nusu (Central) | nɯ$^{33}$ nɯ$^{31}$ | breast | DQ-NusuB:118. |
| Nusu (Central/Zhizhiluo) | nɯ$^{35}$ nɯ$^{31}$ | breast | DQ-NusuA:118. |
| Nusu (Central) | nɯ$^{55}$ nɯ$^{31}$ | breast | JZ-Nusu |
| Nusu (Southern) | nɯ$^{55}$ nɯ$^{31}$ | breast | JZ-Nusu |
|  | nɯ$^{55}$ nɯ$^{31}$ ɹ$^{55}$ | milk | JZ-Nusu |
| Nusu (Bijiang) | nɯ$^{55}$nɯ$^{31}$ | breast; milk | ZMYYC:259.45,281.45 |
| Sani [Nyi] | ɑ$^{44}$ ŋ$^{33}$ | milk (from breast) | MXL-SaniQ:368.2 |
| Phunoi | nù lá̰ | milk | DB-PLolo |
| Ugong | nʊ̀ | breast | DB-Ugong:5.4 |
|  | nʊ̀ wŭŋ | milk | DB-Ugong:5.4.3 |
|  | nʊ̀ ʔa lɛ | nipple | DB-Ugong:5.4.1 |
| Yi (Mile) | A$^{33}$nɯ$^{33}$ | milk | ZMYYC:281.25 |

## 6.3. Naxi

|  |  |  |  |
|---|---|---|---|
| Naxi (Lijiang) | no$^{33}$ | milk | ZMYYC:281.28 |
| Naxi (Eastern) | ṇu$^{31}$bi$^{33}$ | breast | JZ-Naxi |
| Naxi (Yongning) | ṇu$^{31}$bi$^{33}$ | breast; milk | ZMYYC:259.29,281.29 |

## 6.4. Jinuo

|  |  |  |  |
|---|---|---|---|
| Jinuo (Buyuan) | ɑ$^{31}$ na$^{11}$ | milk | JZ-Jinuo |

## 7. Karenic

|  |  |  |  |
|---|---|---|---|
| *Karen | *nu' | breast | AW-TBT:926 |
| *Karen (Pho) | *nú' | breast | RBJ-KLS:23 |
| *Karen (Sgaw) | *nỳ | breast | RBJ-KLS:23 |
| *Karen (Pho-Sgaw) | *nỳ | breast | RBJ-KLS:23 |
| Bwe | -nu | breast | EJAH-BKD |
|  | dɛ nu chi | milk | EJAH-BKD |

---

[8]The -u vowel has been completely swallowed up by the nasal initial in this Gazhuo form, a phenomenon which is typical of Loloish: e.g. the Lahu phonemic syllable /mu/ is pronounced as a syllabic labiodental nasal [ɱ] (see Matisoff 1973b, *The Grammar of Lahu*, pp. 3-4).

| | | | |
|---|---|---|---|
| | nù | breast | AW-TBT:926 |
| | nu-chi | milk | EJAH-BKD |
| Bwe (Western) | nu² | breast | AW-TBT:926 |
| | nũ² | breasts; nipple | GHL-PPB:G.53 |
| Geba | nũ² | breasts; nipple | GHL-PPB:G.53 |
| Palaychi | nù | breast | RBJ-KLS:23 |
| Pho (Delta) | nu¹ | breasts; nipple | GHL-PPB:G.53 |
| Pho (Tenasserim) | nu⁴ | breasts; nipple | GHL-PPB:G.53 |
| Pho (Bassein) | núʔ | breast | RBJ-KLS:23 |
| Pho (Moulmein) | nú | breast | AW-TBT:926; RBJ-KLS:23 |
| Paku | nu³ | breasts; nipple | GHL-PPB:G.53 |
| | nɤ³ | breasts; nipple | GHL-PPB:G.53 |
| Sgaw | nɤ⁶ | breasts; nipple | GHL-PPB:G.53 |
| | ¹nü | breast | AW-TBT:926 |
| Sgaw (Bassein) | nỳ | breast | RBJ-KLS:23 |
| Karen (Sgaw/Hinthada) | da³¹ ny³¹ tʰi⁵⁵ | milk | DQ-KarenB:161 |
| | ny³¹ | breast | DQ-KarenB:121 |
| Sgaw (Moulmein) | nỳ | breast | RBJ-KLS:23 |
| Karen (Sgaw/Yue) | ta³¹ nu³¹ tʰi⁵⁵ | milk | DQ-KarenA:161 |

## 9. Sinitic

| | | | |
|---|---|---|---|
| Chinese (Mandarin) | naai | milk | JS-Ch:486 |
| Chinese (Middle) | ńźju: | nipple, milk, suckle | WSC-SH:48 |
| Chinese (Old) | ńi̯u | breasts; nipple; suckle | GHL-PPB:G.53,U.9,W.75 |
| | njugx | breast / nipple / milk | WSC-SH:48 |
| Chinese (Old/Mid) | ńi̯u/ńźi̯u: | breast, nipple; milk, suckle; hatch | GSR:135a |

## Chinese comparandum

乳 **rǔ** 'breast'

*GSR*: 135a          Karlgren: *ńi̯u          Li: *njugx          Baxter: *njoʔ

This is a long-recognized cognate (see Shafer IST 1966:38, *STC* p. 184, Bodman 1980:171 set 444, Coblin 1986:48, Gong 1995 sets 16 and 70, Schuessler 2007:446).

The correspondence of TB final *-əw (or *-u) to OC *-ug (Li)/*-o (Baxter) is regular. (Examples: 'head' OC 頭 *dug (Li)/*do Baxter, TB *d-bu; 'fog' OC 霧 *mjugh (Li)/*m(r)jos (Baxter), TB *r-məw; 'steal' OC 寇 *khugs (Li)/*kh(r)os (Baxter), TB *r-kəw). This TB final also corresponds to OC *-əgw (Li)/*-u (Baxter), as seen in **(102)** *r-bu ⪤ *pru NEST / WOMB / PLACENTA.

[ZJH]

(53b)          \*s-nəw ᵗₙ          **BREAST / MILK / SUCK**

### 1.1. North Assam

| | | | |
|---|---|---|---|
| Padam-Mising [Abor-Miri] | a **nyun** | breast milk | JAM-Ety |

### 1.2. Kuki-Chin

| | | | |
|---|---|---|---|
| Thanphum | ʃə̆nū⁵ | breasts | GHL-PPB:P.17 |
| Tiddim | nɔ̃i³ | breasts; nipple | GHL-PPB:G.53,P.17 |
| Xongsai | nɔ̃i² | breasts | GHL-PPB:P.17 |

### 1.3. Naga

| | | | |
|---|---|---|---|
| Rengma | **nyun** | chest | GEM-CNL |

### 2.1.2. Bodic

| | | | |
|---|---|---|---|
| Tibetan (Written) | **nud**-pa | breasts; nipple; suckle | GHL-PPB:G.53,U.9,W.75 |
| | **snun**-pa | suckle | STC:p.100 |

### 3.2. Qiangic

| | | | |
|---|---|---|---|
| Pumi (Jinghua) | **niãu**¹³ | milk | JZ-Pumi; ZMYYC:281.11 |
| | **niãu**¹³ po¹³ | breast | JZ-Pumi; ZMYYC:259.11 |

## (53c)     *s-nəw $\frac{k}{ŋ}$     BREAST / MILK

### 1.1. North Assam

| | | | |
|---|---|---|---|
| Padam-Mising [Abor-Miri] | a-**nyuk** | breast milk | JAM-Ety | |
| Milang | a**ɲuŋ** | breast | AT-MPB | |
| | **ɲun**-pi | nipple | AT-MPB | 9 |

### 1.2. Kuki-Chin

| | | | |
|---|---|---|---|
| Lai (Hakha) | **hnʊk**¹ | breasts; nipple | GHL-PPB:G.53,P.17 |

### 2.1.4. Tamangic

| | | | |
|---|---|---|---|
| Manang (Gyaru) | **nyog**¹ ro¹ nyɛ:⁴ | breast (woman) | YN-Man:034 | 10 |
| Manang (Prakaa) | ²**ɲok** ro: | breast | HM-Prak:0025 | |

### 3.2. Qiangic

| | | | |
|---|---|---|---|
| Pumi (Taoba) | **n̩õ**³⁵ | breast | JZ-Pumi; ZMYYC:259.10 | 11 |

### 4.2. Nungic

| | | | |
|---|---|---|---|
| Trung [Dulong] | **nuŋ**⁵⁵ | breast; milk | ZMYYC:259.46,281.46 |
| Trung [Dulong] (Du-longhe) | **nuŋ**⁵⁵ | milk; breast | JZ-Dulong |

### 6.2. Loloish

| | | | |
|---|---|---|---|
| Lisu (Putao) | no²**nʊʔ**⁶ | breasts; nipple | GHL-PPB:G.53,U.9 |
| Lisu (Northern) | nɔ³⁵**nɔʔ**²¹ | milk; breast | DB-Lisu |

### 7. Karenic

| | | | |
|---|---|---|---|
| *Karen (TP) | *****náun'** | breast | RBJ-KLS:23 |

---

[9]Despite the final dental nasal in this form, it is assigned to the present set because of the doublet in -ŋ.

[10]This Manang form proves the independence of etyma **(53c) *s-nəwk/ŋ** BREAST / MILK (first syllable) and **(54) *s-nye-n** BREAST / MILK / SUCK (third syllable).

[11]This form is rather arbitrarily assigned to this set, rather than to **(53b) *s-nəwt/n** BREAST / MILK / SUCK.

| | | | | |
|---|---|---|---|---|
| *Karen | *náun' | breast | RBJ-KLS:23 | 12 |
| Pho (Bassein) | nú? | breast | AW-TBT:926 | |

## (54)  *s-nye-n                    BREAST / MILK / SUCK

This etymon, which frequently occurs reduplicated, may have a hypocoristic (baby-talk) flavor. It is sometimes difficult to distinguish reflexes of this etymon from those of **(53a) *s-nəw** BREAST / MILK / SUCK, which also often appear reduplicated. Particularly problematic are the Qiangic forms, many of which have front vowels, but which after much vacillation I have finally assigned to **(53a) *s-nəw** BREAST / MILK / SUCK instead of to the present set. Both **(53) *s-nəw(-)** BREAST / MILK / SUCK and **(54) *s-nye-n** BREAST / MILK / SUCK occasionally take a nasal suffix, which further complicates the picture (cf. the *Tamang, Chepang, Hayu, and Pa-O forms, below).

A couple of Himalayish languages (Gurung, Thakali) have a velar initial, which appears to be a secondary development from the palatal nasal *ny-. A pair of other forms with voiceless nasals (Lushai, E. Chepang) reflect the *s- prefix.

### 1.1. North Assam

| | | | |
|---|---|---|---|
| Apatani | a-ñi | milk | JS-Tani |
| | à-ñi ñi-pe | nipple | JS-Tani |
| | a-ñíŋ | milk | JS-Tani |
| | ñim-pɯr | nipple | JS-Tani |
| Darang [Taraon] | nye cei | breast milk | JAM-Ety |
| | nye ma: cei | breast milk | JAM-Ety |
| Sulung | a³³niɛ¹¹ | breast | SHK-Sulung; ZMYYC:259.52 |
| | mə³³niɛ¹¹ | milk | SHK-Sulung; ZMYYC:281.52 |

### 1.2. Kuki-Chin

| | | | |
|---|---|---|---|
| Lushai [Mizo] | hne | suck | GEM-CNL |
| Thado | nɔi mù? | nipple | THI1972:66 |

### 1.3. Naga

| | | | |
|---|---|---|---|
| Mao | ne | suck | GEM-CNL |
| | o ne | breast | GEM-CNL |
| Nocte | ni po | breast | WTF-PNN:490 |
| Sema | ni | suck | GEM-CNL |

### 1.4. Meithei

| | | | |
|---|---|---|---|
| Moyon | ni | nipple | DK-Moyon:5.4.1 |
| | ni mówr | nipple | DK-Moyon:5.4.1 |

### 2.1.1. Western Himalayish

| | | | |
|---|---|---|---|
| Kanauri | nu ni | nipple | DS-Kan:12 |

### 2.1.2. Bodic

| | | | |
|---|---|---|---|
| Baima | ne¹³ ne³⁵ | breast | SHK-BaimaQ:5.4 |
| | ne¹³ po³⁵ | breast | SHK-BaimaQ:5.4 |
| | no³⁵ ne¹³ ne³⁵ | milk | SHK-BaimaQ:5.4.3 |

---

[12]These Karenic forms are assigned to this set because of the final glottal stop in Weidert's Pho (Bassein) form.

| | | | |
|---|---|---|---|
| Tibetan (Batang) | ŋə¹³ | suck | DQ-Batang:5.4.5 |

**2.1.4. Tamangic**

| | | | |
|---|---|---|---|
| *Tamang | *ᴬne: | milk | MM-Thesis:555 |
| | *ᴬŋjan | milk | MM-Thesis:213 |
| Chantyal | nfie | milk | NPB-ChanQ:5.4.3 |
| Gurung | ³ŋĕ = ŋĕh | breasts | MM-Thesis:213 |
| | ³ŋe = ŋeh | milk | MM-Thesis:561 |
| | ³ŋe- = ŋeh ba | milk (cow)(v.t.) | MM-Thesis:561 |
| Gurung (Ghachok) | ŋĕh | breasts | SIL-Gur:1.51 |
| | ŋeh | milk | SIL-Gur:7.A.16 |
| | ŋeh pip ba | wean | SIL-Gur:6.B.2.3 |
| | ŋeh tĩq ba | nurse | SIL-Gur:6.B.2.1 |
| | ŋeh ba | milk (cow) | SIL-Gur:3.B.41 |
| | ŋeh kra | nipple | SIL-Gur:2.A.35 |
| Manang (Gyaru) | nyog¹ ro¹ nyɛ:⁴ | breast (woman) | YN-Man:034 |
| | nyɛ:³ ba | suck | YN-Man:087 |
| | nyɛ:¹ | milk | YN-Man:079 |
| | nyɛ:⁴ bɯn¹ | nipple | YN-Man:034-01 ¹³ |
| Manang (Prakaa) | ²ɲe: | milk | HM-Prak:0528 |
| | ³ɲe: | milk | MM-Thesis:561 |
| | ⁴ɲe:- | suck | HM-Prak:0287 |
| Tamang (Risiangku) | ³ne-²tʰun | nipple | MM-TamRisQ:5.4.1 |
| | ³ne: | breast; teat; milk; udder | MM-TamRisQ:5.4, 5.4.2; MM-Thesis:555 |
| Tamang (Sahu) | nyeh cʰuT Tai' ti-pa | suck | SIL-Sahu:17.B.2 |
| | ³ɲe | milk | MM-Thesis:561 |
| | ³ɲe=pa = nyeh-pa | milk (a cow) | MM-Thesis:561 |
| Tamang (Taglung) | ³ɲe | milk | MM-Thesis:561 |
| | ³ɲe-ba | milk | MM-Thesis:561 |
| Thakali (Syang) | ¹nje = Xnjeᶜ | milk | MM-Thesis:561 |
| Thakali (Tukche) | ³ŋje = ŋjeh | breasts | MM-Thesis:561 |
| | ŋjeh | breasts; milk | SIL-Thak:1.51,7.A.16 |
| | ŋjeh coh | nipple | SIL-Thak:2.A.35 |
| | ŋjeh kʰa-lɔ | nurse | SIL-Thak:6.B.2.1 |
| | ŋjeh pi-la | wean | SIL-Thak:6.B.2.3 |

**2.3.1. Kham-Magar-Chepang-Sunwar**

| | | | |
|---|---|---|---|
| Chepang | nyonʔ-sa | suck | SIL-Chep:6.B.2.2 |
| Chepang (Eastern) | hnyonh naʔ | suck | RC-ChepQ:5.4.5 |
| | nyonʔ naʔ | suck | RC-ChepQ:5.4.5 |
| Kham | nwi:səy | nipple | DNW-KhamQ:2.A.35 |

**2.3.2. Kiranti**

| | | | |
|---|---|---|---|
| Hayu | nyen | breast milk | JAM-Ety |
| Limbu | nE | nipple | BM-Lim |

**3.1. Tangut**

| | | | |
|---|---|---|---|
| Tangut [Xixia] | nẹ² | breast | MVS-Grin |

---

¹³The second syllable is probably from **(H:252) *s-bwam ≍ *s-bwap** PLUMP / SWOLLEN / PROTU-BERANCE.

### 3.2. Qiangic

| | | | | |
|---|---|---|---|---|
| Muya [Minyak] | nɯ³³nø⁵³ | breast | SHK-MuyaQ:5.4; ZMYYC:259.15 | 14 |
| | nɯ³⁵nø³⁵ | nipple | SHK-MuyaQ:5.4.1 | |

### 6.1. Burmish

| | | | |
|---|---|---|---|
| Achang (Lianghe) | n̠ɛ̃³¹ | breast; milk | JZ-Achang |
| Achang (Luxi) | n̠ɛn³¹ | breast; milk | JZ-Achang |
| Achang (Xiandao) | ɲɔn³⁵ | breast | DQ-Xiandao:118 |

### 6.2. Loloish

| | | | | |
|---|---|---|---|---|
| Lolo (Ni) | a gni | breasts | GHL-PPB:U.9 | |
| Ahi | ɑ³³ nɯ³³ ni²¹ | nipple | LMZ-AhiQ:5.4.1 | |
| Nesu | a⁵⁵ n̠i²¹ z̩²¹ | nipple | CK-YiQ:5.4.1 | |
| | a⁵⁵ n̠i²¹ ʐ̩²¹ | milk | CK-YiQ:5.4.3 | |
| Nosu | a⁴⁴ne³³ | breast; milk | CK-YiQ:5.4,5.4.3 | |
| | a⁴⁴ne³³ma⁴⁴ma³³ | nipple | CK-YiQ:5.4.1 | |
| Nusu (Northern) | nə̃³¹ nə̃⁵⁵ ɹɯ³⁵ a⁵⁵ | milk | JZ-Nusu | |
| Sani [Nyi] | A³³ni³³ | milk | YHJC-Sani | |
| | A³³ni³³to³³ | nurse (v.) | YHJC-Sani | |
| | a⁴⁴ n̠³³ o⁵⁵ qo¹¹ | nipple | MXL-SaniQ:368.3 | 15 |
| | a⁴⁴n̠³³ | milk | CK-YiQ:5.4.3 | |
| | a⁴⁴n̠³³o⁵⁵qo²¹ | nipple | CK-YiQ:5.4.1 | |
| Phunoi | lã⁵⁵ cu¹¹ ɲi²⁵⁵ | suck | DB-Phunoi | |
| Yi (Mojiang) | A⁵⁵nɛ²¹zi²¹ | milk | ZMYYC:281.26 | |
| Yi (Xide) | a³⁴-nɛ³³ | breasts, milk | CSL-YIzd | |
| | a³⁴-nɛ³³ ma³⁴-ma³³ | nipple | CSL-YIzd | |
| | a³⁴-nɛ³³ to²¹ | breast feed | CSL-YIzd | |
| | a⁴⁴ ne³³ | milk; breast | JZ-Yi; ZMYYC:259.21,281.21 | |
| | n̠i²¹ | breasts, milk | CSL-YIzd | |

### 6.3. Naxi

| | | | |
|---|---|---|---|
| Naxi (Eastern) | n̠i³¹bi³³ | milk | JZ-Naxi |
| Naxi (Western) | n̠i⁵⁵n̠i³³ | milk | JZ-Naxi |

### 7. Karenic

| | | | |
|---|---|---|---|
| Pa-O (Northern) | nɛn² | breasts; nipple | GHL-PPB:G.53 |
| Pa-O | nên | breast | RBJ-KLS:23 |

(55)  **\*m-dzup ≍ \*m-dzip**  SUCK / SUCKLE / MILK / KISS

This widespread etymon is set up as **\*dzo:p** in *STC* #69, on the basis of forms from four Barish and Kuki-Chin languages: (Barish) Dimasa **dźop** and (Kuki-Chin) Lushai **fo:p**, Thado **tsop**, and Siyin **tuop** 'suck; kiss'. (Cf. also Kom Rem **məjop**, Tiddim **to:p**, and Lai Chin **doop**.) However, the rhymes *-op and *-o:p are extremely rare in TB, with virtually no other examples (see *HPTB*, pp. 381-2), and it seems preferable to consider these forms with -o(:)- vocalism to reflect a localized secondary development. (On the other hand, there is a parallel form in NW rGyalrong **kantsʰrop**, alongside Ma'erkang

---

[14]It seems to be the second syllable of these Muya forms which belongs in this set. See the note under **(53a)**.

[15]Literally "breast-head".

rGyalrong **kɑ mə sccup.**) The vast majority of the reflexes point to a high proto-vowel, either *-u- or *-i-. The alternation between these two vowels is especially frequent in the environment of labial consonants, and indeed this is one of the best attested patterns of variation in TB, as well as in Chinese. (See *VSTB* pp. 41-2, *HPTB* pp. 493-505. See also **(58a)** *m-pup KISS / SUCK and **(107)** *(t)sip ⋊ *(t)sup NEST / WOMB / SCROTUM, below.) Several languages show internal variation between these vowels (e.g. Dimasa **dźop** 'suck' ⋊ **sep** 'milk'; Tiddim **teːp¹** 'suck' ⋊ **toːp¹** 'kiss').

The nasal prefix *m- has been added to the reconstruction since it occurs in many Kamarupan languages (e.g. Sema **mtsü**, Ao Chungli **mechep**, Kom Rem **məjop**, Moyon **njúp**, etc.), as well as in Qiangic (e.g. Ergong **ndʑip⁵³**, Namuyi **ntshu⁵³**), and WT **ḥjib(s)-pa**, where *a-chung* "ḥ" is interpreted as a nasal prefix (see *HPTB* pp. 115-6).

Reflexes of the allofam with *-u- vocalism are presented in **(55a)**, and those from the *-i- variant in **(55b)**.

I also recognize an opened-syllable allofam *dz(y)əw MILK/BREAST, treated separately below **(56)**.

A few languages show secondary variants with final stops other than -p. Jingpho has a doublet, one with the expected -p (**tšùp** 'suck, kiss, absorb'), and one that reflects final *-k (**tšúʔ** 'breast'; -ʔ is the regular Jg. reflex of *-k). Similar forms appear in several other languages: Sherpa (Helambu) **chuk pekin** 'kiss', Tamang (Sahu) **cyok-pa** 'kiss', Lashi **tʃu:k⁵⁵** 'nurse; suckle', Bisu **tʃhɔk** 'suck'. All these languages seem to have doublets with both -p and -k. WB has an aberrant form with a final dental (**cut** 'suck'), paralleled by Dulong **tsut⁵⁵** 'suckle' and Tamang (Sahu) **nyeh** *cʰuT* Tai' ti-pa.[16]

For other etyma with similar variation in final position, cf. **(58a)** *m-pup KISS / SUCK and **(107)** *(t)sip ⋊ *(t)sup NEST / WOMB / SCROTUM.

The semantic connection between SUCK and KISS is paralleled by the vulgar English expression *suck face* for 'kiss'.

There is a possible Chinese comparison, 嚵 (Mand. **căn ~ zăn**); this character has two OC readings, *ts'əm 'have in the mouth' and *tsəp 'bite; sting and suck (as a mosquito)' [*GSR* 660f, 660o]; see also Coblin 1986:144. TB also shows some variation between final stop and nasal in this etymon: cf. Sunwar **cim-cā** 'milk a cow' ⋊ **yup-** 'suck'; Tsangla (Motuo) **jum** 'suck (milk)' ⋊ **tɕup⁵⁵ a⁵⁵** 'kiss'. The final nasal in the Milang form **ɟim-ma** seems clearly to be due to assimilation of the initial to the suffix. See the discussion by ZJH, below.

See *HPTB* *dz(y)oːp ⋊ *ts(y)oːp, pp. 31, 371, 382; *dzyuk, p. 382; *dzyup ⋊ *dzyip, pp. 382, 500; *dzyut, p. 382; *tsyup ⋊ *tsyip, p. 500; PLB *C-tšup^L, p. 316; PLB *tšuk^L, p. 30.

## (55a)                    *m-dzup                    SUCK / SUCKLE / MILK / KISS

| 0. Sino-Tibetan | | | |
|---|---|---|---|
| *Sino-Tibetan | *tsop ~ dzop | suck | WSC-SH:144 |

[16]Cf. JAM-*TSR* #73, which contains several typos corrected in *VSTB*, p. 32 and p. 239, n. 41.

## IV. Breast

| | | | |
|---|---|---|---|
| *Tibeto-Burman | *dzo:p | suck; kiss | AW-TBT:963; BM-PK7:171; STC:69; WSC-SH:144 |
| **1.1. North Assam** | | | |
| Apatani | mó-čù | kiss | JS-Tani |
| | mo-ču (sú) | kiss | JS-Tani |
| | mo-čʰuʔ (sú) | kiss | JS-Tani |
| Bokar | bjuŋ-čup | suck | JS-Tani |
| Damu | dzup-ra | suck | JS-Tani |
| Kaman [Miju] | tʌ́-yə̀p | suck | AW-TBT:963 |
| | yə̀p | suck | AW-TBT:963 |
| | yə́p | suck | AW-TBT:1221 |
| **1.2. Kuki-Chin** | | | |
| Khoirao | chup | kiss | GEM-CNL |
| Kom Rem | məǰop | kiss | T-KomRQ:3.9.5 |
| | mə čop | suck | T-KomRQ:5.4.5 |
| Lai (Hakha) | doop | suck | KVB-Lai |
| Lushai [Mizo] | fâwp | kiss | GEM-CNL |
| | fo:p | suck, kiss | STC:69; WSC-SH:144 |
| Maring | chup | kiss | GEM-CNL |
| Siyin | tuop | suck, kiss | STC:69; WSC-SH:144 |
| Thado | cóp | kiss | THI1972:57 |
| | có́p | kiss | THI1972:57 |
| | cèp | suck | THI1972:57 |
| | tsop | suck, kiss | STC:69; WSC-SH:144 |
| Tiddim | to:p[1] | kiss | PB-TCV |
| **1.3. Naga** | | | |
| *Northern Naga | *C_VD-cu:p | suck | WTF-PNN:561 |
| | *C_VD-cʰup | kiss | WTF-PNN:561 |
| Ao (Chungli) | tebang-mesap | kiss | GEM-CNL |
| Chang | shap, ship | suck | GEM-CNL |
| | šʌ̀p | suck | AW-TBT:1114 |
| Konyak | hüp | suck | GEM-CNL |
| | həp | suck | WTF-PNN:561 |
| Konyak (Tamlu) | jup | suck / kiss | AW-TBT:1114 |
| Lotha Naga | ntsap | suck | GEM-CNL |
| | Ntsup | kiss | VN-LothQ:3.9.5 |
| | Ntsup a | suck | VN-LothQ:5.4.5 |
| | zua | nurse (v.) / suckle | VN-LothQ:5.4.6 |
| Nocte | a cup | kiss | WTF-PNN:561 |
| | a cup (jok) | kiss | WTF-PNN:561 |
| | tšup | suck | AW-TBT:963 |
| Phom | jüp | kiss | GEM-CNL |
| | jəp | kiss | WTF-PNN:561 |
| Rengma | sü shi | suck | GEM-CNL |
| Sangtam | mü thsüp | kiss | GEM-CNL |
| Sema | mtsü | suck; kiss | GEM-CNL |
| **1.4. Meithei** | | | |
| Meithei | chap | suck | GEM-CNL |
| | chup | kiss | GEM-CNL |
| | cup pə | kiss | CYS-Meithei:3.9.5 |

| Moyon | cu cu? mówr | nipple | DK-Moyon:5.4.1 |
|---|---|---|---|
| | njup | suck | DK-Moyon:5.4.5 |
| | njup ~ njúp | kiss | DK-Moyon:3.9.5 |

### 1.5. Mikir

| Mikir | ing jup | kiss | GEM-CNL |
|---|---|---|---|
| | ing jùp- | suck | KHG-Mikir:20 |

### 1.7. Bodo-Garo = Barish

| Bodo | sᵣp | suck | AW-TBT:1114 |
|---|---|---|---|
| Dimasa | džop | suck, kiss | STC:69 |
| | dźop | suck, kiss | WSC-SH:144 |
| | job ji | suck | GEM-CNL |
| Lalung | khu jub a | suck | MB-Lal:88 [17] |
| Meche | cop | suck | AW-TBT:1114 |

### 2.1.1. Western Himalayish

| Pattani [Manchati] | cug tʃʰi | suckle, suck | DS-Patt |
|---|---|---|---|
| | cəpu | kiss | DS-Patt |
| | cəpu rəndri | kiss | DS-Patt |

### 2.1.2. Bodic

| Dzongkha | džup | suck | AW-TBT:664 |
|---|---|---|---|
| Tsangla (Motuo) | jum | suck (milk) | SLZO-MLD [18] |
| | tɕup⁵⁵ a⁵⁵ | kiss | JZ-CLMenba |
| | tɕup ?a | kiss | SLZO-MLD |
| Tshona (Mama) | ?o⁵⁵ tʰɔp⁵³ | kiss | SLZO-MLD |
| Tibetan (Sherpa:Helambu) | chuk pekin | kiss | B-ShrpaHQ:3.9.5 |

### 2.1.4. Tamangic

| Tamang (Risiangku) | ¹tsjo: | kiss | MM-TamRisQ:3.9.5 |
|---|---|---|---|
| Tamang (Sahu) | cyok-pā | kiss | AH-CSDPN:10b1.51 |
| | nyeh cʰuT Tai' ti-pa | suck | SIL-Sahu:17.B.2 |

### 2.2. Newar

| Newar | cup-ā na-ye | be kissed ("eat a kiss") | KPM-pc |
|---|---|---|---|
| | cup ā-nala | he kissed | AH-CSDPN:10b1.51 |
| | cup pa nɔ egu | kiss ("have a kiss") | SH-KNw:3.9.5 |

### 2.3.1. Kham-Magar-Chepang-Sunwar

| Sunwar | yup- | suck | BM-PK7:170 |
|---|---|---|---|

### 2.3.2. Kiranti

| Bantawa | chUp | suck up | NKR-Bant |
|---|---|---|---|
| | cup ma | kiss | NKR-Bant |
| Khaling | cūp mū-ne | kiss | AH-CSDPN:10b1.51 |
| Limbu | tsup mEtt- | kiss | BM-Lim |
| Yakha | cup pa cok ma | kiss | TK-Yakha:3.9.5 |

### 3.2. Qiangic

| Ergong (Danba) | wɯ mtsɯ mtsi | suck | SHK-ErgDQ:5.4.5 |
|---|---|---|---|

---

[17]The -b in -jub- represents an unreleased (not truly voiced) stop. Lalung has a doublet chu-ma 'kiss', from the open-syllable allofam (56) *dz(y)əw MILK / BREAST, below.

[18]The final nasal in this form is unexplained, but is perhaps due to assimilation to a now-lost suffix with nasal initial: cf. Milang ɟim-ma.

| | | | |
|---|---|---|---|
| Ergong (Daofu) | ҫhuə | milk | DQ-Daofu:5.4.3 |
| Ergong (Danba) | ҫhɯ | milk | ZMYYC:281.14 |
| | ҫʰɯ | milk | SHK-ErgDQ:5.4.3 |
| Ergong (Daofu) | ʔtsɑu | suck | DQ-Daofu:5.4.5 |
| Namuyi | ntshu⁵³ | milk (v.) | ZMYYC:611.19 |
| | tʂu⁵⁵tʂu⁵⁵mɯ⁵⁵ | kiss | SHK-NamuQ:3.9.5 |
| Pumi (Jinghua) | nə¹³tsə⁵⁵ | milk (v.) | ZMYYC:611.11 |
| Qiang (Mawo) | tsəp | milk | JS-Mawo; JZ-Qiang; SHK-MawoQ:5.4.3; ZMYYC:281.8 |
| | tʂhə | suck / inhale | JZ-Qiang |
| | tʂʰə (tʂʰə la) | suck | SHK-MawoQ:5.4.5 |
| Qiang (Taoping) | ȵy⁵⁵ȵy⁵⁵tsuə⁵⁵ | milk | ZMYYC:281.9 |
| Shixing | tshu³³ | milk (v.) | ZMYYC:611.20 |

3.3. rGyalrongic

| | | | |
|---|---|---|---|
| rGyalrong (NW) | ka ntsʰrop | suck | SHK-rGNWQ:5.4.5 |
| rGyalrong | kə mə scup | suck | DQ-Jiarong:5.4.5 |
| rGyalrong (Maerkang) | kɑ mə scҫup | suck | TBL:1648.11 |

4. Jingpho-Nung-Luish

| | | | |
|---|---|---|---|
| Ganan | tsup³ | suck | GHL-PPB:L.294 |
| | tsɔ⁴ | suck | GHL-PPB:L.294 |
| Kadu (Kantu) | soʔ¹ | suck | GHL-PPB:L.294 |
| | sʻup¹ | suck | GHL-PPB:L.294 |
| Sak (Dodem) | su³ | suck | GHL-PPB:L.294 |
| | tsô?² | suck | GHL-PPB:L.294 |
| Sak (Bawtala) | tsô⁴ | suck | GHL-PPB:L.294 |

4.1. Jingpho

| | | | |
|---|---|---|---|
| Jingpho | chu | milk; breast | GEM-CNL [19] |
| | chu, chyup | suck | GEM-CNL |
| | chup | kiss | GEM-CNL |
| | chyu | breasts of a female | OH-DKL:90 |
| | chyup | suck, as through a straw | OH-DKL:92 |
| | tšúʔ | breast | JAM-TSR:#73 |
| | tʃup³¹ | suck up, absorb | JCD:98 |
| | tʃuʔ⁵⁵ | breast; suck; milk | JCD:96; JZ-Jingpo; ZMYYC:259.47,281.47 |
| | ¹tšup | kiss; suck | AW-TBT:1114,1144 |
| | ʃup³¹ | milk (v.) | ZMYYC:611.47 |

4.2. Nungic

| | | | |
|---|---|---|---|
| Trung [Dulong] (Du-longhe) | tsut⁵⁵ | suckle (milk) | JZ-Dulong [20] |
| Trung [Dulong] (Nujiang) | tҫʰŭʔ⁵⁵ | milk; breast | JZ-Dulong |

6. Lolo-Burmese

| | | | |
|---|---|---|---|
| *Lolo-Burmese | *C-cup | suck / milk | JAM-TSR:73(c) |
| | *ʔcup | suck / milk | JAM-TSR:73(a) |

[19]These Jingpho forms are transcribed as if they were open syllables in Hanson (and sources which recopied his data), but they really have a final glottal stop -ʔ (< *-k), as noted in *ZMYYC* and other more modern sources.

[20]See also WB **cut**.

|  | *ʔcup ≍ *ʔjup ≍ *C-cup | suck / milk | JAM-TSR:69a |
|  | *ʔjup | suck / milk | JAM-TSR:73(b) |

**6.1. Burmish**

| Achang (Xiandao) | ṣuʔ⁵⁵ | suck (milk) | DQ-Xiandao:2262 |  |
|---|---|---|---|---|
| Bola | tʃap⁵⁵ | suck (milk) | DQ-Bola:2262 |  |
| Burmese (Modern) | cut | suck | GHL-PPB:V.108 |  |
| Burmese (Written) | (cut) | suck / kiss | JAM-MLBM:42 |  |
|  | cut | suck, absorb, imbibe | GEM-CNL; JAM-Ety; PKB-WBRD | 21 |
| Hpun (Northern) | ă nù' s(h)ù' | suck (the breast) | EJAH-Hpun |  |
|  | s(h)àʔ | suck | EJAH-Hpun |  |
| Lashi | tʃu:k⁵⁵ | nurse / suckle | DQ-Lashi:5.4.6 |  |
| Maru [Langsu] | tʃap⁵⁵ | suck (as babe at breast); milk (v.) | DQ-Langsu:add3; ZMYYC:611.43 |  |
| Atsi [Zaiwa] | tʃup⁵⁵ | milk (v.) | ZMYYC:611.42 |  |

**6.2. Loloish**

| *Loloish | *C-cutᴸ | suck | DB-PLolo:633 | 22 |
|---|---|---|---|---|
| Akha | cu HS | suck up (e.g. bird sucking nectar, vampire) | JAM-TSR:73(a) |  |
|  | cu LS | suck up (e.g. through small bamboo tube) / kiss | JAM-TSR:73(b) |  |
|  | cu˴ | suck / kiss | JAM-MLBM:42 |  |
| Bisu | kjū | suck / milk | JAM-TSR:73(a) |  |
|  | tšù ~ kjù | suck / milk | JAM-TSR:73(b) | 23 |
|  | tʃhù | suck at the breast | PB-Bisu:35 |  |
|  | tʃhɔk | suck | PB-Bisu:35 |  |
|  | tʃup | kiss | PB-Bisu:32 |  |
| Hani (Hu T'an) | tsu 33c | suck / milk | JAM-TSR:73(a) |  |
| Hani (Shuikui) | a⁵⁵ tʃv̄³³ | breast | JZ-Hani |  |
|  | a⁵⁵ tʃv̄³³ | milk | JZ-Hani |  |
|  | a⁵⁵tʃv̄³³ | breast; milk | ZMYYC:259.32,281.32 |  |
|  | tʃhɤ³¹ | milk (v.) | ZMYYC:611.32 |  |
| *Common Lahu | *chaw˴/htsuh˴ | suck | DB-PLolo:633 |  |
| Lahu (Banlan) | cu: g'i˴ | milk | DB-Lahu:155 |  |
|  | cu: pehˆ | breast | DB-Lahu:119 |  |
| *Common Lahu | *cu⁻ | milk | DB-PLolo:155A |  |
| Lahu (Bakeo) | cu⁻ pehˆ | breast | DB-Lahu:119 |  |
| Lahu (Black) | cú-phû | breast | JAM-II |  |
|  | chɔʔ | suck; kiss | JAM-MLBM:42; JAM-TSR:73(c) |  |
|  | cú | milk | JAM-TSR:73(b) | 24 |

---

[21] This final **-t** is unexplained. See also Dulong **tsut⁵⁵**.

[22] This PLB form set up by Bradley (#633) has only WB for support; elsewhere all Lolo-Burmese forms point to **\*-p**. See e.g. the Bisu, Bola, Maru, and Zaiwa cognates. In general it is difficult to distinguish the PLB rhymes **\*-ut** and **\*-up** based entirely on Loloish (as opposed to Burmish) evidence.

[23] Note the Bisu doublet with **tš-** ≍ **kj-**.

[24] Lahu **cú**, despite its non-checked tone synchronically, reflects a PLB prototype with final stop, **\*ʔjup**;

| | cú phâʔ | wean | JAM-DL:p.466 |
|---|---|---|---|
| | cú-phô | breast | JAM-II |
| | cha-cú-ni | clitoris | JAM-DL:517 [25] |
| | dzɣ³⁵ fɣ⁵³ | breast | JZ-Lahu |
| | tsu³⁵fu³³ | breast | ZMYYC:259.33 |
| | tsu³⁵ɣɯ³¹ | milk | ZMYYC:281.33 |
| | tsɣ³⁵ ɣɯ³¹ | milk | JZ-Lahu |
| Lahu (Yellow) | tsɣ³⁵ pɛʔ⁵⁴ | breast | JZ-Lahu |
| | tsɣ³⁵ ɣɯ³¹ | milk | JZ-Lahu |
| Lolopho | tʂhɯ³¹ | nurse; suckle; suck | DQ-Lolopho:5.4.5,5.4.6 |
| Mpi | tɕhuʔ¹ | suck / kiss | JAM-MLBM:42 |
| Noesu | tʂɤ¹³ | suck | CK-YiQ:5.4.5 |
| Nusu (Bijiang) | tsʅ⁵³ | milk (v.) | ZMYYC:611.45 |

6.3. Naxi

| Naxi (Lijiang) | tʂhuɑ³¹ | milk (v.) | ZMYYC:611.28 |
|---|---|---|---|

6.4. Jinuo

| Jinuo (Baya/Banai) | tʃ h u⁵⁵ | suck (milk) | DQ-JinA:2360 |
|---|---|---|---|
| Jinuo (Baka) | tʃ h ɣ⁵⁵ | suck (milk) | DQ-JinB:2360 |

7. Karenic

| *Karen (Sgaw) | *shuʔ | suckle / nurse | RBJ-KLS:562 |
|---|---|---|---|
| *Karen (Pho) | *shɔ́ʔ | suckle / nurse | RBJ-KLS:562 |
| Bwe | á-dǯù | suck | AW-TBT:963 |
| Pa-O | có? | suckle / nurse | JAM-Ety; RBJ-KLS:562 |
| Palaychi | có | suckle / nurse | JAM-Ety; RBJ-KLS:562 |
| Pho (Bassein) | shɔ̀ʔ | suckle / nurse | JAM-Ety; RBJ-KLS:562 |
| Pho (Moulmein) | shàuʔ | suckle / nurse | JAM-Ety; RBJ-KLS:562 |
| Sgaw | ⁴shuʔ | suck | AW-TBT:963 |
| Sgaw (Bassein) | shuʔ | suckle / nurse | JAM-Ety; RBJ-KLS:562 |
| Sgaw (Moulmein) | shuʔ | suckle / nurse | JAM-Ety; RBJ-KLS:562 |

9. Sinitic

| Chinese (Middle) | tsəp | sting and suck (sc. mosquito) | WSC-SH:144 |
|---|---|---|---|
| Chinese (Old) | tsəp | suck | WSC-SH:144 |

## Chinese comparandum

嘈 **cǎn, zǎn** 'have in mouth; bite; sting'

*GSR*: 660f; 660o    Karlgren: *ts'əm / *tsəp    Li: *tshəm/p    Baxter: *tshim/p

Neither Li nor Baxter reconstructs this word. As Baxter notes (1992:555), this phonetic series presents unusual difficulties for OC reconstruction. Baxter reconstructs some words with *o and others with *i/ɨ.

---

the high-rising tone is the result of "glottal dissimilation", which occurred in pre-Lahu syllables that had both a *glottalized initial and a *final stop (which was reduced to -ʔ in Lahu). For a detailed account of this phenomenon, see Matisoff 1970 ("Glottal dissimilation and the Lahu high-rising tone"). Cf. also Matisoff 1972a #73b.

[25]Literally "vagina-nipple". The last syllable probably means 'red'. Cf. also Lahu **ha-cú-ni** 'uvula' (lit. "tongue-nipple").

It is not clear why Karlgren lists the character twice in *GSR* 660. At *GSR* 660f he reconstructs *ts'əm for the meaning 'have in mouth' and *tsəp for the meaning 'bite', while at *GSR* 660o he reconstructs *tsəp meaning 'sting and suck'. Karlgren's usual practice in *GSR* is to group multiple readings of a single character together, listing that character only once.

On the apparent mismatch between the voiceless PTB initial and the voiced OC initial, see the discussion under **(1b) *pu** EGG.

Vowel correspondences between OC and PTB before labial codas are difficult to pin down. In Li's system, OC *-ə- regularly corresponds to TB *-u- and/or *-i-. Examples include 'three' 三 OC *səm, PTB *gsum; 'enter / sink' 入 OC *njəp, PTB *nup x *nip; and 'sleep' 寢 OC *tshjəm, WT **gzim** (Coblin 1986:134). Using Baxter's system, however, where six vowels (as opposed to just *a, *ə in Li's system) occur before bilabial consonants, correspondences are less regular. This is in part because in many cases there is ambiguity in the reconstruction of vowels before bilabial codas in his system. At the present state of our knowledge, the proposed cognate set is viable.

[ZJH]

## (55b)        *m-dzip        SUCK / KISS

| | | | |
|---|---|---|---|
| **1.1. North Assam** | | | |
| Kaman [Miju] | **jip**[55] | suck (milk) | SLZO-MLD |
| Milang | **ɟim**-ma | suck | AT-MPB |
| **1.2. Kuki-Chin** | | | |
| Tiddim | **teːp**[1] | suck fluids | PB-TCV |
| **1.3. Naga** | | | |
| Ao (Chungli) | me **sep** | suck | GEM-CNL |
| Ao (Mongsen) | **mechep** | suck; kiss | GEM-CNL |
| Chang | **šep** | kiss; suck | WTF-PNN:561,561 |
| | shap, **ship** | suck | GEM-CNL |
| | **shep** | kiss | GEM-CNL |
| Konyak | **jep** | kiss | GEM-CNL; WTF-PNN:561 |
| Lotha Naga | chon **chi** | kiss | GEM-CNL |
| Rengma | sü **shi** | suck | GEM-CNL |
| Sema | a ke **chi** | breast | GEM-CNL |
| | a ke **chi** zü | milk | GEM-CNL |
| **1.5. Mikir** | | | |
| Mikir | ing **sip** | suck | GEM-CNL |
| **1.7. Bodo-Garo = Barish** | | | |
| Dimasa | **sep** | milk | GEM-CNL |
| Garo | caʔ-**sip**-a | suck | AW-TBT:1114 |
| Garo (Bangladesh) | -**srip**- | slurp, swirl with the mouth | RB-LMMG:154 |
| Khiamngan | [12]a[23]**džɛɩʔ** | suck | AW-TBT:1114 |
| | [12]a[12]**tšẹp** | kiss; suck | AW-TBT:1114,1144 |

### 2.1.1. Western Himalayish

| | | | |
|---|---|---|---|
| Pattani [Manchati] | cug tʃʰi | suckle, suck | DS-Patt |
| | tsip tsi | suck | STP-ManQ:5.4.5 |
| | Tùn d̪ʐi | nurse (v.) / suckle | STP-ManQ:5.4.6 |

### 2.1.2. Bodic

| | | | |
|---|---|---|---|
| Baima | pɛ⁵³ tɕi¹³ | kiss | SHK-BaimaQ:3.9.5 |
| Bumthang | zip | suck | AW-TBT:664 |
| Kurtey | džip | suck | AW-TBT:664 |
| Tshona (Mama) | dʑip¹³ | suck (milk) | SLZO-MLD |
| Tibetan (Sherpa:Helambu) | jip ken | nurse; suckle; suck | B-ShrpaHQ:5.4.5,5.4.6 |
| Spiti | jip ce | suck | CB-SpitiQ:5.4.5 |
| Tibetan (Written) | 'jibs | suck | BM-PK7:171 |
| | 'jibs-pa | suck | GEM-CNL |
| | bźibs | suck | AW-TBT:664 |
| | bzip | suck | AW-TBT:664 |
| | ɦjib(s)-pa | suck | AW-TBT:664 |

### 2.1.4. Tamangic

| | | | |
|---|---|---|---|
| Tamang (Bagmati) | 'sip | suck | AW-TBT:664 |
| Tamang (Risiangku) | ³sip | suck (milk, fingers) | MM-TamRisQ:5.4.5 |

### 2.3. Mahakiranti

| | | | |
|---|---|---|---|
| *Dum-Thu-Kha | *chip- | suck | BM-PK7:171 |

### 2.3.1. Kham-Magar-Chepang-Sunwar

| | | | |
|---|---|---|---|
| Magar | cip-ke | milk a cow | AH-CSDPN:03b.41 |
| Sunwar | cim-cā | milk a cow | AH-CSDPN:03b.41 |

### 2.3.2. Kiranti

| | | | |
|---|---|---|---|
| Thulung | chip- | suck (marrow); encroach (on another's land) | BM-PK7:171; NJA-Thulung |

### 3.1. Tangut

| | | | |
|---|---|---|---|
| Tangut [Xixia] | ndĭʊɦi | kiss / suck | NT-SGK:255-122 |
| | Tĭu̞ | suckle / breastfeed / nourish | NT-SGK:7-145 |

### 3.2. Qiangic

| | | | |
|---|---|---|---|
| Ergong (Northern) | ndʑip⁵³ | suck | SHK-ErgNQ:5.4.5 |
| Ergong (Danba) | ntʂhɛ | milk (v.) | ZMYYC:611.14 |
| | wɯ mtsɯ mtsi | suck | SHK-ErgDQ:5.4.5 |
| Ersu (Central) | tsɹ⁵⁵ | nurse / suckle | SHK-ErsCQ |
| Ersu | tʃɛ³³ | milk (v.) | ZMYYC:611.18 |
| Guiqiong | ntʃɦŋ⁵⁵ | milk (v.) | ZMYYC:611.17 |
| | tsy⁵⁵ tsy³³ | kiss; suck | SHK-GuiqQ |
| Muya [Minyak] | nɐ³³tsyi³⁵ | milk (v.) | ZMYYC:611.15 |
| Pumi (Taoba) | nə³⁵tsi⁵³ | milk (v.) | ZMYYC:611.10 |
| Qiang (Mawo) | tʂhi tʂhi | milk (v.) | ZMYYC:611.8 |
| Qiang (Yadu) | tʂʰe | suck (milk) | DQ-QiangN:2262 |
| Queyu (Yajiang) [Zhaba] | lə³⁵dʑe⁵³ | milk (v.) | ZMYYC:611.16 |

### 4.2. Nungic

| | | | |
|---|---|---|---|
| Anong | ɑ³¹tʂhu⁵⁵tʂɦŋ³¹ | milk | ZMYYC:281.44 |

5. Tujia

| | | | |
|---|---|---|---|
| Tujia | tɕi²¹ | milk (v.) | ZMYYC:611.38 |

6.1. Burmish

| | | | |
|---|---|---|---|
| Lashi | ʃɛː³³ | suck | DQ-Lashi:5.4.5 |
| Maru [Langsu] | ʃɛ³¹ | suck | DQ-Langsu:5.4.5 |

6.2. Loloish

| | | | | |
|---|---|---|---|---|
| Ahi | tʂi̱⁵⁵ | nurse / suckle | LMZ-AhiQ:5.4.6 | |
| | tʂɻ 55 | suck / milk | JAM-TSR:73(b) | |
| | tʂɿ̄⁵⁵ | suck | CK-YiQ:5.4.5 | |
| | ɑ³³ nɯ³³ tʂi̱⁵⁵ | suck | LMZ-AhiQ:5.4.5 | |
| Gazhuo | sɻ²⁴ | suck | DQ-Gazhuo:5.4.5 | |
| Lalo | tsɻ⁵⁵ | kiss | CK-YiQ:3.9.5 | |
| | tʂʰɿ̠²¹ | suck | CK-YiQ:5.4.5 | |
| | ɑ⁵⁵ tʂɿ̄³³ | milk | CK-YiQ:5.4.3 | |
| | ɑ⁵⁵ tʂɿ̄³³ bɪ̠³³ | breast | CK-YiQ:5.4 | |
| | ɑ⁵⁵ tʂɿ̄³³ bɪ̠³³ y²¹ dy⁵⁵ | nipple | CK-YiQ:5.4.1 | 26 |
| Lipho | pa̱²¹dʐɻ³³ | breast | CK-YiQ:5.4 | |
| | pa̱²¹dʐɻ³³vi³³ | milk | CK-YiQ:5.4.3 | |
| | tʂhɿ̄²¹ | suck | CK-YiQ:5.4.5 | |
| Lisu (Central) | a⁵-chï² | milk | JF-HLL | |
| Lisu | a⁵chï² | milk | DB-PLolo:155A | |
| Lisu (Northern) | a⁵⁵tʃɻ³⁵ | milk | DB-Lisu | |
| | a⁵⁵tʃɻ³⁵ ɔ⁵⁵dy³³ | nipple | DB-Lisu | 27 |
| | a⁵⁵tʃɻ³⁵hɤ²¹ | milk powder | DB-Lisu | |
| Lisu (Putao) | chʻɿʔ⁶ | suck | GHL-PPB:V.108 | |
| Lisu | hchï⁶ | suck | DB-PLolo:633 | |
| Lisu (Theng-yüeh) | hchï⁶ | suck | GHL-PPB:V.108 | |
| Lisu | hchï⁶ | suck | JAM-TSR:73(c) | |
| Lisu (Central) | hchï⁶ | suck | JF-HLL | |
| Lisu | tshɻ³⁵ | milk (v.) | ZMYYC:611.27 | |
| Lisu (Nujiang) | tʃhɿ̄⁴² | suck | JZ-Lisu | |
| | a⁵⁵ tʃɻ³⁵ | breast; milk | JZ-Lisu | |
| Lisu | a⁵⁵tʃɻ³⁵ | breast; milk | ZMYYC:259.27,281.27 | |
| Nasu | tʂɻ 44 | suck / milk | JAM-TSR:73(b) | |
| | tʂɿ̄⁵⁵ | suck | CK-YiQ:5.4.5 | |
| Nesu | tʂɿ̄²¹ | suck | CK-YiQ:5.4.5 | |
| Nosu | bu⁵⁵tɕɿ̄⁵⁵ | kiss | CK-YiQ:3.9.5 | |
| | tɕɿ̄⁵⁵ | suck | CK-YiQ:5.4.5 | |
| Sani [Nyi] | tʂz̩ 55 | suck / milk | JAM-TSR:73(b) | |
| Yi (Mojiang) | tɕi̥²¹ | milk (v.) | ZMYYC:611.26 | |
| Yi (Nanhua) | bɯ³³dzi̱³³ | breast | ZMYYC:259.24 | |
| | bɯ³³dzi̱³³ʑi³³ | milk | ZMYYC:281.24 | |
| Yi (Nanjian) | a⁵⁵ tʂɿ̄³³ pi³³ | breast | JZ-Yi | |
| | a⁵⁵ tʂɿ̄³³ | milk | JZ-Yi | |
| | a⁵⁵tʂɿ̄³³ | milk | ZMYYC:281.23 | |
| | a⁵⁵tʂɿ̄³³pi³³ | breast | ZMYYC:259.23 | |
| | ɕȳ³³ | milk (v.) | ZMYYC:611.23 | |
| Yi (Xide) | tshi³³ | milk (v.) | ZMYYC:611.21 | |

---

[26] Literally "breast-head".
[27] Literally "breast-head".

| | | | |
|---|---|---|---|
| | tɕɿ⁵⁵-ɕo⁵⁵ | suck | CSL-YIzd |
| 8. Bai | | | |
| Bai | pa̱⁴² tɕi̱⁴⁴ | breast | ZYS-Bai:5.4 |
| | tɕi̱⁴⁴ | suck | ZYS-Bai:5.4.5 |
| | tɕui̱²¹ | kiss | ZYS-Bai:3.9.5 |
| Bai (Dali) | tsue⁴⁴ | milk (v.) | ZMYYC:611.35 |
| Bai (Jianchuan) | tsui⁴⁴ | milk (v.) | ZMYYC:611.36 |

## (56)   *dz(y)əw   MILK / BREAST

This root frequently occurs reduplicated, for obvious hypocoristic reasons, occasionally with voicing of the second reduplicate (cf. the Lalung form). This root is allofamically connected to (55) *m-dzup ≍ *m-dzip SUCK / SUCKLE / MILK / KISS. It is sometimes difficult to distinguish reflexes of the various allofams, especially in branches like Loloish that have reduced final consonantism. Many languages have allofamic doublets in any case.

See *HPTB* *dz(y)əw, p. 382.

### 1.1. North Assam

| | | | | |
|---|---|---|---|---|
| Bengni | a-ču | breast; milk | JS-Tani | |
| Bokar Lhoba | a tɕu: | breast | ZMYYC:259.51 | |
| Bokar | a-ču | breast | JS-Tani | |
| | a-ču: | breast | JS-Tani | |
| Bokar Lhoba | dʐu: | milk (v.) | ZMYYC:611.51 | |
| | tɕu rə | milk dregs | SLZO-MLD | 28 |
| Gallong | a co | breasts | KDG-IGL | |
| | a co cu: cir: | nipple | KDG-IGL | |
| Idu | no ci e co ga | suckle | JP-Idu | |
| | nu ci | milk | JP-Idu | |
| Miri, Hill | o ci | milk | IMS-HMLG | |
| Tagin | a cu | breast | KDG-Tag | |

### 1.2. Kuki-Chin

| | | | | |
|---|---|---|---|---|
| Kom Rem | ču ču | breast | T-KomRQ:5.4 | |
| | ču ču mur | nipple | T-KomRQ:5.4.1 | 29 |
| Maring | chu chu | breast | GEM-CNL | |
| | chu chu yui | milk | GEM-CNL | |

### 1.3. Naga

| | | | |
|---|---|---|---|
| Angami (Khonoma) | nu dzü | milk | GEM-CNL |
| Angami (Kohima) | nou³¹ dzü⁵⁵ | milk | VN-AngQ:5.4.3 |
| | nu dzü | milk | GEM-CNL |
| Ao (Chungli) | ma ma tzü | milk | GEM-CNL |
| Ao (Mongsen) | ma ma tzü | milk | GEM-CNL |
| Chokri | no³¹ dzü³⁵ | milk | VN-ChkQ:5.4.3 |
| | tho no zü | milk | GEM-CNL |

[28]This is a loanword from Tibetan, referring actually to a kind of dried cheese. Cf. WT **ru-ma** 'curdled milk, used as a ferment' (Jäschke 1881/1958:531). See also the Tsangla forms (Motuo; Mama) similarly glossed.

[29]The last syllable means MOUTH.

| Khezha | ňu **juú** | suck | SY-KhözhaQ:5.4.3 |
| | me **tsuú** | suck | SY-KhözhaQ:5.4.4 |
| Mao | o ne **dzü** | milk | GEM-CNL |
| Rengma | nyu **ju** | breast | GEM-CNL |

### 1.4. Meithei

| Moyon | **cu cuʔ** | breast | DK-Moyon:5.4 |

### 1.5. Mikir

| Mikir | **chù**-bōng | breast | KHG-Mikir:74 |
| | **chù**-bōng-chethè | nipple | KHG-Mikir:74 [30] |
| | **chū**-lāng | milk | KHG-Mikir:74 |

### 1.7. Bodo-Garo = Barish

| Deuri | **ce²** | milk | Deuri |
| | **che** | milk | WBB-Deuri:73 |
| Lalung | **chu ju** | breast | MB-Lal:9 |
| | **chu ju** cha na | suck breast | MB-Lal:9 |
| | **chu** ma | kiss | MB-Lal:9 |
| | **chu** ma cha na | kiss | MB-Lal:9 |

### 2.1.1. Western Himalayish

| Bunan | pel **tsi** | milk | SBN-BunQ:5.4.3 |
| Kanauri | **ču ču** | nipple | DS-Kan:29 |
| Pattani [Manchati] | **cu cu** | breast | DS-Patt; STP-ManQ:5.4 |

### 2.1.2. Bodic

| Tsangla (Motuo) | **tçʰu** ra | milk dregs | SLZO-MLD [31] |
| Tshona (Wenlang) | **jo³⁵** | milk | JZ-CNMenba |
| Tshona (Mama) | **jo¹³** | milk | SLZO-MLD; ZMYYC:281.6 |
| | **tçʰu⁵⁵** ru⁵³ | milk dregs | SLZO-MLD |
| Tibetan (Balti) | **ču ču·** | nipple | RAN1975:67 |
| Tibetan (Written) | **bẓo** | milk (v.) | ZMYYC:611.1 [32] |
| | **ḥjo**-ba | milk (v.) | HAJ-TED:179 |
| | **ʒo** | milk | GEM-CNL |

### 2.1.4. Tamangic

| Tamang (Risiangku) | ¹**tsju**-¹**tsju** | milk (baby-talk) | MM-TamRisQ:5.4.3 |
| Tamang (Sahu) | **cya** | milk | SIL-Sahu:7.20 |

### 2.2. Newar

| Newar | **cu cu** pyae gu | suck | SH-KNw:5.4.5 |

### 2.3.2. Kiranti

| Bahing | ny **tsy** | milk | BM-PK7:117 [33] |
| Hayu | **tshux tsu** | breast | BM-PK7:28 |

[30] The Mikir word **chethè** is defined as 'life, breath, stature; pipe' in Walker 1925:31, as in **chethè ari** 'larynx, windpipe'. Thus this form seems to mean 'breast-pipe'. For reasons of space, this semantic association is not diagrammed in the chart at the beginning of this chapter.

[31] This is a loanword from Tibetan, referring to a kind of dried cheese. Cf. the Bokar Lhoba form (above) similarly glossed.

[32] This is actually the future form of the verb, whose principal parts are **ḥjo-ba** (Pres.). **bẓos** (Perf.), **bẓo** (Fut.), **ḥjos** (Impv.). See Jäschke 1881/1958:179.

[33] Bahing **ny-tsy** is glossed as 'nipple' by Hodgson (1857-8); Michailovsky (1991) suggests a connection of the second syllable with an etymon for 'point, tip'.

| | tshʊ | breast, nipple | BM-Hay:84.171 |
|---|---|---|---|

**4. Jingpho-Nung-Luish**

| Sak (Bawtala) | ă tsô² | breasts | GHL-PPB:L.146 |
|---|---|---|---|

**4.2. Nungic**

| Anong | ɑ³¹tʂhu⁵⁵ | breast | ZMYYC:259.44 |
|---|---|---|---|
| | ɑ³¹tʂhu⁵⁵tʂhŋ³¹ | milk | ZMYYC:281.44 |

**6.1. Burmish**

| Achang (Longchuan) | nau³⁵ tʂu³⁵ | breast | JZ-Achang; ZMYYC:259.41 |
|---|---|---|---|
| Burmese (Written) | **cui'** | suck | GEM-CNL |
| Maru [Langsu] | **tʃauk⁵⁵** | nurse / suckle | DQ-Langsu:5.4.6 [34] |

**6.2. Loloish**

| *Loloish | ***co¹** | milk | DB-PLolo:155A |
|---|---|---|---|
| Akha | a˕ **coeˇ** | breast; milk | PL-AED:50 |
| Gazhuo | **ço³³ pɣ³⁵** | breast | DQ-Gazhuo:5.4 |
| Hani (Dazhai) | a³¹ **tɕʰu⁵⁵** | breast; milk | JZ-Hani |
| | a³¹tɕhu⁵⁵ | breast; milk | ZMYYC:259.31,281.31 |
| Hani (Gelanghe) | a³¹ **tɕʰø⁵⁵** | milk | JZ-Hani |
| | a³¹ **tɕʰø⁵⁵ bɛ³³** | breast | JZ-Hani |
| Phunoi | lã⁵⁵ **cu¹¹ ɲiʔ⁵⁵** | suck | DB-Phunoi |
| Sangkong | loŋ³³ **tɕhø⁵⁵** | breast milk | LYS-Sangkon |
| Yi (Dafang) | **tsɒ¹³ mo²¹** | breast | JZ-Yi |
| | **tsɒ¹³ ʑi²¹** | milk | JZ-Yi |
| | tsɒ¹³mo²¹ | breast | ZMYYC:259.22 |
| | tsɒ¹³ʑi²¹ | milk | ZMYYC:281.22 |

## (57)  *pa  BREAST / NIPPLE / MILK

This root appears mostly in Lolo-Burmese, Qiangic, and Baic. It frequently occurs reduplicated, and its simple phonological shape makes it likely that it is hypocoristic in origin. (The same may be said for **(60) *mam** BREAST, below.) Some Lolo-Burmese and Bai forms have been recorded with vowel constriction, but it is not yet clear whether these reflect an allofam with final stop.

**1.7. Bodo-Garo = Barish**

| Deuri | **pu-pu-ti¹** | breast of a female | Deuri |
|---|---|---|---|
| | **pu-pu²** | breast of male | Deuri |

**2.1.1. Western Himalayish**

| Pattani [Manchati] | **pa pa** | breast; nipple | DS-Patt; STP-ManQ:5.4.1 |
|---|---|---|---|

**3.1. Tangut**

| Tangut [Xixia] | **phə** | nipple | DQ-Xixia:5.4.1 |
|---|---|---|---|
| | **phə²** | nipple | MVS-Grin |

**3.2. Qiangic**

| Qiang (Mawo) | **pa pa** | breast | SHK-MawoQ:5.4 |
|---|---|---|---|

---

[34]Note the secondary final velar, the regular Maru reflex of the rhyme *-əw. See note under **(53a)** *s-nəw BREAST / MILK / SUCK, above.

| | | | |
|---|---|---|---|
| | pa pa qǝsti | nipple | SHK-MawoQ:5.4.1 |
| | pɑ pɑ | breast | ZMYYC:259.8; JZ-Qiang; JS-Mawo |
| Qiang (Yadu) | pɑ pǝ | breast | DQ-QiangN:121 |

6.2. Loloish

| | | | |
|---|---|---|---|
| Lipho | pa̠²¹dʐ̩³³ | breast | CK-YiQ:5.4 |
| | pa̠²¹dʐ̩³³vi³³ | milk | CK-YiQ:5.4.3 |
| Lolopho | pɒ³¹ pɒ³¹ | breast; milk | DQ-Lolopho:5.4,5.4.3 |
| | pɒ³¹ pɒ³¹ ɣ⁵⁵ dɯ³³ | nipple | DQ-Lolopho:5.4.1 [35] |
| Mpi | m⁴po²⁴ | breast | DB-PLolo |
| | m⁴po²⁴ʔɯ⁶ | milk | DB-PLolo |
| Nasu | a⁵⁵ pa̠²¹ | breast | CK-YiQ:5.4 |
| | a⁵⁵ pa̠²¹ ȵe⁵⁵ | nipple | CK-YiQ:5.4.1 |
| | a⁵⁵ pa̠²¹ ʑi²¹ | milk | CK-YiQ:5.4.3 |
| Noesu | pa⁵⁵ | breast; milk | CK-YiQ:5.4,5.4.3 |
| | po⁵⁵mo⁵⁵ | nipple | CK-YiQ:5.4.1 |
| Yi (Nanhua) | bɯ³³dʑi̠³³ | breast | ZMYYC:259.24 |
| | bɯ̠³³dʑi̠³³ʑi³³ | milk | ZMYYC:281.24 |

6.3. Naxi

| | | | |
|---|---|---|---|
| Naxi (Western) | ǝ⁵⁵po³¹ | breast | JZ-Naxi |
| Naxi (Lijiang) | ǝ⁵⁵po³¹ | breast | ZMYYC:259.28 |

8. Bai

| | | | |
|---|---|---|---|
| Bai | pa̠⁴² | milk | ZYS-Bai:5.4.3 |
| | pa̠⁴² tu⁵⁵ tʂ̩³³ | nipple | ZYS-Bai:5.4.1 |
| | pa̠⁴² tɯ²¹ po²¹ | nipple | ZYS-Bai:5.4.1 |
| | pa̠⁴² tɕi⁴⁴ | breast | ZYS-Bai:5.4 |
| Bai (Bijiang) | pɑ̠⁴² | breast; milk | JZ-Bai |
| | pɑ̠⁴² | breast; milk | ZMYYC:259.37,281.37 |
| Bai (Dali) | pɑ̠⁴² | breast | JZ-Bai |
| | pɑ̠⁴² tsi̠⁴⁴ | milk | JZ-Bai |
| | pɑ̠⁴² | breast | ZMYYC:259.35 |
| | pɑ̠⁴²tsi⁴⁴ | milk | ZMYYC:281.35 |
| Bai (Jianchuan) | pɑ̠⁴² | breast | JZ-Bai |
| | pɑ̠⁴² tsɛ⁴⁴ | milk | JZ-Bai |
| | pɑ̠⁴² | breast | ZMYYC:259.36 |
| | pɑ̠⁴²tsɛ⁴⁴ | milk | ZMYYC:281.36 |

(58)                     *m-pup ⪢ *pip                     **SUCK / KISS**

This etymon displays the same *-u- ⪢ *-i- variation found with (55) *m-dzup ⪢ *m-dzip SUCK / SUCKLE / MILK / KISS, as well as a similar variation in the position of articulation of the final stop: compare Bengni **mu:-pup**, Rongmei **ka-pút**, and Sunwar **'pu:k pu 'pā-cā**. Weidert 1987 (#651, #1017) sets up "Kuki-Naga-Chin" *m-but, and J. Sun 1993 reconstructs Proto-Tani *pup ⪢ *puk, but in TB generally -p seems to be the most widespread final consonant.

The two labials (initial and final) in this root have an imitative flavor, apparently mimicking the labial activity involved in sucking and kissing.

---

[35]The second element **ɣ⁵⁵ dɯ³³** means 'head'.

## (58a)             *m-pup             KISS / SUCK

This allofam with -u- vocalism is more common, and so far it is only before this variant that the nasal prefix is attested. This prefix should be set up for PTB as a whole, since it occurs in Himalayish (Bunan) **a mbok də ca** and Qiangic (rGyalrong) **kəwu nəpok**, as well as widely in Naga languages.

This variant frequently occurs in compounds after reflexes of **(72)** *m-ʔum ⋇ *mum KISS / HOLD IN THE MOUTH, below (e.g. Milang **mum-pup-ma**), and this may in fact be the source of the prefixal *m- in my reconstruction.

### 1.1. North Assam

| | | | |
|---|---|---|---|
| *Tani | **\*pup ~ puk** | kiss | JS-HCST:224 |
| Padam-Mising [Abor-Miri] | mam-**puk** | kiss | JS-HCST [36] |
| Bengni | mu:-**pup** | kiss | JS-HCST; JS-Tani |
| Bokar | a-**pup** | kiss | JS-HCST; JS-Tani |
| Damu | ʔa-**put**-nə | kiss | JS-Tani |
| Gallong | **buː**-nam | sucking | KDG-IGL |
| | mum-**puk**-nam | kiss | KDG-IGL |
| Kaman [Miju] | **bʉp**[55] | kiss | SLZO-MLD |
| Milang | mum-**pup**-ma | kiss | AT-MPB |
| Tagin | mo **pup**-nam | kiss | KDG-Tag |

### 1.2. Kuki-Chin

| | | | |
|---|---|---|---|
| *Kuki-Naga | **\*m-but** | kiss | AW-TBT:1017 |
| *Kuki-Naga-Chin | **\*m-but** | kiss / suck | AW-TBT:651 |
| Liangmei | ka-**pût** | kiss | AW-TBT:1017 |

### 1.3. Naga

| | | | |
|---|---|---|---|
| Angami Naga | **[2]me[1]bo** | kiss | AW-TBT:1017 |
| Angami (Khonoma) | **mebo** | kiss | GEM-CNL |
| Angami (Kohima) | **mebo** | kiss | GEM-CNL |
| | **me[31] bo[11]** | kiss | VN-AngQ:3.9.5 |
| Chokri | **bo** | kiss | GEM-CNL |
| | **mü[31] bo[11]** | kiss | VN-ChkQ:3.9.5 |
| | **m[31] bo[11]** | kiss | VN-ChkQ:3.9.5 |
| Rengma | **bo** | kiss | GEM-CNL |
| Rengma (Southern) | **[1]n[2]bo** | kiss | AW-TBT:1017 |
| Rongmei | ka-**pút** | kiss | AW-TBT:1017 |
| | kü **put** | kiss | GEM-CNL |
| Zeme | ke **put** | kiss | GEM-CNL |

### 2.1.1. Western Himalayish

| | | | |
|---|---|---|---|
| Bunan | a **mbok** də ca | kiss | SBN-BunQ:3.9.5 |
| Pattani [Manchati] | **pok** | kiss, love | DS-Patt |

### 2.1.2. Bodic

| | | | |
|---|---|---|---|
| Spiti | **po** lenje | kiss | CB-SpitiQ:3.9.5 |

### 2.3.1. Kham-Magar-Chepang-Sunwar

| | | | |
|---|---|---|---|
| Sunwar | **'puːk** pu 'pā-cā | kiss | AH-CSDPN:10b1.51 |

---

[36]The first syllable of this form looks like **(60)** *mam BREAST, but the gloss 'kiss' shows that it belongs here.

2.3.2. Kiranti

| | | | |
|---|---|---|---|
| Khaling | √phəp- | suck | BM-PK7:170 |

3.2. Qiangic

| | | | |
|---|---|---|---|
| Ergong (Daofu) | **bo** pa | kiss | DQ-Daofu:3.9.5 |
| Ergong (Danba) | **bo** pa | kiss | SHK-ErgDQ:3.9.5 |
| Ergong (Northern) | pau⁵³ (**pɔk⁵³**) | kiss | SHK-ErgNQ:3.9.5 |

3.3. rGyalrongic

| | | | |
|---|---|---|---|
| rGyalrong (Northern) | kəwu **nəpok** | kiss | SHK-rGNQ:3.9.5 |
| rGyalrong | po **pok** kapa | kiss | DQ-Jiarong:3.9.5 |
| rGyalrong (NW) | **pox** | kiss | SHK-rGNWQ:3.9.5 |
| rGyalrong (Eastern) | po **pot** | kiss | SHK-rGEQ:3.9.5 |

4.1. Jingpho

| | | | |
|---|---|---|---|
| Jingpho | **pùp** | kiss | GEM-CNL |

6.1. Burmish

| | | | |
|---|---|---|---|
| Maru [Langsu] | **pɔ̰³¹** | kiss | DQ-Langsu:3.9.5 |

6.2. Loloish

| | | | |
|---|---|---|---|
| Ahi | **bu̱²¹** | kiss | CK-YiQ:3.9.5; LMZ-AhiQ:3.9.5 |
| Lisu (Central) | **baw⁶** | kiss | JF-HLL |
| Lisu (Northern) | **bɔʔ²¹** | kiss | DB-Lisu |
| | **bɔʔ²¹** læ²¹hɔ³³ | kiss | DB-Lisu |
| Nasu | **bo̠⁵⁵** | kiss | CK-YiQ:3.9.5 |
| Noesu | **bie¹³** | kiss | CK-YiQ:3.9.5 |
| Nosu | **bu⁵⁵tɕ̍⁵⁵** | kiss | CK-YiQ:3.9.5 |

# (58b)        *pip        SUCK / SUCKLE

This allofam has so far only been found in Himalayish. The variation in position of articulation of the final consonant seems clearly to have been caused by the influence of suffixal material. Cf. the consonantal sequences across morpheme boundary in forms like Bantawa **phïpt-** and Chamling **pips-**, which seem to lie behind forms like Limbu **pi:tt-**, where the labial final has been assimilated to an earlier dental suffix. Note also the variation between final stop and nasal in Thulung.

2.1.2. Bodic

| | | | |
|---|---|---|---|
| Tibetan (Balti) | **pipi·** | breast | RAN1975:47 |

2.3. Mahakiranti

| | | | |
|---|---|---|---|
| *Kiranti | *Pip- | suck | BM-PK7:170 |

2.3.1. Kham-Magar-Chepang-Sunwar

| | | | |
|---|---|---|---|
| Kham | **pi**-nya | suck | DNW-KhamQ:6.B.2.2 |

2.3.2. Kiranti

| | | | | |
|---|---|---|---|---|
| Bahing | **bip-** | suck | BM-PK7:170 | |
| | **biŋ** khu ma | suck | BM-Bah | [37] |
| Bantawa | **phïpt-** | suck | BM-PK7:170 | [38] |

---

[37] The final velar in the first syllable is due to assimilation to the initial of the second syllable.
[38] Note the internal Bantawa vocalic variation between this form and **phüpt-**.

| | phïpʈ- | suck | BM-PK7:170 |
|---|---|---|---|
| | phUp | suck / sip | NKR-Bant |
| | phüpt- | suck / absorb | WW-Bant:60 |
| Chamling | pibd-(u) | suck | WW-Cham:28 |
| | pibd-yu | suck | BM-PK7:170 |
| | pips-(u) | suck | WW-Cham:28 |
| | pips-yu | suck | BM-PK7:170 |
| Dumi | phip- | suck | BM-PK7:170 |
| | phip nɨ | suck, draw (through a straw) | SVD-Dum |
| Hayu | pip- | suck, to nurse, to smoke (tobacco) | BM-PK7:170 |
| | pip i ra | suck, nurse, smoke (tobacco) | BM-Hay:84.15 |
| Kulung | phipp-u | suck | BM-PK7:170; RPHH-Kul |
| Limbu | pi:tt- | suck | BM-Lim; BM-PK7:170 |
| Thulung | phim- | suck | NJA-Thulung |
| | phip- | suck | NJA-Thulung |
| | phip-/phim- | suck | BM-PK7:170 |
| Yakha | pi:ʔ ma: | suck | TK-Yakha:5.4.5 |

## (59)           *m-boŋ           BREAST / MILK

This root is solidly attested in Kamarupan. There is also an excellent match between the Kaman reflex and the reconstructed Tangut form, on the basis of which we set up a nasal prefix for the etymon. W.T. French (1983:490-1) suggests that this root shows an association in Northern Naga between BREAST and FLOWER ("flower" = tree + breast).

**1.1. North Assam**

| Kaman [Miju] | tɕin⁵⁵mphɑuŋ⁵³ | breast | ZMYYC:259.48 |
|---|---|---|---|
| Idu | nu **pũ** | breasts | NEFA-PBI |

**1.3. Naga**

| *Northern Naga | ***pu:ŋ** | breast / flower | WTF-PNN:490 |
|---|---|---|---|
| Yogli | **pauŋ** | breast | WTF-PNN:490 |
| | pil **pauŋ** | flower | WTF-PNN:490 |
| Tangsa (Yogli) | **paung** | breast | GEM-CNL |

**1.5. Mikir**

| Mikir | chù-**bōng** | breast | KHG-Mikir:74 |
|---|---|---|---|
| | chù-**bōng**-chethè | nipple | KHG-Mikir:74 |

**1.7. Bodo-Garo = Barish**

| Bodo | **bun** dəy | breast milk | JAM-Ety |
|---|---|---|---|

**3.1. Tangut**

| Tangut [Xixia] | new **mbụo** | breast | DQ-Xixia:5.4 |
|---|---|---|---|

## (60)           *mam           BREAST

This root is evidently hypocoristic in origin (see also **(57)** **\*pa** BREAST / NIPPLE / MILK, above), and in fact is practically identical to the Indo-European root **\*mā-** 'mother;

breast' (> e.g. Latin *mamma*), of which the *American Heritage Dictionary* (1981:1527) says "An imitative root derived from the child's cry for the breast (a linguistic universal found in many of the world's languages, often in reduplicated form)." The final nasal in this etymon might have arisen through the reduction of an earlier reduplicated form *ma-ma (as in Ao, Sangtam, and Bunan).

There is a phonologically similar but apparently unrelated root (72) *m-ʔum ⪤ *mum KISS / HOLD IN THE MOUTH, below.

### 1.2. Kuki-Chin

| | | | |
|---|---|---|---|
| Paangkhua | **ma** ʹír | breast | LL-PRPL |

### 1.3. Naga

| | | | |
|---|---|---|---|
| Ao (Chungli) | **ma ma** | breast | GEM-CNL |
| | **ma ma** tzü | milk | GEM-CNL |
| Ao (Mongsen) | **ma ma** | breast | GEM-CNL |
| | **ma ma** tzü | milk | GEM-CNL |
| Phom | a **ma** | breast | GEM-CNL |
| Sangtam | **ma ma** | breast | GEM-CNL |
| Yacham-Tengsa | **mam** tü | milk | GEM-CNL |

### 2.1.1. Western Himalayish

| | | | |
|---|---|---|---|
| Bunan | **ma ma** | breast | SBN-BunQ:5.4 |

### 5. Tujia

| | | | |
|---|---|---|---|
| Tujia | **man$^{21}$** | breast | ZMYYC:259.38 |
| | **man$^{21}$tshie$^{21}$** | milk | ZMYYC:281.38 |
| | **mã$^{21}$** | breast | CK-TujBQ:5.4 |
| Tujia (Northern) | **mã$^{21}$** | milk | JZ-Tujia |
| Tujia | **mã$^{21}$ pu$^{35}$ li$^{55}$** | nipple | CK-TujBQ:5.4.1 |
| Tujia (Northern) | **mã$^{21}$ pʰɨe$^{21}$** | breast | JZ-Tujia |
| Tujia | **mã$^{21}$ tsʰe$^{21}$** | milk | CK-TujBQ:5.4.3 |
| | **mã$^{55}$** | breast | CK-TujMQ:5.4 |
| | **mã$^{55}$ tsʰe$^{35}$** | milk | CK-TujMQ:5.4.3 |

### 6.4. Jinuo

| | | | |
|---|---|---|---|
| Jinuo (Baya/Banai) | **mɛ$^{44}$ po$^{31}$** | breast | DQ-JinA:121 |
| Jinuo (Youle) | **mɛ$^{44}$ po$^{42}$** | breast | JZ-Jinuo |
| Jinuo | **mɛ$^{44}$ji$^{33}$** | milk | ZMYYC:281.34 |
| | **mɛ$^{44}$po$^{42}$** | breast | ZMYYC:259.34 |

## (61)  *s(y)ok  BREAST / SUCK / DRINK

This root is quite widespread, and covers a broad semantic range, from BREAST to SUCK to DRINK (any liquid). By a relatively recent extension of meaning, this root is also used for SMOKE (tobacco), and thence for TOBACCO itself (as in Lahu).[40]

There is a promising Chinese comparandum 欶 proposed by Coblin (1986:144). In Matisoff 1970 (#57) I suggested that WB **sok** (also transcribable as **sauk**) 'drink, smoke'

---

[39]The second syllable means 'water'.

[40]The extension of 'drink/suck' to 'smoke (tobacco)' is common in the world's languages. Cf. e.g. Japanese *nomu* 'drink', *tabako wo nomu* 'smoke a cigarette'.

and Lahu **šú** 'tobacco' were cognate. I still believe that to be correct, even though in Matisoff 1988a:1192 I entertained an alternative comparison with WB **hrup** 'snuff up; sniff; sip; sup'. It now looks as if WB **hrup** might be related rather to Chinese 呷 (OC *hrap) 'to drink in with a sucking movement', cited in Coblin 1986:43. This seems preferable semantically and phonologically to Coblin's comparison of the Chinese form to WB **hap** 'bite at' < PTB *hap [*STC* #89].

| | | | |
|---|---|---|---|
| 0. Sino-Tibetan | | | |
| *Sino-Tibetan | *sr + uk | suck / drink | WSC-SH:144 |
| 1.2. Kuki-Chin | | | |
| Matupi | s'uk² | breasts | GHL-PPB:P.17 |
| Tha'oa | s'uk⁴ | breasts | GHL-PPB:P.17 |
| Womatu | soʔ³ | breasts | GHL-PPB:P.17 |
| 1.5. Mikir | | | |
| Mikir | cho-sòk- | suck | KHG-Mikir:73 |
| 1.7. Bodo-Garo = Barish | | | |
| Garo (Bangladesh) | sok | breast; man's nipple | RB-GB |
| | sok-bit-chi | breast milk; mother's milk | RB-GB |
| | sok-kit-ti | nipple | RB-GB |
| 2.1.1. Western Himalayish | | | |
| Bunan | thruk ca | nurse (v.) / suckle | SBN-BunQ:5.4.6 |
| 2.3.1. Kham-Magar-Chepang-Sunwar | | | |
| Chepang | syuŋʔ-sa | suck | SIL-Chep:6.B.2.2 |
| 2.3.2. Kiranti | | | |
| Bantawa | soN | drink in a gulp | NKR-Bant |
| 3.3. rGyalrongic | | | |
| rGyalrong (Eastern) | ka mə scçok | suck | SHK-rGEQ:5.4.5 |
| 4. Jingpho-Nung-Luish | | | |
| Ganan | sɔʔ²⁴ʃi¹ | breasts | GHL-PPB:L.146 |
| Kadu (Kantu) | sôk³ʃi³ | breasts | GHL-PPB:L.146 |
| Sak (Dodem) | ă suʔ² | breasts | GHL-PPB:L.146 |
| 6.1. Burmish | | | |
| Achang (Lianghe) | suʔ⁵⁵ | drink | JZ-Achang |
| Achang (Longchuan) | ʂoʔ⁵⁵ | drink | JZ-Achang |
| Achang (Luxi) | suʔ⁵⁵ | drink | JZ-Achang |
| Achang (Xiandao) | ʂuʔ⁵⁵ | drink | DQ-Xiandao:1895 |
| Bola | ʃauʔ⁵⁵ | drink | DQ-Bola:1895 |
| Burmese (Written) | sok | to drink, smoke | PKB-WBRD; WSC-SH:144 |
| | ə-sok- | to drink, smoke | PKB-WBRD |
| Lashi | ʃu:k⁵⁵ | drink | DQ-Lashi:3.7.7 |
| Maru [Langsu] | ʃauk⁵⁵ | drink | DQ-Langsu:3.7.7 |
| Atsi [Zaiwa] | ʃuʔ⁵⁵ | drink | JZ-Zaiwa |
| 6.2. Loloish | | | |
| *Loloish | *C-ʃuk^L | tobacco | DB-PLolo:406B |

| Akha | shuˆ | sniff up (as salt water for runny nose) | PL-AED |
|------|------|------|------|
| | sjuq | sniff; smell; suck | ILH-PL |
| Lahu (Black) | šú | tobacco | JAM-DL:1192 |
| | su³⁵ | tobacco | ZMYYC:217.33 |
| Lahu (Yellow) | su⁴ | tobacco | JZ-Lahu |
| Nusu (Bijiang) | ɕhu̠⁵⁵ | drink | ZMYYC:534.45 |
| Nusu (Southern) | ɕu³¹ | drink | JZ-Nusu |
| Nusu (Central/Zhizhiluo) | ɕu³¹ | drink | DQ-NusuA:1895. |
| Nusu (Central) | ɕʰu̠⁵⁵ | drink | JZ-Nusu |
| | ʂu̠⁵³ | drink | DQ-NusuB:1895. |
| Nusu (Northern) | ʂu̠⁵⁵ | drink | JZ-Nusu |
| 9. Sinitic | | | |
| Chinese (Middle) | ʂåk | suck, inhale | WSC-SH:144 |
| Chinese (Old) | sruk | suck / drink | WSC-SH:144 |

## Chinese comparanda

欶 **shù, shuò** 'suck'

*GSR*: 1222o        Karlgren: *sŭk        Li: *sruk        Baxter: *srok

Gong 1995 set 279 reconstructed *rsuk. In Li's system another possibility is *sthruk, by analogy with 束 **shù** 'bundle' which is reconstructed *sthjuk to account for the presence in this series of 諫/促 **cù** 'urge on' < *tshjuk. Schuessler 1987:567 reconstructed **shù** 'bundle' as *?-juk to indicate that the initial is uncertain, and in 2007:473 suggests a pre-Old Chinese form *C-sok.

This comparison is made in Coblin 1986:144.

The vowel correspondence is problematic. OC *-uk (Li)/*-ok (Baxter) normally corresponds to PTB *-uk, as in 'bend /crooked' PTB *guk~ *kuk, OC 曲 *khjuk (Li)/*kh(r)jok (Baxter).

[ZJH]

呷 **xiā, xiá** 'to drink with a sucking movement'

*GSR*: not in *GSR* 629        Karlgren: *χap        Li: *hrap        Baxter: *xrap

The Middle Chinese vocalism dictates an Old Chinese reconstruction with medial *-r-, but Schuessler 2007:526 has *hap, arguing that the MC vocalism may be due to "sound symbolism or archaistic colloquialism". This enables him to make a comparison with PTB *hap [*STC* #89] as well as with Austroasiatic forms of similar shape.

Matisoff's proposal that 呷 is instead cognate to WB **hrup** 'snuff up; sniff; sip; sup' provides a better match for Chinese *-r-, but the vocalism is problematic. We would expect a Burmese cognate in -ap < PTB *-ap. Of course, given the likelihood of sound symbolism in words with these semantics, irregular correspondences are to be expected. It is therefore not an easy matter to decide if Chinese 呷 is better compared to PTB *hap or WB **hrup**, or if the similarity of phonological shape is not due to cognacy at all.

[ZJH]

## (62)               *s-loŋ              BREAST

This root appears mainly in Southern Loloish. It is reconstructed as PLB *loŋ$^2$ in Bradley 1979, #119A. The putative Womatu (Kuki-Chin) cognate with voiceless lateral leads me to reconstruct this etymon as *s-loŋ at the PTB level. This etymon bears some resemblance to *b-raŋ CHEST, but we are keeping them separate for now, despite the similarity between, e.g. WB raŋ-pat 'chest' and Bisu lɔŋ-pét 'breast', where the second syllables are both assigned to (65) *b(y)at BREAST / CHEST.

| 1. Kamarupan | | | |
|---|---|---|---|
| Miji | loŋ-kʰjuʔ | chest | IMS-Miji |
| 1.2. Kuki-Chin | | | |
| Womatu | hloʔ³ | breasts | GHL-PPB:P.17 |
| 6.2. Loloish | | | |
| *Loloish | *loŋ² | breast | DB-PLolo:119A |
| Bisu | lɔŋ pét | breast | DB-PLolo |
| | lɔŋ pɛt | breast | PB-Bisu:13 |
| | lɔŋ pɛt láŋ | milk | PB-Bisu:15 [41] |
| Phunoi | lã sì | breast | DB-PLolo |
| | lõ si³¹ | breast | MF-PhnQ:5.4 |
| | lã̄³³ si¹¹ | breast | DB-Phunoi |
| | lã̄⁵⁵ cu¹¹ ɲiʔ⁵⁵ | suck | DB-Phunoi |
| Sangkong | loŋ³³ tɕhø⁵⁵ | breast milk | LYS-Sangkon |

## (63)             *wa        SUCKLE / MILK / BREAST

This etymon is particularly well attested in Himalayish. Most of the Kamarupan forms (especially those with -ma as final syllable) look like loans from Tibetan. The root also occurs in Baic. There are several possible explanations for the final -m in certain Himalayish forms (Bantawa, Chamling, Hayu), as well as the nasalization in Bai ũ 'nurse; suckle': (a) they could be due to rhinoglottophilia[42] because of the zero or glottal-stop initial; (b) they could have arisen by assimilatory epenthesis to the initial p- of the following syllable; or (c) they could have been metanalyzed from the initial of the second syllable of the binome *o-ma, which might originally have been borrowed from Tibetan as a unit before being reduced to a single syllable in the new Bantawa/Chamling compounds. The development of *wa > WT o is regular, e.g. *swa TOOTH > WB swâ/WT so; *g-lwat ≍ *s-lwat LOOSEN / FREE > WB lwat/hlwat ≍ kywat/khywat/WT glod-pa ≍ hlod-pa.

This root appears principally in Himalayish and contiguous Kamarupan languages, but also in Bai, so that it must be set up for PTB.

| 1.1. North Assam | | | |
|---|---|---|---|
| Bokar | *o-ma | milk | JS-Tani |

---

[41]The last element láŋ in this form means 'water'; cf. (165) *laŋ WATER / FLUID / RIVER / VALLEY, below.

[42]See Matisoff 1975.

| | | | |
|---|---|---|---|
| Bokar Lhoba | o ma | milk | ZMYYC:281.51; SLZO-MLD |
| Damu | ʔu-ma | milk | JS-Tani |
| Darang [Taraon] | wo³¹ ma⁵⁵ | milk | SLZO-MLD |
| | wa³¹ma⁵⁵ | milk | ZMYYC:281.49 |
| Miri, Hill | o ci | milk | IMS-HMLG |

**2.1.2. Bodic**

| | | | |
|---|---|---|---|
| Tibetan (Amdo:Bla-brang) | o ma | milk | ZMYYC:281.4 |
| Tibetan (Amdo:Zeku) | o ma | milk | ZMYYC:281.5 |
| | o-mæ | milk | JS-Amdo:486 |
| Tibetan (Batang) | ɣo¹³ ma⁵⁵ | milk | DQ-Batang:5.4.3 |
| Tibetan (Khams:Dege) | o¹³ma⁵³ | milk | ZMYYC:281.3 |
| Tibetan (Lhasa) | o¹³ma¹³ | breast; milk | ZMYYC:259.2,281.2 |
| Tibetan (Sherpa:Helambu) | ō ma | milk | B-ShrpaHQ:5.4.3 |
| Spiti | o ma | milk | CB-SpitiQ:5.4.3 |
| Tibetan (Written) | 'o ma | milk | GEM-CNL |
| | o-ma | milk | ZLS-Tib:61 |
| | o-ma ḥtshir-ba | milk (v.) | HAJ-TED:459 |
| | o.ma | milk | JS-Tib:486 |
| | ɦo ma | milk | ZMYYC:281.1 |

**2.3.1. Kham-Magar-Chepang-Sunwar**

| | | | |
|---|---|---|---|
| Chepang | ʔoh | breasts | SIL-Chep:1.51 |
| | ʔoh-sayʔ | nipple | SIL-Chep:2.A.35 |
| Chepang (Eastern) | ʔoh (lay) tiʔ | milk | RC-ChepQ:5.4.3 |
| | ʔoh sayʔ | nipple | RC-ChepQ:5.4.1 |

**2.3.2. Kiranti**

| | | | |
|---|---|---|---|
| Bantawa | ʔom pi yang ma | milk | WW-Bant:5 |
| Chamling | om pʌy ma | milk | WW-Cham:27 |
| | om pi yang ma | milk | WW-Cham:27 |
| Hayu | pel um pol um(-ha) | milk | BM-Hay:84.142, 84 |

**8. Bai**

| | | | |
|---|---|---|---|
| Bai | o⁵⁵ | nurse / suckle | ZYS-Bai:5.4.6 |
| | ũ³³ | nurse / suckle | ZYS-Bai:5.4.6 |

| (64) | *kom | BREAST / MILK |
|---|---|---|

This root has so far been identified only in a few Kamarupan languages, though there is a possible Dumi (Himalayish) cognate. Several languages (Kom Rem, Meithei, Moyon) have compounds where this root occurs as second element, after a syllable səŋ-/sʌŋ-. This latter element bears a resemblance to **(89) *seŋ** VAGINA, below.

**1.2. Kuki-Chin**

| | | | |
|---|---|---|---|
| Kom Rem | səŋ kʰom | milk | T-KomRQ:5.4.3 |

**1.4. Meithei**

| | | | |
|---|---|---|---|
| Meithei | khom | breast; udder (of cow, goat); milk | CYS-Meithei:5.4,5.4.2,5.4.3; GEM-CNL |
| | khôm | breast milk | JAM-Ety |
| | khom khaynə bə | wean | CYS-Meithei:5.4.7 [43] |

[43]The Meithei verb **khaynə** in this expression means 'to part, to separate'.

|  | khom pi thək pə | nurse / suckle | CYS-Meithei:5.4.6 |  |
|  | khom-pi | nipple | JAM-Ety |  |
|  | khom jin | nipple | CYS-Meithei:5.4.1 |  |
|  | san gom | milk | GEM-CNL |  |
|  | səŋ gom | milk | CYS-Meithei:5.4.3 |  |
| Moyon | sʌŋ ŋom | milk | DK-Moyon:5.4.3 | 44 |

**1.5. Mikir**

| Mikir | kúm bú | breast (poetic) | KHG-Mikir:50 |

**2.3.2. Kiranti**

| Dumi | dɨ dhɨ kwam | nipples (human) | SVD-Dum |

## (65)   *b(y)at   BREAST / CHEST

The semantic range of this etymon is similar to that of English 'breast'; i.e. it can refer
to the general thoracic area (like 'chest'), or specifically to a woman's mammary gland.
In Southern Loloish this root typically occurs after **(62)** *s-loŋ BREAST [q.v.]. The
phonological resemblance of this root to **(81)** *b(y)at VAGINA [q.v.] seems entirely
fortuitous.

**1.1. North Assam**

| Kaman [Miju] | bit³⁵niŋ⁵⁵ | milk (v.) | ZMYYC:611.48 |

**1.2. Kuki-Chin**

| Lailenpi | mə̆ hnɑu¹ bɛʔ¹ | breasts | GHL-PPB:P.17 |

**1.7. Bodo-Garo = Barish**

| Garo (Bangladesh) | sok-bit-chi | breast milk; mother's milk | RB-GB |

**2.3.2. Kiranti**

| Yakha | nu: piʔ meʔmana | nurse (v.) / suckle | TK-Yakha:5.4.6 |

**6.1. Burmish**

| Burmese (Written) | raṅ pat | chest | GEM-CNL | 45 |
|  | raŋ-pat | chest | JAM-Ety |  |

**6.2. Loloish**

| Bisu | lɔŋ pét | breast | DB-PLolo |  |
|  | lɔŋ pɛt | breast | PB-Bisu:13 |  |
|  | lɔŋ pɛt lán | milk | PB-Bisu:15 | 46 |
| Hani (Gelanghe) | a³¹ tɕʰø⁵⁵ bɛ³³ | breast | JZ-Hani |  |
| Lahu (Banlan) | cu: peh^ | breast | DB-Lahu:119 |  |
| Lahu (Bakeo) | cu⁻ peh^ | breast | DB-Lahu:119 |  |
| Lahu (Yellow) | tsɤ³⁵ pɛʔ⁵⁴ | breast | JZ-Lahu |  |
| Lalo | ɑ⁵⁵ tʂɿ³³ bɻ̩³³ | breast | CK-YiQ:5.4 |  |
| Nusu (Central/Zhizhiluo) | ɣɨoŋ³¹ pʰɯ˞⁵⁵ | chest | DQ-NusuA:117. |  |
| Nusu (Central) | ɣɨɚ³¹ pʰɯ˞³³ | chest | DQ-NusuB:117. |  |

---

[44] The nasal initial in the second syllable of this Moyon form has undoubtedly arisen due to assimilation
with the final nasal in the first syllable of the compound.

[45] The first syllables of the WB, Naxi, and Nusu compounds come from *b-raŋ CHEST / BREAST.

[46] The last element lán in this form means 'water'; cf. **(165)** *laŋ WATER / FLUID / RIVER / VALLEY,
below.

| | | | |
|---|---|---|---|
| Nusu (Northern) | ɹɑ³¹ pʰɐ⁵⁵ | chest (of body) | JZ-Nusu |
| Nusu (Southern) | ɹɔ̃³¹ pʰa⁵⁵ | chest (of body) | JZ-Nusu |
| Yi (Nanjian) | a⁵⁵ tʂɹ̄³³ pi̱³³ | breast | JZ-Yi |

### 6.3. Naxi

| | | | |
|---|---|---|---|
| Naxi (Yongning) | ɣɑ³³pv³³ | chest | ZMYYC:257.29 |

## (66)         *tsyur ≍ *tsyir         MILK / SQUEEZE / WRING

This etymon is set up as **\*tsyur** ( = **\*tśur**) in *STC* #188 with the proto-gloss SQUEEZE / WRING, on the basis of the Bahing, Bunan, Hakha, and Kanauri forms, the latter glossed as 'to milk'. There does not seem to be any allofamic connection between this root and **(56) \*dz(y)əw** MILK / BREAST.

See *HPTB* **\*tsyir ≍ \*tsyuːr**, pp. 397, 426, 498.

### 1.1. North Assam

| | | | |
|---|---|---|---|
| Gallong | a co cu: **cir:** | nipple | KDG-IGL |
| Kaman [Miju] | **tɕin⁵⁵** | milk (n.) | SLZO-MLD; ZMYYC:281.48 |

### 1.2. Kuki-Chin

| | | | |
|---|---|---|---|
| Lai (Hakha) | **śur** | wring | STC:188 |
| Lai (Falam) | **sûur/sǔur** | squeeze, milk; rain | KVB-PKC:694 |
| Lakher [Mara] | **sào** | squeeze, wring | KVB-PKC:694 |

### 1.7. Bodo-Garo = Barish

| | | | |
|---|---|---|---|
| Deuri | **dir** bu | milk (human) | WBB-Deuri:67 |

### 2.1.1. Western Himalayish

| | | | |
|---|---|---|---|
| Bunan | **tśhur** | squeeze out | STC:188 |
| Kanauri | **tsür** | milk (v.) | STC:188 |

### 2.1.2. Bodic

| | | | |
|---|---|---|---|
| Tshona (Mama) | **tɕir⁵⁵** | milk (v.) | ZMYYC:611.6 |
| Tibetan (Amdo:Zeku) | **ptsər** | milk (v.) | ZMYYC:611.5 |
| Tibetan (Written) | o-ma ḥtshir-ba | milk (v.) | HAJ-TED:459 |

### 2.1.4. Tamangic

| | | | |
|---|---|---|---|
| Tamang (Sahu) | **'tʰur-pa** | milk (a cow) | SIL-Sahu:14.41 |

### 2.3.2. Kiranti

| | | | |
|---|---|---|---|
| Bahing | **tśyur** | wring | STC:188 |

## (67)         *s-lu         MILK

This root so far seems to be confined to Qiangic (including Tangut). The **\*s-** prefix is reconstructed on the basis of the voiceless liquids in Ergong, NW rGyalrong, and (Sofronov's) Tangut. The aspirated dental stops in Ergong and NW rGyalrong appear to be secondary "extrusions" of the previous liquids. There is no apparent connection with **(62) \*s-loŋ** BREAST, which always means BREAST, not MILK.

### 3.1. Tangut

| | | | |
|---|---|---|---|
| Tangut [Xixia] | **lhi̭u¹** | milk | MVS-Grin |

| | žįu² | milk | MVS-Grin |
|---|---|---|---|
| **3.2. Qiangic** | | | |
| Ergong (Northern) | ɬtʰə⁵³ | milk | SHK-ErgNQ:5.4.3 |
| Muya [Minyak] | lɐ³⁵ | milk | SHK-MuyaQ:5.4.3 |
| | lɐ³⁵ | milk | ZMYYC:281.15 |
| **3.3. rGyalrongic** | | | |
| rGyalrong (Northern) | ta **lu** | milk | SHK-rGNQ:5.4.3 |
| rGyalrong (NW) | ta r̥tʰə | milk | SHK-rGNWQ:5.4.3 |
| rGyalrong (Northern) | ta ʃtok **lu** | colostrum | SHK-rGNQ:5.4.4 [47] |
| rGyalrong | tə **lo** | milk | DQ-Jiarong:5.4.3; |
| | | | ZMYYC:281.12 |
| rGyalrong (Eastern) | tə **lo** | milk | SHK-rGEQ:5.4.3 |

## (68)  IA *du-t  MILK / BREAST

This etymon is certainly of Indo-Aryan origin, from a root *duh- (cf. Nepali **dudh** 'milk', *CSDPN* p.166). See the series of entries beginning with **dugdhá-** in Turner 1966 (*A Comparative Dictionary of the Indo-Aryan Languages*), pp. 365-6.

| | | | |
|---|---|---|---|
| **1.1. North Assam** | | | |
| Milang | (gakir) **tut**-ma | milk | AT-MPB |
| **1.2. Kuki-Chin** | | | |
| Khoirao | a **tu** thui | milk | GEM-CNL |
| **1.7. Bodo-Garo = Barish** | | | |
| Kokborok | **du** | milk | PT-Kok |
| **2.1.5. Dhimal** | | | |
| Dhimal | **du du** | breast | JK-Dh |
| | **du du** no si | nipple | JK-Dh |
| **2.2. Newar** | | | |
| Newar (Kathmandu) | **du-du**-pwa-(la) | breast | KPM-pc [48] |
| Newar (Dolakhali) | **du du** | vagina / breast / milk | CG-Dolak [49] |
| **2.3.1. Kham-Magar-Chepang-Sunwar** | | | |
| Chepang | **dut**-say? | nipple | SIL-Chep:2.A.35 |
| Chepang (Eastern) | **dut** | breast; milk | RC-ChepQ:5.4,5.4.3 |
| | **dut**.say? | nipple | RC-ChepQ:5.4.1 |
| **2.3.2. Kiranti** | | | |
| Dumi | **di dhi** kwam | nipples (human) | SVD-Dum |
| Thulung | **diu diu** | milk | NJA-Thulung |

---

[47]Colostrum is the thin secretion produced by the mother of a newborn for a few days before actual milk is produced.

[48]**pwala** means 'round object; container'; thus the breasts are viewed as "milk containers".

[49]According to K. P. Malla (p.c. 2007), the basic meaning of this form is 'breast', although it is also used euphemistically for 'vagina'.

(69)  $*\ {N \atop s}$ -tuŋ                                      DRINK / SUCKLE

This widespread etymon is attested all over TB (Kamarupan, Himalayish, Lolo-Burmese, Qiangic). It comprises both a simplex and a causative variant, i.e. DRINK (with under-lying nasal prefix) vs. GIVE TO DRINK (with underlying *s- prefix), and by extension SMOKE (tobacco) vs. GIVE TO SMOKE. (Cf. Japanese *tabako wo nomu* 'smoke ("drink") tobacco'.)

The nasal prefix is clearly reflected in Himalayish (Baima, Amdo Tibetan), Qiangic (Namuyi, Tangut), and Loloish (e.g. Yi Dafang, Luquan, Nasu, Xide), sometimes with an actual nasal segment, sometimes more indirectly (as in Lahu **dɔ̀**, where the voiced initial is a reliable reflex of PLB *prenasalization).

There is a phonologically excellent Chinese comparandum with the meaning MILK: 渾 [*GSR* 1188c]. See below.

See *HPTB* PLB *m-daŋ¹ ≍ *m-doŋ¹, p. 123.

### 1.1. North Assam

| | | | |
|---|---|---|---|
| Bokar Lhoba | tuɯŋ | drink | SLZO-MLD |
| Gallong | tuɯ-nam | drink | KDG-IGL |
| Kaman [Miju] | tauŋ⁵⁵ | drink | SLZO-MLD |
| | tʌ́n-tʻàuŋ | drink | AW-TBT:812 |
| | tʻàuŋ | drink | AW-TBT:812 |
| Idu | tioŋ⁵⁵ | drink | SHK-Idu:3.7.7 |
| | tõ | drink | NEFA-PBI |
| | tõ ga | drink | JP-Idu |
| Miri, Hill | ish'-tuɯ-nam | drink water | IMS-HMLG |
| | tuɯ-nam | drink; pluck | IMS-HMLG |
| Tagin | teŋ-nam | drink | KDG-Tag |

### 1.3. Naga

| | | | |
|---|---|---|---|
| Zeme | tung | suck | GEM-CNL |
| | tung dui | milk | GEM-CNL |

### 1.4. Meithei

| | | | | |
|---|---|---|---|---|
| Meithei | thək pə | drink | CYS-Meithei:3.7.7 | 50 |

### 1.5. Mikir

| | | | |
|---|---|---|---|
| Mikir | tong | suck | GEM-CNL |
| | tòng- | suck | KHG-Mikir:90 |

### 2.1.1. Western Himalayish

| | | | |
|---|---|---|---|
| Bunan | tuŋ re | drink (v.) | SBN-BunQ:3.7.7 |
| Pattani [Manchati] | Tùn ḍẓi | nurse (v.) / suckle | STP-ManQ:5.4.6 |
| | tuŋg mi | drink, smoke | DS-Patt |
| | tuŋ mi | drink (v.) | STP-ManQ:3.7.7 |

### 2.1.2. Bodic

| | | | |
|---|---|---|---|
| Baima | ndo³⁵ | drink | SHK-BaimaQ:3.7.7 |
| Dzongkha | thũ: | drink | AW-TBT:812 |
| Tshona (Wenlang) | tʰoŋ⁵⁵ ŋɑ⁵⁵ | drink | JZ-CNMenba |

---

[50]The final stop probably arose via assimilation to the stop initial of the "infinitive nominalizer" **-pə**.

| | | | |
|---|---|---|---|
| Tshona (Mama) | toŋ⁵⁵ | drink | SLZO-MLD |
| Tibetan (Amdo:Zeku) | ntʰoŋ | drink | JS-Amdo:544 |
| Tibetan (Batang) | tʰõ¹³ | drink | DQ-Batang:3.7.7 |
| Tibetan (Central) | thũṅ- | drink | AW-TBT:812 |
| Tibetan (Sherpa:Helambu) | **thung** en | drink (v.) | B-ShrpaHQ:3.7.7 |
| Spiti | **thuŋ** je | drink (v.) | CB-SpitiQ:3.7.7 |
| Tibetan (Written) | **'thuṅ**-ba | suck | GEM-CNL |
| | **thung** | drink | JS-Tib:544 |
| | **ɦthuŋ**-ba | drink | AW-TBT:812 |

### 2.1.4. Tamangic

| | | | |
|---|---|---|---|
| Chantyal | **thũ**-wa | drink (v.) | NPB-ChanQ:3.7.7 |
| Gurung (Ghachok) | **tʰũq**-m | drink | SIL-Gur:1.54 |
| | **tʰũq** ba | drink | SIL-Gur:7.B.2.28 |
| | ŋeh **tĩq** ba | nurse | SIL-Gur:6.B.2.1 |
| Manang (Gyaru) | **tuŋ²** ba | drink | YN-Man:086 |
| Manang (Prakaa) | **¹tʰuŋ**- | drink | HM-Prak:0329 |
| | **¹tʰuŋ** pə | drink | HM-Prak:0525 |
| Tamang (Bagmati) | **'thuŋ** | drink | AW-TBT:812 |
| Tamang (Risiangku) | **²tʰuŋ** | drink | MM-TamRisQ:3.7.7 |
| Thakali (Tukche) | **tʰuŋ**-pɔ | drink | SIL-Thak:1.54 |

### 2.2. Newar

| | | | |
|---|---|---|---|
| Newar | **ton** egu | drink | SH-KNw:3.7.7 |
| Newar (Kathmandu) | **twan**-e | drink | KPM-pc |
| Newar (Dolakhali) | **twɔn**- | drink | CG-Dolak |
| Newar (Kathmandu) | **twɔn**- | drink | CG-Kath |

### 2.3. Mahakiranti

| | | | |
|---|---|---|---|
| *Kiranti | *tuŋ- | drink | BM-PK7:49 |

### 2.3.1. Kham-Magar-Chepang-Sunwar

| | | | |
|---|---|---|---|
| Chepang | **tuŋ** | drink | AW-TBT:7 |
| | **tuŋ**-sa | drink | SIL-Chep:1.54 |
| Chepang (Eastern) | **tuŋ** na? | drink (v.) | RC-ChepQ:3.7.7 |
| Sunwar | **tu:**- | drink | BM-PK7:49 |

### 2.3.2. Kiranti

| | | | |
|---|---|---|---|
| Bahing | **tuŋ**- | drink | BM-PK7:49 |
| | **tuŋ** ku luŋ ma | drink, smoke | BM-Bah |
| Bantawa | **DuN** | drink | NKR-Bant |
| | **duŋ**- | drink | BM-PK7:49 |
| Chamling | **diŋ**-u | drink | BM-PK7:49 |
| | **dung**- | drink | WW-Cham:11 |
| | **dung**-u | drink | BM-PK7:49 |
| Dumi | **tiŋ**- | drink | BM-PK7:49 |
| Hayu | **tun** | drink (except water) | BM-Hay:84.245 |
| Khaling | √**tuŋ**- | drink | BM-PK7:49 |
| Kulung | **duŋŋ**- | drink | BM-PK7:49 |
| | **duŋŋ**-u | drink | RPHH-Kul |
| Limbu | **thuŋ**- | drink | BM-Lim |
| Thulung | **Du(ŋ)**- | drink | NJA-Thulung |
| | **ɖu(ŋ)**- | drink | BM-PK7:49 |

## 3.1. Tangut

| | | | | |
|---|---|---|---|---|
| Tangut [Xixia] | ndefi | drink | JAM-MLBM:70 | 51 |
| | ndǐ | drink | DQ-Xixia:3.7.7 | |

## 3.2. Qiangic

| | | | |
|---|---|---|---|
| Ergong (Daofu) | nu nu sthei | nurse / suckle | DQ-Daofu:5.4.6 |
| Ergong (Northern) | sthə³³ | nurse / suckle | SHK-ErgNQ:5.4.6 |
| | thə¹³ | drink | SHK-ErgNQ:3.7.7 |
| Ergong (Danba) | wthi | drink | SHK-ErgDQ:3.7.7 |
| Ergong (Daofu) | ʔthu | drink | DQ-Daofu:3.7.7 |
| Ersu (Central) | tshɛ⁵⁵ | drink | SHK-ErsCQ |
| Guiqiong | tɕha³⁵ | drink | SHK-GuiqQ |
| Muya [Minyak] | tɕhyɯ⁵³ | drink | SHK-MuyaQ:3.7.7 |
| Namuyi | ndʐ̩³⁵ | drink | SHK-NamuQ:3.7.7 |
| Pumi (Jinghua) | thiɛ̃⁵⁵ | drink | JZ-Pumi |
| Pumi (Taoba) | thiɛ̃³⁵ | drink | JZ-Pumi |
| Qiang (Mawo) | sti | nurse / suckle | SHK-MawoQ:5.4.6 |
| | thi | drink | JZ-Qiang; SHK-MawoQ:3.7.7 |
| Qiang (Taoping) | thie³³ | drink | JZ-Qiang |
| Qiang (Yadu) | tɕhə | drink | DQ-QiangN:1964 |
| Shixing | tɕhĩ³⁵ | drink | SHK-ShixQ |
| Queyu (Yajiang) [Zhaba] | kə³⁵ thũ⁵⁵ | drink | SHK-ZhabQ:3.7.7 |

## 3.3. rGyalrongic

| | | | |
|---|---|---|---|
| rGyalrong (NW) | ka thi | drink | SHK-rGNWQ:3.7.7 |
| rGyalrong (Northern) | kəwu ʃthi | nurse / suckle | SHK-rGNQ:5.4.6 |
| | kə wu thi | drink | SHK-rGNQ:3.7.7 |

## 6. Lolo-Burmese

| | | | |
|---|---|---|---|
| *Lolo-Burmese | *ndaŋ¹ ≍ ʔdaŋ¹ | drink | JAM-MLBM:70 |

## 6.2. Loloish

| | | | |
|---|---|---|---|
| *Loloish | *m-daŋ¹ | drink | DB-PLolo:631; ILH-PL:245 |
| Ahi | tu²² | nurse; drink | CK-YiQ:5.4.6; LMZ-AhiQ:3.7.7 |
| Akha (Thai) | dɔ́ | drink | ILH-PL:245 |
| Akha | dɔ́ | drink | ILH-PL:245 |
| Akha (Yunnan) | dɔ́ | drink | ILH-PL:245 |
| Bisu | táŋ | drink | DB-Bisu |
| Gazhuo | to²¹³ | drink | DLF-Gazhuo |
| | to³²³ | drink | DHFRL; DQ-Gazhuo:3.7.7 |
| | to³³ | nurse; suckle; drink | DLF-Gazhuo; DQ-Gazhuo:5.4.6 |
| Hani (Lüchun) | dó | drink | ILH-PL:245 |
| Hani (Dazhai) | do⁵⁵ | drink | JZ-Hani |
| Hani (Pijo) | tú | drink | ILH-PL:245 |
| Hani (Caiyuan) | tu⁵⁵ | drink | JZ-Hani |
| Hani (Gelanghe) | dɔ⁵⁵ | drink | JZ-Hani |
| Hani (Wordlist) | ddol | drink | ILH-PL:245 |
| Haoni | tɣ⁵⁵ | drink | ILH-PL:245 |

[51] This form is originally from Nishida 1964-66:415.

| | | | |
|---|---|---|---|
| Hani (Shuikui) | tɤ⁵⁵ | drink | JZ-Hani |
| Hani (Khatu) | tú | drink | ILH-PL:245 |
| *Common Lahu | *daw˯ | drink | DB-PLolo |
| Lahu (Black) | dɔ³¹ | drink | JZ-Lahu; ZMYYC:534.33 |
| | dɔ̀ | drink | JAM-MLBM:70 |
| | šú dɔ̀ ve | smoke tobacco | JAM-DL:1193 |
| | tɔ | give to drink; give to smoke | JAM-DL:649 |
| Lahu (Yellow) | dɔʔ²¹ | drink | JZ-Lahu |
| Lalo | du⁵⁵ | drink | CK-YiQ:3.7.7 |
| | tu³³ | nurse / suckle | CK-YiQ:5.4.6 |
| Lipho | ta³³ | nurse | CK-YiQ:5.4.6 |
| Lisu | daw⁴ | drink | DB-PLolo:631 |
| Lisu (Nujiang) | do³³ | drink | JZ-Lisu |
| Lisu | do³³ | drink | ZMYYC:534.27 |
| Lisu (Northern) | hwa²¹si²¹ dɔ⁴⁴ | suck blood wine | DB-Lisu |
| Lolopho | dʋ³³ | drink | DQ-Lolopho:3.7.7 |
| Luquan | nt'ɐ¹¹ | drink | JAM-MLBM:70 |
| Mpi | toŋ⁵/taŋ⁵ | drink | ILH-PL:245 |
| Nasu | d'ɔ¹³ | drink | JAM-MLBM:70 |
| | ndʰɔ²¹ | drink | CK-YiQ:3.7.7 |
| | tɔ²¹ | nurse / suckle | CK-YiQ:5.4.6 |
| Nesu | da²¹ | drink | CK-YiQ:3.7.7 |
| Noesu | to²¹ | nurse | CK-YiQ:5.4.6 |
| Nosu | to²¹ | nurse | CK-YiQ:5.4.6 |
| Sani [Nyi] | A³³ni³³to³³ | nurse (v.) | YHJC-Sani |
| | to³³ | nurse | CK-YiQ:5.4.6 |
| | tʂi⁵⁵ | drink | CK-YiQ:3.7.7; YHJC-Sani |
| | tʂʅ⁵⁵ | drink, smoke | MXL-SaniQ:341.1 |
| Phunoi | tǎ⁵⁵ sə¹¹ | drink | DB-Phunoi |
| Yi (Dafang) | ndɔ²¹ | drink | JZ-Yi; ZMYYC:534.22 |
| Yi (Lishan) | dɔ³¹ | drink | DLF-Gazhuo |
| Yi (Mile) | tu³³ | drink | ZMYYC:534.25 |
| Yi (Mojiang) | dʋ²¹ | drink | ZMYYC:534.26 |
| Yi (Nanhua) | dʌ³³ | drink | ZMYYC:534.24 |
| | tʌ³¹ | give to drink | ZMYYC:534.24 |
| Yi (Nanjian) | du⁵⁵ | drink | JZ-Yi; ZMYYC:534.23 |
| Yi (Xide) | a³⁴-nᴇ³³ to²¹ | breast feed | CSL-YIzd |
| | ndo³³ | drink | CSL-YIzd; JZ-Yi; ZMYYC:534.21 |

## 6.3. Naxi

| | | | |
|---|---|---|---|
| Naxi (Lijiang) | thɯ³¹ | drink | ZMYYC:534.28 |
| Naxi (Eastern) | tʰɯ³¹ | drink | JZ-Naxi |
| Naxi (Western) | tʰɯ³¹ | drink | JZ-Naxi |

## 6.4. Jinuo

| | | | |
|---|---|---|---|
| Jinuo (Youle) | tə⁴² | drink | JZ-Jinuo |
| Jinuo | tɐ⁴² | drink | ZMYYC:534.34 |
| Jinuo (Baya/Banai) | tʌ³¹ | drink | DQ-JinA:1964 |
| Jinuo (Baka) | tʌ³¹ | drink | DQ-JinB:1964 |

## 9. Sinitic

| | | | |
|---|---|---|---|
| Chinese (Mandarin) | tung | milk | GSR:1188c |

| Chinese (Old/Mid) | tịung/t̂ịwong- | milk | GSR:1188c |
| | tung/tung- | milk | GSR:1188c |

## Chinese comparandum

浱 **zhòng** 'milk'

*GSR*: 1188c  Karlgren: **\*tịung** / **\*tung**  Li: **\*tjungh** / **\*tungh**  Baxter: **\*tjongs** / **\*tongs**

The correspondences are a perfect match. OC **\*u** (Li)/**\*o** (Baxter) regularly corresponds to PTB **\*u** before velar codas.

However, there is a competing etymology suggesting that this word is an early borrowing from a Central Asian language (Pulleyblank 1962:250ff). This etymology is supported by the fact that this is not the ordinary Chinese word for 'milk'; early glosses define it as 'milk (of cows and mares)'. The Chinese themselves did not drink such milk, so it would not be surprising if this word were borrowed from nomadic peoples.

[ZJH]

## (70)                    *pil                    MILK (v.) / SQUEEZE / PRESS OUT

This etymon has so far been identified only in Himalayish.

2.1.1. Western Himalayish
| Bunan | **pel** tsi | milk | SBN-BunQ:5.4.3 |

2.3.1. Kham-Magar-Chepang-Sunwar
| Kham | **pi**:-nyā | milk a cow | AH-CSDPN:03b.41 |

2.3.2. Kiranti
| Bantawa | **bitt**- | milk | WW-Bant:10 |
| | ʔom **pi** yang ma | milk | WW-Bant:5 |
| Chamling | om **pAy** ma | milk | WW-Cham:27 |
| | om **pi** yang ma | milk | WW-Cham:27 |
| Hayu | **pel** | milk, press (e.g. oil) | BM-Hay:84.142, 84 |
| | **pel** um **pol** um(-ha) | milk | BM-Hay:84.142, 84 |
| Khaling | **pal**-ne | milk a cow | AH-CSDPN:03b.41 |
| Kulung | **bill**-u | milk | RPHH-Kul |
| Limbu | **phi**:nt- | milk | BM-Lim |

## (71)                    *bruŋ                    SUCK

This root is set up for "Proto-Tani" (part of the traditional "Mirish" or "Abor-Miri-Dafla" group) by Jackson T. Sun (1993). The possible Kanauri cognate suggests that it might actually be more widely distributed in TB.

1.1. North Assam
| *Tani | **\*bruŋ** | suck | JS-HCST:406 |
| Padam [Abor] | **bu** | suck | JS-HCST |
| Apatani | **bju** | suck | JS-Tani |
| | **brju** | suck; suckle | JS-HCST; JS-Tani |
| | ha-**brjã** | breast | JS-Tani |

| | <sup>2</sup>**bryu:** (²) | suck | AW-TBT:651 |
|---|---|---|---|
| Bengni | (dɯ)-**bjuŋ** | suck | JS-Tani |
| | **bjuŋ** | suck | JS-HCST |
| Bokar | **bjuŋ** | suck | JS-HCST |
| | **bjuŋ**-čup | suck | JS-Tani |
| Gallong | **ˆbu:**- | suck | AW-TBT:651 |
| Idu | **pɹoŋ**³⁵ | nurse / suckle | SHK-Idu:5.4.6 |
| | ɲo⁵⁵**bɹɑ**⁵⁵ | milk | ZMYYC:281.50 |
| Miri, Hill | **bu**-nam | suck | IMS-HMLG |

2.1.1. Western Himalayish

| Kanauri | khe **rən** | milk | DS-Kan |
|---|---|---|---|

## (72)      *m-ʔum ⪥ *mum      KISS / HOLD IN THE MOUTH

This root frequently occurs in Kamarupan compounds before **(58a)** *m-pup KISS / SUCK (e.g. Milang **mum-pup**). In fact several of the forms treated under **(58a)** as having prefixal *mV- (e.g. Angami **me³¹bo¹¹**) might be better analyzed as compounds with *mum as the first constituent.

*STC* reconstructs a root *um (#108), later changed to *(m)-u·m 'hold in the mouth / mouthful' on the basis of a group of zero/glottal stop-initialled forms like WT **(ʔ)um** and the prefixed Jingpho form **məūm**. These have been combined with a group of Kamarupan forms meaning 'kiss' to form the present set.

See *HPTB* *m-ʔu:m, pp. 276, 308.

1.1. North Assam

| Padam-Mising [Abor-Miri] | **mam**-puk | kiss | JS-HCST | 52 |
|---|---|---|---|---|
| Apatani | **mó**-čù | kiss | JS-Tani | |
| | **mo**-ču (sú) | kiss | JS-Tani | |
| | **mo**-čʰuʔ (sú) | kiss | JS-Tani | |
| Bengni | **mu:**-pup | kiss | JS-HCST; JS-Tani | |
| Milang | **mum**-pup-ma | kiss | AT-MPB | |
| Mising [Miri] | **um**-bom | hold (as inside the mouth) | STC:108 | |
| Tagin | **mo** pup-nam | kiss | KDG-Tag | |

1.2. Kuki-Chin

| Kom Rem | **m̥om** | hold in mouth (v.) | T-KomRQ:3.7.14 | |
|---|---|---|---|---|
| Lai (Hakha) | **hmoom** | hold in the mouth | KVB-Lai | |
| Liangmei | **mun** rui | kiss | GEM-CNL | |
| Lushai [Mizo] | **hmuam** | hold in the mouth; suck; chew | JHL-Lu:164 | 53 |

1.3. Naga

| Mao | **momu** | kiss | GEM-CNL | |
|---|---|---|---|---|
| Sangtam | **mü** thsüp | kiss | GEM-CNL | |
| Mzieme | **mam** | kiss | GEM-CNL | 54 |

---

[52]The first syllable of this form looks like **(60)** *mam BREAST, but the gloss 'kiss' shows that it belongs here.

[53]The Lushai and Lai forms with voiceless nasals reflect a variant with the *s- prefix.

[54]This form looks like **(60)** *mam BREAST, but the gloss 'kiss' shows that it belongs here.

| | | | |
|---|---|---|---|
| Yimchungrü | a **man** ji | kiss | GEM-CNL |
| **1.4. Meithei** | | | |
| Meithei | **um** bə | hold in mouth | CYS-Meithei:3.7.14 |
| **1.5. Mikir** | | | |
| Mikir | **om** | chew; mouthful | STC:108 |
| **2.1.2. Bodic** | | | |
| Tsangla (Motuo) | **jum**⁵⁵ | hold in mouth; suck | JZ-CLMenba |
| Tibetan (Written) | **ʔum** | a kiss | STC:108 |
| **2.1.3. Lepcha** | | | |
| Lepcha | **ŭm** | receive into mouth without swallow- ing | STC:108 |
| **2.3. Mahakiranti** | | | |
| *Kiranti | *****um-** | eat | BM-PK7:54 |
| **2.3.1. Kham-Magar-Chepang-Sunwar** | | | |
| Chepang (Eastern) | **ʔumh** na? | hold in mouth (v.) | RC-ChepQ:3.7.14 |
| **2.3.2. Kiranti** | | | |
| Bantawa | **um** t- | eat | BM-PK7:54 |
| Chamling | **up**-s-yu | eat | BM-PK7:54 |
| Yakha | **u:m** ma: | hold in mouth (v.) | TK-Yakha:3.7.14 |
| **4.1. Jingpho** | | | |
| Jingpho | **məum** | hold, as water or smoke in the mouth | STC:108 |
| **4.2. Nungic** | | | |
| Anong | **im** | mouthful | STC:108 |
| **6.1. Burmish** | | | |
| Achang (Longchuan) | **mam**³¹ | chew | JZ-Achang |
| | **om**⁵⁵ | hold in mouth | JZ-Achang |
| Atsi [Zaiwa] | **ŋum**⁵¹ | hold in mouth | JZ-Zaiwa |
| **6.2. Loloish** | | | |
| Hani (Dazhai) | **ɔ**³¹ | hold in mouth | JZ-Hani |
| Hani (Gelanghe) | **m(u)m̩**⁵⁵ | hold in mouth | JZ-Hani |
| Hani (Shuikui) | **mu**³¹ | hold in mouth | JZ-Hani |
| Lahu (Yellow) | **mɔ**³¹ | hold in mouth | JZ-Lahu |
| Lalo | **ʔm̩**²¹ | hold in mouth | CK-YiQ:3.7.14 |
| **6.4. Jinuo** | | | |
| Jinuo (Youle) | **mo**⁴² | hold in mouth | JZ-Jinuo |
| **9. Sinitic** | | | |
| Chinese (Middle) | **ʔəm:** | hold in the mouth | WSC-SH:95 |
| Chinese (Old) | **ʔəmx** | hold in the mouth | WSC-SH:95 |

## Chinese comparandum

A Chinese comparandum was recognized already in *STC* #181: 唵 **ʔəm**. This form does not occur in *GSR* #614, but is to be found in Karlgren 1923 (*Analytic Dictionary*, set #238, p. 96).

[JAM]

唵 **ǎn** 'hold in the mouth, put in the mouth'

*GSR*: not in *GSR* 614    Karlgren: \*·əm    Li: \*·əm    Baxter: \*ʔɨ/um?

In Baxter's system the vowel cannot be determined from the Middle Chinese vocalism, and in this case there is also insufficient rhyming or phonetic-series evidence.

The correspondence between OC \*ə (Li)/\*ɨ/u (Baxter) and PTB \*u before labials is regular. See under **(55a)** \*m-dzup SUCK / SUCKLE / MILK / KISS for examples.

[ZJH]

## (73)        *dum        KISS / SUCK

This root is firmly established for Kamarupan, with cognates in the Tani, Northern Naga, and Barish subgroups. There are also convincing but so far isolated cognates in Himalayish (Chepang) and Loloish (Nesu).

**1.1. North Assam**

| | | | |
|---|---|---|---|
| Bengni | (dɯ)-bjuŋ | suck | JS-Tani |
| Darang [Taraon] | du⁵⁵ | suck (milk) | SLZO-MLD |
| Idu | do ga | suck | JP-Idu; NEFA-PBI |

**1.3. Naga**

| | | | |
|---|---|---|---|
| Nocte | tum | kiss | GEM-CNL |
| Tangsa (Yogli) | den | suck | GEM-CNL |

**1.7. Bodo-Garo = Barish**

| | | | |
|---|---|---|---|
| Bodo | ku dúm? | kiss | AW-TBT:35 |
| Dimasa | khu dum | kiss | GEM-CNL |

**2.3.1. Kham-Magar-Chepang-Sunwar**

| | | | |
|---|---|---|---|
| Chepang | tum? | kiss | AW-TBT:35 |
| | tum?-sa | kiss | SIL-Chep:10.B.1.51 |
| | tum?.sā | kiss | AH-CSDPN:10b1.51 |
| Chepang (Eastern) | tum? na? | kiss | RC-ChepQ:3.9.5 |

**6.2. Loloish**

| | | | |
|---|---|---|---|
| Nesu | du²¹ | kiss | CK-YiQ:3.9.5 |

## (74)    *pi ✕ *bi    ROUNDED PART / NIPPLE / FOREHEAD / SHOULDER

This root typically occurs as the last syllable in compounds for such bodyparts as CHEST / BREAST, SHOULDER, FIST, FOREHEAD, and BUTTOCK (cf. Lahu **ni-ma-qa-pɨ**, **làʔ-qá-pɨ**, **làʔ-chîʔ-pɨ**, **nā-qā-pɨ**, and **qhê-qhɔ-pɨ**, respectively).

Hayu **phi** and the Jinuo forms with aspirated initials may descend from a separate root, especially since these morphemes do not occur as the final member in compounds.

**1.1. North Assam**

| | | | |
|---|---|---|---|
| Apatani | à-ñi ñi-**pe** | nipple | JS-Tani |

| Darang [Taraon] | n̩i⁵⁵kha³¹**bi**³⁵ | breast | ZMYYC:259.49 |
| Gallong | lɤ **bi** | shoulder | KDG-IGL |
| Milang | ɲun-**pi** | nipple | AT-MPB |

### 1.3. Naga

| Mao | ka **phe** | shoulder | GEM-CNL |

### 1.4. Meithei

| Meithei | khom-**pi** | nipple | JAM-Ety |
| | seŋ **bi** | clitoris | CYS-Meithei:10.4.4 |

### 2.1.2. Bodic

| Tibetan (Written) | **pi-pi** | nipple / teat | HAJ-TED:323 |

### 2.2. Newar

| Newar | duru **pi pi** ca | nipple | SH-KNw:5.4.1 [55] |
| Newar (Kathmandu) | **pi-pi** | nipple | KPM-pc |
| | **pi-pi**-li | nipple (archaic) | KPM-pc |
| | **pi**-si | breast | KPM-pc [56] |
| Newar (Dolakhali) | **pi** ci | breast, milk; (euph.) vagina | CG-Dolak |

### 2.3.2. Kiranti

| Hayu | **phi** | shoulder | BM-Hay:84.229 |
| Thulung | kup **pi** | forehead | BM-PK7:77; NJA-Thulung |

### 3.2. Qiangic

| Ersu (Central) | vɛ³³ **bi**⁵⁵ | shoulder | SHK-ErsCQ |
| Ersu | vɛ³³**bi**⁵⁵ | shoulder | ZMYYC:250.18 |
| Qiang (Taoping) | la³¹ χa⁵⁵ **pi**³³ | shoulder | JZ-Qiang; ZMYYC:250.9 |
| Qiang (Yadu) | ji **pi** | shoulder | DQ-QiangN:117 |

### 6.2. Loloish

| Ahi | a³³nɯ³³**pi**⁵⁵ | breast | CK-YiQ:5.4 |
| | a³³ nɯ³³ **pi**⁵⁵ | breast | LMZ-AhiQ:5.4 |
| Gazhuo | ço³³ **pɣ**³⁵ | chest | DLF-Gazhuo [57] |
| Hani (Shuikui) | çiõ³³**phɣ**³¹ | chest | ZMYYC:257.32 |
| *Common Lahu | *hpeh:/**pui:** | shoulder | DB-PLolo:107 |
| Lahu (Black) | là?-chî?-**pi** | fist | JAM-Ety |
| | là?-qá-**pi** | shoulder | JAM-Ety |
| | ni-ma-**pi**(šɨ) | chest | JAM-Ety |
| | ni-ma-qa-**pi** | chest | JAM-Ety |
| | ni³³ ma³³ **pɯ**³³ | chest (of body) | JZ-Lahu |
| | ni: ma [**pui:**] | breast; chest; heart | GHL-PPB:U.9 |
| | pɛ³¹**pɯ**³³ | chest | ZMYYC:257.33 [58] |
| | qhɛ̂-qhɔ-**pi** | buttock | JAM-Ety |
| Lahu (Yellow) | n̩i³³ **pɯ**³³ | chest (of body) | JZ-Lahu |
| Lisu | lá⁶-**hprgh**⁴ | shoulder; arm | JAM-Ety; DB-PLolo:107,108 |

[55]**duru** 'milk' is < Skt. (cf. *dugdha-*). See **(68)** *du-t MILK / BREAST. The last constituent **ca** has a diminutive meaning (see note under **(40b)** *s-tay NAVEL / ABDOMEN / CENTER / SELF).

[56]The last element **si** means 'round object; fruit' < PTB *sey.

[57]The first syllables of the Gazhuo and Shuikui forms are probably < Chinese 胸 (Mand. **xiōng**) 'chest'.

[58]This form is also cited in JAM-DL:852 as **pɛ̀-pi** 'crop of bird; (human) breast, chest'. It is co-allofamic with **pɛ̀-pì(-qu)** 'chicken' s breast'. Cf. also **pɛ̀-qu** 'goiter'.

| | | | |
|---|---|---|---|
| Lisu (Northern) | læʔ²¹phɤ³³ | shoulder | DB-Lisu |
| | læʔ²¹phɤ³³ nɔ⁵⁵du³³ | shoulder pad | DB-Lisu |
| | læʔ²¹phɤ³³phi²¹ | shoulder blade | DB-Lisu |
| Lisu (Nujiang) | lɛ³¹ pʰɯ³³ | shoulder | JZ-Lisu |
| Lisu | lɛ³¹pʰɯ⁴⁴ | shoulder | ZMYYC:250.27 |
| Nesu | n̠i³³ mo²¹ po³³ | chest | CK-YiQ:5.1 |
| Sani [Nyi] | ŋ⁴⁴ ma³³ pɿ⁴⁴ be⁴ | heartbeat | MXL-SaniQ:323.4 |
| | ŋ⁴⁴ma³³pɿ⁴⁴be⁴⁴ | heartbeat | CK-YiQ:9.3.1 |
| Yi (Dafang) | la¹³ bɯ²¹ | shoulder | JZ-Yi; ZMYYC:250.22 |
| Yi (Mile) | ᴀ³³nɯ³³pi⁵⁵ | breast | ZMYYC:259.25 |
| Yi (Mojiang) | lɛ²¹pʰu³³ | shoulder | ZMYYC:250.26 |
| Yi (Nanjian) | a⁵⁵tʂɹ̄³³pi³³ | breast | ZMYYC:259.23 |
| **6.3. Naxi** | | | |
| Naxi (Eastern) | n̠u³¹bi³³ | breast | JZ-Naxi |
| Naxi (Yongning) | n̠u³¹bi³³ | breast | ZMYYC:259.29 |
| Naxi (Eastern) | ɑ¹³pv³³ | chest (of body) | JZ-Naxi |
| **6.4. Jinuo** | | | |
| Jinuo | phi³³tha⁵⁵ | shoulder | ZMYYC:250.34 |
| Jinuo (Baya/Banai) | pʰi³¹ tʰa⁵⁵ | shoulder | DQ-JinA:117 |
| Jinuo (Youle) | pʰi⁴²tʰɑ⁵⁵ | shoulder | JZ-Jinuo |

(75)                     ***prat ⪤ *brat***                     **BREAK / WEAN**

Jingpho **pràt**, **šə pràt** 'bear, give birth' are probably to be assigned to this etymon, the semantic connection being the separation of the child from the mother.

Likely comparanda are 裂 (OC *l̥i̯at, *GSR* 291f) 'tear asunder; divide' and 別 (OC ***b'i̯ăt**, *GSR* 292a) 'divide, separate, distinguish, different'.

See ***brat ⪤ *prat*** 'cut apart, cut open', *HPTB*:330,334.

| | | | |
|---|---|---|---|
| **3.2. Qiangic** | | | |
| Qiang (Mawo) | pʰᵘæ | wean | SHK-MawoQ:5.4.7 |
| **3.3. rGyalrongic** | | | |
| rGyalrong | ka pr̥et | wean | DQ-Jiarong:5.4.7 |
| rGyalrong (Eastern) | ka sə pʰʃit | wean | SHK-rGEQ:5.4.7 |
| rGyalrong (Northern) | no prɐt | wean | SHK-rGNQ:5.4.7 |
| **4.1. Jingpho** | | | |
| Jingpho | **pràt** | bear, give birth | JAM-II |
| | **šə pràt** | bear, give birth | JAM-II |
| **6. Lolo-Burmese** | | | |
| *Lolo-Burmese | · *(ʔ-)**brat ⪤** C_{VD}-**prat** | cut (open) | JAM-GSTC:027 |
| **6.1. Burmish** | | | |
| Burmese (Written) | nui' **phrat** | wean | JAM-II |
| | **phrat** | cut something in two (causative) | JAM-GSTC:027 |
| | **prat** | cut in two (simplex) | JAM-GSTC:027 |

6.2. Loloish

| Lahu (Black) | pè? | split, crack, get cracked | JAM-DL:1072 | |
| | phè? | cut open; perform a surgical opera-tion | JAM-GSTC:027 | 59 |

## Chinese comparanda

別 **bié** 'divide, separate'

*GSR*: 292a  Karlgren: *p̯iat  Li: *pjiat  Baxter: *prjat

There is a related Chinese word with voiced initial, *GSR* *b'i̯at (*ibid.*), also written 別, meaning 'to be different'. This voicing alternation is a common Old Chinese morphological process seen in transitive/intransitive verb pairs. Although the TB etymon also has a voicing alternation, this is likely to be an independent phenomenon.

The Chinese and PTB forms correspond perfectly. This cognate set has been proposed by Gong (1995 set 209). Gong 2001 reconstructs the intransitive Chinese verb as *N-brjat > *brjat and the transitive counterpart as *s-brjat > *s-prjat > *prjat.

列 **liè** 'divide, distribute; arrange; rank'

*GSR*: 291a  Karlgren: *l̯iat  Li: *ljat  Baxter: *C-rjat

裂 **liè** 'tear asunder, divide'

*GSR*: 291f  Karlgren: *l̯iat  Li: *ljat  Baxter: *C-rjat

These two homophonous Chinese words are clearly related. Gong (2001) relates 裂 **liè** to the two words written with 別 **bié**, while Schuessler (2007:167) says that 別 **bié** is probably cognate to 列 **liè**.[60] Gong reconstructs 裂 **liè** as *brjat > *rjat, treating it as the root from which the two words written with 別 **bié** are derived.

On Baxter's *C-r-, see the discussion under (5) *rum ⋊ *lum EGG. The relationship to 別 **bié** suggests that in Baxter's reconstruction the consonant represented by *C would most likely be reconstructed as *b.

[ZJH]

---

[59]The Lahu expression **cú phâ?** means 'to wean', but the second syllable descends from PLB *pak 'take apart; dismantle; separate from' (*TSR* #64), not from *prat. (The regular Lahu reflex of *-at is -e?.)

[60]Schuessler gives the Baxter system reconstruction of 別 as *prjet. While this is a possible reconstruction, *prjat is more likely given the word-family connections.

# V. Vagina

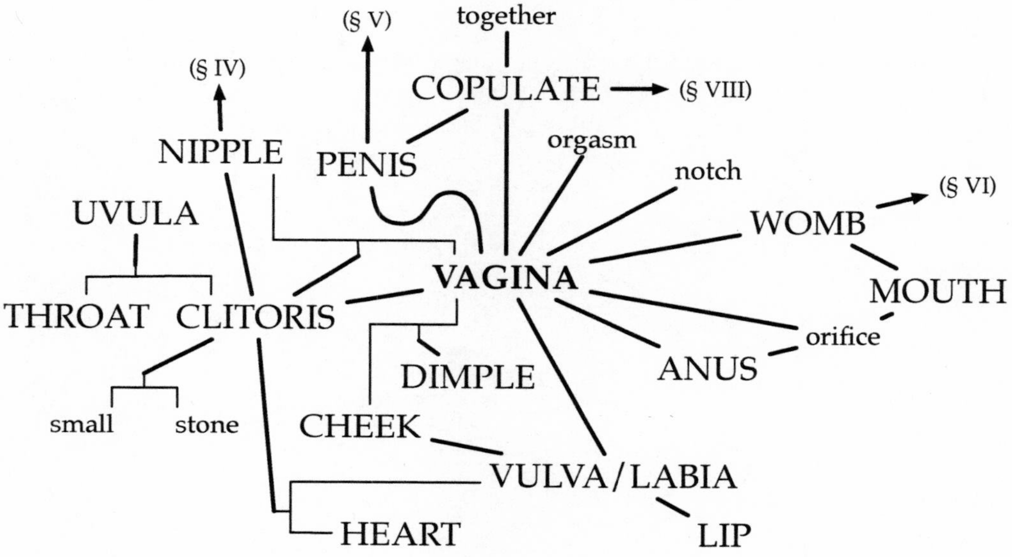


Etyma for VAGINA and PENIS show frequent interchange and/or phonological similarity, by a phenomenon felicitously dubbed "genital flipflop" by Benedict.[1] The roots where this interchange is most evident include: **(76) *s-tu ⪤ *tsu** VAGINA : **(116a) *k-tu-k** PENIS; **(84) *li-n** VAGINA : **(114a) *m-ley ⪤ *m-li** PENIS; **(91) *s-ti ⪤ *m-ti** CLITORIS / VAGINA / NIPPLE : **(117) *ti-k** PENIS; **(86) *mo** VAGINA : **(123) *ma:k** PENIS / MALE / SON-IN-LAW. This relationship is indicated by a *yin-yang* curve in the semantic diagram.

Roots for VAGINA also show interchange with etyma for MOUTH. See especially **(77a) *dzyuk ⪤ *tsyuk** VULVA; **(79) *siŋ ⪤ *sik** MOUTH / LIP; and **(80) *tsyin** VAGINA / CLITORIS / MOUTH / LIP.

There is also an association between VAGINA and ANUS (see, e.g. **(92) *hoŋ** VAGINA / RECTUM / HOLE and **(94) *kwar ⪤ *kor** CONCAVITY / HOLE / EAR / VAGINA).

An association between CLITORIS and UVULA is shown by Lushai **daŋ-mɔn** 'uvula', literally "palate-clitoris". See *VSTB*, p. 67.

[1]Benedict 1979, "A note on Karen genital flipflop" (*LTBA* 5.1:21-24); 1981 "A further (unexpurgated) note on Karen genital flipflop" (*LTBA* 6.1:103); 1991 "Genital flipflop: a Chinese note" (*LTBA* 14.1:143-6).

(76)                              **\*s-tu ≍ \*tsu**                      **VAGINA**

This is by far the best-attested root for VAGINA in TB, with reflexes in Kamarupan, Himalayish, Lolo-Burmese, Karenic, and Qiangic. While most of the supporting forms point to a prefixal **\*s-** plus **\*t-** root-initial, a few reflexes seem to have undergone metathesis, e.g. Hayu **pep-tshu**, Lakher **³tshu**, etc.

Some of the reflexes are transcribed with high front vowel **-i** instead of **-u**, but this fronting seems to be secondary. Compare, e.g. the Abor-Miri, Apatani, and Gallong forms; or the Chepang, Dumi, and Bantawa reflexes, etc.

See *HPTB* **\*s-tu**, p. 247.

1.1. North Assam

| | | | |
|---|---|---|---|
| \*Tani | **\*tɯ** | vulva / vagina | JS-HCST:450 |
| Padam-Mising [Abor-Miri] | ít-tí | vulva | JAM-Ety |
| | tí-muit | hair (pubic) | JAM-Ety |
| | ɯt-tɯ | vulva / vagina | JS-HCST |
| Apatani | a-tú | vagina | JS-Tani |
| | ²a²tu | vagina | AW-TBT:526 |
| Bengni | ti: | vulva / vagina | JS-HCST |
| Gallong | ˆɯt-tɤ | vagina | AW-TBT:526 |
| Sulung | a³¹ tɯi⁵⁵ | vagina | JAM-II |

1.2. Kuki-Chin

| | | | |
|---|---|---|---|
| \*Chin | **\*tshuu** | vagina | KVB-PKC:609 |
| Kuki-Chin | **su** | vagina | Qbp-KC:10.4.1 |
| Kom Rem | **su** | vagina | T-KomRQ:10.4.1 |
| | **su**-də | hymen | T-KomRQ:10.4.3 |
| | **su**-mih | female pubic hair | T-KomRQ:10.4.5 |
| | **su**-mətʰer | clitoris | T-KomRQ:10.4.4 |
| | **su**-ner | vulva / labia | T-KomRQ:10.4.2 |
| Lai (Hakha) | bêel-**tshùu** | dimple (lit. "cheek vagina") | KVB-Lai |
| | tshùu | vagina | KVB-Lai |
| Lakher [Mara] | chhu-khao | vulva | JAM-Ety |
| | ³tshu | vagina | AW-TBT:62 |
| Lushai [Mizo] | chhu | vulva | JAM-Ety |
| | tshû | vagina | AW-TBT:526 |
| | tśhu | vulva / notch (v.) | STC:53n178 |
| Tiddim | sú | vagina | AW-TBT:526 |

1.3. Naga

| | | | |
|---|---|---|---|
| Lotha Naga | ¹o²šɯ(ʔ) | vagina | AW-TBT:526 |
| Nocte | ¹thu | vagina | AW-TBT:526 |
| Phom | ʃɯʔ³³ | vagina | JAM-II |
| Yimchungrü | (¹)tšuʔ | vagina | AW-TBT:526 |

1.4. Meithei

| | | | |
|---|---|---|---|
| Meithei | **thù** | vagina | AW-TBT:62; JAM-Ety |
| | **thu** ban | vulva / labia | CYS-Meithei:10.4.2 |
| | **thu** məkhun | vagina | CYS-Meithei:10.4.1 |

---

[2]*STC* tentatively assigns this Lushai form to **\*tsyuk** (below, (77a)), though I prefer the present analysis.

| Moyon | sòw | vagina | DK-Moyon:10.4.1 |
|---|---|---|---|
| | sòw khùr ~ sowr khùr | vulva / labia | DK-Moyon:10.4.2 |
| | sòw mòwr ~ sow mòwr | female pubic hair | DK-Moyon:10.4.5 |

### 1.7. Bodo-Garo = Barish

| Khiamngan | [12]tauʔ | vagina | AW-TBT:62 |
|---|---|---|---|
| Meche | ki ʈuʔ | vagina | AW-TBT:62 |

### 2.1.1. Western Himalayish

| Bunan | pha šu | vagina | SBN-BunQ:10.4.1 | |
|---|---|---|---|---|
| Kanauri | shik ts | vagina | JAM-Ety | [3] |
| Pattani [Manchati] | pha ṣu | vagina | STP-ManQ:10.4.1 | |
| | pʰə ṣu | vagina | DS-Patt | |

### 2.1.2. Bodic

| Tsangla (Central) | thu | vagina | SER-HSL/T:34 5 | |
|---|---|---|---|---|
| Spiti | tu˜ kup | vagina | CB-SpitiQ:10.4.1 | [4] |
| Tibetan (Written) | stu | vagina; orifice of vagina (vulg.) | BM-PK7:195; JAM-Ety | |

### 2.1.3. Lepcha

| Lepcha | tŭ | *pudenda muliebria* | JAM-Ety |
|---|---|---|---|

### 2.1.4. Tamangic

| Manang (Gyaru) | dɯ[1] | vulva | YN-Man:042-09 |
|---|---|---|---|
| Tamang (Risiangku) | [2]tsjum ʈu | vagina, vulva | MM-TamRisQ:10.4.4 |
| Tamang (Sahu) | [2]cjum-ʈu | vagina | JAM-Ety |
| Thakali (Tukche) | tu-cham | hair (pubic) | JAM-Ety |
| | tu-cʰɔm | hair (pubic, female) | SIL-Thak:2.A.10.2 |

### 2.1.5. Dhimal

| Dhimal | cu cu | vagina | JK-Dh |
|---|---|---|---|

### 2.3. Mahakiranti

| *Kiranti | *tu | vagina | BM-PK7:195 |
|---|---|---|---|

### 2.3.1. Kham-Magar-Chepang-Sunwar

| Chepang | tuʔ | vagina | AW-TBT:62 |
|---|---|---|---|
| Chepang (Eastern) | tuʔ | genitalia / pudenda (female) | RC-ChepQ:10.1 |
| | tuʔ bleŋ | vulva / labia | RC-ChepQ:10.4.2 |
| | tuʔ ghaŋ | vagina | RC-ChepQ:10.4.1 |
| | tuʔ menʔ | female pubic hair | RC-ChepQ:10.4.5 |

### 2.3.2. Kiranti

| Bantawa | dhï | vagina | BM-PK7:195 |
|---|---|---|---|
| | dhi | vagina | BM-PK7:195 |
| | dhï | vagina | JAM-Ety |
| | DhU | vagina | NKR-Bant |
| | dhü | vagina | WW-Bant:27 |
| | phu ci dhü | vagina | WW-Bant:60 |
| | ɖhï | vagina | BM-PK7:195 |

---

[3]Notice the reduction of the vowel to zero in the second syllable.
[4]The second syllable is the Spiti word for "buttocks".

| | | | | |
|---|---|---|---|---|
| Dumi | ka: **di?** | vagina | BM-PK7:195; SVD-Dum | 5 |
| Hayu | pep **tshu** | vagina | BM-Hay:84.142, 84 | |
| Limbu | **tsu** tsup ma | penis; vagina; child's sex organ | SVD-LimA | |
| Thulung | teor **ciu** | vagina | NJA-Thulung | |
| | **thiu** | vagina | BM-PK7:195; NJA-Thulung | |

## 3.1. Tangut

| | | | |
|---|---|---|---|
| Tangut [Xixia] | **tə**$^1$ | vulva | MVS-Grin |

## 3.2. Qiangic

| | | | |
|---|---|---|---|
| Ergong (Northern) | **stə**$^{53}$ | vagina | SHK-ErgNQ:10.4 |
| | **stə**$^{53}$ k$^h$ɐ$^{13}$ | vulva / labia | SHK-ErgNQ:10.4.2 |
| | **stə**$^{53}$ no$^{13}$ | vagina | SHK-ErgNQ:10.4.1 |
| | **stə**$^{53}$ qrə$^{53}$ | hymen | SHK-ErgNQ:10.4.3 |
| | **stə**$^{53}$ rmo$^{53}$ | female pubic hair | SHK-ErgNQ:10.4.5 |
| | **stə**$^{53}$ si$^{53}$ | menstrual blood | SHK-ErgNQ:10.4.7 |
| | **stə**$^{53}$ si$^{53}$ nə$^{53}$ t$^h$ie$^{13}$ | menstruate | SHK-ErgNQ:10.4.6 |
| | **stə**$^{53}$ sqrə$^{53}$ | clitoris | SHK-ErgNQ:10.4.4 |

## 3.3. rGyalrongic

| | | | |
|---|---|---|---|
| rGyalrong | tə **ɕtu** | genitalia; pudenda; vagina | DQ-Jiarong:10.1,10.4.1 |
| | tə **ɕtu** mo rɲ̟ɛ | female pubic hair | DQ-Jiarong:10.4.5 |
| | tə **ɕtu** ɕi | menstrual blood | DQ-Jiarong:10.4.7 |
| | tə **ɕtu** ɕi kə ɕut | menstruate | DQ-Jiarong:10.4.6 |
| rGyalrong (NW) | tə **stə** | female; female organ | SHK-rGNWQ:10.4 |
| | tə **stə** ku | vagina | SHK-rGNWQ:10.4.1 |
| | tə **stə** mtɕ$^h$i | vulva / labia | SHK-rGNWQ:10.4.2 |
| | tə **stə** rme | female pubic hair | SHK-rGNWQ:10.4.5 |
| | tə **stə** tɕ$^h$im | hymen | SHK-rGNWQ:10.4.3 |
| rGyalrong (Eastern) | tə **ʃtu** | female; female organ | SHK-rGEQ:10.4 |
| rGyalrong (Northern) | tə **ʃtu** | female; female organ | SHK-rGNQ:10.4 |
| | tə **ʃtu** k$^h$uŋ du | vagina | SHK-rGNQ:10.4.1 |
| rGyalrong (Eastern) | tə **ʃtu** mor | female pubic hair | SHK-rGEQ:10.4.5 |
| rGyalrong (Northern) | tə **ʃtu** rme | female pubic hair | SHK-rGNQ:10.4.5 |
| | tə **ʃtu** ʴq$^h$u | vulva / labia | SHK-rGNQ:10.4.2 |

## 6.1. Burmish

| | | | |
|---|---|---|---|
| Hpun (Northern) | **tsù** má? | vulva | EJAH-Hpun |

## 6.2. Loloish

| | | | |
|---|---|---|---|
| Ahi | **to**$^{55}$ bi̠$^{21}$ | genitalia / pudenda (general) | LMZ-AhiQ:10.1 |
| | **to**$^{55}$ bi̠$^{21}$ ne$^{33}$ ba$^{55}$ | vagina | LMZ-AhiQ:10.4.1 |
| | **to**$^{55}$ bi̠$^{21}$ ni$^{21}$ | vulva / labia | LMZ-AhiQ:10.4.2 | 6 |
| | **to**$^{55}$ bi̠$^{21}$ tʂ'ɛ$^{22}$ | copulate | LMZ-AhiQ:10.2 |
| | **to**$^{55}$ lo$^{22}$ zo$^{21}$ | clitoris | LMZ-AhiQ:10.4.4 |
| | **to**$^{55}$ nɯ$^{33}$ | female pubic hair | LMZ-AhiQ:10.4.5 |
| | **to**$^{55}$ tɕi$^{22}$ zo$^{21}$ | hymen | LMZ-AhiQ:10.4.3 |
| | **to**$^{55}$bi̠$^{21}$ | vagina | CK-YiQ:10.4.1 |
| Bisu | tɔ hɔ́ŋ | vagina | PB-Bisu:16 |

---

[5] For the front vowel, cf. also the variously transcribed Bantawa forms, probably actually with [i̠].
[6] The third syllable is the same as the first syllable of Ahi **ni**$^{21}$ **tɕi**$^{22}$ "lip".

|  | tɔ pé | vulva | PB-Bisu:16 |
|---|---|---|---|
|  | tɔ tshìŋ | clitoris | PB-Bisu:13 |
| Lalo | tù | vagina | SB-Lalo |
|  | tṳ²¹ | vagina | CK-YiQ:10.4.1 |
|  | tṳ²¹ tɕʰy⁵⁵ | female pubic hair | CK-YiQ:10.4.5 |
| Lipho | tu⁵⁵bi²¹ | vagina | CK-YiQ:10.4.1 |
| Lisu | tu¹-bi⁶ | vagina; vulva | JAM-Ety; JAM-TSR:5 |
| Lisu (Central) | tu¹-bi⁶ | vagina | JF-HLL |
| Lisu | tu¹bi⁶ | vulva | DB-PLolo:123 |
| Lisu (Northern) | tɔ⁵⁵bi²¹ | pudenda | DB-Lisu |
|  | tɔ⁵⁵khu³³ | vagina; orifice | DB-Lisu |
| Lolopho | tɤ⁵⁵ bi³¹ | vagina | DQ-Lolopho:10.4.1 |
|  | tɤ⁵⁵ mɯ³³ | female pubic hair | DQ-Lolopho:10.4.5 |
| Mpi | to²phe² | vagina | SD-MPD |
| Nusu (Central/Zhizhiluo) | tɯ⁵⁵ | vagina | DQ-NusuA:143. |
| Phunoi | pə̀ tò | vulva | JAM-Ety |
| **7. Karenic** |  |  |  |
| Palaychi | zu | vagina | JAM-Ety |
|  | zù | vagina | RBJ-KLS:17 |

## (77)  *dzyuk ⋎ *tsyuk  MOUTH / LIP / VULVA

This etymon ranges semantically between VAGINA/VULVA and MOUTH/LIP. Reflexes with the latter meanings are assembled separately below as **(77b)** *tsyuk MOUTH / LIP. Another root with similar semantic range is **(78)** *tsiŋ ⋎ *tsik VAGINA [q.v.].

This etymon is well-attested in Burmish, with good-looking but scattered cognates in Loloish, Kamarupan, and Himalayish. It seems best to reconstruct this root with a palatal (rather than dental) affricate, as demonstrated in Matisoff 1969.[7] Some reflexes of this etymon are cited in Bauer's far-ranging article (Bauer, R. 1991. "Sino-Tibetan *vulva", *LTBA* 14.1:147-172).

See *HPTB* **\*dzyuk**, p. 66.

## (77a)  *dzyuk ⋎ *tsyuk  VULVA

| **1.3. Naga** |  |  |  |
|---|---|---|---|
| Chang | su·k | vulva | STC:53n178 |
| **2.1.1. Western Himalayish** |  |  |  |
| Kanauri | tsŭk s̲hi | copulate | JAM-Ety |
| **6. Lolo-Burmese** |  |  |  |
| *Lolo-Burmese | *dźuk | vulva | STC:53n178 |
| **6.1. Burmish** |  |  |  |
| Achang (Xiandao) | cuʔ⁵⁵ | vagina | DQ-Xiandao:143 |
| Bola | tʃauʔ³¹ | vagina | DQ-Bola:143 |
| Burmese (Written) | cok | vagina; female private parts (vulg.) | JAM-Ety; PKB-WBRD |

---

[7]"Lahu and Proto-Lolo-Burmese." Cf. the discussion in *STC*, n. 178 (p. 53).

| | cok-ce' | vagina | JAM-Ety |
|---|---|---|---|
| | cok-khôŋ | female urethra | JAM-Ety |
| | cok-khyê | vagina | JAM-Ety |
| | cok-pat | vagina | JAM-Ety |
| | cok-phut | vagina | JAM-Ety |
| | tsauk | vulva | STC:53n178 |
| Hpun (Northern) | só? | vagina | EJAH-Hpun |
| | zù?-mà | vagina / vulva | EJAH-Hpun |
| Lashi | tʃu?$^{31}$ | genitalia / pudenda | DQ-Lashi:10.1 |
| | tʃu?$^{31}$ mou$^{55}$ | female pubic hair | DQ-Lashi:10.4.5 |
| Maru [Langsu] | dźok | vulva | STC:53n178 |
| | tʃauk$^{31}$ | genitalia / pudenda | DQ-Langsu:10.1 |
| | tʃauk$^{31}$ muk$^{55}$ | female pubic hair | DQ-Langsu:10.4.5 |
| Atsi [Zaiwa] | dźu? | vulva | STC:53n178 |

6.2. Loloish

| Nasu | tṣo$^{21}$ pi̠$^{21}$ | vagina | CK-YiQ:10.4.1 |
|---|---|---|---|

## (77b)        *tsyuk        MOUTH / LIP

This is undoubtedly the same etymon as (77a) *dzyuk ⪥ *tsyuk VULVA, with obvious semantic connections. Reflexes with meanings like MOUTH or LIP have so far been found in Kamarupan (including Barish [Atong] and the outlying Sulung language), Himalayish (including Bodic [Tshona] and Kiranti), and Burmese (which has homophonous forms with both the VAGINA and MOUTH meanings).

1.1. North Assam

| Sulung | çək$^{33}$ | mouth | SHK-Sulung |
|---|---|---|---|

1.7. Bodo-Garo = Barish

| Atong | ku-cuk | mouth | JAM-Ety |
|---|---|---|---|

2.1.2. Bodic

| Tshona (Wenlang) | tɕʰuŋ$^{55}$ min$^{55}$ | lip | JZ-CNMenba |
|---|---|---|---|

2.3. Mahakiranti

| *Kiranti | *cok siŋ | lip | BM-PK7:108 | [8] |
|---|---|---|---|---|

2.3.2. Kiranti

| Bantawa | do si ja | lip | JAM-Ety |
|---|---|---|---|
| | Do si wa | lip | NKR-Bant |
| Dumi | kəm tsok si | lips (human); mouth (buccal cavity) and lips; beak, bill | SVD-Dum |
| | tsok si | lip | BM-PK7:108; SVD-Dum |

6.1. Burmish

| Burmese (Written) | ?a-cok | bottom of mouth | JAM-Ety |
|---|---|---|---|

---

[8]These Kiranti forms demonstrate the independence of the present etymon from (79) *siŋ ⪥ *sik MOUTH / LIP.

# (78)          *tsiŋ ⪥ *tsik          VAGINA

This etymon is also best attested in Himalayish, with some support from Kamarupan, and perhaps from Qiangic.

For the moment it seems best to keep this set of forms distinct from **(79)** *siŋ ⪥ *sik MOUTH / LIP. In spite of the plausible phonosemantic association between these etyma, the reflexes are different in languages like Garo (Bangladesh), Kokborok, Bahing, Bantawa, and Chepang [qq.v.].

Evidence for a final velar consonant comes from Barish (especially Lalung), Hayu, and Kanauri.

Complicating the picture is the fact that in some languages the putative cognate is an open syllable that occurs as the second element of compounds with **(85)** *pu VAGINA or **(81)** *b(y)at VAGINA. In such forms, it is possible that the second syllable may actually represent PTB **(H:206)** *sey FRUIT / ROUND OBJECT. (Cf. e.g. Bantawa si 'bear fruit', Newar **maa-si** 'vagina; breast; milk', si 'morpheme in fruit names'.)

### 1.7. Bodo-Garo = Barish

| | | | | |
|---|---|---|---|---|
| Garo (Bangladesh) | **si** | vagina | RB-GB | |
| | **si'-** | vagina | RB-GB | |
| | **si'-i** | vagina | RB-GB | |
| Kokborok | **ši-pa?** | vagina | PT-Kok | |
| Lalung | **she?** | vagina | MB-Lal:63 | |

### 2.1.1. Western Himalayish

| | | | | |
|---|---|---|---|---|
| Kanauri | **s̱hik** ts | vagina | JAM-Ety | 9 |

### 2.1.4. Tamangic

| | | | |
|---|---|---|---|
| Chantyal | ti **si** | clitoris | NPB-ChanQ:10.4.4 |
| Tamang (Risiangku) | ¹pit **si** | vagina | MM-TamRisQ:10.4.1 |
| Tamang (Sahu) | ¹pi-**ci** | vagina | JAM-Ety |

### 2.2. Newar

| | | | |
|---|---|---|---|
| Newar (Dolakhali) | pi **ci** | breast, milk; (euph.) vagina | CG-Dolak |

### 2.3.1. Kham-Magar-Chepang-Sunwar

| | | | |
|---|---|---|---|
| Kham | ti **si:** | clitoris | DNW-KhamQ |

### 2.3.2. Kiranti

| | | | | |
|---|---|---|---|---|
| Bahing | pi-**si** | vagina | JAM-Ety | |
| Bantawa | phu **ci** | vagina; vulva; vagina (baby talk) | NKR-Bant; WW-Bant:60 | |
| | phu **ci** dhü | vagina | WW-Bant:60 | |
| Hayu | pu-**tsing** | vagina | JAM-Ety | 10 |
| | pu **tshi** | vagina | BM-Hay:84.189 | |
| Yakha | **si:** | vagina | TK-Yakha:10.4.1 | |

---

[9]Notice the reduction of the vowel to zero in the second syllable.

[10]Note the variation between final velar nasal and zero-final in the Hayu forms. See also the similar Hayu reflexes of **(79)** *siŋ ⪥ *sik MOUTH / LIP.

---

3.2. Qiangic

| | | | | |
|---|---|---|---|---|
| Qiang (Yadu) | pʰo ʂ | vagina | DQ-QiangN:146 | 11 |

## (79)         *siŋ ≍ *sik         MOUTH / LIP

This etymon is best attested in Himalayish, with some support also from Kamarupan and Luish, and perhaps Qiangic and/or WB. The reflexes have either simple sibilant or affricate initials. I presume the proto-initial to have been *s-, in view of the natural tendency to develop secondary affrication before -i-.

It is very possible that this etymon belongs together with (78) *tsiŋ ≍ *tsik VAGINA (previous etymon), in a single word-family, in view of the similar semantic range of (77) *dzyuk ≍ *tsyuk MOUTH / LIP / VULVA.

A particularly interesting form is Newar **mhu tu si**, where **mhu tu** means 'mouth', and **si** means 'corner (of the mouth)'. The basic meaning of **si** is 'border, margin, bank', as in **khu-si** 'riverbank', **mi-kha-pu-si** 'eyebrow' (K. P. Malla, p.c.). Thus Newar **si** has nothing to do with the present etymon.

1.1. North Assam

| | | | | |
|---|---|---|---|---|
| Milang | caŋ-**ci** | mouth | AT-MPB | |
| | **cip**-pa | beak / bill | AT-MPB | 12 |

1.3. Naga

| | | | |
|---|---|---|---|
| Rengma | meng **si** | lip | GEM-CNL |
| Rongmei | **ci** | lip | GEM-CNL |
| Sema | a ki **chi** | mouth | GEM-CNL |

1.7. Bodo-Garo = Barish

| | | | |
|---|---|---|---|
| Garo | ku-**sik** | mouth | JAM-Ety |
| Garo (Bangladesh) | ku'-**sik** | mouth; language; opening (e.g. of a pot) | RB-GB |
| Kokborok | kʰoʔ-**či** | lip | PT-Kok |

2.1.2. Bodic

| | | | |
|---|---|---|---|
| Tsangla (Central) | lep **chi** | lip | SER-HSL/T:32 14 |

2.1.4. Tamangic

| | | | |
|---|---|---|---|
| Manang (Gyaru) | swɯŋ² man² ji² | lip | YN-Man:011 |
| Manang (Prakaa) | ²mə̀ **ci** | lip | HM-Prak:0010 |

2.3. Mahakiranti

| | | | | |
|---|---|---|---|---|
| *Kiranti | *cok **siŋ** | lip | BM-PK7:108 | 13 |
| | *siŋ (?*ciŋ) | lip | BM-PK7:107 | |

---

[11] The final consonant in this form looks like the fused initial consonant of the second syllable of an original compound, descended from the current etymon. (Compare, e.g. the Bantawa, Hayu, and Tamang compounds.) Fusion of compounds into monosyllables is a striking characteristic of the Qiangic languages. See, e.g., Benedict 1983, "Qiang monosyllabization: a third phase in the cycle", *LTBA* 7.2:113-4.

[12] The labial stop in the first syllable is evidently due to assimilation to the suffix.

[13] These Kiranti forms demonstrate the independence the present etymon from (77b) *tsyuk MOUTH / LIP.

### 2.3.1. Kham-Magar-Chepang-Sunwar

| | | | |
|---|---|---|---|
| Chepang (Eastern) | **səyk** | beak / bill | RC-ChepQ:3.9.3 |

### 2.3.2. Kiranti

| | | | |
|---|---|---|---|
| Bahing | **soe** goe loe | mouth | BM-Bah |
| | **sœ** | mouth | BM-PK7:121 |
| Bantawa | do **si** ja | lip | JAM-Ety |
| | Do **si** wa | lip | NKR-Bant |
| Dumi | kəm tsok **si** | lips (human); mouth (buccal cavity) and lips; beak, bill | SVD-Dum |
| | tsok **si** | lip | BM-PK7:108; SVD-Dum |
| Hayu | kum **dzʊŋ** | lip | BM-Hay:84.244 |
| | kum **tshiŋ** | lip | JAM-Ety |
| | kum **tsiŋ** | lip | BM-PK7:107,122 |
| | tak **siŋ** | skin | BM-Hay:84.246 |
| Limbu | **si** daŋ ba | mouth | BM-PK7:121 |
| | wɔ **se** | lip | BM-Lim |
| Thulung | **si** | mouth; beak; edge (of basket); entry (of bridge) | BM-PK7:121; NJA-Thulung |
| | **si** kok te | lip | NJA-Thulung |
| | **sī** ko ka? te | lip | JAM-Ety |
| | **si** seom | moustache | NJA-Thulung |
| | **si** syom a | moustache | JAM-Ety |

### 3.2. Qiangic

| | | | |
|---|---|---|---|
| Ersu (Central) | **ʂ**ɻ⁵⁵ mpha⁵⁵ ndʐo⁵⁵ pi⁵⁵ | lip | SHK-ErsCQ [14] |
| | **ʂ**ɻ⁵⁵ npha⁵⁵ | mouth | SHK-ErsCQ |
| Namuyi | mi³³ mpʰ **ʂ**ɻ⁵⁵ | mouth | SHK-NamuQ:3.7 |
| | mpʰ **ʂ**ɻ⁵ ⁵ fiə˩³³ qu⁵⁵ | lip | SHK-NamuQ:3.9 |

### 4. Jingpho-Nung-Luish

| | | | |
|---|---|---|---|
| Sak | áng-**sí** | mouth | JAM-Ety |
| | ang-**sy** | mouth | JAM-Ety |
| Sak (Bawtala) | aŋ³**sɤ**³ | mouth | GHL-PPB:K.54 |

### 6.1. Burmish

| | | | |
|---|---|---|---|
| Burmese (Written) | nut-**sî** | beak / bill | JAM-Ety |

## (80)   *tsyin   VAGINA / CLITORIS / MOUTH / LIP

This etymon, with final dental nasal, seems so far to be relatively rare; yet its occurrence in widely separated languages like Jingpho, Meithei, and Chepang require us to set it up for PTB. Like the previous three etyma, **(77) *dzyuk ≍ *tsyuk** MOUTH / LIP / VULVA, **(79) *siŋ ≍ *sik** MOUTH / LIP, **(78) *tsiŋ ≍ *tsik** VAGINA, the semantic range of the present etymon includes both VAGINA and MOUTH/LIP; but all of these etyma, despite their phonosemantic similarity, may well be independent.

---

[14] **ʂ**ɻ⁵⁵ **mpha**⁵⁵ 'mouth' + **ndʐo**⁵⁵ **pi**⁵⁵ 'skin'.

1.4. Meithei

| Meithei | chim ban | lip | GEM-CNL | 15 |
|---|---|---|---|---|
| | chin | mouth | GEM-CNL | |
| | chin bân | lip | JAM-Ety | |
| | cin | mouth | CYS-Meithei:3.7 | |
| | cin ban | lip | CYS-Meithei:3.9 | |
| | mə cin | beak / bill | CYS-Meithei:3.9.3 | |

2.3.1. Kham-Magar-Chepang-Sunwar

| Chepang (Eastern) | cin | clitoris | RC-ChepQ:10.4.4 |
|---|---|---|---|

4.1. Jingpho

| Jingpho | jìn | vagina | JAM-Ety | |
|---|---|---|---|---|
| | jìn-bāw | nymphae clitoris | JAM-Ety | |
| | jìn-dì | vagina | JAM-Ety | |
| | jìn-hkū | vaginal canal | JAM-Ety | 16 |
| | jìn-hkyí | mucus of vagina | JAM-Ety | 17 |
| | jìn-kāu | orifice of vagina | JAM-Ety | |
| | jìn-mūn | female pubic hair | JAM-Ety | |
| | jìn-sìn | nymphae clitoris | JAM-Ety | 18 |
| | jìn-tī | labia pudenda | JAM-Ety | |

(81)                           *b(y)at                           VAGINA

This root is quite widely distributed in TB, appearing in Kamarupan, Himalayish, Lolo-Burmese (including Jinuo), and Bai. It was reconstructed as PLB *b(y)et in Matisoff 1972a #5 and *HPTB* p. 375, but that has been revised here to *b(y)at to accommodate those reflexes that have -a- vocalism (e.g. WB, Kokborok, Bunan). Bradley's (1979) PLB reconstruction without medial glide, *bat, does not account for certain Loloish reflexes with front vowels (e.g. Lahu cha-pè?, since the regular Lahu reflex of *-at is -e?). Bauer 1991 (*LTBA* 14.1) treats this etymon as part of a binome *dzu(k)-byet (see (77a) *dzyuk ≍ *tsyuk VULVA for the first element), and adduces parallels in Hmong-Mien languages and Chinese. Benedict (1990) hypothesizes a "Proto-Austro-Kadai" binome *tu-pi (for the first element see (76) *s-tu ≍ *tsu VAGINA). These freewheeling proposals remain to be evaluated by future generations. There does not seem to be any connection between this etymon and (85) *pu VAGINA, which is confined mostly to Himalayish, and whose reflexes have back vowels.

The Bai forms listed below may well be loans from Chinese.

K. P. Malla suggests that the first syllable of Newar (Dolakhali) pi-ci 'vagina' really means 'breast' (see Kathmandu Newar pi-si 'breast' under (74) *pi ≍ *bi ROUNDED PART / NIPPLE / FOREHEAD / SHOULDER above), but can be used euphemistically to mean 'vagina'. In the other Himalayish forms cited here, however, this morpheme does definitely seem to mean 'vagina'.

---

[15]Note the optional assimilation of the final consonant of the first syllable to the initial consonant of the second.

[16]These Jingpho forms seem to reflect an open-syllable allofam *ku.

[17]The second element means 'excrement'.

[18]Literally "heart of vulva".

See *HPTB* *b(y)et, p. 375.

**1.1. North Assam**

| | | | | |
|---|---|---|---|---|
| Kaman [Miju] | kɯ³¹biat⁵⁵ | love | ZMYYC:719.48 | 19 |

**1.3. Naga**

| | | | |
|---|---|---|---|
| Zeme | ¹pe⁵mu | vagina | AW-TBT:474 |

**1.7. Bodo-Garo = Barish**

| | | | |
|---|---|---|---|
| Kokborok | ši-pa? | vagina | PT-Kok |

**2.1.1. Western Himalayish**

| | | | |
|---|---|---|---|
| Bunan | pha šu | vagina | SBN-BunQ:10.4.1 |
| Kanauri | phɛːts | vulva | RSB-STV |
| Pattani [Manchati] | pha ṣu | vagina | STP-ManQ:10.4.1 |
| | pʰə ṣu | vagina | DS-Patt |

**2.1.2. Bodic**

| | | | |
|---|---|---|---|
| Tibetan (Batang) | pi⁵⁵ pi⁵³ | vagina | DQ-Batang:10.4.1 |

**2.1.4. Tamangic**

| | | | | |
|---|---|---|---|---|
| Tamang (Risiangku) | ¹pit si | vagina | MM-TamRisQ:10.4.1 | 20 |
| Tamang (Sahu) | ¹pi-ci | vagina | JAM-Ety | |

**2.3.2. Kiranti**

| | | | | |
|---|---|---|---|---|
| Bahing | pi-si | vagina | JAM-Ety | |
| Hayu | bi la | genitals | BM-Hay:84.245 | |
| | bi mli | genitals | BM-PK7:138; JAM-Ety | 21 |

**4. Jingpho-Nung-Luish**

| | | | |
|---|---|---|---|
| Ganan | pɑ?⁴ | vulva | GHL-PPB:L.150 |
| Kadu (Kantu) | pɑ?³ | vulva | GHL-PPB:L.150 |
| Sak (Bawtala) | ă paʊ² | vulva | GHL-PPB:L.150 |
| Sak (Dodem) | ă pɛt | vulva | GHL-PPB:L.150 |
| Sak (Bawtala) | ă pɑ?² | vulva | GHL-PPB:L.150 |

**6. Lolo-Burmese**

| | | | |
|---|---|---|---|
| *Lolo-Burmese | *b(y)et | vulva | JAM-TSR:5 |
| Moso (Weixi) | pi³⁵ | vulva | RSB-STV |

**6.1. Burmish**

| | | | |
|---|---|---|---|
| Burmese (Written) | cok-pat | vagina | JAM-Ety |

**6.2. Loloish**

| | | | | |
|---|---|---|---|---|
| *Loloish | *batᴸ | vulva | DB-PLolo:123 | |
| Ahi | to⁵⁵ bi̠²¹ | genitalia / pudenda (general) | LMZ-AhiQ:10.1 | |
| | to⁵⁵ bi̠²¹ ne̠³³ ba⁵⁵ | vagina | LMZ-AhiQ:10.4.1 | |
| | to⁵⁵ bi²¹ ni²¹ | vulva / labia | LMZ-AhiQ:10.4.2 | 22 |
| | to⁵⁵ bi̠²¹ tʂʻɛ²² | copulate | LMZ-AhiQ:10.2 | |
| | to⁵⁵bi̠²¹ | vagina | CK-YiQ:10.4.1 | |

[19]The semantic association VAGINA ⟷ love has not been noted elsewhere, but the phonological fit of this form with the present etymon is perfect.

[20]This Tamang form is of key importance in establishing the -t final for Himalayish.

[21]This is an antonymic compound meaning literally "vagina-penis". See (114a) *m-ley ≍ *m-li PENIS below.

[22]The third syllable is the same as the first syllable of Ahi ni²¹ tɕi²² "lip".

| | | | |
|---|---|---|---|
| Akha | a-**beh** L-LS | vulva | JAM-TSR:5 |
| | a̬ **beh̭** | vulva (impolite child's term) | JAM-Ety |
| Bisu | tɔ **pɛ́** | vulva | PB-Bisu:16 |
| Gazhuo | **pi**$^{21}$ **pi**$^{53}$ mɛ$^{33}$ | genitalia / pudenda | DQ-Gazhuo:10.1 |
| *Common Lahu | ***peh̭** | vulva | DB-PLolo:123 |
| Lahu (Black) | cha(-**pɛ̀ʔ**) | vagina; vulva | JAM-Ety; JAM-TSR:5 |
| | **pɛ̀ʔ** | be horny, randy | JAM-DL:p. 856 |
| Lipho | tu$^{55}$**bi**$^{21}$ | vagina | CK-YiQ:10.4.1 |
| Lisu | tu$^{1}$-**bi**$^{6}$ | vagina; vulva | JAM-Ety; JAM-TSR:5 |
| Lisu (Central) | tu$^{1}$-**bi**$^{6}$ | vagina | JF-HLL |
| Lisu | tu$^{1}$**bi**$^{6}$ | vulva | DB-PLolo:123 |
| Lisu (Northern) | tɔ$^{55}$**bi**$^{21}$ | pudenda | DB-Lisu |
| Lolopho | tv̩$^{55}$ **bi**$^{31}$ | vagina | DQ-Lolopho:10.4.1 |
| Mpi | to$^{2}$**phe**$^{2}$ | vagina | SD-MPD |
| Nasu | tʂo̱$^{21}$ **pi̱**$^{21}$ | vagina | CK-YiQ:10.4.1 |
| Nesu | **pi**$^{55}$ | vagina | CK-YiQ:10.4.1 |
| | **pi**$^{55}$ nu̱$^{33}$ | female pubic hair | CK-YiQ:10.4.5 |
| Noesu | **pe**$^{33}$ | vagina | CK-YiQ:10.4.1 |
| | **pe**$^{33}$ɬɪ$^{33}$ | copulate | CK-YiQ:10.2 |
| Sani [Nyi] | **pæ**$^{55}$ | vagina | CK-YiQ:10.4.1; MXL-SaniQ:303.4 |
| | **pæ**$^{55}$no$^{44}$ | female pubic hair | CK-YiQ:10.4.5 |
| | **pɛ**$^{55}$ | vulva, female genitals | YHJC-Sani |
| | **pɛ**$^{55}$qhɪ$^{33}$ | copulate | YHJC-Sani |
| Phunoi | **pə̀** tò | vulva | JAM-Ety |
| Yi (Southern) | **pi**$^{55}$ | vulva | RSB-STV |
| 6.4. Jinuo | | | |
| Jinuo (Baya/Banai) | tso$^{55}$ **pɛ**$^{55}$ | vagina | DQ-JinA:146 |
| 8. Bai | | | |
| Bai | **pi̱**$^{44}$ | vulva / labia | ZYS-Bai:10.4.2 |
| | **pi̱**$^{44}$ ma̱$^{21}$ | female pubic hair | ZYS-Bai:10.4.5 |
| | **pi̱**$^{44}$ ma̱$^{21}$ tsɿ$^{33}$ | female pubic hair | ZYS-Bai:10.4.5 |
| | **pi̱**$^{44}$ ɕĩ$^{55}$ tɯ̱$^{21}$ | clitoris | ZYS-Bai:10.4.4 |
| | **pi̱**$^{44}$ ʔuĩ$^{33}$ | vagina | ZYS-Bai:10.4.1 |

## Chinese comparandum

According to H. Stimson 1966,[23] the taboo word 屄 (Mand. **bī**) does not appear in dictionaries until the 17th century. Benedict 1988[24] posits OC ***b'iĕt**, underlying such modern dialect forms as Hakka **piet**$^{8}$ and Min Kienyang **pie**$^{7}$. This Chinese word may well be the source of the Baic and some of the Loloish forms listed above.

[JAM]

Chinese dialect forms of this word point to both open and closed-syllable ancestral forms, for example Schuessler 2007:161 notes Amoy (= Xiamen) **tsi**$^{A1}$**-pai**$^{A2}$. This sug-

[23] Hugh Stimson, "A taboo word in the Peking dialect" (*Language* 42.2:285-294). Cited in Bauer 1991:150.

[24] Untitled manuscript circulated as a handout at ICSTLL #21, Lund, Sweden.

gests early Chinese variants *pe and *pet, the latter of which corresponds well to PTB *byat. (For the correspondence between OC *e and PTB *ya, cf. 'eight' 八 OC *pret (Baxter), PTB *b-ryat.) However Schuessler believes that this word is derived from 'to open' (PST *pe), with the addition of *-t marking "nouns of naturally occurring objects". See Schuessler 2007:161, 414. This hypothesis could also explain the etymology of the PTB etymon under discussion here.

[ZJH]

## (82)  *hay ≍ *kay  VAGINA

This root is fairly well attested in Kamarupan, appearing in three sub-branches: Barish (Meche), Naga (Tangkhul), and Mru (Mruic), and apparently also in Himalayish. The alternation between h- and k- is paralleled in a number of other etyma, including STEAL *hu ≍ *r-ku, ROLL *hil ≍ *kil, HIDE *hway ≍ *kway, GAG/CHOKE *hak ≍ *kak, EARTH *ha ≍ *r-ka, (150) LOVE/COPULATE *huŋ ≍ *kuŋ. See Matisoff 1997[25] and *HPTB* p. 57.

| | | | | |
|---|---|---|---|---|
| **1.3. Naga** | | | | |
| Tangkhul | **hai** khur | vulva | JAM-Ety | |
| | **hai** ra | semen | JAM-Ety | 26 |
| | **hay**(-khur) | vulva | JAM-GSTC:184 | |
| **1.6. Mru** | | | | |
| Mru | **kai** | vagina; vulva | JAM-Ety;<br>JAM-GSTC:184 | |
| **1.7. Bodo-Garo = Barish** | | | | |
| Meche | **ki** ʈu? | vagina | AW-TBT:62 | |
| **2.3.2. Kiranti** | | | | |
| Limbu | **hi**-rā | vulva | JAM-Ety;<br>JAM-GSTC:184 | 27 |
| | **hi**-rā-hong | vagina | JAM-Ety;<br>JAM-GSTC:184 | 28 |
| | **hi**-rā-mu-rik | female pubic hair | JAM-Ety | |
| | **hi** ra | vagina | BM-Lim | |

## (83)  *tsya  VAGINA / COPULATE

This etymon is so far sparsely attested, with the best putative cognates occurring in Loloish (Lahu, Jinuo), Chin (Lakher), and perhaps West Himalayish (Pattani).

| | | | |
|---|---|---|---|
| **1.2. Kuki-Chin** | | | |
| Lakher [Mara] | **cha** nô-tao | copulate | JAM-Ety |

---

[25]"Primary and secondary laryngeal initials in Tibeto-Burman."

[26]This certainly looks like a case of "genital flipflop", i.e. semen is viewed as "vagina-semen", since that is its destination. See (157) *ra ≍ *wa SEMEN.

[27]The first syllable **hi**- is a lookalike of the vulgar Siamese word **hĭi**.

[28]The last syllable means 'hole' (see (92) *hoŋ VAGINA / RECTUM / HOLE, below). See G. van Driem, *A Grammar of Limbu* (1987), p. 426.

| | cha-ku | copulate | JAM-Ety | |
|---|---|---|---|---|
| **2.1.1. Western Himalayish** | | | | |
| Pattani [Manchati] | tsek **tsa** | clitoris | STP-ManQ:10.4.4 | 29 |
| **2.3.1. Kham-Magar-Chepang-Sunwar** | | | | |
| Kham | **ca** kə | vagina | DNW-KhamQ | 30 |
| **6.2. Loloish** | | | | |
| Lahu (Black) | **cha** pàʔ ve | copulate with a woman | JAM-DL:517,814 | |
| | **cha** thû | feel sexual desire (woman); lubricate | JAM-DL:681 | |
| | **cha**(-pɛ̀ʔ) | vagina; vulva | JAM-Ety; JAM-TSR:5 | |
| | **cha**-cú-ni | clitoris | JAM-DL:517 | 31 |
| | **cha**-mu | female pubic hair | JAM-Ety | |
| | **cha**-mə̂ | labia | JAM-Ety | 32 |
| | **cha**-ɣ̀ɪ | vaginal secretion | JAM-Ety | |
| **6.4. Jinuo** | | | | |
| Jinuo (Baya/Banai) | **tso**⁵⁵ pɛ⁵⁵ | vagina | DQ-JinA:146 | |

## (84)         \*li-n        VAGINA

This root is confined mostly to Karenic, with possible cognates in Kamarupan and Himalayish. The Lotha form with nasal prefix makes this root look very much like **(114a)** **\*m-ley ⪰ \*m-li** PENIS, suggesting that this might be yet another example of "genital flipflop" (see Benedict 1979, *LTBA* 5.1). For the moment, I regard the final nasal in some Karenic forms as suffixal.

| | | | |
|---|---|---|---|
| **1.3. Naga** | | | |
| Lotha Naga | **Nre** | vagina | VN-LothQ:10.4.1 |
| | **Nre** hum | female pubic hair | VN-LothQ:10.4.5 |
| **2.1.5. Dhimal** | | | |
| Dhimal | **li** | vagina | JK-Dh |
| | **li** muĩ | woman's pubic hair | JK-Dh |
| **2.3.1. Kham-Magar-Chepang-Sunwar** | | | |
| Kham | pə **re:** | vagina | DNW-KhamQ |
| **2.3.2. Kiranti** | | | |
| Bantawa | phu **ri** | vagina | NKR-Bant |
| **7. Karenic** | | | |
| \*Karen (Pho) | **\*lén'** | vagina | RBJ-KLS:17 |
| \*Karen (Sgaw) | **\*lì** | vagina | RBJ-KLS:17 |

---

²⁹The second syllable bears a resemblance to **(90)** **\*tsaŋ** CLITORIS (below), but the usual Pattani reflex of \*-aŋ is -aŋ (e.g. **hraŋ** 'horse' < **(H:267)** **\*s-raŋ**; *maŋ*-api 'dream' < **(H:268)** **\*maŋ**).

³⁰The analysis here is tentative.

³¹Literally "vagina-nipple". The last syllable probably means 'red'. Cf. also Lahu **ha-cú-ni** 'uvula' (lit. "tongue-nipple").

³²The second syllable means "lip".

| *Karen | *ljén' | vagina | RBJ-KLS:17 |
|---|---|---|---|
| *Karen (TP) | *ljén' | vagina | RBJ-KLS:17 |
| *Karen (Pho-Sgaw) | *ljì | vagina | RBJ-KLS:17 |
| Bwe (Western) | li² | vagina | GHL-PPB:I.192 |
| Geba | a²li² | vagina | GHL-PPB:I.192 |
| Pa-O | lîn | vagina | JAM-Ety; RBJ-KLS:17 |
| Pa-O (Northern) | lin² | vagina | GHL-PPB:I.192 |
| Pho (Delta) | lẽ¹ | vagina | GHL-PPB:I.192 |
| Pho (Tenasserim) | lẽ⁴ | vagina | GHL-PPB:I.192 |
| Pho (Bassein) | lénʔ | vagina | JAM-Ety; RBJ-KLS:17 |
| Pho (Moulmein) | lén | vagina | JAM-Ety; RBJ-KLS:17 |
| Paku | li³ | vagina | GHL-PPB:I.192 |
| Sgaw | li⁶ | vagina | GHL-PPB:I.192 |
| Sgaw (Bassein) | lì | vagina | JAM-Ety; RBJ-KLS:17 |
| Karen (Sgaw/Hinthada) | li³³ | vagina | DQ-KarenB:146 |
| Sgaw (Moulmein) | lì | vagina | JAM-Ety; RBJ-KLS:17 |

## (85)　　　　　　　　*pu　　　　　　　　VAGINA

This root appears mostly in Himalayish, with a possible cognate from Qiangic. The second syllable of Mikir **mak-phu** 'mons Veneris' seems unrelated. In view of the gloss it probably means something like 'swelling; protuberance'. It bears a resemblance to other reflexes of the well-attested root **\*bwam ≍ \*pwam** PLUMP / SWOLLEN (*STC* #172; *HPTB* pp. 249, 252, 341, 518).

2.1.4. Tamangic

| Chantyal | ku **pu** | vagina | NPB-ChanQ:10.4.1 | |
|---|---|---|---|---|
| | ku **pu**-ye gala | vulva / labia | NPB-ChanQ:10.4.2 | 33 |

2.3.1. Kham-Magar-Chepang-Sunwar

| Kham | pə re: | vagina | DNW-KhamQ |
|---|---|---|---|

2.3.2. Kiranti

| Bantawa | **phu** ci | vagina; vulva; vagina (baby talk) | NKR-Bant; WW-Bant:60 | |
|---|---|---|---|---|
| | **phu** ci dhü | vagina | WW-Bant:60 | |
| | **phu** ri | vagina | NKR-Bant | |
| Hayu | **pu**-tsing | vagina | JAM-Ety | |
| | **pu** tshi | vagina | BM-Hay:84.189 | |

3.2. Qiangic

| Qiang (Yadu) | pʰo ṣ | vagina | DQ-QiangN:146 | 34 |
|---|---|---|---|---|

## (86)　　　　　　　　*mo　　　　　　　　VAGINA

This root is confined strictly to the Naga branch of Kamarupan with the meaning VAGINA. Several of the reflexes in this set resemble forms that have been assigned to **(123)**

---

[33] The last element means 'cheek'; **-ye** is a genitive marker. The compound means "vagina's cheeks".

[34] The final consonant in this form looks like the fused initial consonant of the second syllable of an original compound. See **(78) \*tsiŋ ≍ \*tsik** VAGINA, above.

**\*maːk** PENIS / MALE / SON-IN-LAW; GENITALS / VAGINA [q.v.], a root which also has several reflexes that mean 'vagina'.

1.2. Kuki-Chin

| | | | |
|---|---|---|---|
| Liangmei | ka-**mo** | vagina | AW-TBT:474 |

1.3. Naga

| | | | | |
|---|---|---|---|---|
| Angami Naga | $^5$u$^2$**mie** | vagina | AW-TBT:474 | 35 |
| Angami (Kohima) | (u) **mie**$^{31}$ | vagina | VN-AṅgQ:10.4.1 | |
| Khezha | $^1$e$^2$**mo** | vagina | AW-TBT:474 | |
| Mao | $^2$o$^5$**mo** | vagina | AW-TBT:474 | |
| Rengma (Southern) | $^5$a$^1$**mo** | vagina | AW-TBT:474 | |
| Rongmei | **mǽu** | vagina | AW-TBT:474 | |
| Sema | $^1$a$^1$**mo** | vagina | AW-TBT:474 | |
| Zeme | $^1$pe$^5$**mu** | vagina | AW-TBT:474 | |

## (87)          \*tsyum          VAGINA / COPULATE

This etymon has been found in a few Himalayish languages (Bantawa, Lepcha, Tamang, and perhaps Newar), as well as in Kamarupan. The basic meaning seems to be 'come together'. There is a perfect fit between the Mikir and Lepcha forms. The analysis of the Mikir form is as follows: **i** 'sleep' + **rap** 'befriend; be together' (see **(151)** \*l(y)ap ≍ \*l(y)am ≍ \*rap COPULATE / LOVE / GET TOGETHER) + **chom** 'suffix indicating action performed together' (Walker 1925:37).

1.3. Naga

| | | | |
|---|---|---|---|
| Tangkhul | kha ŋa **shām** | copulate | JAM-Ety |

1.5. Mikir

| | | | |
|---|---|---|---|
| Mikir | i rap-**chom** | copulate | JAM-Ety |

2.1.3. Lepcha

| | | | | |
|---|---|---|---|---|
| Lepcha | **čʻo** | harmonize; be congruous with | GBM-Lepcha:92 | |
| | **čʻo** da | lie together | GBM-Lepcha:92 | 36 |
| | **čʻom** | have carnal connection with women | GBM-Lepcha:92 | |

2.1.4. Tamangic

| | | | |
|---|---|---|---|
| Tamang (Risiangku) | $^2$**tsjum** ʈu | vagina, vulva | MM-TamRisQ:10.4.4 |
| Tamang (Sahu) | $^2$**cjum**-ʈu̥ | vagina | JAM-Ety |

2.2. Newar

| | | | |
|---|---|---|---|
| Newar (Dolakhali) | **cũ** | vagina / breast / milk | CG-Dolak | 37 |

---

[35]The first syllable is a general body-part prefix in Angami. The vowel of $^2$**mie** seems an unlikely reflex of \*-o; yet the alternative of assigning this form to **(123)** \*maːk PENIS / MALE / SON-IN-LAW; GENITALS / VAGINA seems no better, since the regular Angami reflex of \*-ak seems to be -o (e.g. WEAVE \*dak > Ang. **do**; ANT \*-rwak > Ang. **cho**).

[36]The last element **da** is a reflexive morpheme; cf. Lahu **dàʔ** < PTB \*m-dak. See *HPTB* pp. 318, 320.

[37]Although this Newar form resembles reflexes of **(56)** \*dz(y)əw MILK / BREAST (q.v.), the nasalization of the vowel leads me to include it in the present set.

2.3.2. Kiranti

| | | | |
|---|---|---|---|
| Bantawa | sen **com** | vagina | NKR-Bant |

# (88)   *wen   VAGINA

This is a speculative root, occurring only in Mikir, Tangut, and Bai.

1.5. Mikir

| | | | |
|---|---|---|---|
| Mikir | **ven**-the | vagina | JAM-Ety |
| | **wen** the | vagina | KHG-Mikir:217 |

3.1. Tangut

| | | | | |
|---|---|---|---|---|
| Tangut [Xixia] | tɪ **wə̣**¹ | vagina? | MVS-Grin | 38 |

8. Bai

| | | | |
|---|---|---|---|
| Bai | pi̱⁴⁴ ʔuĩ³³ | vagina | ZYS-Bai:10.4.1 |

# (89)   *seŋ   VAGINA

This root, though so far sparsely attested, seems certainly to occur in three separate branches of TB: Kamarupan (Meithei), Himalayish (Bantawa), and Lolo-Burmese (Ugong), and perhaps in Baic as well.

1.4. Meithei

| | | | |
|---|---|---|---|
| Meithei | **seŋ** bi | clitoris | CYS-Meithei:10.4.4 |

2.3.2. Kiranti

| | | | |
|---|---|---|---|
| Bantawa | **sen** com | vagina | NKR-Bant |

6.2. Loloish

| | | | |
|---|---|---|---|
| Ugong | **sɛŋ** kɔŋ | vagina | DB-Ugong:10.4.1 |
| | **sɛŋ** ʔa lɛ | clitoris | DB-Ugong:10.4.4 |

8. Bai

| | | | |
|---|---|---|---|
| Bai | pi̱⁴⁴ ɕĩ⁵⁵ tṳ²¹ | clitoris | ZYS-Bai:10.4.4 |

# (90)   *tsaŋ   CLITORIS

This root apparently occurs in three branches of TB: Kamarupan (Mikir), Himalayish (Limbu), and Lolo-Burmese (Bisu), with the consistent meaning of CLITORIS.

1.5. Mikir

| | | | |
|---|---|---|---|
| Mikir | ing **chàng** | clitoris | KHG-Mikir:19 |

2.3.2. Kiranti

| | | | |
|---|---|---|---|
| Limbu | nāp-**coŋ** | clitoris | JAM-Ety |
| | nep **caŋ** | clitoris | SVD-LimA:478 |

---

[38]According to M. V. Sofronov 1978, there is some doubt as to the exact meaning of the Tangut graph he reconstructs here.

| | nEp **tsɔŋ** | clitoris | BM-Lim | 39 |
|---|---|---|---|---|
| **6.2. Loloish** | | | | |
| Bisu | tɔ **tshìŋ** | clitoris | PB-Bisu:13 | |

## (91)      *s-ti ≍ *m-ti      CLITORIS / VAGINA / NIPPLE

This root is quite well attested, appearing in Kamarupan, Himalayish, Jingpho, Qiangic, Bai, and Tujia, mostly with the meaning CLITORIS, sometimes VAGINA.

The Qiangic forms (Mawo, NW rGyalrong, and N. rGyalrong) point to Proto-Qiangic **s/m-dzi-s/k**, i.e. a prototype with affricated root-initial, either a sibilant or nasal prefix, and either a sibilant or velar suffix. Chantyal (Tamangic) **ti si** and Kham **ti si:** are borrowings from Nepali (M. Mazaudon, p.c. 2008).

| | | | | |
|---|---|---|---|---|
| **1.1. North Assam** | | | | |
| Darang [Taraon] | **aː-teb** | vagina | JAM-Ety | 40 |
| **1.5. Mikir** | | | | |
| Mikir | ven-**the** | vagina | JAM-Ety | |
| | wen **the** | vagina | KHG-Mikir:217 | |
| **1.7. Bodo-Garo = Barish** | | | | |
| Garo (Bangladesh) | ro'ng-**ti** pi'-sa | clitoris | RB-GB | 41 |
| | sok-kit-**ti** | nipple | RB-GB | |
| Lalung | khin **di** | clitoris | MB-Lal:14 | |
| **2.3.2. Kiranti** | | | | |
| Limbu | neːt **ti** | clitoris | SVD-LimA:p. 477 | |
| **3.1. Tangut** | | | | |
| Tangut [Xixia] | **tɪ** wə̣¹ | vagina? | MVS-Grin | 42 |
| **3.2. Qiangic** | | | | |
| Qiang (Mawo) | khə **sti** | clitoris | JS-Mawo | |
| | kʰæ **sti** | clitoris | SHK-MawoQ:10.4.4 | |
| **3.3. rGyalrongic** | | | | |
| rGyalrong (NW) | tə **mdzis** | clitoris | SHK-rGNWQ:10.4.4 | |
| rGyalrong (Northern) | tə **mdzək** | clitoris | SHK-rGNQ:10.4.4 | |
| **4.1. Jingpho** | | | | |
| Jingpho | jìn-**dì** | vagina | JAM-Ety | |
| | jìn-**tī** | *labia pudenda* | JAM-Ety | |
| **5. Tujia** | | | | |
| Tujia | **tʰe²¹** | vagina | CK-TujBQ:10.4.1 | |

---

[39]PTB *-aŋ seems to yield Limbu -o(ː)ŋ in other cases, e.g. BORN (21) *braŋ BORN / BIRTH > Lb. *po:ŋ-ma?*.

[40]The final labial stop is unexplained.

[41]According to Burling (1992), the literal meaning of this word is "small stone"; it can also refer to the smaller of the two grindstones in a ricemill.

[42]According to M. V. Sofronov 1978 there is some doubt as to the exact meaning of the Tangut graph he reconstructs here.

| | | |
|---|---|---|
| tʰe³⁵ | vagina | CK-TujMQ:10.4.1 |

8. Bai
Bai                    pi̱⁴⁴ çĩ⁵⁵ tṳ²¹         clitoris         ZYS-Bai:10.4.4

## (92)                    *hoŋ                    VAGINA / RECTUM / HOLE

This root has so far been uncovered only in a few widely separated languages, which paradoxically seems to assure that it can be reconstructed for PTB. The basic meaning seems to be HOLE/ORIFICE, which is the gloss of the Limbu cognate syllable in isolation.

This root may be allofamically related to **(93)** *guŋ ≍ *kuŋ HOLE / ORIFICE / ROUNDED PART.

The Mikir form **ke hot** is not related to this root; the morpheme **hot** is glossed as 'niche, groove' in Walker 1925, p. 57. Cf. Lahu **nī-qhὲʔ** 'penis', where the second syllable means 'notch (as a stick); chip; break off a piece'. The semantic association lies evidently in the notched appearance of the glans.

2.3.2. Kiranti
| | | | |
|---|---|---|---|
| Limbu | hi-rā-**hong** | vagina | JAM-Ety; |
| | | | JAM-GSTC:184 |
| | le **hoŋ** | hole of penis; *meatus urinarius* | JAM-Ety |
| | ne bo **hoŋ** | nostril | JAM-Ety |
| | nE bu **hoŋ** | nostril | BM-Lim |
| Yakha | na bu? ka: ɔ **hɔŋ** | nostril | TK-Yakha:3.5.2 |
| 3.2. Qiangic | | | |
| Shixing | qhɑ⁵⁵ **huŋ³³** | anus / rectum | SHK-ShixQ |
| 6.2. Loloish | | | |
| Bisu | tɔ **hɔ́ŋ** | vagina | PB-Bisu:16 |
| Ugong | ḥoŋ-dǔŋ-yέ | placenta | DB-Ugong |

## (93)          *guŋ ≍ *kuŋ          HOLE / ORIFICE / ROUNDED PART

This widespread etymon is similar to **(94)** *kwar ≍ *kor CONCAVITY / HOLE / EAR / VAGINA (below), in that it typically occurs as the second morpheme in binomes referring to orifices of the body, especially EAR, NOSTRIL, and ANUS; occasionally it occurs in compounds for VAGINA.

This etymon is certainly allofamically related to *s-koŋ ≍ *s-kok HOLLOW OBJECT/HEAD, as in the last syllable of, e.g. Lahu **ó-qō** 'head' < PLB *bʷu²-ʔgoŋ².

It is also very possible that it is allofamically related to **(92)** *hoŋ VAGINA / RECTUM / HOLE. For remarks on velar/laryngeal interchange in TB, see **(82)** *hay ≍ *kay VAGINA above.

There are excellent Chinese comparanda: 空 [*GSR* 1172h] *k'ung 'hollow, empty' and 孔 [*GSR* 1174a-b] *k'ung 'very, greatly; empty'. Another likely Chinese relative is

肛 'anus', Mand. **gāng** (not in *GSR* series 1172), though this might fit better with **\*kaŋ** HIPS / BUTTOCKS; and/or **\*k(l)oŋ** BACKSIDE / BUTTOCKS / HIPS / ANUS. See ZJH's discussion, below.

See *HPTB* **\*guŋ ≍ \*kuŋ**, pp. 285, 310; PLB **\*guŋ² ≍ \*kuŋ²**, p. 285.

**0. Sino-Tibetan**

| | | | |
|---|---|---|---|
| *Tibeto-Burman | \*na ku:ŋ | nostril | WTF-PNN:527 |

**1.1. North Assam**

| | | | |
|---|---|---|---|
| Apatani | rù-**kó** | hole | JS-Tani |
| Bengni | uŋ-**ko:** | hole | JS-Tani |

**1.3. Naga**

| | | | |
|---|---|---|---|
| Konyak (Tamlu) | **goŋ**-ka | anus | AW-TBT:1 |
| Rongmei | nu **kong** | ear | GEM-CNL |

**1.4. Meithei**

| | | | |
|---|---|---|---|
| Meithei | na **kong** | ear | GEM-CNL |
| | nâ **kông** | ear | JAM-Ety |
| | na **koŋ** nəp thi | earwax | CYS-Meithei:3.6.6 |

**2.1.2. Bodic**

| | | | |
|---|---|---|---|
| Tashigang | khi-**gaŋ** | anus ("feces-hole") | AW-TBT:1 |
| Tibetan (Amdo:Zeku) | k\ʰoŋ-wə | hole (small) | JS-Amdo:367 |
| | kʰəŋ | hole | JS-Amdo:366 |
| Tibetan (Batang) | na⁵⁵ khõ⁵⁵ | ear canal | DQ-Batang:3.6.4 |
| Tibetan (Written) | **khung** | hole | JS-Tib:366 |
| | **khung**.bu | hole (small) | JS-Tib:367 |
| | **kuṅ** | hole | JAM-II |
| | mig-**khuŋ** | eyehole / eye socket | JAM-Ety |
| | rna-**kuṅ** | earhole | JAM-Ety |

**2.1.4. Tamangic**

| | | | |
|---|---|---|---|
| *Tamang | **\*khuŋ²** | hole | MM-K78:26 |
| Gurung (Ghachok) | **kʰũq** | hole | SIL-Gur:5.A.62 |
| | **²khũ** | hole | MM-K78:26 |
| Tamang (Sahu) | na.'**kʰuŋ** | eyeball | SIL-Sahu:2.22 |
| | **²khuŋ** | hole | MM-K78:26 |
| Thakali (Marpha) | **²khuŋ** | hole | MM-K78:26 |
| Thakali (Syang) | **ᴴkhũŋ** | hole | MM-K78:26 |
| Thakali (Tukche) | **kho** toŋ | hole | MM-K78:26 |
| | **kʰo** toŋ | hole | SIL-Thak:5.A.62 |

**2.3.1. Kham-Magar-Chepang-Sunwar**

| | | | |
|---|---|---|---|
| Chepang | **gʰaŋ** | hole | SIL-Chep:5.A.62 |
| | por-**ghaŋ** | anus / rectum | AW-TBT:1 |
| | porʔ **ghāng** | anus | JAM-Ety |
| | porʔ-**gʰaŋ** | anus / rectum | SIL-Chep:2.A.46 |
| Chepang (Eastern) | no **ghaŋ** | ear canal | RC-ChepQ:3.6.4 |
| | por **ghaŋ** | anus / rectum | RC-ChepQ:9.12 |
| Kham | 'ki **kũ:** | anus / rectum | DNW-KhamQ:2.A.46 |
| | ki **ku** | anus | JAM-Ety |

**2.3.2. Kiranti**

| | | | |
|---|---|---|---|
| Kulung | **khu** lum_ | hole (in the ground) | RPHH-Kul |

## 3.2. Qiangic

| | | | |
|---|---|---|---|
| Ersu (Central) | htʃɛ⁵⁵ **ku**⁵⁵ | anus / rectum | SHK-ErsCQ |
| | nɑ⁵⁵ **ku**⁵⁵ | ear | SHK-ErsCQ |
| Qiang (Mawo) | nə **ku** | ear | JZ-Qiang |
| | nə **kuə̯** | ear | SHK-MawoQ:3.6 |
| | nə **kuə̯** tsʰæ n̩ʂə̯ | earwax | SHK-MawoQ:3.6.6 |
| | nə **kṳ** | ear | JS-Mawo |
| | nə **kṳ** staba | earlobe | JS-Mawo |
| | nə **ku** tsha χʂ | earwax | JZ-Qiang |
| Qiang (Taoping) | ȵi³¹ **kie**³³ | ear | JZ-Qiang |
| Qiang (Yadu) | ȵu **k** | ear | DQ-QiangN:107 ⁴³ |

## 3.3. rGyalrongic

| | | | |
|---|---|---|---|
| rGyalrong (NW) | tə stə **ku** | vagina | SHK-rGNWQ:10.4.1 |
| rGyalrong (Northern) | tə ʃtu **kʰuŋ** du | vagina | SHK-rGNQ:10.4.1 |

## 4.1. Jingpho

| | | | |
|---|---|---|---|
| Jingpho | jìn-**hkū** | vaginal canal | JAM-Ety ⁴⁴ |
| | lədî **hkū** | nostril | JAM-Ety |
| | nā ləshîng **hkū** | earhole | JAM-Ety |
| | ¹daŋ²kaŋ-²**khu** | anus | AW-TBT:1 |

## 6. Lolo-Burmese

| | | | |
|---|---|---|---|
| *Lolo-Burmese | *****kuŋ¹** | hole in ground / pit | JAM-MLBM:2 |

## 6.1. Burmish

| | | | |
|---|---|---|---|
| Achang (Lianghe) | na³¹ **kɯ**³¹ | ear | JZ-Achang |
| Burmese (Written) | hna-**khôŋ** | nose | JAM-II |
| | **khôŋ**- | to be hollow; trough; canoe | PKB-WBRD |
| | ə-**khôŋ** | hollow, cavity | PKB-WBRD |
| | ʔə **kʰôŋ** | hollow / cavity | JAM-MLBM:3 |
| Lashi | tʃhɹ̌⁵⁵ **khuŋ**⁵⁵ tuaŋ³³ | anus / rectum | DQ-Lashi:9.12 |

## 6.2. Loloish

| | | | |
|---|---|---|---|
| Hani (Pijo) | **khú** | hole | ILH-PL:554 |
| | ɔ **khú** | hole | ILH-PL:554 |
| Hani (Khatu) | à **khú** | hole | ILH-PL:554 |
| | **khú** | hole | ILH-PL:554 |
| Lahu (Black) | nā-qhɔ̂-**qhɔ** | nostril | JAM-Ety |
| | qhɛ̂-**qhɔ** | anus; buttock | JAM-Ety |
| | qhɛ̂-**qhɔ**-dì | buttock | JAM-Ety |
| | qhɛ̂-**qhɔ**-pɨ | buttock | JAM-Ety |
| | qhɛ̂-tû-**qhɔ** | anus | JAM-Ety |
| | ɔ²¹**qhɔ**³³ | hole | ZMYYC:34.33 |
| | ɔ̂-**qʰɔ** | hole in ground, pit | JAM-MLBM:2 |
| Lalo | tɕʰi²¹ **kʰṳ**⁵⁵ | anus, rectum | CK-YiQ:9.12 |
| | ʔna⁵⁵ **kʰṳ**³³ **kʰṳ**⁵⁵ dṳ⁵⁵ | nostril | CK-YiQ:3.5.2 |
| Lisu | e⁵⁵**khu**⁴⁴ | hole | ZMYYC:34.27 |
| | hhi⁵-**hku**⁴ | anus | JAM-Ety |
| | na¹-paw³ **hku**⁴ | earhole | JAM-Ety |

---

⁴³Note the radical reduction of the second element in the compound.
⁴⁴These Jingpho forms seem to reflect an open-syllable allofam **ku**.

| | | | |
|---|---|---|---|
| Lisu (Northern) | tɔ⁵⁵khu³³ | vagina; orifice | DB-Lisu |
| Mpi | ʔa²-kʰuŋ² | cavity / hollow (as in tree, rock) | JAM-MLBM:3 |
| | ʔa²-kʰuŋ⁶ | hole in ground / pit | JAM-MLBM:2 |
| Nasu | ɬi³³ xo³³ du³³ | anus / rectum | CK-YiQ:9.12 |
| Ugong | ní kɔŋ | penis hole | DB-Ugong |
| | sɛŋ kɔŋ | vagina | DB-Ugong:10.4.1 |
| | ʔéŋ kɔŋ | anus / rectum | DB-Ugong:9.12 |
| Yi (Nanjian) | khu̱⁵⁵du̱⁵⁵ | hole | ZMYYC:34.23 |

**6.3. Naxi**

| | | | |
|---|---|---|---|
| Naxi (Lijiang) | kho³³lo³³ | hole | ZMYYC:34.28 |

**6.4. Jinuo**

| | | | |
|---|---|---|---|
| Jinuo | na³³kho⁵⁵ | ear | ZMYYC:241.34 |
| Jinuo (Baya/Banai) | na⁴⁴ kʰo⁵⁵ | ear | DQ-JinA:107 |
| Jinuo (Baka) | n̥a⁴⁴ kʰu⁵⁵ | ear | DQ-JinB:107 |
| Jinuo (Youle) | n̥a³³ kʰo⁵⁵ | ear | JZ-Jinuo |

**7. Karenic**

| | | | |
|---|---|---|---|
| Bwe | nɛ-kú | ear | EJAH-BKD |
| Bwe (Western) | nɛ²ku¹ | ear | AW-TBT:931; GHL-PPB:G.45 |
| Bwe | nè-kú | ear | AW-TBT:931 |
| Geba | ñĩ²gu² | ear | GHL-PPB:G.45 |
| Pho (Tenasserim) | nɑ⁴ [ku⁵] | ear | GHL-PPB:G.45 |

**9. Sinitic**

| | | | |
|---|---|---|---|
| Chinese (Mandarin) | ěr-kǒng | earhole | JAM-II |
| | kǒng | hole | JAM-II |
| | kuung duhng | hole | JS-Ch:366 |
| | shaau kuung | hole (small) | JS-Ch:367 |
| Chinese (Old/Mid) | k'ung/k'ung | hollow; empty | GSR:1172h |
| | k'ung/k'ung: | very, greatly; empty | GSR:1174a |

## Chinese comparanda

空 **kōng** 'hollow, empty'

*GSR*: 1172h          Karlgren: *k'ung          Li: *khung          Baxter: *khong (p. 771)

孔 **kǒng** 'very, greatly; empty'

*GSR*: 1174a          Karlgren: *k'ung          Li: *khungx          Baxter: *khong?

This OC-PTB comparison is long-recognized. See for example Simon 1929, Gong 1995 set 75, Coblin 1986:71.

The Chinese forms are a perfect match for the TB reconstruction. For another example of this final correspondence, cf. **(44a)** *t/duŋ NAVEL. On the aspiration mismatch in the initial corresponce, see the discussion under **(1b)** *pu EGG.

The two Chinese forms are clearly etymological doublets. Schuessler (2007:335) speculates that 孔 **kǒng** may be an 'endoactive' derivation meaning 'hole', from 空 **kōng** 'hollow, empty', lit. 'that which is hollow, empty'.

肛 **gāng** 'lower intestines / anus'

*GSR*: not in 1172

This word is not attested until the Middle Chinese period. The Old Chinese reconstruction would be *krung (Li)/*krong (Baxter) if we assume membership in *GSR* 1172; however, it is possible that the Old Chinese source is *krong (Li)/*krung (Baxter), and that the phonetic element of the character was chosen after the merger of these two OC finals. (The Mandarin pronunciation is irregular; we would expect *jiāng*.)

Schuessler (2007:251) suggests a comparison with WT **gźaŋ** 'anus'; however, the vowel correspondence is not good (unless a late borrowing is involved). It is certainly possible that this word is in the same family as 空 and 孔, although the function of *-r- is not clear.

[ZJH]

(94)         ***kwar ≍ *kor***         **CONCAVITY / HOLE / EAR / VAGINA**

*STC* makes an artificial distinction between two groups of forms, one reconstructed *kor 'valley; pit; cave' (#349) and the other *kwar 'hole' (#350), here combined into a single etymon. This etymon is widely distributed in Kamarupan, with scattered cognates elsewhere (Himalayish, Qiangic, Nungish, Bai). It appears as the last syllable in compounds referring to orifices of the body, especially EAR, NOSTRIL, ANUS, and VAGINA; occasionally also in compounds for EYE.

Sometimes, however, a similar morpheme appears as a monosyllable or as the first syllable in a compound; these cases I refer to a separate (but perhaps allofamically related) etymon *kon/r EAR, with the specific meaning EAR. A key form here is Kom Rem **kōr khur** 'ear canal', with the structure *kon/r EAR + *kor.

While I occasionally reconstruct **kwar ≍ *kor** for the second syllables of compounds meaning EYE (e.g. Wancho **mǝk-ǝr**), there is a group of Bodo-Garo forms meaning EYE where I set up a separate (but again perhaps allofamic) etymon *gon EYE, with the specific meaning EYE. Compare Bodo **ha-khor** 'hole, valley' vs. **me-gon** 'eye'; Garo **ging-kol** 'nostril' vs. **mik-on** 'eye'. There is also some evidence from Monpa Tsangla for the independence of this etymon and *gon EYE: **miŋ-khor** 'eye' vs. **miŋ-khoŋ-(taŋ)** 'eye (< **(H:324)** *s-mik EYE + *gon EYE).

See *HPTB* *kor ≍ *kwar, pp. 395, 401.

| 0. Sino-Tibetan | | | | |
|---|---|---|---|---|
| *Tibeto-Burman | *kor | pit, valley, cave | STC:349 | |
| | *kwar | hole, cavity | STC:350 | |
| 1.2. Kuki-Chin | | | | |
| Kom Rem | kōr kʰur | ear canal | T-KomRQ:3.6.4 | 45 |
| | nar kʰur | nostril | T-KomRQ:3.5.2 | |
| Lailenpi | mɷ̆ nɑ⁴ kuɑ¹ | ear | GHL-PPB:N.2 | |

---

[45]This form constitutes good evidence for the independence of etyma **(94)** *kwar ≍ *kor CONCAVITY / HOLE / EAR / VAGINA and *kon/r EAR.

## V. Vagina

| | | | |
|---|---|---|---|
| Lakher [Mara] | chhu-**khao** | vulva | JAM-Ety |
| | hna-pasu-**khao** | nostril | JAM-Ety |
| | na-cha-**kao** | ear | JAM-Ety |
| | na-**khao** | earhole | JAM-Ety |
| | sisi-**khor** | armpit ("tickle-hole") | STC:265 |
| | ¹nə²ko | ear; earhole | AW-TBT:108,162 |
| Liangmei | cha **kun** | ear | GEM-CNL |
| | ka-**kŭan** | ear | AW-TBT:162 |
| Lothvo (Hiranpi) | nɑ¹**küɛ³** | ear | GHL-PPB:N.2 |
| Lushai [Mizo] | hnâr-**kua** | nostril | JAM-Ety |
| | **khuar ⪥ khur** | hole, cavity | STC:350 |
| | **kor** | small valley, ravine | STC:349 |
| | **kùa** | hole / inside of abdomen | AW-TBT:431 |
| | mong-**kua** | anus | JAM-Ety |
| Zotung | nă⁴**kuɑ⁴** | ear | GHL-PPB:N.2 |

### 1.3. Naga

| | | | |
|---|---|---|---|
| *Northern Naga | ***gor** | hole / cave | WTF-PNN:504 |
| Chang | kuŋ **kan** | nostril | WTF-PNN:527 |
| Lotha Naga | kheno **kvu** | nostril | VN-LothQ:3.5.2 |
| Nocte | kho **kan** | nostril | WTF-PNN:504 |
| | kʰo **kan** | nostril | WTF-PNN:527 |
| | loŋ **kan** | cave | WTF-PNN:504 |
| | na **kan** | earhole | WTF-PNN:504 |
| Ntenyi | a **khwe** la | ear | GEM-CNL |
| Rongmei | nu-**kúan** | ear; earhole | AW-TBT:162,162 |
| Sangtam | nang **khi** | ear | GEM-CNL |
| | ¹naŋ¹**ki** | ear | AW-TBT:162 |
| Tangkhul | hai **khur** | vulva | JAM-Ety |
| | hay(-**khur**) | vulva | JAM-GSTC:184 |
| | khanā **khur** | earhole | JAM-Ety |
| | kharaŋ **khur** | anus | JAM-Ety |
| | laŋ **khor** | anus | JAM-Ety |
| Wancho | ha **kon** | cave | WTF-PNN:504 |
| | **kan** yet | den | WTF-PNN:504 |
| | ko **kan** | doorway, gate | WTF-PNN:504 |
| | kuŋ **kan** | nostril | WTF-PNN:504 |
| | mək-**ər** | eye | JAM-Ety |
| | na-**kor** | ear | JAM-Ety |
| Yimchungrü | ²nu²**gu** | ear | AW-TBT:108,162 |
| | ²nɯ²**kɯn** | ear; earhole | AW-TBT:162,162 |
| | nü **khün** | ear | GEM-CNL |
| Zeme | mi **kun** | ear | GEM-CNL |
| | ³mi³**kən** | ear | AW-TBT:162 |
| | ³mi³**kən** | ear | AW-TBT:162 |
| Mzieme | pe **kün** | ear | GEM-CNL |

### 1.4. Meithei

| | | | |
|---|---|---|---|
| Meithei | na-gi mə **khun** | ear canal | CYS-Meithei:3.6.4 |
| | na ton mə **khun** | nostril | CYS-Meithei:3.5.2 |
| | thi **gun** | anus / rectum | CYS-Meithei:9.12 [46] |

---

[46]Contrast the last syllables of Meithei **thi-gun** 'anus' (< ***kləy** SHIT + ***kor**) and **nâ-kông** 'ear'

|  | ²ma²**gu** | hole | AW-TBT:431 |
| Moyon | nar **khùr** ~ | nostril | DK-Moyon:3.5.2 |
|  | nàr **khùr** |  |  |
|  | nà bʌ **kòwrl** | ear canal | DK-Moyon:3.6.4 |
|  | sòw **khùr** ~ | vulva / labia | DK-Moyon:10.4.2 |
|  | sowr **khùr** |  |  |

### 1.5. Mikir

| Mikir | **kàn**-chêng | nose bridge | KHG-Mikir:40 |
|  | no **kan** | nose; nostril | GEM-CNL; JAM-Ety |
|  | nò **kàn** | nose; nostril | KHG-Mikir:115,115 |
|  | no **kan** ang lhor | nostril | JAM-Ety |
|  | no **ku** | ear | JAM-Ety |

### 1.7. Bodo-Garo = Barish

| Atong | na-**kur** | ear | JAM-Ety |
| Bodo | ha-**khor** | hole, valley | STC:349 |
| Dimasa | ha-**khor** | cave | STC:349 |
| Garo | a-**khol** | cave | STC:349 |
| Garo (Bangladesh) | ging a'-**kil**-ok | nostril | RB-GB |
|  | ging-**kil**-ok | nostril | RB-GB |
|  | ging-**kol** | nostril | RB-GB |
|  | na'-chil a'-**kil**-ok | earhole | RB-GB |
|  | na-chil a'-**kil**-ok | earhole | RB-GB |
|  | na-chil a'-**kol** | earhole | RB-GB |
|  | na-chil-ni a'-**kil**-ok | earhole | RB-GB |
|  | na-**kol** | earhole | RB-GB |
| Khiamngan | nǫu²kan | ear | AW-TBT:350 |
|  | ²nǫu²**kan** | ear | AW-TBT:162 |
|  | ²nǫu **kan** | earhole | AW-TBT:162 |
|  | ²nou-²**kan** | ear | AW-TBT:162 |
| Kokborok | kʰi-**kor** | anus | PT-Kok |

### 2.1.2. Bodic

| Tsangla (Motuo) | miŋ kʰ**or** | eye | SLZO-MLD |
|  | miŋ kʰ**u** | eye | SLZO-MLD |
| Tibetan (Written) | **kor** | round, circular; hollow in the ground, pit | STC:349 |

### 2.1.4. Tamangic

| Manang (Gyaru) | k**ɯɯ**² | hole | YN-Man:324 |
| Tamang (Risiangku) | ¹na **kal** | nostril | MM-TamRisQ:3.5.2 |

### 2.3.2. Kiranti

| Hayu | no **gu** no **gu**-ha | ear | BM-Hay:[72.1.78], |
| Limbu | nɛk **khoʔ** ba | ear | AW-TBT:162 |
|  | nɛk **koʔ** ba | ear | BM-PK7:50 |
| Thulung | no **ka** phlā | ear | JAM-Ety |

### 3.2. Qiangic

| Qiang (Mawo) | nə **kuǎ** ʐu | ear canal | SHK-MawoQ:3.6.4 |

### 3.3. rGyalrongic

| rGyalrong | ta sop kʰ**oi** jdu | anus / rectum | DQ-Jiarong:9.12 |

(< *r/g-na EAR / HEAR / LISTEN + **(93)** *guŋ ≍ *kuŋ HOLE / ORIFICE / ROUNDED PART).

| | | | |
|---|---|---|---|
| | tə rɲa **kʰoi** jdu | ear canal | DQ-Jiarong:3.6.4 |
| | tə çna **kʰoi** jdu | nostril | DQ-Jiarong:3.5.2 |
| rGyalrong (Eastern) | tə ʃna **kʰɐ** jdu | nostril | SHK-rGEQ:3.5.2 |

4.2. Nungic

| | | | | |
|---|---|---|---|---|
| Anong | duŋ-**khr** | hole | STC:169,350 | 47 |

8. Bai

| | | | |
|---|---|---|---|
| Bai | jũ³³ tɯ²¹ **kuã**⁵⁵ sʰ³³ | earwax | ZYS-Bai:3.6.6 |
| | jũ³³ tɯ²¹ **kuã**⁵⁵ tçi³³ ne²¹ | eardrum | ZYS-Bai:3.6.5 |
| | jũ³³ tɯ²¹ **kuã**⁵⁵ tçĩ⁵⁵ ne²¹ | earlobe | ZYS-Bai:3.6.1 |
| | jũ³³ tɯ²¹ **kuã**⁵⁵ ʔuĩ³³ xɯ³¹ | ear canal | ZYS-Bai:3.6.4 |
| Bai (Jianchuan) | jũ³³ tɯ²¹ **kuã**⁵⁵ | ear | JZ-Bai |

# (95)  *rik  PUBIC HAIR

This curious etymon has so far been found only in a couple of Kiranti languages, Limbu and Hayu. The meaning seems to be specifically PUBIC HAIR (of either sex). It seems to bear no relationship to any etymon reconstructed with the general meaning BODY HAIR. It is included in this section for convenience, since Limbu **hi-rā-mu-rik** contains VAGINA as its first element.

2.3.2. Kiranti

| | | | |
|---|---|---|---|
| Hayu | **rik** | pubic hair | BM-Hay:84.249 |
| Limbu | hi-rā-mu-**rik** | female pubic hair | JAM-Ety |
| | le mu **rik** | hair (pubic) | JAM-Ety |

* * *

We are not including roots for FEMALE/WOMAN in this volume, since they seem quite independent of etyma for the "female organs". (Apparent exceptions are a few forms from rGyalrong, e.g. NW rGyalrong **tə stə** 'female' < **(76)** *s-tu ✕ *tsu VAGINA; but these may be misglossed.) On the other hand, words for MALE do frequently interchange with words for the male genitals; some of these etyma are accordingly discussed in Chapter VII below.

---

[47]The first syllable is from PTB *dwaŋ (STC #169; HPTB p. 269). Cf. WT **doŋ**, WB **twâŋ** 'hole', **re-twâŋ** 'well'; Lahu **yɨ̀-tû** 'well'; Tiddim Chin **waːŋ** 'hole; make a hole'. The second syllable is analyzed as **khər** in STC.

# VI. Womb

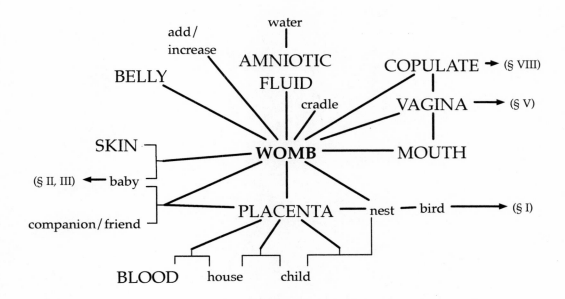

Words for WOMB or PLACENTA are frequently associated with notions of NEST, HOUSE, or BELLY. A slightly different metaphor is exemplified by Kanauri **chaŋ khŭl**, lit. "child skin", with the second element < PTB *gul ⋉ *gil ⋉ (H:58) *ʔul SKIN.

(96)                     ***s-b-rum***                     **WOMB / PLACENTA**

This etymon is not reconstructed in *STC*, but appears in *VSTB* pp. 225-6 and Matisoff 1983[1] #52.

This root occurs in Kamarupan, Himalayish, and perhaps Lolo-Burmese (Ugong). There is a possible Chinese comparandum (below). WT shows variation between **-r-** and **-l-**. The **b-** has been treated as a prefix and dropped everywhere but in WT and Chinese. For a similar doubly prefixed form set up for PTB, cf. ***s-b-rul*** SNAKE. WT **hlums** reflects an alternant ***s-lum***. This ***s-*** prefix seems to have preempted the initial consonant in Tsangla **shum, wak tsa çum** 'placenta'.

I now consider this etymon to be independent of ***s-lam*** (next etymon), even though I treated them as allofams in *VSTB* and *TIL*.

---

[1]"Translucent insights: a look at Proto-Sino-Tibetan through Gordon H. Luce's *Comparative Wordlist.*" *BSOAS* 46.3:462-76.

1.3. Naga

| | | | |
|---|---|---|---|
| Tangkhul | **rəm** | afterbirth; placenta | Bhat-TNV:84; JAM-Ety; JAM-VSTB |

2.1.2. Bodic

| | | | | |
|---|---|---|---|---|
| Tsangla (Central) | **shum** | placenta | SER-HSL/T:35 16 | |
| Tsangla (Motuo) | **wak tsa çum** | placenta | SLZO-MLD | |
| Tibetan (Amdo:Bla-brang) | **rəm** | hatch | ZMYYC:786.4 | |
| Tibetan (Written) | **hlums** | womb (resp.) | JAM-TIL:52 | |
| | **lhums** | womb | GHL-PPB:X.213; JAM-Ety; JAM-VSTB | |
| | **rum** | womb | GHL-PPB:X.213; JAM-Ety; JAM-TIL:52; JAM-VSTB | |
| | **sbrum**-pa | pregnant | JAM-VSTB; GEM-CNL | 2 |

6.2. Loloish

| | | | |
|---|---|---|---|
| Ugong | **lə̆ŋ** yέʔ | placenta | DB-Ugong:10.4.11 |

9. Sinitic

| | | | |
|---|---|---|---|
| Chinese (Old) | **b'i̯wăm** | mould, matrix | JAM-TIL:52 | 3 |

## Chinese comparandum

妊 **rèn** 'pregnant'

*GSR*: 667i    Karlgren: *ńi̯əm    Li: *njəmh    Baxter: *njɨms

Gong (1995 set 368) proposed that this Chinese word was cognate to WT **sbrum** < *smrum. However, the vowel and initial correspondences are not regular, and the comparison is not found in Gong's later publications. Schuessler (2007:441) treats 妊 **rèn** 'pregnant' as an internal Chinese derivation from 任 **rén** 'carry on the shoulder, to load'.

[ZJH]

### (97)                              *s-lam                         WOMB / PLACENTA

I now consider this to be a separate etymon from the phonologically similar root **(96)** ***s-b-rum** WOMB / PLACENTA. The Chinese comparandum 範 (see below) fits better with ***s-lam** with respect to the vowel, but there is no evidence within TB for a ***b**-prefix. See *VSTB* pp. 224-227; *HPTB* p. 250.

This etymon ***s-lam** may well be allofamically related to a group of roots with the same proto-rhyme, **(98)** ***pʷam** WOMB / PLACENTA / NEST / BELLY (next etymon).

See *HPTB* ***s-lam**, p. 250.

1.2. Kuki-Chin

| | | | |
|---|---|---|---|
| Lushai [Mizo] | **hlam** | placenta | JAM-Ety; JAM-VSTB |

[2]The word-family relationship between WT **rum** 'womb' and **sbrum-pa** 'pregnant' was already recognized by W. Simon (1975:250).

[3]The credit for recognizing the cognacy of this Chinese word with forms in Tibetan belongs to G.H. Luce (1981). See Matisoff 1983 #52. The labial initial is paralleled in WT **sbrum-pa** 'pregnant'.

| Tiddim | lam | placenta | JAM-VSTB |
| | ˋlam | placenta | JAM-Ety |
| **6.2. Loloish** | | | |
| Lahu | ɔ̀-lò | womb | JAM-VSTB |
| Lahu (Black) | ɔ̀-lò | womb; placenta | JAM-Ety; |
| | | | JAM-MLBM:89 |
| Mpi | loʔ⁶ | womb / placenta | JAM-MLBM:89 |
| **6.4. Jinuo** | | | |
| Jinuo (Baya/Banai) | a³³ lo⁴⁴ | placenta | DQ-JinA:147 |
| **7. Karenic** | | | |
| *Karen (Pho) | *də̀nˈlánˈ | womb | RBJ-KLS:442 |
| *Karen (Pho-Sgaw) | *də̀ hlɔ̀ | womb | RBJ-KLS:442 |
| *Karen (Sgaw) | *dɔ́ lɔ̀ | womb | RBJ-KLS:442 |
| Palaychi | də̀q-lɔ̀ | womb | JAM-VSTB; JAM-Ety; |
| | | | RBJ-KLS:442 |
| Pho (Bassein) | dɔ́n-lánʔ | womb | JAM-VSTB; JAM-Ety; |
| | | | RBJ-KLS:442 |
| Pho (Moulmein) | dən-lán | womb | JAM-VSTB; JAM-Ety; |
| | | | RBJ-KLS:442 |
| Karen (Sgaw) | dɔ́-lɔ̀ | womb | JAM-VSTB |
| Sgaw (Bassein) | dɔ́ lɔ̀ | womb | JAM-Ety; RBJ-KLS:442 |
| Sgaw (Moulmein) | dɔ́ lɔ̀ | womb | JAM-Ety; RBJ-KLS:442 |

The note marker "4" appears to the right of the Lahu (Black) JAM-MLBM:89 line.

## Chinese comparandum

範 **fàn** 'mould; rule, law'

*GSR*: 626d    Karlgren: *b'i̯wăm    Li: *bjamx    Baxter: *bjamʔ / *b(r)jomʔ

Baxter does not reconstruct this word. There are several possible reconstructions in his system, as indicated above. The Chinese word may be related to 凡 **fán** 'general rule, pattern' and 法 **fǎ** 'law, model', reconstructed *b(r)jom and *pjap respectively by Baxter, but this does not clarify the Old Chinese vocalism.

Although the semantics can be explained[5], the comparison with the PTB root is difficult to justify because of the mismatch of initial consonants.

[ZJH]

(98)        *pʷam        **WOMB / PLACENTA / NEST / BELLY**

Like **(1) *pʷu** EGG / BIRD / ROUND OBJECT above, some of the reflexes of ***pʷam** have initial w- **(98a)**, while others have an initial labial stop or derivative thereof **(98b)**. All these forms meaning 'womb / placenta / nest / belly' clearly represent the same etymon as **\*p-wam** BELLY, presented separately as **(98c)**. A further group of forms with nasal initials **(98d)** may also be brought into this word family. Finally,

---

[4]Lahu -o is the regular reflex of PTB and PLB *-am.

[5]For the semantic connection, cf. Latin and English *matrix* 'womb; a situation or surrounding substance in which something originates', ult. < *mater* 'mother'. [JAM]

there is a strong likelihood that **(97)** **\*s-lam** WOMB / PLACENTA is also allofamically related.

Some languages (e.g. Jingpho, Lashi, Zaiwa) show internal variation between stop and semivowel. The semantic association between WOMB and BELLY is too obvious to belabor. *Belly* was used frequently in early Mod. Eng. to mean WOMB: "As yet my wife hath not laid her belly" (*Plumpton Correspondence* 1549-50); "My belly did not blab, so I was still a Mayde" (William Warner, *Albion's England*, 1592); "Why, she may plead her belly at worst" (John Gay, *The Beggar's Opera*, 1728).[6]

See *HPTB* **\*pʷam**, pp. 47, 61; PLB **\*p-wam²**, pp. 46, 253.

### (98a)  \*wam  PLACENTA / WOMB

| | | | |
|---|---|---|---|
| 2.3. Mahakiranti | | | |
| *BSDTK | **\*wam** | placenta | BM-PK7:139 |
| 2.3.2. Kiranti | | | |
| Bahing | **wam** | placenta | BM-PK7:139; JAM-Ety; JAM-VSTB |
| | **wamt-** | placenta | BM-Bah |
| Khaling | **wäm** | placenta | BM-PK7:139 |
| Limbu | **a-wam** | placenta | JAM-Ety |
| Thulung | **wam** | placenta | BM-PK7:139 |
| | **wãm** | placenta | JAM-Ety; JAM-VSTB |
| | **wam** | placenta | NJA-Thulung |
| 6.1. Burmish | | | |
| Burmese (Written) | **wam** | womb / belly | JAM-TIL:52 |
| | **wam⁴** | womb | GHL-PPB:X.213 |

### (98b)  \*pam  WOMB / PLACENTA / NEST

| | | | |
|---|---|---|---|
| 1.3. Naga | | | |
| Tangkhul | **nao-pam** | womb | JAM-Ety |
| 1.4. Meithei | | | |
| Meithei | **naw phəm** | placenta | CYS-Meithei:10.4.11 |
| 1.7. Bodo-Garo = Barish | | | |
| Lalung | **pum** ba | womb | MB-Lal:56 |
| 2.3.2. Kiranti | | | |
| Hayu | tsã: **pim** | womb | BM-Hay:84.23,35 |
| 6.2. Loloish | | | |
| Sangkong | **pam³¹** | nest | LYS-Sangkon |

---

[6]In former times, a pregnant female criminal condemned to death was allowed to bring the baby to term before being executed. This practice was known as "pleading one's belly". See *OED* 1971:789.

# (98c)            *pʷam           BELLY

Several languages have compounds for BELLY where the first element is from *wam and the second apparently from (1c) *pu BALL / EGG / ROUND OBJECT: Hani (Caiyuan) ɔ³¹ pʰu³¹, Jinuo (Baya/Banai) vu⁵⁵ pʰu⁴⁴, Jinuo (Youle) ɣo⁵⁵ pʰu⁴⁴, and Karen u⁵⁵ pʰɤ⁵⁵.

See the long discussion of this etymon in *VSTB* pp. 124-7.

| | | | | |
|---|---|---|---|---|
| 0. Sino-Tibetan | | | | |
|   *Tibeto-Burman | **\*pam** | belly; stomach | JAM-VSTB:4a | |
| | **\*wam** | belly; stomach | JAM-VSTB:4b | |
| 1.1. North Assam | | | | |
|   Milang | mak-**pap** | abdomen | AT-MPB | 7 |
| 1.2. Kuki-Chin | | | | |
|   *Kuki-Naga-Chin | **\*pum** | belly | AW-TBT:857 | |
|   Lushai [Mizo] | **pum** | abdomen / belly | JAM-Ety | |
| | **pùm**~ pùŋ | belly | JAM-VSTB | |
| 1.3. Naga | | | | |
|   Konyak (Tamlu) | **hwum** | belly | JAM-VSTB:4b | |
|   Tangkhul | ā phur ā **phām** | abdomen / belly | JAM-Ety | |
| | ā phur ā **pham** | belly | JAM-VSTB:4a | |
| 3.1. Tangut | | | | |
|   Tangut [Xixia] | (ɣɔɦ) tefi | navel | NT-SGK:191 | |
| | ʔo | belly / abdomen | DQ-Xixia:5.7 | |
| | ʔo tī | navel | DQ-Xixia:5.7.1 | |
| 3.2. Qiangic | | | | |
|   Ergong (Northern) | **vəu⁵³** | belly / abdomen (outer bulge) | SHK-ErgNQ:5.7 | |
|   Ergong (Danba) | **vɛu** | belly / abdomen | SHK-ErgDQ:5.7 | |
|   Ergong (Daofu) | **vɑu** | belly / abdomen | DQ-Daofu:5.7 | |
|   Muya [Minyak] | **vu³⁵lø⁵³** | belly / abdomen | SHK-MuyaQ:5.7 | |
| 4.1. Jingpho | | | | |
|   Jingpho | pù-**hpam** | stomach | JAM-Ety | |
| | **wàm**-pūm | stomach complaint | JAM-TJLB:247 | |
| | **wun**-bu | navel | JAM-Ety | |
| 6.1. Burmish | | | | |
|   Achang (Lianghe) | oŋ³¹ tʂɑ³¹ | full, satiated | JZ-Achang | |
|   Achang (Longchuan) | ɔm³¹ tau³¹ | belly | JZ-Achang | |
|   Achang (Luxi) | ɔm⁵¹ tau⁵¹ | belly | JZ-Achang | |
| | ɔm⁵¹ tsa⁵¹ | full, satiated | JZ-Achang | |
|   Bola | vɛ³¹ tau³¹ | belly | DQ-Bola:119 | |
| | vɛ̃³¹ pɔt⁵⁵ | pregnant | DQ-Bola:1912 | |
|   Burmese (Written) | **wâm** | abdomen; belly | JAM-Ety; JAM-TJLB:247; JAM-VSTB:4b; PKB-WBRD | |

---

[7]The stop final in this compound may be due to assimilation to the initial **p-**.

| | | | |
|---|---|---|---|
| | **wâm**-pân | abdomen / belly | JAM-Ety |
| Lashi | khjei$^{55}$ **pham**$^{55}$ | stomach | DQ-Lashi:9.10 |
| | **wɔm**$^{33}$ pu:t$^{31}$ | pregnant | DQ-Lashi:10.4.14 |
| | **wɔm**$^{33}$ tou$^{33}$ | belly / abdomen | DQ-Lashi:5.7 |
| Maru [Langsu] | **vɛ̃**$^{35}$ pat$^{55}$ | pregnant | DQ-Langsu:10.4.14 |
| | **vɛ̃**$^{35}$ tuk$^{31}$ | belly / abdomen | DQ-Langsu:5.7 |
| | **wɛn** | belly | JAM-VSTB:4b |
| | **wɛn**-tok | abdomen, stomach | JAM-VSTB:4b |
| Atsi [Zaiwa] | khji$^{21}$ **pham**$^{21}$ | stomach | JZ-Zaiwa |
| | **vàm** | belly | JAM-VSTB:4b |
| | **vam**$^{21}$ | belly | JZ-Zaiwa |
| 6.2. Loloish | | | |
| *Loloish | ***wam**$^{2}$ | belly | DB-PLolo:133 |
| Akha | **ù**-máʔ | abdomen | JAM-VSTB |
| | **u**ˬ maˆ | abdomen / belly | JAM-Ety |
| Hani (Dazhai) | **u**$^{31}$ de$^{31}$ | belly | JZ-Hani |
| Hani (Caiyuan) | **ɔ**$^{31}$ p$^{h}$u$^{31}$ | belly | JZ-Hani |
| Hani (Gelanghe) | **u**$^{31}$ ma̱$^{33}$ | belly | JZ-Hani |
| Hani (Shuikui) | **ɣu**$^{31}$ mɔ$^{33}$ | belly | JZ-Hani |
| Lahu (Nyi) | **g'aw**ˇ tu: shi_ | navel | DB-Lahu:120 |
| *Common Lahu | ***g'o**ˇ | belly | DB-PLolo:133 |
| Lahu (Bakeo) | **g'u**ˇ tu: shi_ | navel | DB-Lahu:120 |
| Lahu (Shehleh) | **g'u**ˬ tu: | navel | DB-Lahu:120 |
| Lahu | **g̈ô**-pè | belly | JAM-VSTB:4b |
| Lahu (Banlan) | **u**ˇ tu: shi_ | navel | DB-Lahu:120 |
| Lahu (Black) | **g̈ô**- | belly | JAM-TJLB:247 |
| | **g̈û**(~ **g̈ɔ̂**)-tu-câʔ | umbilical cord | JAM-DL:1138 |
| | **g̈û**(~ **g̈ɔ̂**)-tu-šī | navel | JAM-DL:1138 |
| | **ɣô**-pè~ **ɣû**-pè | abdomen / belly | JAM-Ety |
| | **ɣû**-tu-šī-câʔ | umbilical cord | JAM-DL:1129 |
| | **ɣu**$^{53}$ pe$^{31}$ | belly | JZ-Lahu |
| | **ɣu**$^{53}$ ty̩$^{33}$ si$^{11}$ | navel | JZ-Lahu |
| Lahu (Yellow) | **ʔu**$^{55}$ piʔ$^{21}$ | belly | JZ-Lahu |
| | **ʔu**$^{55}$ tu$^{33}$ ɕiʔ$^{21}$ | navel | JZ-Lahu |
| Nusu (Central/Zhizhiluo) | **va**$^{31}$ lɔ̱$^{53}$ | belly | DQ-NusuA:119. |
| Nusu (Central) | **va**$^{31}$ lɔ$^{53}$ | belly | DQ-NusuB:119. |
| Nusu (Northern) | **vɔ**$^{35}$ | belly | JZ-Nusu |
| Nusu (Central) | **vɑ**$^{31}$ lɔ$^{53}$ | belly | JZ-Nusu |
| Nusu (Southern) | **yɛ**$^{31}$ dʐɔ$^{55}$ | full, satiated | JZ-Nusu |
| Yi (Dafang) | **ɣɔ**$^{13}$ mo$^{55}$ | belly | JZ-Yi |
| Yi (Xide) | **vu**$^{55}$-dʑi$^{21}$ ko$^{33}$ | belly | CSL-YIzd |
| | **vu**$^{55}$-ȵi$^{33}$ | pregnant | CSL-YIzd |
| 6.4. Jinuo | | | |
| Jinuo (Buyuan) | **vu**$^{42}$ mɔ$^{44}$ | belly | JZ-Jinuo |
| Jinuo (Baya/Banai) | **vu**$^{55}$ pø$^{33}$ | pregnant | DQ-JinA:1981 |
| | **vu**$^{55}$ p$^{h}$u$^{44}$ | belly | DQ-JinA:122 |
| Jinuo (Youle) | **ɣo**$^{55}$ pø$^{44}$ | pregnant | JZ-Jinuo |
| | **ɣo**$^{55}$ pɹɤ$^{33}$ | full, satiated | JZ-Jinuo |
| | **ɣo**$^{55}$ p$^{h}$u$^{44}$ | belly | JZ-Jinuo |
| 7. Karenic | | | |
| Karen (Sgaw/Hinthada) | **u**$^{55}$ p$^{h}$ɤ$^{55}$ | belly | DQ-KarenB:122 |

| (98d) | *mam | **WOMB / PLACENTA / NEST** |
|---|---|---|

This etymon probably also stands in an allofamic relationship with **(98)** **\*pʷam** WOMB / PLACENTA / NEST / BELLY, in view of the identical rhymes that they share. Perhaps these forms with initial **m-** descend from fusions with the bodypart prefix **\*mi-** (< **\*mi-n** 'person') **(H:449)** **\*r-mi(y)** PERSON / MAN, i.e. **\*mi-wam** or **\*mi-pam**.

1.1. North Assam

| *Tani | *mam | placenta | JS-HCST:295 | |
|---|---|---|---|---|
| Padam [Abor] | a-**mam** | placenta | JS-HCST | |
| Padam-Mising [Abor-Miri] | a **mam** | placenta | JAM-Ety | |
| | **mam**-ruk | womb | JAM-Ety | |
| Bengni | nɯ-**mam** | placenta | JS-HCST | |
| Bokar | nə-**mam** | placenta; womb | JS-HCST; JS-Tani | |
| Bokar Lhoba | nə **mam** | placenta | SLZO-MLD | |

2.1.2. Bodic

| Tshona (Mama) | n**ʌm**¹³ nʌŋ⁵⁵ | placenta | SLZO-MLD | |
|---|---|---|---|---|

2.3.1. Kham-Magar-Chepang-Sunwar

| Magar | **mim** | nest | AH-CSDPN:03a.013 | |
|---|---|---|---|---|

2.3.2. Kiranti

| Bantawa | **mon** | placenta | JAM-Ety | 8 |
|---|---|---|---|---|
| Hayu | tsat-**nom**-ri | placenta; womb | JAM-Ety | 9 |

| (99) | *ba(:)y ≍ *pa(:)y | **WOMB / PLACENTA / PREGNANT** |
|---|---|---|

This root has been identified in Kamarupan and Himalayish. The reconstructed rhyme **\*-ay** is directly reflected by the Mru, Tiddim, Mizo, and Chepang reflexes, and indirectly by Written Tibetan and Mikir **-e**, which are also the regular reflexes of **\*-ay**. See Matisoff 1985a #140 and *HPTB* pp. 206-219 for many corroborative cognate sets. I am also tentatively including the Lakher (Mara) word for 'add; increase' in this set, since the same association between WOMB/PLACENTA and ADD/INCREASE is found in the etymon (**(101)** **\*tsat** WOMB / PLACENTA / NEST, below).

See *HPTB* **\*pa:y**, p. 210.

1.2. Kuki-Chin

| Lakher [Mara] | **bai** | add to | JAM-GSTC:107 |
|---|---|---|---|
| Lushai [Mizo] | p**ăi** | conceive / pregnant | JAM-GSTC:140 |
| Tiddim | ´**pa:i** | conceive / pregnant | JAM-GSTC:140 |
| Tiddim Chin | ´**pa:i**/´pa:i | conceive / pregnant / carry a child | EJAH-TC |
| Tiddim | `**pa:i** | conceive / pregnant | JAM-GSTC:140 |

1.5. Mikir

| Mikir | o so-a **pe** | placenta | JAM-Ety |
|---|---|---|---|
| | **pe** | womb | JAM-Ety |

---

⁸This form apparently shows dissimilation of the second nasal.

⁹This form, on the other hand, seems to show dissimilation of the first nasal, as does the Tshona (Mama) form below.

1.6. Mru

| | | | | |
|---|---|---|---|---|
| Mru | a⁴bɑi² | placenta, afterbirth | GHL-PPB:Q.73 | |

1.7. Bodo-Garo = Barish

| | | | | |
|---|---|---|---|---|
| Bodo | **pi** sá kó | womb | JAM-Ety | |
| Garo (Bangladesh) | **bi**-bil | womb | RB-GB | |

2.1.2. Bodic

| | | | | |
|---|---|---|---|---|
| Tibetan (Batang) | **bi**¹³ khõ⁵⁵ | womb | DQ-Batang:10.4.8 | 10 |
| | **bi**¹³ tsho⁵³ | amniotic fluid | DQ-Batang:10.4.10 | |
| Tibetan (Written) | **be**-snabs | vaginal mucus at childbirth | JAM-Ety | 11 |

2.3.1. Kham-Magar-Chepang-Sunwar

| | | | | |
|---|---|---|---|---|
| Chepang (Eastern) | **pay?** | placenta | RC-ChepQ:10.4.11 | |

2.3.2. Kiranti

| | | | | |
|---|---|---|---|---|
| Limbu | sāi **be**-rā | placenta | JAM-Ety | |
| | sara **phe** | womb | BM-Lim | |

(100)   * $\frac{m}{l}$ -ŋal   **WOMB / PLACENTA**

This etymon is well-represented in Himalayish (with the *m- prefix in WT) and in Qiangic (with a lateral prefix in Ergong and rGyalrong). The root-initial *ŋ- has become n- in several languages.

The first syllables of Meithei **naw phəm** 'placenta' and Tangkhul **nao-pam** 'womb' are apparently not cognate, since *-al > Meithei -al or -an (cf. *m-kal ≍ *s-gal SMALL OF BACK > Meithei **nam-gal ~ nam-gan**) and > Tangkhul -ay (cf. *baːl FILTH / EXCREMENT > Tangkhul **páy**). S. Imoba 2004 (*Manipuri to English Dictionary*, p. 202) records **-naw** 'small, little', **naw-wà** 'baby', **nawsum** 'cradle', and **nawpu-bə** 'gestation, pregnancy'.

2.1.1. Western Himalayish

| | | | | |
|---|---|---|---|---|
| Bunan | **ŋal** | womb | SBN-BunQ:10.4.8 | |

2.1.2. Bodic

| | | | | |
|---|---|---|---|---|
| Tibetan (Written) | **mn̥al** | womb | JAM-Ety | |

2.3.1. Kham-Magar-Chepang-Sunwar

| | | | | |
|---|---|---|---|---|
| Chepang (Eastern) | so **nal?** | womb | RC-ChepQ:10.4.8 | 12 |

2.3.2. Kiranti

| | | | | |
|---|---|---|---|---|
| Limbu | siŋ **nā** | womb | JAM-Ety | |
| Thulung | **ŋe** le | womb | NJA-Thulung | |

3.2. Qiangic

| | | | | |
|---|---|---|---|---|
| Ergong (Northern) | **lŋa**⁵³ jo¹³ | womb | SHK-ErgNQ:10.4.8 | |
| | **lŋa**⁵³ ɕip⁵³ | amniotic sac / bag of waters | SHK-ErgNQ:10.4.9 | |

[10]The second syllable probably means 'house' (cf. WT **khaŋ-pa**).
[11]The second element means 'snot; nasal mucus'.
[12]The first syllable means 'child'.

| Ergong (Daofu) | ɬŋɑ tɕho | pregnant | DQ-Daofu:10.4.14 |
| 3.3. rGyalrongic | | | |
| rGyalrong (NW) | tə lŋa ktɕʰim | amniotic sac / bag of waters | SHK-rGNWQ:10.4.9 |
| | tə lŋa sa scçe | womb | SHK-rGNWQ:10.4.8 |

# (101)  *tsat  WOMB / PLACENTA / NEST

This root is well distributed among the subgroups of TB, with strong (though rather scattered) cognates in Kamarupan, Himalayish, Lolo-Burmese, Jingpho, and Karenic. The basic meaning of this etymon may be 'add, increase; breed, bear young', since that is the meaning of the free Jingpho verb **jàt** (Hanson, p. 206; Dai Qingxia et al., 1983:345), as well as of the Thulung form.

1.2. Kuki-Chin
| Tha'oa | tat¹ | womb | GHL-PPB:O.13 |
| | tat⁴ | womb | GHL-PPB:O.13 |

2.1.3. Lepcha
| Lepcha | a yeñ čot | placenta | JAM-Ety |

2.3.1. Kham-Magar-Chepang-Sunwar
| Chepang | chyut | nest | AH-CSDPN:03a.013 |
| | cʰyut | nest | SIL-Chep:3.A.13 |

2.3.2. Kiranti
| Hayu | tsat-nom-ri | placenta; womb | JAM-Ety |
| Thulung | cat- | add, put on top | NJA-Thulung |

4.1. Jingpho
| Jingpho | jàt | add, increase, augment; breed, bear young, multiply (of beasts) | OH-DKL:206 |
| | pù-jàt | womb | JAM-Ety |
| | pū-jàt | snake's nest | JCD:673 [13] |
| | pə jàt | womb | JAM-Ety |

6.1. Burmish
| Achang (Xiandao) | tʂʰɔʔ⁵⁵ | placenta | DQ-Xiandao:144 |
| Bola | tʃauʔ³¹ tui⁵⁵ | womb | DQ-Bola:146 |
| Lashi | tso³³ sɔt⁵⁵ | womb | DQ-Lashi:10.4.8 [14] |
| Maru [Langsu] | tsɔ³⁵ sat⁵⁵ | womb | DQ-Langsu:10.4.8 |

6.2. Loloish
| Ahi | i³³ tɕʻe³³ | placenta | LMZ-AhiQ:10.4.11 |
| | i³³tɕhe³³ | placenta | CK-YiQ:10.4.11 |
| Bisu | aŋ-jàt-ja-húm | womb | PB-Bisu:16 |

7. Karenic
| Karen (Sgaw/Hinthada) | la⁵⁵ tθa³¹ | placenta | DQ-KarenB:147 |

[13]Cf. Jingpho **pū ~ ləpū** 'snake'.
[14]Lashi **tso³³** and Maru **tsɔ³⁵** mean 'child'.

## (102)      *r-bu ⪥ *pru      NEST / WOMB / PLACENTA

This etymon is quite widely distributed, appearing in Kamarupan, Lolo-Burmese, Jingpho-Nung, Qiangic, and Karenic, with a key Himalayish cognate in Written Tibetan.

There is a good Chinese comparandum, 胞 *GSR* 1113b (see below).

The root shows metathetic variants, with the *r- treated either as a prefix (*r-bu; cf. the Aimol, Kom Rem, and Moyon reflexes) or as a post-initial glide (*pru; cf. the WT reflex). This is similar to **(104)** *r-ku ⪥ *kru NEST / UTERUS / AMNIOTIC SAC, below. It also shows variation in the voicing of the initial consonant, both in TB and in Chinese (*GSR* gives two OC readings, *pộg and *p'ộg).

In passing, *STC* (p. 102) gives a few forms meaning NEST from Kuki-Chin languages, without offering any reconstruction. See also **(113)** *bu CHILD, quite distinct from the present etymon.

See *HPTB* *pru(w), p. 199.

### 0. Sino-Tibetan

| | | | |
|---|---|---|---|
| *Sino-Tibetan | *prəɣw/phrəɣw | womb | WSC-SH:161 |

### 1.1. North Assam

| | | | | |
|---|---|---|---|---|
| Padam-Mising [Abor-Miri] | mi-**bu** | placenta | JAM-Ety | 15 |
| | mib-**bo** | placenta | JAM-Ety | |
| | mib-**bu** | placenta | JAM-Ety | |
| Apatani | paro **pu**-wa | nest (hen's) | JS-Tani | |
| | paro **pɯ**-a | nest (hen's) | JS-Tani | |
| Damu | **bu**-la | placenta | JS-Tani | |
| | **pu**-ra | placenta | JS-Tani | |
| Darang [Taraon] | ɑ⁵⁵ **po**⁵⁵ | placenta | SLZO-MLD | |
| Kaman [Miju] | **mphău**⁵³ | nest | ZMYYC:368.48 | |
| Milang | ta-**pyu**-ap | nest | AT-MPB | |

### 1.2. Kuki-Chin

| | | | | |
|---|---|---|---|---|
| Aimol | **rəbu** | nest | STC:p.102 | |
| Ashö [Sho] | ə **bü** | nest | STC:p.102 | |
| Khami | tə **bu** | nest | STC:p.102 | |
| Awa Khumi | ă tă **buʔ²** | womb / placenta | GHL-PPB:O.13 | |
| Kom Rem | nəi **rəbu** | placenta; womb | T-KomRQ:10.4.11,10.4.8 | |
| Lai (Hakha) | **bu**· θ | build a nest | STC:p.102 | 16 |
| | ə **bu** | nest | STC:p.102 | |
| Lushai [Mizo] | **bu** | nest | GEM-CNL; STC:p.102 | |
| Thado | ʌ **bú** | nest | THI1972:59 | |

### 1.3. Naga

| | | | |
|---|---|---|---|
| Rongmei | **bou** | nest | GEM-CNL |

### 1.4. Meithei

| | | | |
|---|---|---|---|
| Moyon | næ̀ **rubów** | womb | DK-Moyon:10.4.8 |

---

[15]The first syllable probably means 'person' (see **(H:449)** *r-mi(y) PERSON / MAN), i.e. PLACENTA = PERSON + NEST.

[16]The last consonant is from suffixal *-t (see *STC* pp. 102-3).

**1.7. Bodo-Garo = Barish**

| | | | | |
|---|---|---|---|---|
| Dimasa | **bu** thup | nest | GEM-CNL | |
| Kokborok | **bə**-tʰɔ | nest | PT-Kok | |

**2.1.2. Bodic**

| | | | | |
|---|---|---|---|---|
| Tibetan (Written) | (ḥ)**phru**-ba | uterus; placenta | WSC-SH:161 | |
| | (ḥ)p'**ru**-ma | womb of animals | JAM-Ety | 17 |

**3.1. Tangut**

| | | | |
|---|---|---|---|
| Tangut [Xixia] | **mbu**¹ | womb | MVS-Grin |

**3.2. Qiangic**

| | | | |
|---|---|---|---|
| Qiang (Mawo) | wuk nə:¹ **bu** | nest | ZMYYC:368.8 |
| Qiang (Taoping) | i³¹tshie⁵⁵χ**bu**²⁴¹ | nest | ZMYYC:368.9 |

**3.3. rGyalrongic**

| | | | |
|---|---|---|---|
| rGyalrong | ta **pu** ktɕɛm | womb | DQ-Jiarong:10.4.8 |
| rGyalrong (Northern) | ta **po** tso fkəm | womb | SHK-rGNQ:10.4.8 |
| | ta **po** tso ɻqʰu | amniotic sac / bag of waters | SHK-rGNQ:10.4.9 |
| rGyalrong (Eastern) | ta **pu** wan dʑi | placenta | SHK-rGEQ:10.4.11 |
| | ta **pu** kəstʃiwutʂitətʃi | amniotic fluid | SHK-rGEQ:10.4.10 |
| | ta **pꞏ** sta | amniotic sac / bag of waters | SHK-rGEQ:10.4.9 |
| | ta **pꞏ** tʃʰem | womb | SHK-rGEQ:10.4.8 |

**4.1. Jingpho**

| | | | |
|---|---|---|---|
| Jingpho | **pù**-jàt | womb | JAM-Ety |
| | **pə** jàt | womb | JAM-Ety |

**4.2. Nungic**

| | | | |
|---|---|---|---|
| Trung [Dulong] | **pɯ**³¹tɕiʔ⁵⁵dăŋ⁵³ | nest | ZMYYC:368.46 |

**6.2. Loloish**

| | | | | |
|---|---|---|---|---|
| Bisu | ʔaŋ **pʰò** | nest | DB-Bisu | |
| Gazhuo | **pao**³³ | placenta | DQ-Gazhuo:10.4.11 | 18 |
| Hani (Dazhai) | **bɯ**³¹ | nest | ZMYYC:368.31 | |
| Lipho | **po**⁵⁵lo³³ | placenta | CK-YiQ:10.4.11 | |
| Nasu | **bɤ**³³ | placenta | CK-YiQ:10.4.11 | |

**7. Karenic**

| | | | |
|---|---|---|---|
| Pa-O | **pò** khròŋ | uterus | DBS-PaO |

**8. Bai**

| | | | | |
|---|---|---|---|---|
| Bai | ji⁵⁵ **pao**⁵⁵ | placenta / afterbirth | ZYS-Bai:10.4.11 | 19 |

**9. Sinitic**

| | | | |
|---|---|---|---|
| Chinese (Mandarin) | **pɑo** | womb | GSR:1113b |
| | **p'ɑo** | womb | GSR:1113b |
| Chinese (Middle) | **pau** | womb | WSC-SH:161 |
| | **phau** | womb | WSC-SH:161 |

---

¹⁷Quite distinct etymologically is WT **bu-snod** 'womb', where the first syllable is a morpheme meaning 'child' **(113) *bu** CHILD and the second syllable is from **(111) *s-nut ≍ *s-not** MOUTH / VESSEL / WOMB, below.

¹⁸This is evidently a loan from Chinese 胞 (see below).

¹⁹This Bai forms looks like a loan from Chinese (cf. Mandarin 胞 **bāo**).

| Chinese (Old) | phrəgw | womb | WSC-SH:161 |
| | prəgw | womb | WSC-SH:161 |
| Chinese (Old/Mid) | pộg/pɑu | womb | GSR:1113b |
| | p'ộg/p'ɑu | womb | GSR:1113b |

## Chinese comparandum

胞 **bāo** 'womb'

*GSR*: 1113b          Karlgren: *pộg          Li: *prəgw          Baxter: *pru

This cognate set is in Bodman 1980:142 set 310, Coblin 1986:161, Gong 1995 set 61, and Schuessler 2007:157.

The regular correspondence between OC final *-əgw (Li), *-u (Baxter) and TB *-əw (or *-u) is well-attested. Examples include 'nine' TB *d-kəw, OC *kjəgw (Li)/*kʷjuʔ (Baxter); 'dove/pigeon' TB *khəw, OC *kjəgw/*k(r)ju (Baxter); and (1b) *pu EGG (elsewhere in this volume).

The TB final also corresponds to OC *-ug (Li)/*-o (Baxter), as seen in (53a) *s-nəw BREAST / MILK / SUCK.

[ZJH]

# (103)                     *tsaŋ                     NEST / WOMB / PLACENTA

This root seems solidly established for Himalayish, where it means mostly NEST, but sometimes CRADLE, CAGE, or WOMB. However, many of these forms may be loans from Tibetan. The etymon also clearly appears in Lolo-Burmese, where it means WOMB / PLACENTA, and in at least one Qiangic language (Queyu), where it means NEST.

### 2.1.2. Bodic

| Kaike | chāng | nest | AH-CSDPN:03a.013 |
| Tshona (Mama) | tshʌŋ⁵⁵ | nest | ZMYYC:368.6 |
| Tibetan (Amdo:Bla-brang) | tshaŋ | nest | ZMYYC:368.4 |
| Tibetan (Amdo:Zeku) | tshaŋ | nest | ZMYYC:368.5 |
| | tṣʰaŋ | nest | JS-Amdo:635 |
| Tibetan (Jirel) | chāngq | nest; cradle | AH-CSDPN:03a.013,06a.38 |
| Tibetan (Khams:Dege) | tshaŋ⁵³ | nest | ZMYYC:368.3 |
| Tibetan (Lhasa) | tshaŋ⁵⁵ | nest | ZMYYC:368.2 |
| Tibetan (Sherpa) | čhāng | nest | AH-CSDPN:03a.013 |
| | chāng | cradle | AH-CSDPN:06a.38 |
| Tibetan (Written) | tshaṅ | nest | GEM-CNL |
| | tshang | nest | JS-Tib:635 |
| | tshaŋ | nest | ZMYYC:368.1 |
| | tshaŋ-ŋu | cradle | HAJ-TED:444 |

### 2.1.4. Tamangic

| *Tamang | *dzaŋ³ | nest | MM-K78:43 |
| | *ᴬdzaŋ | nest | MM-Thesis:348 |
| Gurung (Ghachok) | cõh | nest | SIL-Gur:3.A.13 |
| Gurung | cọh | nest | AH-CSDPN:03a.013 |
| Gurung (Ghachok) | ³cõ | nest | MM-K78:43 |

| | | | |
|---|---|---|---|
| Gurung | ³tsõ = tsõh | nest | MM-Thesis:348 |
| Manang (Gyaru) | dzaŋ² | nest | YN-Man:318 |
| Manang (Ngawal) | ³tsaŋ | nest | MM-K78:43 |
| Manang (Prakaa) | ²tsaŋ | nest | HM-Prak:0066 |
| | ³tsaŋ | nest | MM-Thesis:348 |
| Tamang (Risiangku) | ³tsaŋ | nest | MM-K78:43; |
| | | | MM-Thesis:348 |
| Tamang (Sahu) | cāhng | nest | AH-CSDPN:03a.013 |
| | ³caŋ | nest | MM-K78:43 |
| | ³tsaŋ | nest | MM-Thesis:348 |
| Tamang (Taglung) | tsaŋ | nest | MM-Thesis:348 |
| | ³tsaŋ | nest | MM-K78:43; |
| | | | MM-Thesis:348 |
| Thakali | ʼneme cāhng | nest | AH-CSDPN:03a.013 |
| Thakali (Marpha) | ³tsaŋ | nest | MM-K78:43 |
| | ¹¹dzaŋ | nest | MM-Thesis:348 |
| Thakali (Syang) | ³tsaŋ | nest | MM-K78:43 |
| | ³¹tsaŋ, ³¹tsaᶠŋ | nest | MM-Thesis:348 |
| Thakali (Tukche) | ʼneme cahŋ | nest; cage | SIL-Thak:3.A.13,6.A.12 |
| | ³caŋ | nest | MM-K78:43 |
| | ¹neme ³tsaŋ | nest | MM-Thesis:348 |

**2.3.2. Kiranti**

| | | | |
|---|---|---|---|
| Hayu | tsã: pim | womb | BM-Hay:84.23,35 |

**3.2. Qiangic**

| | | | |
|---|---|---|---|
| Queyu (Yajiang) [Zhaba] | tshã⁵³ | nest | ZMYYC:368.16 |

**6.1. Burmish**

| | | | |
|---|---|---|---|
| Bola | ŋji⁵⁵ tʃʰɔ³⁵ | placenta | DQ-Bola:144 |
| Burmese (Written) | chaṅ-ʔim | womb | JAM-Ety |

**6.2. Loloish**

| | | | |
|---|---|---|---|
| Bisu | tʃhàŋ tʃhàŋ | placenta | PB-Bisu:15 |

## (104)      *r-ku ≍ *kru      NEST / UTERUS / AMNIOTIC SAC

This root is set up on slender but rather convincing evidence, if we are willing to admit relationship via metathesis between Angami forms with **kr-**, and Qiangic forms with **ɹaq-**. (For another etymon that shows a similar metathesis of prefixal and medial -**r**-, cf. **(102) *r-bu ≍ *pru** NEST / WOMB / PLACENTA, above. The semantic scope of the Qiangic forms extends to AMNIOTIC SAC. In many TB languages, as in English, the amniotic fluid is referred to simply by the word for WATER (cf. Eng. "Her water broke"), e.g. Maru **ɣək³¹** 'water; amniotic fluid' (< **(164) *rəy** WATER / LIQUID, below), Baima **ʃuɛ³⁵** 'amniotic fluid' (< Chinese; cf. Mand. 水 **shuǐ** 'water').

**1.3. Naga**

| | | | |
|---|---|---|---|
| Angami (Khonoma) | pera **kru** | nest | GEM-CNL |
| Angami (Kohima) | **kru** | nest | GEM-CNL |

**3.2. Qiangic**

| | | | |
|---|---|---|---|
| Qiang (Mawo) | tʃə **ɹaqu** | amniotic sac / bag of waters | SHK-MawoQ:10.4.9 |

| | tʂə ɹaqu | womb | JS-Mawo |
|---|---|---|---|
| 3.3. rGyalrongic | | | |
| rGyalrong (Northern) | ta po tso ɻ̥qʰu | amniotic sac / bag of waters | SHK-rGNQ:10.4.9 |

## (105)  *tsyul ≍ *tsywal   WOMB / PLACENTA / UMBILICAL CORD

Some reflexes of this etymon have simple sibilant initials (e.g. Paangkhua **sùul**, Kham **sal**), while some have dental or palatal affricates, others have dental stops (e.g. Matupi and Maru) or even prefixed affricates (e.g. Pumi **stʃuɑ⁵⁵**). The vocalism of the reflexes ranges from **-u-** to **-wa-** to **-o-** to **-a-**. Semantically, this etymon varies in meaning from WOMB/PLACENTA to NEST and UMBILICAL CORD. This etymon is found throughout Chin and sporadically elsewhere in Kamarupan (Mru), and is also solidly attested in Qiangic. Several resemblant forms in TB languages of Nepal are loans from Nepali: Chantyal **sal** 'placenta', Thakali **sāl** 'umbilical cord', Kham **'sāl** 'id.', Limbu **sāi be-rā** 'placenta' (M. Mazaudon, p.c. 2008). Pattani (Western Himalayish) **šwal** 'placenta, umbilical cord' may also be a borrowing from Indo-Aryan.

| 1.2. Kuki-Chin | | | | |
|---|---|---|---|---|
| Hwalngau | sʻuːl⁴ | womb | GHL-PPB:O.13 | |
| Khualsim | sʻuːl⁴ | womb | GHL-PPB:O.13 | |
| Lai (Hakha) | sʻul² | womb | GHL-PPB:O.13 | 20 |
| Lailenpi | məˊcʻuʔ⁴ | womb | GHL-PPB:O.13 | |
| Lakher [Mara] | chhi < tshuul | womb | LL-PRPL | 21 |
| | ²tshi | womb | AW-TBT:487 | |
| Lothvo (Hiranpi) | tsə⁴ | womb | GHL-PPB:O.13 | |
| | tsʻɤ⁴ | womb | GHL-PPB:O.13 | |
| Lushai [Mizo] | chhûl | womb; placenta | JAM-Ety | |
| | chul | womb | JAM-Ety; JAM-VSTB | |
| | chʻuːl⁴ | womb | GHL-PPB:O.13 | |
| | tshùul | womb | AW-TBT:487; LL-PRPL | |
| Matupi | tʻul² | womb | GHL-PPB:O.13 | |
| Mera | ă tsʻiʔ¹ | womb | GHL-PPB:O.13 | |
| | ă tsʻiʔ⁵ | womb | GHL-PPB:O.13 | |
| Paangkhua | ma sùul | womb | LL-PRPL | |
| | sùul-ìn | womb | LL-PRPL | |
| Thanphum | ăˋtʻuːn¹ | womb | GHL-PPB:O.13 | |
| Tiddim | sʻul⁴ | womb | GHL-PPB:O.13 | |
| Zotung | sʻwɛ⁵ | womb | GHL-PPB:O.13 | 22 |
| 1.6. Mru | | | | |
| Mru | **thua** | womb | JAM-Ety; JAM-VSTB | 23 |

---

[20]It is not clear what phonetic feature Luce was attempting to transcribe with his symbol "sʻ" (e.g. in Hakha, Hwalngau, Khualsim, Tiddim, and Zotung); a Hakha consultant in Berkeley pronounces this word with what sounds like an ordinary [s]. In general, PTB *s- > Proto-Chin *t(h)-, while PTB *ts- > Proto-Chin *s-.

[21]Contra Löffler 1966, I do not assign the Lushai and Mru forms to (76) *s-tu ≍ *tsu VAGINA.

[22]Luce gives another Zotung form **ʃɯ¹** for WOMB that I include under (107) *(t)sip ≍ *(t)sup NEST / WOMB / SCROTUM, below.

[23]Contra Löffler 1966, I do not assign the Lushai and Mru forms to (76) *s-tu ≍ *tsu VAGINA.

### 2.1.2. Bodic

| | | | | |
|---|---|---|---|---|
| Tibetan (Written) | **śa**-ma | placenta, afterbirth | HAJ-TED:556 | 24 |

### 2.1.3. Lepcha

| | | | | |
|---|---|---|---|---|
| Lepcha | a yeň **tyól** | placenta | JAM-Ety | |
| | bam-**tyól** mat | copulate | JAM-Ety | 25 |
| | kŭp-**tʻor** | womb | JAM-Ety | 26 |
| | tă-a'yŭ **tyól** | menses | JAM-Ety | 27 |

### 2.2. Newar

| | | | |
|---|---|---|---|
| Newar | **swạ/swạn**- | nest | AH-CSDPN:03a.013 |

### 3.2. Qiangic

| | | | | |
|---|---|---|---|---|
| Ergong (Danba) | **mdʐo** | nest | ZMYYC:368.14 | 28 |
| Ergong (Northern) | **tɕʰə**⁵³ | placenta | SHK-ErgNQ:10.4.11 | |
| Ersu | **xuɑi⁵⁵ntʂhɛ⁵⁵** | nest | ZMYYC:368.18 | |
| Pumi (Jinghua) | **stʃuɑ⁵⁵** | nest | ZMYYC:368.11 | |
| | tsy⁵⁵ **tsuɑ̃⁵⁵** | placenta | JZ-Pumi | |
| Pumi (Taoba) | **ɕua⁵³** | nest | ZMYYC:368.10 | |
| Qiang (Mawo) | **tsʌ** | amniotic fluid | SHK-MawoQ:10.4.10 | |
| Qiang (Taoping) | i³¹**tshie⁵⁵**χbu²⁴¹ | nest | ZMYYC:368.9 | |
| Shixing | **dʐyɛ³³khuɐ⁵⁵** | nest | ZMYYC:368.20 | |

### 3.3. rGyalrongic

| | | | |
|---|---|---|---|
| rGyalrong | ta **lɟja** | placenta | DQ-Jiarong:10.4.11 |

## (106)                   *toŋ                   NEST / WOMB

This sparsely attested and speculative etymon rests on the Jingpho-Nung and Tujia forms. Apparently distinct is Bahing **dzok-** 'nest'. The WB form "**thok**" cited in *ZMYYC* #368 appears to be spurious.

### 4.1. Jingpho

| | | | |
|---|---|---|---|
| Jingpho | hkrì **tung** | womb; abdomen | JAM-Ety |

### 4.2. Nungic

| | | | |
|---|---|---|---|
| Anong | tɕha⁵⁵**dɑŋ³¹** | nest | ZMYYC:368.44 |
| Trung [Dulong] | pɯ³¹tɕi?⁵⁵**dăŋ⁵³** | nest | ZMYYC:368.46 |

### 5. Tujia

| | | | | |
|---|---|---|---|---|
| Tujia (Northern) | **thũ⁵⁵** | nest | JZ-Tujia | |
| Tujia | ȵie³⁵pi⁵⁵**thoŋ⁵⁵** | nest | ZMYYC:368.38 | 29 |
| Tujia (Southern) | **?a³³tʉ³³** | nest | JZ-Tujia | |

²⁴The cognacy of this WT form is not certain, since WT does preserve final *-l. The first syllable is homophonous with **śa** ( < **(H:448)** *sya FLESH / MEAT / GAME ANIMAL), though Jäschke (p.556) does not include it under that lemma, evidently considering it to be a separate morpheme. The Newar form **sa:** 'placenta' apparently means "house", but Newar **swạ** 'nest' seems to be a genuine reflex of *tsywal.

²⁵The first word **bam-tyól** means 'concubine' (Mainwaring p. 255).

²⁶This Lepcha syllable **-tʻor** may in fact descend from a separate etymon than Lepcha **-tyól** (cf. Mikir **tar** 'nest').

²⁷The first three syllables **tă-a'yŭ** mean 'female'.

²⁸Qiangic shows evidence both for a nasal prefix (Ergong **mdʐo**, Ersu **xuɑi⁵⁵ntʂhɛ⁵⁵**) and prefixal *s- (Pumi Jinghua).

²⁹The first two syllables mean 'bird'.

## (107)       *(t)sip ≍ *(t)sup      NEST / WOMB / SCROTUM

This etymon displays the most pervasive variational pattern in TB vowels, between *-u- and *-i- (see Wolfenden 1929:114-5, *STC* pp. 80-4, *VSTB* pp. 41-2, *HPTB* pp. 493-505).[30] It is well distributed, occurring widely in Kamarupan (but not in Chin), with convincing cognates in Himalayish, Jingpho, and Qiangic. The Burmish cognates point to different final consonants: WB has **-k**, while Achang and Zaiwa have **-t**. W.T. French (1983:526) suggests an etymology (which appears fanciful), deriving this root from a compound **\*sa-yip** ANIMAL + SLEEP ( < **(H:448) \*sya** FLESH / MEAT / GAME ANIMAL and **(H:354) \*s-yip ≍ \*s-yup** SLEEP).

### 1.1. North Assam

| | | | |
|---|---|---|---|
| *Tani | **\*sup** | nest / lair | JS-HCST:271 |
| Padam-Mising [Abor-Miri] | a-**sup** | nest / lair | JS-HCST |
| Apatani | a-**si?** | nest / lair | JS-HCST |
| | à-**sɯ** | nest | JS-Tani |
| | pɯta a-**si?** | nest (bird's) | JS-Tani |
| Bengni | a-**sup** | nest, den | JS-Tani |
| | ta:-**šup** | nest / lair | JS-HCST |
| Bokar | a-**šup** | nest / lair | JS-HCST |
| | a-**sup** | nest | JS-Tani |
| Damu | ʔa-**ɕup** | nest | JS-Tani |
| Darang [Taraon] | ɑ³¹**jɯ**⁵⁵ | nest | ZMYYC:368.49 |
| Gallong | pɤta-a **sup** | nest | KDG-IGL |
| Kaman [Miju] | sɑ⁵⁵ **sɑp**⁵⁵ | placenta | SLZO-MLD |
| Idu | **su**⁵⁵ | nest | ZMYYC:368.50 |
| Milang | ta-pyu-**ap** | nest | AT-MPB |
| Tagin | ta **sep** | nest | KDG-Tag |

### 1.2. Kuki-Chin

| | | | |
|---|---|---|---|
| Liangmei | pa **sib** | nest | GEM-CNL |
| Zotung | **ʃɯ**¹ | womb | GHL-PPB:O.13 |

### 1.3. Naga

| | | | |
|---|---|---|---|
| *Northern Naga | **\*siup** | nest | WTF-PNN:526 |
| Ao (Chungli) | te **sep** | nest | GEM-CNL |
| Ao (Mongsen) | tü **sep** | nest | GEM-CNL |
| Chang | **hap** | nest | GEM-CNL |
| Konyak | ü **lep** | nest | GEM-CNL |
| Lotha Naga | o **shab** | nest | GEM-CNL |
| Nocte | a **rup** | nest | GEM-CNL |
| Phom | **jep** | nest | GEM-CNL |
| Rengma | a **se** | nest | GEM-CNL |
| Sangtam | a **süp** | nest | GEM-CNL |
| Sema | pü **sü** | nest | GEM-CNL |
| Tangkhul | a **thip** | nest | GEM-CNL |
| Wancho | ao **zap** | nest | GEM-CNL |
| Yimchungrü | **sap** | nest | GEM-CNL |
| Zeme | **chip** | nest | GEM-CNL |
| Mzieme | **tsip** | nest | GEM-CNL |

---

[30]For other etyma with similar variation, see e.g. **(55) \*m-dzup ≍ \*m-dzip** SUCK / SUCKLE / MILK / KISS, **(112) \*k-yim ≍ \*k-yum** HOUSE / WOMB, **(H:354) \*s-yip ≍ \*s-yup** SLEEP.

1.7. Bodo-Garo = Barish

| | | | |
|---|---|---|---|
| Dimasa | bu **thup** | nest | GEM-CNL |
| Garo (Bangladesh) | bi-**tip** | nest | RB-LMMG:24 |
| | ri-**sip**-il | testicles | RB-GB |
| | sa'-**tip** | womb, uterus | RB-GB |
| Kokborok | bə-tʰɔ | nest | PT-Kok |

2.3.1. Kham-Magar-Chepang-Sunwar

| | | | |
|---|---|---|---|
| Kham | '**sip** | nest | AH-CSDPN:03a.013 |
| | 'za **sip** | womb | DNW-KhamQ |

2.3.2. Kiranti

| | | | |
|---|---|---|---|
| Limbu | **hap** | nest | BM-Lim |

3.2. Qiangic

| | | | |
|---|---|---|---|
| Ergong (Northern) | lŋa⁵³ ɕip⁵³ | amniotic sac / bag of waters | SHK-ErgNQ:10.4.9 |
| | lʁo³³ ɕip⁵³ | scrotum | SHK-ErgNQ:10.3.4 [31] |

4.1. Jingpho

| | | | |
|---|---|---|---|
| Jingpho | **tsip** | nest | GEM-CNL |
| | u̱³¹**tsi̱p**⁵⁵ | nest | ZMYYC:368.47 |

6.1. Burmish

| | | | |
|---|---|---|---|
| Achang (Lianghe) | ɑ³¹**sut**³¹ | nest | JZ-Achang |
| Achang (Longchuan) | **sut**⁵⁵ | nest | ZMYYC:368.41 |
| Achang (Luxi) | **sut**⁵⁵ | nest | JZ-Achang |
| Burmese (Spoken Rangoon) | tθɑi?⁴⁴ | nest | ZMYYC:368.40 |
| Burmese (Written) | a **suik** | nest | GEM-CNL |
| | ə-**suik** | nest ( of bird or beast ) | PKB-WBRD |
| Atsi [Zaiwa] | ŋo̱?⁵⁵**sut**⁵⁵ | nest | ZMYYC:368.42 |

6.2. Loloish

| | | | |
|---|---|---|---|
| Hani (Shuikui) | ɔ⁵⁵ʒu⁵⁵ | nest | ZMYYC:368.32 |

6.4. Jinuo

| | | | |
|---|---|---|---|
| Jinuo (Baya/Banai) | jo⁴⁴ sɯ⁵⁵ | womb | DQ-JinA:149 |

## (108)  *kʷəy  NEST / WOMB / PLACENTA

Besides Lolo-Burmese, where it is widely attested (even in Jinuo), this etymon has solid reflexes in Qiangic (Shixing) and Bai. The suggested Kamarupan cognate (in Mao) is uncertain; this form might better be assigned to **(104)** *r-ku ≍ *kru NEST / UTERUS / AMNIOTIC SAC (above), like Angami **kru**. This root was reconstructed for PLB in Matisoff 1978b:6; cf. also Matisoff 1988a:917-8. This is a good example of the development of *labiovelar initials into Lahu labials, as also in DOG (PTB *kʷəy > Lahu **phî**); see also *STC* n. 83 (p. 26). Note the doublets in Hani (Khatu) and Naxi (Lijiang); the Naxi forms clearly show alternative labial and velar reflexes of the complex *labiovelar initial. Compounds for WOMB/PLACENTA typically have the structure CHILD + NEST. Compounds for SCROTUM have the structure TESTICLE + NEST.

---

[31]Literally, TESTICLE + NEST.

See *HPTB* \*$k^w$əy, p. 196; PLB \*$k^w$əy[1], p. 25.

| 1.3. Naga | | | |
|---|---|---|---|
| Mao | o **kre** | nest | GEM-CNL |
| 3.2. Qiangic | | | |
| Shixing | dʑyɛ³³**khuɐ**⁵⁵ | nest | ZMYYC:368.20 |
| 6. Lolo-Burmese | | | |
| \*Lolo-Burmese | \*$k^w$**iy**[1] | nest | JAM-MLBM:7 |
| 6.2. Loloish | | | |
| Akha | **gý** | nest | ILH-PL:303 |
| Hani (Khatu) | **khý/tjhí** | nest | ILH-PL:303 |
| Lahu (Black) | nī-sī-**phi** | scrotum | JAM-Ety |
| | **phɯ**³³ | nest | ZMYYC:368.33 |
| | yâ-**phi**(-tɛ) | placenta ("child-nest") | JAM-Ety |
| | za⁵³ **phɯ**³³ | placenta | JZ-Lahu |
| | ɔ̀-**p**ʰ**i** | nest | JAM-MLBM:7 |
| Lisu (Northern) | a⁵⁵næ⁵⁵**khɤ**³³ | nest of crow | DB-Lisu |
| Lisu | **khɯ**³³ | nest | ZMYYC:368.27 |
| Lisu (Northern) | **khɤ**³³ | nest; brood | DB-Lisu |
| Lisu (Central) | nyá²-**hkrgh**⁵ | nest (bird's) | JF-HLL |
| Lisu | ra⁵ **hkrgh**⁵ | womb | JAM-Ety |
| Lisu (Central) | ra⁵ **hkrgh**⁵ | womb | JF-HLL |
| Lisu (Northern) | za²¹**khɯ**³³ | womb | DB-Lisu |
| Mpi | **khɯ**⁶ | nest | ILH-PL:303 |
| | ʔa²-**k**ʰ**ɯ**⁶ | nest | JAM-MLBM:7 |
| Yi (Dafang) | ŋa³³**tɕhy**³³ | nest | ZMYYC:368.22 |
| Yi (Mile) | (xe³³zo²¹)i³³**tɕhi**³³ | nest | ZMYYC:368.25 |
| Yi (Nanhua) | ŋʌ³³**tɕhi**³³ | nest | ZMYYC:368.24 |
| Yi (Nanjian) | **khɯ**⁵⁵ty⁵⁵ | nest | ZMYYC:368.23 |
| Yi (Xide) | he³³tsɿ̄ **khɯ**⁴⁴**khɯ**³³ | nest | ZMYYC:368.21 |
| 6.3. Naxi | | | |
| Naxi (Yongning) | **khv**¹³ | nest | ZMYYC:368.29 |
| Naxi (Lijiang) | **khɯ**³¹; **phy**³¹ | nest | ZMYYC:368.28 |
| 6.4. Jinuo | | | |
| Jinuo | a³³**khɯ**³³ | nest | ZMYYC:368.34 |
| 8. Bai | | | |
| Bai (Dali) | tso⁴⁴**khv**³¹ | nest | ZMYYC:368.35 |
| Bai (Jianchuan) | **khv**³¹ | nest | ZMYYC:368.36 |

32

33

---

[32]The last element occurs in many other Lahu compounds, including **á-thɔ-phi** 'scabbard; sheath' ("knife-nest"), **ú-gê-phi** 'pillow-case', **khá-cè-phi** 'quiver for arrows', **yɨ̀ʔ-phi** 'bed' ("sleep-nest"), **lì?-phi** 'envelope', etc.

[33]Note the alternation between velar and labial initials, not surprising in view of the proto-labiovelar \*$k^w$- reconstructed for this root.

# Chinese comparandum

窠 **kē** 'burrow, nest'

*GSR*: not in 351          Karlgren: --          **Li**: *****khwar**          Baxter: *****kʷhaj**

This character is not in *GSR* and is not reconstructed by either Li or Baxter. Based on its phonetic element and its Middle Chinese reading, however, its OC reconstruction is not in doubt. The word occurs in the *Shuowen Jiezi*, attesting to its existence in the first century AD. The *Shuowen* entry reads 空也。從穴。果聲。一曰鳥巢也。在樹曰巢。在穴曰窠。 "Empty. [The character is formed] from [semantic element] 穴 and 果 is the phonetic. Another meaning is bird's nest. When in a tree it is called *cháo*, in a cave it is called *kē*.") The element 果 depicts an object in a tree and is part of the pictograph in 巢 **cháo** 'nest'. In 窠 it may be serving as a semantic as well as a phonetic element.

The connection with PTB was proposed by Handel (1998). It establishes a correspondence between PTB labiovelar initials and Chinese labiovelar initials. The vowel correspondence, however, is problematic, since PTB final *-əy usually corresponds to OC *-id (Li)/*-əj (Baxter); see the examples under the discussion for **(2a) *d(w)əy** EGG / TESTICLE.

[ZJH]

## (109)                    *****k-yaŋ**                    **PLACENTA / NEST**

This etymon is firmly reconstructible for PTB on the basis of the excellent fit between the Himalayish and Lolo-Burmese cognates. The velar prefix is reconstructed to accommodate the WB and Pa-O forms, as well as a group of Himalayish forms that mean CRADLE. For a similar association with CRADLE see **(103) *tsaŋ** NEST / WOMB / PLACENTA, below.

**2.1.3. Lepcha**

| Lepcha | a **yen̊** čot | placenta | JAM-Ety |
|---|---|---|---|
| | a **yen̊** tyól | placenta | JAM-Ety |

**2.1.4. Tamangic**

| Tamang (Sahu) | **kohyong** | cradle | AH-CSDPN:06a.38 |
|---|---|---|---|
| | **kʰyaŋ** | cradle | SIL-Sahu:6.33 |

**2.3.1. Kham-Magar-Chepang-Sunwar**

| Chepang | **khoyong** | cradle | AH-CSDPN:06a.38 |
|---|---|---|---|
| | **kʰoyoŋ** | cradle | SIL-Chep:6.A.38 |
| Magar | **koyo** | cradle | AH-CSDPN:06a.38 |

**2.3.2. Kiranti**

| Chamling | **yON** | nest | WW-Cham:40,63 |
|---|---|---|---|
| Khaling | **yāng** | nest | AH-CSDPN:03a.013 |
| Kulung | **yoŋ_** | nest | RPHH-Kul |
| Yakha | pica: **yaŋ** dɔŋ | placenta | TK-Yakha:10.4.11 |

[34] The last syllable **-dɔŋ** of the Yakha form matches well with the middle syllable **-dŭŋ-** of one of the Ugong forms in this set [q.v.], though there is still insufficient data to etymologize them.

6.1. Burmish

| | | | |
|---|---|---|---|
| Burmese (Written) | ə-**khyâŋ** | afterbirth | PKB-WBRD |
| | ʔə **khyâng** | placenta | JAM-Ety |

6.2. Loloish

| | | | |
|---|---|---|---|
| Ugong | ḥoŋ-dǔŋ-yɛ́ | placenta | DB-Ugong |
| | lɛ̌ŋ yɛ́ʔ | placenta | DB-Ugong:10.4.11 |

7. Karenic

| | | | |
|---|---|---|---|
| Pa-O | pò **khròŋ** | uterus | DBS-PaO |


# (110)  *(d)zyi  PLACENTA / NEST

This etymon is tentatively set up for PTB on rather shaky evidence: several forms from Loloish, and a single putative cognate from Qiangic (rGyalrong).

3.3. rGyalrongic

| | | | |
|---|---|---|---|
| rGyalrong (Eastern) | ta pu wan **dẓi** | placenta | SHK-rGEQ:10.4.11 |

6.2. Loloish

| | | | |
|---|---|---|---|
| Hani (Pijo) | **sjhí** | nest | ILH-PL:303 |
| Lalo | **ẓi**³³ | placenta | CK-YiQ:10.4.11 |
| Nosu | pha⁵⁵**ẓi**³³ | placenta | CK-YiQ:10.4.11 |
| Yi (Xide) | pʰa⁵⁵-**çi**³³ | placenta, afterbirth | CSL-YIzd |


# (111)  *s-nut ⪥ *s-not  MOUTH / VESSEL / WOMB

This etymon is widely distributed with the meaning MOUTH in Burmish and Karenic, with good-looking cognates in Qiangic (Pumi) and Bai. The Tibetan cognate gives a clue to its more general meaning of VESSEL; the expression **snod drug** 'the six vessels' refers in traditional Tibetan anatomy to the gall-bladder, stomach, small and large intestines, urinary bladder, and uterus (in females) or spermatic vessels (in males).[36] The Tibetan compound **bu-snod**, literally "child-vessel", refers specifically to the womb. See *STC* (pp. 144, 145, 150) for references to the Burmese, Karen, and Tibetan cognates.

See *HPTB* *s-not ⪥ *s-nut, p. 381.

2.1.2. Bodic

| | | | |
|---|---|---|---|
| Spiti | pui **net** | womb | CB-SpitiQ:10.4.8 |
| Tibetan (Written) | bu-**snod** | womb | JAM-Ety |
| | **snod** | vessel | HAJ-TED:319 |

3.2. Qiangic

| | | | |
|---|---|---|---|
| Pumi (Taoba) | ŋʚ³⁵ pu³⁵ la⁵³ | lip | JZ-Pumi |

6.1. Burmish

| | | | |
|---|---|---|---|
| Achang (Lianghe) | **nut**⁵⁵ ɯ⁵⁵ | lip | JZ-Achang |

---

[35]There is a homophonous WB word ʔəkhyâŋ 'one who is connected with another', cognate to Lahu ɔ̀-chɔ̂ 'friend' (*HPTB* p. 265). it is possible that there is a genuine semantic assocation between these two WB words, with the placenta conceived of as the "child's friend".

[36]See Jäschke 1881/1958, p. 319.

| | | | |
|---|---|---|---|
| | ŋ̊ut⁵⁵ | mouth | JZ-Achang |
| | ŋ̊ut⁵⁵ tshaʔ⁵⁵ | tongue | JZ-Achang |
| Achang (Longchuan) | ŋ̊ot⁵⁵ | mouth | JZ-Achang |
| | ŋ̊ot⁵⁵ mui³¹ | beard | JZ-Achang |
| | ŋ̊ot⁵⁵ tuŋ⁵⁵ | lip | JZ-Achang |
| Achang (Luxi) | nut⁵⁵ | mouth | JZ-Achang |
| | nut⁵⁵ tɔŋ⁵¹ | lip | JZ-Achang |
| Achang (Xiandao) | ŋ̊ut⁵⁵ | mouth | DQ-Xiandao:107 |
| | ŋ̊ut⁵⁵ mui³¹ | beard | DQ-Xiandao:109 |
| | ŋ̊ut⁵⁵ ʐ̩⁵⁵ | lip | DQ-Xiandao:108 |
| | ŋ̊ɔt⁵⁵ mui³¹ | beard | DQ-Xiandao:109.1 |
| Bola | nɔt⁵⁵ | mouth | DQ-Bola:107 |
| | nɔt⁵⁵ kau̯ʔ | lip | DQ-Bola:108 |
| | nɔt⁵⁵ mø³¹ | beard; whiskers | DQ-Bola:109,110 |
| Burmese (Modern) | nhut | mouth, snout | GHL-PPB:V.109 |
| Burmese (Written) | hnut | mouth; womb | JAM-Ety; PKB-WBRD |
| | hnut-khâm | lip, brim; upper edge of vessel | JAM-Ety; JAM-TJLB:185 |
| | hnut-khàm | lip | STC:329 |
| | nhut | mouth, snout | GHL-PPB:V.109 |
| | nhut kham: | lip | GEM-CNL |
| | nut-sî | beak / bill | JAM-Ety |
| Lashi | nua̱t⁵⁵ | beak; bill; mouth | DQ-Lashi:3.7,3.9.3 [37] |
| | nua̱t⁵⁵ ku̱k⁵⁵ | lip | DQ-Lashi:3.9 |
| | nua̱t⁵⁵ mou⁵⁵ | moustache; whiskers (of animal) | DQ-Lashi:8.1.2.3,8.1.7 |
| | nua̱t⁵⁵ mə³³ | beard | DQ-Lashi:8.1.2.1 |
| | vuʔ³¹ nŏ³³ | snout (pig) | DQ-Lashi:3.5.5 |
| Maru [Langsu] | na̱t⁵⁵ | beak; bill; mouth | DQ-Langsu:3.7,3.9.3 |
| | na̱t⁵⁵ ka̱uk⁵⁵ | lip | DQ-Langsu:3.9 |
| | na̱t⁵⁵ muk⁵⁵ | whiskers (of cat) | DQ-Langsu:8.1.7 |
| | na̱t⁵⁵ mɔi³¹ | beard; moustache | DQ-Langsu:8.1.2.1,8.1.2.3 |
| | vɔʔ³¹ nŏ³¹ | snout (pig) | DQ-Langsu:3.5.5 |
| | ɔ³¹ nat⁵⁵ ka̱uk⁵⁵ | lower lip | DQ-Langsu:3.9.2 |
| Atsi [Zaiwa] | nu̱t⁵⁵ | mouth | JZ-Zaiwa |
| | nu̱t⁵⁵ ku̱ʔ⁵⁵ | lip | JZ-Zaiwa |
| | nu̱t⁵⁵ mui²¹ | beard | JZ-Zaiwa |

## 6.2. Loloish

| | | | |
|---|---|---|---|
| Lisu (Putao) | mɯ⁵nɯ² | mouth, snout | GHL-PPB:V.109 |

## 7. Karenic

| | | | |
|---|---|---|---|
| *Karen (Pho) | *nòʔ | beak; bill; mouth | RBJ-KLS:668,691 |
| *Karen (Sgaw) | *nɔʔ | mouth | RBJ-KLS:668 |
| | *nɔ̀ʔ | beak / bill | RBJ-KLS:691 |
| Pho (Bassein) | nòʔ | beak; bill; mouth | JAM-Ety; RBJ-KLS:668,691 |
| | nò' | beak / bill | JAM-Ety |

---

[37] These Lashi forms bear a strong surface resemblance to Siamese **nùat** (< Proto-Tai **\*hn-**) 'beard'. This word is not widely distributed in Tai. "Except Tay (a Central Tai dialect) **nuôt D1L** this word seems restricted to the SW dialects" (Li Fang Kuei 1977:116). The Northern and Central Tai dialects generally have forms descending from Proto-Tai **\*mum** (*HCT* pp. 72-73). It seems possible that this is a loan from Burmish into SW Tai.

| | | | |
|---|---|---|---|
| Pho (Moulmein) | **noʔ** | beak; bill; mouth | JAM-Ety; RBJ-KLS:668,691 |
| Sgaw (Bassein) | **nɔʔ** | mouth | JAM-Ety; RBJ-KLS:668 |
| | **nɔ̀ʔ** | beak / bill | JAM-Ety; RBJ-KLS:691 |
| Karen (Sgaw/Hinthada) | **nɔ³³ tsʰu³¹** | beard | DQ-KarenB:112 |
| Sgaw (Moulmein) | **nɔʔ** | mouth | JAM-Ety; RBJ-KLS:668 |
| | **nɔ̀ʔ** | beak / bill | JAM-Ety; RBJ-KLS:691 |
| Karen (Sgaw/Yue) | **nɔ̰ʔ⁵⁵ pʰoʔ⁵⁵** | lip | DQ-KarenA:111 |
| | **nɔ̰ʔ⁵⁵ sʰu³¹** | beard | DQ-KarenA:112 |
| 8. Bai | | | |
| Bai | **nḛ²¹** | mouth | ZYS-Bai:3.7 |

## (112)                    *k-yim ≍ *k-yum                    HOUSE / WOMB

This etymon is extremely widespread in TB with the meaning HOUSE (see *STC* #53). In the present set I am including only those compounds (typically of the structure CHILD + HOUSE) that mean WOMB/PLACENTA. This root shows vocalic variation between *-u- and *-i-. Some languages have reflexes with initial velar stop, but others (e.g. Lushai, WB) point to a variant beginning with y- or i-; that is, some languages have treated the velar as a prefix.

See *HPTB* **\*k-yim ≍ \*k-yum**, pp. 21, 35, 273, 498, 504, 531, 533.

| | | | | |
|---|---|---|---|---|
| 0. Sino-Tibetan | | | | |
| *Tibeto-Burman | **\*kim** | house | STC:53 | |
| 1.1. North Assam | | | | |
| Mising [Miri] | **əkum** | house | STC:53 | |
| 1.2. Kuki-Chin | | | | |
| Chinbok | **im** | house | STC:53 | |
| Lushai [Mizo] | **in** | house | STC:142n384 | |
| Paangkhua | sùul-**ìn** | womb | LL-PRPL | |
| 1.3. Naga | | | | |
| Nocte | **hum** | house | STC:53 | |
| Tangsa (Moshang) | **yim ≍ yüm** | house | STC:53 | |
| 1.4. Meithei | | | | |
| Meithei | **yum** | house | STC:53 | |
| 1.5. Mikir | | | | |
| Mikir | arlo a **hem** | womb | JAM-Ety | 38 |
| | **hem** | womb; house | JAM-Ety; JAM-VSTB; STC:53 | 39 |
| | o sô a-**hêm** | placenta / afterbirth | KHG-Mikir:36 | |
| | o so-a **hem** | placenta | JAM-Ety; JAM-VSTB | |
| 1.6. Mru | | | | |
| Mru | **kim** | house | STC:53 | |

---

[38]Compare to **oso ahem** 'placenta' ("child house").
[39]This Mikir form has nothing to do with **(96) \*s-b-rum** WOMB / PLACENTA above, contra *VSTB*, pp. 226-7.

### 1.8. Chairel

| | | | |
|---|---|---|---|
| Chairel | **him** | house | STC:53 |

### 2.1.2. Bodic

| | | | |
|---|---|---|---|
| Tibetan (Written) | **khyim** | house | STC:53 |

### 2.1.3. Lepcha

| | | | |
|---|---|---|---|
| Lepcha | **khyŭm** | house | STC:25n82 |

### 2.3.1. Kham-Magar-Chepang-Sunwar

| | | | |
|---|---|---|---|
| Chepang | **kyim ⋇ tim** | house | STC:53 |
| Magar | **im ⋇ yum** | house | STC:53 |

### 2.3.2. Kiranti

| | | | |
|---|---|---|---|
| Bahing | **khyim ⋇ khim** | house | STC:53 |
| Dumi | mori-ki:m | womb, uterus | SVD-Dum |
| Hayu | **kim ⋇ kem** | house | STC:53 |
| Limbu | **him** | house | STC:53 |

### 3.3. rGyalrongic

| | | | |
|---|---|---|---|
| rGyalrong | ta pu **ktɕɛm** | womb | DQ-Jiarong:10.4.8 |
| rGyalrong (Northern) | ta po tso **fkəm** | womb | SHK-rGNQ:10.4.8 |
| rGyalrong (Eastern) | ta pʲ **tʃʰem** | womb | SHK-rGEQ:10.4.8 |
| rGyalrong (NW) | tə lŋa **ktɕʰim** | amniotic sac / bag of waters | SHK-rGNWQ:10.4.9 |

### 4. Jingpho-Nung-Luish

| | | | |
|---|---|---|---|
| Andro | **kem** | house | STC:53 |
| Kadu | **tyem** | house | STC:53 |

### 4.2. Nungic

| | | | |
|---|---|---|---|
| Anong | **kyim ⋇ tśim ⋇ tśum** | house | STC:53 |

### 6.1. Burmish

| | | | |
|---|---|---|---|
| Burmese (Written) | chaṅ-**ʔim** | womb | JAM-Ety |
| | **im** | house | STC:53 |
| | swê-**ʔim** | placenta | JAM-Ety [40] |

### 6.2. Loloish

| | | | |
|---|---|---|---|
| Bisu | aŋ-jàt-ja-**húm** | womb | PB-Bisu:16 |
| Lahu | **yɛ̀** | house | STC:53 |

# (113)            *bu            CHILD

This etymon means CHILD. It is included here because of the important WT form **bu-snod** 'womb' ("child-vessel"). Care is required to distinguish this etymon from reflexes of **(102) *r-bu ⋇ *pru** NEST / WOMB / PLACENTA, above. Coblin (1986:164) suggests the Chinese comparandum 僕 (below).

### 0. Sino-Tibetan

| | | | |
|---|---|---|---|
| *Sino-Tibetan | **\*buʔ** | boy / servant | WSC-SH:47 |

### 2.1.2. Bodic

| | | | |
|---|---|---|---|
| Spiti | **pui** net | womb | CB-SpitiQ:10.4.8 |

[40]Literally BLOOD + HOUSE. See **\*s-hwiy ~ \*s-hywəy-t** BLOOD.

| | | | | |
|---|---|---|---|---|
| Tibetan (Written) | **bu**-snod | womb | JAM-Ety | 41 |
| 9. Sinitic | | | | |
| Chinese (Old) | **buk** | servant, male slave | WSC-SH:164 | 42 |

## Chinese comparandum

僕 **pú** 'servant, groom, male slave'

*GSR*: 1211b Karlgren: ***b'uk / *b'ôk** Li: ***buk** Baxter: ***bok**

The vowel correspondence is regular, as OC ***-uk** (Li)/***-ok** (Baxter) normally corresponds to PTB ***-uk**, as in 'bend /crooked' PTB ***guk~ *kuk**, OC 曲 ***khjuk** (Li)/***kh(r)jok** (Baxter). However, the presence of coda ***-k** in the Chinese form is unexplained.

Peiros and Starostin (1996.1:57 set 203) relate this Chinese word to Tibetan **phrug** 'child' and Burmese **pauk** 'young of animals'.

[ZJH]

[41]For the second element, see **(111) *s-nut ⋉ *s-not** MOUTH / VESSEL / WOMB, above.
[42]Chinese 僕.

# VII. Penis

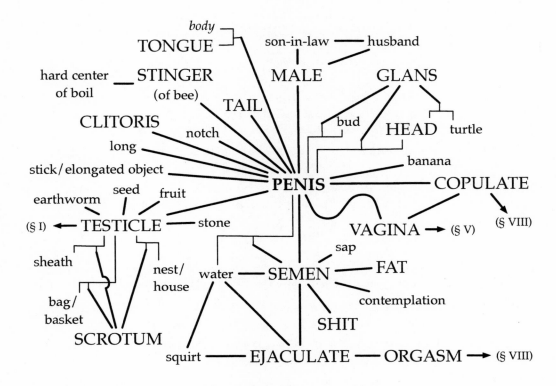

The various components of the male genitalia show semantic associations with a number of other bodyparts, as well as with a wide range of objects in other semantic fields. Some of these associations are widespread or universal in the world's languages; others seem more idiosyncratic to ST or the SEA'n linguistic area.

Among the universal semantic associations we may list the following:

(1) PENIS ⟷ TAIL: The English word *penis* itself is from Lat. *pēnis* 'tail' (cf. also Fr. *queue* < Lat. *cauda* 'tail'), among countless other examples. The widespread TB etymon for TAIL **(H:216)** *may ⪥ *mey ⪥ *mi (cf. also Chinese 尾 OC *mi̯wər) has similar associations, e.g. Jingpho **mài, ǹ-mài** 'tail; a euphemistic name for the male private parts' (Hanson 1906/1954, p. 400).

(2) PENIS ⟷ BANANA: This connection is made explicitly in Kokborok **tʰa-li** (see **(114a)** *m-ley ⪥ *m-li PENIS below) and in Newar **mwā-e** 'banana; penis'.

(3) GLANS PENIS ⟷ PENIS + HEAD: This is a universal association (cf. WT **mje-mgo**; Lahu **ni-ó-qō**; Lisu (Northern) ɔ⁵⁵dy³³ 'head', hɔ̃²¹ɔ⁵⁵dy³³ 'penis'; Yakha **tu khəruk**

'head', **li: go: u tu kəruk** 'glans'; Qiang (Mawo) **qə̌ pæʈʂ** 'head', **li qə̌ pæʈʂ** 'glans'; Eng. *dick-head*).

(4) TESTICLE ⟷ EGG: This is also a universal association (cf. e.g. Russian *jajtsy* 'eggs; testicles', Hebrew *beytsim* 'id.'). The same etymon may have some reflexes meaning EGG and others meaning TESTICLE. Several TB etyma showing this association have been treated above under EGG (Chapter I); others will be treated below in this chapter. Alternatively a language may have a compound word for TESTICLE of the structure PENIS + EGG.

(5) TESTICLE ⟷ FRUIT / BALL / ROUNDED OBJECT: TB compounds for TESTICLE frequently take the form PENIS + FRUIT/ROUND OBJECT, e.g. Lahu **ni-ši** 'testicle' (2nd syll. < **(H:206) *sey** FRUIT / ROUND OBJECT).[1]

Cf. also Newar **kwaa-si** 'testicles' (lit. "hot-fruit"), reminiscent of the vulgar English simile "hot as balls".

(6) TESTICLE ⟷ STONE: Also a widespread association in the world's languages, including archaic English slang. In TB, cf. formations like Monpa **khong-lung** 'testicle' (**lung** 'stone').

(7) SCROTUM ⟷ BASKET / BAG / POUCH / NEST: This obvious association occurs in Lat. *scrōtum* < *scrautum* 'leather pouch for arrows', and is also found in TB, e.g. Lahu **ni-si-phɨ** 'scrotum', **phɨ** 'nest; receptacle' < **(108) *kʷəy** NEST / WOMB / PLACENTA. Cf. also **(131) *s-bloŋ** SCROTUM / POUCH, **(136) *ʔip ≍ *ʔi:t** BAG / SCROTUM.

(8) SEMEN ⟷ PENIS + LIQUID: Cf. Nesu **ler³³ ʐ̩²¹** and Noesu **ɬu⁵⁵ʑi²¹**, where the second element < **(164) *rəy** WATER / LIQUID, and WB **lî-rañ**.

Semantic associations that seem more peculiar to the SEA'n linguistic area include the following:

(9) PENIS ⟷ VAGINA: Many etyma have some reflexes which refer to the male organ, but others which refer to the female counterpart, a phenomenon that has been dubbed 'genital flipflop' (see chapter note under VAGINA). Etyma like this should perhaps be assigned the gender-neutral gloss GENITALS at the proto-level. Several have been treated under VAGINA (Chapter V, above); others will be treated below in this chapter.

(10) PENIS ⟷ BODY + TONGUE: Cf. Garo **maŋ-sre** 'penis' < **(H:265) *s-maŋ** BODY / CORPSE + **(H:215) *s-lya** TONGUE. This form was cited in Benedict 1979:24.

(11) TESTICLE ⟷ SEED: Cf. WB **lî-ce'**, lit. "penis-seed".

(12) GLANS ⟷ NOTCH: Cf. WB **lî-thac** 'corona glandis', lit. "penis-notch", and Lahu **ni-qhὲʔ** 'penis', where the second syllable means 'notch (as a stick); chip; break off a piece'.

---

[1]Note that TESTICLE ⟷ NUT is not characteristic of SEA, since languages in this region generally lack a word for NUT distinct from FRUIT. Cf. Chinese 果 (Mand. **guǒ**), used equally well for FRUIT (more specifically 水果 Mand. **shuǐguǒ** "water-fruit") and NUT, e.g. 開心果 Mand. **kāixīnguǒ** 'pistachio' (lit. "open-heart-fruit").

(13) GLANS ⟶ BUD: Cf. WB **lî-ŋum** 'glans', lit. "penis-bud".

(14) GLANS ⟶ TURTLE: While Latin *glāns* means 'acorn', Mandarin **guī-tóu** 'glans penis' means literally "turtle-head". (For obvious reasons, this formation is especially appropriate for the uncircumcised organ.) The data is so far insufficient to establish whether this same metaphor occurs in TB languages.

(15) SEMEN ⟶ SHIT: A few languages associate semen with SHIT / BODY DIRT / EX-CRETION. Cf. Lahu **nī-qhê** "penis-shit", Chepang **təyŋ-kliʔ** 'id.', and Bantawa **lü-khü-wa** (**khü** 'stool, excreta'). In Jingpho **ne³¹khji⁵⁵**, however, this combination of morphemes means SMEGMA.

(16) SEMEN ⟶ FAT: Cf. Lahu **nī-chu** 'semen' (lit. "penis-fat").

Few monomorphemic etyma are reconstructible for SEMEN, with three possibilities offered below: **(157) *ra ≍ *wa** SEMEN, **(158) *ŋya** SEMEN, and **(159) *bo** SEMEN.

Words for FORESKIN/PREPUCE, naturally enough, are compounds of PENIS + SKIN, and are beyond the scope of this volume.

Expressions for COPULATE frequently involve PENIS plus a verb. See Chapter VIII.

**(114)**             **\*m-ley ≍ \*m-li ≍ \*m-ney**            **PENIS**

This is by far the most widely attested etymon for PENIS in TB, occurring in Kamarupan, Himalayish, Lolo-Burmese (including Jinuo), and Qiangic. (See *STC* #262, which cites reflexes from the first three of these groups.) The nasal prefix is well-established, appearing e.g. in WT and other Himalayish languages. This prefix has caused nasalization of the root-initial lateral in several languages (e.g. Meithei and Jingpho), or even driven out or "preempted" the root-initial entirely (as in Chang Naga or Lahu). Those forms which have developed a secondary nasal root-initial are presented separately below as set **(114b) *m-ney** PENIS. A couple of Loloish languages (Lalo, Lisu) have reflexes in **h-**. It is possible that these point to an alternant with sibilant prefix, **\*s-ley** (as is reflected more directly in Phunoi **hle¹¹** and Lepcha **săli**). Several Loloish languages (Lalo, Lipho, Lolopho, Nesu, Sani/Nyi) have words for PENIS and TESTICLE with initial **d-**. Since it is true that there is much interplay between **l-** and **d-** in ST,[2] and it is also the case that palatalized labial initials are sometimes dentalized in Loloish languages like Sani,[3] it might seem reasonable to assign these reflexes in **d-** to **\*m-ley** if we posit an intermediate palatalized prototype like **\*myey**. However, Lalo has forms with both **d-** and **h-** (**de³³se²¹** 'testicle', **he²¹** 'penis'), which suggests that two separate etyma are involved. I am therefore assigning the reflexes in **d-** to **(117) *ti-k** PENIS, below.

Several languages have forms that resemble reflexes of this etymon, but which are really loans from Indo-Aryan (cf. Skt. *lingam*): WB **lin-khu'** 'scrotum', Kanauri **liṅ** 'penis (polite)'.

---

[2]See the note under **(40) *m/s-la(:)y ≍ *s-tay** NAVEL, above.

[3]E.g. PTB/PLB **\*my-** > Sani **n-** (e.g. **(H:324) *s-myak ≍ *s-mik** EYE > Sa. **ne⁴⁴**); **\*by-** > Sani **dl-** (e.g. **(H:171) *bya** BEE > Sa. **dla-ma**); **\*py-** > Sa. **tl-** (e.g. **(H:532) *pyam ≍ *byam** FLY (v.) > Sa. **tlö**); see *STC*, n. 93, p. 29.

## (114a)  *m-ley ≍ *m-li  PENIS

There is apparently a slight variation in the rhyme of this etymon between *-ey and
*-i, although the reflexes of these two rhymes are not distinguishable for many TB lan-
guages at present. *STC* (#262 and note 197) recognizes "vowel gradation" in this root,
assigning Kanauri **kut-li**, Bahing **bli**, WB **lî**, Garo **ri-gaŋ**, and Dimasa **li** to PTB *li*, but
WT **mdźe** to *m-ley. For convenience, we are grouping all the reflexes of this etymon
with lateral initials together in **(114a)**, regardless of the precise proto-rhyme to which
they may eventually be assigned.

See also *HPTB* *m-ley ≍ *m-li, pp. 47, 49, 153, 219, 509.

| | | | |
|---|---|---|---|
| 0. Sino-Tibetan | | | |
| *Tibeto-Burman | *li | penis | STC:262 |
| | *li ~ *m-ley | penis | BM-PK7:138 |
| | *m-ley | penis | AW-TBT:142 |
| | *m-ley ≍*li | penis | JAM-GSTC:049 |
| | *mlye | penis | AW-TBT:142 |
| 1.4. Meithei | | | |
| Meithei | bu **ri** khaw | testicle | CYS-Meithei:10.3.5 |
| 1.7. Bodo-Garo = Barish | | | |
| Dimasa | **li** | penis | JAM-Ety; |
| | | | JAM-GSTC:049; |
| | | | STC:262 |
| Garo | **ri** | penis | AW-TBT:142 |
| | **ri**-gaŋ | penis | JAM-Ety; |
| | | | JAM-GSTC:049; |
| | | | STC:262 |
| Garo (Bangladesh) | **ri**-gong | penis | RB-GB |
| | **ri**-ku-chil | foreskin | RB-GB |
| | **ri**-sim-ang | male pubic hair | RB-GB |
| | **ri**-sip-il | testicles | RB-GB |
| Kokborok | **bələy** | penis | PT-Kok |
| | tʰa-**li** | banana | PT-Kok  4 |
| 2.1.1. Western Himalayish | | | |
| Kanauri | kut-**li** | penis | JAM-GSTC:049; |
| | | | STC:262 |
| | kut **lī** | penis (less polite) | JAM-Ety |
| | **les** | penis | DS-Kan:27  5 |
| 2.1.2. Bodic | | | |
| Baima | kha$^{13}$ **ndʐ̩**$^{53}$ | penis | SHK-BaimaQ:10.3.1 |
| | **li**$^{53}$ dʑ$^{341}$ | testicle | SHK-BaimaQ:10.3.5 |
| Tibetan (Amdo:Zeku) | **ndʑe** | penis | JS-Amdo:743 |
| | **ndʑe** ŋo | glans penis | JS-Amdo:304 |
| Tibetan (Balti) | **že·** | penis | RAN1975:74 |
| Tibetan (Batang) | **dʑɛ**$^{55}$ ba?$^{53}$ | foreskin | DQ-Batang:10.3.3 |
| | **dʑɛ**$^{55}$ ngo$^{53}$ | glans penis | DQ-Batang:10.3.2 |

---

[4]Literally "penis-fruit" (p.c., Prashanta Tripura, 1987).
[5]The suffixal **-s** in this form is unexplained.

| Tibetan (Written) | gsaṅ-**mje** | penis (respectful) | JAM-Ety | 6 |
| | **mdźe** | penis | JAM-GSTC:049 | |
| | **mje** | penis | GHL-PPB:X.35; JS-Tib:743 | |
| | **mje** mgo | glans penis | JS-Tib:304 | |
| | **mje** | penis | JAM-Ety | |
| | **mje**-mgo | glans penis | JAM-Ety | |
| | **mje**-rlig | penis and testicles | JAM-Ety | |

### 2.1.3. Lepcha

| Lepcha | **săli** krik | penis | JAM-Ety | 7 |

### 2.1.4. Tamangic

| *Tamang | *[A]**mlai** | penis | MM-Thesis:768 | |
| | *[A]**mle:** | penis | MM-Thesis:768 | |
| Chantyal | mɦio **le** | penis | NPB-ChanQ:10.3.1 | |
| Gurung (Ghachok) | **mrĩ** la baq | copulate | SIL-Gur:2.B.2.13 | |
| | **mrį̄** lā bāq | copulate | JAM-Ety | |
| Manang (Gyaru) | **ml**ɛ[1] | penis | YN-Man:042-07 | |
| Manang (Prakaa) | [2]**mle** | penis | HM-Prak:0510 | |
| | [3]**mle** | penis | MM-Thesis:768 | |
| Tamang | **mle**[ɦ]-ka | penis | AW-TBT:631 | |
| Tamang (Risiangku) | [3]**mlē** ka | penis | MM-TamRisQ:10.3.1 | |
| Tamang (Sahu) | **mlē**-ka | penis | JAM-Ety | |
| Thakali (Syang) | [51]**mle** = [51]**mle**[ɦ] | penis | MM-Thesis:768 | |
| Thakali (Tukche) | **mleh**-cham | hair (pubic) | JAM-Ety | |
| | **mleh**-cʰɔm | hair (pubic, male) | SIL-Thak:2.A.10.1 | |
| | [3]**mle** | penis | MM-Thesis:768 | |
| | [3]**mle**-[H]tsʰəm | pubic hair (male) | MM-Thesis:768 | |

### 2.3. Mahakiranti

| *BSDTK | *__bli__ | penis | BM-PK7:138 | |
| *Kul-Cham-Ban | *__li__ | penis | BM-PK7:138 | |
| Athpare (Rai) | **le** wa ḍin | testicle | AW-TBT:617b | |

### 2.3.2. Kiranti

| Bahing | **bli** | penis | BM-PK7:138; STC:262 | |
| Bantawa | **li** | penis | BM-PK7:138; JAM-Ety; NKR-Bant; WW-Bant:45 | |
| | **li**-wa-din | testicle | WW-Bant:46 | 8 |
| | **lü**-khü-wa | semen | WW-Bant:47 | |
| | **lU** khU wa | semen | NKR-Bant | |
| | **l** Ua Din | testicle | NKR-Bant | |
| Belhare | **li** | penis | BB-Belhare | |
| Dumi | **li:** | penis | BM-PK7:138; SVD-Dum | |
| Hayu | bi **mli** | genitals | BM-PK7:138; JAM-Ety | 9 |
| Khaling | '**li** swām | hair (pubic) | JAM-Ety | |
| | **li** | penis | BM-PK7:138 | |

---

[6]First syllable means 'secret thing; hidden thing'.

[7]This form reflects an alternate prototype with sibilant prefix, *s-ley. Cf. also Bisu **hlè**, where the voiceless lateral also points to *s- instead of *m-.

[8]Literally "penis + bird + egg". Cf. also the Athpare form.

[9]This is an antonymic compound meaning literally "vagina-penis". See **(81)** *b(y)at VAGINA above.

| Limbu | le | penis; top of penis | BM-Lim; BM-PK7:138; JAM-Ety | |
| | le hoŋ | hole of penis; *meatus urinarius* | JAM-Ety | 10 |
| | le: | penis | AW-TBT:142 | |
| | le bong | testicle | JAM-Ety | |
| | lɛ dwa | glans penis | BM-Lim | |
| | le hek | top of penis | JAM-Ety | |
| | lɛ khaŋ | glans penis | BM-Lim | |
| | le mu rik | hair (pubic) | JAM-Ety | |
| | lɛ nt- | glans penis | BM-Lim | |
| | lɛ suŋ | male genitals | BM-Lim | |
| | le thim ba | testicle | BM-Lim | |
| | le wā | semen | JAM-Ety | |
| | lɛ dhi:m ba | testicle ("penis-egg") | AW-TBT:142,617b | |
| Thulung | ble | penis | BM-PK7:138; NJA-Thulung | |
| | le- | copulate | NJA-Thulung | |
| | le koak ti | testicle | NJA-Thulung | |
| Yakha | li: | penis | TK-Yakha:10.3.1 | |
| | li: geŋ | testicle | TK-Yakha:10.3.5 | |
| | li: go: u muŋ | male pubic hair | TK-Yakha:10.3.6 | |
| | li: go: u tu kəruk | glans penis | TK-Yakha:10.3.2 | 11 |
| | li: gəu: wə ha rik | foreskin | TK-Yakha:10.3.3 | |

## 3.1. Tangut

| Tangut [Xixia] | be le | penis | DQ-Xixia:10.3.1 | |
| | l dai¹ | testicle | MVS-Grin | 12 |

## 3.2. Qiangic

| Qiang (Mawo) | liq | penis | JS-Mawo | |
| | li hu̜ | pubic hair (male) | JS-Mawo | |
| | li hu̜ŋ | male pubic hair | SHK-MawoQ:10.3.6 | |
| | li qə̜ pæts | glans penis | SHK-MawoQ:10.3.2 | 13 |
| Qiang (Yadu) | læq | penis | DQ-QiangN:144 | |

## 6. Lolo-Burmese

| *Lolo-Burmese | *(n)-li² | penis | AW-TBT:142 | |

## 6.1. Burmish

| Achang (Xiandao) | li⁵⁵ tsi³¹ | testicles | DQ-Xiandao:142 | |
| Burmese (Written) | lî | penis; penis (vulgar) | JAM-Ety; JAM-GSTC:049; JAM-TJLB:260; PKB-WBRD | |
| | lì | penis | STC:262 | |
| | lî khyôŋ | glans penis | JAM-Ety | |
| | lî-ce' | testicle | JAM-Ety | 14 |
| | lî-chan | testicle | JAM-Ety | |

---

[10] For the second syllable, see **(92) *hoŋ** VAGINA / RECTUM / HOLE.

[11] **tu kəruk** means 'head'.

[12] The first element **l-** 'penis' appears in reduced form in this "crypto-compound".

[13] Second element **qə̜ pæts** means "head".

[14] Second element means 'seed' < **(133) *dzəy** SEED / TESTICLE / ROUND OBJECT, below.

| | | | |
|---|---|---|---|
| | lî-rañ | semen | JAM-Ety |
| | lî-thac | *corona glandis* | JAM-Ety |
| | lî-ŋum | glans penis | JAM-Ety | 15 |
| | li⁴ | penis | GHL-PPB:X.35 |
| | lə ʔu | scrotum | JAM-Ety | 16 |

### 6.2. Loloish

| | | | |
|---|---|---|---|
| *Loloish | *(n)-li² | penis | AW-TBT:294; DB-PLolo:122 |
| Akha | beu^ leu^ | penis (polite) | PL-AETD | 17 |
| Bisu | hlè | penis | DB-PLolo | 18 |
| | hlɜ̌ ʔu³³ | testicles | DB-PLolo | 19 |
| | lè thɛ | penis | PB-Bisu:15 |
| | lè ʔu | testicles | PB-Bisu:15 | 20 |
| Lalo | hè | penis | SB-Lalo |
| | he²¹ | penis | CK-YiQ:10.3.1 |
| Lisu | h'aw⁵ | penis | DB-PLolo:122; JAM-GSTC:049 |
| Lisu (Northern) | hɜ̌²¹ɔ⁵⁵dy³³ | glans penis | DB-Lisu |
| Lisu (Central) | h'aw⁵ | penis | JF-HLL |
| Lisu (Northern) | la⁵⁵fu³³ | testicle | DB-Lisu | 21 |
| Mpi | tɕhɑ²lɑʔ⁴ | penis | DB-PLolo | 22 |
| Nesu | ler³³ ʐ̩²¹ | semen | CK-YiQ:10.3.7 | 23 |
| Noesu | ɫu⁵⁵ʑi²¹ | semen | CK-YiQ:10.3.7 |

### 6.4. Jinuo

| | | | |
|---|---|---|---|
| Jinuo (Baya/Banai) | li⁵⁵ tsɿ³³ | testicles | DQ-JinA:145 |

## (114b)         *m-ney         PENIS

This etymon is obviously an allofam of **(114a) *m-ley ⪥ *m-li** PENIS. The reflexes in this set arose through assimilation of the lateral root-initial to the nasal prefix. In some cases (e.g. Jingpho, Meithei) the prefix still co-occurs with the secondary nasal root-initial. In other languages (e.g. Lahu) the prefix has disappeared as such, after supplanting the original root-initial ("prefix preemption").[24] This allofam occurs in Jingpho, and is widely attested in Lolo-Burmese; there are also a few scattered reflexes in Kamarupan languages (Chang, Meithei, Mru).

---

[15] The second syllable means 'flower bud'.

[16] The first syllable is reduced to schwa in this compound. This atonic syllable is a reduction of **lî** 'penis', and is not to be identified with the first syllable of WB **lin-khu'** 'scrotum', which is ultimately from Skt. *lingam*.

[17] The stopped tone in the second syllable is unexplained. Note, however, the final -q in some Qiang forms. Akha **a͜loe͜** has been tentatively assigned to **(144) *ləw-k** COPULATE, below.

[18] The voiceless lateral reflects an **\*s-** prefix. Cf. also Lepcha **săli**.

[19] Literally "penis+egg".

[20] Literally "penis + egg".

[21] Lit. "penis+egg".

[22] According to Bradley (1978:304-5), this form is apparently a doublet of Mpi **ne²**; see **(114b)**.

[23] The second element in the Nesu and Noesu compounds < **(164) *rəy** WATER / LIQUID.

[24] For the first use of the term "prefix preemption" see Matisoff 1972b, "Tangkhul Naga and comparative TB".

---

1.3. Naga

| Chang | **nè** | penis | AW-TBT:294 |
|---|---|---|---|

1.4. Meithei

| Meithei | **mənu** | penis | CYS-Meithei:10.3.1 |
|---|---|---|---|

1.6. Mru

| Mru | **nia-** | penis | JAM-Ety |
|---|---|---|---|
| | **niaɑ¹** | penis | GHL-PPB:Q.51 |
| | **niaɑ⁴** | penis | GHL-PPB:Q.51 |

4.1. Jingpho

| Jingpho | **mənē** | penis | JAM-Ety; JAM-TJLB:260 |
|---|---|---|---|
| | **mənè~ məné?** | penis | JAM-GSTC:049 |
| | **nē** | penis | JAM-Ety |
| | **ne**-di | testicle | JAM-Ety |
| | **ne**-rú-rú | masturbation | JAM-Ety |
| | **ne**-um | foreskin / prepuce | JAM-Ety |
| | **ne**-zu | semen | JAM-Ety |
| | **ne³¹kha?⁵⁵** | *corona glandis* | JCD |
| | **ne³¹khji⁵⁵** | smegma | JCD [25] |
| | **ne³¹kjo̲³¹** | sexually dysfunc- tional male | JCD |
| | **ne³¹laŋ³³** | penis | JCD |
| | **ne³¹mun³³** | male pubic hair | JCD |
| | **ne³¹phji?³¹** | foreskin / prepuce | JCD |
| | **ne³¹po̲t³¹** | penis shaft | JCD |
| | **ne³¹si³³** | impotence | JCD |
| | **ne³¹tan³¹** | large penis | JCD |
| | **ne³¹than³³** | glans penis | JCD |
| | **ne³¹ti³¹** | scrotum | JCD |
| | **ne³¹tsu³³** | semen | JCD |
| | **ne³¹tu̲m³³** | testicles | JCD |
| | **ne³¹tʃin³¹** | circumcised penis | JCD |
| | **ne³¹up⁵⁵** | uncircumcised penis | JCD |
| | **ne³¹ʒaŋ³³** | sexually potent male | JCD [26] |
| | **ne³¹ʒu?⁵⁵** | masturbation | JCD |
| | **nè?-ūm** | foreskin / prepuce | JAM-TJLB:126 |
| | **¹mə¹nye** | penis | AW-TBT:294 |

6.1. Burmish

| Achang (Xiandao) | **ŋ̊i³¹** | penis | DQ-Xiandao:141 |
|---|---|---|---|
| Bola | **ŋ̊ji³⁵** | penis | DQ-Bola:141 |
| | **ŋ̊ji³⁵ tʃi̱³⁵** | testicles | DQ-Bola:142 |
| Lashi | **ŋ̊ji⁵⁵ mou⁵⁵** | male pubic hair | DQ-Lashi:10.3.6 |
| | **ŋ̊ji⁵⁵ tʃei⁵⁵** | testicle | DQ-Lashi:10.3.5 |
| Maru [Langsu] | **n?yī** | penis | AW-TBT:294; JAM-GSTC:049 |
| | **ŋ̊ji³⁵ muk⁵⁵** | male pubic hair | DQ-Langsu:10.3.6 |
| | **ŋ̊ji̱³⁵ tʃi̱k⁵⁵** | testicle | DQ-Langsu:10.3.5 |

---

[25] Lit. "penis-shit".

[26] For the second syllable, see **(115)** ***N-yaŋ** PENIS / TESTICLE / STINGER (of bee).

| Atsi [Zaiwa] | nʔyì | penis | AW-TBT:294; JAM-GSTC:049 | |
|---|---|---|---|---|
| 6.2. Loloish | | | | |
| Lahu (Banlan) | ni_ | penis | DB-Lahu:122 | |
| *Common Lahu | *ni_ | penis | DB-PLolo:122 | |
| Lahu (Shehleh) | ni_ hk'eh˯ | penis | DB-Lahu:122 | |
| Lahu (Bakeo) | ni_ hk'eh˯ | penis | DB-Lahu:122 | |
| Lahu (Nyi) | nyi_ hk'eh˯ | penis | DB-Lahu:122 | |
| Lahu (Black) | nɨ thû | have an erection; be aroused | JAM-DL:681,769 | |
| | nɨ(-qhɛ̀ʔ) | penis | JAM-Ety | |
| | nɨ-chu | semen | JAM-TJLB:83 | 27 |
| | nɨ-mu | male pubic hair | JAM-DL:769 | |
| | nɨ-ó-qō | glans penis | JAM-Ety | 28 |
| | nɨ-qhɛ̀ʔ | penis | JAM-GSTC:049; JAM-TJLB:260 | 29 |
| | nɨ-qhɛ̂ | smegma; semen | JAM-Ety | 30 |
| | nɨ-šī | testicle | JAM-Ety | |
| | nɨ-sī-phɨ | scrotum | JAM-Ety | 31 |
| | nɨ-sī-u | testicle | JAM-Ety | |
| | nɨ-u-tɛ́ | testicle | JAM-Ety | |
| Mpi | ne² | penis | DB-PLolo | 32 |
| Phunoi | nè | penis | DB-PLolo | |
| Ugong | ní | penis | DB-Ugong:10.3.1 | |
| | ní khû | testicle | DB-Ugong:10.3.5 | |
| | ní kɔŋ | penis hole | DB-Ugong | |
| | ní mɛ́ŋ | male pubic hair | DB-Ugong:10.3.6 | |
| | ní wŭŋ | semen | DB-Ugong:10.3.7 | |

# (115)    *N-yaŋ    PENIS / TESTICLE / STINGER (of bee)

This etymon has so far been uncovered almost exclusively in Kamarupan, where it is widely attested. The Lailenpi and Lotha forms point to a prototype with nasal prefix, *N-yaŋ. Many of the daughter languages have developed initial z- in this etymon. In several languages, the meaning of this word extends to 'stinger of bee', which perhaps is the original meaning. For the stinging semantics, cf. vulgar English *prick*.

An excellent extra-Kamarupan candidate for cognacy is Jingpho **rāŋ** 'to be concupiscent; to be driven by sexual desires; to burn with lust' (Hanson 1906/1954:564), recorded as **ʒaŋ³³** in Dai, et al. 1983:684, where it is glossed 性冲动 'sexual impulse'.

---

[27] Second element means 'fat; grease'.

[28] Literally "penis-head". The last syllable is from Proto-Loloish *ʔguŋ² 'hollow object; head'.

[29] Lahu **qhɛ̀ʔ** means 'to be notched'; probably so called because of the notched appearance of the *corona glandis*.

[30] The second element means 'shit; body waste'.

[31] The last element means 'nest; receptacle'. See **(108)** *kʷəy NEST / WOMB / PLACENTA, Chapter VI. It occurs in many other Lahu compounds, including **yâ-phɨ** 'placenta' ("child-nest"), **á-thɔ-phɨ** 'scabbard; sheath' ("knife-nest"), **ú-gê-phɨ** 'pillow-case', **khá-cè-phɨ** 'quiver for arrows', **yɨʔ-phɨ** 'bed' ("sleep-nest"), **lɨʔ-phɨ** 'envelope', etc.

[32] According to Bradley (1978:304-5), this form is apparently a doublet of Mpi **tɕhɑ²lɑʔ⁴**; see **(114a)**.

See the compound **ne**[31] **ʒaŋ**[33] 'sexually potent male', under **(114b)** ***m-ney** PENIS, above.

### 1.1. North Assam

| | | | |
|---|---|---|---|
| Darang [Taraon] | **sã:** brã | scrotum | JAM-Ety |
| | **sha:** brẽ | scrotum | JAM-Ety |
| Milang | **ɲaŋ**-ke | male | AT-MPB |

### 1.2. Kuki-Chin

| | | | |
|---|---|---|---|
| *Chin | ***yaŋ** | penis / stinger (of bee) | KVB-PKC:1224 |
| Ashö [Sho] (Sandoway) | **ă`yauŋ2** | penis | GHL-PPB:P.20 |
| Cho (Mindat) | **yang** | penis | KVB-PKC:1224 |
| Khualsim | **zaŋ²** | penis | GHL-PPB:P.20 |
| Awa Khumi | **ă yã²** | penis | GHL-PPB:P.20 |
| Khumi | **jaang** | penis; stinger (of bee) | KVB-PKC:1224 |
| Khumi (Bangladesh) | **yaang** kduy | male genitals ("penis + testicles") | DAP-Chm |
| Awa Khumi | **yã³dü²** | testicles | GHL-PPB:P.13 |
| Khumi (Ahraing) | **yã¹** | penis | GHL-PPB:P.20 |
| Kom Rem | **j̆əŋ** | penis | T-KomRQ:10.3.1 |
| | **j̆əŋ** kəti mu | testicle | T-KomRQ:10.3.5 |
| | **j̆əŋ** mih | male pubic hair | T-KomRQ:10.3.6 |
| | **j̆əŋ** mətʰer | glans penis | T-KomRQ:10.3.2 |
| | **j̆əŋ** vun | foreskin ("penis-skin") | T-KomRQ:10.3.3 |
| Lai (Hakha) | **zâŋ** | penis; stinger (of bee) | KVB-Lai |
| Lai (Falam) | **záŋ** | penis; stinger (of bee) | KVB-PKC:1224 |
| Lai (Hakha) | **zaŋ⁵** | penis | GHL-PPB:P.20 |
| Lailenpi | **mə yə'¹** | penis | GHL-PPB:P.20 |
| Lakher [Mara] | **zá** | penis | KVB-PKC:1224 |
| | **za**-vo | foreskin ("penis-skin") | JAM-Ety |
| | **za**-vo-tai | circumcision | JAM-Ety |
| Lothvo (Hiranpi) | **yuə³** | penis | GHL-PPB:P.20 |
| | **ʒuə³** | penis | GHL-PPB:P.20 |
| Lushai [Mizo] | **zang** | penis | JAM-Ety |
| | **zang** tan | circumcise | JAM-Ety |
| | **zăŋ** | penis; stinger (of bee) | KVB-PKC:1224 |
| | **zaŋ³** | penis | GHL-PPB:P.20 |
| Matupi | **yɑŋ⁴** | penis | GHL-PPB:P.20 |
| Mera | **zɑ'¹** | penis | GHL-PPB:P.20 |
| Sizang | **zang** | penis | KVB-PKC:1224 |
| Tha'oa | **yaŋ²** | penis | GHL-PPB:P.20 |
| Thado | **záŋ** | penis | KVB-PKC:1224 |
| Thanphum | **ʒɑŋ⁵** | penis | GHL-PPB:P.20 |
| Tiddim | **zang¹** | penis | KVB-PKC:1224 |
| | **zaŋ³** | penis | GHL-PPB:P.20 |

---

[33]The initial **ɲ-** looks like a fusion of the nasal prefix plus the root-initial **y-**.

| | | | | |
|---|---|---|---|---|
| Womatu | yak¹tui⁴ | testicles | GHL-PPB:P.13 | 34 |
| | yaŋ¹ | penis | GHL-PPB:P.20 | |
| Xongsai | zaŋ² | penis | GHL-PPB:P.20 | |
| | ʒaŋ² | penis | GHL-PPB:P.20 | |
| Zotung | zã⁵ | penis | GHL-PPB:P.20 | |

**1.3. Naga**

| | | | | |
|---|---|---|---|---|
| Lotha Naga | Njo | penis | VN-LothQ:10.3.1 | |
| | Njo hum | male pubic hair | VN-LothQ:10.3.6 | |
| | njo tsung | testicle | VN-LothQ:10.3.5 | |
| Phom | daŋ³³ | penis | JAM-II | |
| Tangkhul | shaŋ hon | ring on the penis; *corona glandis* | JAM-Ety | |
| | shaŋ khā | testicle | JAM-Ety | |
| | shaŋ kui | penis | JAM-Ety | 35 |

**1.4. Meithei**

| | | | |
|---|---|---|---|
| Moyon | jʌŋ | penis | DK-Moyon:10.3.1 |
| | jʌŋ bów | semen | DK-Moyon:10.3.7 |
| | jʌŋ bów isòw? | ejaculate (v.) | DK-Moyon:10.3.8 |
| | jʌŋ brí | glans penis | DK-Moyon:10.3.2 |
| | jʌŋ brí khùm | foreskin | DK-Moyon:10.3.3 |
| | jʌŋ mówr | male pubic hair | DK-Moyon:10.3.6 |

**4.1. Jingpho**

| | | | |
|---|---|---|---|
| Jingpho | ne³¹ʒaŋ³³ | sexually potent male | JCD |

## (116a)  *k-tu-k  PENIS

This root, which has allofams both with and without a final velar stop, is found in several different subgroups of TB: Kamarupan, Himalayish, Luish (Sak), Qiangic (including Xixia), and Baic. It has so far not been discovered in Lolo-Burmese or Karenic.

This root resembles **(116b) *tsu** PENIS. The possibility that these two etyma might be one and the same is reinforced by the natural tendency of /t/ to become affricated before /u/, as witnessed by Japanese, where /tu/ is realized as [tsɯ].

This etymon also bears a perhaps accidental resemblance to **(76) *s-tu ≍ *tsu** VAGINA.

An apparently prefixal **k-** is attested in Kham and Spiti. Cf. also the Tangut binome **khǐu thu**.

**1.1. North Assam**

| | | | |
|---|---|---|---|
| Damu | mak-**tuk** | penis | JS-Tani |

**1.3. Naga**

| | | | |
|---|---|---|---|
| Angami (Kohima) | (u) tho⁵⁵ | penis | VN-AngQ:10.3.1 |
| Chokri | thü³¹ la³¹ | penis | VN-ChkQ:10.3.1 |
| Chakrü | ²u²tho²la | penis | AW-TBT:142 |

---

[34]Note the denasalization of the final consonant of the first syllable before the voiceless stop onset of the second syllable. For the second syllable, see **(2a) *d(w)əy** EGG / TESTICLE, above.

[35]The second syllable is homophonous with Tangkhul **kui** 'head', though this seems to be fortuitous, since the form does not mean 'glans'. It assigned below to **(127) *s-kyu** MALE / PENIS.

1.7. Bodo-Garo = Barish

| | | | | |
|---|---|---|---|---|
| Lalung | **tu** dar | penis | MB-Lal:78 | 36 |
| | **tu** khi sha la | scrotum | MB-Lal:78 | |
| | **tu** ki ku thi | testicle | MB-Lal:78 | |

2.1.2. Bodic

| | | | |
|---|---|---|---|
| Spiti | **koto** | penis | CB-SpitiQ:10.3.1 |

2.1.5. Dhimal

| | | | |
|---|---|---|---|
| Dhimal | **tau** | penis | JK-Dh |
| | **ta** muĩ | man's pubic hair | JK-Dh |
| | **ta** tui | penis | JK-Dh |

2.2. Newar

| | | | |
|---|---|---|---|
| Newar (Dolakhali) | **tuk** la | penis | CG-Dolak |

2.3.1. Kham-Magar-Chepang-Sunwar

| | | | |
|---|---|---|---|
| Kham | **katu** | penis; penis (child's) | DNW-KhamQ |

3.1. Tangut

| | | | |
|---|---|---|---|
| Tangut [Xixia] | khĭ̱ **thu** | penis | DQ-Xixia:10.3.1 |
| | **thu²** | penis | MVS-Grin |
| | **Tu** | penis | NT-SGK:269-052 |

3.3. rGyalrongic

| | | | |
|---|---|---|---|
| rGyalrong (Northern) | tə skʰər **dok** | testicle | SHK-rGNQ:10.3.5 |

8. Bai

| | | | | |
|---|---|---|---|---|
| Bai | **tu³³** | penis | ZYS-Bai:10.3.1 | |
| | **tu³³ tu̱²¹ po̱²¹ kʰo³³** | glans penis | ZYS-Bai:10.3.2 | 37 |

# (116b)　　　　　　　　　*tsu　　　　　　　　PENIS

This allofam is only shakily attested. The Spiti and Ergong forms look parallel, and it is possible that the latter is a borrowing from a western Tibetan dialect (no similar form has been uncovered in Written Tibetan). The fit between the Hayu form and the others is excellent.

1.3. Naga

| | | | |
|---|---|---|---|
| Ao Naga | ²ta³**tsɯ**³tšaŋ | testicle | AW-TBT:617a |

2.1.2. Bodic

| | | | |
|---|---|---|---|
| Spiti | bu **tsu** | penis | CB-SpitiQ:10.3.1 |

2.3.2. Kiranti

| | | | |
|---|---|---|---|
| Hayu | **tsu** | penis | BM-Hay:72.1.109, |

3.2. Qiangic

| | | | |
|---|---|---|---|
| Ergong (Daofu) | pə **tsə** | penis | DQ-Daofu:10.3.1 |

---

[36] A Lalung subtlety should be noted: the first elements of **tu-dar** 'penis' and **tu ki ku-thi** 'testicle' are to be assigned to (116a) *k-tu-k PENIS; on the other hand, the first element of Lalung **tu-di** 'egg' is from (H:226-7) *daw BIRD 'bird'. This is somewhat confusing, since (2a) *d(w)əy EGG / TESTICLE (see above, Chapter I) sometimes means 'testicle' rather than 'egg'.

[37] Cf. Bai **tu̱²¹ po̱²¹** 'head'.

# (117)        *ti-k        PENIS

This etymon is well-attested in Karenic and apparently also in Lolo-Burmese (see note above under **(114a)** ***m-ley** ⩨ ***m-li** PENIS), with scattered but good-looking cognates in Kamarupan (Meithei), Himalayish, and Luish (Jingpho-Nungish-Luish).

In Chart L (Sak-Luish Group) of Luce 1996, under the confusing gloss "Penis/Testicles", two forms are given from Bawtala Sak, one from Dodem Sak, two from Ganan, and two from Kadu (Kantu). Where two forms are given from the same language, separated by a semicolon, I have assumed that the first one means 'penis' and the second one 'testicles', and have reglossed them accordingly. Under this interpretation, some syllables are assigned to the present root; while others, phonologically quite similar, are taken to mean 'testicle', and are assigned to **(2a)** ***d(w)əy** EGG / TESTICLE, above [q.v.].

Rather arbitrarily, I assign reflexes with stop initials to this root and those with fricated or palatalized initials to **(118)** ***dzi** PENIS.

Like the previous etymology **(116a)** ***k-tu-k** PENIS, some reflexes of this root have a final **-k**.

The resemblance to English *dick* appears entirely accidental.

| | | | | |
|---|---|---|---|---|
| **1.4. Meithei** | | | | |
| Meithei | **ti** | penis | CYS-Meithei:10.3.1 | |
| **2.1.1. Western Himalayish** | | | | |
| Bunan | **tig** pa | testicle | SBN-BunQ:10.3.5 | |
| **2.1.2. Bodic** | | | | |
| Tibetan (Written) | **tʻig-le** | *semen virile*; contemplation | JAM-Ety | 38 |
| **2.1.3. Lepcha** | | | | |
| Lepcha | **tʻik-ṅak** | glans penis | GBM-Lepcha:151 | |
| | **tʻik-uṅ** | *sperma genitale*; semen | GBM-Lepcha:151 | |
| | **tʻik** | penis | JAM-Ety | |
| **6.2. Loloish** | | | | |
| Bisu | **lɛ̀ thɛ** | penis | PB-Bisu:15 | |
| Lalo | **de-fu** | testicle | SB-Lalo | |
| | **de³³ tɕʰy⁵⁵** | male pubic hair | CK-YiQ:10.3.6 | |
| | **de³³se²¹** | testicle | CK-YiQ:10.3.5 | 39 |
| Lipho | **dɛ³³** | penis | CK-YiQ:10.3.1 | |
| | **dɛ³³fu³³** | testicle | CK-YiQ:10.3.5 | |

[38] This curious form receives four glosses in Jäschke, p. 231: (1) 'spot (as on a leopard)'; (2) 'zero, naught'; (3) *'semen virile'*; (4) 'contemplation'. Jäschke remarks that the last two senses are "mystically connected with each other" in Buddhist thought. (The sense of 'naught' seems like a recent extension of 'spot', since a small zero looks like a dot.) On *a priori* semantic grounds, another WT word, **tʻigs-pa** 'drop (of liquid)' also looks like it might be related; but in other Himalayish languages similar forms have no liquid associations, e.g. Bunan **tig-pa** 'testicle' and Lepcha **tʻik** 'penis'. It looks as if 'spot/zero' and 'semen/contemplation' are mere homophones.

[39] The second syllable means 'round object' < **(H:206)** ***sey** FRUIT / ROUND OBJECT.

| | | | | |
|---|---|---|---|---|
| | dɛ³³vi³³ | semen | CK-YiQ:10.3.7 | 40 |
| Lolopho | dæ³³ muɯ³³ | male pubic hair | DQ-Lolopho:10.3.6 | |
| | dæ³³ sæ³¹ | testicle | DQ-Lolopho:10.3.5 | 41 |
| | dæ³³ vi³³ | semen | DQ-Lolopho:10.3.7 | 42 |
| | dæ³³ ɣ⁵⁵ dɯ³³ | glans penis | DQ-Lolopho:10.3.2 | 43 |
| | dæ³³ zo³¹ | penis | DQ-Lolopho:10.3.1 | |
| Nesu | der²¹ fu²¹ | testicle | CK-YiQ:10.3.5 | |
| Sani [Nyi] | dæ³³ | penis | YHJC-Sani:78.1 | |
| | dæ³³ ɬɑ³³ n̩⁴⁴ ma³³ | testicles | YHJC-Sani:78.2 | |
| | dɛ³³ | penis | CK-YiQ | |
| | dɛ³³ɬɒ³³nɪ³³mɒ³³ | testicles | YHJC-Sani | |
| | tæ³³ ɬɑ³³ ma³³ | penis | MXL-SaniQ:314.5 | |
| | tæ³³ ɬɑ³³ n̩⁴⁴ | testicles | MXL-SaniQ:314.6 | |
| | tæ³³ɬɑ³³ma³³ | penis | CK-YiQ:10.3.1 | |
| | tæ³³ɬɑ³³ma³³no⁴⁴ | male pubic hair | CK-YiQ:10.3.6 | |
| | tæ³³ɬɑ³³n̩⁴⁴ | testicle | CK-YiQ:10.3.5 | |

**7. Karenic**

| | | | |
|---|---|---|---|
| *Karen (Pho) | *théq | penis | RBJ-KLS:531 |
| *Karen (Sgaw) | *thé? | penis | RBJ-KLS:531 |
| Bwe (Western) | cʻɪ² | penis | GHL-PPB:J.220 |
| Geba | ă tʻi² | penis | GHL-PPB:J.220 |
| Pa-O | tê | penis | JAM-Ety; RBJ-KLS:531 |
| Pa-O (Northern) | te¹ | penis | GHL-PPB:J.220 |
| Pho (Tenasserim) | tʻe¹ | penis | GHL-PPB:J.220 |
| Pho (Delta) | tʻe⁴ | penis | GHL-PPB:J.220 |
| Pho (Bassein) | thè | penis | JAM-Ety; RBJ-KLS:531 |
| Pho (Moulmein) | thé? | penis | JAM-Ety; RBJ-KLS:531 |
| Paku | tʻe³ | penis | GHL-PPB:J.220 |
| Sgaw | tʻe⁴ | penis | GHL-PPB:J.220 |
| Sgaw (Bassein) | thè | penis | JAM-Ety; RBJ-KLS:531 |
| Karen (Sgaw/Hinthada) | tʰe³¹ | penis | DQ-KarenB:144 |
| Sgaw (Moulmein) | thé? | penis | JAM-Ety; RBJ-KLS:531 |

# (118)　　　　　　　　　*dzi　　　　　　　　　PENIS

This etymon seems solid enough, though it has a rather strange distribution, occurring in scattered languages of the Himalayish, Lolo-Burmese (including Jinuo), and Jingpho-Nungish groups, as well as in the unclassified Tujia. There is not yet enough evidence to decide whether to reconstruct a *voiced or *voiceless initial, or both *voiced and *voiceless allofams.

This root looks as if it might stand in an allofamic relationship with **(117) *ti-k** PENIS. Note, however, that the reflexes of **(117)** and the present root are quite different in Nesu and Sani.

---

[40] Literally "penis-water".
[41] The second syllable means 'round object' < **(H:206) *sey** FRUIT / ROUND OBJECT.
[42] Literally "penis-water".
[43] The second element **ɣ⁵⁵ dɯ³³** means 'head'.

2.3.2. Kiranti

| | | | |
|---|---|---|---|
| Hayu | tsɪːpɪ | penis | BM-Hay:72.1.109, |

4. Jingpho-Nung-Luish

| | | | |
|---|---|---|---|
| Kadu (Kantu) | ti¹ | penis | GHL-PPB:L.149 |
| Sak (Bawtala) | ă tji² | penis | GHL-PPB:L.149 |
| | ă tji² tu⁴ | testicles | GHL-PPB:L.149 |
| Sak (Dodem) | ă tji⁴ | penis | GHL-PPB:L149 |

5. Tujia

| | | | |
|---|---|---|---|
| Tujia | zi²¹ | penis | CK-TujBQ:10.3.1 |
| | ʐi³⁵ | penis | CK-TujMQ:10.3.1 |

6.2. Loloish

| | | | |
|---|---|---|---|
| Ahi | a⁵⁵ɕi²¹ | penis | CK-YiQ:10.3.1 |
| | a⁵⁵ɕi²¹nɯ³³ | male pubic hair | CK-YiQ:10.3.6 |
| | dzi³³ | penis | LMZ-AhiQ:10.3.1 |
| | dzi³³ nɯ³³ | male pubic hair | LMZ-AhiQ:10.3.6 |
| Nasu | dzi²¹ | penis | CK-YiQ:10.3.1 |
| Nesu | dzi²¹ | penis | CK-YiQ:10.3.1 |
| | dzi³¹ nu³³ | male pubic hair | CK-YiQ:10.3.6 |
| Nosu | dze²¹ɲe³³ | male pubic hair | CK-YiQ:10.3.6 |
| Sani [Nyi] | dzi³³ | penis | YHJC-Sani |
| | dzɿ³³ | penis | MXL-SaniQ:351.5 |

6.4. Jinuo

| | | | |
|---|---|---|---|
| Jinuo (Baya/Banai) | tʃʰɤ⁵⁵ lɤ³¹ | penis | DQ-JinA:144 |

# (119)            *m-be            PENIS

On the basis of the data so far available, this etymon has a fairly wide though scattered distribution, with reflexes in a single Himalayish language (Hayu), a few closely related Loloish languages (Noesu, Nosu, Nusu), and a couple of Qiangic languages (rGyalrong and Xixia). It is noteworthy that the nasal prefix is overtly attested in Hayu, rGyalrong, and Xixia, so that it may confidently be set up for PTB. This etymon is quite distinct from the most widely attested root for PENIS with nasal prefix, **(114a) *m-ley ≍ *m-li** PENIS above, as proven e.g. by the Hayu reflexes: ***m-ley** > Hayu **mli**, ***m-be** > Hayu **-(m)be**.

2.3.2. Kiranti

| | | | | |
|---|---|---|---|---|
| Hayu | khõːbe | penis | JAM-Ety | |
| | kho mbe | penis | BM-PK7:138 | |
| | tsɪːpɪ | penis | BM-Hay:72.1.109, | 44 |

3.1. Tangut

| | | | |
|---|---|---|---|
| Tangut [Xixia] | mbefi | penis | NT-SGK:211-112 |
| | mbɪn² | penis | MVS-Grin |

3.3. rGyalrongic

| | | | |
|---|---|---|---|
| rGyalrong (NW) | tə mbi | penis | SHK-rGNWQ:10.3.1 |
| | tə mbi ku | glans penis | SHK-rGNWQ:10.3.2 |
| | tə mbi r̥tʰə | semen | SHK-rGNWQ:10.3.7 |

[44] The relationship between the apparent Hayu doublets, **-pɪ** and **-(m)be**, is not clear.

|  | tə **mbi** r̥tʰə kətə | ejaculate | SHK-rGNWQ:10.3.8 |
|---|---|---|---|
|  | tə **mbi** tɕʰim | foreskin | SHK-rGNWQ:10.3.3 |
| rGyalrong (Northern) | tə **mbu** ndzom | glans penis | SHK-rGNQ:10.3.2 |
|  | tə **mbu** r̥qʰu | foreskin | SHK-rGNQ:10.3.3 |
|  | tə **mbu** tɕi | semen | SHK-rGNQ:10.3.7 |

6.2. Loloish

| Noesu | **be³³** | penis | CK-YiQ:10.3.1 |
|---|---|---|---|
|  | **be³³mi²¹** | male pubic hair | CK-YiQ:10.3.6 |
| Nosu | **be³³** | penis | CK-YiQ:10.3.1 |
| Nusu (Central/Zhizhiluo) | **bɯ⁵⁵** | penis | DQ-NusuA:141. |

# (120)         *pot         PENIS

This etymon is of very restricted distribution, occurring only in the Jingpho-Luish group. It appears unrelated to the equally restricted etymon *pok, below (121). A Lepcha form tălam-pót 'testicles' is not to be brought in here, since the last element (pót, a-pót) means 'fruit; ball', and recurs in other bodypart compounds like nyen-pót 'woman's breast; cow's udder' and anyor-pót 'dewlap'.

4. Jingpho-Nung-Luish

| Ganan | kăpɔ³ ti¹ | testicles | GHL-PPB:L.149 | 45 |
|---|---|---|---|---|
|  | kăpɔ¹ pɔʔ krɔʔ⁴ | penis | GHL-PPB:L.149 |  |
| Kadu (Kantu) | kăpɔt³ ti¹ | testicles | GHL-PPB:L.149 |  |

4.1. Jingpho

| Jingpho | ne³¹**pot³¹** | penis shaft | JCD |
|---|---|---|---|

# (121)         *pok         SCROTUM

This root has only been found in a few languages, two Himalayish (Dumi, Tamang) and one Qiangic (rGyalrong), though the phonological and semantic fit among them is excellent.

There is a probably fortuitous resemblance between this root and (120) *pot PENIS.

2.1.4. Tamangic

| Tamang (Risiangku) | ⁴**pak** si | testicle | MM-TamRisQ:10.3.5 |
|---|---|---|---|

2.3.2. Kiranti

| Dumi | **phok** sɨ | scrotum | SVD-Dum | 46 |
|---|---|---|---|---|

3.3. rGyalrongic

| rGyalrong (Eastern) | tə rgo **pok** cco | scrotum | SHK-rGEQ:10.3.4 | 47 |
|---|---|---|---|---|

---

[45] For the last syllable of the Ganan and Kadu forms, see (2a) *d(w)əy EGG / TESTICLE, above.

[46] The second syllables of the Dumi and Tamang (Risiangku) forms are < (H:206) *sey FRUIT / ROUND OBJECT.

[47] rGyalrong tə rgo means 'testicle'; see (7) *s/r-go-ŋ EGG / TESTICLE, above.

(122)                          *teŋ                    PENIS / CLITORIS / LONG

This etymon has been discovered in Himalayish (Chepang and Lepcha) and Kamarupan (Mikir). A pair of superficially resemblant forms must be banished from this etymon:

Garo **go'l-teng** 'penis' is analyzed by Burling as STICK + LONG. The gloss of **go'l** or **gol dik** as 'stick' is confirmed in K. W. Momin's *English-Achikku Dictionary* (n.d.:227). I have no independent evidence that **teng** means 'long' in Garo, although several other Kamarupan languages have similar forms with that meaning: Khoirao **ka tang ba**, Liangmei **ka-theŋ-bu**, Maram **tang**, Mikir **ke ding**, Rengma **ka thong**, Tangkhul **ka sang**, etc.

Lepcha **tălam t'yeṅ** 'testicle' must also be rejected. According to Mainwaring/Grünwedel (1898:164), the second element **t'yeṅ** actually means 'the chief or most precious part', as in **să-bŭr t'yeṅ** 'the musk bag or gland of the musk-deer'. The true Lepcha cognate is probably the first syllable of **čeṅ pă-tiṅ**.

1.5. Mikir
| Mikir | ing **teng** | clitoris | JAM-Ety | |
|---|---|---|---|---|

2.1.3. Lepcha
| Lepcha | **čeṅ** pă-tiṅ | penis | JAM-Ety | 48 |
|---|---|---|---|---|

2.3.1. Kham-Magar-Chepang-Sunwar
| Chepang | təiŋ | penis | AW-TBT:617a | |
|---|---|---|---|---|
| Chepang (Eastern) | təyŋ | genitalia; pudenda (male); penis | RC-ChepQ:10.1,10.3.1 | |
| | təyŋ kli? | semen | RC-ChepQ:10.3.7 | 49 |
| | təyŋ ta laŋ | glans penis | RC-ChepQ:10.3.2 | |
| | təyŋ thyo reŋ | foreskin | RC-ChepQ:10.3.3 | |
| | təŋ | penis | RC-ChepQ:10.3.1 | |

(123)       *ma:k    PENIS / MALE / SON-IN-LAW; GENITALS / VAGINA

This etymon seems basically to belong in masculine semantic space, since most TB reflexes mean PENIS. The likely Chinese comparandum 牡 means MALE (of certain birds and animals; see below), and this sense also occurs in TB (see Taraon **mau-a**, below), implying that MALE is the more original meaning.

Benedict 1979[50] suggests a connection with PTB *ma:k (better *s-ma:k) 'son-in-law' [STC #324; HPTB p. 325]: cf. WT **mag-pa**, Lepcha **myok**, Dhimal **hma-wa**, Miri **mak-bo** ~ **mag-bo**, Jingpho **dà-má?**, WB **səmak**, Lahu **ɔ̀-má-pā**, Lushai [Mizo] **ma:k-pa**. The long vowel is supported by the Mizo form, and the *s- prefix is evidenced indirectly by Lepcha (where -y- < *s-), and directly by Dhimal and WB. This *s- prefix is in turn undoubtedly a reduction of PTB *za SON / CHILD.

Nevertheless, this root has undergone an enantiodromic shift or "genital flipflop" to

---

[48]The last morpheme, **pă-tiṅ**, seems to mean 'small stick, switch' (Mainwaring, pp. 127-8).
[49]Literally "penis-shit".
[50]"A note on Karen genital flipflop", *LTBA* 5.1:22-23, n. 36.

mean VAGINA in both Mikir and (probably) Newar (neither of these forms was cited in Benedict 1979), so that it was evidently reinterpreted in some areas as 'genitals (of either sex)'. This makes one wonder whether the root **(86)** ***mo** VAGINA presented above on the basis of forms from Naga languages might also be somehow related to the present etymon.

### 1.1. North Assam

| | | | | |
|---|---|---|---|---|
| Padam [Abor] | **ma:g**-re:k | man's girdle or belt | JHL-AM | |
| Padam-Mising [Abor-Miri] | e **mâk** | penis | JAM-Ety | |
| | **mait** | penis | JAM-Ety | |
| | **mâk**-pop | male pubes | JAM-Ety | |
| | **mâk**-shik | foreskin; skin; to hide, shelter | JAM-Ety:84 | |
| | **mâng**-mî | semen | JAM-Ety | 51 |
| | **mâng**-muit | male pubic hair | JAM-Ety | |
| | ə-**mak** | penis | JS-HCST | |
| Bokar | **mok** | penis | JS-HCST:131 | |
| Damu | **mak**-tuk | penis | JS-Tani | |
| Gallong | ˆɤ **mak** | penis | AW-TBT:631 | |
| Mising [Miri] | **ma:k**-bo ~ **ma:g**-bo | cousin; son-in-law; brother-in-law | JHL-AM | 52 |
| Darang [Taraon] | **mau**-a: | male (human) | NEFA-Taraon | |

### 1.3. Naga

| | | | |
|---|---|---|---|
| Ao Naga | ³ta³**mi?** | penis | AW-TBT:142 |

### 1.5. Mikir

| | | | | |
|---|---|---|---|---|
| Mikir | **mak** | *os Veneris* (female pubic bone) | GDW-DML:98 | |
| | **mák** | vulva; labia; vagina | KHG-Mikir:160,160 | |
| | **mak**-phu | *mons Veneris* | JAM-Ety | 53 |

### 2.1.4. Tamangic

| | | | |
|---|---|---|---|
| Chantyal | **mfio** le | penis | NPB-ChanQ:10.3.1 |

### 2.2. Newar

| | | | |
|---|---|---|---|
| Newar (Kathmandu) | **maa** si | vagina / breast / milk | CG-Kath |
| Newar | **ma** si | vulva; labia; vagina | SH-KNw:10.4.1,10.4.2 |

### 3.3. rGyalrongic

| | | | |
|---|---|---|---|
| rGyalrong | **mo** | penis | DQ-Jiarong:10.3.1 |

## Chinese comparandum

A likely Chinese comparandum has been suggested by Benedict 1979, pp. 22-23 and n. 36: 牡 OC **môg**/MC **mə̪u** [irreg.] 'male'.

[JAM]

---

[51] The final nasals in the first syllables of Abor-Miri 'semen' and 'male pubic hair' have evidently arisen via assimilation to the initial of the following syllables.

[52] A cousin is a prospective brother-in-law in cross-cousin marriages.

[53] In view of the gloss, the last syllable might mean something like 'swelling; protuberance'; it bears a resemblance to other reflexes of the well-attested root **(H:252) *bwam** PLUMP/SWOLLEN.

牡 **mǔ** 'male (quadruped)'

*GSR*: 1063a       Karlgren: **\*môg**       Li: **\*məgwx**       Baxter: **\*m(r)juʔ**

The Middle Chinese reflex of this word has irregular vocalism. This accounts for the discrepancy between Baxter's reconstruction (with medial **\*-j-**) and Li's (without medial **\*-j-**). The presence of **\*-j-** in Baxter's form accounts regularly for vocalic development, but the medial itself must then be assumed to drop irregularly in Middle Chinese.

The proposed connection to PTB **\*maːk** presents some difficulties. The Chinese vocalism would normally correspond to a rounded PTB vowel. (See examples in Gong 1995 sets 61-69.) Although those open syllables in OC reconstructed with **\*-g** by Karlgren and Li sometimes correspond to syllables with coda **\*-k** in PTB, more generally we find OC **\*-k** corresponding to PTB **\*-k** and open syllables corresponding to open syllables.

Schuessler (2007:391) argues that the Chinese word is related to Austroasiatic forms meaning 'male animal'.

[ZJH]

## (124)               \*s-nyak ⋊ \*s-nik               **PENIS / COPULATE**

This root seems basically to mean PENIS, with extensions into the meaning COPULATE. Some reflexes resemble those of **(114b)** **\*m-ney** PENIS, although Jingpho has distinct reflexes of both: **mənè ~ mənyè** 'penis' vs. **nèʔ ~ nyèʔ** 'copulate'. Evidence for the **\*s-** prefix is to be found in Lakher, Kom Rem, and Moyon.

Some likely reflexes have initial laterals, rather than nasals. Most of the Tani forms cited in J. Sun 1993:131 have labial rather than dental nasal clusters, but it seems more plausible to assign them to this etymon than to any other.

In *GSTC* #172, I compared the Lakher and Jingpho forms, but offered no reconstruction.

### 1.1. North Assam

| | | | |
|---|---|---|---|
| *Tani | **\*mrak** | penis | JS-HCST:289 |
| Apatani | à-**mja** | penis | JS-Tani |
| | ¹a²**mrya** | penis | AW-TBT:631 |
| Bengni | ñak | penis | JS-HCST |
| Tagin | (a-)**mlak** | penis | JS-HCST:131 |
| Bangru | mə³³lɔʔ⁵³ | penis | JS-HCST:334 |
| Sherdukpen | **lak** | penis | JS-HCST:334 |
| Sulung | a³³ la?⁵³ | penis | JS-HCST:334 |
| Yano | **mlak** | penis | JS-HCST:131 |

### 1.2. Kuki-Chin

| | | | |
|---|---|---|---|
| Kom Rem | ə **nho** | copulate | T-KomRQ:10.2 |
| Lakher [Mara] | **hnei** | copulate | JAM-GSTC:172 |

### 1.3. Naga

| | | | |
|---|---|---|---|
| Angami Naga | ⁴**na** | copulate | AW-TBT:155 |
| Angami (Kohima) | ke³¹ na³³ | copulate | VN-AngQ:10.2 |
| Ao Naga | ³ni³tɯp | copulate | AW-TBT:155 |
| Chokri | kü³¹ na⁵⁵ | copulate | VN-ChkQ:10.2 |

| Yimchungrü | [1]ne | copulate | AW-TBT:155 | |
|---|---|---|---|---|
| **1.4. Meithei** | | | | |
| Meithei | **na** nə bə | copulate | CYS-Meithei:10.2 | |
| Moyon | **ŋho?** | copulate | DK-Moyon:10.2 | |
| **2.1.3. Lepcha** | | | | |
| Lepcha | a-**ṅak** | penis | JAM-Ety | |
| | gar-**nek** | penis | JAM-Ety | 54 |
| | t'ik-**ṅak** | glans penis | GBM-Lepcha:151 | |
| **2.2. Newar** | | | | |
| Newar (Kathmandu) | **na** ku | penis | CG-Kath | |
| Newar | **na** ku | penis | SH-KNw:10.3.1 | 55 |
| | **na** ku gwara | glans penis | SH-KNw:10.3.2 | |
| **2.3.1. Kham-Magar-Chepang-Sunwar** | | | | |
| Chepang (Eastern) | lu? **na?** | copulate | RC-ChepQ:10.2 | |
| Kham | **ne:**h-nya | copulate | DNW-KhamQ:2.B.2.13 | |
| | **ne:**h-nyā | copulate | JAM-Ety | |
| | **ne:**ɦ-nyā | copulate | AW-TBT:155 | |
| **2.3.2. Kiranti** | | | | |
| Khaling | le-**ne** | copulate | JAM-Ety | |
| Limbu | **nik**-t(u) | copulate | AW-TBT:155 | |
| | **nik** ma | copulate | AW-TBT:155 | |
| | **nik** t- | copulate with | BM-Lim | |
| **4.1. Jingpho** | | | | |
| Jingpho | **nè? ~ nyè?** | copulate | JAM-Ety; JAM-GSTC:172 | 56 |

# (125) $*\genfrac{}{}{0pt}{}{b}{m}$-laŋ        PENIS / MALE / HUSBAND

This etymon has been identified in Himalayish, Jingpho, and Qiangic, though more support from the latter group would be welcome. The PTB root initial is taken to have been a *lateral, with both a labial nasal and a labial stop prefix attested.

According to K. P. Malla, the second syllable of Newar **mijɔ̃** 'male' is from Skt. *jana* 'man', not from the present root. The first syllable is from the widespread TB morpheme **(H:449) *r-mi(y)** PERSON / MAN.

J. Sun 1993:131 reconstructs Proto-Tani ***mrak**, but the forms he cites are better assigned to **(124) *s-nyak ≍ *s-nik** PENIS / COPULATE, above.

This root seems distinct from **(137) *la** MALE.

---

[54]The first syllable of this form resembles the second syllable of Kham or-'**kal** 'penis'. However, according to Mainwaring/Grünwedel 1898:53, the morpheme **gar** actually means 'curved, crooked at one end, bent'.

[55]According to K. P. Malla (p.c. 2007), -**ku** serves as a classifier for "a piece with some magnitude in girth or depth".

[56]The *Jinghpo-Chinese Dictionary* (Dai, et al. 1983:566) cites the form ne[31] 性交 [have sexual congress]' with no final glottal stop, making it look identical to the word for 'penis'.

Also to be brought into this etymon is WB **lâŋ**, which (as suggested in Matisoff 1995:52-3) is to be compared with Chinese 郎 (Mand. **láng**) [WHB **\*C-rāŋ**], now meaning 'young man; bridegroom; clf. for sons'. This word is glossed only as 'place name (Tso); double roof, one roof above the other' in *GSR* #735r. However, it would be rash to infer that the synchronic meaning did not exist at all in spoken OC.

See the remarks by Handel, below.

1.1. North Assam

| | | | | |
|---|---|---|---|---|
| Darang [Taraon] | **mlŏ** | penis | JAM-Ety | |
| Mising [Miri] | mil-**bong** | husband | PKB-KSEA:129 | 57 |
| Padam [Abor] | mi-**long** | husband; masculine suffix | PKB-KSEA:129 | 58 |

1.2. Kuki-Chin

| | | | |
|---|---|---|---|
| Liangmei | ka-lɛ̃ | penis | AW-TBT:142 |

2.1.2. Bodic

| | | | |
|---|---|---|---|
| Tsangla | **long** | penis | KDG-ICM:67 |
| Tsangla (Central) | **long** | penis | SER-HSL/T:34 3 |

2.1.3. Lepcha

| | | | |
|---|---|---|---|
| Lepcha | tyang-mo **long** | male elephant | PKB-KSEA:137 |

2.1.4. Tamangic

| | | | |
|---|---|---|---|
| Manang (Gyaru) | **byuŋ²** | male | YN-Man:147 |

3.2. Qiangic

| | | | |
|---|---|---|---|
| Muya [Minyak] | ʁo³⁵ | male | SHK-MuyaQ:10.3 |

3.3. rGyalrongic

| | | | |
|---|---|---|---|
| rGyalrong (NW) | tə ʁʑa | male | SHK-rGNWQ:10.3 |

4.1. Jingpho

| | | | |
|---|---|---|---|
| Jingpho | ne³¹laŋ³³ | penis | JCD |

6.1. Burmish

| | | | |
|---|---|---|---|
| Burmese (Written) | **lâŋ** | husband | PKB-WBRD |

## Chinese comparandum

郎 **láng** 'husband, young man'

| | | | |
|---|---|---|---|
| *GSR*: 735r | Karlgren: **\*lâng** | Li: **\*lang** | Baxter: **\*C-rang** |

The meaning 'husband, young man' is not attested until quite late. It appears to be derived from the basic sense 'veranda or corridor (of a palace or mansion)' via 'official (doing duty there)', making it an improbable cognate to PTB roots meaning 'male'. (See Schuessler 2007:344.)[59] Furthermore, nearly all scholars are now in agreement that Middle Chinese **l-** derives from earlier **\*r-**, and does not normally correspond to PTB **\*l-**.

[ZJH]

---

[57]Benedict 1941/2008:129 observes that this form "appears to be metathesized", implying an earlier form **mi-b-long**.

[58]The first syllable means 'person' < **(H:449) \*r-mi(y)** PERSON / MAN.

[59]Schuessler suggests that WB **laŋ** 'husband' is actually a loan from Chinese, though this seems unlikely in view of the paucity of Chinese loanwords in Burmese. [JAM]

**(126)**                      **\*gaŋ**                     **PENIS / MALE**

This etymon has solid reflexes in Kamarupan (Garo, Mikir) and Himalayish (Lepcha, Manchati). Several Chinese comparanda suggest themselves: 雄 OC **\*gi̯ŭng** 'male' [*GSR* 887-L] and/or 犅 OC **\*kâng** 'bull' [*GSR* 697f-g]. A less plausible comparison is with 公 **\*kung** 'father; prince' (although Karlgren notes that 'some of these forms seem to suggest a phallic interpretation') [*GSR* 1173a-f]. *STC* (n. 488, p. 190) suggests comparing this last Chinese morpheme to TB forms like Rawang **əkhaŋ** 'grandfather'; WB **pha'-khaŋ** 'father', **mi'-khaŋ** 'mother', **khaŋ-pwân** 'spouse', and **khaŋ-bhya** 'sir; madam'. It seems unlikely, however, that this group of forms has anything specifically to do with maleness; it seems rather to have been an honorific appellation for an elder or respected relative of either sex.

| | | | |
|---|---|---|---|
| 1.5. Mikir | | | |
| Mikir | chò-**kàng** | penis | KHG-Mikir:69 |
| 1.7. Bodo-Garo = Barish | | | |
| Garo | ri-**gaŋ** | penis | JAM-Ety; JAM-GSTC:049; STC:262 |
| Garo (Bangladesh) | ri-**gong** | penis | RB-GB |
| 2.1.1. Western Himalayish | | | |
| Pattani [Manchati] | **gàŋ** mì | male | STP-ManQ:10.3 |
| 2.1.3. Lepcha | | | |
| Lepcha | suň-**gaň** | penis | JAM-Ety |
| 9. Sinitic | | | |
| Chinese (Old) | **wjɨng** | male of birds and small animals | WHB-OC:1348 |

## Chinese comparanda

雄 **xióng** 'male'

*GSR*: 887l      Karlgren: **\*gi̯ŭng**      Li: **\*gwjəng**      Baxter: **\*wjɨng** (1348)

This proposed cognate is doubtful. The OC labialized initial plus schwa vocalism would normally correspond to a rounded vowel in PTB.

犅 **gāng** 'bull'

*GSR*: 697f-g      Karlgren: **\*kâng**      Li: **\*kang**      Baxter: **\*kang**

The proposed cognacy works phonetically, but one must also note a competing etymology with equally persuasive semantics that relates this Chinese word to WT **glang** 'cow, elephant'. (Gong 1995 and 2001 instead relate WT **glang** to OC 'elephant' 象 **\*gljangx** > **\*ljangx**.)

Schuessler (2007:251) suggests that 犅 may come from earlier **\*klaŋ**, and posits a relationship with Mru **klaŋ** 'male' and Lushai **tlaŋ** 'male', as well as with WT **glang**. He proposes a PTB root *laŋ with animal prefix *s- or *k-.[60]

Note the parallel etymology with a homophonous member of the same phonetic series 岡 'ridge', which has been compared to WT **sgang** 'hill, spur' and WB **khang** 'strip of high ground' (see for example Coblin 1986:94-2).[61]

[ZJH]

## (127)               *s-kyu                          MALE / PENIS

This etymon is represented by convincing cognates in Himalayish (Bunan, Kanauri) and Qiangic (rGyalrong, Xixia), though it is so far sparsely represented in TB as a whole.

**1.3. Naga**

| | | | | |
|---|---|---|---|---|
| Tangkhul | shaŋ **kui** | penis | JAM-Ety | 62 |

**2.1.1. Western Himalayish**

| | | | |
|---|---|---|---|
| Bunan | **khyua** | male | SBN-BunQ:10.3 |
| Kanauri | **skyo** | male | DS-Kan:37,41 |

**2.3.1. Kham-Magar-Chepang-Sunwar**

| | | | |
|---|---|---|---|
| Chepang (Eastern) | **goyʔ** co? | male | RC-ChepQ:10.3 |

**3.1. Tangut**

| | | | |
|---|---|---|---|
| Tangut [Xixia] | **khĭu̱** thu | penis | DQ-Xixia:10.3.1 |
| | **khi̱u²** | penis | MVS-Grin |
| | **kĭuɦ** | penis | NT-SGK:269-052 |

**3.3. rGyalrongic**

| | | | |
|---|---|---|---|
| rGyalrong (Northern) | tə **sku** | penis | SHK-rGNQ:10.3.1 |

## (128)      *səw-t      TESTICLES / PENIS / VIRILITY / SEMEN

This etymon is firmly established in Lolo-Burmese (Burmese itself has reflexes of both the stopped and non-stopped allofams) and Jingpho. The first syllable of Kham **zuh-ri:** 'testicle' is probably to be assigned to **(4) *dz(y)u** EGG rather than to the present root, in view of the 2nd syllable of the compound **'ba-zu-ri:** '(non-human) egg', where the first syllable means 'bird'. Palaychi (Karenic) **shóq** 'penis' seems unrelated.

The semantic center of the root seems to be VIRILITY. It occurs especially in compounds for intact (as opposed to castrated) male animals, with extensions into SEMEN, TESTICLES, and PENIS. This root was reconstructed for PLB in Matisoff 1988a:1225.

See *HPTB* PLB **\*səw¹/²**, p. 182.

**1.3. Naga**

| | | | |
|---|---|---|---|
| Khezha | **'è sò** | penis | SY-KhözhaQ:10.3.1 |

**4.1. Jingpho**

| | | | |
|---|---|---|---|
| Jingpho | ne-**zu** | semen | JAM-Ety |

[60] See the previous etymon **(125) *b/m-laŋ** PENIS / MALE / HUSBAND.

[61] See also *HPTB*:266, 303. [JAM]

[62] The second syllable is homophonous with Tangkhul **kui** 'head', though this seems to be fortuitous, since the form does not mean 'glans'.

| | ne³¹tsu³³ | semen | JCD | |
|---|---|---|---|---|
| | zū | semen | JAM-Ety; JAM-TJLB:83 | |
| | ə zu | semen | JAM-Ety | |
| 6.1. Burmish | | | | |
| Burmese (Written) | sui | penis; penis ( of animals ) | JAM-Ety; PKB-WBRD | 63 |
| | sut | semen | JAM-Ety; PKB-WBRD | |
| | ʔə sûi | testicle | JAM-Ety | |
| 6.2. Loloish | | | | |
| Lahu (Black) | ğâʔ-phu-šɔ̄ | uncastrated cock | JAM-DL:1225 | |
| | í-mû-šɔ̄ | stallion | JAM-DL:1225 | |
| | nû-šɔ̄ | bull | JAM-DL:1225 | |
| | nû-ɔ̀-pā-šɔ̄ | bull | JAM-Ety | |
| | vàʔ-šɔ̄ | uncastrated boar | JAM-DL:1225 | |
| | ɔ̀-pā-šɔ̄ | intact male animal | JAM-DL:1225 | |
| | ɔ̀-phu-šɔ̄ | intact male | JAM-Ety | |
| | ɔ̀-šɔ̄-tɔ̂ | castrated animal | JAM-Ety | |

## (129)  *r-lik  TESTICLE / EGG / PENIS

This etymon was already set up in Matisoff 1972a #170 as PLB *r-lek, on the basis of a single Loloish form (Akha) and WT **rlig-pa**. It is solidly attested in Himalayish, with possible cognates in Xixia and Kamarupan (esp. Mikir).

See *HPTB* *r-lik, pp. 344, 374.

| 1.5. Mikir | | | | |
|---|---|---|---|---|
| Mikir | che lèk | glans penis; penis | KHG-Mikir:64,64 | |
| 2.1.1. Western Himalayish | | | | |
| Kanauri | lik pā | penis (polite) | JAM-Ety | |
| | liṭ | egg | DS-Kan:28 | 64 |
| | līṭ(h) | egg | JAM-Ety | |
| | li:ṭ | egg | DS-Kan:29 | |
| Pattani [Manchati] | Tig **lhig** | egg (of animal) | STP-ManQ:10.4.16 | |
| | ṭig **lʰig** | egg, boil (sore) | DS-Patt | |
| 2.1.2. Bodic | | | | |
| Spiti | lik pa | testicle | CB-SpitiQ:10.3.5 | |
| Tibetan (Written) | gsaň-**rlig** | testicle (hon.) | JAM-Ety | |
| | mǰe-**rlig** | penis and testicles | JAM-Ety | |
| | **rlig**-bu | scrotum | JAM-Ety | |
| | **rlig**-pa | testicle | JAM-Ety | |
| | **rlig**-ṡubs | scrotum | JAM-Ety | 65 |
| 2.3.1. Kham-Magar-Chepang-Sunwar | | | | |
| Kham | zuh **ri:** | testicles | DNW-KhamQ | 66 |

[63]This form goes back to PLB Tone *1. It is the allofam **sûi** ( < PLB Tone *2) which is directly cognate to Lahu **šɔ̄**.

[64]The relationship of this Kanauri form for EGG to Kanauri **lik-pa** 'penis' is uncertain.

[65]Last syllable means 'case, covering, sheath'.

[66]For the first syllable, see **(4) *dz(y)u** EGG, above.

### 2.3.2. Kiranti

| | | | | |
|---|---|---|---|---|
| Belhare | la **lik** | semen, sperm | BB-Belhare | 67 |

### 3.1. Tangut

| | | | |
|---|---|---|---|
| Tangut [Xixia] | **le** | testicle | DQ-Xixia:10.3.5 |
| | **Le** | testicle | NT-SGK:269-111 |

### 6. Lolo-Burmese

| | | | |
|---|---|---|---|
| *Lolo-Burmese | *(**r-**)**lek** | testicle | JAM-TSR:170 |

### 6.2. Loloish

| | | | | |
|---|---|---|---|---|
| Akha | **leh LS** | testicle | JAM-TSR:170 | |
| | **leh‿ uˆ** | scrotum | JAM-Ety | |
| | **leh‿ uˆ leh‿ si˅** | scrotum | PL-AETD | 68 |
| Nasu | **ɬo²¹** | testicle | CK-YiQ:10.3.5 | |

# (130)                    *sen                    TESTICLE / EGG

This etymon is still not well established, with only scattered reflexes in Himalayish, Lolo-Burmese, Karenic, and Baic. The final nasal is reconstructed on the basis of the vowel nasalization in some Bai dialects.

### 2.1.5. Dhimal

| | | | |
|---|---|---|---|
| Dhimal | **syeq, syeq** guli | testicle | JK-Dh |

### 2.3.2. Kiranti

| | | | | |
|---|---|---|---|---|
| Hayu | **se: thoŋ** | testicle | JAM-Ety | 69 |

### 6.2. Loloish

| | | | |
|---|---|---|---|
| Nosu | **sɻ²¹pa³³** | testicle | CK-YiQ:10.3.5 |
| Phunoi | **shɛ̀ ʔu** | testicle | JAM-Ety |
| | **sʰɛ¹¹ ʔu³³** | testicles | DB-Phunoi |

### 7. Karenic

| | | | |
|---|---|---|---|
| Pho (Tenasserim) | **sʻɔ̃⁴ ɗi¹** | egg, tuber, testicles | GHL-PPB:G.80 |
| Pho (Delta) | **sʻɔ̃ ɗi⁴** | egg, tuber, testicles | GHL-PPB:G.80 |

### 8. Bai

| | | | |
|---|---|---|---|
| Bai | **sẽ⁴²** | egg (of animal) | ZYS-Bai:10.4.16 |
| Bai (Bijiang) | **sẽ⁴²** | egg | JZ-Bai |
| | **sẽ⁴²** | egg | ZMYYC:170.37 |
| Bai (Dali) | **se̲⁴²** | egg | JZ-Bai |
| | **se⁴²** | egg | ZMYYC:170.35 |
| | **sɛ⁵** | egg | FD-Bai:pp.150-169 |
| Bai (Jianchuan) | **sẽ̲⁴²** | egg | JZ-Bai |
| | **sẽ⁴²** | egg | ZMYYC:170.36 |

---

[67] For the first syllable, see **(157)** *ra ⪥ *wa SEMEN.

[68] Last syllable < **(H:206)** *sey FRUIT / ROUND OBJECT.

[69] It is possible that the first syllable of this Hayu form is rather < **(H:206)** *sey FRUIT / ROUND OBJECT.

## (131)                    *s-bloŋ                    SCROTUM / POUCH

This root has only been identified in three languages (Darang, Lepcha, and Bai), though the semantic and phonological fit is good among them. The basic meaning of the etymon is 'purse, small pouch' (cf. French *la bourse* 'purse; stock market', *les bourses* 'testicles'). The resemblance to **(125)** ***b/m-laŋ** PENIS / MALE / HUSBAND is due to chance.

1.1. North Assam

| | | | |
|---|---|---|---|
| Darang [Taraon] | sã: **brã** | scrotum | JAM-Ety |
| | sha: **brẽ** | scrotum | JAM-Ety |

2.1.3. Lepcha

| | | | |
|---|---|---|---|
| Lepcha | tă-**blyoŋ** | purse, pouch | JAM-Ety |
| | tălam să **tăblyóṅ** | scrotum | JAM-Ety |

8. Bai

| | | | |
|---|---|---|---|
| Bai | kuã³³ lõ²¹ | scrotum | ZYS-Bai:10.3.4 |

## (132)            *s-mu            SEED / TESTICLE / ROUND OBJECT

This etymon appears to be confined to Kamarupan and Monpa (Mama Tshona), with the basic meaning 'ball; round object', appearing in such transparent compounds as Lushai **mit-mu** 'eyeball' and **til-mu** 'testicle'. There is perhaps a cognate in Bisu.

1.2. Kuki-Chin

| | | | | |
|---|---|---|---|---|
| Anal | wɔ̀-**hmú** | seed | AW-TBT:299 | |
| Kom Rem | ǰəŋ kəti **mu** | testicle | T-KomRQ:10.3.5 | |
| Lakher [Mara] | mo **hmô** | eyeball | JAM-Ety | |
| | ti **hmô** | scrotum | JAM-Ety | 70 |
| | ²ə³**hmou** | seed | AW-TBT:299 | |
| Lushai [Mizo] | mit-**mu** | eyeball | JAM-Ety | |
| | **mû** | seed | AW-TBT:299 | |
| | **mu** | seed | GEM-CNL | |
| | til-**mu** | testicle | JAM-Ety | 71 |

1.5. Mikir

| | | | |
|---|---|---|---|
| Mikir | a **mū**(?) | seed | AW-TBT:299 |
| | mék a-**mū** | eyeball | KHG-Mikir:167 |
| | mek a **mu** | eyeball | JAM-Ety |
| | **mu** | seed | GEM-CNL |

1.7. Bodo-Garo = Barish

| | | | |
|---|---|---|---|
| Dimasa | bu **mu** | seed | GEM-CNL |

2.1.2. Bodic

| | | | |
|---|---|---|---|
| Tshona (Mama) | sir⁵⁵ sir⁵⁵ **mo**⁵³ | egg | SLZO-MLD |

6.2. Loloish

| | | | |
|---|---|---|---|
| Bisu | ʔaŋ **hnɯ** | seed | DB-Bisu |

---

[70] The first element is from **(2b)** *dil ✕ *dul EGG / TESTICLE.
[71] The first element is from **(2b)** *dil ✕ *dul EGG / TESTICLE.

## (133)  *dzəy  SEED / TESTICLE / ROUND OBJECT

The basic meaning of this etymon seems to be SEED, with extensions into SMALL
ROUND OBJECT, and thence to TESTICLE.

See *HPTB* *dzəy, pp. 31, 190.

### 1.2. Kuki-Chin

| | | | |
|---|---|---|---|
| Lakher [Mara] | $^2$ə$^3$tsi | seed | AW-TBT:148b |
| Lushai [Mizo] | chi | seed | GEM-CNL |
| | tsî | seed | AW-TBT:148b |
| Tiddim | tsĭ | seed | AW-TBT:148b |

### 1.3. Naga

| | | | |
|---|---|---|---|
| Angami (Khonoma) | tsa | seed | GEM-CNL |
| Angami (Kohima) | tsie | seed | GEM-CNL |
| Ao (Chungli) | me tsü | seed | GEM-CNL |
| Chokri | tsa | seed | GEM-CNL |
| Phom | šei-li | seed | JAM-GSTC:114 |
| | shei li | seed | GEM-CNL |

### 2.1.2. Bodic

| | | | |
|---|---|---|---|
| Tshona (Mama) | tɕu$^{13}$ | seed | ZMYYC:220.6 |

### 3.2. Qiangic

| | | | |
|---|---|---|---|
| Qiang (Mianchi) | zuì | pit, stone; bullet | JAM-II |
| | zuì zuí | testicles | JAM-II |

### 6.1. Burmish

| | | | |
|---|---|---|---|
| Achang (Xiandao) | li$^{55}$ tsi$^{31}$ | testicles | DQ-Xiandao:142 |
| | ɲɔʔ$^{55}$ tsi$^{31}$ | eyeball | DQ-Xiandao:101.3 |
| Bola | ŋji$^{35}$ tʂ$^{35}$ | testicles | DQ-Bola:142 |
| Burmese (Written) | a ce' | seed | GEM-CNL |
| | hwê-ce' ~ gwê-ce' | testicles | JAM-Ety |
| | hwê-ce'-ʔit | scrotum | JAM-Ety |
| | lî-ce' | testicle | JAM-Ety |
| | mjo$^3$se$^1$ | seed | ZMYYC:220.39 |
| | myui:ce' | seed | GEM-CNL |
| | ə-ce' | a seed | PKB-WBRD |
| Lashi | ŋji$^{55}$ tʃei$^{55}$ | testicle | DQ-Lashi:10.3.5 |
| Maru [Langsu] | ŋji$^{35}$ tʃik$^{55}$ | testicle | DQ-Langsu:10.3.5 |

### 6.2. Loloish

| | | | |
|---|---|---|---|
| Hani (Pijo) | à tzy | seed | ILH-PL:368 |
| Hani (Caiyuan) | a$^{31}$tsɻ$^{33}$ | seed | ZMYYC:220.30 |
| Hani (Wordlist) | al ssyuq | seed | ILH-PL:368 |
| Hani (Khatu) | à tzy | seed | ILH-PL:368 |

### 6.4. Jinuo

| | | | |
|---|---|---|---|
| Jinuo | a$^{33}$tsi$^{44}$ | seed | ZMYYC:220.34 |
| Jinuo (Baya/Banai) | li$^{55}$ tsɻ$^{33}$ | testicles | DQ-JinA:145 |
| Jinuo (Youle) | tʃɤ$^{35}$ | seed | JZ-Jinuo |
| Jinuo (Buyuan) | ɑ$^{44}$tsi$^{33}$ | seed | JZ-Jinuo |

### 8. Bai

| | | | |
|---|---|---|---|
| Bai (Dali) | tsv$^{33}$ | seed | ZMYYC:220.35 |
| Bai (Jianchuan) | tsṽ$^{33}$ | seed | ZMYYC:220.36 |

## (134)                  *ka               BALL / TESTICLE / EGG

This root seems basically to have meant 'ball', with natural extensions to EGG and TES-TICLE. A number of Himalayish compounds meaning PENIS have similar-looking morphemes (e.g. Baima **kha**$^{13}$ **ndʐ**$^{53}$, Bunan/Manchati **kha**-ṭa, Tamang **mlē**-**ka**) though the semantic development BALL → TESTICLE → PENIS is improbable, and these syllables must be assumed to reflect a separate etymon.

The Newar form **kwaa-si** does not belong in this set. According to K. P. Malla, it means literally "hot-fruits" (**si** < **(H:206)** ***sey** FRUIT / ROUND OBJECT). The true Newar cognate is represented by the second syllable of **mi-kha** 'eyeball', below.

| | | | | |
|---|---|---|---|---|
| **1.2. Kuki-Chin** | | | | |
| Liangmei | mai-tiŋ-**kha** | testicle | AW-TBT:617a | |
| **1.3. Naga** | | | | |
| Tangkhul | shaŋ **khā** | testicle | JAM-Ety | |
| **2.1.2. Bodic** | | | | |
| Kaike | **kā** pum | egg | JAM-Ety | |
| Tsangla (Central) | ming **khu** | pupil | SER-HSL/T:32 4 | |
| Tshona (Wenlang) | k$^h$a$^{55}$ lum$^{55}$ | egg | JZ-CNMenba | 72 |
| Tshona (Mama) | khAʔ$^{53}$lum$^{53}$ | egg | ZMYYC:170.6 | |
| | k$^h$Aʔ$^{53}$ lum$^{53}$ | egg | SLZO-MLD | |
| **2.2. Newar** | | | | |
| Newar | mi-**kha** | eyeball | KPM-pc | |
| **2.3.2. Kiranti** | | | | |
| Thulung | mī **ka** sī | eye | JAM-Ety | |
| Yakha | miʔ **ka**: makurna | iris | TK-Yakha:3.4.2.1 | |
| **.3.2. Qiangic** | | | | |
| Muya [Minyak] | mi$^{55}$kɯ$^{33}$lø$^{35}$ | eyeball | SHK-MuyaQ:3.4.2 | |
| **4.1. Jingpho** | | | | |
| Jingpho | myìʔ **hka** | eye-socket; eye-lid | JAM-Ety | |
| **4.2. Nungic** | | | | |
| Trung [Dulong] | ka$^{55}$lŭm$^{53}$ | egg | ZMYYC:170.46 | 73 |
| Trung [Dulong] (Dulonghe) | ka$^{55}$ lŭm$^{53}$ | egg | JZ-Dulong | |
| Trung [Dulong] (Nujiang) | k$^h$a$^{31}$ lŭm$^{53}$ | egg | JZ-Dulong | |
| **6.2. Loloish** | | | | |
| Lahu (Black) | mɛ̂ʔ-**qha**-lɛ̂ | eyeball | JAM-Ety:DL 1022 | |
| | mɛ̂ʔ-**qha**-phu | eyeball | JAM-Ety:DL 1022 | |
| **7. Karenic** | | | | |
| Bwe | mù-**ká** ə-phlú-θɛ | eyeball | EJAH-BKD | |
| **8. Bai** | | | | |
| Bai | ŋuĩ$^{33}$ **kæ**$^{55}$ çĩ$^{55}$ k$^h$o$^{33}$ | eyeball | ZYS-Bai:3.4.2 | |

---

[72]For the second syllable, see **(5)** ***rum** ⋉ ***lum** EGG, above.
[73]For the second syllable, see **(5)** ***rum** ⋉ ***lum** EGG, above.

# (135)           *kuk           POUCH / BASKET / SCROTUM

This root was reconstructed as meaning 'bag; basket; receptacle' in *STC* #393. It seems to refer often to a pannier, or hanging basket for transporting goods on an animal's back.

See *HPTB* *kuk, pp. 356, 359, 361.

| | | | | |
|---|---|---|---|---|
| 0. Sino-Tibetan | | | | |
| *Tibeto-Burman | *kuk | pouch, little bag | STC:393 | |
| 1.2. Kuki-Chin | | | | |
| Kom Rem | kəti kok | scrotum | T-KomRQ:10.3.4 | 74 |
| 1.3. Naga | | | | |
| *Northern Naga | *C$_{VD}$-kʰuk | bag | WTF-PNN:454 | |
| Konyak | ni khok | bag | GEM-CNL; WTF-PNN:454 | |
| Nocte | chi khok | small basket | WTF-PNN:454 | |
| Tangsa (Moshang) | ya khak | bag | GEM-CNL | |
| 1.5. Mikir | | | | |
| Mikir | hok | small hanging basket | STC:393 | |
| 1.7. Bodo-Garo = Barish | | | | |
| Dimasa | baiŋ-kho | basket carried on a load | STC:393 | |
| | bo kho | receptacle | STC:393 | |
| Garo | khok | basket | RJL-DPTB:3; STC:393 | |
| 2.1.2. Bodic | | | | |
| Tibetan (Amdo:Zeku) | kʰəg mæ | bag (small) | JS-Amdo:39 | |
| Tibetan (Written) | khug-ma | pouch; little bag | RJL-DPTB:3; STC:393; JS-Tib:39 | |
| 2.1.3. Lepcha | | | | |
| Lepcha | kóm ba-guk | purse | RJL-DPTB:3 | |
| | kóm ba-gŭk | purse | STC:393 | 75 |

# (136)           *ʔip ≍ *ʔiːt           BAG / SCROTUM

This etymon is firmly attested in Kamarupan and Burmese, and may be confidently set up for PTB. The basic meaning seems to be 'bag, pouch'. The final -p (instead of -t) in the Lushai form is unexplained.

See *HPTB* *ʔip ≍ *ʔiːt, p. 533.

| | | | |
|---|---|---|---|
| 1.1. North Assam | | | |
| Padam-Mising [Abor-Miri] | 'et-tum | testes and scrotum | JAM-Ety |
| Gallong | ˆɯt-tum `a pɤ | testicle | AW-TBT:617a |
| 1.2. Kuki-Chin | | | |
| Lushai [Mizo] | ip | bag | GEM-CNL |

---

[74] For the first element, see (2b) *dil ≍ *dul EGG / TESTICLE.
[75] The first element means 'silver; money'.

6.1. Burmish

| Burmese (Written) | hwê-ce'-ʔit | scrotum | JAM-Ety |
| | it | bag | GEM-CNL; PKB-WBRD |
| | kap-pay-ʔit | scrotum | JAM-Ety |

# (137)                          *la                          MALE

This etymon is very well attested in Kamarupan, Lolo-Burmese, and Jingpho, with possible cognates also in Himalayish. *STC* (p. 96) recognizes a 'masculine suffix' *-la, "used with words for animals (in Tsangla, Digaro, Nung, Kachin, Burmese-Lolo, Konyak, Garo-Bodo, Mikir, and Meithei)".

1.1. North Assam

| Nishi [Dafla] | nyĕ-**lo** | husband | PKB-KSEA:135 |
| Tagen | nyo-**lĕ** | husband | PKB-KSEA:135 |
| Tagin | nyi **lo** | male | KDG-Tag |

1.3. Naga

| *Northern Naga | *la[A] | male (of animals) | WTF-PNN:520 |
| Chang | kei **lo** | male dog | WTF-PNN:520 |
| | ok **lo** šou | domestic boar | WTF-PNN:520 |
| Chokri | thü³¹ **la**³¹ | penis | VN-ChkQ:10.3.1 |
| Chakrü | ²u²tho²**la** | penis | AW-TBT:142 |
| Khezha | ¹e²**lɯ** | male | AW-TBT:288 |
| Konyak (Tamlu) | **la** | male | AW-TBT:288 |
| Mao | ¹**lo** | male | AW-TBT:288 |
| Nocte | da **la** | male | WTF-PNN:531 |
| | vak **la** | male pig | WTF-PNN:520 |
| | ²**la**(ʔ) | male | AW-TBT:288 |
| | ¹dʌ¹**la** | male | AW-TBT:288 |
| Nocte (Namsang) | de-**la** | husband | PKB-KSEA:243 |
| Rengma (Southern) | ²**lø** | male | AW-TBT:288 |
| Rongmei | ka-**lû** | male | AW-TBT:288 |
| Sema | ²a²**li** | male | AW-TBT:288 |
| Tableng | kui-**la** | male dog | PKB-KSEA:243 |
| Tangsa | ¹**la**(ʔ) | male | AW-TBT:288 |
| Tangsa (Moshang) | gui-hẽ **la** | male dog | PKB-KSEA:243 |
| | gui hen **la** | male dog | WTF-PNN:520 |
| Wancho | vak **la** | boar | WTF-PNN:520 |

1.4. Meithei

| Meithei | **la** bə | male | AAAM-SSM |

1.7. Bodo-Garo = Barish

| Bodo | jɤ **la** | male | AW-TBT:288 |
| Khiamngan | ²mẹ¹**lọu** | male | AW-TBT:288 |
| Kokborok | čə-**la** | male | PT-Kok |
| | **la** | male suffix | PT-Kok |
| | šəy-**la** | male dog | PT-Kok |

2.2. Newar

| Newar (Dolakhali) | tuk **la** | penis | CG-Dolak |

### 4. Jingpho-Nung-Luish

| | | | |
|---|---|---|---|
| Ganan | -la¹ | male of animals | GHL-PPB:K.39 |
| Kadu (Kantu) | -la¹ | male of animals | GHL-PPB:K.39 |
| Sak (Bawtala) | ă la³ | male of animals | GHL-PPB:K.39 |

### 4.1. Jingpho

| | | | |
|---|---|---|---|
| Jingpho | là | male | JAM-TJLB:249 |
| | ²la | male | AW-TBT:288 |
| | ʔə là | male | JAM-TJLB:249 |

### 4.2. Nungic

| | | | |
|---|---|---|---|
| Nung (Rawang) | nang-la | husband; male | PKB-KSEA:166 |

### 6.1. Burmish

| | | | |
|---|---|---|---|
| Burmese (Written) | là | male | AW-TBT:288 [76] |
| | ə-lâ | not castrated | PKB-WBRD |
| | ʔə lâ | not castrated | JAM-TJLB:249 |
| Lashi | lo³³ | male | DQ-Lashi:10.3 |
| Maru [Langsu] | lɔ³⁵ | male | DQ-Langsu:10.3 |
| Atsi [Zaiwa] | à lò | male | AW-TBT:288 |

### 6.2. Loloish

| | | | |
|---|---|---|---|
| Lisu | la⁵htsaw⁴ | man | DB-PLolo:161 |

### 6.4. Jinuo

| | | | |
|---|---|---|---|
| Jinuo (Baya/Banai) | tʃʰɤ⁵⁵ lɤ³¹ | penis | DQ-JinA:144 |

## (138)     *m-tun ⪦ *m-dun     FOREPART / FORESKIN

This root has the general meaning of FOREPART. In combination with etyma for TOOTH it means FRONT TOOTH/INCISOR. In combination with SKIN it can mean FORESKIN (cf. WT **mdun-lpags**). The Lepcha form requires special comment (see note).

### 1.2. Kuki-Chin

| | | | |
|---|---|---|---|
| Kom Rem | **kətu** hə | tooth (incisor) | T-KomRQ:3.10.1 |

### 2.1.1. Western Himalayish

| | | | |
|---|---|---|---|
| Bunan | **du** suà | tooth (incisor) | SBN-BunQ:3.10.1 |

### 2.1.2. Bodic

| | | | |
|---|---|---|---|
| Spiti | **dun** sò | tooth (incisor) | CB-SpitiQ:3.10.1 |
| Tibetan (Written) | **mdun** | before; at; to; front | GEM-CNL; ZMYYC:51.1 |
| | **mdun**-lpags | foreskin (vulg.) | JAM-Ety |
| | **mdun**-n̊os | front of body | JAM-Ety |
| | **mdun**-so | tooth (front) | JAM-Ety |

### 2.1.3. Lepcha

| | | | |
|---|---|---|---|
| Lepcha | a t'un | foreskin | JAM-Ety [77] |

### 2.3.1. Kham-Magar-Chepang-Sunwar

| | | | |
|---|---|---|---|
| Chepang (Eastern) | **jun?** səyk | tooth (incisor) | RC-ChepQ:3.10.1 |

[76]This word is not to be found in the dictionaries of Judson 1893/1953/1966 or Bernot 1978-92.

[77]The Lepcha morpheme **t'un** means 'skin; hide' in isolation (GBM-Lepcha p. 154), though the prefixed form **a-t'un** is glossed either 'skin' (pp. 154, 532) or 'foreskin' (p. 491).

3.2. Qiangic

| | | | |
|---|---|---|---|
| Qiang (Mawo) | ʂə **zdu** | tooth (incisor) | SHK-MawoQ:3.10.1 |

## (139)              *tsyaŋ              TESTICLE

This root has so far only been found in a few Naga and Kuki-Chin languages.

1.2. Kuki-Chin

| | | | |
|---|---|---|---|
| Thado | tīl **cáŋ** | testicle | THI1972:30 |

1.3. Naga

| | | | |
|---|---|---|---|
| Ao Naga | ²ta³tsɯ³**tšaŋ** | testicle | AW-TBT:617a |
| Lotha Naga | njo **tsung** | testicle | VN-LothQ:10.3.5 |
| Nocte | ¹**tšʌŋ** | testicles; testicle | AW-TBT:16,617a |

# VIII. Copulate

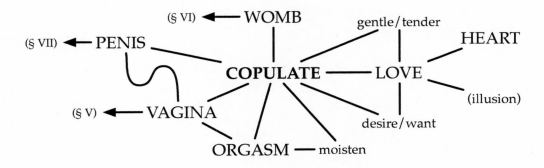

It should come as no surprise that verbs meaning COPULATE are closely associated with notions of LOVE and DESIRE. Most etyma in this section have a semantic range which encompasses both the physical act of love and its emotional concomitant. At least one root makes an overt connection between COPULATE and PENIS (cf. (124) *s-nyak ≍ *s-nik PENIS / COPULATE, above). Innumerable euphemisms for the act of sexual congress occur, but most of these are best treated in a separate study devoted to verbs. Typical verbs extended to a sexual sense include: PUSH (Mikir **dòy** 'push', **che-dóy** 'copulate'); DO (Jingpho **dī** 'do, make, form, fashion; be guilty of illicit intercourse'); MEET (Jingpho **khrúm** 'meet, converge; have sexual intercourse'), etc.

## (140)     *ŋ-(w)a:y     COPULATE / MAKE LOVE / LOVE / GENTLE

This root is well-attested in TB, occurring in Kamarupan, Lolo-Burmese, Jingpho-Nung, Karenic, and Baic. There is an excellent Chinese comparandum, 愛 'love' [*GSR* 508a]. *STC* (pp. 150, 192) compares Proto-Karen **\*ʔai** to the Chinese word, but does not cite any other TB forms. In Matisoff 1985a (*GSTC*) #126, I reconstructed PTB **\*ŋ-(w)ay**, on the basis of forms from Jingpho, Tiddim, Lushai, and Tangkhul. Another set of forms, reconstructed separately in *STC* #315 as **\*ŋoy**, with the gloss GENTLE / QUIET / MODERATE, I believe to be allofamically related to the present etymon (see *GSTC* #92). Also to be brought in here are Northern Naga forms meaning EASY and SOFT (French 1983:481, 554).

There is a look-alike in Proto-Tai: **\*ŋaay**$^{B2}$ 'easy' (*HCT*:204) > Siamese **ŋâay**.

See *HPTB* **\*ŋ-(w)a:y**, pp. 210, 217, 220.

| 0. Sino-Tibetan | | | |
|---|---|---|---|
| *Tibeto-Burman | *ŋ-(w)ay | love; make love | JAM-GSTC:126; RJL-DPTB:206 |
| | *ŋoy | gentle / quiet / moderate | STC:315 |

1.1. North Assam

| | | | |
|---|---|---|---|
| Padam-Mising [Abor-Miri] | **ngi** | comfort, soothe, cheer, console, pacify (as a child) | JAM-GSTC:092 |
| Idu | **we**⁵⁵thu⁵⁵ | love | ZMYYC:719.50 |
| | **wu** tʰu **wu** ga | love | JP-Idu |

1.2. Kuki-Chin

| | | | |
|---|---|---|---|
| Bawm | **ngàai** | love | LL-PRPL |
| Lushai [Mizo] | hma **ngaih** | love | GEM-CNL |
| | in **uai** | clasp one another and be reluctant to leave | JAM-GSTC:126 |
| | in **uai** lung-leng | make love to one another | JAM-GSTC:126 |
| | in-**ngai** | copulate; long for one another | JAM-Ety |
| | **ngáai/ngài?** | love | LL-PRPL |
| | **ngai** | copulate | JAM-Ety |
| | **ngāi** | long for, miss, feel earnest desire for; copulate | JAM-GSTC:126 |
| | **uai** | pull, drag (as badly balanced load); hang onto; make love | JAM-GSTC:126,126; RJL-DPTB:206 |
| | **ŋoi** | quiet, silent | STC:315 |
| | **ŋuai** | listless, quiet, silent | STC:315 |
| | **ŋui** | downhearted, sad | STC:315 |
| Paangkhua | ra **ngáai** | love | LL-PRPL |
| Tiddim | -**ŋa:i** | love | RJL-DPTB:206 |
| | -**ŋai?** | love; fall in love | JAM-GSTC:126 |
| | -**ŋa:i** | love; fall in love | JAM-GSTC:126 |
| | **ŋa:i²/ŋai?³** | love; listen | PB-TCV |
| | ´**ŋɛ:i** | tenderly | JAM-GSTC:126 |

1.3. Naga

| | | | |
|---|---|---|---|
| *Northern Naga | *C-**ŋuay** | easy | JAM-GSTC:092 |
| | *C$_{VL}$-**ŋuay** | easy | WTF-PNN:481 |
| | *ñ**a:y** | soft | JAM-GSTC:061 |
| | *ɲ**a:y** | soft | WTF-PNN:554 |
| Tangkhul | khə **ŋáy** | desire | JAM-GSTC:126; RJL-DPTB:206 |
| | **ngai** lon | gentle | JAM-GSTC:126 |
| | sa-**ngai** kachi | desire | JAM-GSTC:126 |
| | sa-**ŋai** kachi | that which one likes to do | RJL-DPTB:206 |

4.1. Jingpho

| | | | |
|---|---|---|---|
| Jingpho | **ńwái** | respect, love; love | JAM-GSTC:126; RJL-DPTB:206 |
| | **ŋwì** | gentle, mild, peaceful, quiet | STC:315 |
| | ə **ŋwi**-śa ✕ ə **ŋoi**-śă | gently, peacefully, moderately | STC:315 |

### 6.1. Burmish

| | | | |
|---|---|---|---|
| Achang (Luxi) | ai³⁵ | love | JZ-Achang |
| Burmese (Written) | ŋwé | appear in small measure; gentle, moderate | STC:315 |
| Hpun (Northern) | ŋweʔ | copulate | EJAH-Hpun |

### 6.2. Loloish

| | | | |
|---|---|---|---|
| Sani [Nyi] | vɪ⁴⁴mo⁵⁵ | copulate | CK-YiQ:10.2 |

### 6.4. Jinuo

| | | | |
|---|---|---|---|
| Jinuo | mo⁴⁴e³³ | love | ZMYYC:719.34 |

### 7. Karenic

| | | | |
|---|---|---|---|
| *Karen (Sgaw) | *wέʔ | copulate | RBJ-KLS:474 |
| *Karen | *ʔai | love; make love | JAM-GSTC:126; STC:192n491 |
| *Karen (TP) | *ʔáiq | love | RBJ-KLS:72 |
| *Karen | *ʔáiq | love | RBJ-KLS:72 |
| *Karen (Pho-Sgaw) | *ʔwὲq | copulate | RBJ-KLS:474 |
| | *ʔὲq | love | RBJ-KLS:72 |
| *Karen (Pho) | *ʔέq | love | RBJ-KLS:72 |
| *Karen (Sgaw) | *ʔέʔ | love | RBJ-KLS:72 |
| Karen | ʔɑi | love | ACST:508a |
| Pa-O | ʔái | love | RBJ-KLS:72 |
| | ʔe | love | STC:149n409 |
| | ʔwe | copulate | JAM-Ety; RBJ-KLS:474 |
| Palaychi | ʔwὲq | copulate | JAM-Ety; RBJ-KLS:474 |
| | ʔə | love | STC:149n409 |
| | ʔὲq | love | RBJ-KLS:72 |
| Pho | ai | love / make love | JAM-GSTC:126 |
| Pho (Bassein) | ʔài | love | RBJ-KLS:72 |
| | ʔwὲ | copulate | JAM-Ety; RBJ-KLS:474 |
| Pho (Moulmein) | ʔwέʔ | copulate | JAM-Ety; RBJ-KLS:474 |
| | ʔέʔ | love | RBJ-KLS:72 |
| Sgaw | ε | love / make love | JAM-GSTC:126 |
| Sgaw (Bassein) | wὲ | copulate | JAM-Ety; RBJ-KLS:474 |
| | ʔὲ | love | RBJ-KLS:72 |
| Sgaw (Moulmein) | wέʔ | copulate | JAM-Ety; RBJ-KLS:474 |
| | ʔέʔ | love | RBJ-KLS:72 |

### 8. Bai

| | | | |
|---|---|---|---|
| Bai (Dali) | e⁴⁴ | love | ZMYYC:719.35 |

### 9. Sinitic

| | | | |
|---|---|---|---|
| Chinese (Old) | ậi | love | JAM-GSTC:126 |
| | əd | love | JAM-GSTC:126 |
| | ʔits | love / grudge | WHB-OC:1160,337 |
| Chinese (Old/Mid) | əd/ậi | love | ACST:508a |

## Chinese comparandum

愛 **ài** 'love'

*GSR*: 508a        Karlgren: *·əd        Li: *·ədh        Baxter: *ʔits (337)

The Chinese form most closely resembles the Karen form **ʔai**. Because we expect OC *ʔ-

to correspond to PTB *Ø- and OC *ŋ- to correspond to PTB *ŋ-, the Chinese form must be assumed to relate to a PTB allofam lacking initial *ŋ-.

Baxter reconstructs *ʔits, but a reconstruction of *ʔijs is also possible, as rhyming evidence does not definitvely indicate the presence of a stop coda.

The correspondence between TB final *-ay and OC final *-əd (Li), *-ij (Baxter) is attested, for example in the word for 'tail', TB *r-may, OC *mjədx (Li), *mjij? (Baxter). Elsewhere in this volume, **(40b)** *s-tay NAVEL / ABDOMEN / CENTER / SELF offers additional support for this correspondence.

[ZJH]

## (141)   *r-ga ⪦ *N-ga ⪦ *d-ga ⪦ *s-ga   COPULATE / LOVE / WANT

This etymon is extremely well attested, occurring in Kamarupan, Himalayish, Lolo-Burmese, Nungish, Qiangic, and probably Baic. Its range of meanings extends from WANT/DESIRE to LOVE to COPULATE. This root is notable for the large number of prefixes that it has acquired in various branches of TB: *r- (in Qiangic [rGyalrong, Ergong] and Amdo Tibetan); *N- (in Loloish and perhaps Meluri); *d- (in Written Tibetan), and *s- (in Qiangic [Pumi]).

This etymon has been grammaticalized in Lahu, where it now functions as a desiderative particle, e.g. **qay gâ** 'want to go', **dɔ̀ gâ** 'want to drink', etc. See Matisoff 1988a:399-400.

See *HPTB* PLB *m-ga², p. 163.

| | | | |
|---|---|---|---|
| **1.1. North Assam** | | | |
| Idu | ha³¹**kau**⁵⁵ | like | ZMYYC:720.50 |
| | wu tʰu wu **ga** | love | JP-Idu |
| **1.2. Kuki-Chin** | | | |
| Meluri | **ngü** | want | GEM-CNL |
| **1.3. Naga** | | | |
| Tangkhul | kha ma **kha** | copulate | JAM-Ety |
| **1.7. Bodo-Garo = Barish** | | | |
| Kokborok | **ga** | copulate | PT-Kok |
| **2.1.1. Western Himalayish** | | | |
| Kanauri | **go** s̱hi | copulate | JAM-Ety |
| **2.1.2. Bodic** | | | |
| Tsangla (Tilang) | **gra** | love | JZ-CLMenba |
| Tshona (Wenlang) | do³⁵**go**⁵⁵ | want | JZ-CNMenba |
| Tshona (Mama) | dɔ¹³**gɔ**⁵³ | want | ZMYYC:674.6 |
| Tibetan (Amdo:Bla-brang) | **hga** | like | ZMYYC:720.4 |
| | **ko** kə | want | ZMYYC:674.4 |
| Tibetan (Amdo:Zeku) | **rga** | love; like | ZMYYC:719.5,720.5 |
| | **rgo** | want | ZMYYC:674.5 |
| Tibetan (Khams:Dege) | **ga**³¹ | love; like | ZMYYC:719.3,720.3 |
| | **gø**⁵⁵ | want | ZMYYC:674.3 |
| Tibetan (Lhasa) | **ko**?¹³ | want | ZMYYC:674.2 |

| | | | | |
|---|---|---|---|---|
| Tibetan (Written) | dga | like | JS-Tib:586 | |
| | dga.ba | happy | JS-Tib:343 | |
| | dgafi | love; like | ZMYYC:719.1,720.1 | 1 |
| | dgafi po | glad | ZMYYC:908.1 | |
| | dga ba | glad | GEM-CNL | |
| | dgos | want | GEM-CNL; ZMYYC:674.1 | 2 |
| | dgos pa | necessary | GEM-CNL | |

### 3.2. Qiangic

| | | | |
|---|---|---|---|
| Ergong (Northern) | rgə³³ | copulate | SHK-ErgNQ:10.2 |
| Ergong (Danba) | ʐgia zɛ | love | ZMYYC:719.14 |
| Ersu | ga⁵⁵ | love | ZMYYC:719.18 |
| | ja³³ga⁵⁵ | like | ZMYYC:720.18 |
| Guiqiong | tʂha⁵⁵gi³³ | like | ZMYYC:720.17 |
| Muya [Minyak] | ŋguɯ⁵³ | like | ZMYYC:720.15 |
| Pumi (Jinghua) | giɯu¹³ | like | ZMYYC:720.11 |
| | sgia⁵⁵ | love | ZMYYC:719.11 |
| Pumi (Taoba) | giu³⁵ | like | ZMYYC:720.10 |
| | ɣiɛ³⁵ | love | ZMYYC:719.10 |
| Queyu (Yajiang) [Zhaba] | ga³⁵ | love | ZMYYC:719.16 |

### 3.3. rGyalrongic

| | | | |
|---|---|---|---|
| rGyalrong | ka rga | like | ZMYYC:720.12 |

### 4.2. Nungic

| | | | |
|---|---|---|---|
| Trung [Dulong] | gɯ⁵⁵ | want | ZMYYC:674.46 |
| Trung [Dulong] (Nujiang) | gɯ⁵⁵ | want | JZ-Dulong |

### 6.2. Loloish

| | | | |
|---|---|---|---|
| *Loloish | *m-ga² | want | DB-PLolo:827A |
| Hani (Dazhai) | ga³¹ | love | ZMYYC:719.31 |
| Hani (Gelanghe) | gɤ³¹ | want | JZ-Hani |
| Lahu (Black) | gâ | desiderative particle; want to V | JAM-DL:399-400 |
| Nusu (Bijiang) | gɯ³⁵a⁵⁵ | like | ZMYYC:720.45 |
| Yi (Dafang) | gɯ²¹ | like | ZMYYC:720.22 |
| Yi (Mojiang) | gɯ²¹sɛ²¹ | like | ZMYYC:720.26 |
| Yi (Nanhua) | gɯ³³go³³ | like | ZMYYC:720.24 |
| Yi (Xide) | ŋgu³³ | love | ZMYYC:719.21 |

### 8. Bai

| | | | |
|---|---|---|---|
| Bai (Bijiang) | ko²¹ | love | ZMYYC:719.37 |
| Bai (Jianchuan) | ko²¹ | love | ZMYYC:719.36 |

## (142)                    *m-dza-k                    LOVE

This etymon was reconstructed as PTB **\*m-dza** in *STC* #67, on the basis of forms from Written Tibetan, Jingpho, and Written Burmese (with a note that the Jingpho form actually ends in glottal stop, so that it "may be distinct"). There is in fact ample rea-

---

[1] This form is glossed by Jäschke (pp. 82-3) as 'rejoice; like, be willing; intend, wish'.

[2] Although this Tibetan form implies 'necessity as well as want' (Jäschke p. 87), it looks like an allofam of **dgafi** 'rejoice; like, be willing' [q.v.].

son to set up both open-syllabled and stop-finalled allofams for this root: *m-dza ⟡ *m-dzak. The latter allofam is attested not only in Jingpho, but in Yi Nanhua (note the constricted vowel), and directly in NW rGyalrong (Qiangic group). The nasal prefix is directly reflected in WT, Yi (Dafang), and Jingpho.

0. Sino-Tibetan

| | | | |
|---|---|---|---|
| *Tibeto-Burman | **\*m-dza** | love | STC:67 |

2.1.2. Bodic

| | | | |
|---|---|---|---|
| Tibetan (Amdo:Bla-brang) | xha **tsha** | love | ZMYYC:719.4 |
| Tibetan (Written) | **mdza**-ba | love | STC:67 |

2.3.2. Kiranti

| | | | |
|---|---|---|---|
| Hayu | **tsha** niŋ-kuq li | love | BM-Hay:84.57,58,2 |

3.2. Qiangic

| | | | |
|---|---|---|---|
| Guiqiong | **tṣha⁵⁵gi³³** | love | ZMYYC:719.17 |
| Namuyi | **dza̱⁵⁵** | love | ZMYYC:719.19 |
| Qiang (Mawo) | **χtçi** | love | ZMYYC:719.8 |
| Shixing | **tshi⁵⁵** | love | ZMYYC:719.20 |

3.3. rGyalrongic

| | | | |
|---|---|---|---|
| rGyalrong (NW) | ndot **tçʰak** | copulate | SHK-rGNWQ:10.2 |

4.1. Jingpho

| | | | |
|---|---|---|---|
| Jingpho | **ndža** | show love; affection-ate | STC:67 |
| | **ndžáʔ** | love | STC:28n89 |

6.1. Burmish

| | | | |
|---|---|---|---|
| Burmese (Written) | **ca** | have tender regard for | PKB-WBRD |
| | **tsa** | have tender regard for another | STC:67 |

6.2. Loloish

| | | | |
|---|---|---|---|
| Yi (Dafang) | **ndẓu³³** | love | ZMYYC:719.22 |
| Yi (Nanhua) | **ne̱³³dẓʌ³³** | love | ZMYYC:719.24 |

(143)  **\*krik ⟡ \*kriŋ**  **LOVE / COPULATE**

This root is well attested in Kamarupan and Burmish, with an excellent cognate in Written Tibetan. The correspondence of WT **-ig** to WB **-ac** is perfectly regular. (Cf. *HPTB* pp. 343-348). The Maring form points to an allofam with final nasal.

1.1. North Assam

| | | | |
|---|---|---|---|
| Apatani | **kì** | love | JS-Tani |

1.2. Kuki-Chin

| | | | |
|---|---|---|---|
| Maring | **karing** | love | GEM-CNL |

1.3. Naga

| | | | |
|---|---|---|---|
| Angami (Khonoma) | **khre** | love | GEM-CNL |
| Angami (Kohima) | **khrie** | love | GEM-CNL |
| Chokri | **khrü** | love | GEM-CNL |
| Mao | **khro** | love | GEM-CNL |

## 2.1.2. Bodic

| | | | | |
|---|---|---|---|---|
| Tibetan (Written) | ḥkʻrig-pa | copulate | JAM-Ety | 3 |

## 6.1. Burmish

| | | | |
|---|---|---|---|
| Achang (Lianghe) | kɛ⁵⁵kik⁵⁵ | love | JZ-Achang |
| Arakanese | hcat | love | JO-PB |
| Burmese (Spoken Rangoon) | tɕhiʔ⁴⁴ | love | ZMYYC:719.40 |
| Burmese (Written) | khjas | love | ZMYYC:719.39 |
| | khyac | love; to love | GEM-CNL; JO-PB; PKB-WBRD |
| Burmese (Inscriptional) | khyat | love | JO-PB |
| Burmese (Written) | ə-khyac | love, affection | PKB-WBRD |
| Intha | hyi' | love | JO-PB |
| Maru [Langsu] | c'ít | love | JO-PB |
| Tavoyan | hyi' | love | JO-PB |
| Atsi [Zaiwa] | tʃi̱t⁵⁵ | love | ZMYYC:719.42 |

## (144)    *ləw-k    COPULATE

This etymon is fairly well attested in TB as a whole, especially in Himalayish and Chin, but also in Lolo-Burmese (Burmese), and Qiangic (rGyalrong). Judging from the Burmese gloss in Judson 1893/1966, it seems to be connected with the notion of piercing or penetrating.

The allofam with final -k is attested not only in the Form-II of verbs in several Chin languages, but also in Chepang. The Form-I of Chin verbs, as well as the Kiranti and Burmese forms, reflect the open-syllable allofam.

## 1.2. Kuki-Chin

| | | | |
|---|---|---|---|
| *Chin | *luu ⋈ luuk | copulate | KVB-PKC:1003 |
| Cho (Mindat) | luk ~ luuk | penetrate sexually, possess a woman | KVB-PKC:1003 |
| Khumi | liiw | have intercourse with | KVB-PKC:1003 |
| Lakher [Mara] | lu | copulate | JAM-Ety |
| | lū | copulate | KVB-PKC:1003 |
| Lushai [Mizo] | in-lu-khung | copulate | JAM-Ety |
| | lu | copulate | JAM-Ety |
| | lùu ~ lûuk | copulate | KVB-PKC:1003 |
| Thado | lûu ~ lûʔ | copulate | KVB-PKC:1003 |
| Tiddim | lu:¹ ~ lu:k¹ | copulate | KVB-PKC:1003 |

## 2.1.1. Western Himalayish

| | | | |
|---|---|---|---|
| Pattani [Manchati] | lhù ṣi | copulate | STP-ManQ:10.2 |
| | lui | copulate | DS-Patt |

## 2.3. Mahakiranti

| | | | |
|---|---|---|---|
| *Dum-Thu-Kha | *le- | copulate | BM-PK7:37 |
| *Kiranti | *lu- | copulate | BM-PK7:37 |

---

[3] Jäschke (p. 61) notes that this word is "the usual, not exactly obscene, yet not euphemistic term for it". It also has the non-sexual meanings 'cohere, stick together' and 'be cloudy, overcast (of the sky)'.

## 2.3.1. Kham-Magar-Chepang-Sunwar

| | | | |
|---|---|---|---|
| Chepang | lu?-sa | copulate | SIL-Chep:2.B.2.13 |
| | lu? .sā | copulate | JAM-Ety |
| Chepang (Eastern) | lu? na? | copulate | RC-ChepQ:10.2 |
| Sunwar | lu:- | copulate | BM-PK7:37 |
| | lu:-cā | copulate | JAM-Ety |

## 2.3.2. Kiranti

| | | | | |
|---|---|---|---|---|
| Bahing | lu- | copulate | BM-PK7:37 | |
| Bantawa | lï- | copulate | BM-PK7:37 | |
| | lü ma | copulate | WW-Bant:47 | |
| Khaling | le- | copulate | BM-PK7:37 | 4 |
| | le-ne | copulate | JAM-Ety | |
| Thulung | le- | copulate | BM-PK7:37 | |

## 3.3. rGyalrongic

| | | | |
|---|---|---|---|
| rGyalrong | ta lu ka pa | copulate | DQ-Jiarong:10.2 |
| rGyalrong (Eastern) | ta lu ka pa | copulate | SHK-rGEQ:10.2 |

## 6. Lolo-Burmese

| | | | |
|---|---|---|---|
| *Lolo-Burmese | *ləw² | copulate / penis | JAM-II |

## 6.1. Burmish

| | | | |
|---|---|---|---|
| Burmese (Written) | lûi | pierce in coitus (vulg.) | PKB-WBRD |

## 6.2. Loloish

| | | | | |
|---|---|---|---|---|
| Akha | aˬ loeˬ | penis | JAM-Ety | 5 |

## (145)　　　　　　　*duk ⪧ *tu　　　　　LOVE / DESIRE / WANT

This etymon is well-attested in Kamarupan, with good-looking cognates in Himalayish and Loloish. Two allofams should be reconstructed, one with and one without final *-k. The Idu and Loloish forms point to an allofam with *voiceless initial, while the Moyon form reflects an evidently secondary nasal prefix.

## 1.1. North Assam

| | | | |
|---|---|---|---|
| Idu | we⁵⁵thu⁵⁵ | love | ZMYYC:719.50 |
| | wu tʰu wu ga | love | JP-Idu |

## 1.2. Kuki-Chin

| | | | |
|---|---|---|---|
| *Chin | *ɗu? | want, crave, lack | KVB-PKC:116 |
| Cho (Mindat) | du | be destitute, in want, needy | KVB-PKC:116 |
| Lai (Hakha) | du? | want; desire; crave; like; lack | KVB-Lai |
| Lai (Falam) | dù? | want, crave, like | KVB-PKC:116 |

---

[4]Khaling has -e where other Kiranti languages have -u in at least two other roots: COME/BRING DOWN Hayu ju(t)-, Bahing ju(t)-, Kulung yuw-, yutt-; but Khaling ye(n)-. STEAL Hayu khu(t)-, Bahing ku(s)-, Thulung khu-, Kulung kuss-; but Khaling khe-. See Michailovsky 1991, *Proto-Kiranti*, pp. 15, 34.

[5]This Akha reflex is to be referred to the present etymon, rather than to (114a) *m-ley ⪧ *m-li PENIS, since Akha -oe is the regular reflex of PTB *-əw (e.g. STEAL *r-kəw > Ak. k'oeˬ; WEEP *ŋəw > Ak. ngoeˇ). For the Akha reflex of PLB *r-lik 'testicle', see lehˬ, above (129). See also the note on Akha beuˆ leuˆ 'penis (polite)', above (114a).

| Lakher [Mara] | dū | love (by grand-mother) | KVB-PKC:116 |
|---|---|---|---|
| Lushai [Mizo] | duh | love | GEM-CNL |
| | dùh | want, wish; need, require; desire, like | KVB-Lai:116 |
| | duk | desire | GEM-CNL |
| Paite | duh | crave, like | KVB-PKC:116 |
| Tiddim | du?³ | desire food | PB-TCV |

**1.4. Meithei**

| Moyon | ntu | copulate | DK-Moyon:10.2 |
|---|---|---|---|

**2.1.2. Bodic**

| Tshona (Wenlang) | do³⁵go⁵⁵ | want | JZ-CNMenba |
|---|---|---|---|
| Tshona (Mama) | dɔ¹³gɔ⁵³ | want | ZMYYC:674.6 |

**2.1.4. Tamangic**

| Tamang (Sahu) | tu:h 'ti-pa | love | SIL-Sahu:21.A.52 |
|---|---|---|---|

**2.3.2. Kiranti**

| Hayu | dak | desire, need | BM-Hay:84.34 |
|---|---|---|---|

**6.2. Loloish**

| Lahu (Black) | cha **thû** | feel sexual desire (woman); lubri-cate | JAM-DL:681 |
|---|---|---|---|
| | nī **thû** | have an erection; be aroused | JAM-DL:681,769 |
| | **thû** | feel sexual desire; be horny (man or woman) | JAM-Ety |
| Yi (Nanjian) | **thu²¹** | love | ZMYYC:719.23 |

## (146)                    *yo                    COPULATE

This root was reconstructed for Proto-Tani by J. Sun (1993), but seems to have a wider distribution, both elsewhere in Kamarupan (Konyak) and in Himalayish. The Konyak, Baima, and Spiti compounds look like they all have the same morphemic structure, with **(147) *yaŋ** LOVE / DESIRE / COPULATE [see below] as their second element.

**1.1. North Assam**

| *Tani | *jo | copulate | JS-HCST:81 |
|---|---|---|---|
| Padam-Mising [Abor-Miri] | jo | copulate | JS-HCST |
| | yo | copulate | JAM-Ety |
| | yo-shu | copulate | JAM-Ety [6] |
| Apatani | í | copulate | JS-Tani |
| Bengni | ju | copulate | JS-HCST |
| Bokar | jo | copulate | JS-HCST |
| Gallong | a **ya**-nam | love | KDG-IGL |

**1.3. Naga**

| Konyak | **ya** yiang | love | GEM-CNL |
|---|---|---|---|

---

[6] Abor-Miri **shu** is a reflexive morpheme.

2.1.2. Bodic

| | | | | |
|---|---|---|---|---|
| Baima | $\mathfrak{zo}^{13}$ $\mathfrak{io}^{13}$ | copulate | SHK-BaimaQ:10.2 | 7 |
| Spiti | jo je | copulate | CB-SpitiQ:10.2 | |

## (147)　　　　　　　*yaŋ　　　　　　LOVE / DESIRE / COPULATE

This etymon is fairly well established, occurring in Kamarupan, Baic, and Himalayish. This root is independent of (146) *yo COPULATE above, with which it occurs in binomes (Konyak, Baima, Spiti). There is a longshot Chinese comparandum, 癢 'itch', OC **zi̯ang** [*GSR* #732r], Mand. **yǎŋ**, though the semantic association is doubtful.

1. Kamarupan

| | | | |
|---|---|---|---|
| Miji | luŋ-ʒaŋ | love; be kind to | IMS-Miji |

1.1. North Assam

| | | | |
|---|---|---|---|
| Bokar | a-**jaŋ** | love | JS-Tani |
| Milang | a-**yan**-ma | love | AT-MPB |

1.2. Kuki-Chin

| | | | |
|---|---|---|---|
| Khoirao | nri **ye** | love | GEM-CNL |

1.3. Naga

| | | | |
|---|---|---|---|
| Konyak | ya **yiang** | love | GEM-CNL |

2.1.2. Bodic

| | | | | |
|---|---|---|---|---|
| Baima | $\mathfrak{zo}^{13}$ $\mathfrak{io}^{13}$ | copulate | SHK-BaimaQ:10.2 | 8 |
| Tsangla (Motuo) | **jaŋ** | want | ZMYYC:674.7 | |
| Tshona (Wenlang) | **ʑiŋ**$^{35}$ | love | JZ-CNMenba | |
| Spiti | jo **je** | copulate | CB-SpitiQ:10.2 | |

8. Bai

| | | | |
|---|---|---|---|
| Bai | **jæ̃**$^{44}$ | copulate | ZYS-Bai:10.2 |

## Chinese comparandum

癢 **yǎng** 'itch' ≍ 痒 **yáng** 'disease'

*GSR*: 732i,732r　　　　Karlgren: *z**i̯**ang　　　Li: *rang(x)　　　Baxter: *(l)jang(?)

Setting aside the question of semantics, this is a plausible comparison.

For other members of this phonetic series, Baxter reconstructs *z(l)ang, *k(l)ang and *kh(l)ang. The presence of medial *-l- ties the pronunciation of these words together; but the medial is given in parentheses because it does not affect subsequent development and Baxter is probably doubtful about its presence. Li's initial *r- has been revised to *l- by most scholars. Handel 1998 and Schuessler 2007 both reconstruct initial *j- in this situation.

---

[7]It would not be clear *a priori* which of these phonologically similar Baima syllables should be referred to the present etymon, though the Spiti and Konyak binomial cognates suggest it is the first syllable that belongs here, while the second descends rather from (147) *yaŋ LOVE / DESIRE / COPULATE, below.

[8]The Spiti and Konyak cognates suggest it is the second syllable that belongs here, while the first descends rather from (146) *yo COPULATE, above.

This proposal parallels the comparison of Chinese 'sheep' 羊 *jang (Mand. yáng) with PTB *g-yaŋ.

[ZJH]

## (148)         *m-brel         COPULATE / CONNECT

The basic meaning of this etymon seems to be 'hang together; cohere; be connected; come together; meet, join' (see the range of meanings in WT, Jäschke p. 402). It is attested chiefly in Himalayish, with apparently excellent Qiangic cognates. The nasal prefix is reflected by the WT a-chung (ḥ-), and directly by the Northern rGyalrong form. It is of course quite possible that the rGyalrong and Ergong forms are borrowings from Tibetan.

**2.1.2. Bodic**

| | | | |
|---|---|---|---|
| Tibetan (Written) | ḥbrel-ba | copulate / join / be connected | JAM-Ety |

**2.1.4. Tamangic**

| | | | |
|---|---|---|---|
| Chantyal | pfie-wa | copulate | NPB-ChanQ:10.2 |
| Gurung (Ghachok) | mehq **bral** diba | copulate (animals), have sexual intercourse (cows) | SIL-Gur |
| | **preh** ba | copulate (animals), have sexual intercourse (animals) | SIL-Gur |
| | **prxe**-ba | copulate | JAM-Ety [9] |
| Tamang (Risiangku) | ⁴pja | copulate; copulate (of males) | MM-TamRisQ:10.2; MM-Thesis:702 |
| Tamang (Sahu) | ´pyāh pā | copulate | JAM-Ety |
| Thakali (Tukche) | peh-la | copulate | JAM-Ety |
| | peh-lɔ | copulate | SIL-Thak:2.B.2.13 |

**3.2. Qiangic**

| | | | |
|---|---|---|---|
| Ergong (Daofu) | ʔphǝ phǝ | copulate | DQ-Daofu:10.2 |

**3.3. rGyalrongic**

| | | | |
|---|---|---|---|
| rGyalrong (Northern) | tǝ ka **mbrǝ mbro** | copulate | SHK-rGNQ:10.2 |

## (149)      *m-bak ⋉ *m-baŋ      COPULATE / LOVE / WOMB

This etymon, which seems to cover quite an unusual semantic range, including COPULATE, LOVE, and WOMB/NEST, is fairly broadly distributed, with likely reflexes in Kamarupan, Himalayish, Loloish, and Tangut (Xixia). Allofams with final velar stop and final velar nasal both occur. The nasal prefix is directly attested in Moyon, Bisu, and Tangut.

**1.1. North Assam**

| | | | |
|---|---|---|---|
| Bengni | **pak** | love | JS-Tani |

[9]This Gurung form is cited in Noonan's (1999) *Chantyal Dictionary and Texts* under 'have sex'.

| | | | |
|---|---|---|---|
| Sulung | a$^{33}$pak$^{11}$ | love | ZMYYC:719.52 |
| Tagin | pak-nam | love | KDG-Tag |
| 1.4. Meithei | | | |
| Moyon | mpú? | copulate | DK-Moyon:10.2 |
| 2.1.1. Western Himalayish | | | |
| Pattani [Manchati] | bàŋ | womb | STP-ManQ:10.4.8 |
| | baŋg | nest | DS-Patt |
| 2.1.3. Lepcha | | | |
| Lepcha | tă-băk | womb | JAM-Ety |
| 3.1. Tangut | | | |
| Tangut [Xixia] | mbâ² | copulate | MVS-Grin |
| 6.2. Loloish | | | |
| Bisu | aŋ làp ?mbã | genitals | PB-Bisu:14 |
| Lahu (Black) | cha pà? ve | copulate with a woman | JAM-DL:517,814 |
| | pà? | copulate | JAM-Ety |
| Mpi | po?⁴ | womb | SD-MPD |
| | po?⁴ muŋ?¹ | womb | SD-MPD |

## (150)        *kuŋ ≍ *huŋ             LOVE / COPULATE

This root has been found only in Kamarupan, where it shows variation between initial **k-** and **h-**. (This variation is paralleled in a number of other etyma, including **(82)** *hay ≍ *kay VAGINA; see the note under that reconstruction, Chapter V above.) The final **-n** in the Konyak and Bodo forms is unexplained.[10]

| | | | |
|---|---|---|---|
| 1.2. Kuki-Chin | | | |
| Liangmei | kung | love | GEM-CNL |
| Puiron | kung | love | GEM-CNL |
| 1.3. Naga | | | |
| Konyak | kün | love | GEM-CNL |
| Zeme | hung | love | GEM-CNL |
| Mzieme | hung | love | GEM-CNL |
| 1.5. Mikir | | | |
| Mikir | kang hon | love | GEM-CNL |
| 1.7. Bodo-Garo = Barish | | | |
| Bodo | kón | copulate | JAM-Ety |

## (151)    *l(y)ap ≍ *l(y)am ≍ *rap    COPULATE / LOVE / GET TOGETHER

This etymon is attested in Kamarupan and Himalayish, with a possible cognate in Loloish (Bisu). The initial shows variation between **l-** and **r-**. This root seems to be quite distinct from **(154)** *la COPULATE / LOVE, below. The final **-t** in the Tangkhul forms is unexplained.

---

[10]It is remotely possible that these two forms are related to the second Mikir syllable **hon**, from a separate root *kon ≍ *hon.

1.1. North Assam

| | | | |
|---|---|---|---|
| Darang [Taraon] | **lyeb**-ga: | copulate | JAM-Ety |

1.3. Naga

| | | | | |
|---|---|---|---|---|
| Lotha Naga | **lam** | love | GEM-CNL | |
| Tangkhul | kha ŋa **rāt** | copulate | JAM-Ety | |
| | **rat** | copulate | Bhat-TNV:86 | |

1.5. Mikir

| | | | | |
|---|---|---|---|---|
| Mikir | do **rap rap** | copulate | JAM-Ety | 11 |
| | i **rap**-chom | copulate | JAM-Ety | |
| | i **rap-rap** | copulate | JAM-Ety | |

2.1.1. Western Himalayish

| | | | |
|---|---|---|---|
| Pattani [Manchati] | sem **lep** i | love | DS-Patt |

2.3.1. Kham-Magar-Chepang-Sunwar

| | | | |
|---|---|---|---|
| Chepang | **rāp**-sā | love | AH-CSDPN:10b1.52 |
| | **rap**-sa | love | SIL-Chep:10.B.1.52 |
| Magar | **ro**-ke | love | AH-CSDPN:10a.01,10b1.52 |

6.2. Loloish

| | | | |
|---|---|---|---|
| Bisu | aŋ **làp** ʔmbā | genitals | PB-Bisu:14 |

# (152)        *(t)si        COPULATE / LOVE

This root has scattered but good-looking reflexes in Kamarupan (Maram, Meithei), Himalayish (Kanauri, Manchati), Loloish (Ahi, Nesu), Nungish (Dulong), Qiangic (Muya), and Tujia. Most reflexes have a simple sibilant fricative initial, but the Loloish and Tujia forms have affricates. There does not seem to be any connection with **(117)** *ti-k PENIS or **(118)** *dzi PENIS, above.

1.2. Kuki-Chin

| | | | | |
|---|---|---|---|---|
| Maram | a lung **si** | love | GEM-CNL | 12 |

1.4. Meithei

| | | | |
|---|---|---|---|
| Meithei | nung **si** | love | GEM-CNL |

2.1.1. Western Himalayish

| | | | |
|---|---|---|---|
| Kanauri | go **shi** | copulate | JAM-Ety |
| | tsŭk **shi** | copulate | JAM-Ety |
| Pattani [Manchati] | lhù **ṣi** | copulate | STP-ManQ:10.2 |

3.2. Qiangic

| | | | |
|---|---|---|---|
| Muya [Minyak] | $si^{33}si^{55}$ | love | ZMYYC:719.15 |

4.2. Nungic

| | | | |
|---|---|---|---|
| Trung [Dulong] | $ŋi^{55}çi^{31}$ | love | ZMYYC:719.46 |
| Trung [Dulong] (Du-longhe) | $ŋi^{55}$ $śi^{31}$ | love | RJL-DPTB:206 |

---

[11] The basic meaning of Mikir **rap** is 'to befriend; to be together'. It occurs as an auxiliary after other verbs (e.g. **do** 'be; exist', **i** 'sleep'), meaning 'to V together'.

[12] The second syllable of the Maram form, as well as the first syllable of the Meithei form mean 'heart' < **(H:141)** *m-luŋ HEART.

| Trung [Dulong] (Nujiang) | ńi⁵⁵ śi³¹ | love | RJL-DPTB:206 |
| --- | --- | --- | --- |

5. Tujia

| Tujia (Northern) | a³⁵tshi⁵⁵ | love | JZ-Tujia |
| --- | --- | --- | --- |
| Tujia | a³⁵tshi⁵⁵ | love | ZMYYC:719.38 |
| Tujia (Southern) | ʔa²¹tshi²¹ | love | JZ-Tujia |

6.2. Loloish

| Ahi | tʂhɛ³³ | copulate | CK-YiQ:10.2 |
| --- | --- | --- | --- |
| Nesu | tɕɪ³³ | copulate | CK-YiQ:10.2 |

# (153)      *pam ⪥ *bam      LOVE / DESIRE / COPULATE

This root is solidly attested in Kamarupan (Chin [Lai], Naga [Lotha, Phom] and Meithei), but so far it has not been discovered anywhere else.

1.2. Kuki-Chin

| Lai (Hakha) | pom | copulate, make love | JAM-Ety:D.Van Bik |
| --- | --- | --- | --- |

1.3. Naga

| Lotha Naga | chi pon | love | GEM-CNL |
| --- | --- | --- | --- |
| Phom | bam | love | GEM-CNL |

1.4. Meithei

| Meithei | pam | love; desire | GEM-CNL |
| --- | --- | --- | --- |

# (154)      *la      COPULATE / LOVE

This putative etymon is sparsely attested, appearing only in Himalayish, with a good-looking cognate in Kamarupan (Tangkhul). It seems to be quite independent from the homophonous root (137) *la MALE, Chapter VII above. A Jingpho form meaning 'love, like, esteem', transcribed variously as ra [Hanson p.563; Marrison 1967:157], rà? [JAM-Ety], and ʒaʔ³¹ [ZMYYC #719] does not fit in here, due to the final -ʔ (< *-k). This may be a loan into Jingpho from Tai (cf. Siamese rák, Shan hak [Cushing 1914:630]).[13] There is another unrelated Jingpho morpheme of similar shape (in the low falling tone, without final glottal stop), meaning 'want' in the sense of 'lack; be in need', transcribed variously as ra (Hanson 1906/1954:563 [separate entry from preceding]), rà (JAM-Ety), and ʒa³¹ (ZMYYC #674; Dai et al. 1983:681). This form is certainly cognate to rGyalrong ra (ZMYYC #674) < PTB *ra.

This root seems quite distinct from (151) *l(y)ap ⪥ *l(y)am ⪥ *rap COPULATE / LOVE / GET TOGETHER.

1.3. Naga

| Tangkhul | kha lā | copulate | JAM-Ety |
| --- | --- | --- | --- |

2.1.4. Tamangic

| Gurung (Ghachok) | mrī la baq | copulate | SIL-Gur:2.B.2.13 |
| --- | --- | --- | --- |
| | mrị̄ lā bāq | copulate | JAM-Ety |
| Tamang (Sahu) | ʾhe la la pa | love | SIL-Sahu:10.1 |

---

[13]This Tai etymon is, however, not reconstructed in *HCT*.

| Thakali (Tukche) | peh-**la** | copulate | JAM-Ety |
| | peh-**lɔ** | copulate | SIL-Thak:2.B.2.13 |
| **2.3.2. Kiranti** | | | |
| Dumi | **la** li kha | love | SVD-Dum |

## (155)             *saw             LOVE

This promising root, of limited distribution, has been found in Kamarupan, with an apparent cognate in Himalayish (Chepang). Some reflexes have -**a**, others have a back vowel (-**u** or -**o**); the rhyme is reconstructed as *-**aw** on the testimony of Dimasa.

| **1.1. North Assam** | | | | |
| Apatani | hen-**sú** | love | JS-Tani | |
| **1.2. Kuki-Chin** | | | | |
| Liangmei | lung **sa** | love | GEM-CNL | 14 |
| **1.3. Naga** | | | | |
| Chang | **sa** nou | love | GEM-CNL | |
| Rengma | **so** | love | GEM-CNL | |
| **1.5. Mikir** | | | | |
| Mikir | jin **so** | love | GEM-CNL | |
| **1.7. Bodo-Garo = Barish** | | | | |
| Dimasa | kha **sao** | love | GEM-CNL | |
| **2.3.1. Kham-Magar-Chepang-Sunwar** | | | | |
| Chepang | rāp-**sā** | love | AH-CSDPN:10b1.52 | |
| | rap-**sa** | love | SIL-Chep:10.B.1.52 | |

## (156)             *ʔin ≍ *ʔit             LOVE

This rootlet has so far only been found in three Kamarupan languages, and even these three putative cognates show variation in their rhymes. Lushai has final -**n**, while Tiddim has the homorganic stop -**t**; the final -**m** in Ao Chungli is perhaps due to assimilation to the labial nasal prefix in that language.

| **1.2. Kuki-Chin** | | | |
| Lushai [Mizo] | **in** uai | clasp one another and be reluctant to leave | JAM-GSTC:126 |
| Tiddim | iːt[1] | love deeply | PB-TCV |
| **1.3. Naga** | | | |
| Ao (Chungli) | me **im** | love | GEM-CNL |

---

[14]The first syllable means 'heart'. Cf. the Maram and Meithei forms under (152) *(t)**si** COPULATE / LOVE, above.

# IX. Body Fluids

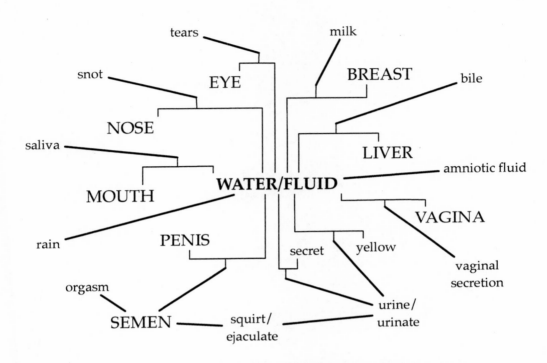

In Sino-Tibetan languages, the words for the various liquids produced by or contained in the body tend to be transparent compounds where the last element is a morpheme meaning 'water; liquid'.[1] Of the many body fluids,[2] only a few relate directly to the reproductive system (AMNIOTIC FLUID, MILK, SEMEN, VAGINAL SECRETIONS). In this section, however, in order to illustrate the scope of the various ST roots for WATER, I include a generous sampling of compounds referring to non-reproductive body fluids.[3]

(157)  *ra ≍ *wa  **SEMEN**

There is no single widespread root for SEMEN to be reconstructed for PTB, though several promising local candidates are attested here and there. Many forms for this

---

[1]Exceptions are BLOOD, URINE, SWEAT, and sometimes BILE, which are usually monosyllabic words.

[2]That is, AMNIOTIC FLUID, BILE, BLOOD, MILK, PHLEGM, PUS, SALIVA, SEMEN, SNOT, SWEAT, TEARS, VAGINAL SECRETIONS.

[3]The numerous roots for water (over ten at last count) in the STEDT database merit a separate study. Words for WATER seldom seem to be used by themselves in ST languages to mean URINE, unlike e.g. English, where *make water* is a common euphemism for 'urinate'; for an exception see the WT form **č'u** below.

IX. Body Fluids

concept are euphemistic (e.g. words that otherwise simply mean 'water'); many others are compounds of the structure PENIS + WATER (e.g. Tangkhul **shaŋ-ra**). Other "sementic" associations include SEMEN ⟷ SAP (Akha **a˘ dzi˛** means both [Lewis p.35]); SEMEN ⟷ SHIT (Lahu **nī-qhê**); SEMEN ⟷ FAT (Lahu **nī-chu**); SEMEN ⟷ CONTEMPLATION (WT **t'ig-le** [Jäschke p. 231]). The present root appears in Kamarupan, Himalayish, and Qiangic.

1.3. Naga

| Tangkhul | hai **ra** | semen | JAM-Ety | 4 |
| | pha **ra** | semen | JAM-Ety | |
| | shaŋ **ra** | semen | JAM-Ety | |

1.7. Bodo-Garo = Barish

| Bodo | pe **da** | semen | JAM-Ety | 5 |

2.3.2. Kiranti

| Bantawa | lü-khü-**wa** | semen | WW-Bant:47 | |
| | lU khU **wa** | semen | NKR-Bant | |
| Belhare | **la** lik | semen, sperm | BB-Belhare | |
| Dumi | ro: **ri** | semen, sperm, seed | SVD-Dum | 6 |
| Limbu | le **wā** | semen | JAM-Ety | |
| Thulung | **la** sa | semen | NJA-Thulung | |

3.1. Tangut

| Tangut [Xixia] | rĭɑr **rĭe** | semen | DQ-Xixia:10.3.7 | 7 |

3.2. Qiangic

| Qiang (Mawo) | ʁliə˩ | semen | JS-Mawo | |

(158)                    \*ŋya                    SEMEN

This root has so far been found only in a few Himalayish languages.

2.1.1. Western Himalayish

| Pattani [Manchati] | **ñya** ri | semen | STP-ManQ:10.3.7 |
| | **ñya** ri hut si | ejaculate (v.) | STP-ManQ:10.3.8 |

2.1.4. Tamangic

| Tamang (Risiangku) | ¹**ŋja** | semen | MM-TamRisQ:10.3.7 |
| Tamang (Sahu) | ¹**ŋja** | semen | JAM-Ety |

2.3.2. Kiranti

| Limbu | **yā** rimbā | semen | JAM-Ety |

---

[4]For the first syllable, see **(82)** \***hay** ✕ \***kay** VAGINA, above. This certainly looks like a case of "genital flipflop", i.e. semen is viewed as "vagina-semen", since that is its destination.
[5]The **-d-** in this form is a plausible Bodo intervocalic reflex of \*-**r**-. The name of this language itself is often transcribed as "Boro". See Bhat 1968.
[6]This form looks exactly parallel to Tangut **rĭar rĭe**.
[7]This compound looks exactly parallel to Dumi **ro: ri**.

228

## (159)  *bo  SEMEN

This etymon has so far been found only in a few Kuki-Chin languages.

1.2. Kuki-Chin

| | | | |
|---|---|---|---|
| Kom Rem | ə **bo** | semen | T-KomRQ:10.3.7 |
| Lushai [Mizo] | **baw** | semen | JAM-Ety |

1.4. Meithei

| | | | |
|---|---|---|---|
| Moyon | jʌŋ **bów** | semen | DK-Moyon:10.3.7 |
| | jʌŋ **bów** isòw? | ejaculate (v.) | DK-Moyon:10.3.8 |

## (160)  *ʔ-bik  SQUIRT / EJACULATE

This is only one of a large number of verbs than can be used to mean EJACULATE.[8]
This particular root has so far been identified only in a couple of Loloish languages. In
Ahi it means specifically 'eject semen', while the Lahu cognate is used to mean 'squirt
urine'. Although this etymon had a *stopped final in Proto-Loloish (as indicated by the
Ahi constriction and the Lahu high-rising tone), it was not reconstructed in Matisoff
1972a.

6.2. Loloish

| | | | |
|---|---|---|---|
| Ahi | **pi̱**$^{55}$ | ejaculate | LMZ-AhiQ:10.3.8 |
| Gazhuo | **pi**$^{35}$ | urinate | DQ-Gazhuo:9.7.2 |
| Lahu (Black) | jî **pí** ve | urinate | JAM-DL:p. 582 |
| | jî **pí** | urinate ("squirt urine") | JAM-DL:818 |
| | **pí** | spurt; squirt out | JAM-DL:818 |
| Lolopho | zi̱$^{31}$ **pi̱**$^{55}$ ʂo$^{31}$ | urinate | DQ-Lolopho:9.7.2 |

## (161)  *tsyu  WATER / BODY FLUID

1.3. Naga

| | | | |
|---|---|---|---|
| Angami (Kohima) | mhi$^{31}$ **dzü**$^{55}$ | tears | VN-AngQ:3.4.6 |
| Chokri | mhü$^{31}$ **dzü**$^{33}$ | tears | VN-ChkQ:3.4.6 |
| Lotha Naga | e sü **tchhü** | tears (weeping) | GEM-CNL |
| | E su **tsu** | tears | VN-LothQ:3.4.6 |
| | shi ro **tchhü** | milk | GEM-CNL |
| | Sho ro **tchu** | milk | VN-LothQ:5.4.3 |
| Mao | o **chü** rü | rain | GEM-CNL |

2.1.1. Western Himalayish

| | | | |
|---|---|---|---|
| Bunan | khu **cu** | semen | SBN-BunQ:10.3.7 |

2.1.2. Bodic

| | | | |
|---|---|---|---|
| Baima | ɲi$^{53}$ **tʃu**$^{53}$ | sweat / perspiration | SHK-BaimaQ:8.2.1 |
| Kaike | kha **jyu** | spittle / saliva | JAM-Ety |
| Tibetan (Amdo:Bla-brang) | hnək **tɕhə** | tear (n.) | ZMYYC:239.4 |
| Tibetan (Amdo:Zeku) | ɣnək **tɕhə** | tear (n.) | ZMYYC:239.5 |

[8]Another such verb is *m-tis 'be wet'. See below, (162) *m-t(w)əy ✕ *m-ti WATER / FLUID / LIQUID
/ SOAK.

| | | | | |
|---|---|---|---|---|
| Tibetan (Batang) | kha⁵⁵ **tɕho**⁵³ | saliva | DQ-Batang:3.7.5 | |
| | mi?⁵⁵ **tɕho**⁵³ | tears | DQ-Batang:3.4.6 | |
| Tibetan (Jirel) | kho **jyuq** | spittle / saliva | JAM-Ety | |
| | mik **cyukq** | tears | JAM-Ety | |
| Tibetan (Khams:Dege) | ɲi⁵⁵**tɕhu**⁵³ | tear (n.) | ZMYYC:239.3 | |
| Tibetan (Lhasa) | mik⁵³**tɕhu**⁵³ | tear (n.) | ZMYYC:239.2 | |
| Tibetan (Sherpa:Helambu) | mē **zhū** | tears | B-ShrpaHQ:3.4.6 | |
| Sherpa | mik **cur** | tears | JAM-Ety | |
| Tibetan (Sherpa:Helambu) | ŋōl **chu** | sweat / perspiration | B-ShrpaHQ:8.2.1 | |
| Tibetan (Written) | **č'u** | water; water in the body; euph. for urine | JAM-Ety | 9 |
| | **č'u**-ser | pus | JAM-Ety | 10 |
| | k'a-**č'ú** | spittle / saliva | JAM-Ety | |
| | mig **tɕhu** | tear (n.) | ZMYYC:239.1 | |
| | mig-**č'u** | tears | JAM-Ety | |
| | mig-**tʃhu** | tears | ZLS-Tib:62 | |
| **2.1.4. Tamangic** | | | | |
| Tamang (Sahu) | khā **cyo** | spittle / saliva | JAM-Ety | |
| Thakali (Tukche) | 'mi-**kju** | tears | SIL-Thak:2.A.65 | |
| | 'mi-**kyu** | tears | JAM-Ety | |
| | chap-**kyu** | sweat | JAM-Ety | |
| | cʰɔp-**kju** | sweat | SIL-Thak:2.A.74 | |
| **3.2. Qiangic** | | | | |
| Muya [Minyak] | mi⁵³**tɕɯ**⁵³ | tears | SHK-MuyaQ:3.4.6 | |

(162)     ***m-t(w)əy ⋉ *m-ti***     **WATER / FLUID / LIQUID / SOAK**

This is a rather complex word family in which all three dental suffixes /-t, -s, -n/ are attested. Reflexes include Kanauri **this** 'wet', Jingpho **mədìt** 'moisten sthg; wet, damp', Lalo **tíq** 'steep, soak', Kanauri **ti** 'water', Jingpho **mədī** 'moist, damp, wet', Lahu **dì** 'moisten due to sexual excitement (of a woman), ejaculate (of a man)'. The nasal prefix is reflected directly in Jingpho, and indirectly by the voiced Lahu initial.

Note the Kanauri form **thiss**, where the -s perhaps reflects the source of the -t to be found in other languages.

As noted above, there is sometimes confusion between this root and **(2a) *d(w)əy** EGG / TESTICLE, as in compounds of BIRD + WATER > EGG. Note the Kom Rem forms **mit ɣətui** 'eyeball' and **nəi tui** 'amniotic fluid', where the second element definitely means 'egg' in the former, but 'liquid' in the latter.

To make the phonosemantic variation in this root more plausible, compare the various English words derived from Proto-Indo-European ***wod ⋉ *wēd ⋉ *we-n-d** etc.:

---

⁹See also WT **gsaṅ-č'ab** 'urine (resp.)', lit. "secret-water". **č'ab** is the respectful form for **č'u** 'water'.
¹⁰Literally "yellow water".

Inherited Germanic material:

1. **\*wod-ōr** [suffixed o-grade] > pGmc **\*watar** > OE *wætar* > *water*
2. **\*wēd-o-** [suffixed lengthened grade] > pGmc **\*wēd-** > OE *wǣt, wēt* > *wet*
3. **\*wod-** [o-grade] > pGmc **\*wat-skan** > OE *wæscan, wacsan* > *wash*
4. **\*we-n-d-** [with nasal infix] > pGmc **\*wintruz** 'wet season' > OE *winter* > *winter*
5. **\*ud-ro-, \*ud-rā** [suffixed zero-grade] 'water animal', in pGmc **\*otraz** > OE *otor* > *otter*

Borrowings from other Indo-European languages:

6. **\*ud-ōr** [suffixed zero-grade] > Greek *hudōr* 'water' > *HYDRO-* (incl. *clepsydra, dropsy*)
7. **\*u-n-d-ā** [suffixed nasalized zero-grade] > Latin *unda* 'wave' > *undulate, inundate, abound, redundant, surround*
8. **\*ud-skio** [suffixed zero-grade] > Scot. and Ir. Gaelic *uisge* 'water' > *uisquebaugh, whiskey*
9. **\*wod-ā-** [suffixed o-grade] > Russ. *voda* 'water', with *-ka* 'diminutive' > *vodka*

See Matisoff 1994a:52-53.

See *STC* #55 and Matisoff 1988a p. 705. *STC* #55, #167, and #168 should be combined as one root.

See *HPTB* **\*twəy**, p. 194; **\*twəy ⪤ \*dwəy**, p. 195; **\*twəy-n**, p. 451; **\*ti(y)**, pp. 193, 194, 471; **\*m-ti-s**, pp. 434, 351.

There are several likely Chinese comparanda, the best of which is probably 涕 OC **t'iər** 'weep, tears' *GSR* 591m. Cf. also 水 OC **śi̯wər** 'water' *GSR* 576a-e, and 川 'river', the latter pointing to an allofam with a nasal final **\*m-twəy-n**.

| 0. Sino-Tibetan | | | |
|---|---|---|---|
| *Tibeto-Burman | *(snɑ-)ti(y)A | snot | ACST:551f |
| | *ti(y) | water | STC:55 |
| **1.1. North Assam** | | | |
| Darang [Taraon] | nye **cei** | breast milk | JAM-Ety |
| | nye ma: **cei** | breast milk | JAM-Ety |
| Idu | te⁵⁵tɕʰi̯⁵⁵ | sweat / perspiration | SHK-Idu:8.2.1 |
| | ti **ci** | sweat | JP-Idu; NEFA-PBI |
| | ti **ci** brõ ga | sweat | JP-Idu |
| **1.2. Kuki-Chin** | | | |
| Khoirao | a tu **thui** | milk | GEM-CNL |
| Kom Rem | mit rətʰi | tears | T-KomRQ:3.4.6 |
| | mit ɣətui | eyeball ("eye-egg") | T-KomRQ:3.4.2 [11] |
| | nəi **tui** | amniotic fluid | T-KomRQ:10.4.10 |
| | **tui** suh | amniotic sac / bag of waters | T-KomRQ:10.4.9 |
| Lakher [Mara] | sa-pi-**ti** | breast milk | JAM-Ety |
| | ti | water, egg | JAM-Ety |
| Liangmei | n **dui**, bui na **dui** | milk | GEM-CNL |
| Lushai [Mizo] | hnu te **tui** | milk | GEM-CNL |
| | mit-**tui** | tears | JAM-Ety |
| Maram | ta na **dui** | milk | GEM-CNL |
| Puiron | se nu **tui** | milk | GEM-CNL |

---

[11]Properly speaking, this compound really belongs under **(2a) \*d(w)əy** EGG / TESTICLE above, but is included here to point out the contrast with **nəi tui** 'amniotic fluid' (see section note).

1.3. Naga

| | | | |
|---|---|---|---|
| Chang | san **tei** | milk | GEM-CNL |
| Rongmei | nau **dui** | milk | GEM-CNL |
| | talân-**dui** | sweat | AW-TBT:471 |
| | tülün **dui** | sweat | GEM-CNL |
| Wancho | cham **ti** | milk | GEM-CNL |
| | hu-**ci** | spittle / saliva | JAM-Ety |
| | tsam **ti** | milk | WTF-PNN:462 |
| | tzam **ti** | milk | WTF-PNN:462 |
| Yacham-Tengsa | mam **tü** | milk | GEM-CNL |
| Zeme | tung **dui** | milk | GEM-CNL |

1.7. Bodo-Garo = Barish

| | | | |
|---|---|---|---|
| Atong | ku-**dəi** | spittle / saliva | JAM-Ety |
| Bodo | bun **dəy** | breast milk | JAM-Ety |
| | ga ga **dəy** | phlegm / sputum / saliva / mucus | JAM-Ety |
| | ga lam **doi** | sweat | STC:381 |
| | gu zu **dəy** | phlegm / sputum / saliva / mucus | JAM-Ety |
| | gə ləm **dəy** | sweat | JAM-Ety |
| | gɤ lɤm-**dɤi** | sweat | AW-TBT:363 |
| | ha gá **dɤiʔ** | phlegm | AW-TBT:641 |
| | mə **də́y** ~ mi **də́y** | tears | JAM-Ety |
| Dimasa | **di** | water | GEM-CNL |
| | **di** khau | draw water | STC:336 |
| | gi lim **di** ≍ gu lum **di** | sweat | STC:381 |
| Garo | ku-**ci** | spittle / saliva | JAM-Ety |
| | t**ɕi** | water | STC:45n149 |
| Garo (Bangladesh) | sok-bit-**chi** | breast milk; mother's milk | RB-GB |
| Kokborok | kləŋ-**təy** | sweat | PT-Kok |
| | məʔ-**təy** | tears | PT-Kok |
| | wa-**təy** | rain | PT-Kok |

2.1.1. Western Himalayish

| | | | |
|---|---|---|---|
| Bunan | mik **ti** | tears | SBN-BunQ:3.4.6 |
| | **thi** | wet | STC:55 |
| Kanauri | dŭs-**tī** | sweat | JAM-Ety |
| | dus **ti** | sweat | DS-Kan:39,60 |
| | mig **sti** | tears | DS-Kan:60 |
| | mĭt **tī** | tears | JAM-Ety |
| | **thi**-ss | wet | STC:16n59 |
| | **ti** | water | STC:55 |
| Pattani [Manchati] | mig **ti** | tears | DS-Patt |
| | mik **ti** | tears | STP-ManQ:3.4.6 |
| | **ti** | water | STC:55 |

2.1.2. Bodic

| | | | |
|---|---|---|---|
| Tibetan (Written) | **mchi**-ma | tears | WSC-SH:147 |

2.1.5. Dhimal

| | | | |
|---|---|---|---|
| Dhimal | hi **ti** | blood | JK-Dh |
| | hna-**thi** | snot | STC:168n449 |

|  | hnɑ-**thi** | snot | ACST:551f |
|---|---|---|---|

**2.2. Newar**

| Newar | **wā** | rain | CG-NewariQ3 |

**2.3.1. Kham-Magar-Chepang-Sunwar**

| Chepang | **tiʔ** | water | AH-CSDPN:01.075; AW-TBT:93; SIL-Chep:1.75 |
| Chepang (Eastern) | hləp rə **tiʔ** | sweat / perspiration | RC-ChepQ:8.2.1 |
|  | mik **tiʔ** | tears | RC-ChepQ:3.4.6 |
|  | ʔoh (lay) **tiʔ** | milk | RC-ChepQ:5.4.3 |
| Magar | **di** | water | STC:55 |
|  | mik **Di** | tears | JAM-Ety |

**2.3.2. Kiranti**

| Bahing | plik **ti** | tears | BM-PK7:178 |
| Hayu | pe ku **ti** | tears | BM-PK7:178; JAM-Ety |
|  | **ti** | water | STC:55 |

**3.2. Qiangic**

| Guiqiong | fu⁵⁵ tʃ̩³³ | sweat | SHK-GuiqQ |
| Qiang (Taoping) | ȵy⁵⁵ ȵy⁵⁵ tsuə³³ | milk | JZ-Qiang |
| Queyu (Yajiang) [Zhaba] | nu⁵³ tɕʰi⁵³ | milk | SHK-ZhabQ:5.4.3 |
|  | nu⁵³tɕhi⁵³ | milk | ZMYYC:281.16 |

**4.1. Jingpho**

| Jingpho | **mədi** | moist | JAM-TJLB:337 |
|  | **mədi** | moist, damp, wet | STC:55 |
|  | **mədìt** | wet, dampen; wet, damp, moist | STC:55 |

**4.2. Nungic**

| Anong | **thi** | water | STC:55 |
|  | tsh̩³¹dzɑŋ⁵⁵ | rain (v.) | ZMYYC:750.44 |
|  | tshɻ̍⁵⁵ | rain | ZMYYC:8.44 |

**5. Tujia**

| Tujia | a²¹ la⁵⁵ tsʰe³⁵ | tears | CK-TujMQ:3.4.6 |
| Tujia (Northern) | lo³⁵ pu³⁵ pʑe⁵⁵ tsʰe²¹ | tears | JZ-Tujia |
| Tujia | lo³⁵ pu⁵⁵ pɰe⁵⁵ tsʰe²¹ | tears | CK-TujBQ:3.4.6 |
|  | man²¹**tshie²¹** | milk | ZMYYC:281.38 |
|  | mã²¹ **tsʰe²¹** | milk | CK-TujBQ:5.4.3 |
|  | mã⁵⁵ **tsʰe³⁵** | milk | CK-TujMQ:5.4.3 |
| Tujia (Southern) | ʔa²¹la⁵⁵ **tsʰe³⁵** | tears | JZ-Tujia |

**6.1. Burmish**

| Achang | **ti** | water | STC:55 |
| Lashi (Lachhe') | pɔ̌⁴-**tjwi²** | sweat | GHL-PPB:T.25 |

**6.2. Loloish**

| Gazhuo | kɤ⁵⁵**tiɛ⁵⁵** | perspiration | DHFRL |
|  | ȵa⁵³ ji³²³ **tiɛ²⁴** | tears | DLF-Gazhuo; DHFRL |

| Lahu (Black) | dì | have an orgasm (man or woman); ejaculate (man) | JAM-DL:705; JAM-TSR:109(a) |
|---|---|---|---|
| | tî? | soak | JAM-TSR:109(b) |
| Lisu | ti² | immerse | JAM-TSR:109(b) |
| Nasu | na̱³³ ndʰɯ³³ | tears | CK-YiQ:3.4.6 |
| Ugong | thi | water | STC:55 |
| Yi (Dafang) | na³³ ndie³³ | tears | JZ-Yi |
| Yi (Nanjian) | mi̱³³ dzɹ̩⁵⁵ ɣɯ⁵⁵ | tears | JZ-Yi |
| Yi (Xide) | m(u)³³ha³³dʑi²¹ | rain (v.) | ZMYYC:750.21 |

### 6.3. Naxi

| Naxi (Yongning) | dʑi³³ | rain (v.) | ZMYYC:750.29 |
|---|---|---|---|

### 7. Karenic

| Bwe | dɛ nu chi | milk | EJAH-BKD |
|---|---|---|---|
| | mo chí | tears | EJAH-BKD |
| | nu-chi | milk | EJAH-BKD |
| Karen (Sgaw/Hinthada) | a³¹ ny³¹ tʰi⁵⁵ | milk (cow's) | DQ-KarenB:328.1 |
| | da³¹ ny³¹ tʰi⁵⁵ | milk; milk (cow's) | DQ-KarenB:161,328.2 |
| | glɔ³¹ ny³¹ tʰi⁵⁵ | milk (cow's) | DQ-KarenB:328 |
| | mi³³ tʰi⁵⁵ | tears | DQ-KarenB:194 |
| Karen (Sgaw/Yue) | mɛ?³¹ tʰi⁵⁵ | tears | DQ-KarenA:194 |
| | ta³¹ nu³¹ tʰi⁵⁵ | milk | DQ-KarenA:161 |

### 8. Bai

| Bai (Dali) | pɑ⁴² tsi̱⁴⁴ | milk | JZ-Bai |
|---|---|---|---|
| | pɑ⁴²tsi⁴⁴ | milk | ZMYYC:281.35 |
| Bai (Jianchuan) | pɑ⁴² tsɛ⁴⁴ | milk | JZ-Bai |
| | pɑ⁴²tsɛ⁴⁴ | milk | ZMYYC:281.36 |

### 9. Sinitic

| Chinese (Mandarin) | bí tì | snot | JAM-Ety |
|---|---|---|---|
| Chinese (Middle) | thiei: | tears, snot (especially that which flows during weeping) | WSC-SH:146 |

## Chinese comparanda

涕 **tì** 'weep, tears'

*GSR*: 591m      Karlgren: *t'iər      Li: *thidx      Baxter: *thij? (p. 792)

The Middle Chinese reading would permit an Old Chinese reconstruction in either the OC 脂 Zhī rhyme group (*-id (Li)/*-ij (Baxter)) or the OC 微 Wēi rhyme group (*-əd (Li)/*-ij (Baxter)). Li does not reconstruct this word, but he assigns other words in *GSR* 591 to the 脂 Zhī group. Words in *GSR* 591 are reconstructed some with one vowel, some with the other by Baxter (see 1992:457ff for an explanation), but 涕 is reconstructed with *-ij because it rhymes unambiguously with a number of 脂 Zhī group words in *Shījīng* #203. Still, it is possible that in Baxter's system the word goes back to

---

[12]The second syllable of the Bai (Bijiang) form **vĩ³³ çui³³** is an obvious loan from Chinese (cf. Mand. **shuǐ**), although the other Bai forms listed seem to reflect the present etymon.

earlier *thij?, with vowel fronting occurring early in the dialect on which the *Shījīng* poem was based. Baxter proposes just such a development for other words in the phonetic series.

If the OC vowel is reconstructed as *i, the vowel correspondence with the proposed TB cognate is regular (see **(2a)** *d(w)əy EGG / TESTICLE for examples). A 微 Wēi group reconstruction of *-əd (Li)/*-ij (Baxter) does not jeopardize the comparison, but this Chinese rhyme seems to correspond to TB *-ay more often than to TB *-əy. It may be that the correspondence with *-ay is regular while that with *-əy is irregular but not uncommon. See **(40b)** *s-tay NAVEL / ABDOMEN / CENTER / SELF and **(140)** *ŋ-(w)aːy COPULATE / MAKE LOVE / LOVE / GENTLE, but note also 'hungry' OC 飢 *krjɨj (Baxter), TB *b-kri-(n/s).

On the aspiration mismatch in the initials, see the discussion under **(1b)** *pu EGG.

[ZJH]

水 **shuǐ** 'water, river'

*GSR* 576a-e          Karlgren: *ɕi̯wər          Li: --          Baxter: *h[l]juj? (1239)

Gong 1995 set 133 reconstructs *hljədx and compares to WT **chu** 'water, brook, river', presumably assuming that the latter derives from an earlier form with a lateral initial. The comparison is, however, not tenable given the reconstruction of the PTB root in this volume (**(161)** *tsyu WATER / BODY FLUID).

This Chinese word is most likely related to PTB *lwi(y) 'flow, stream' (see *STC* #210), as proposed by Coblin (1986:158) and discussed in Handel (1998). A relationship with **(162)** *m-t(w)əy ⪥ *m-ti WATER / FLUID / LIQUID / SOAK seems unlikely because of the mismatch of initial consonants.

[ZJH]

川 **chuān** 'river'

*GSR*: 462a          Karlgren: *t̂'i̯wən          Li: *thjiən (?)          Baxter: *KHju/on (1126)

The reconstruction of this Chinese word is problematic. As Karlgren (*GSR* 462a) notes, the Middle Chinese form is probably irregular. The Old Chinese rhyme group is uncertain, which is why Baxter gives two possibilities for the vowel. Baxter's capital *KH indicates a velar initial that palatalized irregularly in the development of Middle Chinese. Handel (1998) reconstructs *khlun and Schuessler (2007:195) *k-hlun, because *GSR* 462 looks like a lateral series. Schuessler further suggests that the Chinese word is related to PTB *kluːŋ 'river / valley', which has areal connections with Austroasiatic and Tai. However, this does not explain the *-n coda in Chinese.

The proposed PTB comparison in this volume depends on an Old Chinese reconstruction like Li's with a dental initial, which in Baxter's system would look like *thjun. However, the vowel correspondence is still irregular, and the comparison further requires positing an *-n suffix not found in Tibeto-Burman.

[ZJH]

## (163)          *ku          SEMEN / WATER / BODY FLUID

**2.1.1. Western Himalayish**

| | | | |
|---|---|---|---|
| Bunan | khu cu | semen | SBN-BunQ:10.3.7 |

**2.1.2. Bodic**

| | | | |
|---|---|---|---|
| Tibetan (Written) | k'u-ba | *semen virile* | JAM-Ety |
| | k'u-k'rag | semen and uterine blood | JAM-Ety |

**2.3.1. Kham-Magar-Chepang-Sunwar**

| | | | |
|---|---|---|---|
| Sunwar | prek ku | tears | BM-PK7:178; JAM-Ety |

**2.3.2. Kiranti**

| | | | |
|---|---|---|---|
| Bantawa | lü-khü-wa | semen | WW-Bant:47 |
| | lU khU wa | semen | NKR-Bant |
| Hayu | pẽ: khu | tears | BM-Hay:84.98 |
| | pe ku ti | tears | BM-PK7:178; JAM-Ety |
| Thulung | bri ko | tears | BM-PK7:178; NJA-Thulung |

## (164)          *rəy          WATER / LIQUID

See *HPTB* *rəy, p. 250; PLB *rəy[1], pp. 42, 43, 189, 213.

**1.2. Kuki-Chin**

| | | | |
|---|---|---|---|
| Maring | chu chu yui | milk | GEM-CNL |
| | wa yui | egg | GEM-CNL |
| | yui | water | GEM-CNL |

**1.3. Naga**

| | | | |
|---|---|---|---|
| Sema | a ke chi zü | milk | GEM-CNL |
| Tangkhul | ²sai³lən-²rə | sweat | AW-TBT:471 |

**1.4. Meithei**

| | | | |
|---|---|---|---|
| Moyon | mìk rʌ̀ tsə̀ | tears | DK-Moyon:3.4.6 |

**2.1.1. Western Himalayish**

| | | | |
|---|---|---|---|
| Pattani [Manchati] | ñya ri | semen | STP-ManQ:10.3.7 |
| | ñya ri hut si | ejaculate (v.) | STP-ManQ:10.3.8 |

**2.1.2. Bodic**

| | | | |
|---|---|---|---|
| Tsangla (Central) | ming-ri | tears | SER-HSL/T:36 12 |
| Tsangla (Motuo) | miŋ¹³ ri¹³ | tears | JZ-CLMenba |
| | miŋ ri | tears; tear (n.) | SLZO-MLD; ZMYYC:239.7 |
| | ri¹³ naŋ¹³ sop⁵⁵ | thirsty | JZ-CLMenba |
| | ri naŋ sop | thirsty; thirsty (V) | SLZO-MLD; ZMYYC:898.7 |

**3.2. Qiangic**

| | | | |
|---|---|---|---|
| Muya [Minyak] | ʐɯ⁵³ | amniotic sac / bag of waters | SHK-MuyaQ:10.4.9 [13] |
| Namuyi | miɛ⁵⁵ɕiɛ¹³³ | tears | SHK-NamuQ:3.4.6 |
| Qiang (Taoping) | ma³¹ʐɿ⁵⁵ | rain | ZMYYC:8.9 |

[13]Cf. also Muya tɕɯ⁵³ 'water' (*ZMYYC* #10), assigned to (161) *tsyu WATER / BODY FLUID, above.

| | | | |
|---|---|---|---|
| | mi⁵⁵ ʁo³³ | tears | JZ-Qiang |
| Queyu (Yajiang) [Zhaba] | tɕʰu⁵⁵ ʑi⁵⁵ | sweat / perspiration | SHK-ZhabQ:8.2.1 |
| | n̻e⁵⁵ ʑi⁵³ | tears | SHK-ZhabQ:3.4.6 |

## 6.1. Burmish

| | | | |
|---|---|---|---|
| Burmese (Written) | re ŋat | thirst for water | JAM-GSTC:034 |
| Hpun (Northern) | ă nù ʁaíŋ | milk ('breast liquid') | EJAH-Hpun |
| Maru [Langsu] | nuk⁵⁵ ɣək³¹ | milk | DQ-Langsu:5.4.3 [14] |
| | ɣək³¹ | amniotic fluid; water | DQ-Langsu:10.4.10; ZMYYC:10.43 |
| | ɣək³¹lɔ̃³¹ | river | ZMYYC:18.43 |
| Atsi [Zaiwa] | vui⁵¹ ʃit⁵⁵ | thirsty | JZ-Zaiwa |

## 6.2. Loloish

| | | | |
|---|---|---|---|
| Ahi | la̱³³ʑi²² | semen | CK-YiQ:10.3.7 |
| | lɑ̱³³ ʑi²² | semen | LMZ-AhiQ:10.3.7 |
| | ne̱³³ ʑi²² | tears | LMZ-AhiQ:3.4.6 |
| | ni²¹ ʑi²² | saliva | LMZ-AhiQ:3.7.5 |
| Gazhuo | ji³¹ tɕa⁵³ sɻ³⁵ | thirsty | DQ-Gazhuo:3.7.8 |
| | n̻a⁵³ ji²⁴ | tears | DLF-Gazhuo |
| | n̻a⁵³ ji³²³ | tears | DQ-Gazhuo:3.4.6 |
| | n̻a⁵³ ji³²³ tiɛ²⁴ | tears | DLF-Gazhuo; DHFRL |
| Hani (Lüchun) | mja ý | tears | ILH-PL:129 |
| Hani (Dazhai) | ze⁵⁵ | rain (v.) | ZMYYC:750.31 |
| | ɔ³¹ze⁵⁵ | rain | ZMYYC:8.31 |
| Hani (Shuikui) | jɛ⁵⁵(ɣu³¹jɛ⁵⁵) | rain (v.) | ZMYYC:750.32 |
| | u³¹jɛ⁵⁵ | rain | ZMYYC:8.32 |
| Lahu (Banlan) | a ke̱ g'i˯ | sweat | DB-Lahu:151 |
| | cu: g'i˯ | milk | DB-Lahu:155 |
| Lahu (Black) | cha-ɣɨ | vaginal secretion | JAM-Ety |
| | mɛʔ⁵⁴ ɣɯ³¹ | tears | JZ-Lahu |
| | mɛ̂ʔ-ɣɨ | tears | JAM-Ety |
| | tsu³⁵ɣɯ³¹ | milk | ZMYYC:281.33 |
| | tsɣ³⁵ ɣɯ³¹ | milk | JZ-Lahu |
| Lahu (Yellow) | mɛʔ⁵⁴ ɣɯ³¹ | tears | JZ-Lahu |
| | tsɣ³⁵ ɣɯ³¹ | milk | JZ-Lahu |
| Lalo | zjə̀q-ɣə́ | semen | SB-Lalo |
| | za²¹ ɣɯ⁵⁵ | semen | CK-YiQ:10.3.7 |
| | ʔmĩ̄³³ ɣɯ⁵⁵ | tears | CK-YiQ:3.4.6 |
| Lipho | dɛ³³vi³³ | semen | CK-YiQ:10.3.7 |
| | pa̱²¹dzɻ³³vi³³ | milk | CK-YiQ:5.4.3 |
| Lisu (Northern) | hɔ̃²¹ʒɻ³³ | semen | DB-Lisu |
| Lisu | mrgh⁵-rghe⁴ | spittle / saliva | JAM-Ety |
| Lisu (Nujiang) | mɯ³¹ ɣɯ³³ | saliva | JZ-Lisu |
| | tʃi⁵⁵ ʒi³³ | sweat | JZ-Lisu |
| Lisu | tʃi⁵⁵ʒi³³ | sweat | ZMYYC:277.27 |
| Lisu (Northern) | tɕi⁵⁵ji³³ | sweat | DB-Lisu |
| Lolopho | dæ³³ vi³³ | semen | DQ-Lolopho:10.3.7 |
| Mpi | m⁴poʔ⁴²ɯ⁶ | milk | DB-PLolo |
| Nasu | a⁵⁵ pa̱²¹ ʑi²¹ | milk | CK-YiQ:5.4.3 |
| | tɕʰa̱⁵⁵ ʑi²¹ | semen | CK-YiQ:10.3.7 |
| Nesu | le̱r³³ ʐɻ²¹ | semen | CK-YiQ:10.3.7 |

[14]See the note under (53a) *s-nəw BREAST / MILK / SUCK above for discussion of this form.

| | | | |
|---|---|---|---|
| | nɿ³³ zɻ³³ | tears | CK-YiQ:3.4.6 |
| Noesu | ɬu⁵⁵zi²¹ | semen | CK-YiQ:10.3.7 |
| Nosu | bɻ²¹zi³³ | semen | CK-YiQ:10.3.7 |
| Nusu (Northern) | nə̃³¹ nə̃⁵⁵ ɹɯ³⁵ ɑ⁵⁵ | milk | JZ-Nusu |
| Nusu (Southern) | nɯ⁵⁵ nɯ³¹ ɹə̰⁵⁵ | milk | JZ-Nusu |
| Sani [Nyi] | lʌ³³zɿ³³ | semen | YHJC-Sani |
| | la⁴⁴zɿ³³ | semen | CK-YiQ:10.3.7 |
| | ne³³zɿ³³ | tears | YHJC-Sani |
| | ne⁴⁴ zч³³ | tears | MXL-SaniQ:320.5 |
| | tɕæ⁵⁵ zɻ³³ | sweat | YHJC-Sani:227.4 |
| | tɕɛ⁵⁵zɿ³³ | sweat | YHJC-Sani |
| | zч³³ sî²² | thirsty | MXL-SaniQ:355.1 |
| Yi (Dafang) | tsɒ¹³ zi²¹ | milk | JZ-Yi; ZMYYC:281.22 |
| Yi (Mile) | tʂʌ⁵⁵zi³³ | sweat | ZMYYC:277.25 |
| Yi (Mojiang) | ʌ⁵⁵nɛ²¹zi²¹ | milk | ZMYYC:281.26 |
| Yi (Nanhua) | bɯ³³dzɿ³³zi³³ | milk | ZMYYC:281.24 |
| Yi (Nanjian) | mɿ³³ dzɻ⁵⁵ ɣɯ⁵⁵ | tears | JZ-Yi |
| | tɕe²¹ɣɯ⁵⁵ | sweat | ZMYYC:277.23 |
| Yi (Xide) | zɻ³³ sɿ⁵⁵ | thirsty | JZ-Yi; CSL-Ylzd |

**6.4. Jinuo**

| | | | |
|---|---|---|---|
| Jinuo (Baya/Banai) | mja³¹ ji³¹ | tears | DQ-JinA:194 |
| Jinuo (Baka) | mja³¹ ji³¹ | tears | DQ-JinB:194 |
| Jinuo (Youle) | mjɑ⁴² e⁴² | tears | JZ-Jinuo |
| | mɛ³³ e⁴⁴ | milk | JZ-Jinuo |
| Jinuo (Baya/Banai) | mɛ⁴⁴ po³¹ a³³ ji⁴⁴ | milk | DQ-JinA:161 |
| Jinuo | mɛ⁴⁴ji³³ | milk | ZMYYC:281.34 |

**8. Bai**

| | | | |
|---|---|---|---|
| Bai (Dali) | mɿ⁴² jɿ⁴² | tears | JZ-Bai |

## (165)     *laŋ     WATER / FLUID / RIVER / VALLEY

See *HPTB* PLB *laŋ¹, p. 266.

**1.1. North Assam**

| | | | |
|---|---|---|---|
| Padam-Mising [Abor-Miri] | a-pi a **lang** | bile | JAM-Ety:JHL-AM p.255 |
| | ap-pio a **lang** | bile | JAM-Ety:JHL-AM p.255 |
| | pui-ing a **lang** | bile | JAM-Ety:JHL-AM p.255 |
| Apatani | mí-**la** | tears | JS-Tani |
| | miʔ-**la** | tears | JS-Tani |
| Bengni | ñik-**la:** | tears | JS-Tani |
| Bokar | mik-**laŋ** | tears | JS-Tani |
| Gallong | ɲig **la** | tears | KDG-IGL |
| Miri, Hill | ɲik-**la** | tears | IMS-HMLG |

**1.3. Naga**

| | | | |
|---|---|---|---|
| Chang | **lang** | rain | GEM-CNL |
| Tangkhul | hup khǝ-**laŋ** | sweat | JAM-Ety |

**1.4. Meithei**

| | | | |
|---|---|---|---|
| Meithei | pi **raŋ** | tears | CYS-Meithei:3.4.6 |

**1.5. Mikir**

| | | | |
|---|---|---|---|
| Mikir | a mut a **lang** | bile | JAM-Ety; JAM-VSTB:(3) |

|  |  |  |  |
|---|---|---|---|
|  | bùm a-**lāng** | semen | KHG-Mikir:159 |
|  | bum a **lang** | semen ("penis-water") | JAM-Ety |
|  | chū-**lāng** | milk | KHG-Mikir:74 |
|  | mók-**lāng** | milk | KHG-Mikir:172 |
|  | mok **lang** | milk; breast milk | GEM-CNL; JAM-Ety |

**2.3.2. Kiranti**

| Thulung | u ba **la?** | bile | JAM-Ety |
|---|---|---|---|

**6.1. Burmish**

| Maru [Langsu] | ɣək³¹lɔ̃³¹ | river | ZMYYC:18.43 |
|---|---|---|---|

**6.2. Loloish**

| Bisu | khàn **laŋ** | saliva | PB-Bisu:15 |
|---|---|---|---|
|  | **láŋ** bɛ | thirsty | PB-Bisu:27 |
|  | lɔŋ pɛt **láŋ** | milk | PB-Bisu:15 |
|  | pɛ khà **laŋ** | gall | PB-Bisu:14 [15] |
|  | pɛ kʰà (**làŋ**) | bile | DB-Bisu |
| Lahu (Black) | **lɔ̀** | river; valley | JAM-DL:1401-2 |
|  | **lɔ̀**-qá | river, stream | JAM-DL:1402 |
|  | **lɔ̀**-qhò? | valley; dry riverbed | JAM-DL:1402 |
| Phunoi | **lã**⁵⁵ bɑt¹¹ de³³ | thirsty | DB-Phunoi |
|  | mõ³¹ hut **lã**⁵⁵ | sweat / perspiration | MF-PhnQ:8.2.1 |
|  | nù **lá** | milk | DB-PLolo |
| Ugong | nù **wŭŋ** | milk | DB-Ugong:5.4.3 |

---

[15]The first two syllables mean 'liver'; cf. Garo **bi-ka** 'liver'.

# Appendix: Source Abbreviations

AAAM-SSM    Abbi, Anvita and Awadhesh K. Mishra. 1985. "Consonant clusters and syllable structure of Meitei." *LTBA* 8.2:81-92.

ACST    Chou Fa-kao 周法高. 1972. "Archaic Chinese and Sino-Tibetan." *Journal of the Institute of Chinese Studies of the Chinese University of Hong Kong* 5.1:159-237.

AH-CSDPN    Hale, Austin. 1973. *Clause, Sentence, and Discourse Patterns in Selected Languages of Nepal IV: Word Lists.* Summer Institute of Linguistics Publications in Linguistics and Related Fields 40. Kathmandu: SIL and Tribhuvan University Press.

AT-MPB    Tayeng, Aduk. 1976. *Milang phrase book.* Shillong: The Director of Information and Public Relations, Government of Arunachal Pradesh.

AW-TBT    Weidert, Alfons K. 1987. *Tibeto-Burman Tonology: a comparative account. Current Issues in Linguistic Theory*, Vol. 54. Amsterdam and Philadelphia: John Benjamins Publishing Co.

B-ShrpaHQ    Bishop, Naomi. 1989. Body Parts Questionnaire (Sherpa Helambu).

BB-Belhare    Bickel, Balthasar. 1995. "The possessive of experience in Belhare." In David Bradley, ed., *Tibeto-Burman Languages of the Himalayas.* Canberra: Pacific Linguistics (A-86), pp. 135-55.

Bhat-Boro    Bhat, D. N. Shankara. 1968. *Boro Vocabulary, with a grammatical sketch.* Deccan College Building Centenary and Silver Jubilee Series #59. Poona: Deccan College Postgraduate and Research Institute.

Bhat-TNV    Bhat, D. N. Shankara. 1969. *Tankhur Naga Vocabulary.* Deccan College Building Centenary and Silver Jubilee Series #67. Poona: Deccan College Postgraduate and Research Institute.

BM-Bah    Michailovsky, Boyd. 1989. "Bahing." Electronic ms.

BM-Hay    Michailovsky, Boyd. 1989. "Hayu." Electronic ms.

BM-Lim    Michailovsky, Boyd. 1989. "Limbu." Electronic ms.

BM-PK7    Michailovsky, Boyd. 1991. "Proto-Kiranti forms." Unpublished ms.

CB-SpitiQ    Bodh, Sri Chhimed. 1991. Body Parts Questionnaire (Spiti).

CG-Dolak    Genetti, Carol. ca. 1990. Dolakhali (Newari) word list.

CG-Kath    Genetti, Carol. ca. 1990. Kathmandu Newari word list.

CG-NewariQ3    Genetti, Carol. 1990. Natural Objects Questionnaire.

CK-TujBQ    Chen Kang 陈康. 1986. Body Parts Questionnaire (Tujia, Bizika dialect).

CK-TujMQ    Chen Kang 陈康. 1986. Body Parts Questionnaire (Tujia, Mondzi dialect).

CK-YiQ    Chen Kang 陈康. 1986. Body Parts Questionnaire (8 Yi dialects).

CSL-YIzd    Chen Shilin 陈士林, Li Min 李民, et al., eds. 1979. 彝汉字典 *Yí-Hàn zìdiǎn [Yi-Chinese dictionary].* Chengdu: Yi Language Work Unit, People's Committee of Sichuan.

CYS-Meithei    Singh, Chungkham Yashawanta. 1991. Body Parts Questionnaire (Meithei).

DAP-Chm    Peterson, David A. 2008. "Bangladesh Khumi verbal classifiers and Kuki-Chin 'chiming'." *LTBA*, to appear.

DB-Bisu    Bradley, David. ca. 1993. Bisu vocabulary, extracted from DB-PLolo.

| | |
|---|---|
| DB-Lahu | Bradley, David. 1979. *Lahu Dialects.* Oriental Monograph Series, #23. Canberra: Australian National University. |
| DB-Lisu | Bradley, David. 1994. *A Dictionary of the Northern Dialect of Lisu (China and Southeast Asia).* Pacific Linguistics Series C-126. Canberra: Australian National University. |
| DB-Phunoi | Bradley, David. ca. 1993. Phunoi vocabulary, extracted from DB-PLolo. |
| DB-PLolo | Bradley, David. 1979. *Proto-Loloish.* Scandinavian Institute of Asian Studies Monograph Series, #39. London and Malmö: Curzon Press. |
| DB-Ugong | Bradley, David. 1993. Body Parts Questionnaire (Ugong). |
| DBS-PaO | Solnit, David. 1989. Pa-O word list. Electronic ms. |
| Deuri | Anonymous. n.d. Deuri body part terms. |
| DHFRL | Dai Qingxia 戴庆厦 et al., eds. 1991. 藏缅语十五种 *Zàngmiǎnyǔ shíwǔzhǒng [Fifteen Tibeto-Burman languages].* Beijing: 燕山出版社 Yānshān Chūbǎnshè. |
| DK-Moyon | Kosha, Donald. 1990. Body Parts Questionnaire (Moyon). |
| DLF-Gazhuo | Dai Qingxia 戴庆厦, Liu Juhuang 刘菊黄, and Fu Ailan 傅爱兰. 1987. 云南蒙古族嘎卓语研究 "On the Gazhuo language of the Mongolian people of Yunnan Province." 语言研究 *Yǔyán Yánjiū*, No. 1. |
| DNW-KhamQ | Watters, David and Nancy Watters. 1989. Body Parts Questionnaire (Kham). unpublished computer file. |
| DQ-Batang | Dai Qingxia 戴庆厦. 1989. Body Parts Questionnaire (Batang). |
| DQ-Bola | Dai Qingxia 戴庆厦. 1989. Field Notebook on Bola. |
| DQ-Daofu | Dai Qingxia 戴庆厦. 1989. Body Parts Questionnaire (Daofu). |
| DQ-Gazhuo | Dai Qingxia 戴庆厦. 1989. Body Parts Questionnaire (Gazhuo). |
| DQ-Jiarong | Dai Qingxia 戴庆厦. 1989. Body Parts Questionnaire (rGyalrong). |
| DQ-JinA | Dai Qingxia 戴庆厦. 1989. Field Notebook on Jinuo A. |
| DQ-JinB | Dai Qingxia 戴庆厦. 1989. Field Notebook on Jinuo B. |
| DQ-KarenA | Dai Qingxia 戴庆厦. 1989. Field Notebook on Karen A. |
| DQ-KarenB | Dai Qingxia 戴庆厦. 1989. Field Notebook on Karen B. |
| DQ-Langsu | Dai Qingxia 戴庆厦. 1989. Field Notebook on Langsu [Maru]. |
| DQ-Lashi | Dai Qingxia 戴庆厦. 1989. Field Notebook on Leqi [Lashi]. |
| DQ-Lolopho | Dai Qingxia 戴庆厦. 1989. Field Notebook on Lolopho. |
| DQ-NusuA | Dai Qingxia 戴庆厦. 1989. Field Notebook on Nusu A. |
| DQ-NusuB | Dai Qingxia 戴庆厦. 1989. Field Notebook on Nusu B. |
| DQ-QiangN | Dai Qingxia 戴庆厦. 1989. Field Notebook on Northern Qiang. |
| DQ-Xiandao | Dai Qingxia 戴庆厦. 1989. Field Notebook on Achang (Xiandao). |
| DQ-Xixia | Dai Qingxia 戴庆厦. 1989. Body Parts Questionnaire (Xixia = Tangut). |
| DS-Kan | Sharma, D.D. 1988. *A Descriptive Grammar of Kinnauri.* Delhi: Mittal Publications (Studies in Tibeto-Himalayan Languages #1). |
| DS-Patt | Sharma, D.D. 1982. *Studies in Tibeto-Himalayan Linguistics: a descriptive analysis of Pattani (a dialect of Lahaul).* Hoshiarpur: Vishveshvaranand Vishva Bandhu Institute of Sanskrit and Indological Studies, Panjab University. |
| EA-Tsh | Andvik, Eric. 1993. "Tshangla verb inflections." *LTBA* 16.1:75-136. |
| EJAH-BKD | Henderson, Eugénie J. A. 1997. *Bwe Karen Dictionary.* School of Oriental and African Studies, University of London. |

| | |
|---|---|
| EJAH-Hpun | Henderson, Eugénie J. A. 1986. "Some hitherto unpublished material on Northern (Megyaw) Hpun." In John McCoy and Timothy Light, eds., *Contributions to Sino-Tibetan Studies*, pp. 101-34. Leiden: E.J. Brill. |
| EJAH-TC | Henderson, Eugénie J. A. 1965. *Tiddim Chin: a descriptive analysis of two texts.* London Oriental Series #15. London and New York: Oxford University Press. |
| FD-Bai | Dell, François. 1981. *La langue Bai: phonologie et lexique.* Paris: Centre de Recherches Linguistiques sur l'Asie Orientale de l'Ecole des Hautes Etudes en Sciences Sociales. |
| GBM-Lepcha | Mainwaring, G.B. 1898. *Dictionary of the Lepcha Language.* Revised and completed by Albert Grünwedel. Berlin: Unger Brothers. |
| GDW-DML | Walker, George David. 1925. *A Dictionary of the Mikir language, Mikir-English and English-Mikir.* Shillong: Assam Government Press. |
| GEM-CNL | Marrison, G.E. 1967. *The Classification of the Naga Languages of Northeast India.* Ph.D. dissertation, School of Oriental and African Studies, University of London. 2 vols. |
| GHL-PPB | Luce, G. H. 1986. *Phases of Pre-Pagán Burma: languages and history.* Vol. 2. Oxford: Oxford University Press. |
| GSR | Karlgren, Bernhard. 1957. *Grammata Serica Recensa.* Stockholm: Museum of Far Eastern Antiquities, Publication 29. |
| HAJ-TED | Jäschke, Heinrich August. 1881/1958. *A Tibetan-English Dictionary, with special reference to the prevailing dialects.* London. Reprinted (1958) by Routledge and Kegan Paul. |
| HM-Prak | Hoshi Michiyo. 1984. *A Prakaa Vocabulary: a dialect of the Manang language.* Anthropological and Linguistic Studies of the Gandaki Area in Nepal II. (*Monumenta Serindica* #12.) Tokyo: ILCAA. |
| ILH-PL | Hansson, Inga-Lill. 1989. "A comparison of Akha, Hani, Khatu, and Pijo." *LTBA* 12.1:1-91. |
| IMS-HMLG | Simon, Ivan Martin. 1976. *Hill Miri Language Guide.* Shillong: Philological Section, Research Dept., Government of Arunachal Pradesh. |
| IMS-Miji | Simon, Ivan Martin. 1979. "Miji language guide." Shillong: Directorate of Research (Philological Section) Government of Arunachal Pradesh. |
| JAM-DL | Matisoff, James A. 1988. *The Dictionary of Lahu.* UCPL #111. Berkeley, Los Angeles, London: University of California Press. |
| JAM-Ety | Matisoff, James A. 1987. Body part card file. |
| JAM-GSTC | Matisoff, James A. 1985. "God and the Sino-Tibetan copula, with some good news concerning selected Tibeto-Burman rhymes." *Journal of Asian and African Studies* (Tokyo) 29:1-81. |
| JAM-II | Matisoff, James A. 1993. Personal communications from JAM, more recent than the Body Part Card File. |
| JAM-MLBM | Matisoff, James A. 1978. "Mpi and Lolo-Burmese microlinguistics." *Monumenta Serindica* (ILCAA, Tokyo) 4:1-36. |
| JAM-Rong | Matisoff, James A. 1994. Rongmei elicitation. |
| JAM-TIL | Matisoff, James A. 1983. "Translucent insights: a look at Proto-Sino-Tibetan through Gordon H. Luce's comparative word-list." *BSOAS* 46.3:462-76. |
| JAM-TJLB | Matisoff, James A. 1974. "The tones of Jinghpaw and Lolo-Burmese: common origin vs. independent development." *Acta Linguistica Hafniensia* (Copenhagen) 15.2, 153-212. |
| JAM-TSR | Matisoff, James A. 1972. *The Loloish Tonal Split Revisited.* Research Monograph #7. Berkeley: Center for South and Southeast Asian Studies, University of California, Berkeley. |

| | |
|---|---|
| JAM-VSTB | Matisoff, James A. 1978. *Variational Semantics in Tibeto-Burman: the 'organic' approach to linguistic comparison. OPWSTBL* #6. Philadelphia: Institute for the Study of Human Issues. |
| JCD | Dai Qingxia 戴庆厦, Xu Xijian 徐悉艰 , et al. 1983. 景汉辞典 *Jing-Han cidian – Jinghpo Miwa ga ginsi chyum – Jinghpo-Chinese dictionary.* Kunming: Yunnan Nationalities Press. |
| JF-HLL | Fraser, James Outram. 1922. *Handbook of the Lisu (Yawyin) Language.* Rangoon: Office of the Superintendent of Government Printing. |
| JHL-AM | Lorrain, J. Herbert. 1907. *A Dictionary of the Abor-Miri Language, with illustrative sentences and notes.* Shillong: Eastern Bengal and Assam Secretariat Printing Office. |
| JHL-Lu | Lorrain, J. Herbert. 1940. *Dictionary of the Lushai Language.* Bibliotheca Indica 261. Calcutta: Royal Asiatic Society of Bengal. |
| JK-Dh | King, John. 1994. Dhimal body parts. Personal communication. |
| JO-PB | Okell, John. 1971. "K- clusters in Proto-Burmese." Paper presented at ICSTLL #4, Indiana University, Bloomington, IN. |
| JP-Idu | Pulu, Jatan. 1978. *Idu Phrase Book.* Shillong: The Director of Information and Public Relations, Arunachal Pradesh. |
| JS-Amdo | Sun, Jackson 孫天心. 1985. *Aspects of the Phonology of Amdo Tibetan.* M.A. thesis, Institute of English, National Normal University, Taipei. Published 1986, Monumenta Serindica No. 16, Tokyo: ILCAA. |
| JS-Ch | Sun, Jackson 孫天心. 1985. Chinese glosses, excerpted from JS-Amdo. |
| JS-HCST | Sun, Jackson 孫天心. 1993. *A Historical-Comparative Study of the Tani (Mirish) Branch in Tibeto-Burman.* Ph.D. dissertation, University of California, Berkeley. |
| JS-Mawo | Sun, Jackson 孫天心. ca. 1986. Qiang Mawo body part word list. Unpublished ms. |
| JS-Tani | Sun, Jackson 孫天心. 1993. "Tani synonym sets." Electronic ms. |
| JS-Tib | Sun, Jackson 孫天心. 1985. Tibetan glosses, excerpted from JS-Amdo. |
| JZ-Achang | Dai Qingxia 戴庆厦 and Cui Zhichao 崔志超, eds. 1985. 阿昌语简志 *Āchāngyǔ jiǎnzhì [Brief description of the Achang language].* Beijing: 民族出版社 Nationalities Press. |
| JZ-Bai | Xu Lin 徐琳 and Zhao Yansun 赵衍荪, eds. 1984. 白语简志 *Báiyǔ jiǎnzhì [Brief description of the Bai language].* Beijing: 民族出版社 Nationalities Press. |
| JZ-CLMenba | Zhang Jichuan 张济川, ed. 1986. 仓洛门巴语简志 *Cāngluò Ménbāyǔ jiǎnzhì [Brief description of the Cangluo Menba language].* Beijing: 民族出版社 Nationalities Press. |
| JZ-CNMenba | Lu Shaozun 陆绍尊, ed. 1986. 错那门巴语简志 *Cuònà Ménbāyǔ jiǎnzhì [Brief description of the Cuona Menba language].* Beijing: 民族出版社 Nationalities Press. |
| JZ-Dulong | Sun Hongkai 孙宏开, ed. 1982. 独龙语简志 *Dúlóngyǔ jiǎnzhì [Brief description of the Dulong language].* Beijing: 民族出版社 Nationalities Press. |
| JZ-Hani | Li Yongsui 李永燧 and Wang Ersong 王尔松, eds. 1986. 哈尼语简志 *Hāníyǔ jiǎnzhì [Brief description of the Hani language].* Beijing: 民族出版社 Nationalities Press. |
| JZ-Jingpo | Liu Lu 刘璐, ed. 1984. 景颇族语言简志（景颇语）*Jǐngpōzú yǔyán jiǎnzhì (Jǐngpōyǔ) [Brief description of the Jingpo language of the Jingpo people].* Beijing: 民族出版社 Nationalities Press. |
| JZ-Jinuo | Gai Xingzhi 盖兴之, ed. 1986. 基诺语简志 *Jīnuòyǔ jiǎnzhì [Brief description of the Jinuo language].* Beijing: 民族出版社 Nationalities Press. |
| JZ-Lahu | Chang Hong'en 常竑恩 et al., eds. 1986. 拉祜语简志 *Lāhùyǔ jiǎnzhì [Brief description of the Lahu language].* Beijing: 民族出版社 Nationalities Press. |

JZ-Lisu        Xu Lin 徐琳, Mu Yuzhang 木玉璋, Gai Xingzhi 盖兴之, eds. 1986. 傈僳语简志 *Lìsùyǔ jiǎnzhì [Brief description of the Lisu language]*. Beijing: 民族出版社 Nationalities Press.

JZ-Naxi        He Jiren 和即仁 and Jiang Zhuyi 姜竹仪, eds. 1985. 纳西语简志 *Nàxīyǔ jiǎnzhì [Brief description of the Naxi language]*. Beijing: 民族出版社 Nationalities Press.

JZ-Nusu       Sun Hongkai 孙宏开 and Liu Lu 刘璐, eds. 1986. 怒族语言简志（怒苏语） *Nùzú yǔyán jiǎnzhì (Nùsūyǔ) [Brief description of the Nusu language of the Nu people]*. Beijing: 民族出版社 Nationalities Press.

JZ-Pumi       Lu Shaozun 陆绍尊, ed. 1983. 普米语简志 *Pǔmǐyǔ jiǎnzhì [Brief description of the Pumi language]*. Beijing: 民族出版社 Nationalities Press.

JZ-Qiang     Sun Hongkai 孙宏开, ed. 1981. 羌语简志 *Qiāngyǔ jiǎnzhì [Brief description of the Qiang language]*. Beijing: 民族出版社 Nationalities Press.

JZ-Tujia      Tian Desheng 田德生, He Tianzhen 何天贞 et al., eds. 1986. 土家语简志 *Tǔjiāyǔ jiǎnzhì [Brief description of the Tujia language]*. Beijing: 民族出版社 Nationalities Press.

JZ-Yi         Chen Shilin 陈士林, Bian Shiming 边仕明, Li Xiuqing 李秀清, eds. 1985. 彝语简志 *Yíyǔ jiǎnzhì [Brief description of the Yi language]*. Beijing: 民族出版社 Nationalities Press.

JZ-Zaiwa     Xu Xijian 徐悉艰 and Xu Guizhen 徐桂珍, eds. 1984. 景颇族语言简志（载瓦语） *Jǐngpōzú yǔyán jiǎnzhì (Zàiwǎyǔ) [Brief description of the Zaiwa language of the Jingpo people]*. Beijing: 民族出版社 Nationalities Press.

KDG-ICM     Das Gupta, K. 1968. *An Introduction to Central Monpa*. Shillong: Philology Section, Research Department, North-East Frontier Agency.

KDG-IGL     Das Gupta, K. 1963. *An Introduction to the Gallong Language*. Shillong: Philological Section, Research Department, North-East Frontier Agency.

KDG-Tag     Das Gupta, K. 1983. *An Outline on Tagin Language*. Directorate of Research, Government of Arunachal Pradesh.

KHG-Mikir   Grüssner, Karl-Heinz. 1978. *Arleng Alam, die Sprache der Mikir: Grammatik und Texte*. Wiesbaden: Franz Steiner.

KPM-pc      Malla, Kamal P. 2007. Personal communications.

KVB-Lai     Van Bik, Kenneth. 1995-. Personal communications.

KVB-PKC     Van Bik, Kenneth. 2007. *Proto-Kuki-Chin*. Ph.D. dissertation, University of California, Berkeley.

LL-PRPL     Löffler, Lorenz G. 1985. "A preliminary report on the Paangkhua language." In Graham Thurgood, et al., eds., *Linguistics of the Sino-Tibetan area: the state of the art*, pp. 279-286. (Pacific Linguistics Series C, No. 87). Canberra: Australian National University.

LMZ-AhiQ    Luo Meizhen. ca. 1990. Body Parts Questionnaire (Yi: Ahi).

LYS-Sangkon  Li Yongsui 李永燧. 1991. 缅彝语言调查的新收获：桑孔语 "Mian-Yi yuyan diaocha de xin shouhuo: Sangkongyu [A new harvest from research into Burmese-Yi: the Sangkong language]." Presented at the Fifth International Yi-Burmese Conference. Xichang, Sichuan. Beijing: Institute of Nationality Studies, Chinese Academy of Social Sciences.

MB-Lal      Balawan, M. 1965. *A First Lalung Dictionary, with the corresponding words in English and Khasi*. Shillong.

MF-PhnQ     Ferlus, Michel. 1991. Body Parts Questionnaire (Phunoi).

MM-K78      Mazaudon, Martine. 1978. "Consonantal mutation and tonal split in the Tamang sub-family of Tibeto-Burman." *Kailash* 6.3:157-79.

MM-TamRisQ  Mazaudon, Martine. 1991. Body Parts Questionnaire (Tamang: Risiangku).

| | |
|---|---|
| MM-Thesis | Mazaudon, Martine. 1994. *Problèmes de comparatisme et de reconstruction dans quelques langues de la famille tibéto-birmane.* Thèse d'État, Université de la Sorbonne Nouvelle, Paris. |
| MVS-Grin | Sofronov, M.V. ca. 1978. "Annotations to Grinstead 1972." Reconstructions of Tangut body part terms, personally entered into the glossary of Grinstead 1972. |
| MXL-Lolo | Ma Xueliang 马学良. 1948. 倮文作祭獻藥供牲經譯注 *Luǒwén* Zuòjì, xiànyào, gōng-shēngjīng *yìzhù [Annotated Translation of* The Lolo Classic of Rites, Cures, and Sacrifices]. *AS/BIHP* 20:577-666. |
| MXL-SaniQ | Ma Xueliang 马学良. ca. 1989. Field Notebook. |
| NEFA-PBI | Anonymous. 1962. *A Phrase Book in Idu.* Shillong: Philological Section, Research Department, North-East Frontier Agency. |
| NEFA-Taraon | Anonymous. n.d. *Taraon.* Shillong: Philological Section, Research Department, North-East Frontier Agency. |
| NJA-Thulung | Allen, N.J. 1975. *Sketch of Thulung Grammar.* East Asian Papers #6. Ithaca: China-Japan Program, Cornell University. |
| NKR-Bant | Rai, Novel Kishore. 1985. *A Descriptive Study of Bantawa.* Poona: Deccan College Post-Graduate and Research Institute. |
| NPB-ChanQ | Noonan, Michael, W. Pagliuca, and R. Bhulanja. 1992. Body Parts Questionnaire (Chantyal). |
| NT-SGK | Nishida Tatsuo 西田龍雄. 1964, 1966. 西夏語の研究 *Seikago no kenkyū [A Study of the Hsi-Hsia Language: reconstruction of the Hsi-Hsia language and decipherment of the Hsi-Hsia script].* Tokyo: 座右宝刊行会 Zauhō Kankōkai. 2 vols. Vol. I (1964), Vol. II (1966). |
| OH-DKL | Hanson, Ola. 1906. *A Dictionary of the Kachin Language.* Rangoon. Reprinted (1954, 1966), Rangoon: Baptist Board of Publications. |
| PB-Bisu | Beaudouin, Patrick. 1988. *Glossary English-French-Bisu; Bisu-English-French.* Nice, France: Section de Linguistique. U.E.R. Lettres, Université de Nice. |
| PB-CLDB | Bhaskararao, Peri. 1996. "A computerized lexical database of Tiddim Chin and Lushai." In Nara, Tsuyoshi and Machida, Kazuhiko (eds.), A Computer-Assisted Study of South-Asian Languages, pp. 27-143. Report #6. Tokyo: ILCAA. |
| PB-TCV | Bhaskararao, Peri. 1994. "Tiddim Chin verbs and their alternants." *Journal of Asian and African Studies.* Nos. 46-47. |
| PKB-KSEA | Benedict, Paul K. 1941/2008. *Kinship in Southeastern Asia.* Ph.D. dissertation, Department of Anthropology, Harvard University (1941). To be published as STEDT Monograph #6, 2008. |
| PKB-WBRD | Benedict, Paul K. 1976. *Rhyming Dictionary of Written Burmese. LTBA* 3.1:1-93. |
| PL-AED | Lewis, Paul. 1968. *Akha-English Dictionary.* Data Paper #70, Linguistics Series III. Ithaca: Cornell University, Southeast Asia Program. |
| PL-AETD | Lewis, Paul. 1989. *Akha-English-Thai Dictionary.* Chiang Rai, Thailand: Development & Agricultural Project for Akha. |
| PT-Kok | Tripuri, Prashanta and Dan Jurafsky. 1988. *Kokborok Word List.* Unpublished ms. |
| Qbp-KC | Thien Haokip. 1998. Body Parts Questionnaire (Kuki-Chin). |
| RAN1975 | Rangan, K. 1975. *Balti Phonetic Reader.* Phonetic Reader Series, #17. Mysore: CIIL. |
| RB-GB | Burling, Robbins. 1992. *Garo (Bangladesh dialect) Semantic Dictionary.* |
| RB-LMMG | Burling, Robbins. 2003. *The Language of the Modhupur Mandi (Garo). Vol. III: Glossary.* Ann Arbor, Michigan. |

RBJ-KLS       Jones, Robert B., Jr. 1961. *Karen Linguistic Studies: description, comparison, and texts.* UCPL #25. Berkeley and Los Angeles: University of California Press.

RC-ChepQ      Caughley, Ross. 1990. Body Parts Questionnaire (Chepang).

RJL-DPTB      LaPolla, Randy J. 1987. "Dulong and Proto-Tibeto-Burman." *LTBA* 10.1:1-43.

RPHH-Kul      Rai, Krishna Prasad, Anna Holzhausen, and Andreas Holzhausen. 1975. "Kulung body part index from *Kulung-Nepali-English Glossary.*" Kathmandu: SIL and Institute of Nepal and Asian Studies, Tribhuvan University.

RSB-STV       Bauer, Robert S. 1991. "Sino-Tibetan *vulva." *LTBA* 14.1:147-72.

SB-Lalo       Björverud, Susanna. 1994. "The phonology of Lalo." Paper presented at ICSTLL #27, Sèvres/Paris.

SBN-BunQ      Sharma, S.R. 1991. Body Parts Questionnaire (Bunan).

SD-MPD        Srinuan Duanghom. 1976. *An Mpi dictionary.* Ed. by Woranoot Pantupong. Bangkok: Working Papers in Phonetics and Phonology #1, Indigenous Languages of Thailand Research Project, Central Institute of English Language.

SER-HSL/T     Egli-Toduner, Susanna. n.d. *Handbook of the Sharchhokpa-Lo/Tsangla (language of the people of eastern Bhutan).* Thimphu, Bhutan: Helvetas.

SH-KNw        Shakya, Daya Ratna and David Hargreaves. 1989. Body Parts Questionnaire (Newari).

SHK-Anong     Sun Hongkai 孙宏开. 1988. "Notes on Anong, a new language." *LTBA* 11.1:27-63.

SHK-BaimaQ    Sun Hongkai 孙宏开. 1991. Body Parts Questionnaire (Baima).

SHK-ErgDQ     Sun Hongkai 孙宏开. 1991. Body Parts Questionnaire (Ergong: Danba).

SHK-ErgNQ     Sun Hongkai 孙宏开. 1991. Body Parts Questionnaire (Ergong: Northern).

SHK-ErsCQ     Sun Hongkai 孙宏开. 1991. Body Parts Questionnaire (Ersu).

SHK-GuiqQ     Sun Hongkai 孙宏开. 1991. Body Parts Questionnaire (Guiqiong).

SHK-Idu       Sun Hongkai 孙宏开. 1991. Body Parts Questionnaire (Idu).

SHK-MawoQ     Sun Hongkai 孙宏开. 1991. Body Parts Questionnaire (Mawo).

SHK-MuyaQ     Sun Hongkai 孙宏开. 1991. Body Parts Questionnaire (Muya).

SHK-NamuQ     Sun Hongkai 孙宏开. 1991. Body Parts Questionnaire (Namuyi).

SHK-rGEQ      Sun Hongkai 孙宏开. 1991. Body Parts Questionnaire (rGyalrong: Eastern).

SHK-rGNQ      Sun Hongkai 孙宏开. 1991. Body Parts Questionnaire (rGyalrong: Northern).

SHK-rGNWQ     Sun Hongkai 孙宏开. 1991. Body Parts Questionnaire (rGyalrong: Northwest).

SHK-ShixQ     Sun Hongkai 孙宏开. 1991. Body Parts Questionnaire (Shixing).

SHK-Sulung    Sun Hongkai 孙宏开. 1993. Body Parts Questionnaire (Sulong).

SHK-ZhabQ     Sun Hongkai 孙宏开. 1991. Body Parts Questionnaire (Zhaba).

SIL-Chep      Caughley, Ross. 1972. *A Vocabulary of the Chepang Language.* Kirtipur, Kathmandu: SIL, Tribhuvan University.

SIL-Gur       Glover, Warren W. 1972. *A Vocabulary of the Gurung Language.* Kirtipur, Kathmandu: SIL, Tribhuvan University.

SIL-Sahu      Taylor, Doreen, Fay Everitt, and Karna Bahadur Tamang. 1972. *A Vocabulary of the Tamang Language.* Kirtipur, Kathmandu: SIL, Tribhuvan University.

SIL-Thak      Hari, Maria. 1971. *A Vocabulary of the Thakali Language.* Kirtipur, Kathmandu: SIL, Tribhuvan University.

| | |
|---|---|
| SLZO-MLD | Sun Hongkai 孙宏开, Lu Shaozun 陆绍尊, Zhang Jichuan 张济川, and Ouyang Jueya 欧阳觉亚, eds. 1980. 门巴、珞巴、僜人的语言 *Menba, Luoba, Dengren de yuyan [The languages of the Monpa, Lhoba, and Deng peoples]*. Beijing: Social Sciences Press. |
| STC | Benedict, Paul K. 1972. *Sino-Tibetan: a Conspectus*. James A. Matisoff, contributing editor. Princeton-Cambridge Series in Chinese Linguistics, #2. New York: Cambridge University Press. |
| STP-ManQ | Sharma, S.R. 1991. Body Parts Questionnaire (Manchati). |
| SVD-Dum | Driem, George van. 1993. *A Grammar of Dumi*. Mouton Grammar Library #10. Berlin, New York: Mouton de Gruyter. |
| SVD-LimA | Driem, George van. 1987. *A Grammar of Limbu*. Mouton Grammar Library #4. Berlin, New York, Amsterdam: Mouton de Gruyter. |
| SY-KhözhaQ | Yabu, Shiro. 1994. Body Parts Questionnaire (Khözha). |
| T-KomRQ | Toba, Sueyoshi and Allen Kom. 1991. Body Parts Questionnaire (Kom Rem). |
| TBL | Dai Qingxia 戴庆厦, et al., eds. 1992. 藏缅语族语言词汇 *A Tibeto-Burman Lexicon*. Beijing: Central Institute of Minorities. |
| THI1972 | Thirumalai, M.S. 1972. *Thaadou Phonetic Reader*. Phonetic Reader Series #6. Mysore: CIIL. |
| TK-Yakha | Kohn, Tamara. ca. 1990. Body Parts Questionnaire (Yakha). |
| VN-AngQ | Nienu, Vikuosa. 1990. Body Parts Questionnaire (Angami Naga). |
| VN-ChkQ | Nienu, Vikuosa. 1990. Body Parts Questionnaire (Chokri). |
| VN-LothQ | Nienu, Vikuosa. 1990. Body Parts Questionnaire (Lotha). |
| WBB-Deuri | Brown, W.B. 1895. *An Outline Grammar of the Deori Chutiya Language Spoken in Upper Assam, with an introduction, illustrative sentences, and short vocabulary*. Shillong: Assam Secretariat Printing Office. |
| WHB-OC | Baxter, William. 1992. *A Handbook of Old Chinese Phonology*. Berlin, New York: Mouton de Gruyter. |
| WSC-SH | Coblin, Weldon South. 1986. *A Sinologist's Handlist of Sino-Tibetan Lexical Comparisons*. Monumenta Serica Monograph Series, Vol. 18. Nettetal: Steyler Verlag. |
| WTF-PNN | French, Walter T. 1983. *Northern Naga: a Tibeto-Burman Mesolanguage*. Ph.D. dissertation, City University of New York. |
| WW-Bant | Rai, Novel Kishore, Tikka Ram Rai, and Werner Winter. 1984. *A Tentative Bantawa Dictionary*. Unpublished ms. |
| WW-Cham | Winter, Werner. 1985. *Materials Towards a Dictionary of Chamling: I. Chamling-English; II. English-Chamling*. Based on data collected by Dhan Prasad Rai. Preliminary Version. Kiel: Linguistic Survey of Nepal. |
| YHJC-Sani | Wu Zili 武自立, Ang Zhiling 昂智灵, Huang Jianmin 黄健民. 1984. 彝汉简明词典 *Yí-Hàn jiǎnmíng cídiǎn [A Concise Yi-Chinese dictionary]*. Yunnan Nationalities Press. |
| YN-Man | Nagano, Yasuhiko. 1984. *A Manang Glossary*. Anthropological and Linguistic Studies of the Gandaki Area in Nepal II. (*Monumenta Serindica* #12.) Tokyo: ILCAA. |
| ZLS-Tib | Zhang Liansheng 张连生. 1988. *A Handbook of Chinese, Tibetan and English Words*. Unpublished ms. |
| ZMYYC | Sun Hongkai 孙宏开, et al., eds. 1991. 藏缅语语音和词汇 *Zàngmiǎnyǔ yǔyīn hé cíhuì [Tibeto-Burman Phonology and Lexicon]*. Beijing: Chinese Social Sciences Press. |
| ZYS-Bai | Zhao Yansun 赵衍荪. 1990. Body Parts Questionnaire (Bai). |

# References

*American Heritage Dictionary of the English Language.* 2000. J. P. Pickett, et al., eds. Boston: Houghton Mifflin Company.

Balawan, M. 1965. *A First Lalung Dictionary, with the corresponding words in English and Khasi.* Shillong.

Bauer, Robert S. 1991. "Sino-Tibetan \*vulva." *LTBA* 14.1:147-72.

Baxter, William. 1992. *A Handbook of Old Chinese Phonology.* Berlin, New York: Mouton de Gruyter.

Baxter, William H. and Laurent Sagart. 1998. "Word formation in Old Chinese." In *New approaches to Chinese word formation: morphology, phonology and the lexicon in modern and ancient Chinese.* Jerome L. Packard, ed., 35-76. Berlin and New York: Mouton de Gruyter.

Benedict, Paul K. 1939. "Semantic differentation in Indo-Chinese." HJAS 4:213-29.

————. 1941/2008. *Kinship in Southeastern Asia.* Ph.D. dissertation, Department of Anthropology, Harvard University (1941). To be published as STEDT Monograph #6, 2008.

————. 1972. *Sino-Tibetan: a Conspectus.* James A. Matisoff, contributing editor. Princeton-Cambridge Series in Chinese Linguistics, #2. New York: Cambridge University Press.

————. 1975a. *Austro-Thai Language and Culture, with a glossary of roots.* New Haven: HRAF Press.

————. 1975b. "Where it all began: memories of Robert Shafer and the *Sino-Tibetan Linguistics Project*, Berkeley 1939-40." *LTBA* 2.1:81-92.

————. 1976. "Sino-Tibetan: another look." *JAOS* 96.2:167-97.

————. 1979. "Four forays into Karen linguistic history." Edited and expurgated by James A. Matisoff. *LTBA.* 5.1:1-35. ["A note on the loss of final stop in Karen", pp. 4-7; "A note on the reconstruction of Karen preglottalized surd stops", pp. 8-12; "A note on the reconstruction of Karen final \*-s", pp. 13-20; "A note on Karen genital flipflop", pp. 21-24.]

————. 1981. "A further (unexpurgated) note on Karen genital flipflop." *LTBA* 6.1:103.

————. 1983. "Qiang monosyllables: a third phase in the cycle." *LTBA* 7.2:113-14.

————. 1988. Untitled ms. circulated at ICSTLL #21, Lund, Sweden.

————. 1990. *Austro-Tai/Japanese.* Ann Arbor: Karoma Press.

Sources for particular records not mentioned specifically in the text are listed in the Appendix of Source Abbreviations.

————. 1991. "Genital flipflop: a Chinese note." *LTBA* 14.1:143-6.

Bernot, Denise. 1978-92. *Dictionnaire birman-français*. 15 fascicules. Paris: SELAF.

Bhat, D. N. Shankara. 1968. *Boro Vocabulary (with a grammatical sketch)*. Poona: Deccan College Postgraduate and Research Institute.

Bodman, Nicholas C. 1980. "Proto-Chinese and Sino-Tibetan: data towards establishing the nature of the relationship." In Frans van Coetsem and Linda R. Waugh, eds., *Contributions to Historical Linguistics: Issues and Materials*, pp. 34-199. Leiden: E. J. Brill.

————. 1969. "Tibetan *sdud* 'folds of a garment', the character 卒, and the **\*st-** hypothesis." *AS/BIHP* 39:327-45.

Bradley, David. 1979. *Proto-Loloish*. Scandinavian Institute of Asian Studies Monograph Series, no. 39. London and Malmö: Curzon Press.

Buck, Carl Darling. 1949. *A Dictionary of Selected Synonyms in the Principal Indo-European Languages: a contribution to the history of ideas*. Chicago: University of Chicago Press.

Burling, Robbins. 1959. "Proto-Bodo." *Language* 35:433-53.

————. 1966. "The addition of final stops in the history of Maru." *Language* 42.3:581-86.

————. 1967/1968. *Proto-Lolo-Burmese*. Indiana University Research Center in Anthropology, Folkore, and Linguistics, publication 43. The Hague: Mouton. Issued simultaneously as a Special Publication, *IJAL* 33.2, Part II.

————. 1969. "Proto-Karen: a reanalysis." *OPWSTBL* vol. I, Alton L. Becker, ed., pp. 1-116. Ann Arbor: University of Michigan.

————. 1983. "The *sal* languages." *LTBA* 7.2:1-32.

————. 1992. *Garo (Bangladesh dialect) Semantic Dictionary*. Unpublished.

————. 1999. "On Kamarupan." *LTBA* 22.2:169-71.

————. 2003. *The Language of the Modhupur Mandi (Garo). Vol. III: Glossary*. Ann Arbor, Michigan.

Coblin, Weldon South. 1986. *A Sinologist's Handlist of Sino-Tibetan Lexical Comparisons*. Monumenta Serica Monograph Series, Vol. 18. Nettetal: Steyler Verlag.

Cook, Richard S. 1996. *The Etymology of Chinese* 辰 Chén. *LTBA* 18.2:1-238.

Cushing, Josiah N. 1881/1914. *A Shan and English Dictionary*. Second edition (1914). Rangoon: American Baptist Mission Press.

Dai Qingxia 戴庆厦, et al., eds. 1992. 藏缅语族语言词汇 *A Tibeto-Burman Lexicon*. Beijing: Central Institute of Minorities. ("TBL")

Dai Qingxia 戴庆厦, Xu Xijian 徐悉艰 , et al. 1983. 景汉辞典 *Jing-Han cidian – Jinghpo Miwa ga ginsi chyum – Jinghpo-Chinese dictionary*. Kunming: Yunnan Nationalities Press.

Driem, George van. 1987. *A Grammar of Limbu.* Mouton Grammar Library #4. Berlin, New York, Amsterdam: Mouton de Gruyter.

———. 1993. *A Grammar of Dumi.* Mouton Grammar Library #10. Berlin, New York: Mouton de Gruyter.

———. 2003. Review of Graham Thurgood and Randy J. LaPolla (eds.): *The Sino-Tibetan Languages.* London and New York: Routledge. 2003. *BSOAS*, 66.2:282-84.

Duàn Yùcái 段玉裁. 1815. 説文解字注 *Shuōwén Jiězì Zhù [Commentary on the Shuowen Jiezi].* Reprinted 1989 by Shànghǎi Gǔjí Chūbǎnshè.

French, Walter T. 1983. *Northern Naga: a Tibeto-Burman Mesolanguage.* Ph.D. dissertation, City University of New York.

Gong Hwang-cherng 龔煌城. 1989/2002. "The phonological reconstruction of Tangut through examination of phonological alternations." Reprinted in Gong 2002, pp. 75-110. Originally published in: *AS/BIHP* 60.1:1-45.

———. 1990. 從漢藏語的比較看上古漢語若干的擬測 "Cóng Hàn-Zàngyǔ de bǐjiào kàn Shànggǔ Hànyǔ ruògān shēngmǔ de nǐcè [Reconstruction of some initials in Archaic Chinese from the viewpoint of comparative Sino-Tibetan]." In *A Collection of Essays in Tibetan Studies*, Vol. 3, pp. 1-18. Taipei: Committee on Tibetan Studies.

———. 1994. "The first palatalization of velars in Late Old Chinese." In Matthew Y. Chen and Ovid J. L. Tzeng, eds., *Linguistics Essays in Honor of William S.-Y. Wang: inter-disciplinary studies on language and language change*, pp. 131-142. Taipei: Pyramid Press.

———. 1995. "The system of finals in Proto-Sino-Tibetan." In William S.-Y. Wang, ed., *The Ancestry of the Chinese Language*, pp. 41-92. Berkeley: POLA.

———. 1997. 從漢藏語的比較看重紐問題(兼論上古介音對中古韻母演變的影像) "Cóng Hàn-Zàng yǔ de bǐjiào kàn chóngniǔ wèntí (jiān lùn Shànggǔ *-rj-* jièyīn duì Zhōnggǔ yùnmǔ yǎnbiàn de yǐngxiǎng) [The *chongniu* problem from the viewpoint of comparative Sino-Tibetan (with discussion of the effect of the Old Chinese medial *-rj-* on the development of Middle Chinese rhymes)]." In Republic of China Phonology Conference, Taiwan Normal University Chinese Department, and Academia Sinica Institute of History and Philology, eds., 聲韻論叢 *Shēngyùn lùn cóng [Collected essays in Chinese phonology]*, Vol. VI, pp. 195-243. Taipei: 台灣學生書局 Táiwān Xuéshēng Shūjú.

———. 2000. 從漢藏語的比教看上古漢語的詞頭問題 "Cóng Hàn-Zàng yǔ de bǐjiào kàn Shànggǔ Hànyǔ de cítóu wèntí [The problem of Old Chinese prefixes from the perspective of comparative Sino-Tibetan studies]." *Languages and Linguistics* (Taipei) 1.2:39-62.

———. 2002. 漢藏語研究論文集 *Hàn Zàng yǔ yánjiù lùnwén jí [Collected papers on Sino-Tibetan linguistics].* Language and Linguistics Monograph Series, C2-2. Taipei: Institute of Linguistics (Preparatory Office), Academia Sinica.

Grierson, Sir George Abraham and Sten Konow (eds.). 1903-28. *Linguistic Survey of*

*India.* 13 vols. Calcutta: Office of the Superintendent of Government Printing. Reprinted (1967, 1973), Delhi: Motilal Banarsidass.

Grinstead, Eric. 1972. *Analysis of the Tangut Script.* Scandinavian Institute of Asian Studies Monograph Series, #10. Lund: Studentlitteratur.

Hale, Austin. 1973. *Clause, Sentence, and Discourse Patterns in Selected Languages of Nepal IV: Word Lists.* Summer Institute of Linguistics Publications in Linguistics and Related Fields #40. Kathmandu: SIL and Tribhuvan University Press.

Handel, Zev J. 1998. *The Medial Systems of Old Chinese and Proto-Sino-Tibetan.* Ph.D. dissertation, University of California, Berkeley.

Hanson, Ola. 1906. *A Dictionary of the Kachin Language.* Rangoon. Reprinted (1954, 1966), Rangoon: Baptist Board of Publications.

Haudricourt, André-Georges. 1942-5. "Restitution du karen commun." *BSLP* 42.1:103-11.

———. 1975. "Le système de tons du karen commun." *BSLP* 70:339-43.

Henderson, Eugénie J. A. 1997. *Bwe Karen Dictionary.* School of Oriental and African Studies, University of London.

Hodgson, Brian Houghton. 1857. "Comparative vocabulary of the several languages (dialects) of the celebrated people called Kirântis." *JASB* 26.5:333-71.

Hyman, Larry M., ed. 1973. *Consonant Types and Tone.* Southern California Occasional Papers in Linguistics #1. Los Angeles: University of California, Los Angeles.

Imoba, S. 2004. *Manipuri to English Dictionary.* Imphal: S. Ibetombi Devi.

Jäschke, Heinrich August. 1881/1958. *A Tibetan-English Dictionary, with special reference to the prevailing dialects.* London. Reprinted (1958) by Routledge and Kegan Paul.

Jones, Robert B., Jr. 1961. *Karen Linguistic Studies: description, comparison, and texts.* UCPL #25. Berkeley and Los Angeles: University of California Press.

Judson, Adoniram. 1893. *Burmese-English Dictionary.* Rangoon. Revised and enlarged (1953) by Robert C. Stevenson and F. H. Eveleth. Reprinted (1966), Rangoon: Baptist Board of Publications.

Karlgren, Bernhard. 1923. *Analytic Dictionary of Chinese and Sino-Japanese.* Paris: P. Geuthner.

———. 1933. "Word families in Chinese." *BMFEA* 5:5-120.

———. 1957. *Grammata Serica Recensa.* Stockholm: Museum of Far Eastern Antiquities, Publication 29. ("GSR")

Kitamura Hajime 北村甫, Nishida Tatsuo 西田龍雄, and Nagano Yasuhiko 長野泰彦, eds. 1994. *Current Issues in Sino-Tibetan Linguistics.* Osaka: Organizing Committee of 26th ICSTLL. ("CISTL")

Kumar, Braj Bihari and Thimase Pocuri. 1972. *Hindi-Pochury-English Dictionary.* Kohima, Nagaland: Nagaland Bhasha Parishad (Linguistic Circle of Nagaland).

Kumar, Braj Bihari, et al. 1973. *Hindi-Sangtam-English Dictionary.* Kohima, Nagaland: Nagaland Bhasha Parishad (Linguistic Circle of Nagaland).

Li Fang-Kuei 李方桂. 1971/1980. 上古音研究 "Shànggǔyīn Yánjiū [Studies on Old Chinese phonology]." *Tsing Hua Journal of Chinese Studies,* n.s. 9:1-61. Reprinted (1980), Beijing: 商务印书馆 Shāngwù Yìnshūguǎn, pp. 1-83.

———. 1976. 幾個上古聲母問題 "Jǐge Shànggǔ shēngmǔ wèntí [Some problems concerning Old Chinese initials]." In 總統蔣公逝世週年論文集 *Zǒngtǒng Jiǎng gōng shìshì zhōunián lùnwén jí [Collected papers in commemoration of the anniversary of the death of President Chiang],* 1143-50. Taipei: Academia Sinica. Reprinted in Li 1980:85-94.

———. 1977. *A Handbook of Comparative Tai.* Oceanic Linguistics Special Publication #15. Honolulu: University Press of Hawai'i. ("HCT")

———. 1980. See Li 1971.

Löffler, Lorenz G. 1966. "The contribution of Mru to Sino-Tibetan linguistics." *ZDMG* 116.1:118-59.

Lorrain, J. Herbert. 1907. *A Dictionary of the Abor-Miri Language, with illustrative sentences and notes.* Shillong: Eastern Bengal and Assam Secretariat Printing Office.

Luce, G. H. 1981. *A Comparative Word-List of Old Burmese, Chinese, and Tibetan.* London: School of Oriental and African Studies, University of London.

———. 1986. *Phases of Pre-Pagán Burma: languages and history.* Vol. 2. Oxford: Oxford University Press.

Mainwaring, G.B. 1898. *Dictionary of the Lepcha Language.* Revised and completed by Albert Grünwedel. Berlin: Unger Brothers.

Marrison, G.E. 1967. *The Classification of the Naga Languages of Northeast India.* Ph.D. dissertation, School of Oriental and African Studies, University of London. 2 vols.

Matisoff, James A. 1969. "Lahu and Proto-Lolo-Burmese." *OPWSTBL* vol. I, Alton L. Becker, ed., pp. 117-221. Ann Arbor: University of Michigan.

———. 1970. "Glottal dissimilation and the Lahu high-rising tone: a tonogenetic case-study." *JAOS* 90.1:13-44.

———. 1972a. *The Loloish Tonal Split Revisited.* Research Monograph #7. Berkeley: Center for South and Southeast Asian Studies, University of California, Berkeley.

———. 1972b. "Tangkhul Naga and comparative Tibeto-Burman." *TAK* 10.2:1-13.

———. 1973a. "Tonogenesis in Southeast Asia." In L. M. Hyman, ed., pp. 71-96.

———. 1973b/1982. *The Grammar of Lahu.* UCPL #75. Berkeley and Los Angeles: University of California Press. Reprinted 1982.

———. 1974. "The tones of Jinghpaw and Lolo-Burmese: common origin vs. independent development." *Acta Linguistica Hafniensia* (Copenhagen) 15.2, 153-212.

———. 1975. "Rhinoglottophilia: the mysterious connection between nasality and glottality." In C. A. Ferguson, L. M. Hyman, and J. J. Ohala, eds., *Nasálfest* pp. 267-287. Stanford, CA.

———. 1978a. *Variational Semantics in Tibeto-Burman: the 'organic' approach to linguistic comparison.* OPWSTBL #6. Philadelphia: Institute for the Study of Human Issues.

———. 1978b. "Mpi and Lolo-Burmese microlinguistics." *Monumenta Serindica* (ILCAA, Tokyo) 4:1-36.

———. 1980. "Stars, moon, and spirits: bright beings of the night in Sino-Tibetan." *GK* 77:1-45.

———. 1982. "Proto-languages and proto-Sprachgefühl." *LTBA* 6.2:1-64.

———. 1983. "Translucent insights: a look at Proto-Sino-Tibetan through Gordon H. Luce's comparative word-list." *BSOAS* 46.3:462-76.

———. 1985a. "God and the Sino-Tibetan copula, with some good news concerning selected Tibeto-Burman rhymes." *Journal of Asian and African Studies* (Tokyo) 29:1-81.

———. 1985b. "Out on a limb: *arm, hand,* and *wing* in Sino-Tibetan." In Graham Thurgood, et al., eds., *Linguistics of the Sino-Tibetan area: the state of the art,* pp. 421-425. (Pacific Linguistics Series C, No. 87). Canberra: Australian National University.

———. 1986. "The languages and dialects of Tibeto-Burman: an alphabetic/genetic listing, with some prefatory remarks on ethnonymic and glossonymic complications." In John McCoy and Timothy Light, eds., *Contributions to Sino-Tibetan Studies,* pp. 1-75. Leiden: E.J. Brill. Revised and reprinted (1996) as STEDT Monograph #2, with Stephen P. Baron and John B. Lowe.

———. 1988a. *The Dictionary of Lahu.* UCPL #111. Berkeley, Los Angeles, London: University of California Press.

———. 1988b. "Universal semantics and allofamic identification: two Sino-Tibetan case-studies: *straight/flat/full* and *property/livestock/talent.*" In Akihiro Sato, ed., *Languages and History in East Asia: Festschrift for Tatsuo Nishida on the Occasion of his 60th Birthday,* pp. 3-14. Kyoto: Shokado.

———. 1990a. "On megalocomparison." *Language* 66.1:106-20.

———. 1990b. "The dinguist's dilemma: l/d interchange in Sino-Tibetan." Paper presented at ICSTLL #23, University of Texas, Arlington.

———. 1991a. "Areal and universal dimensions of grammatization in Lahu." In Elizabeth C. Traugott and Bernd Heine, eds., *Approaches to Grammaticalization,* Vol. II, pp. 383-453. Amsterdam: Benjamins.

———. 1991b. "The mother of all morphemes." In Martha Ratliff and Eric Schiller, eds. *Papers from the First Annual Meeting of the Southeast Asian Linguistics Society* (SEALS), pp. 293-349. Tempe: Arizona State University.

———. 1991c. "Jiburish revisited: tonal splits and heterogenesis in Burmo-Naxi-Lolo checked syllables." *AO* 52:91-114.

———. 1992. "Following the marrow: two parallel Sino-Tibetan etymologies." *LTBA* 15.1:159-177.

———. 1994a. "Regularity and variation in Sino-Tibetan." In *CISTL*, pp. 36-58.

———. 1994b. "How dull can you get?: *buttock* and *heel* in Sino-Tibetan." *LTBA* 17.2:137-51. Reprinted in Pierre Pichard and François Rabine, eds., *Études birmanes en hommage à Denise Bernot*, pp. 373-83. Paris: EFEO.

———. 1995. "Sino-Tibetan palatal suffixes revisited." In *NHTBM*, pp. 35-91. Osaka: National Museum of Ethnology.

———. 1997. "Primary and secondary laryngeal initials in Tibeto-Burman." In Anne O. Yue and Mitsuaki Endo, eds., *In Memory of Mantaro J. Hashimoto*, pp. 29-50. Tokyo: Uchiyama Books Co.

———. 1999. "In defense of Kamarupan." *LTBA* 22.2:173-182.

———. 2000a. "An extrusional approach to *p-/w- variation in Sino-Tibetan." *Language and Linguistics* (Taipei) 1.2:135-86.

———. 2000b. "Three Tibeto-Burman/Sino-Tibetan word families: *set (of the sun); pheasant/peacock; scatter/pour*." In Marlys Macken, ed., *Papers from the Tenth Annual Meeting of the Southeast Asian Linguistics Society* (SEALS), pp. 215-32. Tempe: Arizona State University.

———. 2003. *Handbook of Proto-Tibeto-Burman: system and philosophy of Sino-Tibetan reconstruction.* UCPL #135. Berkeley and Los Angeles: University of California Press. ("HPTB")

———. 2004. "Areal semantics: is there such a thing?" In Anju Saxena, ed., *Himalayan Languages, Past and Present*, pp. 347-393. Berlin and New York: Mouton de Gruyter.

———. 2007a. "Response to Laurent Sagart's review of *Handbook of Proto-Tibeto-Burman*." *Diachronica* 24.2:435-44.

———. 2007b. "The fate of the Proto-Lolo-Burmese rhyme *-a: regularity and exceptions." Paper presented at ICSTLL #40, Heilongjiang University, Harbin, China.

Mazaudon, Martine. 1978. "Consonantal mutation and tonal split in the Tamang subfamily of Tibeto-Burman." *Kailash* 6.3:157-79.

———. 1994. *Problèmes de comparatisme et de reconstruction dans quelques langues de la famille tibéto-birmane.* Thèse d'État, Université de la Sorbonne Nouvelle, Paris.

Michailovsky, Boyd. 1991. *Proto-Kiranti.* Unpublished ms.

Miller, Roy Andrew. 1968. "Once again, the Maru final stops." Paper presented at ICSTLL #1, Yale University.

Mills, James Philip. 1926/1973. *The Ao Nagas.* London. Reprinted (1973), Delhi: Oxford University Press.

Momin, K. W. n.d. *English-Achikku Dictionary.* Printed by V. N. Bhattacharya at the Inland Printing Works, 60-3, Dharamtala Street, Calcutta-13.

# References

Monier-Williams, Sir Monier. 1899/1970. *A Sanskrit-English Dictionary*. Delhi, Varanasi, Patna: Motilal Banarsidass.

Namkung, Ju, ed. 1996. *Phonological Inventories of Tibeto-Burman Languages*. STEDT Monograph #3. Berkeley: University of California.

Nishi Yoshio 西義郎, James A. Matisoff, and Nagano Yasuhiko 長野泰彦, eds. 1995. *New Horizons in Tibeto-Burman Morphosyntax*. Senri Ethnological Studies #41. Osaka: National Museum of Ethnology. ("NHTBM")

Nishida Tatsuo 西田龍雄. 1964, 1966. 西夏語の研究 *Seikago no kenkyū [A Study of the Hsi-Hsia Language: reconstruction of the Hsi-Hsia language and decipherment of the Hsi-Hsia script]*. Tokyo: 座右宝刊行会 Zauhō Kankōkai. 2 vols. Vol. I (1964), Vol. II (1966).

Noonan, Michael, et al. 1999. *Chantyal Dictionary and Texts*. Berlin and New York: Mouton de Gruyter.

*Oxford English Dictionary*. 1971. Compact Edition, 2 vols. reproduced micrographically. 3rd U.S. Printing, 1973. Oxford University Press.

Pan Wuyun 潘悟云. 2000. 汉语历史音韵学 *Hànyǔ lìshǐ yīnyùnxué [Chinese Historical Phonology]*. Shanghai: 教育出版社 Jiàoyù Chūbǎnshè.

Peiros, Ilia and S.A. Starostin. 1996. *A Comparative Vocabulary of Five Sino-Tibetan Languages*. 5 fascicles. Melbourne: University of Melbourne.

Peterson, David A. 2008. "Bangladesh Khumi verbal classifiers and Kuki-Chin 'chiming'." *LTBA*, to appear.

Pulleyblank, Edwin G. 1962. "The consonantal system of Old Chinese." *AM* 9:58-144, 206-265.

Qu Wanli 屈萬里. 1983. 詩經詮釋 *Shījīng Quánshì [Complete text of the Book of Odes]*. Taipei: 聯經出版公司 Liánjīng Chūbǎn Gōngsī.

Sagart, Laurent. 1999. *The Roots of Old Chinese*. Amsterdam Studies in the Theory and History of Linguistic Science #184. Amsterdam: John Benjamins.

Sagart, Laurent. 2007. "Reconstructing Old Chinese uvulars in the Baxter-Sagart system (ver. 0.97)." Paper presented at ICSTLL #40, Heilongjiang University, Harbin.

———. 2006. Review of Matisoff 2003. *Diachronica* 23.1:206-223

Schuessler, Axel. 1987. *A Dictionary of Early Zhou Chinese*. Honolulu: University of Hawai'i Press.

———. 2007. *ABC Etymological Dictionary of Old Chinese*. Honololu: University of Hawai'i Press.

Sedláček, Kamil. 1970. *Das Gemein-Sino-Tibetische*. Wiesbaden: Franz Steiner Verlag.

Shafer, Robert. 1966-73. *Introduction to Sino-Tibetan*. 5 parts. Wiesbaden: Otto Harrassowitz.

Simon, Walter. 1929. "Tibetisch-chinesische Wortgleichungen: Ein Versuch." *MSOS* 32.1:157-228.

———. 1975. "Tibetan initial clusters of nasal and R." *AM* 19.2:246-51.

Sofronov, M.V. ca. 1978. "Annotations to Grinstead 1972." Reconstructions of Tangut body part terms, personally entered into the glossary of Grinstead 1972.

Stimson, Hugh. 1966. "A taboo word in the Peking dialect." *Language* 42.2:285-294.

Sun Hongkai 孙宏开, et al., eds. 1991. 藏缅语语音和词汇 *Zàngmiǎnyǔ yǔyīn hé cíhuì [Tibeto-Burman Phonology and Lexicon]*. Beijing: Chinese Social Sciences Press.

Sun, Jackson Tianshin 孫天心. 1993. *A Historical-Comparative Study of the Tani (Mirish) Branch in Tibeto-Burman.* Ph.D. dissertation, University of California, Berkeley.

Thurgood, Graham. 1984. "The *Rung* languages: a major new TB subgroup." In *Proceedings of the Tenth Annual Meeting of the Berkeley Linguistics Society*, pp. 338-349. University of California, Berkeley.

Thurgood, Graham and Randy J. LaPolla, eds. 2003. *The Sino-Tibetan Languages.* London: Routledge.

Turner, R.L. 1966. *A Comparative Dictionary of the Indo-Aryan Languages.* London: Oxford University Press.

VanBik, Kenneth. 2003. *Proto-Kuki-Chin.* Ph.D. dissertation, University of California, Berkeley.

Walker, George David. 1925. *A Dictionary of the Mikir Language, Mikir-English and English-Mikir.* Shillong: Assam Government Press.

Weidert, Alfons K. 1975. *Componential Analysis of Lushai Phonology.* Amsterdam: J. Benjamins B. V.

———. 1979. "The Sino-Tibetan tonogenetic laryngeal reconstruction theory." *LTBA* 5.1:49-127.

———. 1981. "Star, moon, spirits, and the affricates of Angami Naga: a reply to James A. Matisoff." *LTBA* 6.1:1-38.

———. 1987. *Tibeto-Burman Tonology: a comparative account. Current Issues in Linguistic Theory* #54. Amsterdam and Philadelphia: John Benjamins.

Wolfenden, Stuart N. 1929. *Outlines of Tibeto-Burman Linguistic Morphology.* With special reference to the prefixes, infixes, and suffixes of Classical Tibetan, and the languages of the Kachin, Bodo, Naga, Kuki-Chin, and Burma groups. Prize Publication #12. London: Royal Asiatic Society.

Yu Nae-wing 余迺永. 2000. 新校互註 · 宋本廣韻 *Xīn Jiào Hù Zhù - Sòng Běn Guǎngyùn [A New Revision of the Sung Edition of the Kuang-yun Rhyming Dictionary].* 上海辭書出版社 Shànghǎi Císhū Chūbǎnshè.

# Index of Chinese Comparanda by Pīnyīn